Hieroglyphic Vocabulary

by

E.A. Wallis Budge

978-1-63923-010-5

Hieroglyphic Vocabulary

Printed June, 2016

Lushena Books, Inc
607 Country Club Drive, Unit E
Bensenville, IL 60106

www.lushenabks.com

Printed in the United States of America

Books on Egypt and Chaldæa.

VOL. XXXI OF THE SERIES.

HIEROGLYPHIC VOCABULARY

WITH AN INDEX
TO ALL THE ENGLISH EQUIVALENTS
OF THE EGYPTIAN WORDS.

Books on Egypt and Chaldæa.

A HIEROGLYPHIC VOCABULARY TO THE THEBAN RECENSION OF THE BOOK OF THE DEAD

WITH AN INDEX TO ALL THE ENGLISH EQUIVALENTS OF THE EGYPTIAN WORDS

BY

E. A. WALLIS BUDGE, M.A., LITT. D., D. LITT., D. LIT.

KEEPER OF THE EGYPTIAN AND ASSYRIAN ANTIQUITIES IN THE BRITISH MUSEUM.

VOL. XXXI.

NEW EDITION. REVISED AND ENLARGED.

LONDON

KEGAN PAUL, TRENCH, TRÜBNER & CO. LTD.

DRYDEN HOUSE, 43, GERRARD STREET, W.

1911

PREFACE TO THE SECOND EDITION.

THE following pages contain a Hieroglyphic Vocabulary to all the texts of the Chapters of the Theban Recension of the Book of the Dead which is printed in this Series (Vols. XXVIII—XXX), and also to most of the supplementary Chapters of the Saïte and Graeco-Roman period which are appended thereto. The whole work has been comprehensively revised, and in the case of characters to which the values given in 1897, when the first edition was compiled, are now obsolete, special care has been taken to place them in the order in which they have since been proved to belong. The arrangement of the words and their various forms is usually alphabetical, and it is hoped that the few exceptions to this rule will cause the reader no difficulty. A very considerable number of words and forms have been added to this edition, and it was necessary, for reasons of space, to omit all references.

A new feature of this edition of the Vocabulary is the Index to all the English equivalents of Egyptian words printed herein. This was prepared in answer to the requests of many who had used the first edition of the Vocabulary.

For the care which Mr. Adolf Holzhausen has given to the printing of this work my sincere thanks are due.

E. A. WALLIS BUDGE

BRITISH MUSEUM,
February 4th, 1911.

VOCABULARY.

 A.

aatā, atitā 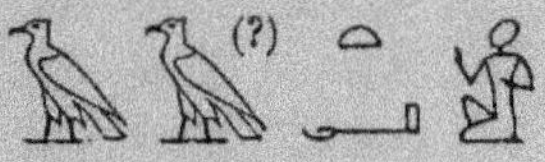 ministrant, celebrant, a kind of priest.

aȧr 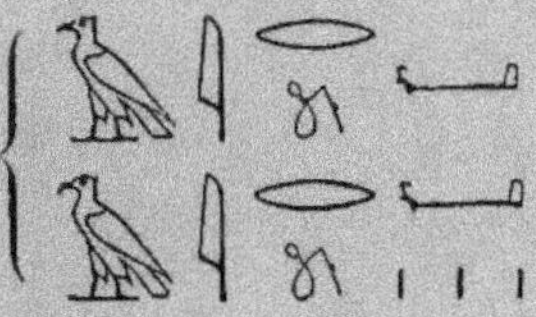 to bind, tie together, to put under restraint, to coerce, to persecute, to oppress.

au  to make a gift or offering, to present.

ait  bread-cakes, loaves of any shape offered for funerary oblations.

aut  offerings of meat and drink, sacrifices, bread-cakes, etc.

aut  light, radiance.

au  to be long, length, the opposite of  *usekh* breadth, to extend, be extended, *e. g.*  extended (*i. e.*, lavish) hand,  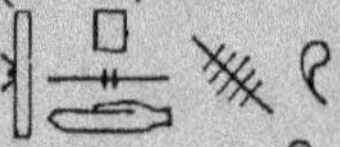 length of the back,  extended of years,  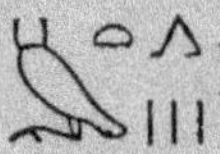 long of strides; compare also 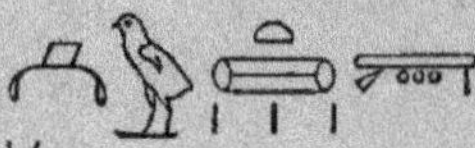, 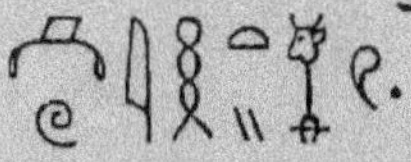.

au  to expand, to dilate (of the heart), hence ,  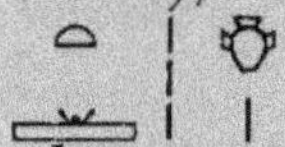 joy, gladness, pleasure, delight.

au  fully, exceedingly, to the utmost, to the full extent.

Au-ā 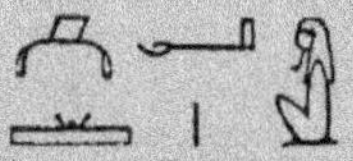 the "god of the extended arm".

au  children, youths, the young, unmarried men, synonym of *sheriu*  children.

ausek 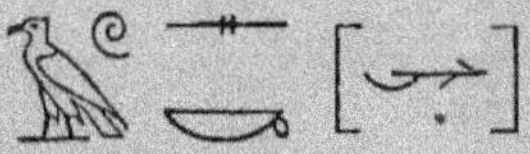 stick, staff, sceptre, symbol of high position and dignity.

abit 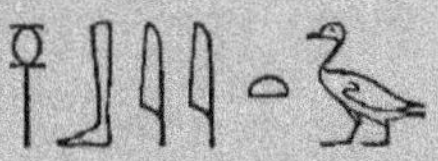 an insect which brought the deceased into the Hall of

Osiris, identified with the praying mantis. A variant gives *bai* .

abu  cessation 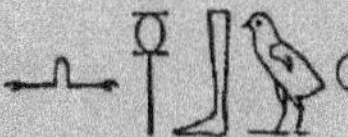 ceaselessly, unremittingly.

Abu  Elephant-city. The Island of Elephantine and the town and district of Syene. The region of the First Cataract.

abka  to shine.

abtu  maternal and paternal ancestors. Heb. אָבוֹת.

Abt-ṭesi-ruṭu-neter 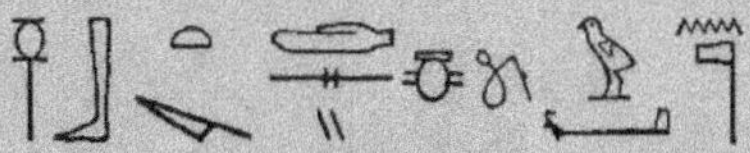 a proper name.

apṭu  geese, ducks, water-fowl in general, and finally birds of any and every kind offered for sacrifices.

afiu  fish offered at funerary feasts.

afu  to injure, to harm.

Amm  flame, fire, heat, blaze, to scorch, to burn, to shrivel up. Var. 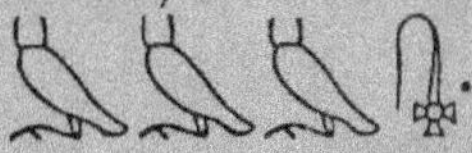.

Am[m]u  the Fire City of the Other World.

amm  to grasp with the hand, to hold in the fist, to seize, take by violence, snatch at, fist, grasp.

amu 

ames  the name of a sceptre, or staff, associated with Àmsu, or Menu, the god of generation and fertility.

Ani  a scribe and treasurer of holy offerings.

Arthikasathika 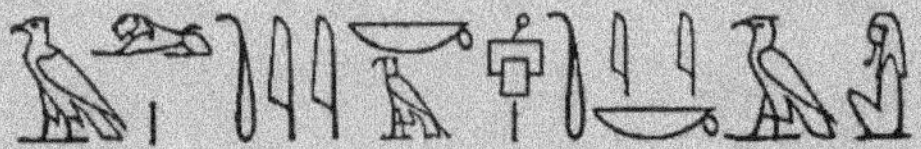 a proper name.

ah  to be troubled, injured, suffering.

aha  evil, injury, harm.

Ahat  an ancient goddess, who was identified with Hathor, and appeared in the form of a cow or a woman.

Ahit 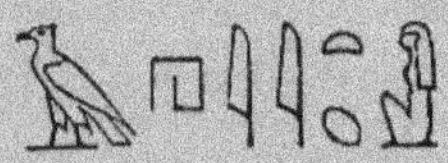 a goddess who supplied the dead with food.

Aḥu 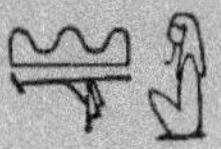 a god who was connected with offerings.

Aḥui (?)  the name of a canal (?).

aḥu 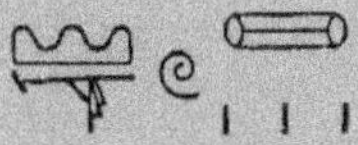 food, bread-cakes, offerings of all kinds.

aḥet 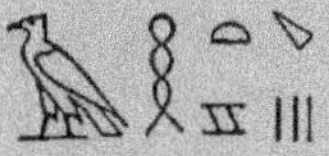 fields, estates, farm, cultivated land.

akh  to bloom, to blossom, flower, bloom.

akhakh  flowers of the sky, *i. e.*, stars.

akhi  reed, water-plant, rushes, marsh flowers.

akhet  the first season of the Egyptian Year.

akhaā  to enter, to penetrate.

akhab 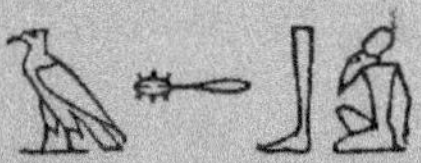 to give to drink.

Akhabiu 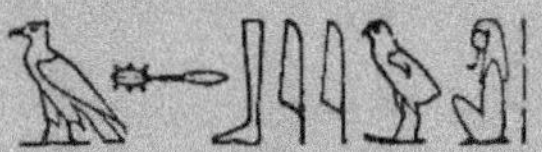 a class of divine beings, or gods, who were associated with the Akeru-gods .

akhetu  *i. e.*, , things, objects, food, bread-cakes.

Aseb 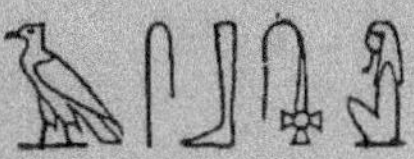 the name of a Fire-god in the Other World.

asbiu 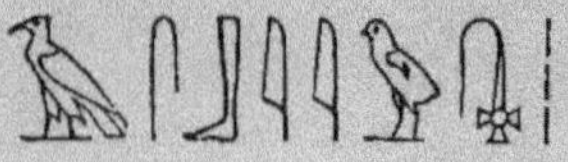 sparks of fire, flames, fiery spirits.

Aseb-ḥer-per-em-khetkhet  a god with a face of fire which advanced and retreated alternately.

askh  to cut a crop, to reap.

asta 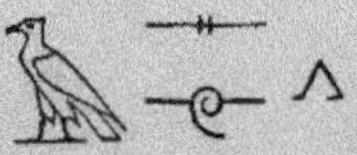 to hasten, to hurry, be swift or rapid.

asta ȧb 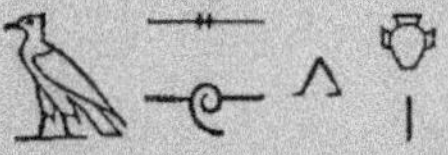 to hurry the heart, to arrive at a hasty judgment.

astu  water in motion, a stream or canal.

Ashu  name of a god.

Ashbu 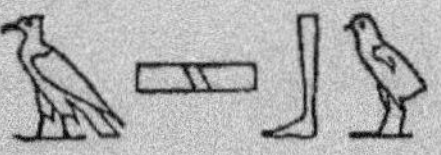 name of the warder of the 5th Ārit.

Asher  name of a city, or temple district, or god.

ashert  roasted flesh of animals, or birds, grilled meat, steaks, joints, etc.

akit  a chamber, or hut, or small house.

Aker  a very ancient name of the Earth-god.

Akeru  The two gods who guarded the western and eastern ends of the tunnel through the earth which the Sun-god passed through nightly. They were the ancestors of the Akhabiu gods, 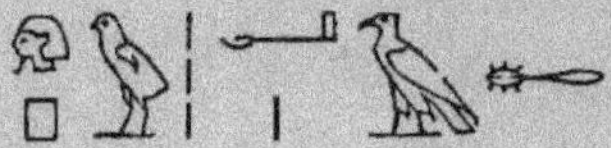 , and also of Rā 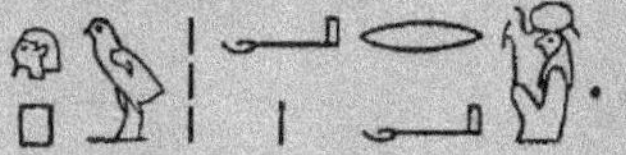.

Akeriu 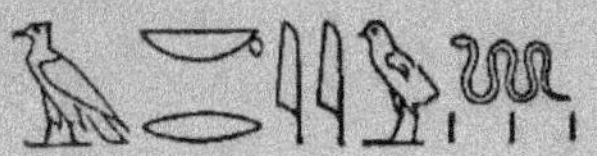 a group of earth-gods who appeared in the form of serpents.

aqa  *i. e.,*  dirt, filth, what is filthy.

Aqeṭqeṭ 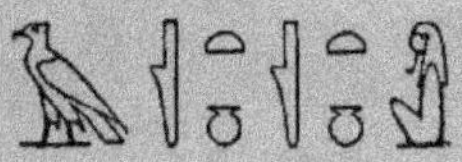 one of a group of seven gods or spirits associated with Osiris.

Aḳab

Aḳb  the great celestial ocean and the god who presided over it, water, flood, celestial Nile.

Akḳbȧ  the great celestial ocean and the god who presided over it, water, flood, celestial Nile.

at 

atu  injury, assault, attack.

at  a support of a god, a perch for a bird, etc. The word is also written with a wrong determinative .

at  the vertebrae, back, the middle of something.

at 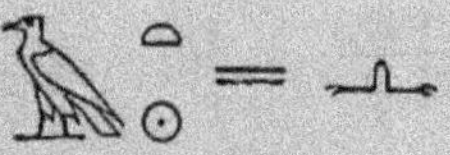 not

at  moment, a period of time, season.

Ati  The ninth nome of Lower Egypt; its capital was Per-Ȧsȧr (Busiris).

atiu  evil beings, fiends, enemies.

atutu  a kind of wood.

atep  a load, a burden, something carried on the head, to carry, to bear, to support.

atef  name of one of the principal crowns of Osiris.
atefu 

Atef-ur  a proper name.

aṭ  to be wounded, injured.

atȧu 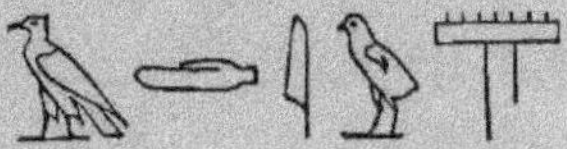 a ceremonial garment with magical properties.

aṭu  crocodile, or water lizard. Plur. .

Ȧtes ḥer-mer (?)  a proper name.

aṭet 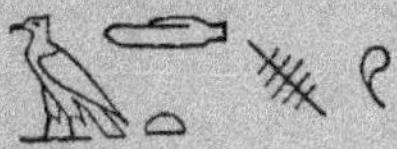 the vertebrae, back. Also written .

 Ȧ.

A  The god Thoth . The form is common in the later period.

ȧ  Personal pronoun. I, me, my.

ȧ  O! Hail!

ȧ  praise, acclamation.

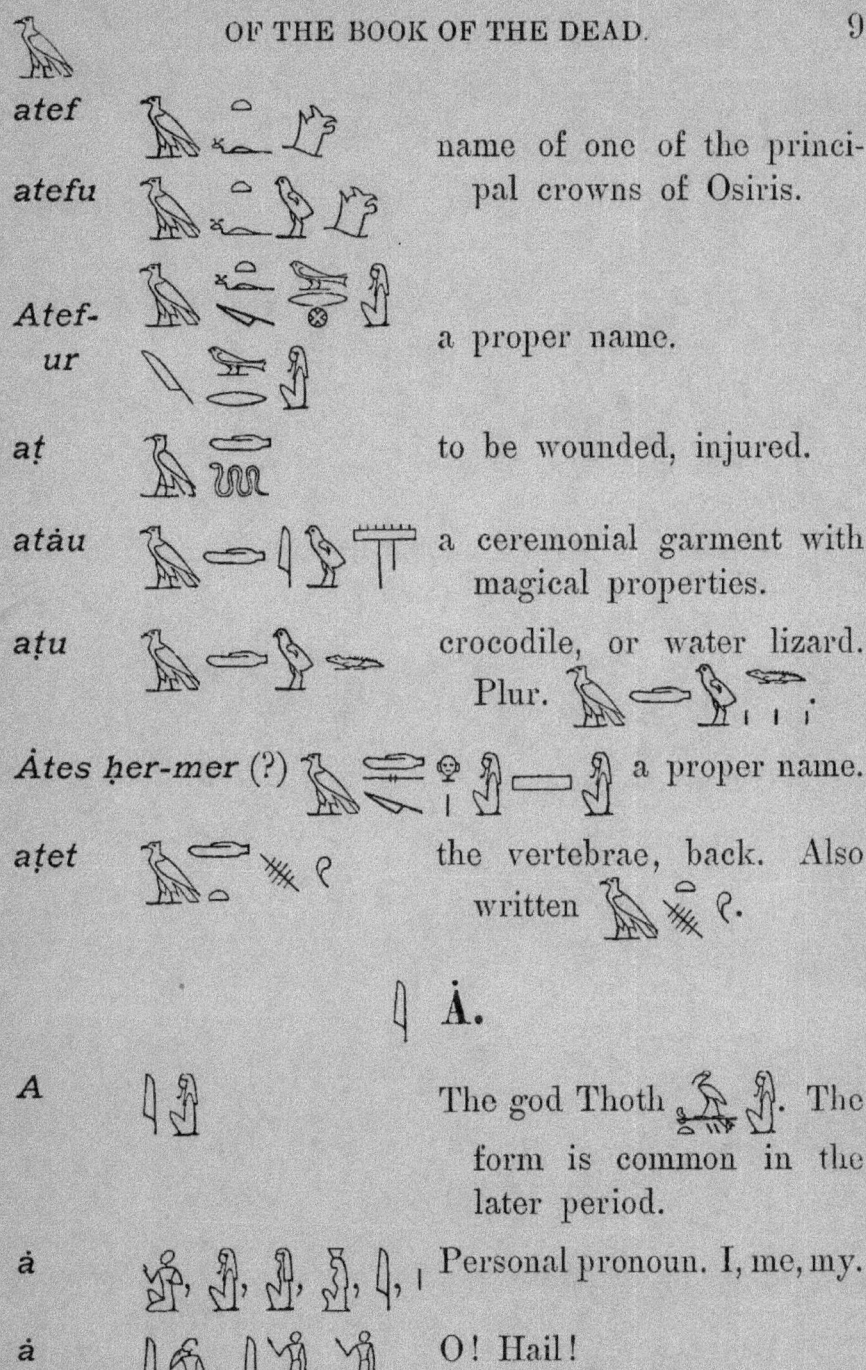

ȧa  boat.

ȧa 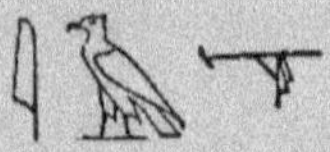 standard, perch for a sacred bird.

ȧaa  plants, flowers, growing crops.

ȧaau  he of the two feathers, plumed one.

ȧaat  standard, perch for a sacred bird.

ȧau
ȧaut  aged one, old age, old man, senior; plur. .

ȧait 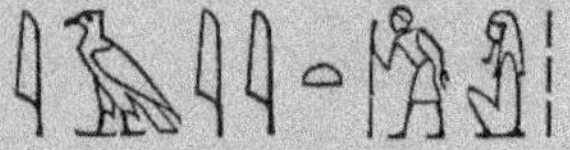 aged gods, divine old men.

ȧau  to praise, to applaud, to ascribe glory to, to acclaim, to rejoice.

ȧaiu  praise, praises, acclamations, rejoicings, glorifyings.

ȧaiu 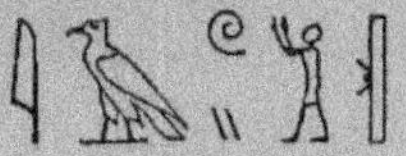

ȧaut  praise, praises, acclamations, rejoicings, glorifyings.

ȧait  tombs, or funerary domains under the charge of priests, sepulchres.

ȧaiti  the gods who preside over the Ȧats; see Chapter CL.

ȧamḥet 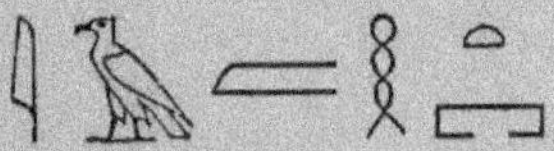 see 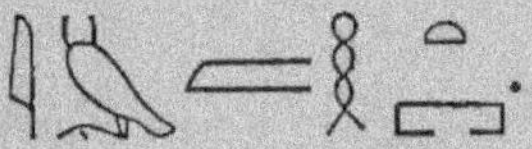.

Ȧaru   a region in the Other World which formed a portion of the abode of the blessed.

ȧarret 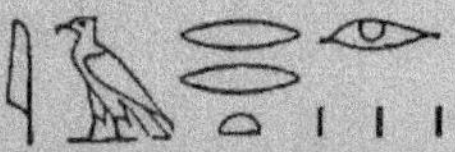 eyes (?).

ȧarret  milk.

ȧaret  vine, vineyard.

Ȧaheṭ  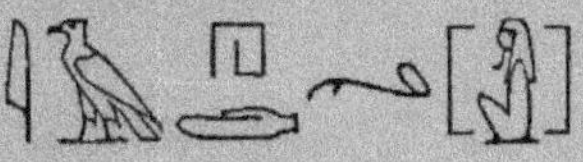 a god whose functions are undefined.

ȧakhu  light, splendour, radiance, brilliance, rays, the god of light or splendour.

Ȧakha-bit  the name of a goddess.

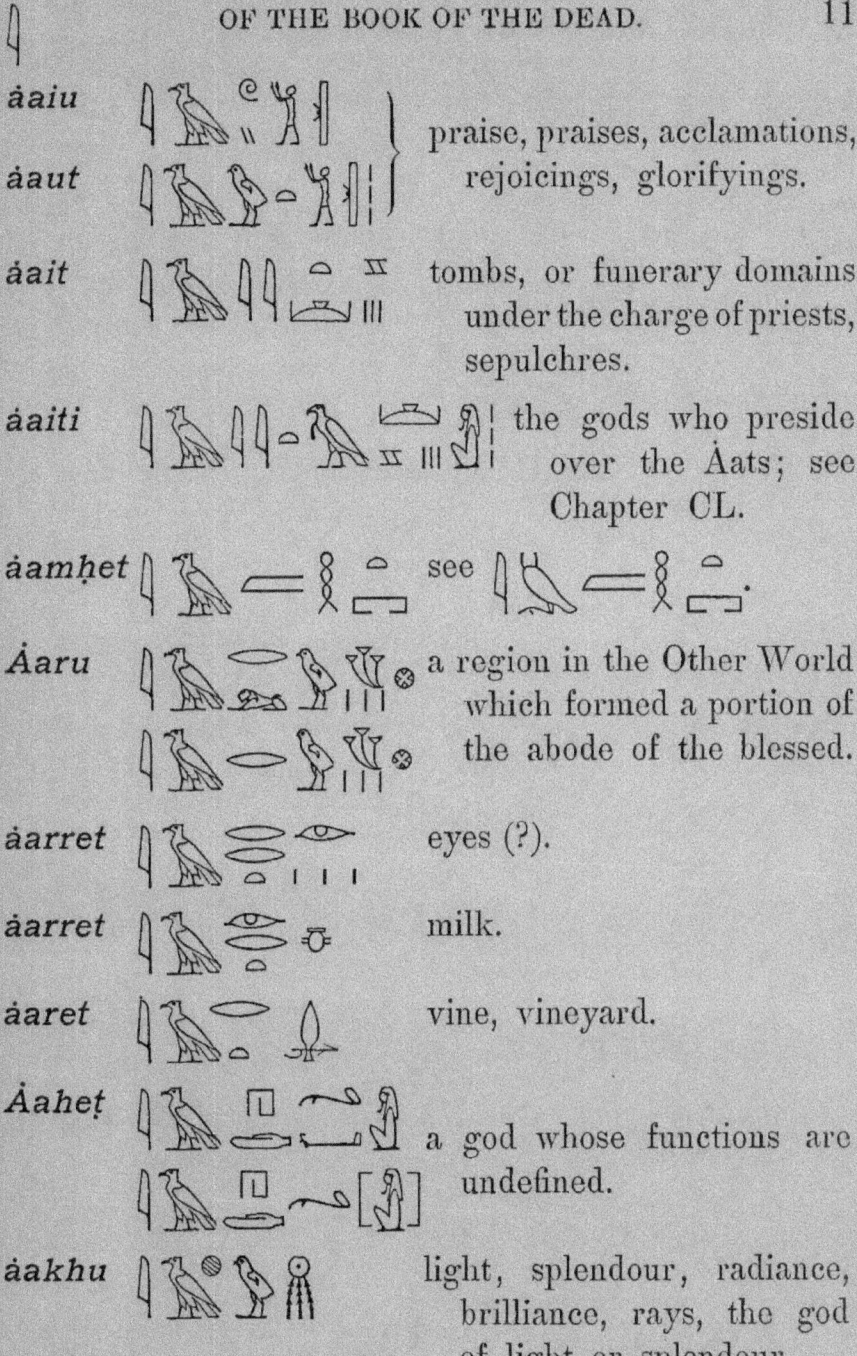

Ȧaku 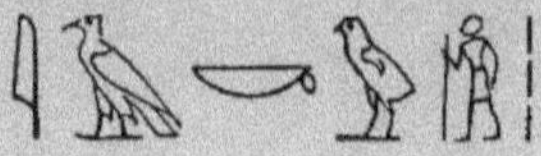 the name of a group of gods or of deified human beings.

ȧakebi 

ȧake-bit 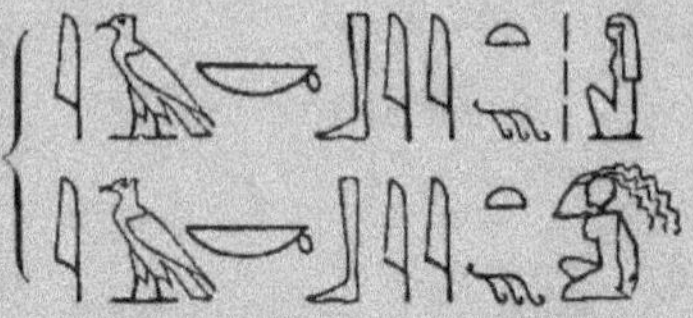

} women who wail and pluck out their hair, professional wailing women or mourners.

ȧakebu  groans, lamentations, mourning, wailings. Another form is 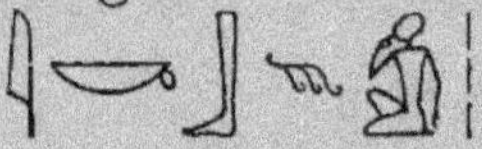.

ȧaqet  flowers, grass, herbs.

Ȧaqeṭ-qeṭ 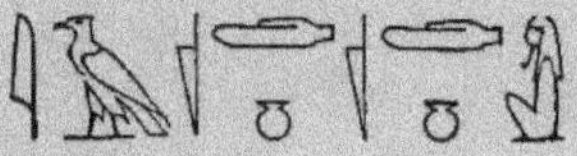 "He who revolves", name of a god.

ȧat  dignity, rank, grade of honour, position, preferment. Plur. .

ȧaat  things possessing a bad or strong smell.

ȧat  an article of dress, part of a girdle (?).

ȧat  the vertebrae, back.

ȧat  to split, to cleave asunder, to break.

ȧat  standard, perch, pedestal.

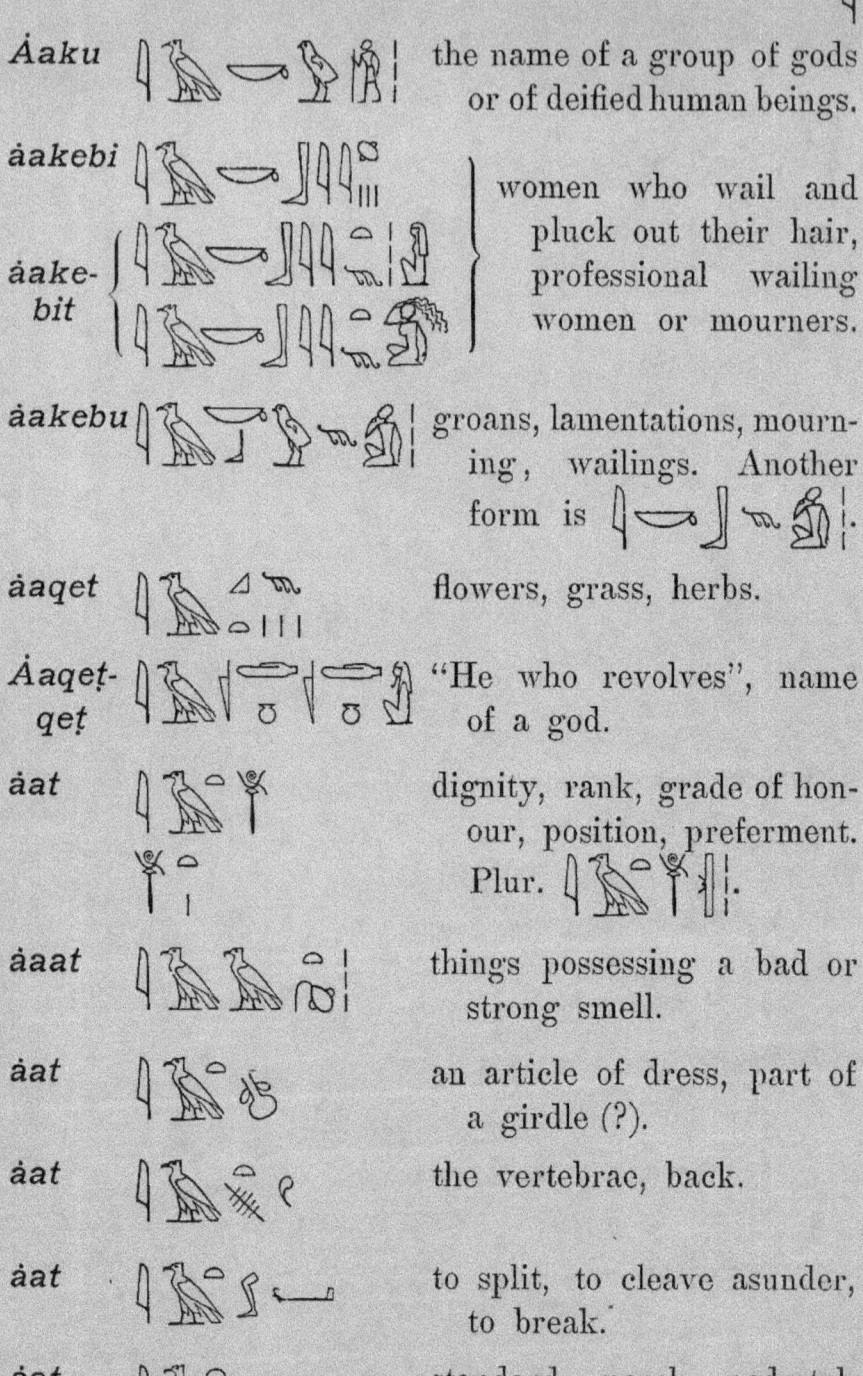

Ȧat ent Ȧp-uat 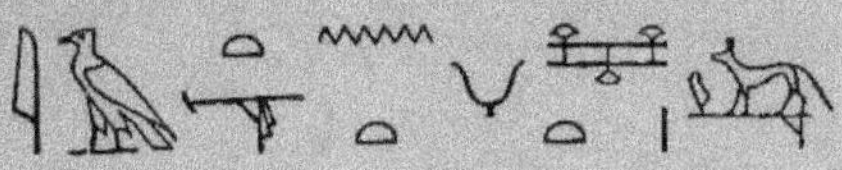 "Standard of Ȧp-uat", name of the lower deck of the magical boat.

ȧat  domain of a god, tomb of a god, funerary district; plur. . The kingdom of Osiris contained 14 Ȧats:—

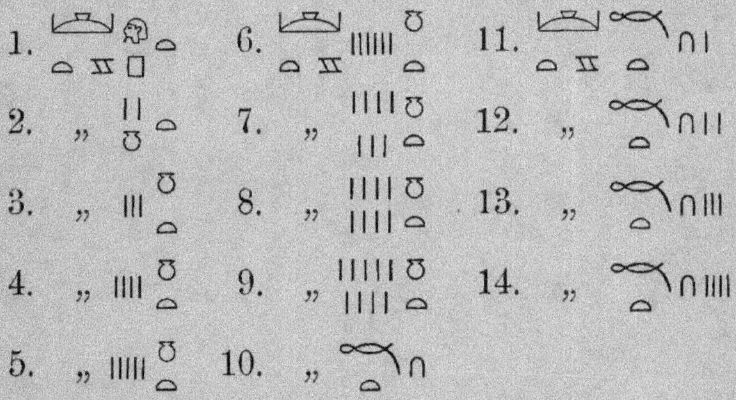

ȧat Ȧmentet  the funerary domain of the West (Ȧmentet).

ȧat khu  the Ȧat of blessed souls.

ȧat en khet 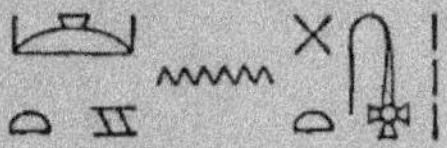 the Ȧat of fire.

ȧati 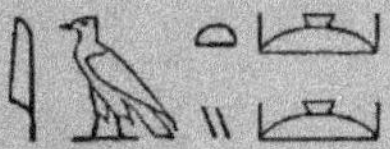 The two Ȧats, *i. e.*, the Ȧat of Horus and the Ȧat of Set, or the two Ȧats of Osiris.

Ȧat-urt 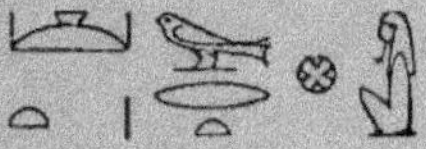 the god of the Great Ȧat.

Åat ent Kher-āḥa The Åat of Kher-āḥa, *i. e.*, the ancient Egyptian city which stood near Old Cairo (Fusṭâṭ).

àatu praise, praisings, adorations.

àati, **àatu** slaughter houses, chambers of tortures; places where the enemies of Rā and Osiris were punished.

àaṭ child, male or female, youth.

àaṭeb flood, storm, rush of water.

àaṭet net for snaring birds or fish, the net in which the Enemy snared souls.

àaṭet rain-storm, dew, moisture.

àaṭti oppression, injury, oppressor.

àā , , to wash, to cleanse, purify, to wash the heart, *i. e.*, to cleanse the heart by taking vengeance.

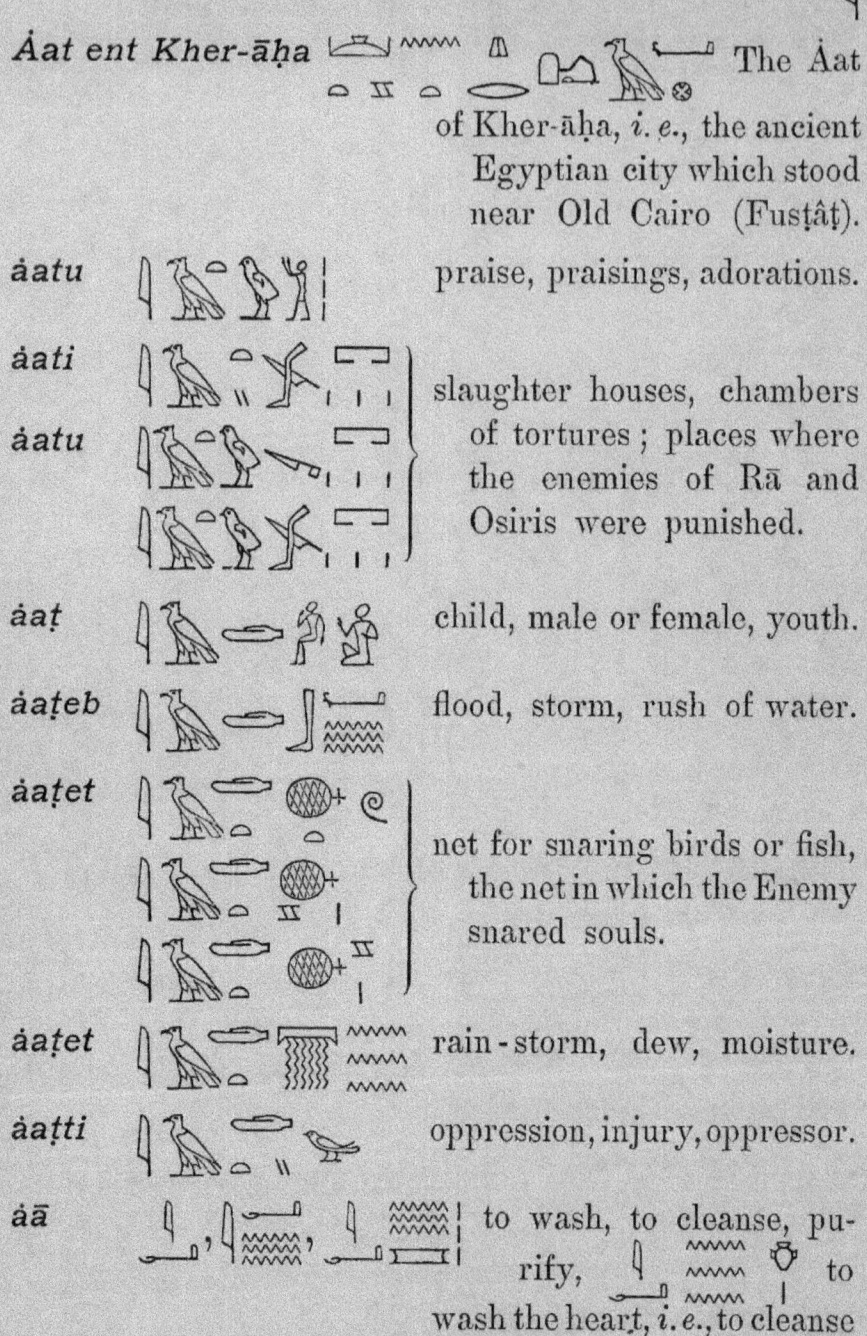

ȧāu  a washing, a cleansing.

ȧā 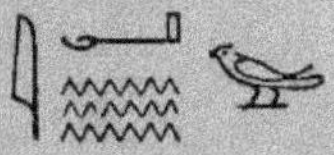 a sinful act.  to sin against the god.

ȧāāu  apes, incarnations of the spirits that praised the rising sun.

ȧāb  to come towards, to meet, to present an offering, one opposite, an offering.

ȧāb 
ȧābet 
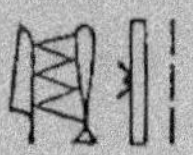
an offering, oblation, ceremonial gift, a vessel of offerings.

ȧāb 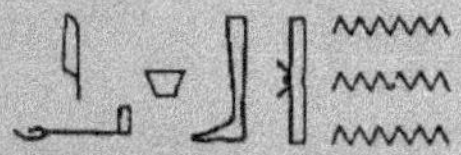 an offering of a libation.

ȧānu 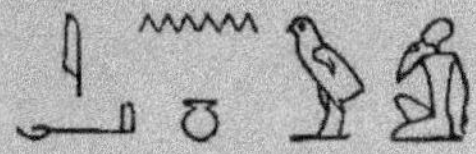 praise, adoration, words of glorification ; plur. 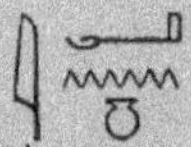 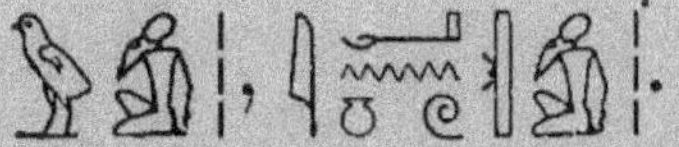.

ȧār 
ȧārt 
ȧārtu 
serpent, snake, cobra. The Greek form is οὐραῖος, uraeus.

ȧārāt 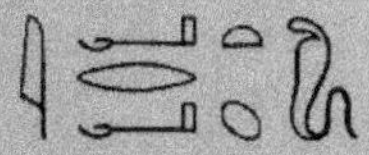 snake goddess; plur. 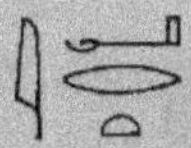 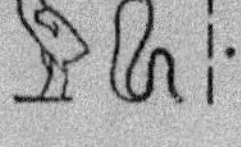.

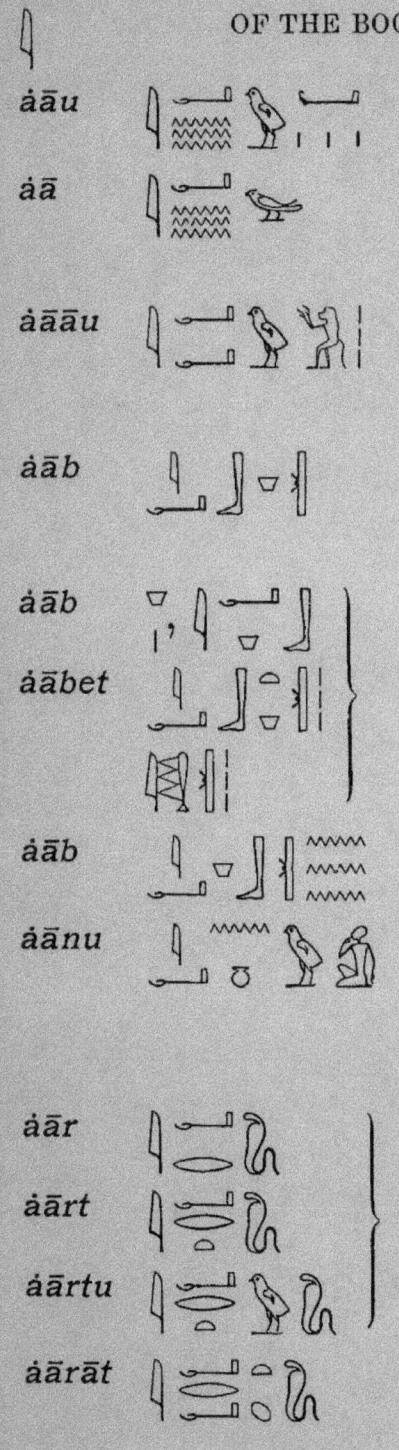

ȧārti 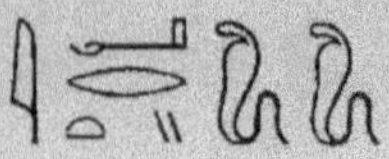 the Two Snake-goddesses, *i. e.*, Isis and Nephthys; the Four Snake-goddesses 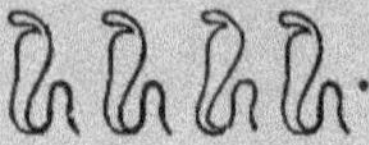.

ȧārtu ānkhu 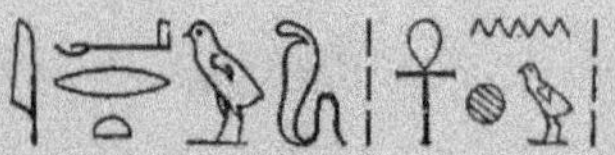 the "living uraei" which lived on the cornice of the shrine of Osiris.

ȧāḥ, ȧāḥu  the moon.

ȧāḥu 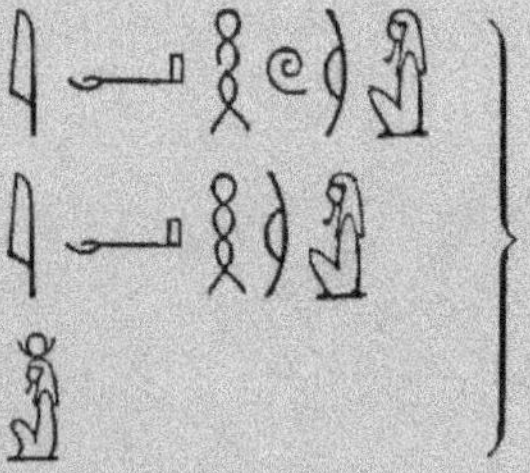 the Moon-god, in later times called Khensu .

ȧātu ent khert  name of a part of the magical boat (Chap. XCIX).

ȧu  praises, rejoicings.

ȧu 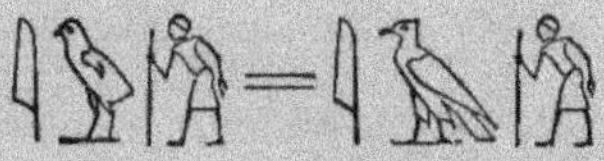 old man.

ȧu  used in later times for  *er* from, to, into, for, at, in, etc.

ȧu  to be, to exist;  I am,  thou art, 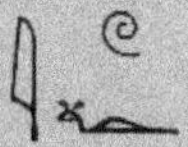 he is,  we are,  she is; as an auxiliary 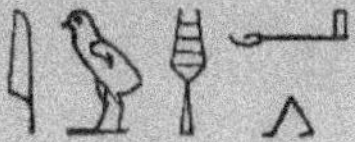, etc., and see *passim.*

àu  to be shipwrecked,

 the shipwrecked man.

àu  offence, sin, crime, iniquity, wickedness, defect, breach of the Law.

àui

àuit

àut

 evil, harm, injury, defects, deceit, to commit wickedness, or sin.

àu  to speak, cry out, utter words.

àu  to conceive a child, be pregnant.

àua  ox (of the Earth-god Seb).

àuai  roof of a building.

àuàu  dogs, jackals.

Àuu-ba  a proper name.

ȧuāu		the living body.
ȧuā		flesh and bone, joint of meat, haunch of an animal, carcase.
ȧuāu		
ȧuā	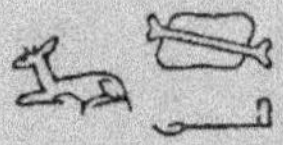	to be flesh and bone of some one, to be the heir, inheritance, the divine Heir.
ȧuāā	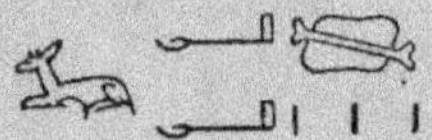	
ȧuāu		
ȧuāu	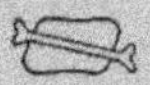	heir.

ȧuāt	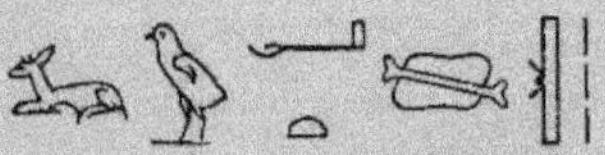	heirship, inheritance.

ȧuāu		heirs, kinsfolk, people of one's own flesh and blood.
ȧuiu		those who lacerate or cut.

àuur  to conceive, conception, pregnant.

àuurt  a pregnant goddess.

 heir.

àuf  flesh, limbs, members.

Àuf-ānkh  a proper name.

àumes  false or deceitful speech, exaggeration in speech, lies.

àun  colour, skin, hair.

àuna  certainly, assuredly.

àunt  a garment, clothed, dressed.

Àurâu-àaqer-sa-ànqrebathi 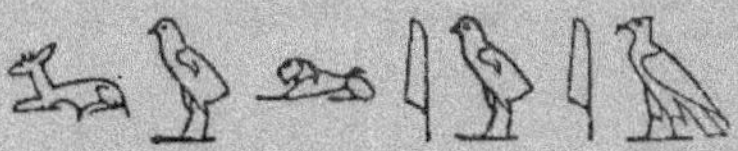

 a proper name.

àuhet  to utter words.

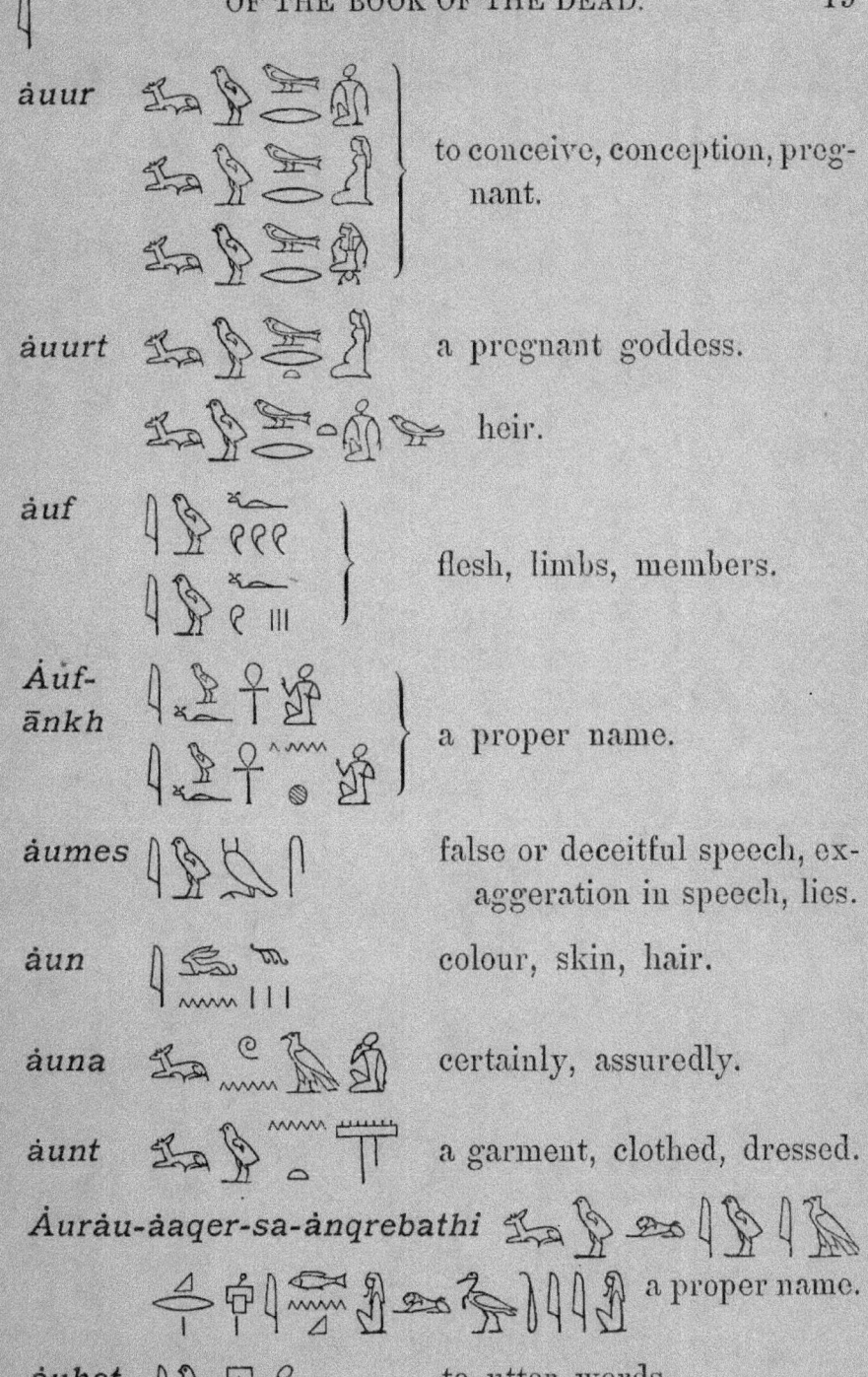

àuheṭ name of a god or divine being.

àuḥ to be submerged, sprinkled. steeped in something.

àukhemu a group of gods, stars.

àukhemu urṭu stars which never rest.

àukhemu seku circumpolar stars which never set.

àukhemu Pen-ḥeseb (?) stars of the god Pen-ḥeseb.

àukhekh night, evening, darkness.

àusu scales, balance.

Àuḳer
Àuḳert the name of the Other World of Heliopolis (Ànnu).

Áuḳeru 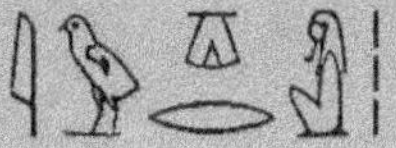 the gods of the Heliopolitan Other World.

Áuḳert 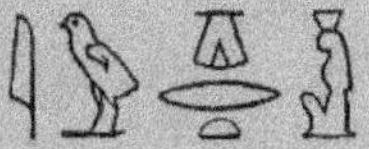 the goddess of Áuḳert.

Áuḳert-khentet-ȧst-s 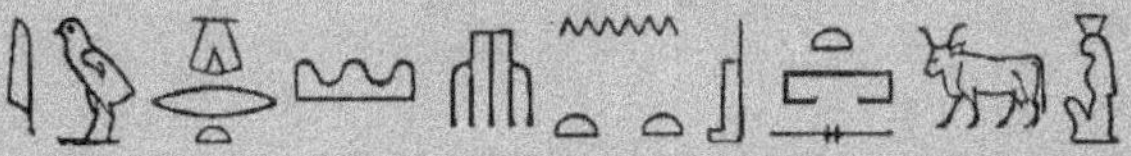 name of one of the seven sacred cows.

ȧuṭ  to travel.

ȧu-t  thou art.

ȧu-ten 

ȧu-then  ye are.

ȧuti  fiends, enemies, foes.

ȧb  desire, wish.

ȧb  pegs, stakes.

ȧb  thirst.

ȧb 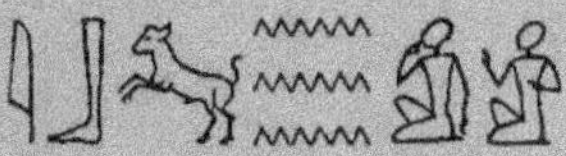 thirsty man.

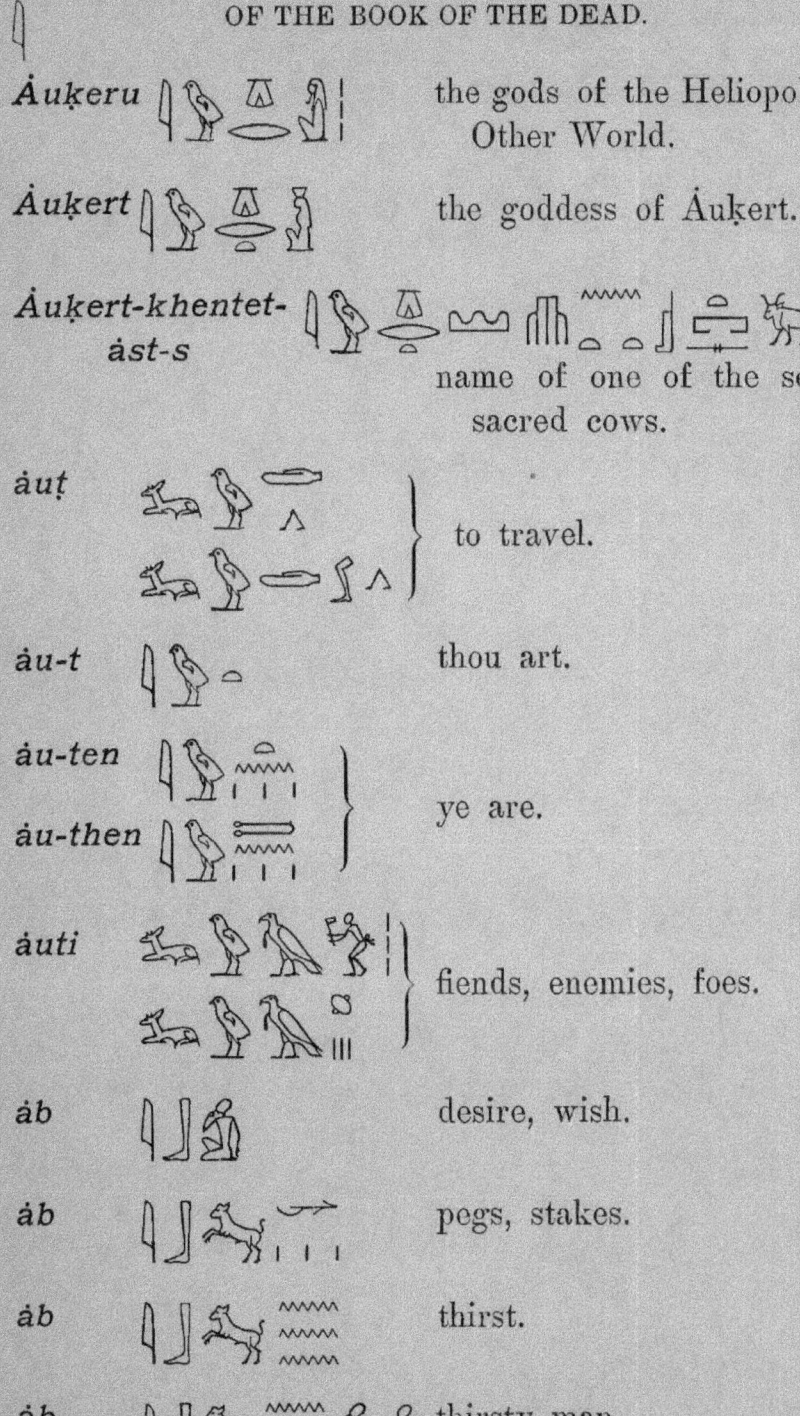

Ȧb 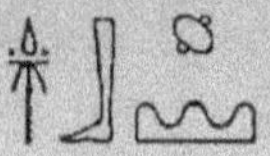 = Abtu 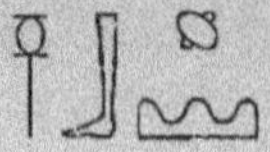 Elephantine.

ȧb  =  name of a fish.

ȧb 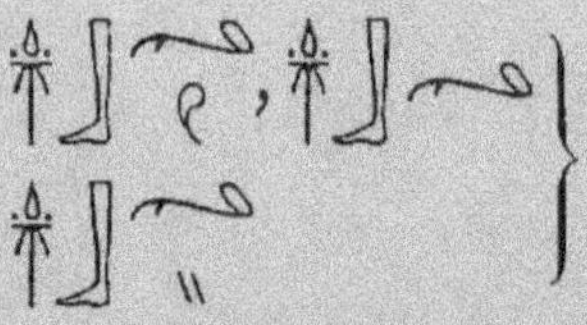 left side.

ȧb 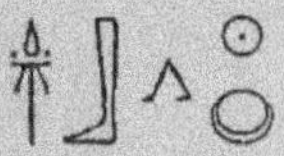 cessation.

ȧb 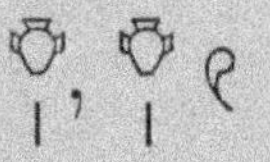 the physical heart, will, wish, love, desire; plur. 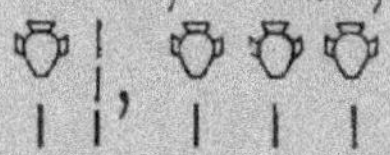

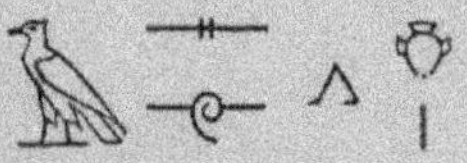 to judge hastily.

 to do as one pleases.

 "great of heart", bold, brave, arrogant, boastful.

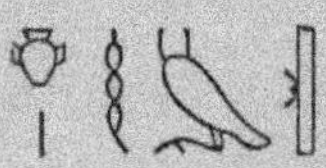 of joyful heart.

 to eat the heart, *i. e.*, to lose the temper, be sorry.

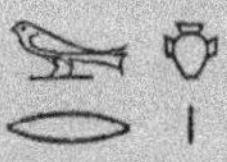 valiant.

 be brave.

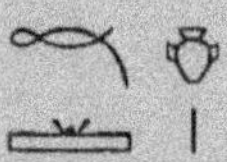 to fill the heart, to satisfy, be satisfied.

 within.

	 with 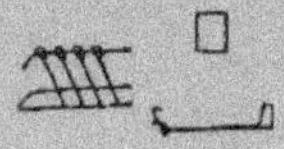	heart's desire.
	 with 	prompting of the heart, desire.
	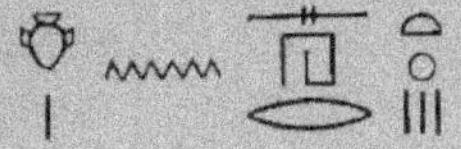	the amulet of the carnelian heart.
àba		heart-soul.
àbu		drink.
àbu		the desired one.
Àbu-ur		a proper name.
àbu	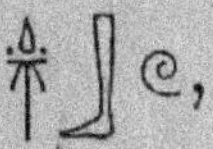, or 	to stop, to cease.
		cessation.
àbui		left side.
àbi	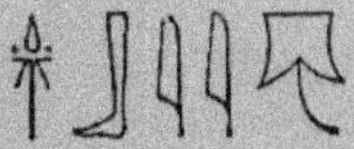	panther or leopard skin.
àbit	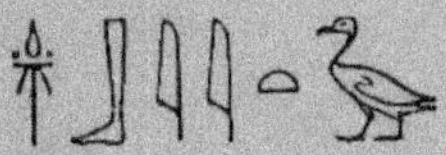	the praying mantis.
àber	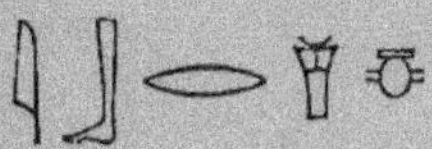	a kind of unguent.
àbḥu	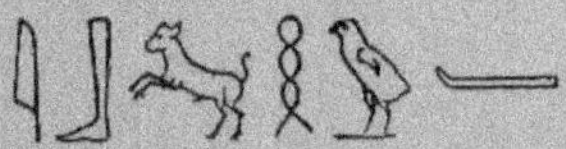	tooth. Plur.  

àbekh 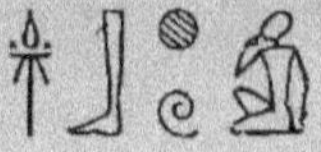 to penetrate, to make a way through.

àbsit 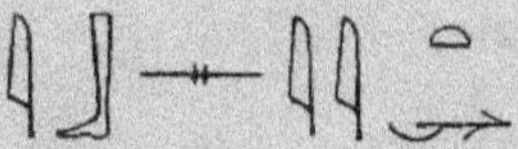 hull of a boat.

Àb-ka
Abt-ka  a proper name.

àbku  grief, to grieve, to weep.

àbt  middle hall, or chamber, of a house.

àbt 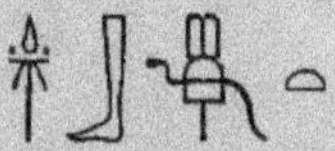 coffer.

àbt  thirst.

àbt  left hand side, the east.

àbt
àbti 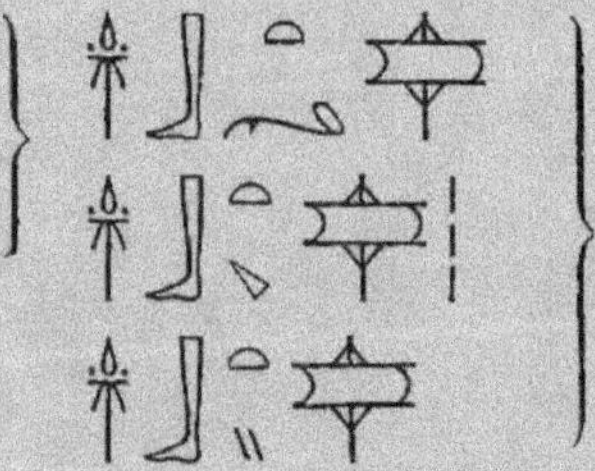 east wind.

àbt
àbti 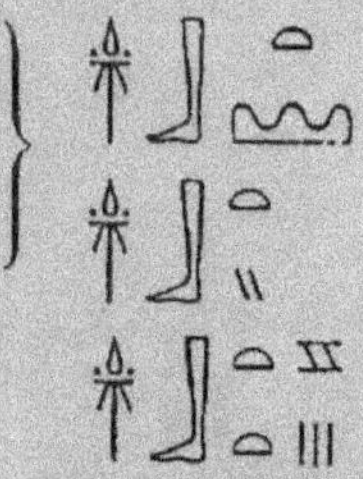 eastern country, or region. 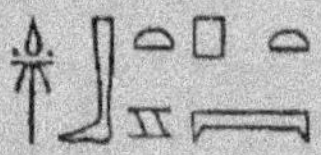 eastern sky, east of heaven;  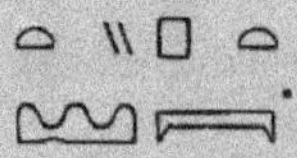.

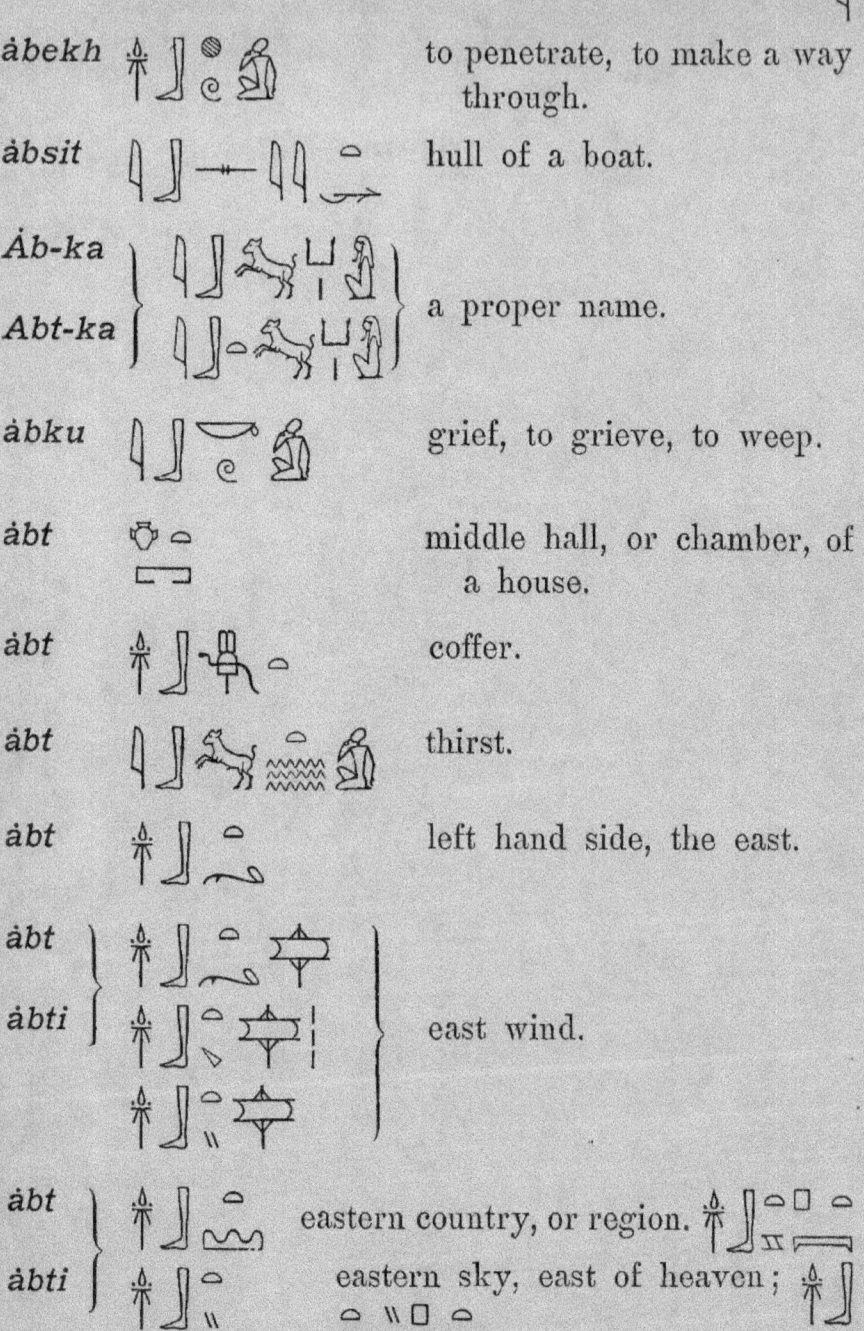

àbti 

àbtet (*àbti*) 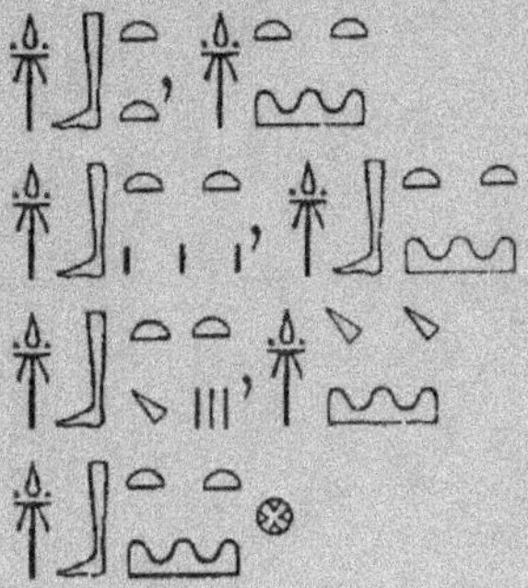 east, eastern country, or region.

àbtet 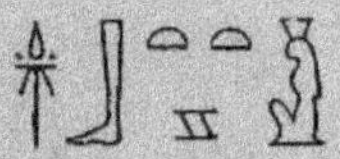 goddess of the east.

àbtiu  gods of the east, eastern deities.

àbt 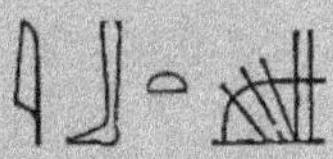 net.

àbtu  slaughter, slaughterings.

Àbṭ 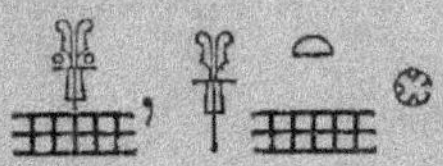 the nome of Abydos.

Àbt 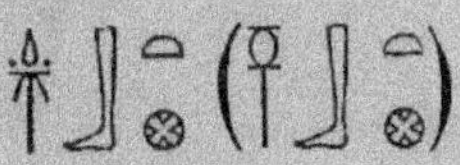 the city of Abydos.

Àbṭu 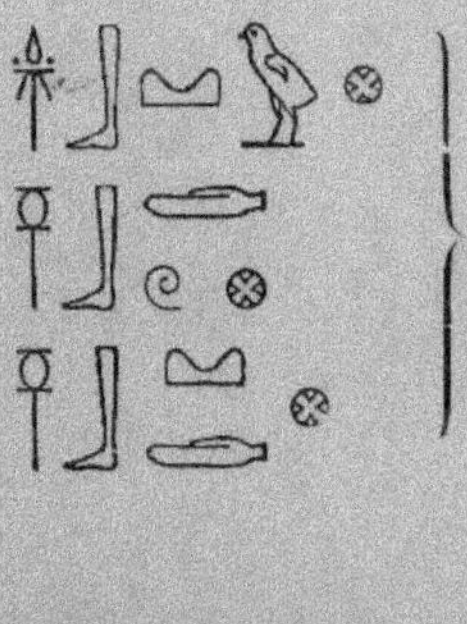 the city of Abydos.

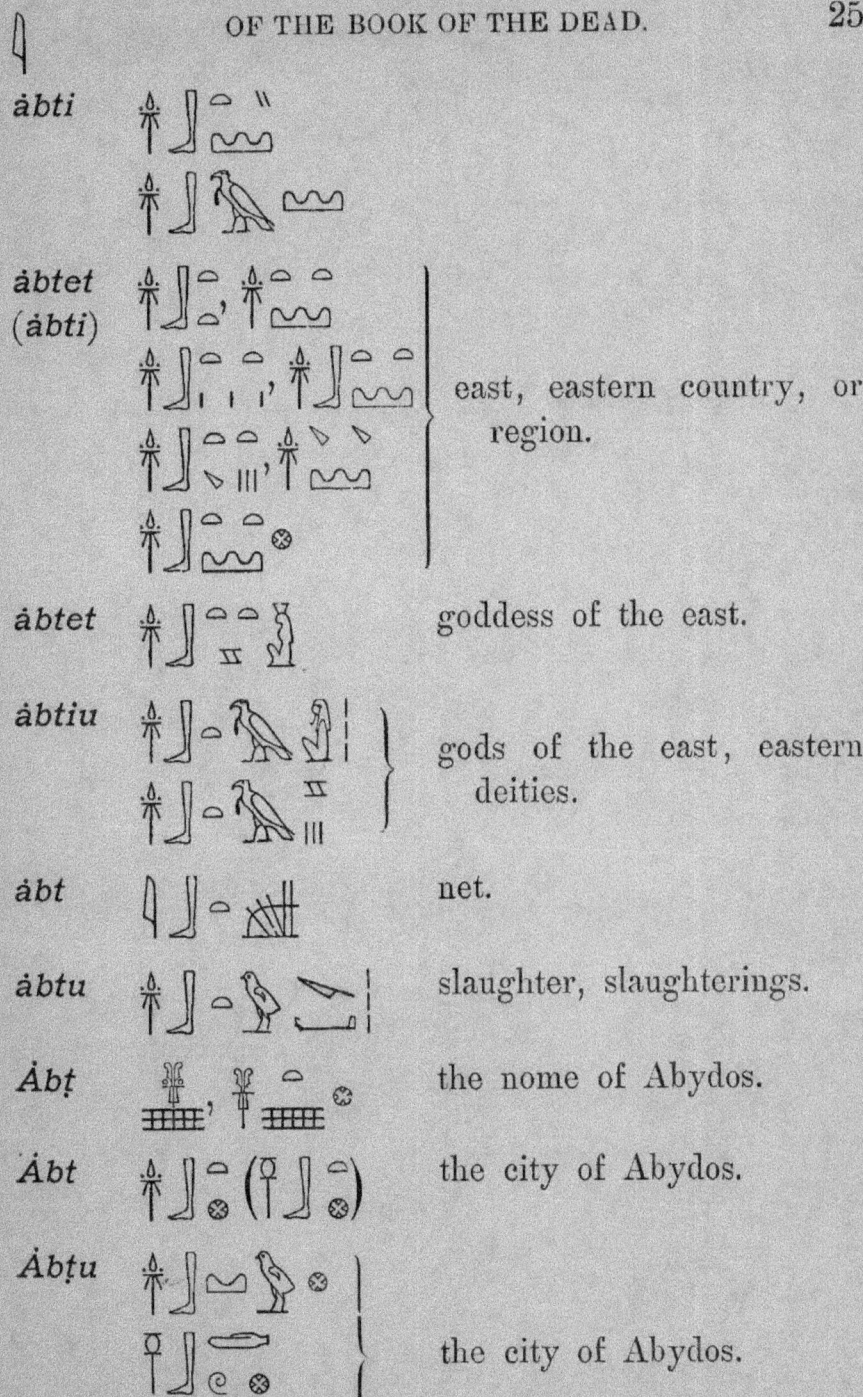

Àbṭu 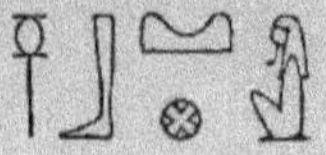 the city god of Abydos.

àbeṭ 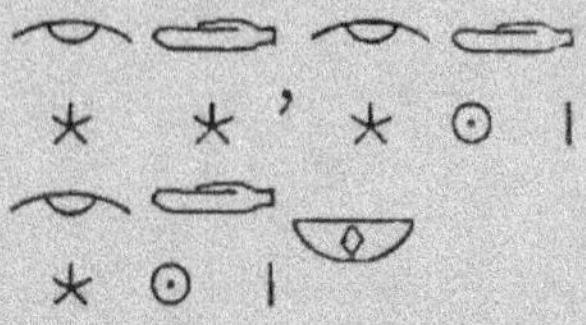 the month of thirty days, plur. ; the monthly festival, plur. .

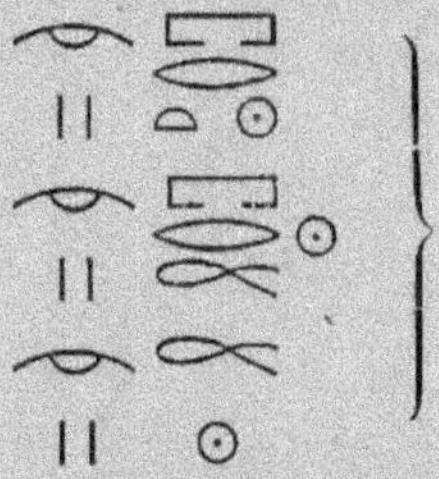 the second month of the season Pert, the last day of the second month of this season.

àbṭ 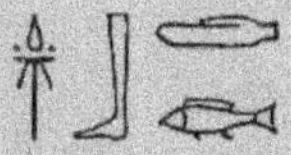

àbṭu  a mythological fish which swam before the Boat of Rā; its companion was the *ànt* fish.

àp  to count up, to reckon, to consider, a reckoning, a counting, 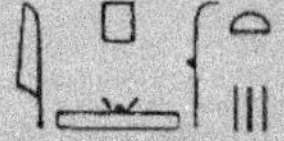 reckoner of years,  counter,  numbered, counted.

àppet  reckoning, account.

àp 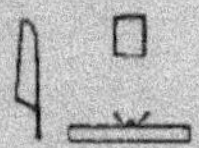 to judge, to be judged, to decree, be decreed, judgment.  great judgment.

àp — judge of dooms.

judged. — judge.

àp, *àpu* — to judge, to dispute or argue with someone, to award, be awarded, to bring a message, to announce tidings. — a judge of words or affairs, — *àp maāt* righteous judge.

àpt — decree, judgment, sentence of doom.

àput mitu — sentence of death.

àp, *àpu*, *àpi*, *àpt* — to open. — open! — opened.

àp re, *àpu re*, *àpt re* — the ceremony of "opening the mouth".

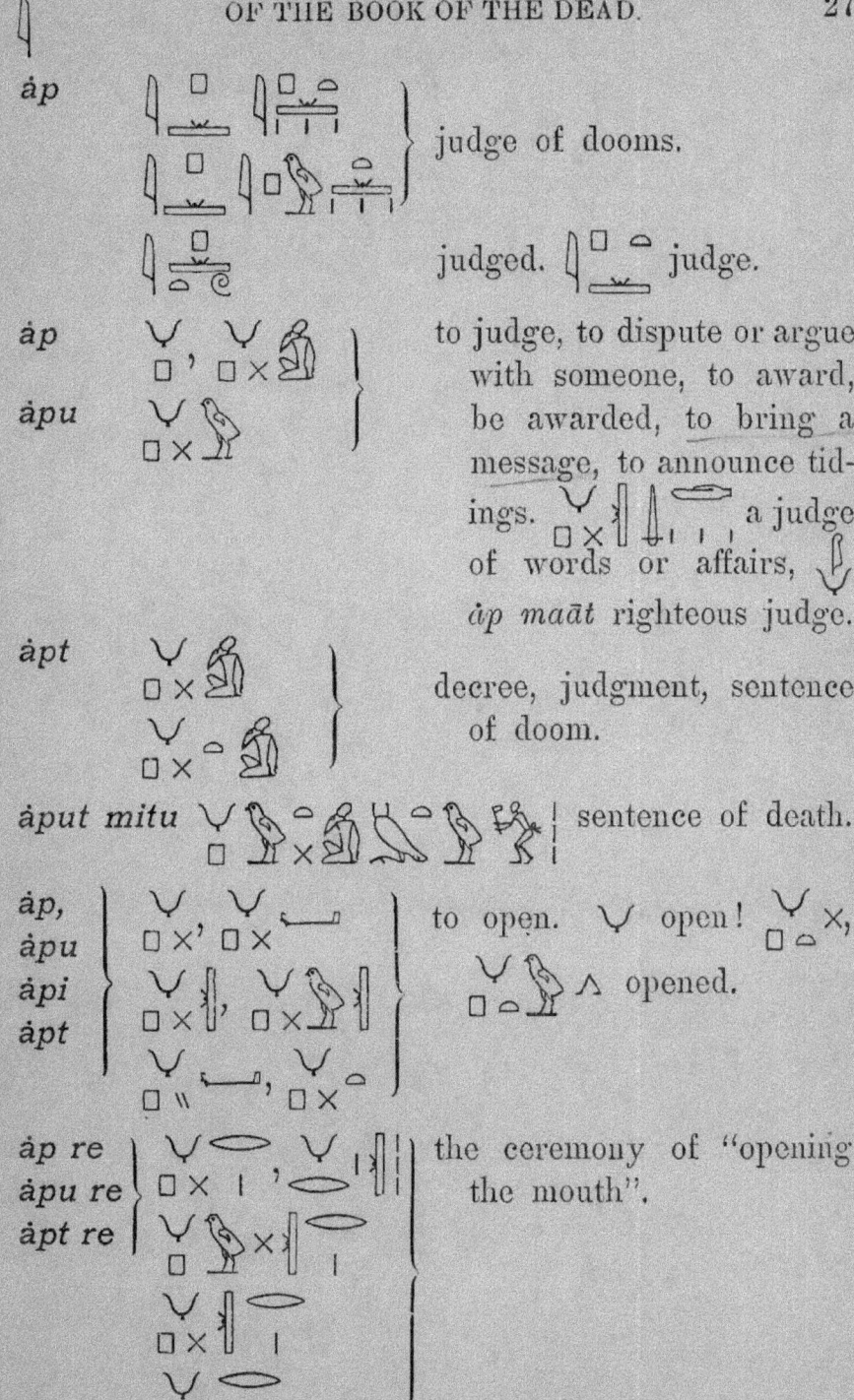

Ȧp-uat
Ȧp-uati
Ȧp-uatu — "Opener of the roads", a name of a wolf-god who was supposed to conduct the deceased over the roads which lead to the Sekhet Ȧaru, or Elysian Fields. Ȧp-uat was a companion of the jackal-god Ȧnpu, with whom he is sometimes confounded.

Ȧp-uat meḥt sekhem pet The god Ȧp-uat of the north as guide to the roads of heaven.

Ȧp-uat resu sekhem taui The god Ȧp-uat of the south as guide to the roads of earth.

Ȧp-ur "great opener", name of a god.

ȧp ḥer except. except thyself.

Ȧpu A city, the Panopolis of the Greeks, the Akhmîm of the Arabs.

ȧpu
ȧpiu — these, these gods, these who dwell in.

ȧpiu — openers, those who make a way.

ȧputi — messenger, envoy, ambassador; plur.

two envoys.

ȧppiu — judges.

ȧpen — (see) these. these gods who dwell in.

Ȧpsi — a name or title of a god.

ȧpt — sacred chamber of a temple, private apartments of a house, sacred or profane *ḥarîm*.

ȧpt — stick, staff, sceptre.

ȧpt ȧst — name of a portion of Eastern Thebes, Karnak (?).

ȧpt — message, envoy.

ȧpt — messengers.

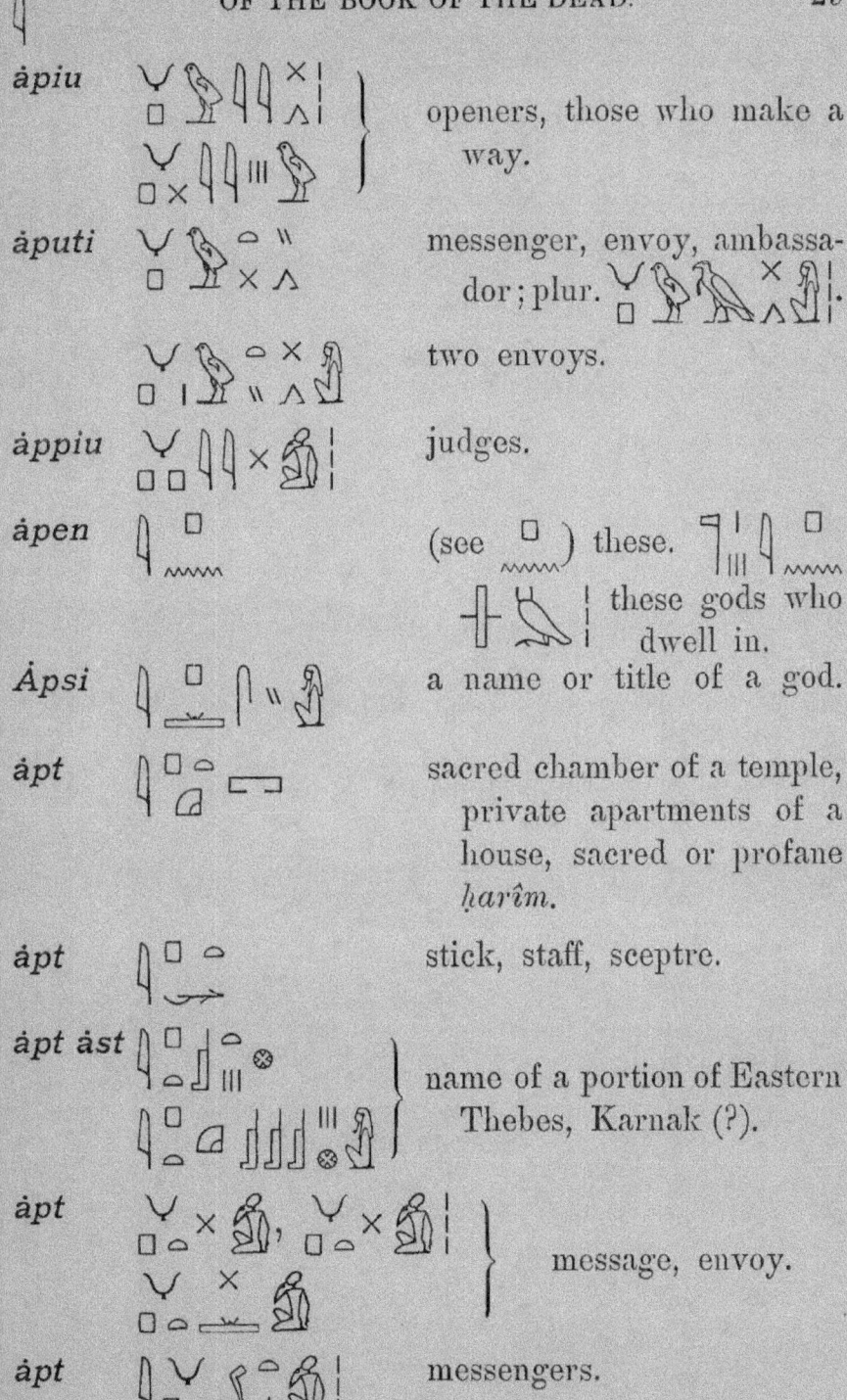

ȧpt 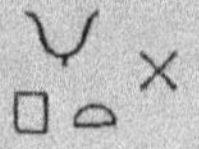 brow, forehead, top of the head (?).

 the hottest part of the fire.

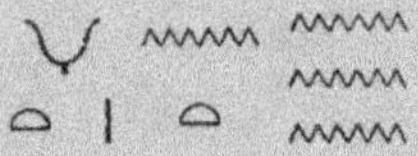 top, surface (?) of the waters.

 brow of the god Qaḥu.

ȧptu 
ȧpten 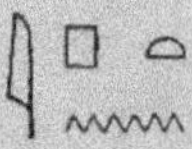 } these.

Ȧp-shāṭ-taui 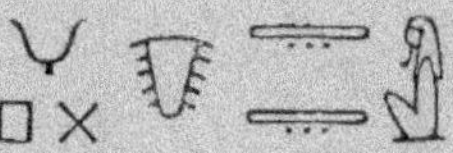 a name of Osiris.

ȧf, afu 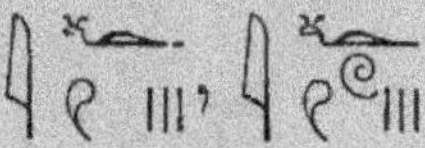 flesh, limbs, members.

ȧfṭ  to rest, to sit down.

ȧfṭu 
ȧfṭet  } four.

ȧfṭi  a kind of cloth or garment.

ȧm  in, into, inside.

ȧm (?)  a standard.

ȧm  a boat.

ȧm  to arrive in safety.

ȧm	flax, a kind of cloth.
ȧm	not, do not.
ȧm / *ȧmu*	to eat, to consume, swallow up, devour.
ȧmi	eating, eater; plur.
ȧmti	eater.
ȧm baiu	eater of heart-souls.
ȧm besku	"Eater of Livers", or intestines.
ȧm sāḥu	"Eater of mummies".
ȧm snef	"Eater of Blood"; one of the Forty-two Judges in the Hall of Osiris.
ȧm (un)	to eat, to consume.
ȧm	bread-cakes, food.
	drink.

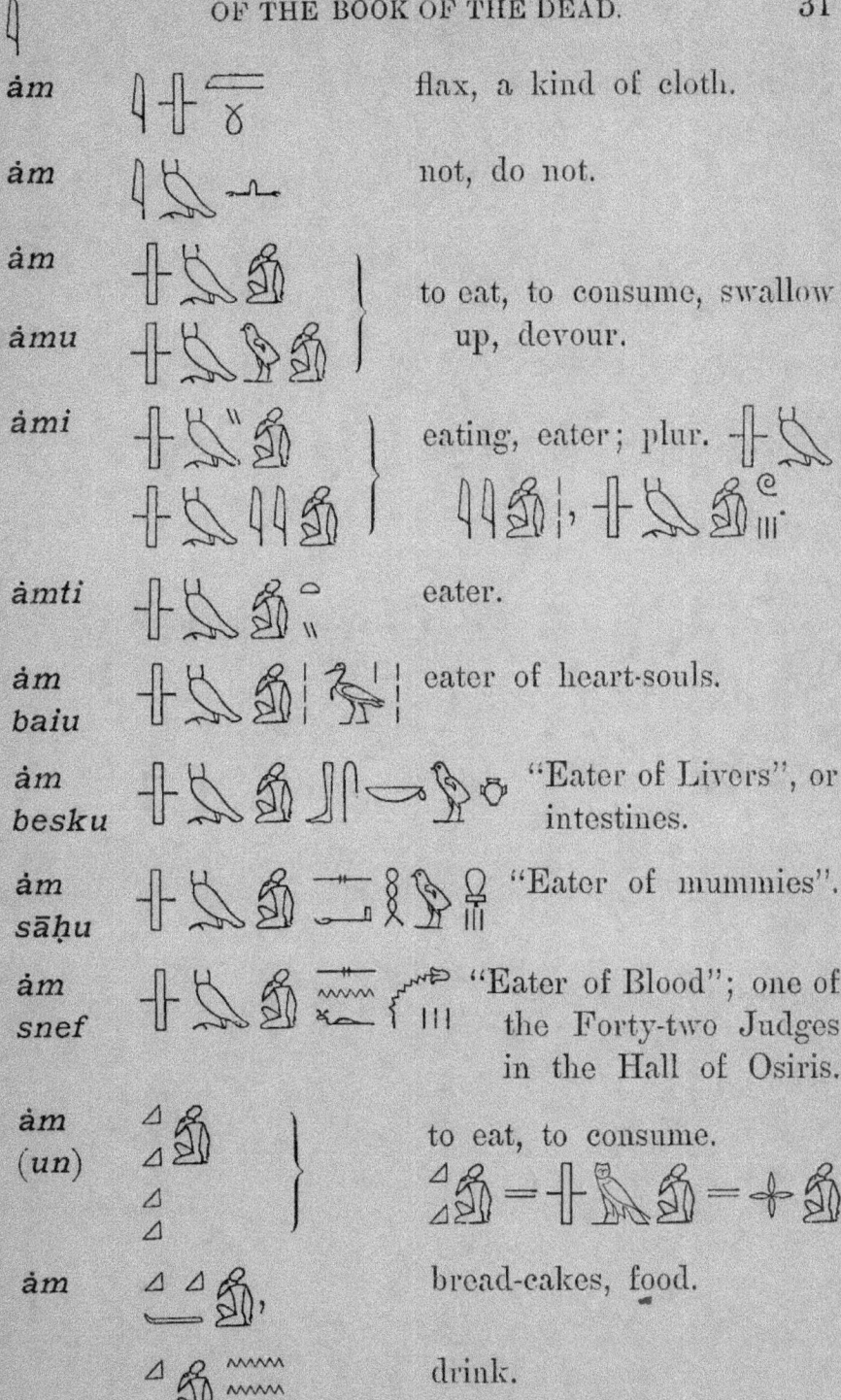

Am-ḥauat-ent-pehui-f  "Eater of the offal of his body"; the name of the doorkeeper of the Third Ārit.

ȧmt, *ȧmtu* 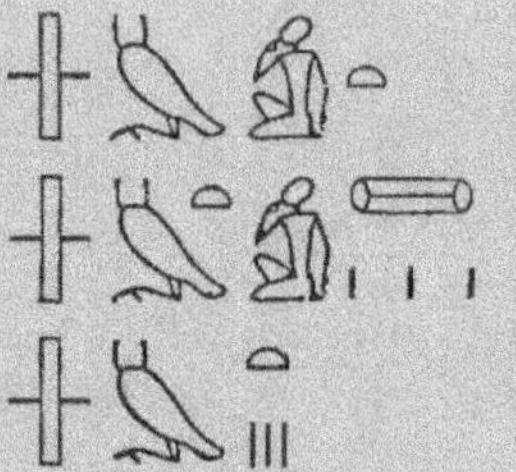 food, something fit or used for food.

ȧm, *ȧmt* 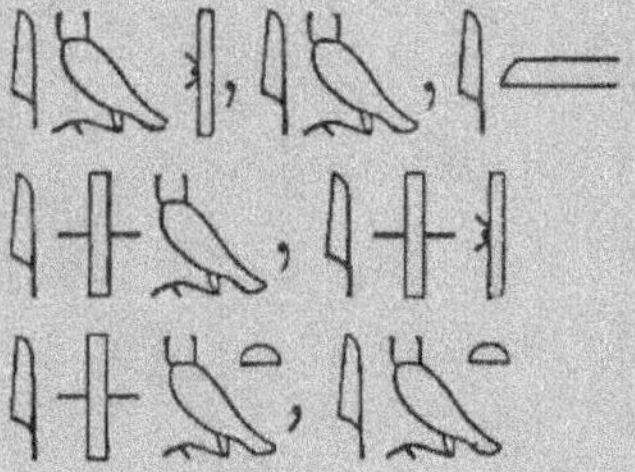 in, among, with, through, upon, by, around, there, therein.  in it (or him),  in it (or her),  by the back of.

ȧm, *ȧmt* 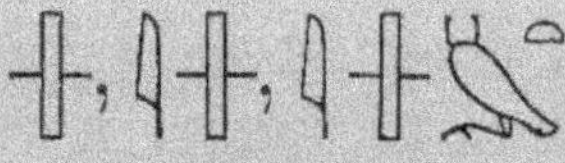 dweller in.

ȧmi 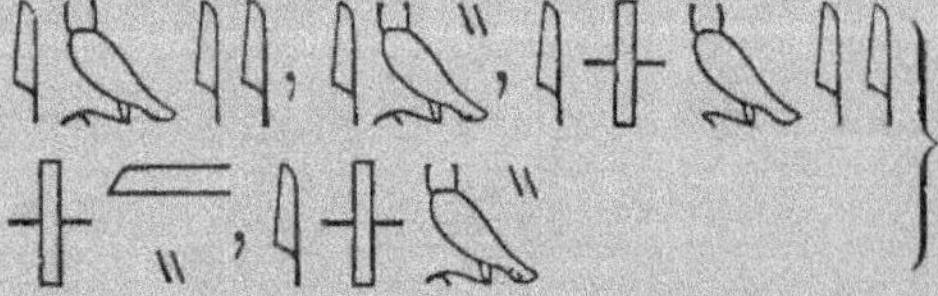 he who is in, dweller in; plur. , 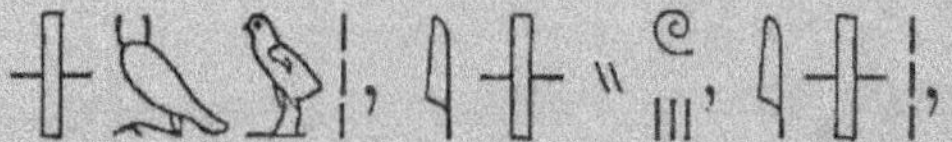  those who are in.

àm-ā

àm àst-ā 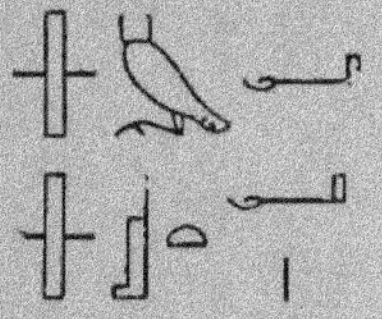 a title of a priest or ministrant.

àm-uḥet (?) ***neb ta Tchesert*** 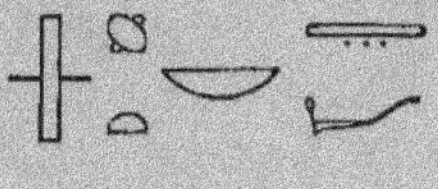 "he who is in the embalmment chamber, Lord of Ta-tchesert", a title of Anubis, the divine physician and embalmer.

àmi-at  one in, or at, the supreme moment.

àmi àb  he who is in the heart. 

àm-àten-f  he who is in his disk, *i. e.*, Rā.

àmi-uàa-f  he who is in his Boat, *i. e.*, Rā.

àmi mu  he who is in the water, *i. e.*, Sebek.

àmi unnut-f  he who is in his hour.

Àmi-meḥen-f

àmi-meḥent-f 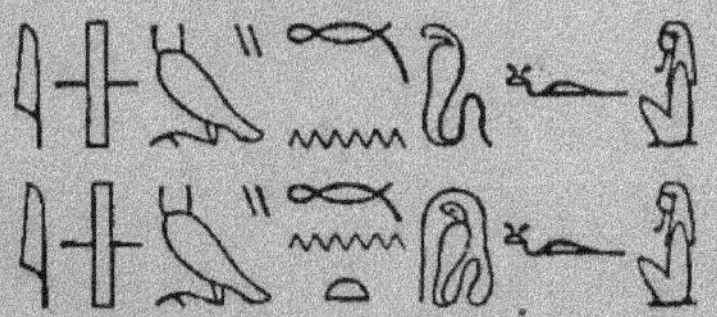 he who is in his Meḥen serpent, *i. e.*, Rā, or Àf; plur. .

àmi-ha-f  he who is in his time, or place.

àmi-hem-f  he who is in his fiery serpent, *i. e.*, Rā.

àmi-khet  he who is in his fiery disk.

àm-khet 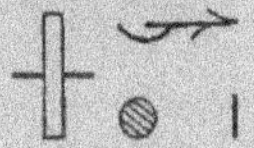

àmi-khet 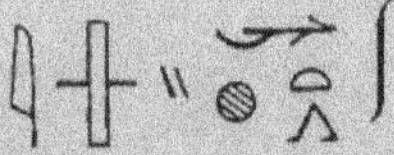 he who is in the following of.

àmi-suḥt 

àm-suḥt  he who is in his egg, *i. e.*, Rā.

àmi-mer-nesert (?) 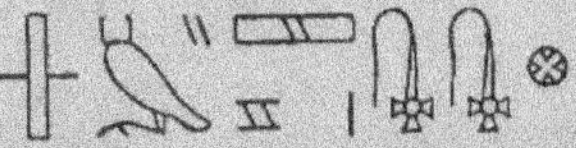 he who is in his fiery Lake, *i. e.*, Rā.

àmi-karà-f  he who is in his shrine, *i. e.*, Rā or Osiris.

àmi-ṭebtu  he who is in his coffin, *i. e.*, Osiris.

àmi-tchetta 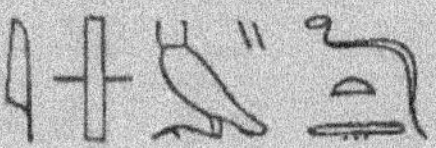 he who dwelleth in eternity.

àmiu-àat-sen  the gods in their domains.

àmiu Àbṭu  those in Abydos.

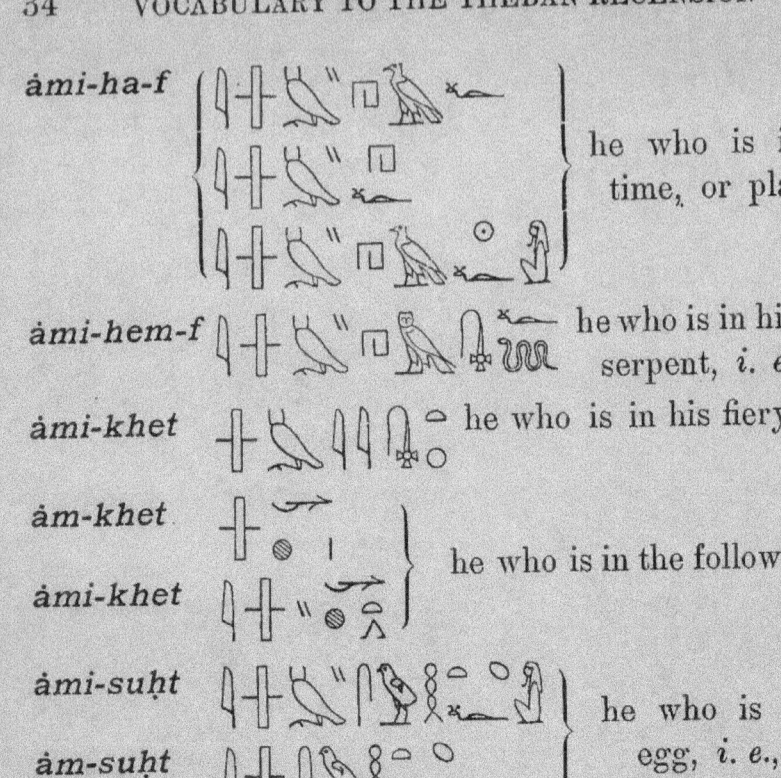

ȧmiu-Ȧnu  the gods in Ȧnu (Heliopolis).

ȧmiu-ȧḥ-ur 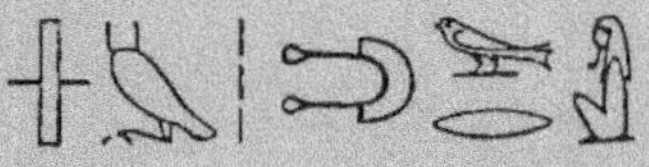 those in the Great Field.

ȧmiu-āāui  those in the hands.

ȧmiu-baḥ  the gods who are in the presence.

ȧmiu-beḳa 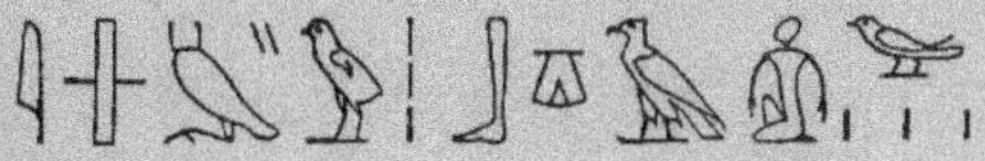 those who are in a weak state.

ȧmiu em-baḥ  the gods who are in the presence.

ȧmiu-hru-sen 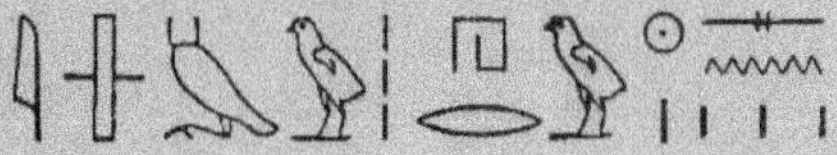 those who are in their days.

ȧmiu-Nekhen  those who dwell in Nekhen.

ȧmiu Kher-neter  those who are in the Other World.

ȧmiu Neṭet  those who dwell in the city of Neṭet.

ȧmiu khet, *ȧmiu khet*  those who are in the following of.

ȧmiu khuti  those who are in the two horizons.

àmiu sāḥu — those who are in their mummied forms.

àmiu-sut-sen — those who are in their hair.

àmiu seḥu-sen — those who are in their halls.

àmiu-shems, *àmiu-shemsu* — those who are in the following of.

àmiu-karà-sen — those who are in their shrines.

àmiu-ta — those who are in the earth.

àmtu, *àmth*, *àmith*, *àmithu* — among, between; Chap. CIV. 1, CIV. 1.

àmt — in

àm àb — what is in the heart, thought? prayer?

àm khent — title of a priest.

àma  tree.

àmam  date-palm.

àmakh 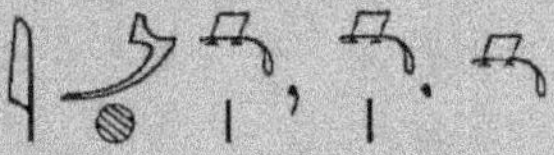 serf, servant, one who venerates another, or is venerated, a beatified being, .

àmakhi 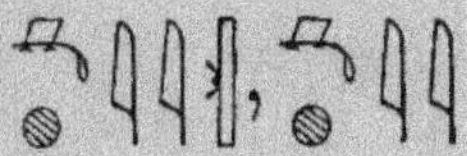 partic. masc.  partic. fem.; plur. , 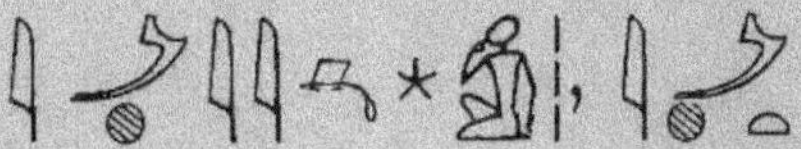 . A late form is .

àmu  divine beings.

àmu  trees, plants.

àmu  flames, fire.

 gods of fire.

àmu  colour, pigment.

Àm-urt  a proper name.

àmi shrine, chamber.

àmuhettu, *àmihettut* apes, incarnations of the spirits of the dawn.

àmuti image, figure.

àmem palm-tree.

àmem to putrefy.

àmem skin, hide.

àmmā grant, give, let there be, prithee, give I pray, open I pray, give water and air, give thy hand, let me pass, give (*i. e.*, incline) thy face.

àmmu beams, rays of light, splendour.

ȧmmu  boats.

ȧmmeḥet  a portion of the Other World of Seker.

ȧmm ḳeḥu 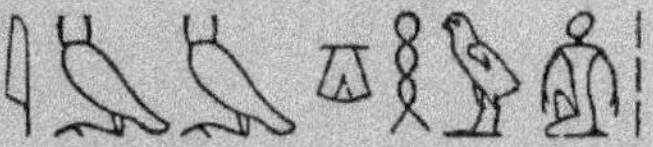 those who are in a state of weakness.

Ȧmen 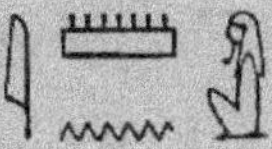 a god of generation and conception, who symbolized the invisible creative forces of Nature.

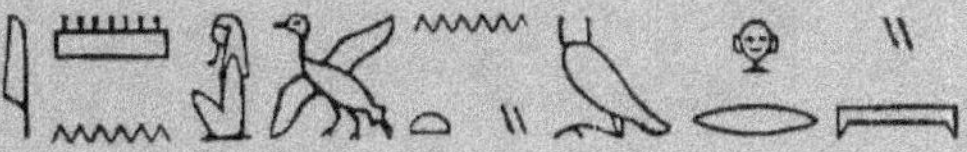 "Ȧmen which art in heaven".

 "Ȧmen the prolific Bull".

Ȧmen-nathk-ruthi-Ȧmen  A Sûdânî form of Ȧmen.

Ȧmen-nau-ȧn-ka-entek-Sharu  A Sûdânî form of Ȧmen.

Ȧmen-Rā 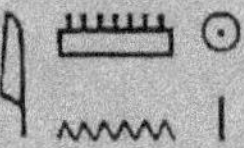 the great god of Thebes, chief element in the triad Ȧmen-Rā, Mut and Khensu.

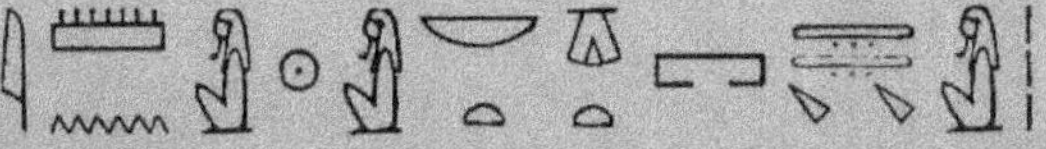 "Ȧmen - Rā, Lord of the throne of the Two Lands".

"King of the South and North, Ȧmen-Rā, king of the gods".

Ȧmen-Rā Ḥeru-khuti Ȧmen-Rā Harmachis.

Ȧmen-ruti Ȧmen and the two lion-gods Shu and Tefnut.

ȧmen to hide, be hidden, hidden one, something hidden. , those who hide, hider, secrecy, in secret, the hidden gods.

ȧmenu-ā those whose arms are hidden.

he whose name is hidden.

those whose bodies are hidden.

those whose mysteries are hidden.

ȧmenḥiu the divine butchers, or gods of slaughter.

Åmen-ḥetep 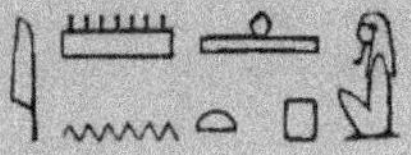 a proper name.

Åment, *Amenti*, *Åmentet* 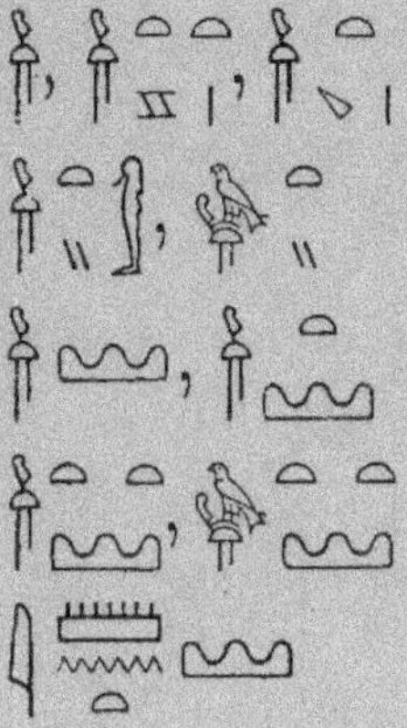 the "hidden" place, or land, the West, the abode of departed spirits, the name of the first division of the Other World. A late form of the name is .

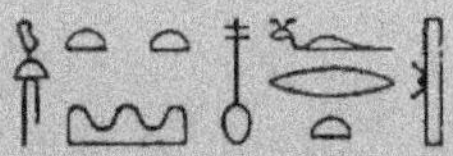 the "beautiful Åmentet".

Ament 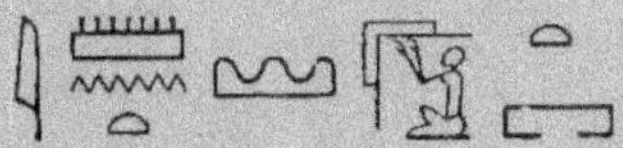 hidden place; plur. .

åmentiu  divine beings who live in Åmenti, or the West;  Åmenti deified,  the goddess of the West, or Åmenti.

åmenti 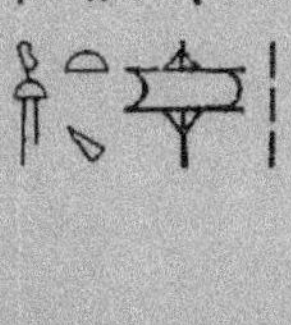 the west wind.

àmsi 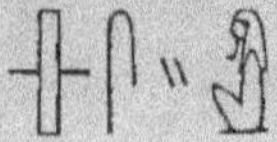 a god of generation, fertility, fecundity, etc. Probably a form of Menu .

Àmseth 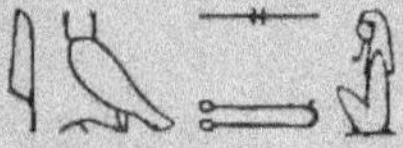 one of the four sons of Horus. The reading appears to be a mistake made by the Egyptians in reading 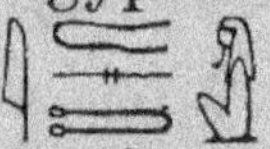 *Àmseth* instead of *Àḳesth*. See Ḳesthà.

àmt 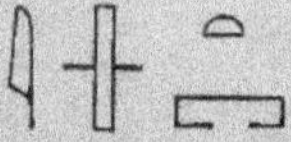 chamber, house, abode.

àmt  possessions, goods of a house.

àmt  the title-deeds of a house or property.

àmt  tree (?), or tent, camp.

àmt  light, radiance, splendour.

àmt 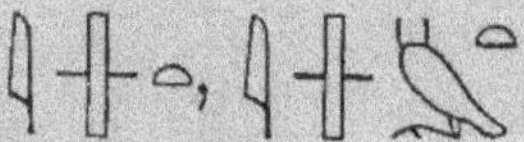 that which is in. 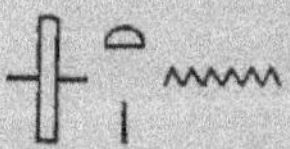 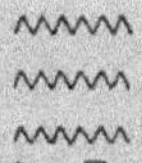 what is in the waters. , etc.

Àmt-ṭehen-f  a proper name.

àmtiu  . . . .

ȧn — a mark of emphasis or interrogation, used sometimes as a preposition, behold! lo! cf.

ȧn ḳert — lo moreover.

ȧn (n) — no, not, mark of the negative. most certainly there cannot be done. I am not.

ȧn ȧs — except, unless.

ȧn ȧbu — ceaselessly.

ȧn urṭ — unresting.

ȧn petrȧ — unobserved.

ȧn maa
ȧn maa-n-tu } unseen, invisible.

ȧn maa-n-tu  } unseen, invisible.
ȧn maatu 

ȧn mu 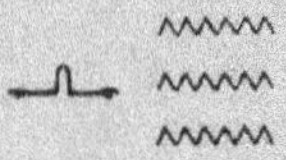 waterless.

ȧn meḥ 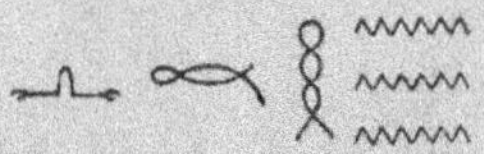 } undipped (?), unwashed (?). Also 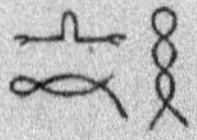 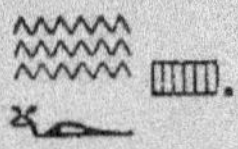.
ȧn meḥ-f 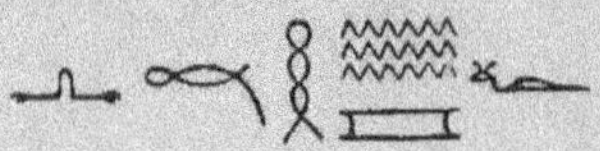

ȧn nifu  airless.

ȧn netchnetchet 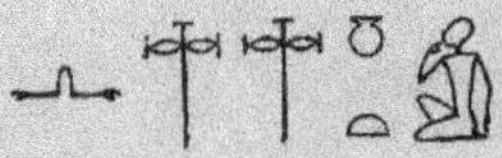 not to be discussed or gainsaid.

ȧn rekh  } unknown.
ȧn rekhtu 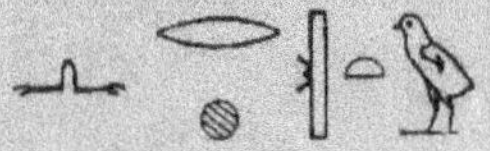

ȧn kheper 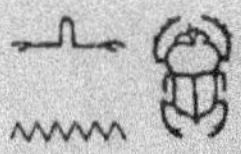 never was.

ȧn sep 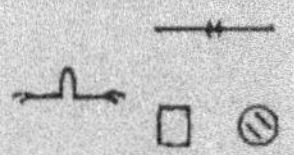 at no time.

ȧn smȧ 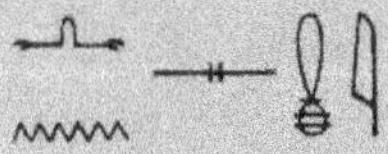 untold.

ȧn sek 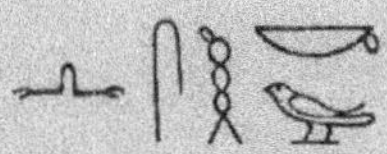 indestructible,

ȧn seṭ 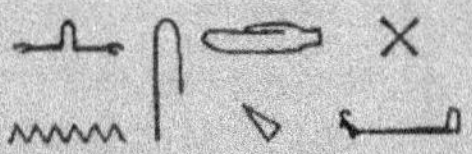 unsplit.

ȧn shenārtu  unturnable.

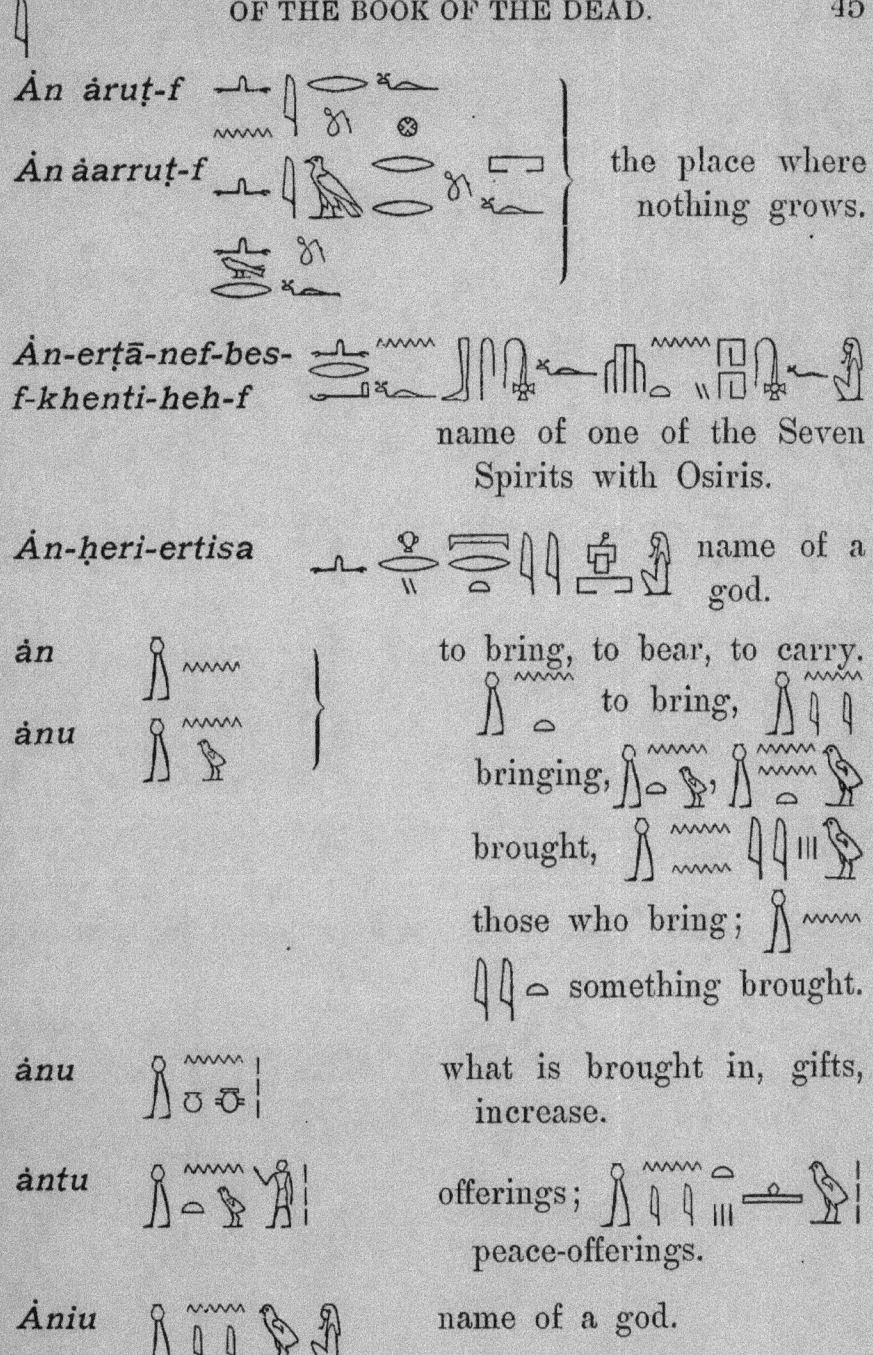

Ȧn ȧruṭ-f
Ȧn ȧarruṭ-f  the place where nothing grows.

Ȧn-erṭā-nef-bes-f-khenti-heh-f 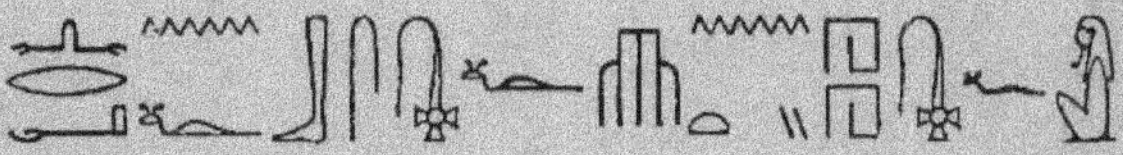 name of one of the Seven Spirits with Osiris.

Ȧn-ḥeri-ertisa 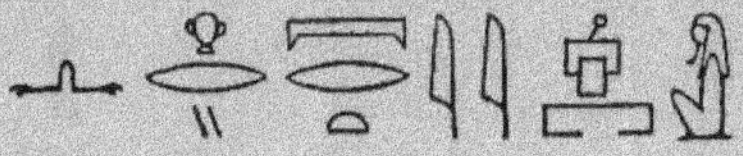 name of a god.

ȧn 
ȧnu  to bring, to bear, to carry.  to bring,  bringing, ,  brought, 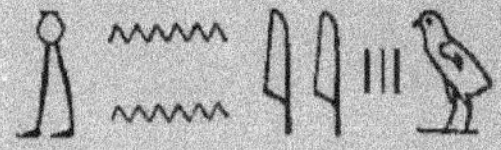 those who bring; 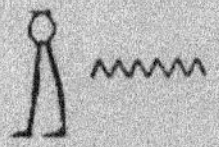  something brought.

ȧnu 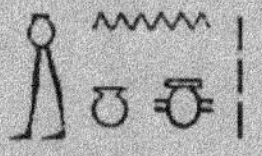 what is brought in, gifts, increase.

ȧntu  offerings;  peace-offerings.

Ȧniu  name of a god.

Ȧn  name of a god.

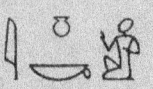

Ȧn-{ṭes / ṭemt} — a proper name.

ȧnit — a dwelling, chamber, house.

ȧnuk — I.

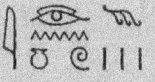

Ȧnu — On, Heliopolis.

ȧnnu — skin.

ȧnnuit — skin, hair, plumage.

Ȧn-ȧtef-f — "Bringer of his father", a proper name.

Ȧn ā-f — "Bringer of his arm"; the name of one of the Forty-two Judges in the Hall of Osiris.

Ȧn-urt-emkhet-uas — name of the mast in the magical boat (Chap. XCIX).

ȧnb — to dance, to rejoice.

ȧneb — wall; plur.

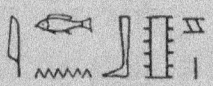

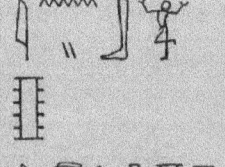

ȧneb 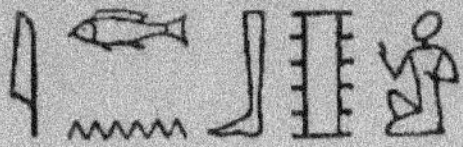 mason.

ȧnep  region, estate, ground.

Ȧnp, **Ȧnpu**  The god Anubis, son of Set and Nephthys, a jackal-god who embalmed the dead, and guided the souls of the blessed to the Other World. Titles: 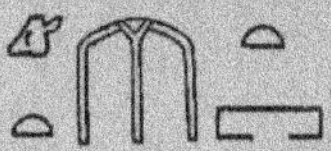, 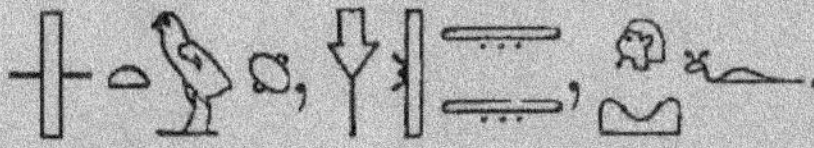.

Ȧn-mut-f  "The pillar of his mother", title of a ministrant or priest.

ȧnem 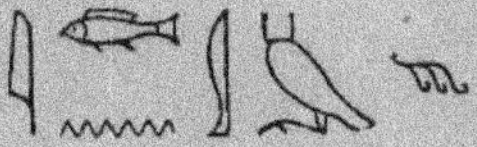

 skin, hide.

ȧnemsit 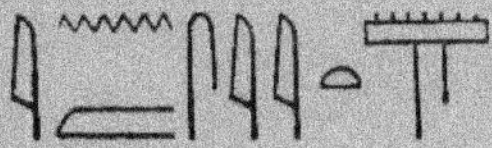 a kind of garment.

ȧnenit 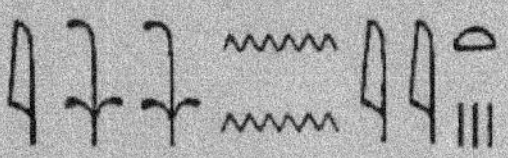 a proper name?

Ȧn-ruṭ-f  the god of the place where nothing grows.

Ȧnreruṭ-f 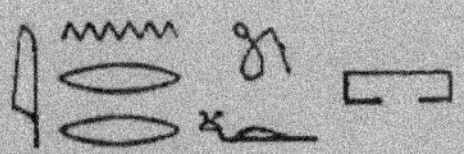 the place where nothing grows.

ȧner 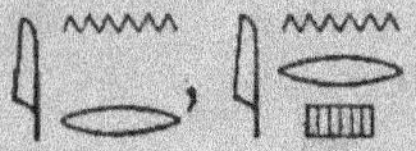 stone.

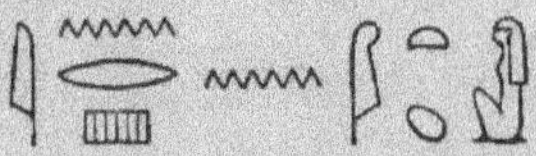 "Stone of Maāt", a proper name.

ȧner 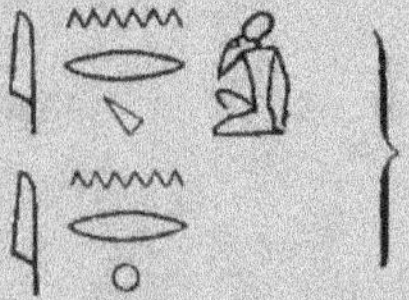 a proper name.

ȧnhetet 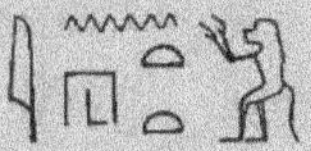 ape.

ȧnḥui  the two eye-brows.

ȧnḥu-tu  surrounded.

Ȧn-ḥer  "Bearer of the sky"; an ancient god of Upper Egypt who is often associated with .

Ȧn-ḥer 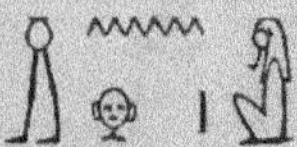 name of the warder of the Sixth Ārit.

Ȧn-ḥetep  one of the Forty-two gods in the Hall of Osiris.

ȧnes
ȧnsi 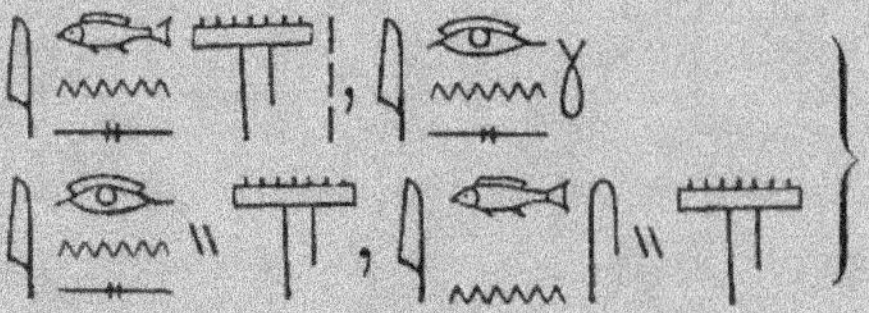 name of a ceremonial garment.

ȧnset 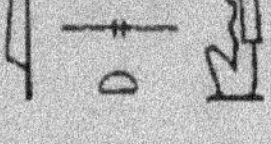 a goddess (?).

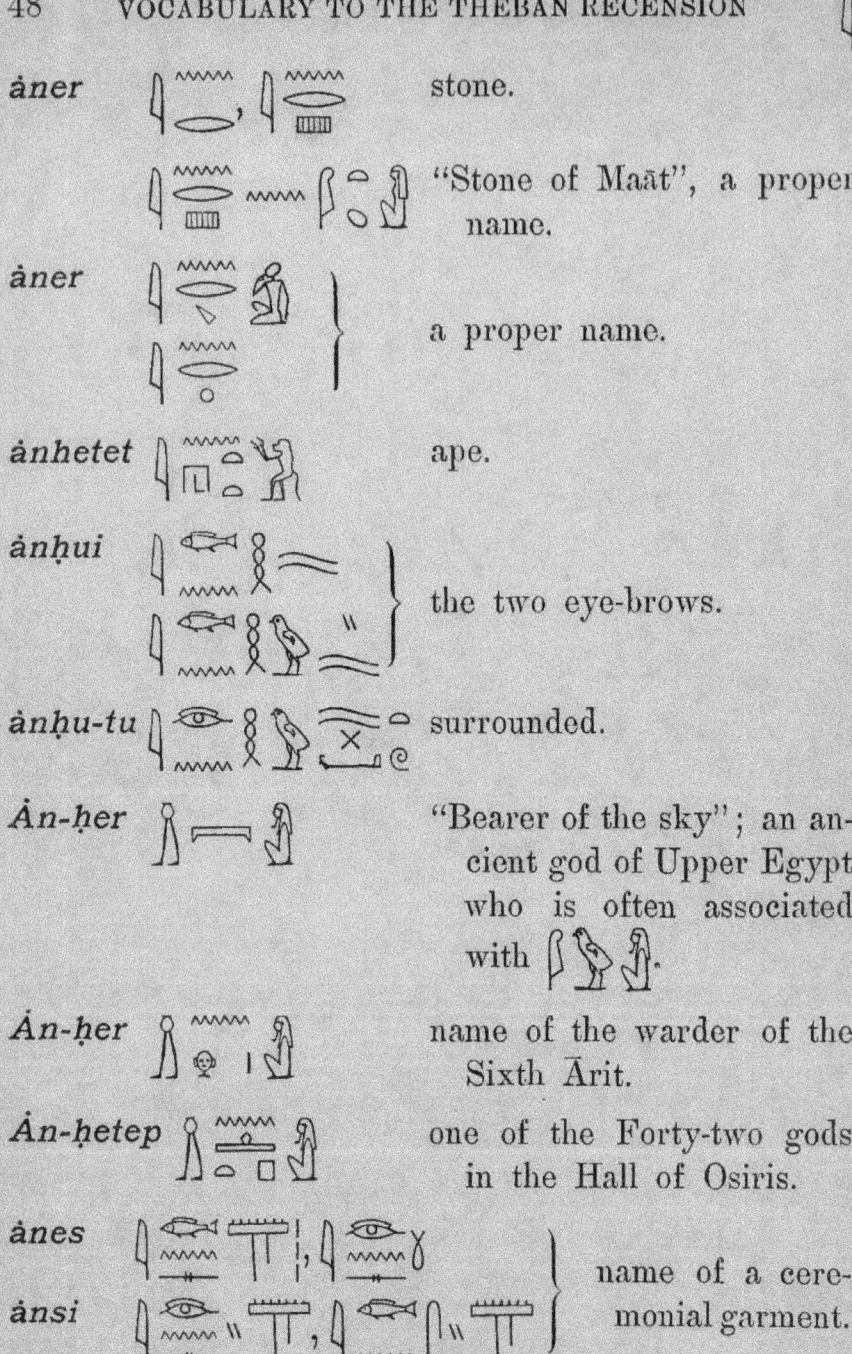

ȧneq 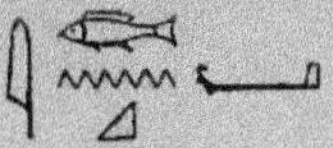 to bind, tie on, to fasten.

ȧnqet  to embrace, to surround.

ȧnqet 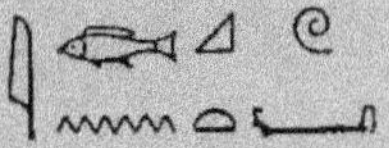 name of a tool, or instrument, "clincher", rope (?).

ȧnt 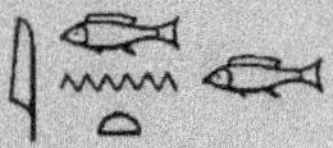 name of a mythological fish which swam before the boat of Rā.

ȧnt 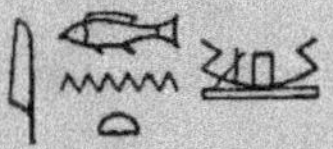 name of a solar boat.

ȧnt 
ȧntet, *ȧnti* 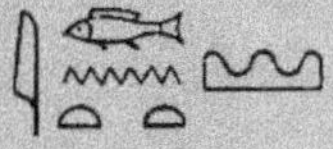
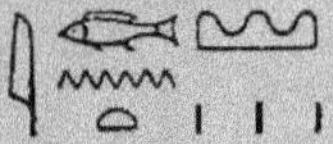
a valley, especially a funerary valley.

ȧnti  pillars, columns.

Ȧnti 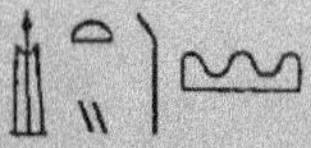 the hill-folk who lived in the Eastern Desert of Ta-sti 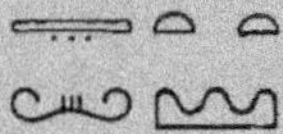, or Nubia.

ȧnti 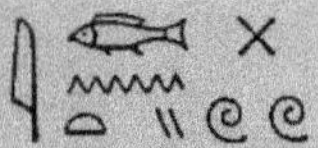 a hindrance, obstruction.

ȧntiu  those who have nothing, the destitute, those who are not, or do not exist.

ȧntet 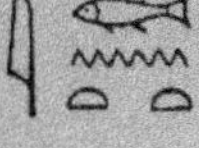 to go back.

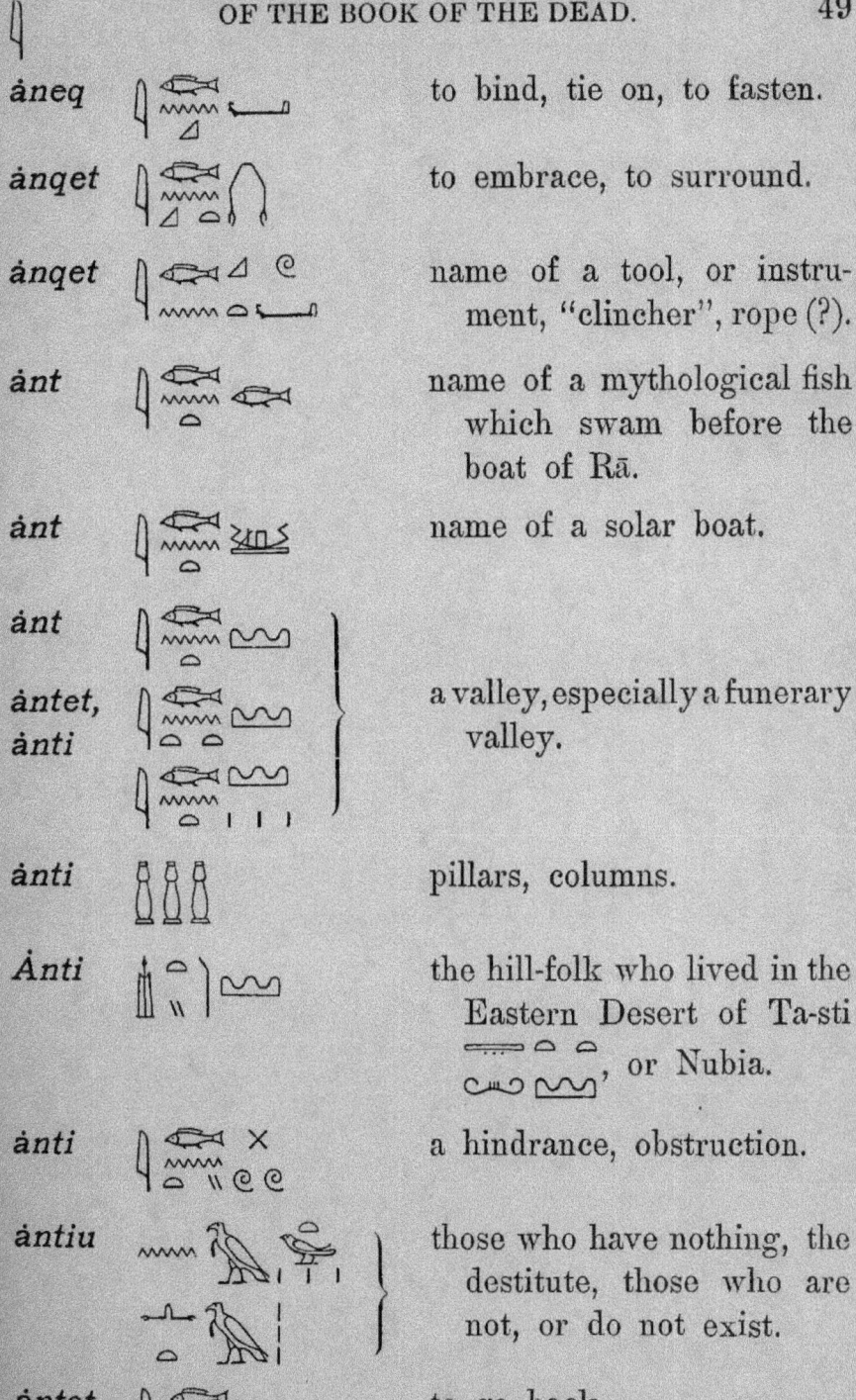

àntet 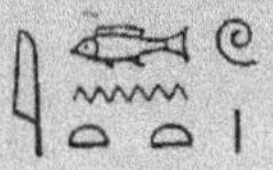 cord, fetter, chain.

Àn-ṭebu  the name of a god.

ànetch 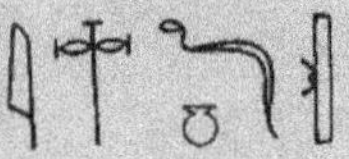 to incline, to bow.

ànetch ḥer 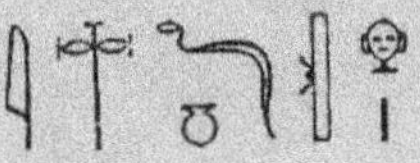 to incline the head to a suppliant, to turn the face towards.

àr  to tie together.

àr  if, now.

àr sa  if after, now as for.

àr ḳert  if moreover, however.

àr
àru
àrit 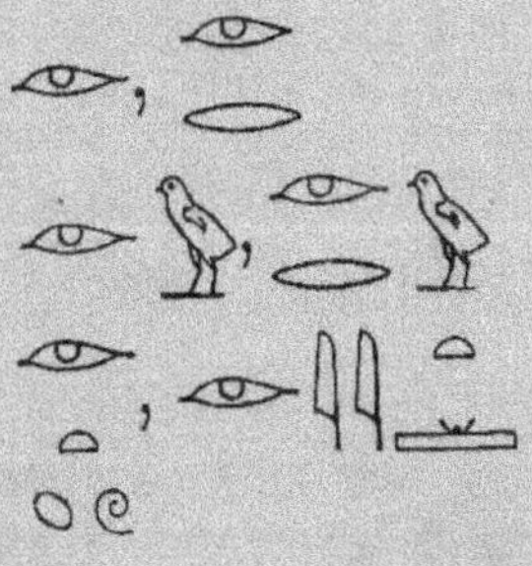 to do, to make, to create, to form, to fashion; ,  doing, making, creator;  made, wrought,  made;  make ye;  things done.

àrit  to work the heart, to think.

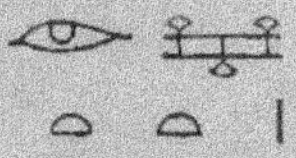 to make or prepare a path or road.

 to prepare food.

 to celebrate the Haker festival.

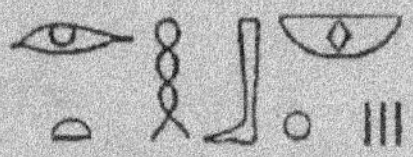 to keep festivals.

 to make protection, to perform ceremonies for the protection of some one.

 to work for successful results, to strive for peace.

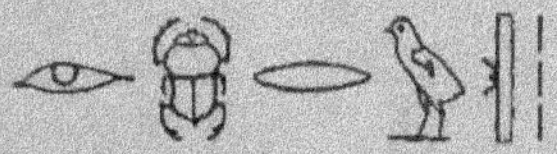 to perform a transformation.

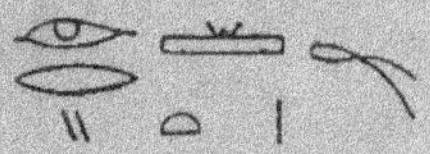 to make, or write, or recite, a book.

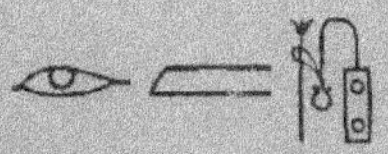 to do into writing, to make a copy, to write.

àriu 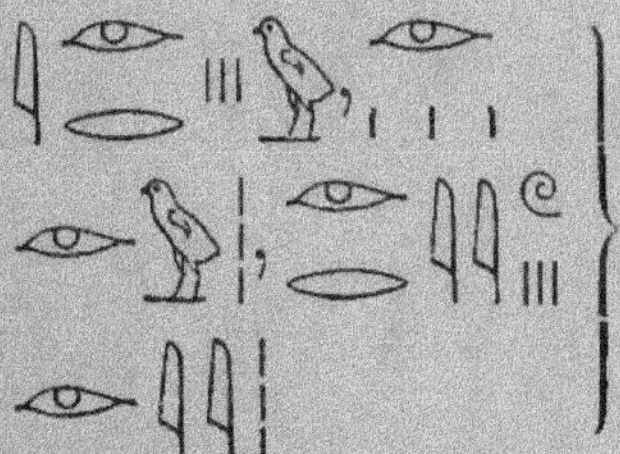 doers, makers, workers.

àriu  workmen; fem. 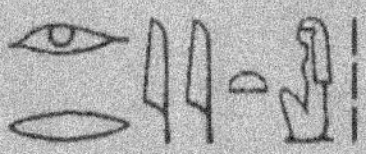.

ȧrit work, something done.

actions, deeds, labours, works, things done or to be done.

ȧr, ȧri used as an auxiliary verb, see *passim*.

ȧri-Maāt "Maker of truth, or righteousness", a title of Osiris, Hathor, and other gods.

Ȧri-em-ȧb-f
Ȧri-en-ȧb-f the name of one of the Forty-two Judges in the Hall of Osiris.

Ȧri-nef-tchesef name of a plank or peg in the magical boat.

Ȧri-entuten-em-meska-en-Mer-ur uṭebtu-en-Suti name of the leather bands in the magical boat.

Ȧri-ḥetch-f a proper name.

Ȧrisi a proper name.

ȧru form, attribute, figure, image; plur.

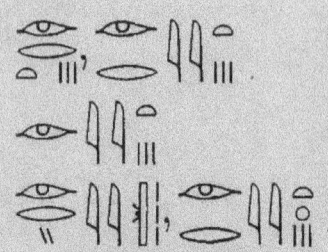

àri 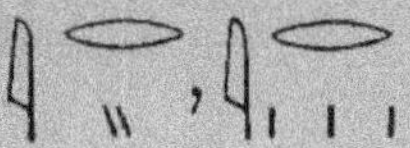 belonging to:  their name; 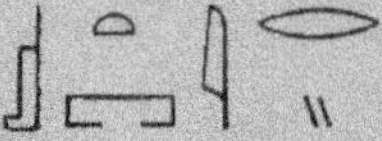 their seat;  their bull (var. 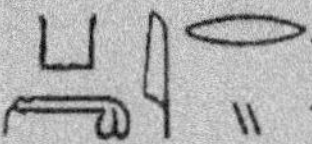);  their length.

àri  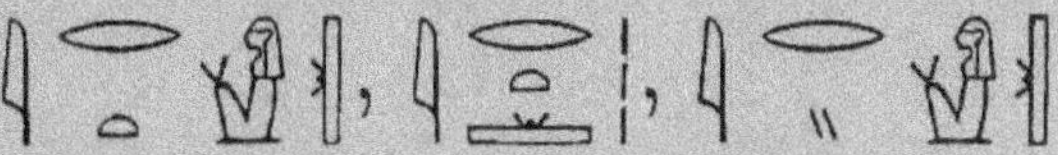 a person in charge of, or belonging to, or attendant upon something, watcher, porter, guardian.

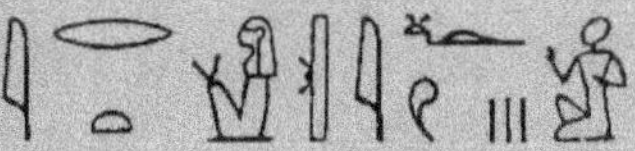 guardian of my flesh.

 guardian, or guardians, of the sky.

 keeping watch about, or around.

 keepers of my mouth.

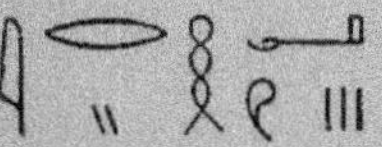 watching the limbs.

 keeping guard over the neck.

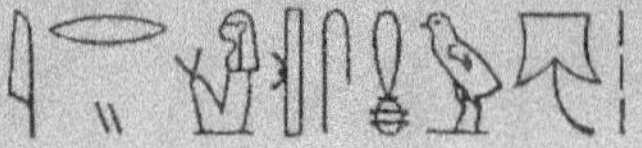 belonging to the leathers.

 guarding the earth.

ȧri āa  porter, doorkeeper, guardian; plur. .

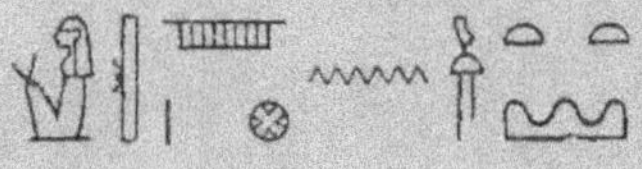 porter of the door of Ȧmentet.

ȧriu ārrtu 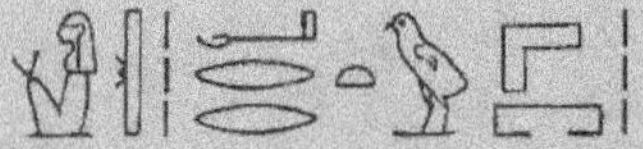 warders of the Ārits.

ȧri mākhait  warder of the Scales.

ȧri ḥemit 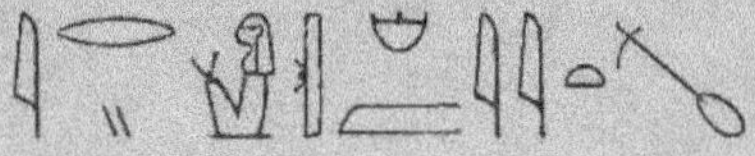 warder of the oar, *i. e.*, steersman.

ȧri ḥenbiu  warder of the cultivated lands.

ȧru khut  guardians of light, *i. e.*, beings of light.

ȧri sȧpu.  keepers of the records, or books of doom.

ȧri sebkhet-f 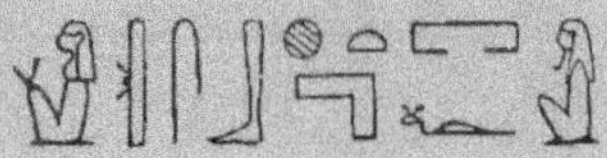 keeper of his pylon.

ȧri qeb en meru en khet	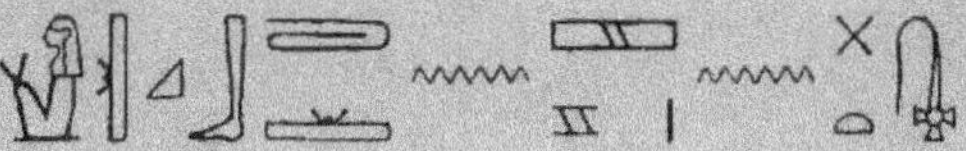	keeper of the Bend of the Lake of Fire.
ȧrārti	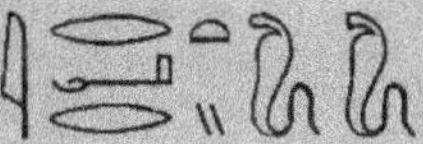	two uraei.
Ȧruhut		a proper name.
ȧrp	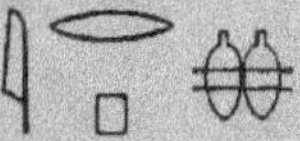	wine.
ȧrpu		... Chap. CLXIX. 1.
ȧref	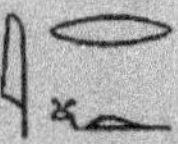	an emphatic particle.
ȧrmā		with.
ȧrek		a particle.
ȧrt	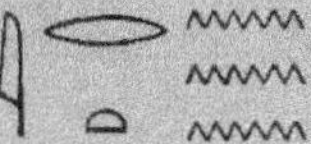	to flow, what flows.
ȧrt	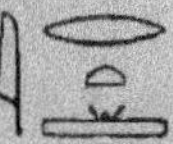	Chapter LB. 1.
ȧrtet	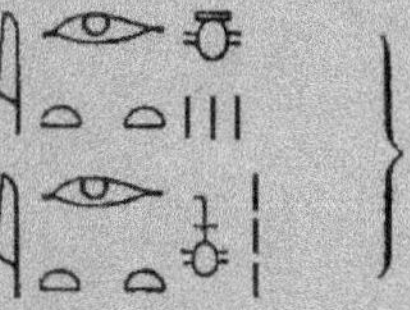	milk.
ȧh		calamity.
ȧhabu		joy, gladness, cries of joy.

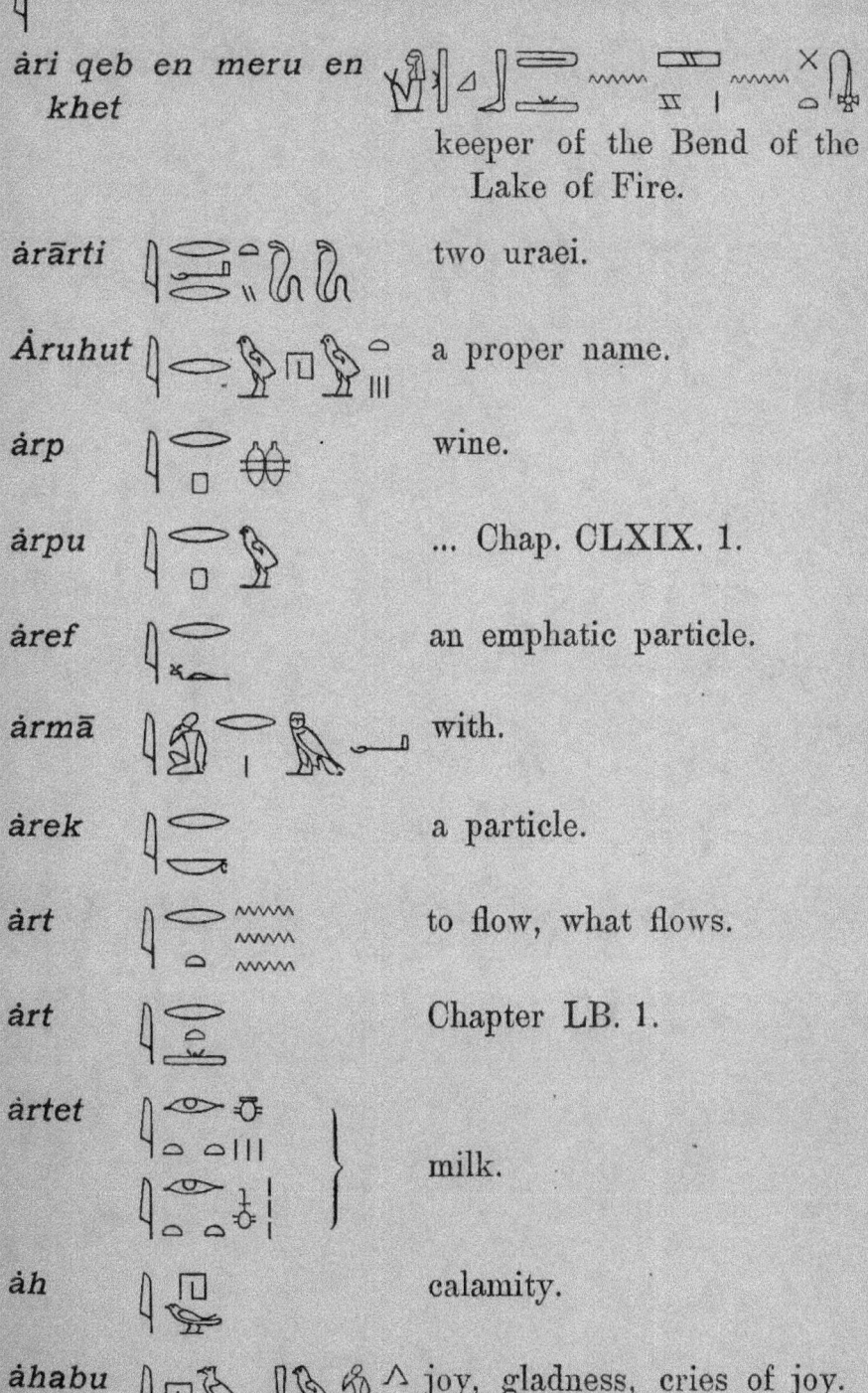

àhen  a kind of wood.

àhehi  rejoicings, cries of joy.

Àḥ  the Moon-god,

àḥ 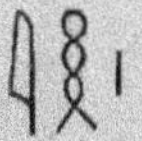 ... Book of Breathings II. 22.

àḥ  collar, embrace, to ward off.

àḥ, àḥu  ox; plur.  oxen, .

àḥai  a sistrum bearer.

àḥāu 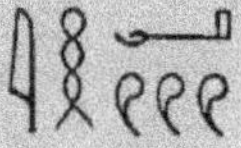 members.

àḥi 
àḥu  the name of one of the Forty-two Judges in the Hall of Osiris; a proper name; .

àḥu  fields (?), measuring cords.

àḥu 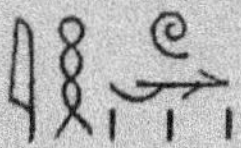 wooden tools or instruments.

àḥui 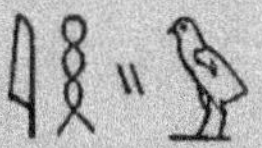 the two *àḥui* gods =  .

Ȧḥibit — name of a god.

ȧḥunnu — youth, child.

ȧḥemu (?) — ... Chap. XCII. 13.

ȧḥti — throat.

Aḥti — a name of Osiris.

Ȧkh — O!, would that, O tell me.

ȧkhabu — grain.

ȧkhib — to speak.

ȧkhemu urṭu — a class of stars.

ȧkhekhu, *ȧkhekhui* — darkness, night.

Ȧkhsesef — a proper name.

Ȧs — a proper name.

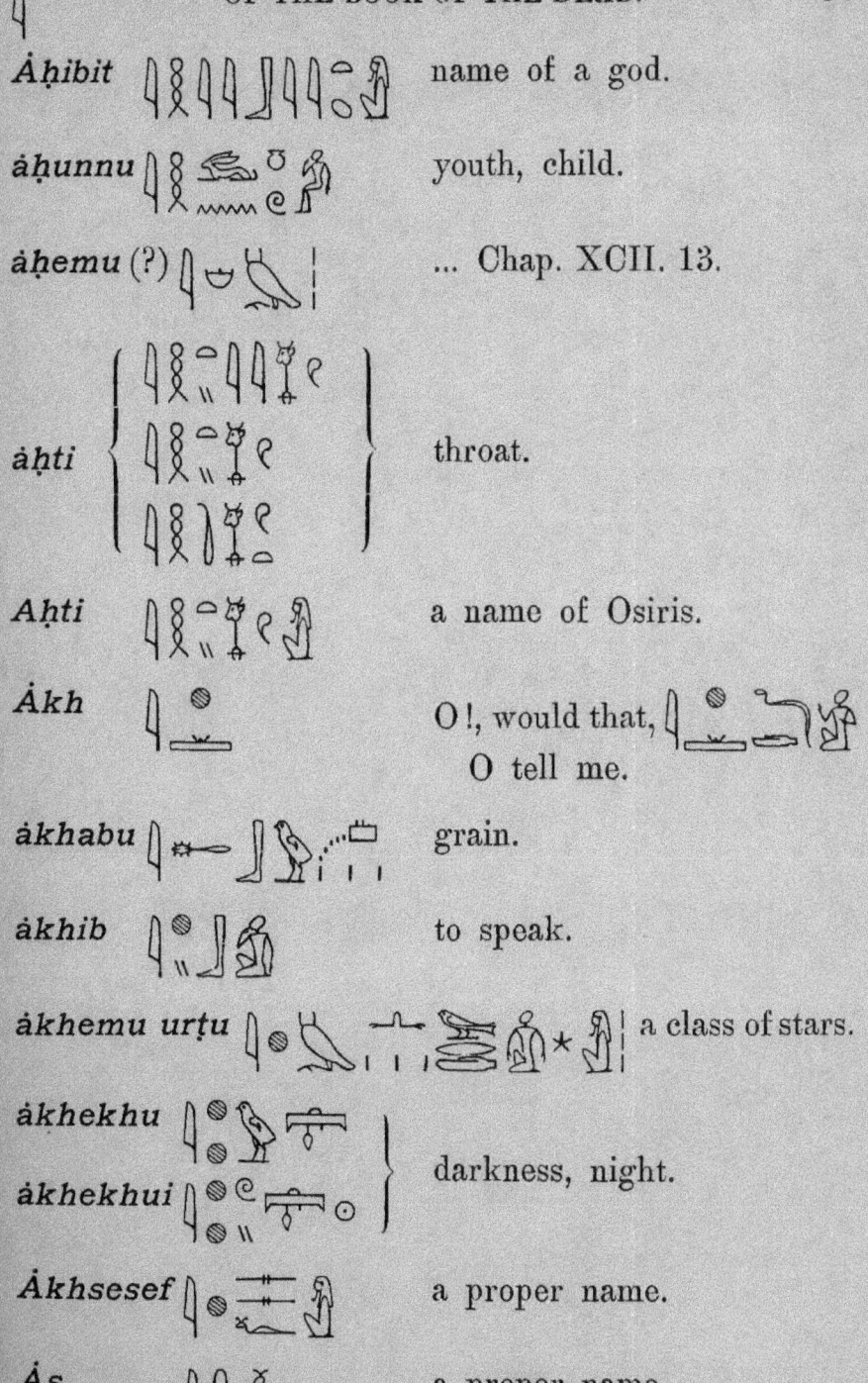

ȧs — behold, to wit, namely, ...

ȧsu — intestines.

ȧsu — winds.

ȧsu (?) — ... Chap. CXXVII B. 17.

ȧsi, ȧsu — tomb, sepulchre.

ȧsu — recompense ... or ... in return for, in place of.

ȧs — to pass forward, to advance.

ȧsu, *ȧsi* — to decay, to rot, destruction. ... decay, ... incorruptible.

Àsàr 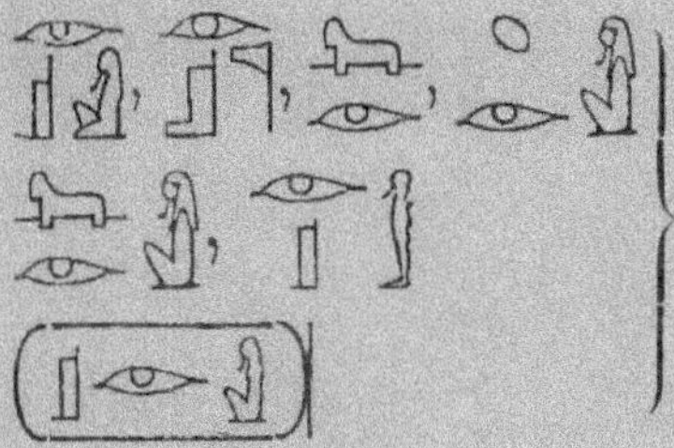 the god Osiris, son of Seb and Nut, husband of Isis, and father of Horus. The deceased is usually identified with Osiris and is called by his name.

Àsàr Ànpu 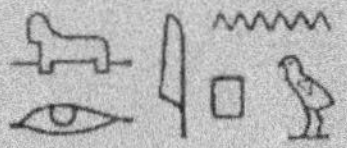 Osiris-Anubis.

Àsàr ānkhti  Osiris the Living One.

Àsàr Unnefer  Osiris Un-Nefer.

Àsàr Utetti  Osiris the begetter.

Àsàr-ba-erpi 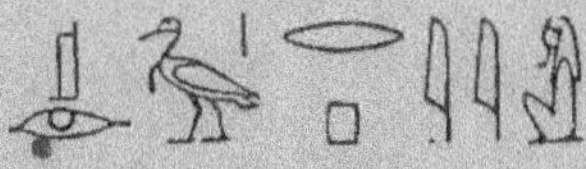 Osiris, soul of the divine Image.

Àsàr-bati-erpit  Osiris, twin soul of the divine image.

Àsàr Ptaḥ neb ānkh  Osiris-Ptaḥ, Lord of Life.

Àsàr-em-pesuru  Osiris in Pesuru.

Àsàr em pesṭ ent nut-f 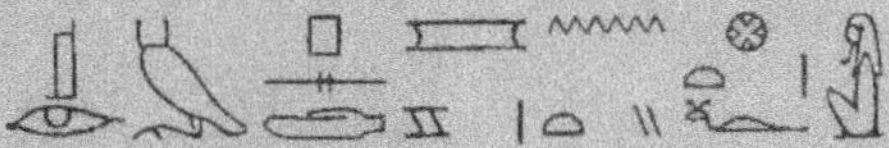

Àsàr em Seḥnen 

Åsår em Ṭenit 

Åsår nub ḥeḥ  Osiris, gold of eternity.

Åsår neb ānkh  Osiris, Lord of Life.

Åsår neb er tcher  Osiris, Lord to the boundary, *i. e.*, of All.

Asår Netchesti 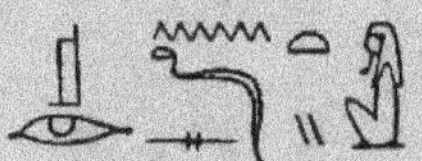 Osiris the Less.

Åsår Ḥenti  Osiris of the two crocodiles.

Åsår Ḥeru  Osiris-Horus.

Åsår Ḥeru-khuti Tem  Osiris-Harmachis.

Åsår ḥer åb semt  Osiris in the funerary mountain.

Åsår ḥer shāu-f  Osiris on his sand.

Åsår khent Åbṭu 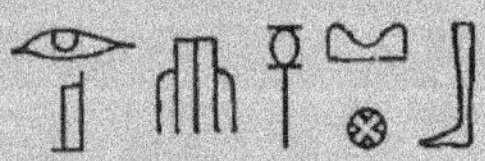 Osiris, President of Abydos.

Åsår khenti Åmenti 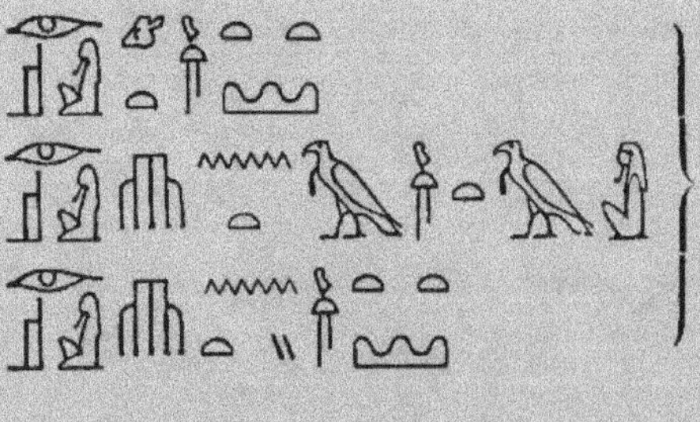 Osiris, President of Amenti, or the Other World.

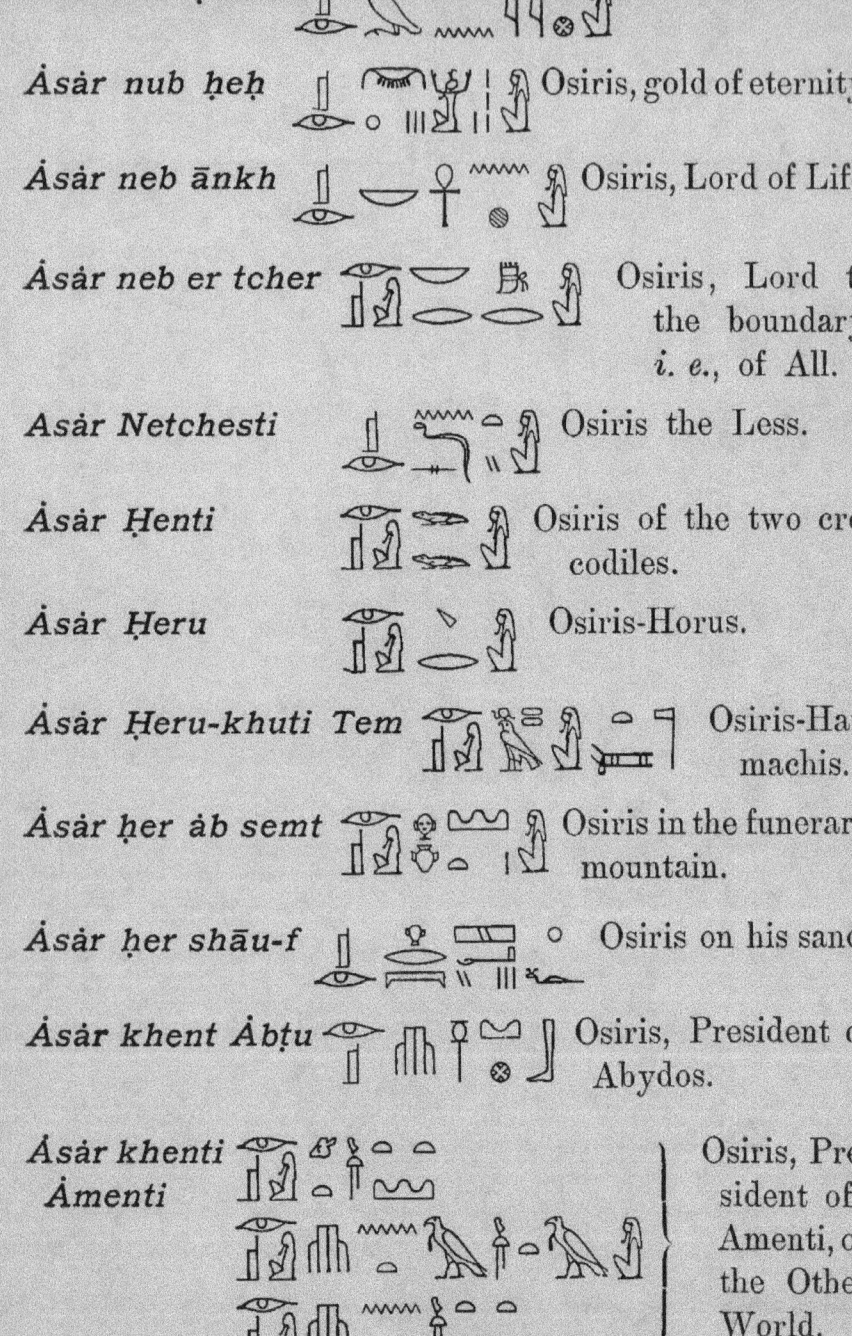

Ȧsȧr khenti Ȧmentiu  Osiris, President of those who dwell in the Other World.

Ȧsȧr khent Un 

Ȧsȧr khenti 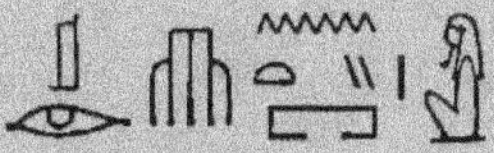

Ȧsȧr khenti Nefer (?) 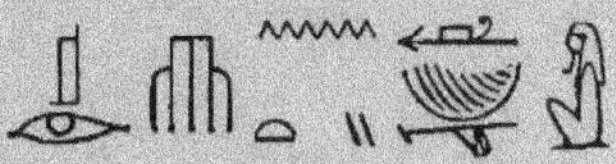

Ȧsȧr khenti nut-f 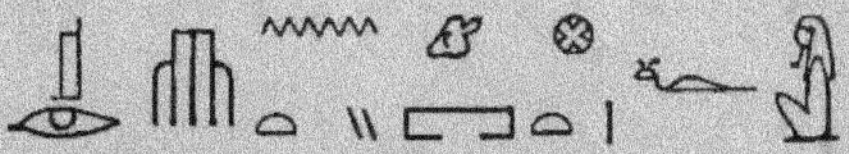

Ȧsȧr khenti nestu 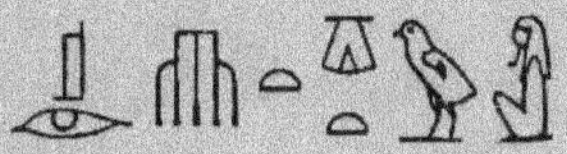

Ȧsȧr khenti Ru-stau 

Ȧsȧr khenti seḥ ḥemt 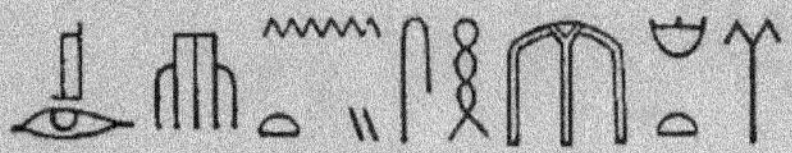

Ȧsȧr sa Nut 

Ȧsȧr saa 

Ȧsȧr Sab (or *Ḳeb*?) 

Ȧsȧr Saḥ 

Àsàr Sekri 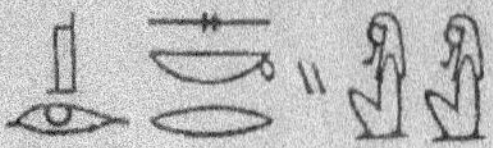

Àsàr Taiti 

Àsàr tua 

Àsàr Ṭem ur 

Àsàr Teḳaiti 

Àsàrtiu  beings like unto Osiris.

àsi 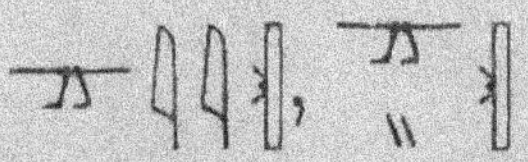 who?, what?

àsp  grief (?), misery, wretchedness.

àsfet, *àsfeti*  faults, sins, evil deeds, sinners, evil ones.

àsfetiu  evil fiends, sinners.

àsentu 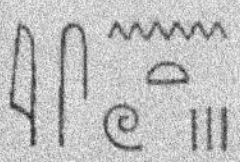 cords, ropes.

àser  tamarisk (?),  plants, herbs, grass.

Àsert 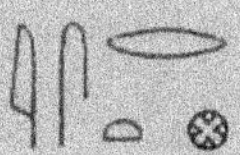 name of a city.

àsha		linen, some kind of woven stuff.
Àses	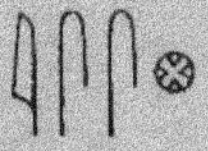	a city in the seventh Àat.
Àsest	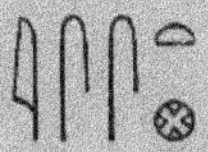	
àses	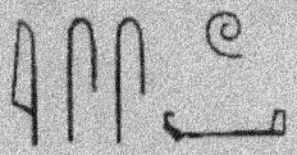	to rope in, to bind.
àsstu	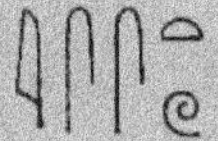	a rope.  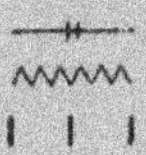 those whose heads are tied.
àsk	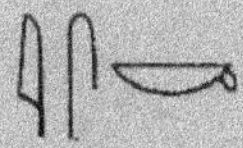	behold, lo!
àst, àstu		behold.
àsth	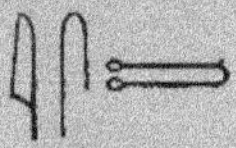	
Àst		the goddess Isis.
àst	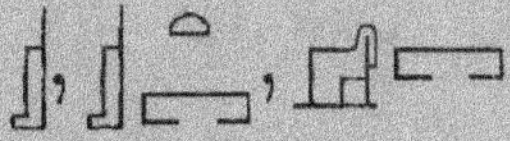	seat, place, habitation, abode, shrine; plur. 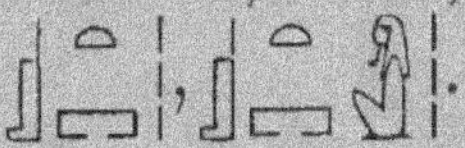.
àst àb	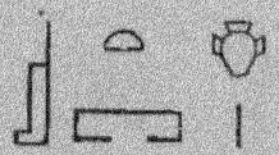	place of the heart, heart's chosen place.
àst āāui	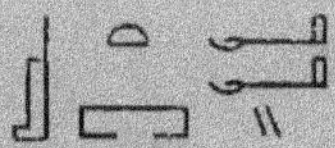	place of the two hands.

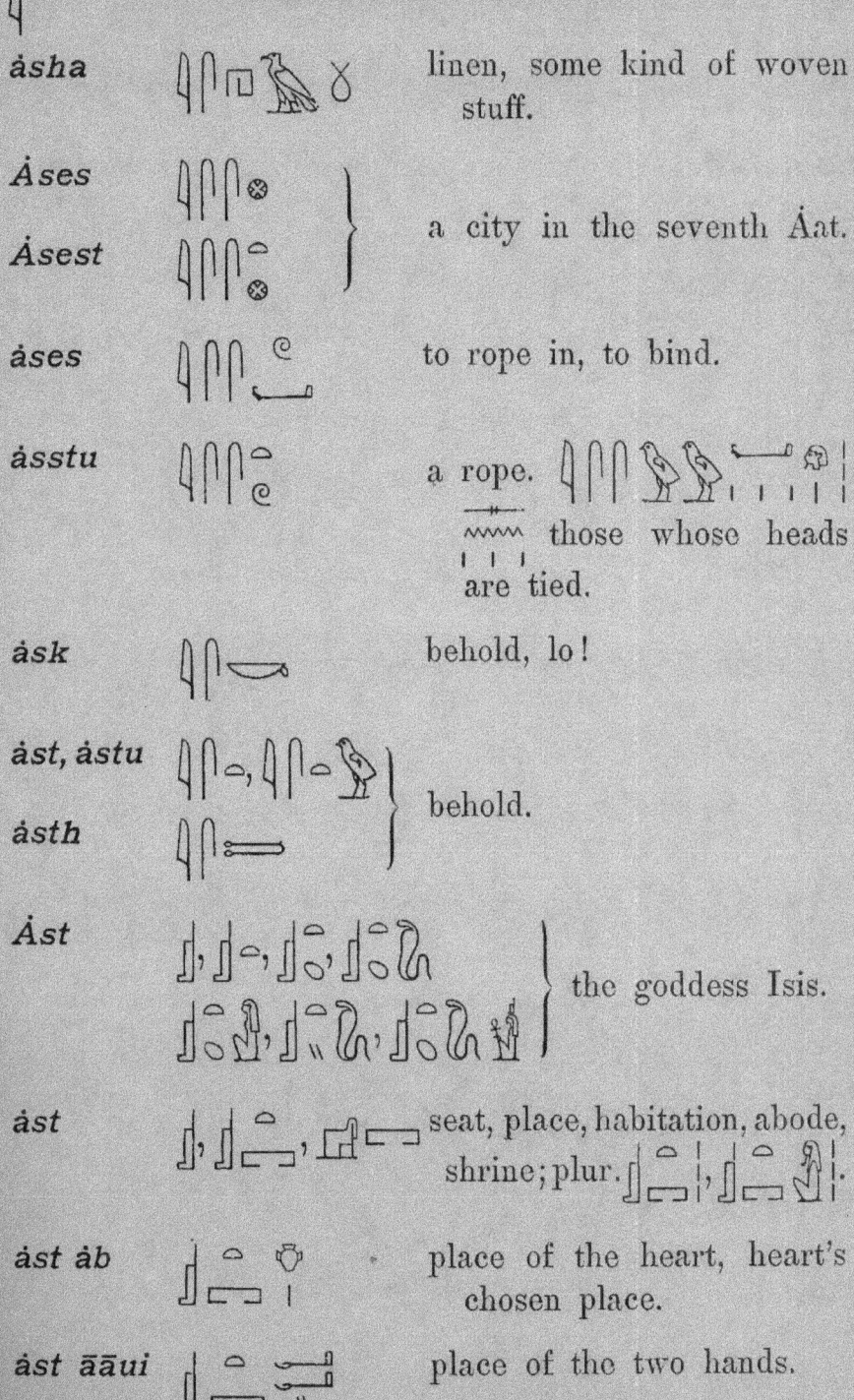

ȧst urt 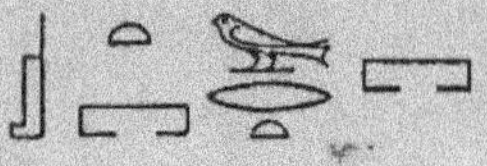 great place, *i. e.*, the sky.

ȧst utchat  seat of the Utchat, resting place of the Eye of Rā.

ȧst maāt  the place where the Law is administered.

ȧst ḥert  heaven.

ȧst ḥeḥ 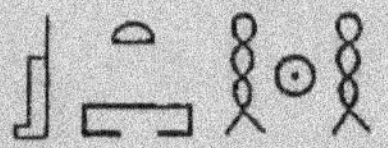 everlasting abode.

ȧst Ḥeqet 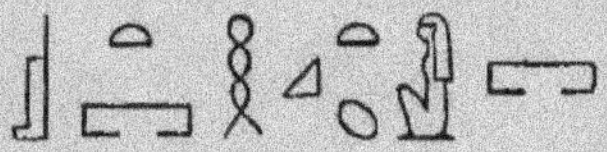 shrine of Ḥeqet.

ȧst ḥetep 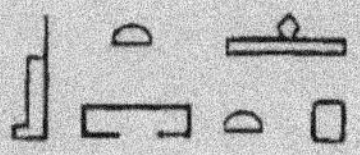 place of repose.

ȧst ḥetep ȧb 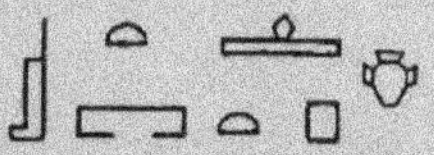 seat of rest of the heart.

ȧst shetau en Ḥeru 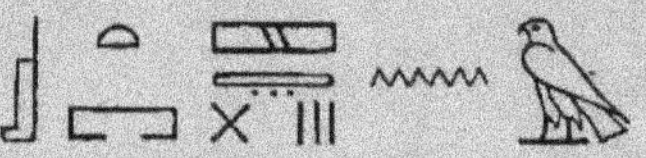 the secret abodes of Horus.

ȧst qebḥ  place of cool water, bath.

ȧst taa  place of fire in the Other World.

ȧst tchesert 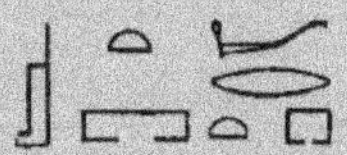 shrine, sanctuary, holy place.

ȧsṭ 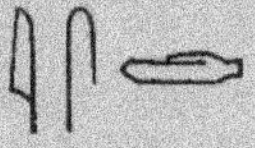 to tremble, make to shake.

Ȧsṭenu 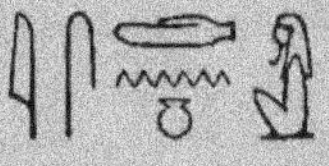 name of a god.

àsteḥ (?) / ***àstheḥt*** (?)	to beat down.
Àsṭes	name of a god.
Àstcheṭet	name of a district.
àshāt	knife, slaughter.
àshep	light, radiance.
àshpit	chamber, hut, house.
àsheset	see àqeset.
àshesh	to be carried away.
àshet	subsistence, oppression, oppressor (?).
àshta	tree.
àsheṭ	persea tree, trees, plants.
àk	injury.

ȧkebu hair.

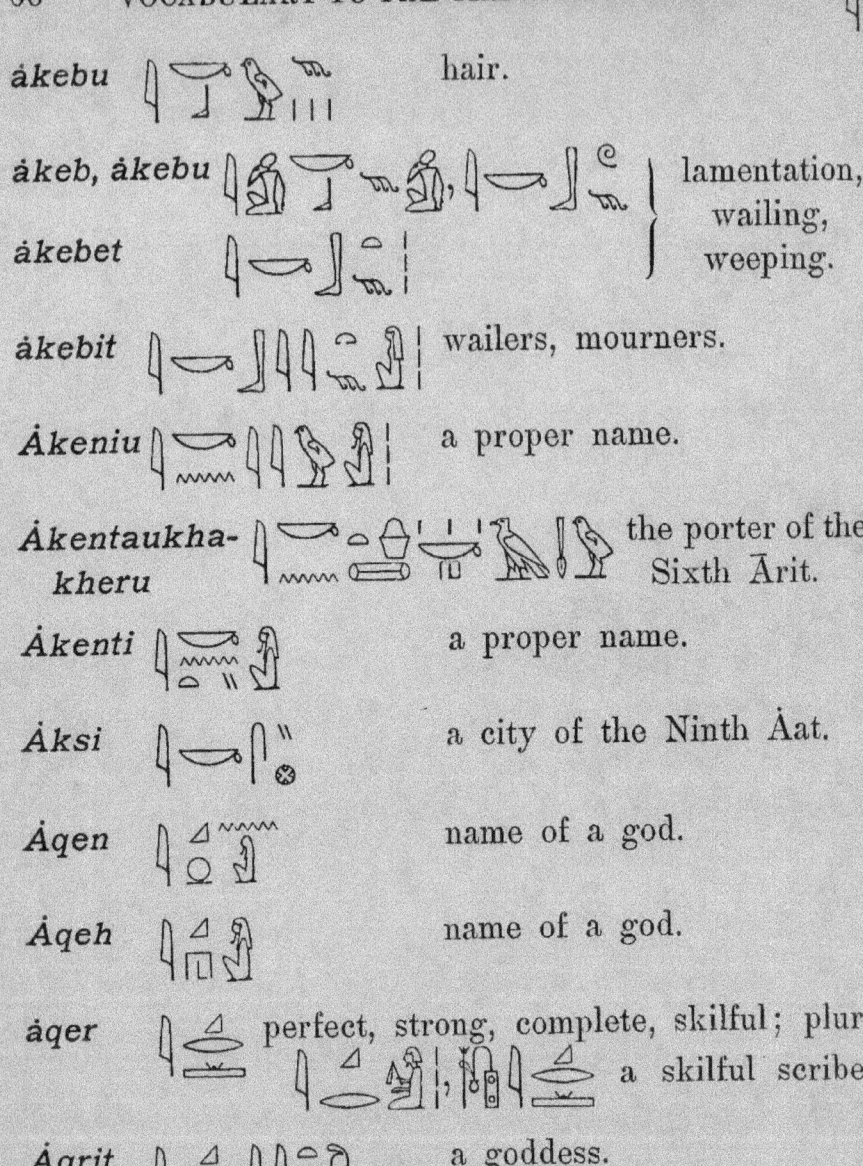

ȧkeb, ȧkebu, **ȧkebet** lamentation, wailing, weeping.

ȧkebit wailers, mourners.

Ȧkeniu a proper name.

Ȧkentaukha-kheru the porter of the Sixth Ārit.

Ȧkenti a proper name.

Ȧksi a city of the Ninth Ȧat.

Ȧqen name of a god.

Ȧqeh name of a god.

ȧqer perfect, strong, complete, skilful; plur. , a skilful scribe.

Ȧqrit a goddess.

Ȧqert-khenti-ḥet-set the name of one of the Seven Cows.

ȧqḥu to enter.

ȧqeset who, what, where,.

ȧqet wine, beer.

ȧqeṭu builders, masons, architects.

ȧqeṭs bad, wicked, evil.

Ȧḳau name of a god.

ȧḳap
ȧḳep } rain-storm, tempest.

Ȧḳeru
Ȧḳeriu } gods of the Other World.

Ȧḳert
Ȧḳertet } the name of the Other World of Heliopolis.

Ȧḳert-khent-Ȧset-s the name of one of the Seven Cows.

ȧḳeḳit a kind of garment, robe.

ȧt father.

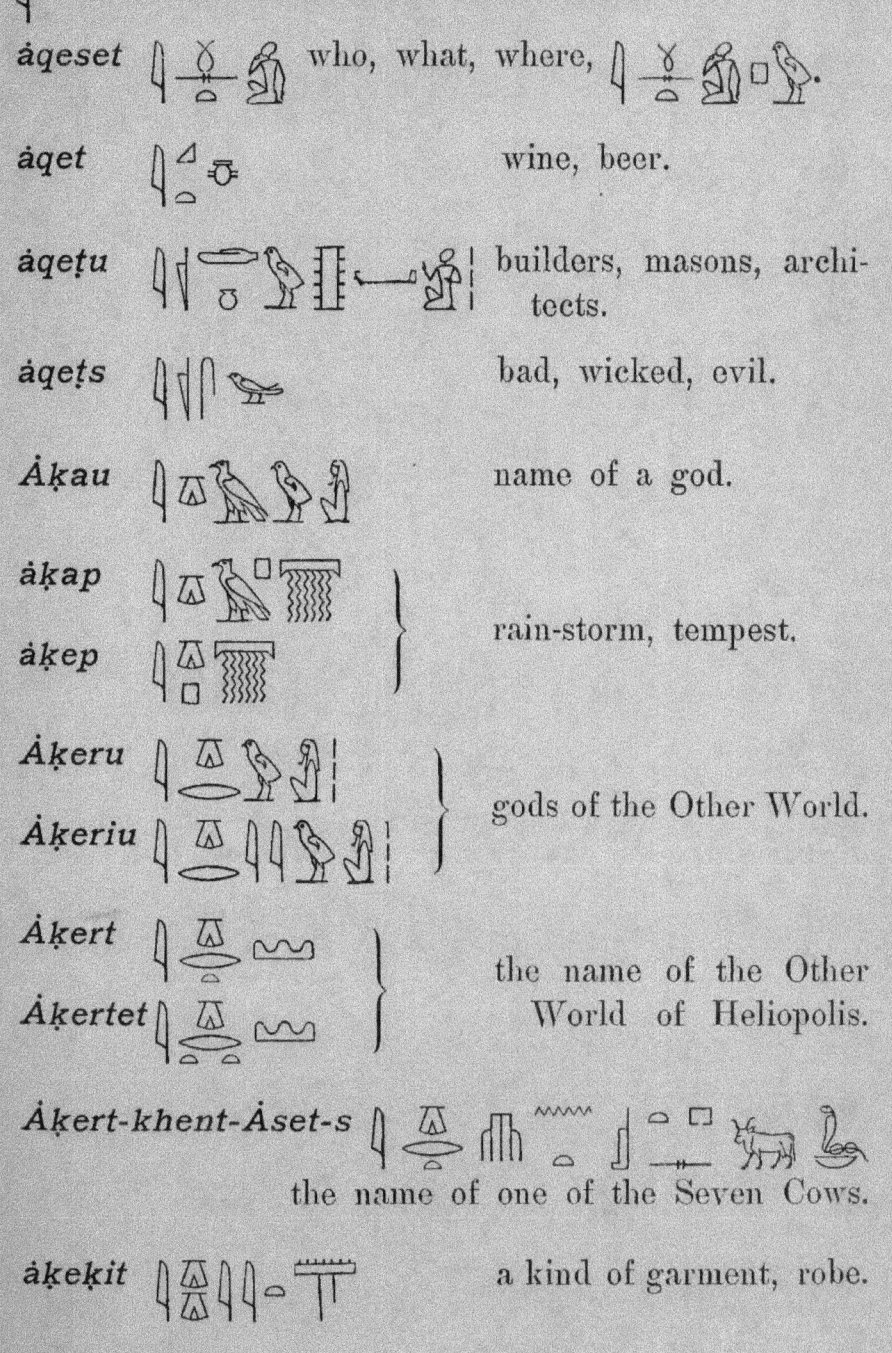

åt (for **ånt**) 

åti (for **ånti**)

åtet

negation, no, none, not, cannot, without, impotence, plur. 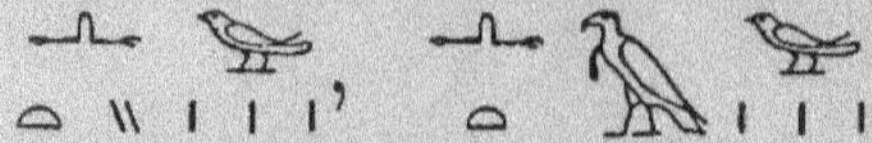 things which are not, evil beings;  without, destitute, abjects.

åti ākhem  unquenchable.

åti uteb  immutable.

åti men 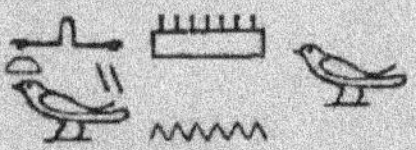 painless.

åti maa  invisible, not seeing, blind.

åtu rekh  unknown.

åtu khesef  irresistible.

åtu åsi  incorruptible.

åti sek 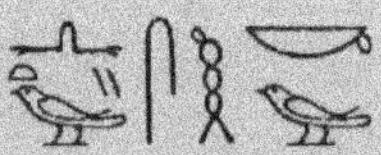 undecaying.

åti shes  impassable.

åt 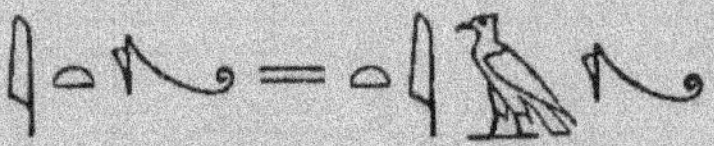 emanation.

Åtaru-åm-tcher-qemtu-renu-par-sheta 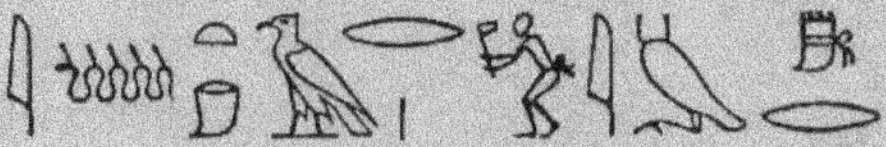  a proper name.

ȧteb territory, region.

ȧtef father; dual , ; plur. , father gods , Father Osiris , Father Kheperȧ .

Ȧtem see under Tem, Temu.

ȧten the solar disk.

the god of the solar disk.

the two-horned disk.

ȧtennu appellations.

ȧter, *ȧtru* river, canal, water-flood, stream; plur. .

ȧtert one half of the sky, or world.

ȧtert meḥt 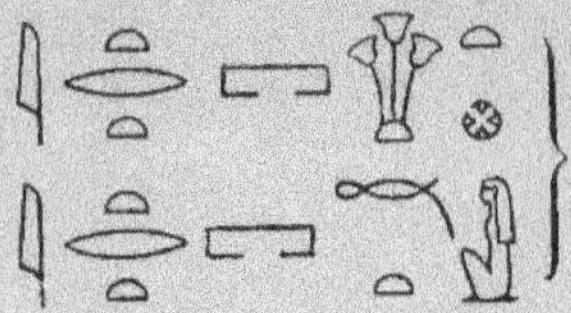 the northern half of the sky.

ȧtert shemā 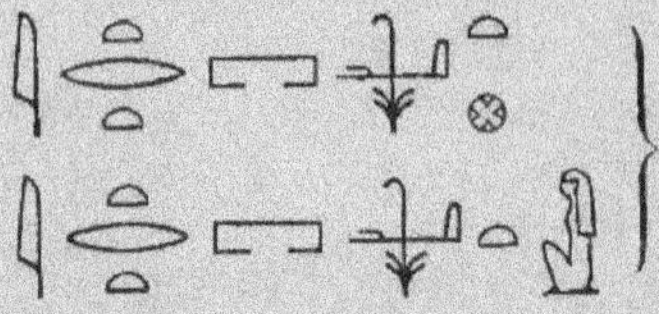 the southern half of the sky.

ȧterti

ȧturti  the two halves of the sky.

Ȧthabu  name of a city.

ȧtḥu 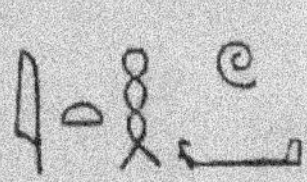 to drag, pull, draw.

Ȧtektaukehaqkheru 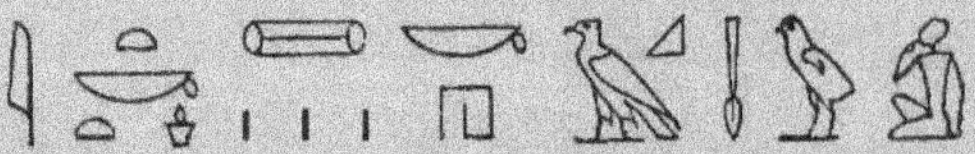 a proper name.

ȧṭ  oppression, oppressed one.

ȧṭ  to be deaf.

Ȧṭu  a city of the Eleventh Ȧat.

ȧṭu  children.

àṭeb  region, domain; plur. .

àṭmà 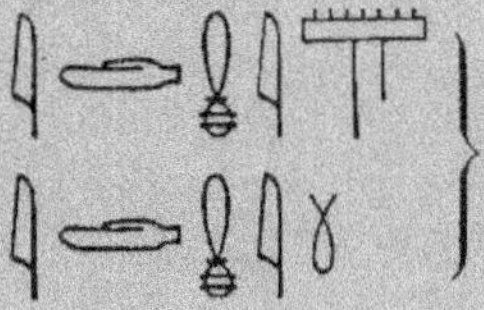 a kind of cloth, a ceremonial garment.

àṭen 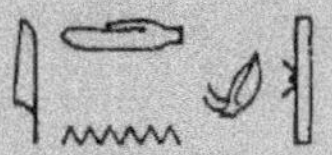 deputy, vicar, chief ?

àṭent 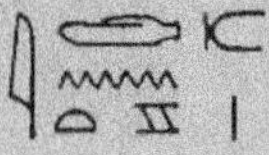 division, a separation.

àṭerit 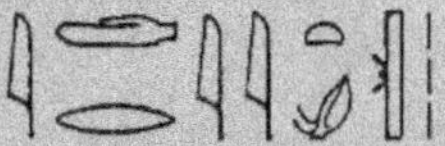 misfortunes, calamities.

àṭḥu  papyrus swamps, the Delta generally.

àṭeṭiu  those who injure.

àthi (**àti**)  prince, sovereign, king.

àthen 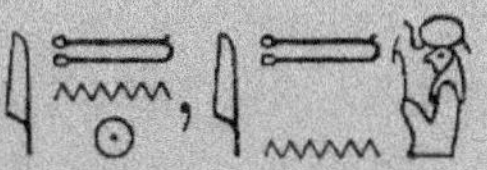 the solar disk, the god of the solar disk.

àtheth 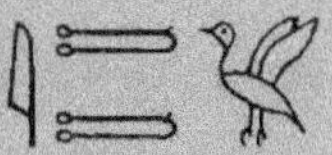 to hover, to alight.

àtcha  robber, man of violence, violence.

Ā.

ā — hand, arm, paw of an animal; dual [hieroglyphs], [hieroglyphs], [hieroglyphs]; plur. [hieroglyphs], power [hieroglyphs], [hieroglyphs] at once, straightway, immediately, [hieroglyphs] ancestor (see ṭep ā); [hieroglyphs] "Eater of the Arm", name of a god, [hieroglyphs] a flight, [hieroglyphs] action of battle, [hieroglyphs] place of yesterday, [hieroglyphs] before.

Āāiu, etc. [hieroglyphs] the name of the posts of the magic net (Chapter XCIX).

ā, āa [hieroglyphs] house, dwelling.

āa [hieroglyphs] to advance, journey onwards.

āa [hieroglyphs] door, gate; plur. [hieroglyphs]

āatu [hieroglyphs]; the two leaves of a door [hieroglyphs].

 gods of the doors.

 the two doors of the sky.

 the two doors of truth.

 the two doors of the sky.

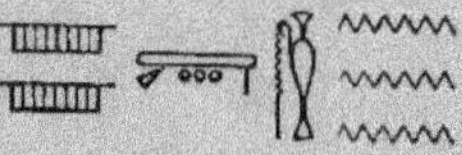 the two doors of Ta-qebḥ.

āa
āat
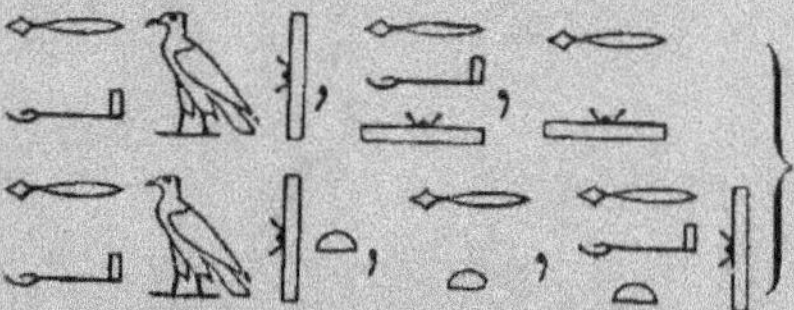 great, large, mighty, to be great;  great one,  great god, 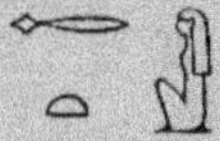 great goddess; plur. 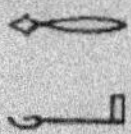  

āaui
āaāa
 twice great.

āati 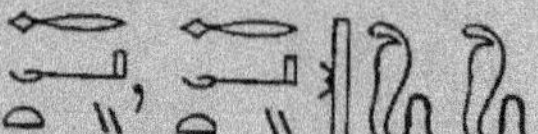 two great goddesses.

āa-ȧb  great of heart, *i. e.*, proud, arrogant.

 great forms, *i. e.*, possessing many forms.

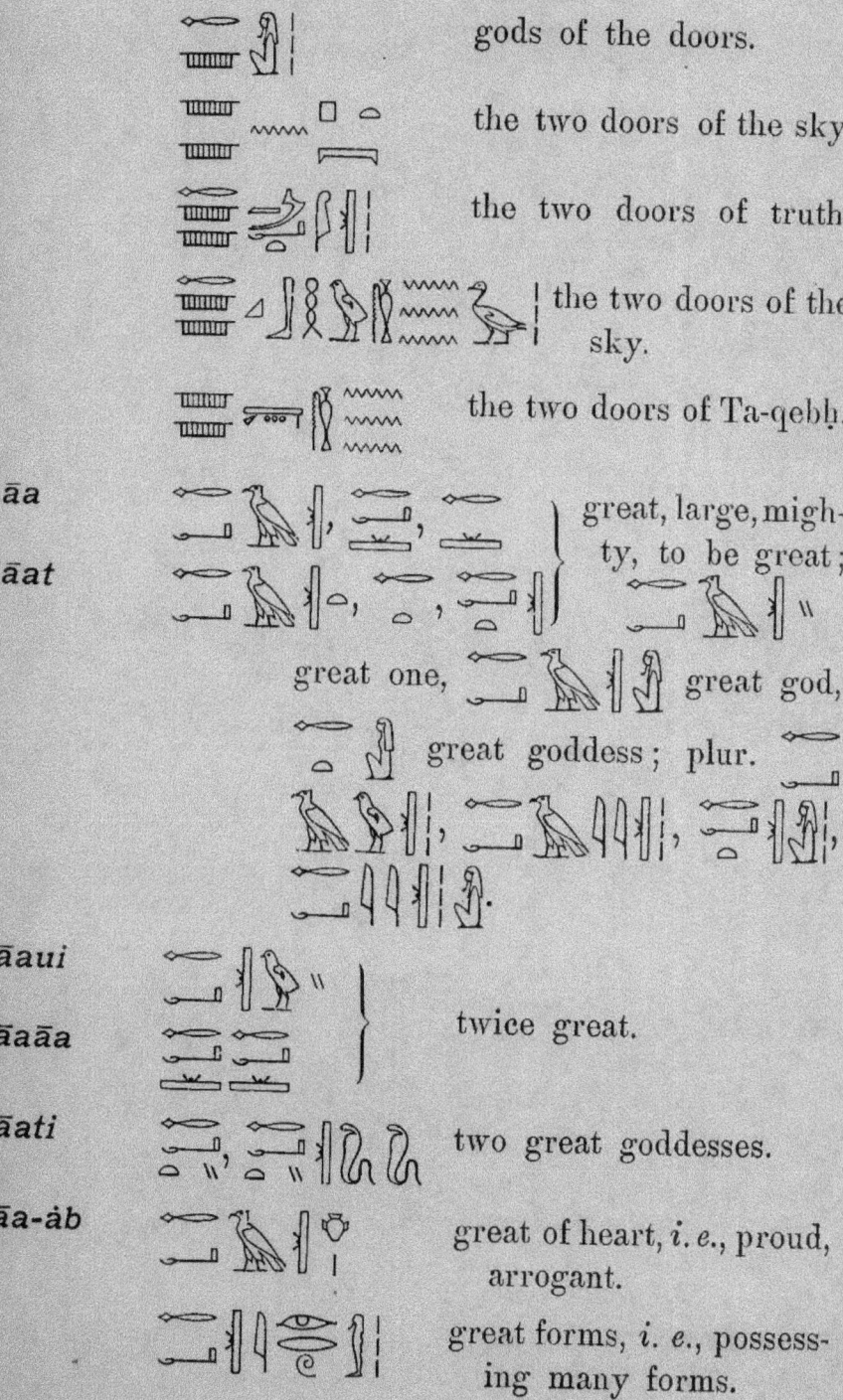

āat ur sep sen  most exceedingly great.

āa baiu  great of souls, *i. e.*, most valorous.

āa mertu 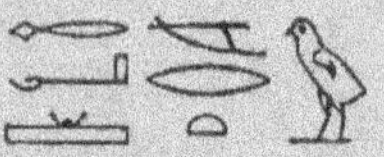 greatly beloved.

āa neruȧ  greatly victorious.

āa rennu  possessing many names.

āa khāu  possessing many crowns.

āa kheperu 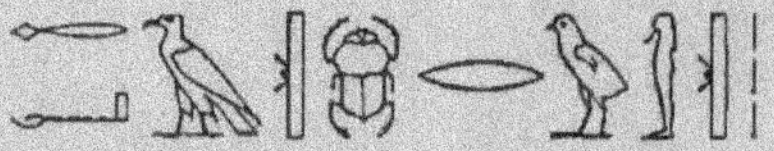 of many transformations.

āa senṭ 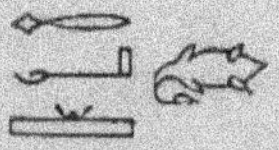 he who is greatly feared.

āa sekhemu  great one of powers.

āa sheps  most holy.

āa shefshefit  most terrible, or awful one.

Āa-kheru  "mighty of speech", the warder of the Seventh Ārit.

Āat-em-khut  "great one in the horizon", a proper name.

āā 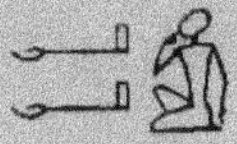 to eat?

āā 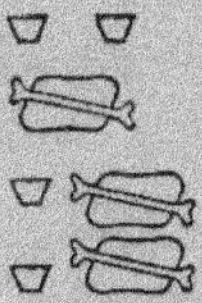 heir, inheritance, heritage, to inherit.

āat  stone amulet, plur. 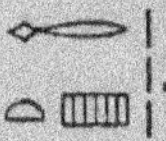.

āt, āāt 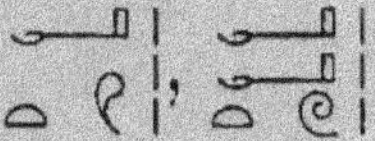 members, limbs, body.

āātu-pu-ent Kher-neter 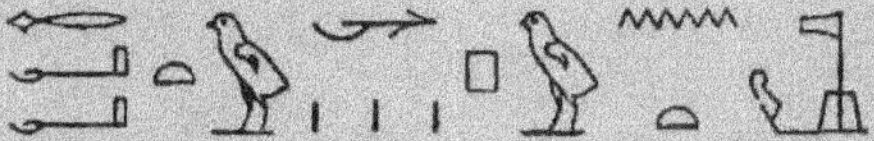 name of the oar-rests in the magic boat (Chap. CXIX).

Āaṭi  the name of one of the Forty-two Judges in the Hall of Osiris.

āu, āāu  ass.

āān, *āānā*, *āānāu* 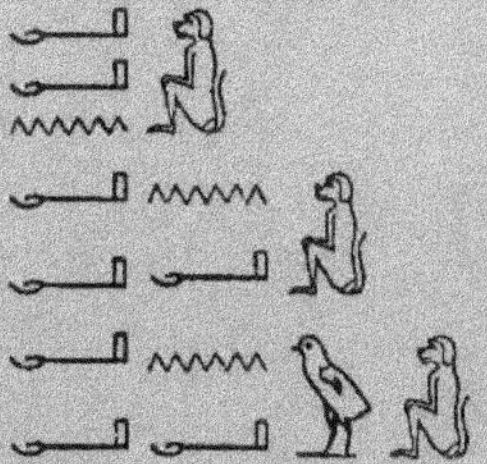 ape, monkey.

āu, *āut*  animals, quadrupeds.

āu  sins, offences (vol. II, 148, 4).

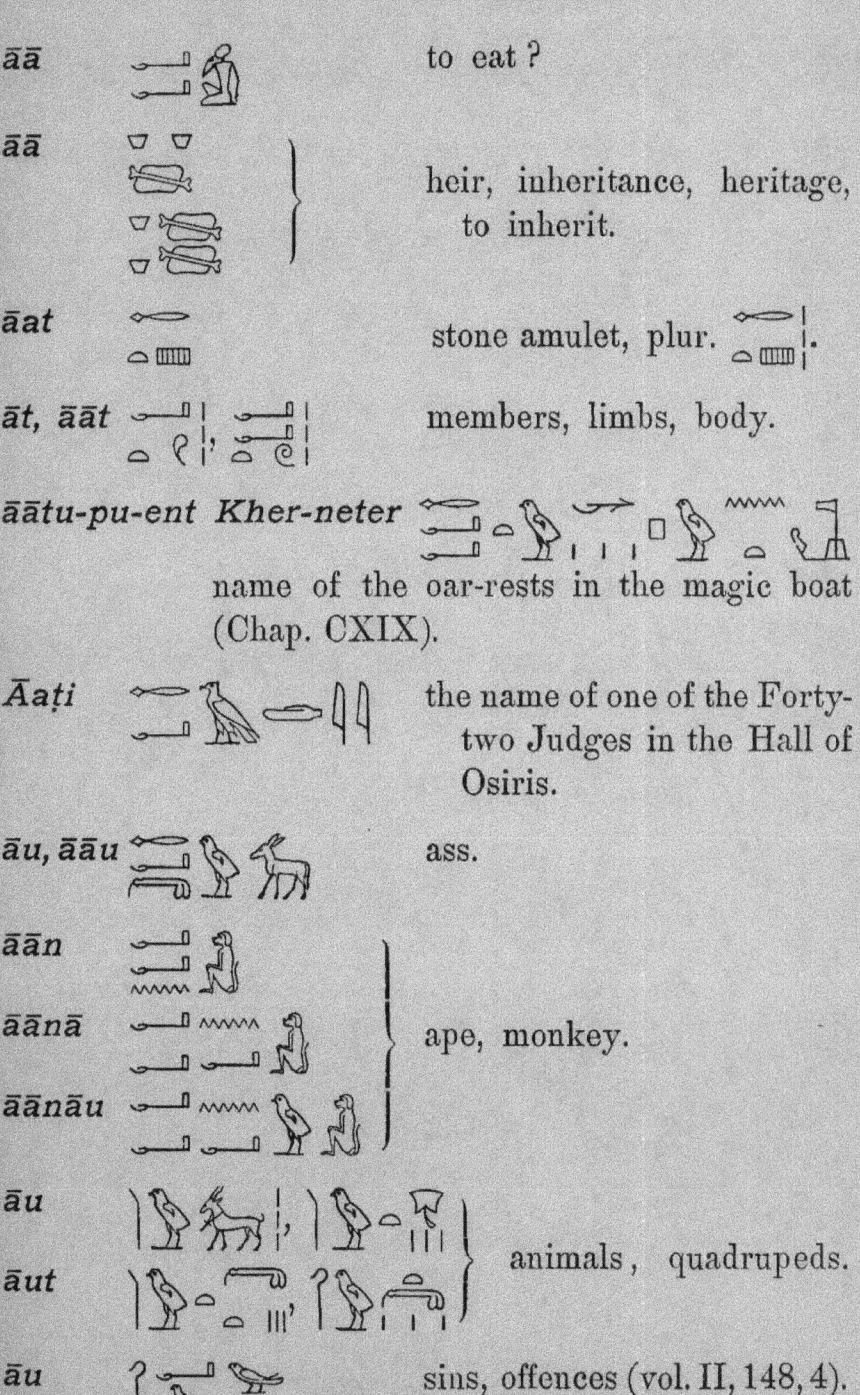

āua, **āuau** — to be strong, to act violently, to plunder, to rob, to oppress, vanquish, etc. , violence, wrong, evil act, evil doer, robber ; ill treated, oppressed ; (Chap. XVII, Nebseni, l. 25).

āuai — violence.

āun, **āunu** — , to be strong, violent, fierce.

āun-āb (?) — to be of a fierce disposition, violence.

āuq — pool, marsh, watery ground.

āb — , with , opposite, before, in front of, thus ; , , , , , .

āba (**uba**) — opposition.

āb — altar, table of offerings.

āb — to present offerings, to offer up a sacrifice.

ābuaa — to bring before, to present.

āab, *āabet*, *ābet* — offering, sacrifice; plur.

ābai (*āabai*) — sacrifice, offering, a priest who read the Liturgies.

āb (*uāb*), *ābu* (*uābu*), *ābet* (*uābet*) — clean, pure, holy, to be pure, to purify, to sprinkle or wash ceremonially.

āb (*uāb*) — libation, purification; plur.

āb (*uāb*) — libationer, a man ceremonially pure.

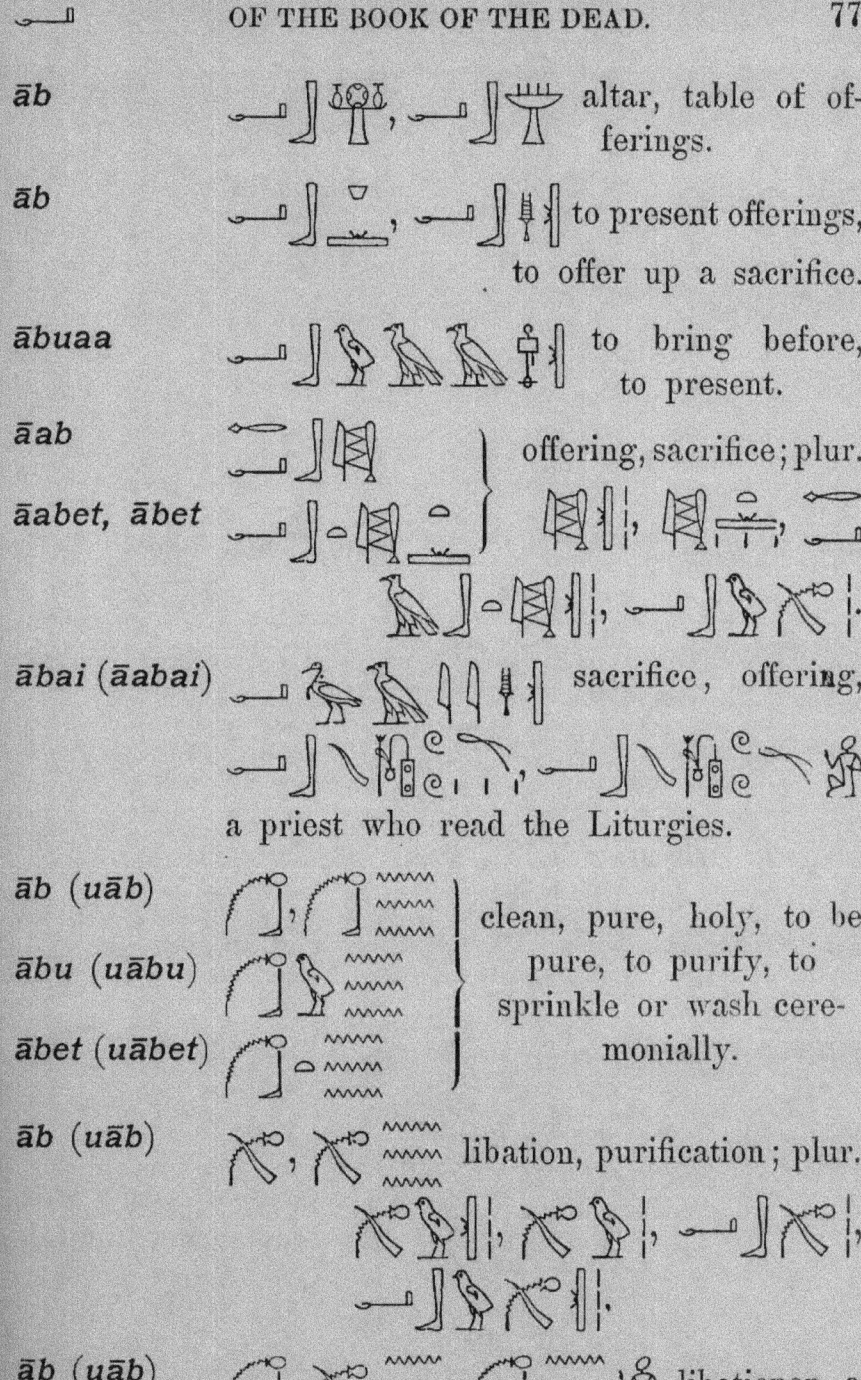

āb (*uāb*) pool of water used for purificatory purposes.

ābu (*uābu*) clean raiment, holy apparel.

ābet (*uābet*) water-house, bath, clean place; plur. ; great pure place

ābti (*uābti*) double holy place.

āb(*uāb*) *āāui* , clean-handed.

āb (*uāb*) *ru* clean-mouthed.

āb (*uāb*) *ḥeru* clean-faced beings.

ābu (*uābu*) propitiatory offerings.

Āb-ur (*Uāb-ur*) a title of Osiris.

āba (*uba*) to open or force a way, or passage, through something.

āba (*uba*) *ru* to open the mouth.

āba (*uba*), **ābet** (*ubet*), **ābata** (*ubata*) — entrance, opening.

āba — to see.

ābat (*ubat*) — fore-court of a temple.

Āba-ta (*Uba-ta*) — "Opener of the Earth", a name of a god.

Ābau-taui — the name of a god.

āb — horn; , two-horned; plur. ; broad-horned; *neb ābui* "lord of two horns" = Dhu 'l-Ḳarnên, a title of Alexander the Great.

ābiu — divine ancestors.

ābeb — to see.

āp (*āap*) , — to fly.

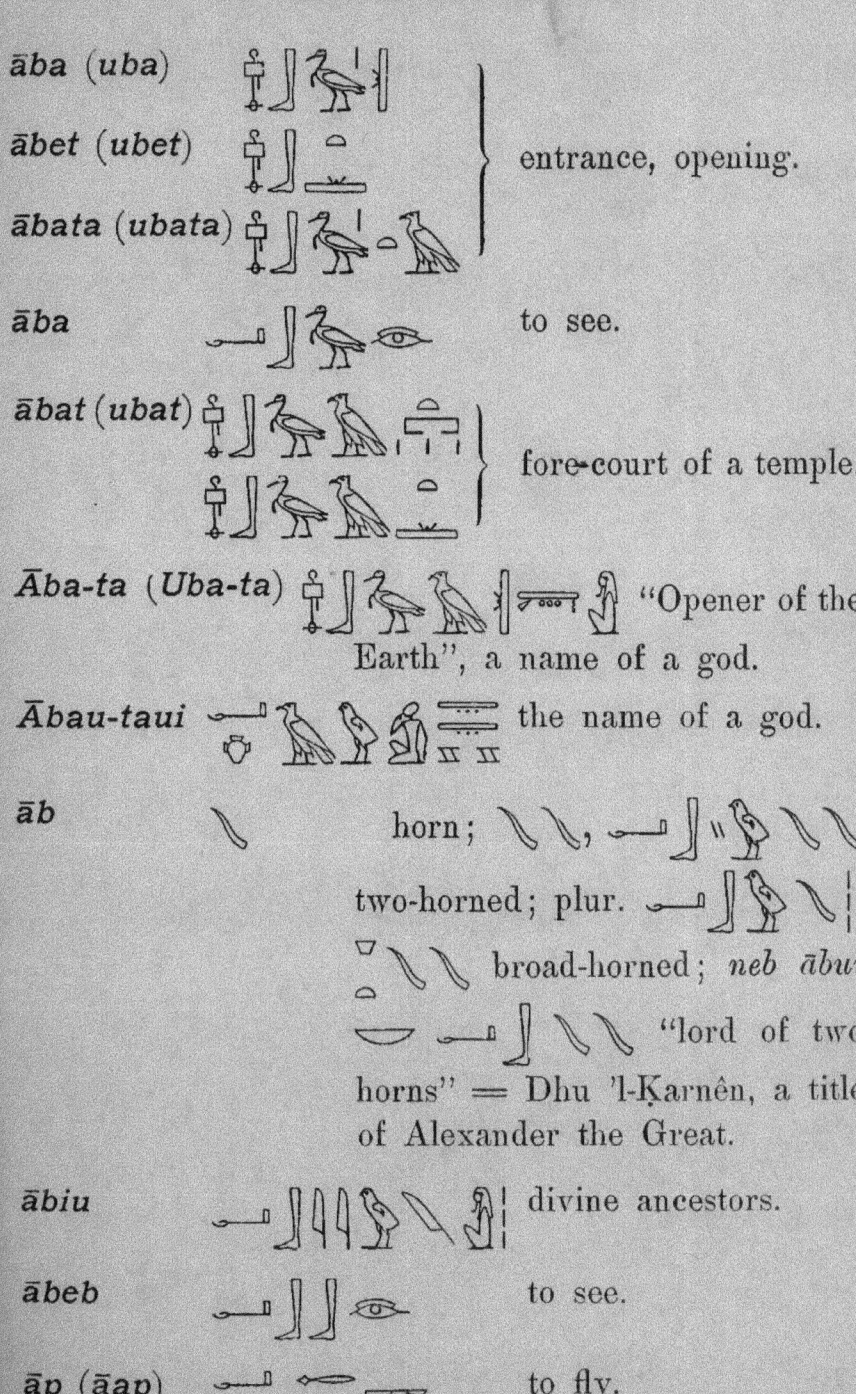

Āpep  the arch-enemy of Rā. Copt. ⲁⲫⲱⲫ "giant".

Āpef 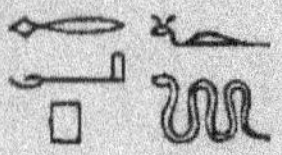 name of a fiend.

āper 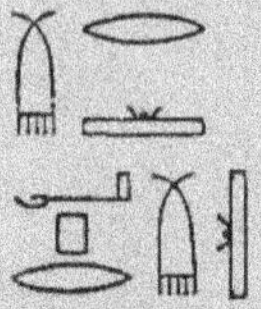 to be equipped or provided with, furnished with; 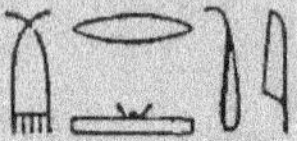 provided.

Āper / ***Āpert***  the name of a city and city-god.

āpesh  tortoise, turtle.

āpshait  a kind of beetle. Perhaps the weevil, the Muta Jambi, or "head of God", of the Bakuba of the Kasai District in the Congo Free State. (See T. A. Joyce in *Man*, vol. IX, No. 1, p. 3.)

āfa  filth.

āfau  food.

āfent 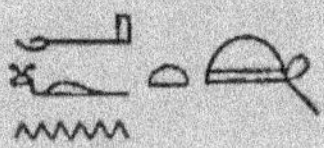 wig, headdress; plur. 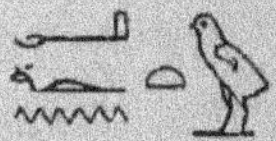

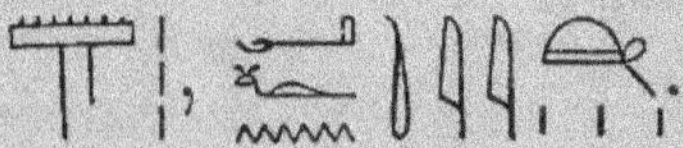.

āftet  place, abode, chest.

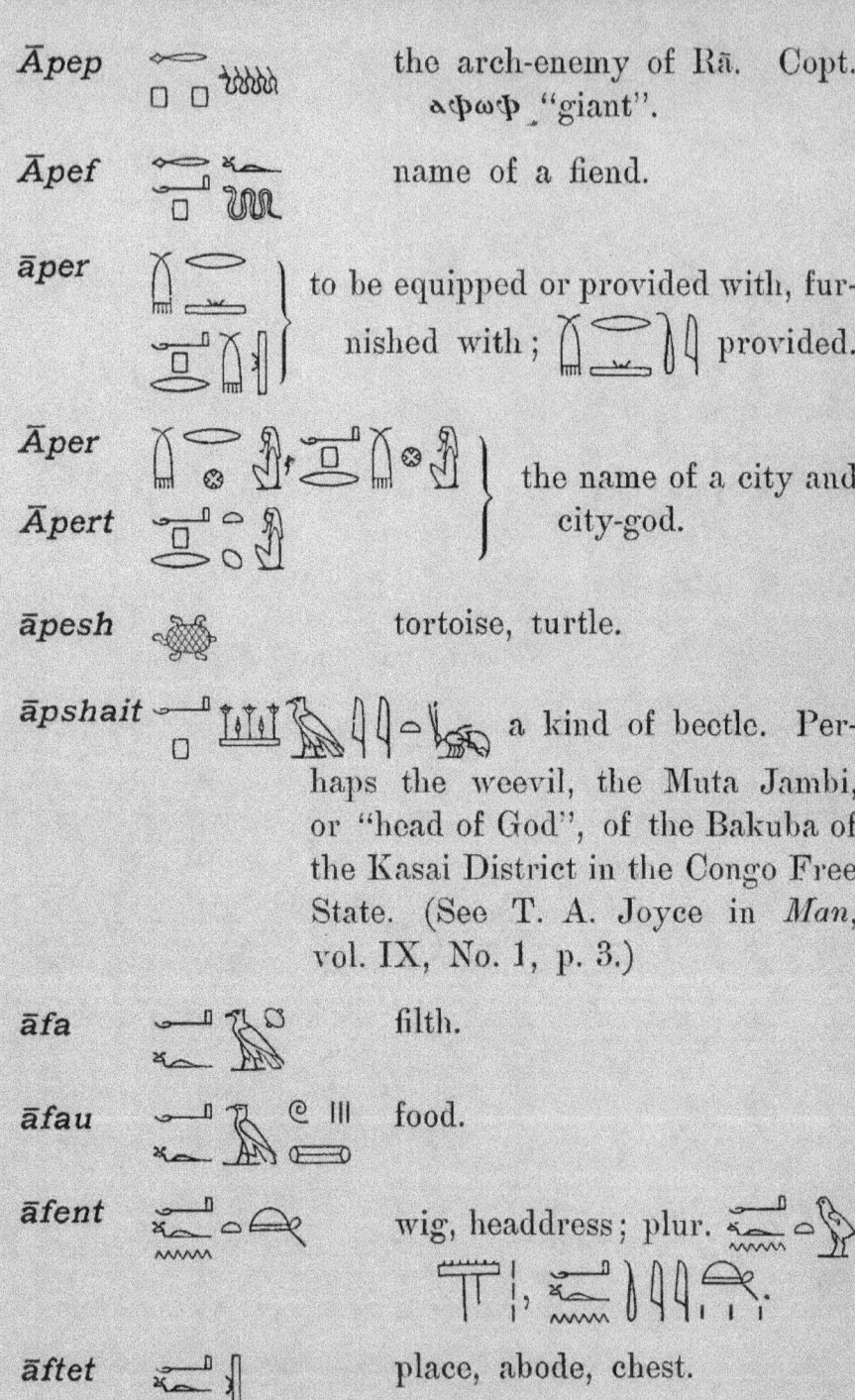

āfṭet 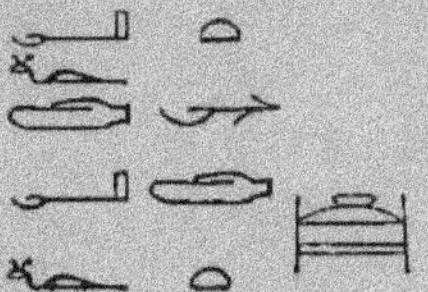 place, abode, chest.

ām  to eat, consume, devour; 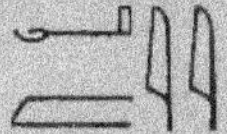  eaters.

āmam 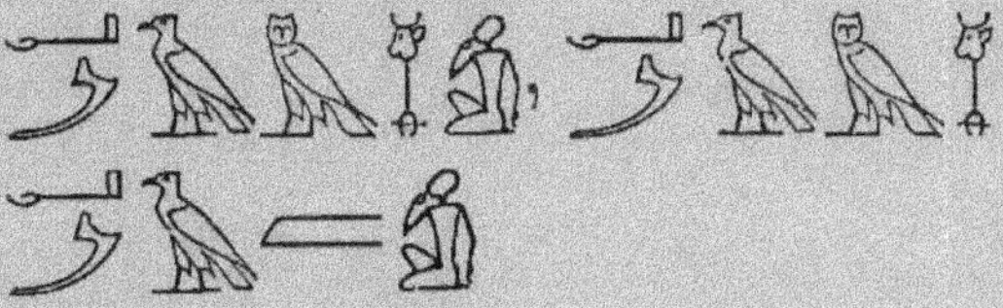 to eat, to understand, to comprehend.

āmt  what is eaten, food.

ām ȧb  "to eat the heart", *i. e.*, become angry and rage.

āmam-ȧrit  "Eater of the Eye"; name of a god.

Ām-āu 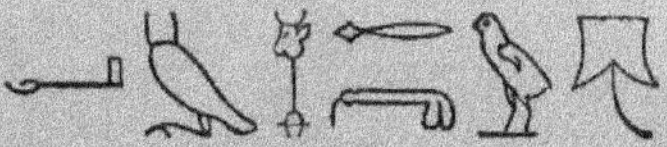 "Eater of the Ass"; name of a fiend and enemy of Rā.

Ām-ȧsfetti 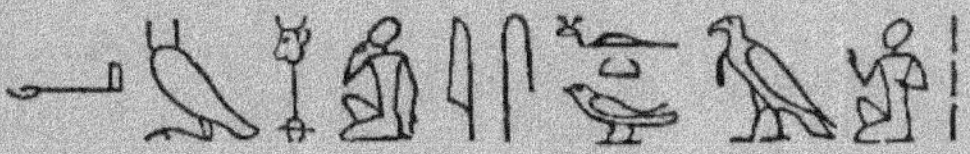 "Eater of Sinners"; name of a god.

Ām-baiu  "Eater of souls"; name of a fiend.

Ām-ḥeḥ  "Eater of eternity".

Ām-khaibitu  "Eater of Shades"; the name of one of the Forty-two Judges in the Hall of Osiris.

Āmām 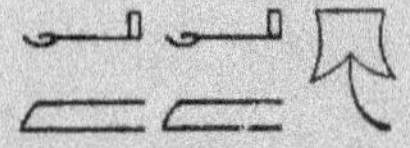 "Devourer"; the name of the Eater of the dead.

Ām-mit  "Devourer of the dead".

Ām-mit  a consuming serpent goddess.

Ān 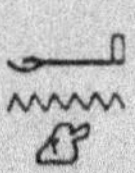 a proper name.

ān 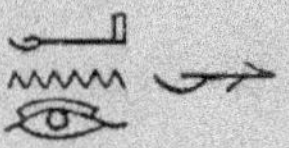
āni 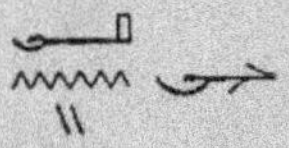 } tablet, board, writing palette.

ān 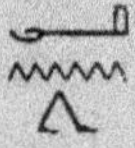 to turn back. Partic. plur.  those who turn away, or return.

ānu  a mythological fish.

Ānpet 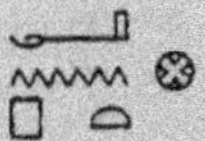 a name of the city of Mendes.

ānkh  to live, to live upon, to feed upon, life, living one, living; 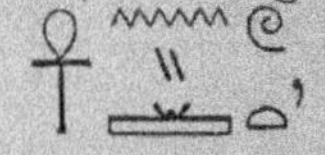, 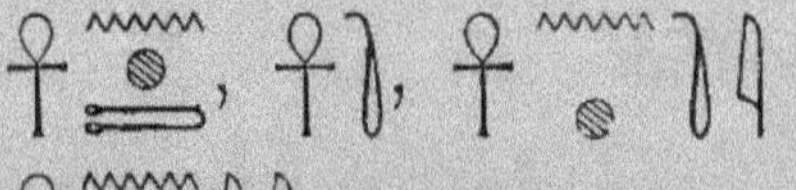 alive. Copt. ⲱⲛϩ.  the living one, a name of Osiris.

ānkhu,
ānkhiu  the living, men and women, title of the blessed dead.

ānkh tchetta 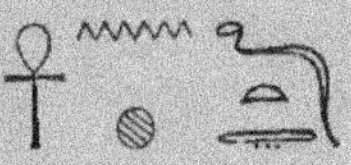 the living for ever. 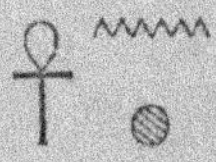 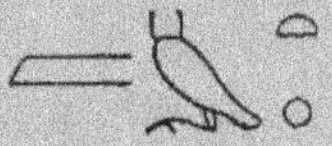 life from death.

ānkh user  life and power.

ānkh utcha senb 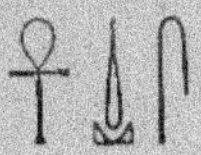 life, strength and health.

ānkhet 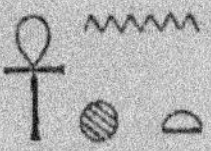 life.

ānkhet 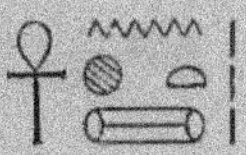 victuals.

Ānkhti 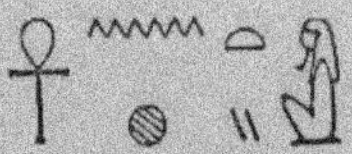 a name of Osiris.

ānkh 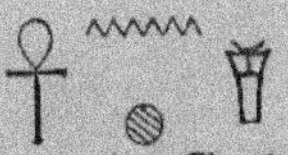 a kind of unguent.

Ānkhet pu ent Sebek neb Bakhau 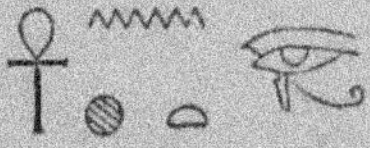 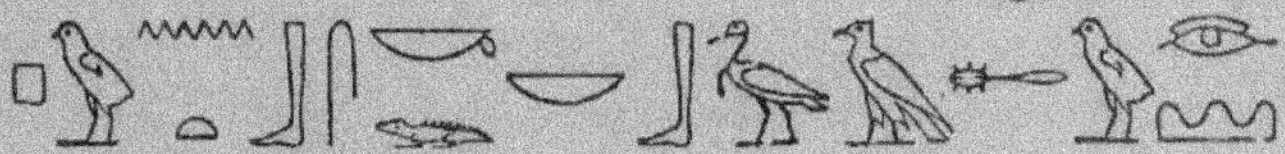 a proper name.

Ānkh-em-bu 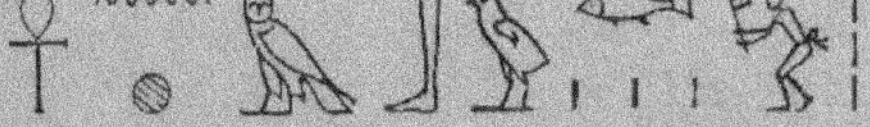 "Eater of abominable things".

Ānkh-em-fentu  "Eater of worms"; name of the warder of the Fifth Ārit.

ānkhui  the two ears.

ānkhâmu 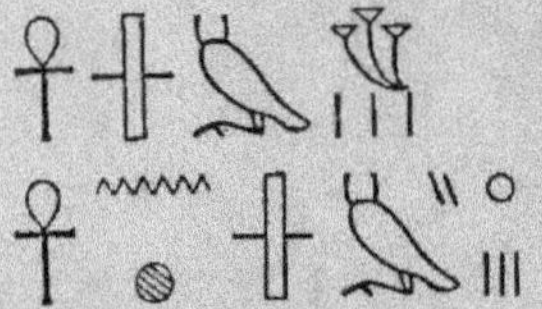 flowers, or aromatic plants.

ānt  ring.

ānt 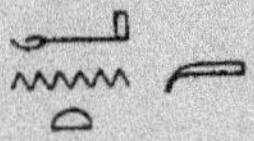 to be covered with something.

ānt 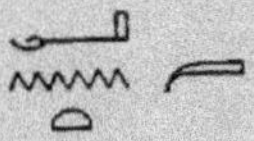 claw, talon, hook, nail of the hand or foot, 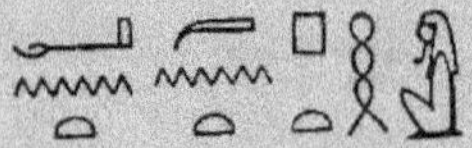 "Claw of Ptaḥ"; a proper name.

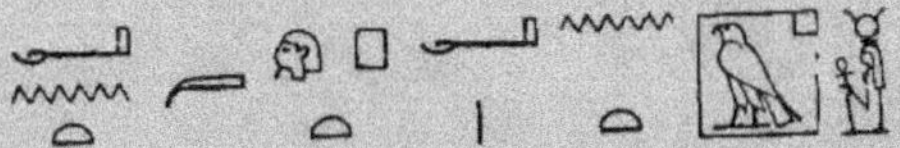 "Claw on the hand of Hathor"; a proper name.

ānti 

ānṭ 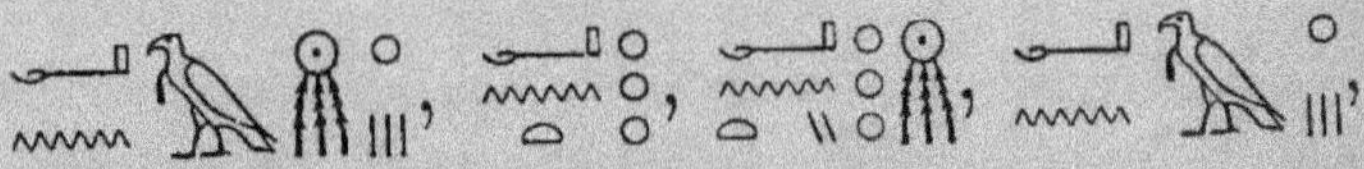 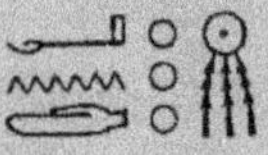 myrrh, unguent (?).

ānti a preparation of myrrh used by women.

ānṭu light, radiance.

ānṭ evil.

ānṭu darkness.

Ānṭi the name of one of the Forty-two Judges in the Hall of Osiris.

ār an animal of the goat species.

ār to approach, to bring, to come, to arrive; ; divine beings who approach.

ārȧ to find (?).

ārār jawbone.

ārārt uraeus.

ārāti two uraei goddesses.

two very large uraei.

the living serpent goddesses.

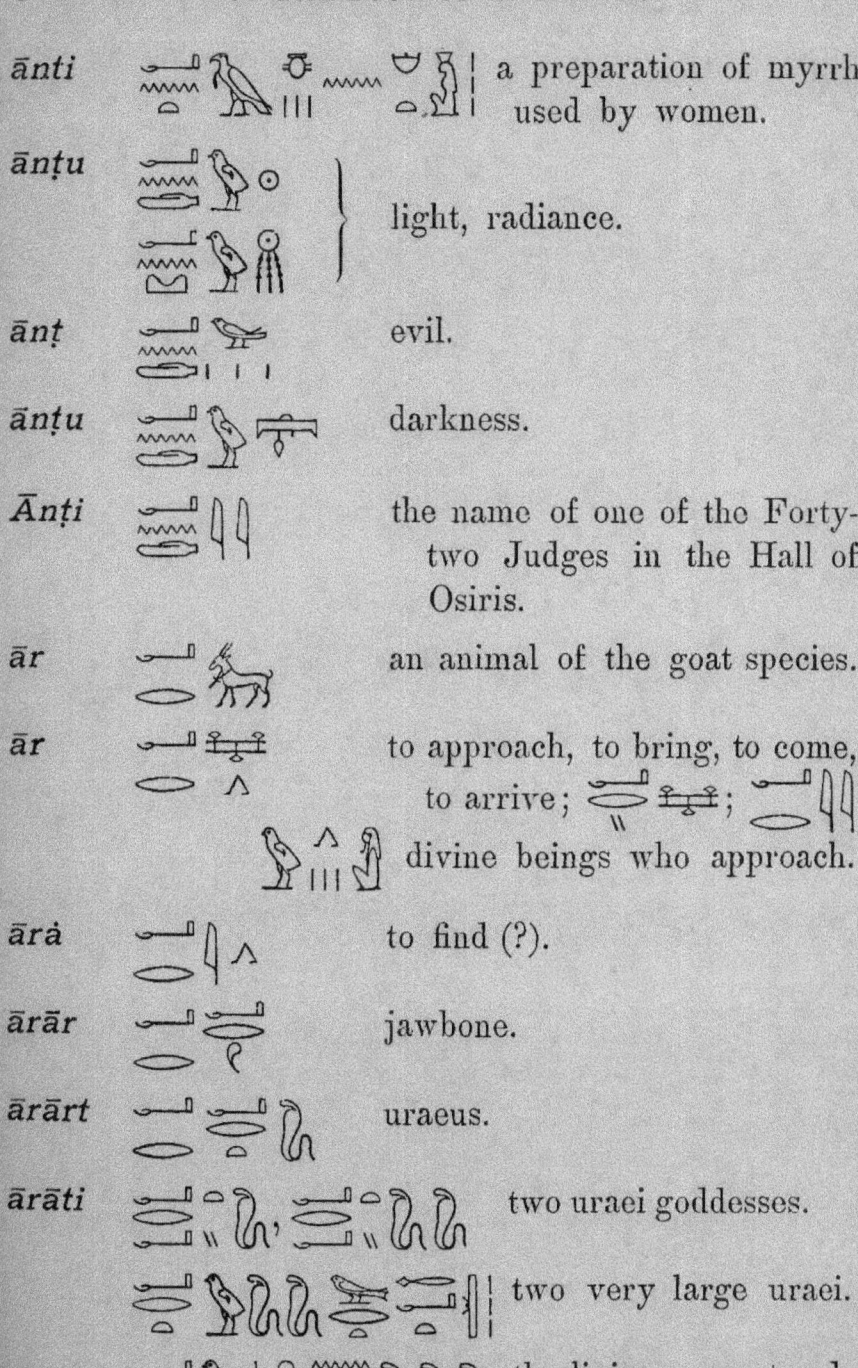

ārit 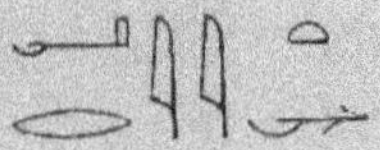 tool, lintel of a door.

ārit 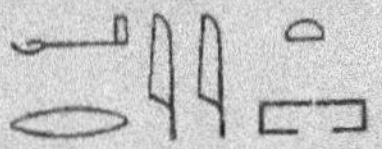 hall, chamber; plur. 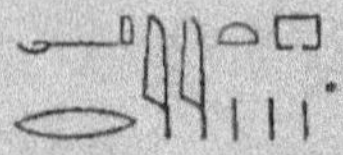

The Seven Ārits 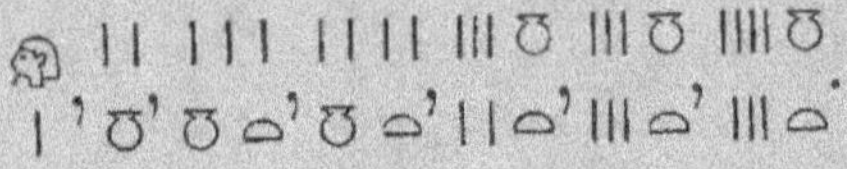

ārfi 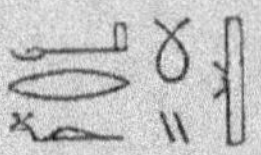 bundle, purse.

ārrt 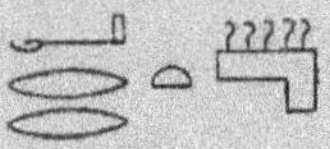
ārrit 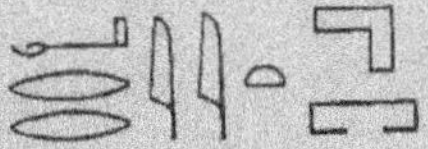 hall, mansion; plur. 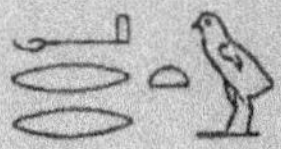 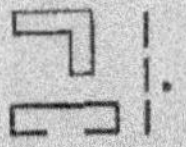

Ārq 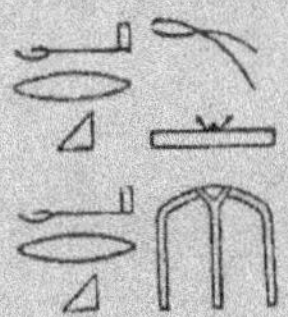 to bind, to tie, girdle, to be completed.

ārq 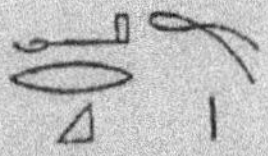 to swear.

Ārq-ḥeḥ  name of a city.

ārq 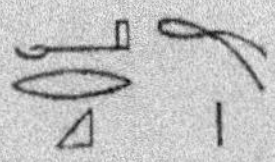 end; 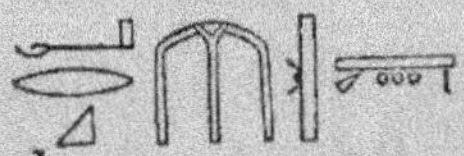 end of the earth.

ārqi  last day of the lunar month.

ārt 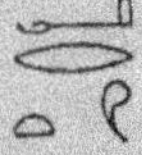 jaw, jawbone.

ārti 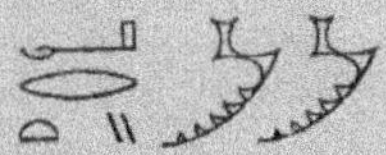 the two jaws.

ārtu  houses, abodes, mansions.

āḥ 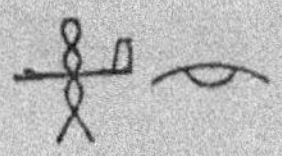 moon.

āḥ 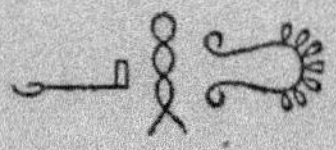 to surround, embrace.

āḥa, *āḥau*  to fight, do battle, wage war;  fighter,  fightings.

āḥa-ā  to fight bravely (?).

āḥa-tu  fight, contest, struggle.

āḥau  fighting implements, weapons.

āḥaui 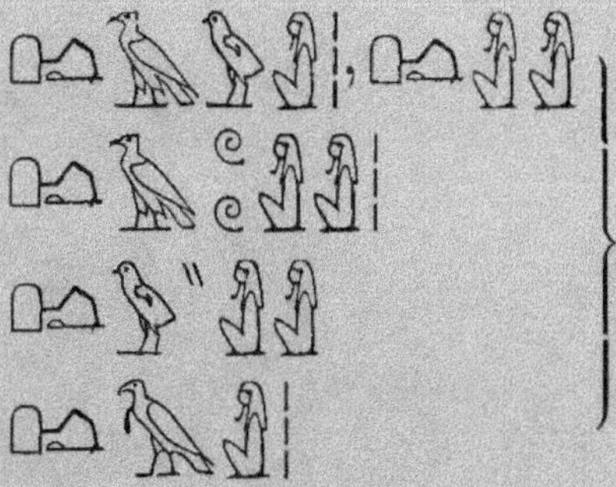 the two Fighters, *i. e.*, Horus and Set.

Āḥau ḥeru  "Fighting faces", a name of certain gods.

āḥāt 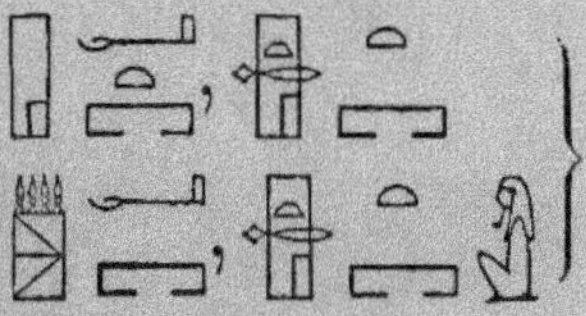 great house, palace.

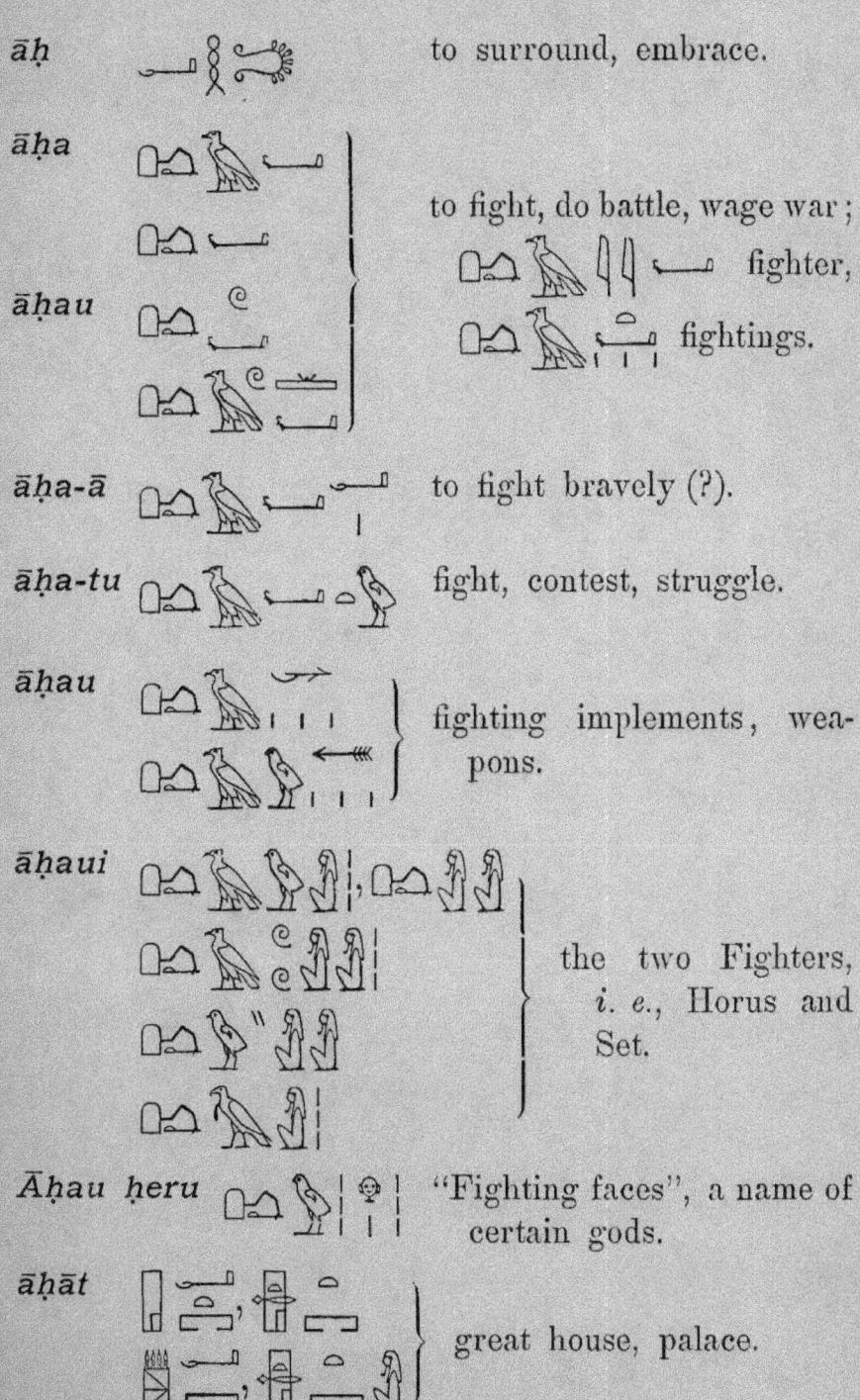

āḥā — to stand up, to withstand.

āḥā — as an auxiliary verb: , and see *passim*.

āḥā — stability.

āḥāu — condition, state, position.

āḥā, āḥāu, āḥāt — time, season or duration of life, life, a contemporary.

period from life, or in life.

period of eternity.

āḥāu — noon-day.

āḥāu — supports.

āḥāu — stores, food, provisions.

folk who are provisioned.

āḥāit boat.

āḥāt tomb.

ākh to spread out the heavens, or sky.

Ākhtuset a class of divine beings. The variants are: *ākhmiu*. *àukhu-seku*. *ākhsemiu*.

ākha to fly, to soar; *ākhai* flying.

ākha to sleep.

ākhan
ākhanet } to close the eye.

ākhu fire-altars.

ākhem
ākhemu } to quench, to extinguish; quenched.

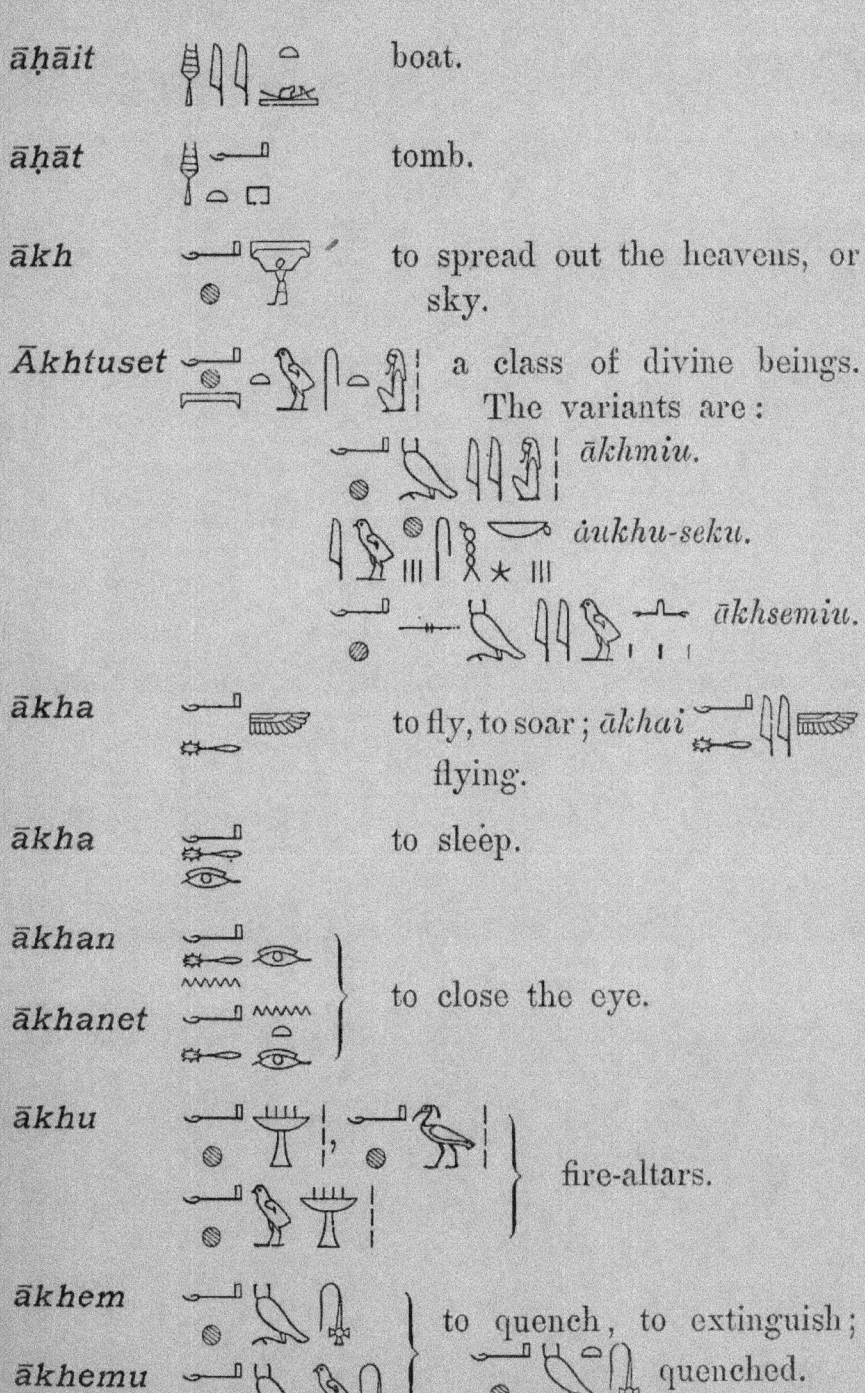

ākhemu 
ākhmiu  quenchers, those who extinguish.

ākhem  figure of a god.

ākhemu  figures of gods.

ākhmet  river banks.

Ākhen-àriti(?)-*f* 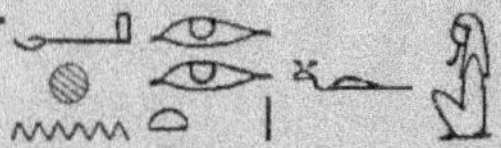 a proper name.

ākhekhau  serpent-fiends, monsters.

ākhekhu  "Darkness"; a proper name.

āsha  to be much or many, manifold.

 many reeded.

 of multitudinous festivals.

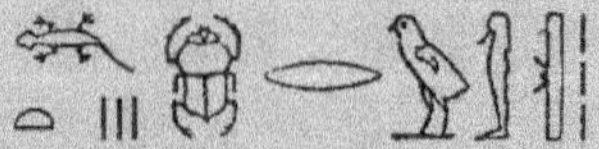 of many forms.

 loud voiced to speak.

āshau
āshat  crowd, multitude.

āshat  crowd, multitude.

āsh  to call, to invoke, to cry out.

āshu ,

 evil speech.

āsh  cedar, or acacia, tree, cedar gum.

āshāsht 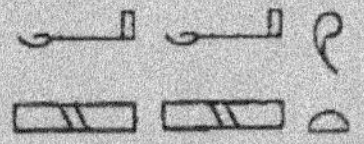 part of the body.

āshāt 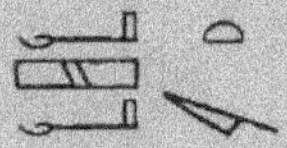 knife.

āshem  the forms in which the gods appear upon earth.

āshemu 

āshemiu  crocodiles. A variant gives  .

āshashat 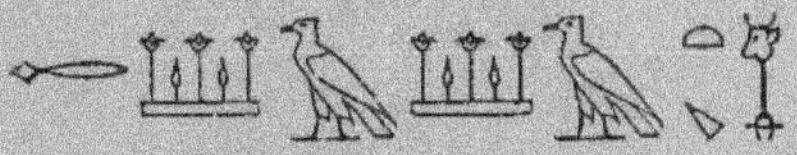 gullet.

Ākesh  name of a city.

āq 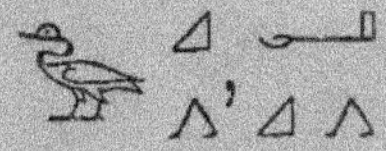 to enter, go in.

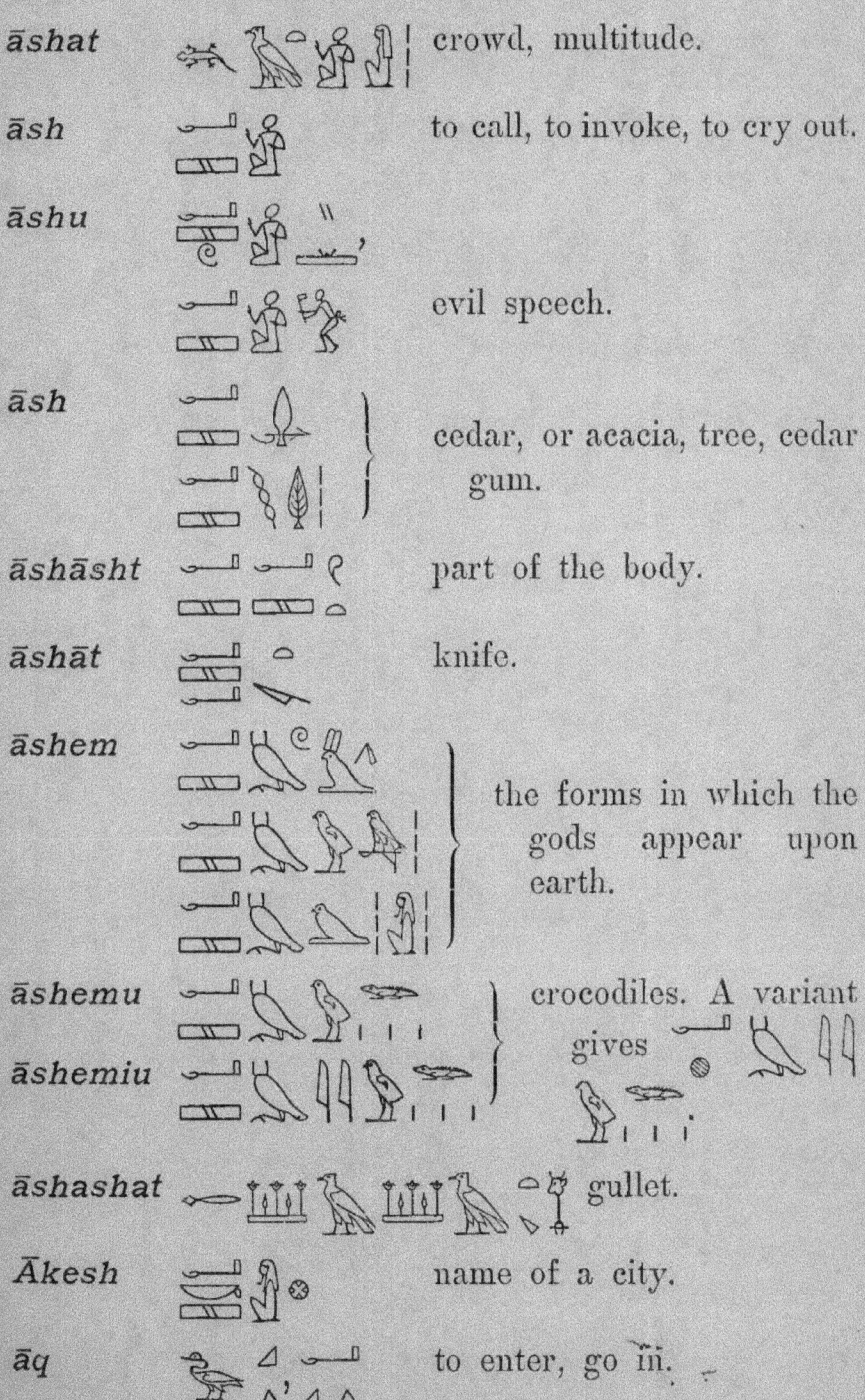

āqiu  those who enter.

āqet 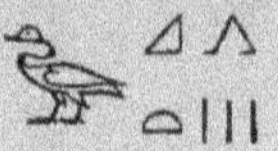 things which enter.

āq pert  entrance and exit.

Āq-ḥer-âmi-unnut-f  "He who enters in his hour"; a proper name.

āqu  cakes, loaves of bread.

āqa  to present bread (?). Chap. XCIX, 3.

āq maāt (?)  exact truth (?), just.

āqa  to keep the mean, right, exact, true, just, truth, to be in the middle.

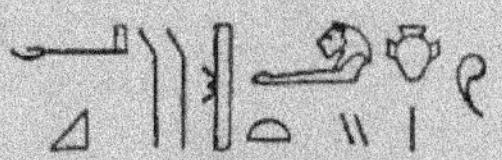 to be exactly over the heart.

āqau  truth, right, justice.

Āqan  the name of a god.

āqi 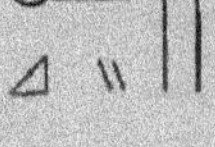 part of a boat.

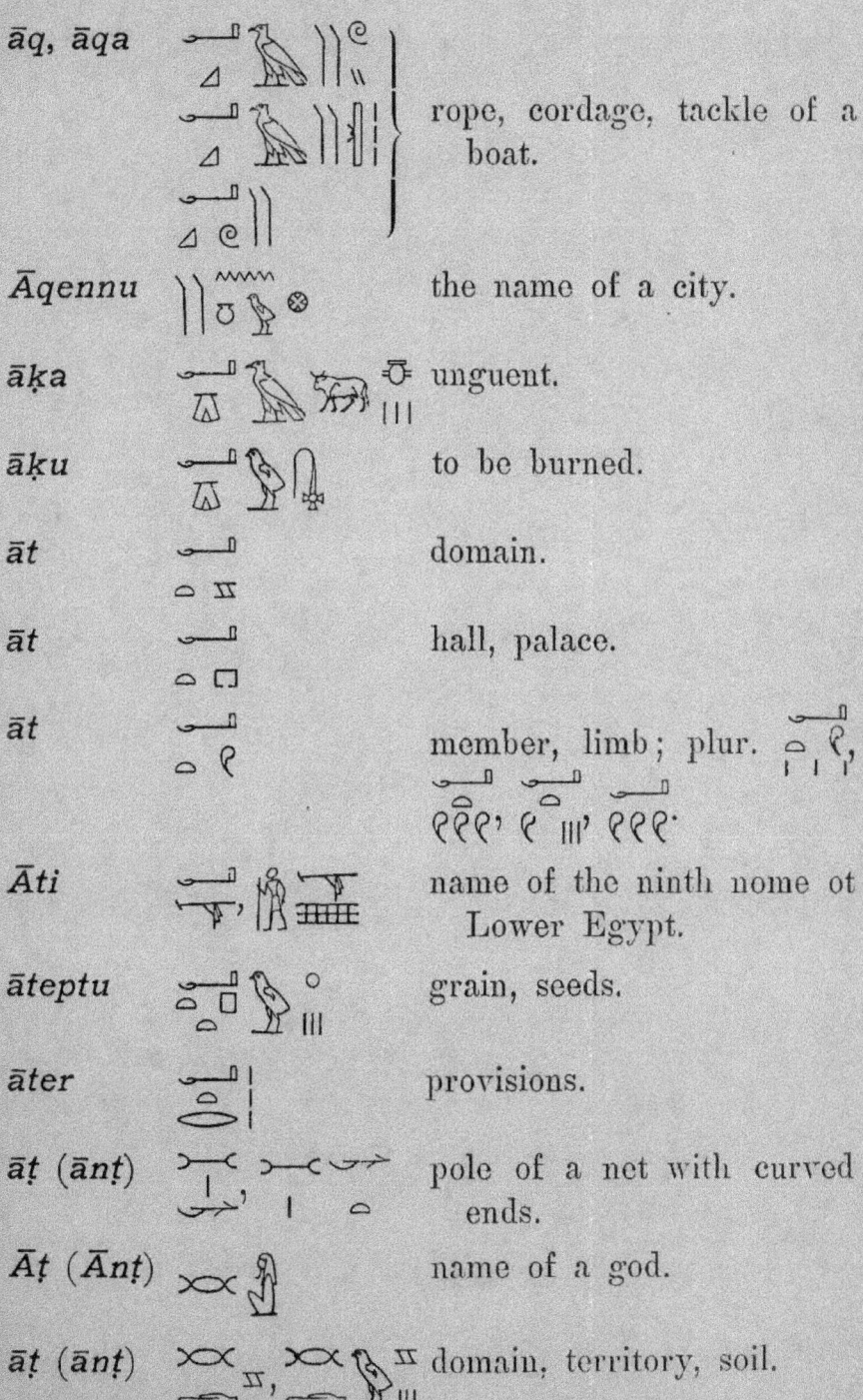

āq, āqa	rope, cordage, tackle of a boat.
Āqennu	the name of a city.
āḳa	unguent.
āḳu	to be burned.
āt	domain.
āt	hall, palace.
āt	member, limb; plur.
Āti	name of the ninth nome ot Lower Egypt.
āteptu	grain, seeds.
āter	provisions.
āṭ (*ānṭ*)	pole of a net with curved ends.
Āṭ (*Ānṭ*)	name of a god.
āṭ (*ānṭ*)	domain, territory, soil.

āṭ (*ānṭ*) to split, to divide.

Āṭ (*Ānṭ*) the morning boat of the sun.

āṭu name of a mythological fish.

āṭurtu (a mistake ?)

Ātch-ur "Great splitter"; name of a god.

ātchet (*āntchet*) fixed, firm.

, U.

. . . . Chap. CLXVIII. Circle X, 14, 2.

u they, them, their.

u district, region.

Ua a proper name.

ua, *uau* to depart, go away, be afar off ; remote.

ua  way, path, road; plur. 

uau

uau  waterway, stream.

uauau  radiance, light.

uau  flame, fire.

uau  chains, fetters.

uauu  to speak evil, blaspheme.

uauiuait  hair.

uai  to destroy, overcome, gain the mastery over.

Uaipu  a cow-goddess.

uab  flower, blossom.

Uamemti  the name of one of the Forty-two Judges in the Hall of Osiris.

uart  ropes, cordage.

Uarekht (?) 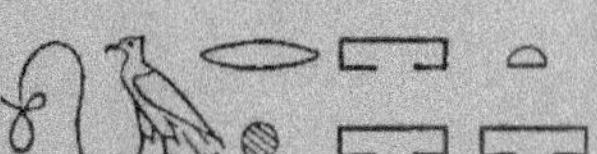 a mythological region.

Uart-neter-semsu a proper name.

uaḥ to place, to set, to fix, to add to, permanent, abiding.

to add to something.

uaḥit libation vessels.

uaḥuu mummy bandages.

uaḥtu to mummify.

uakh
uakhet } "Green"; the name of a pool in the Elysian Fields.

uas sceptre.

uas contentment, happiness.

Uast Thebes.

uash to worship, be adored; two-fold worship.

Uaḳ } the name of a festival.

uat way, road, path; plur. , ; great roads, good roads, all roads, ways of the dead; the two roads.

eastern roads.

western roads.

northern roads.

southern roads.

uatch sceptre, staff, stick.

uatch tablet of green faïence, amulet.

uatch unguent, sulphate of copper eye-paint.

uatchu sulphate of copper.

uatch shemāt sulphate of copper of the south.

uatchet a kind of linen.

uatch  to make to flourish, be green, vigorous, to blossom, be new, fresh.

uatchet 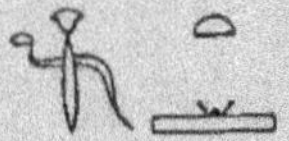 green.

uatchet  green things, plants, herbs.

uatchu 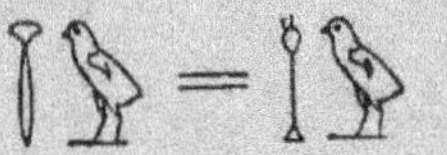 *q. v.*

Uatch-àriti (?) 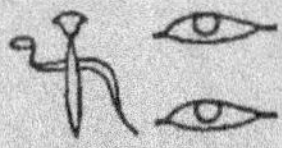 "Green Eyes"; a proper name.

Uatch-ur
Uatch-urà 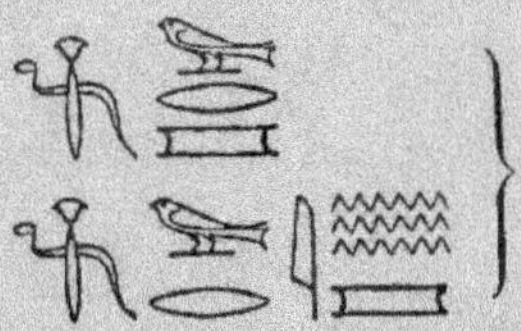 "Great Green Sea"; *i. e.*, the Mediterranean.

Uatch-nesert 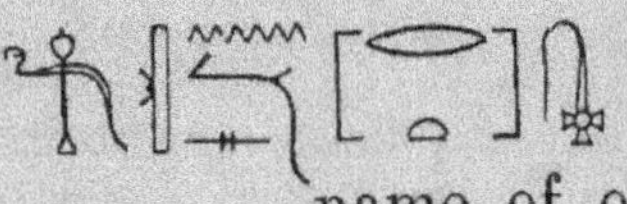 "Green Flame"; the name of one of the Forty-two Judges in the Hall of Osiris.

Uatchit 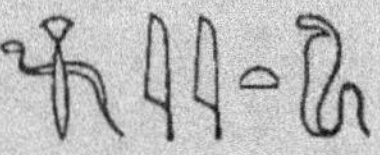 a goddess of fire.

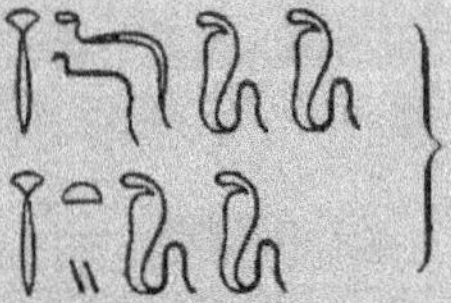 the two fire-goddesses, Isis and Nephthys.

uatchit  abode, house.

uà  I, me.

uȧa — boat, boat of Rā.

uȧaui — the two boats of Rā, the boats of morning and evening.

uȧa en Maāti — the boat of Maāt.

uȧa en ḥeḥ — "Boat of Millions of Years".

uȧn — to become worms.

uā, *uāu* — One, the One, *i. e.*, God. One of the gods;

One God (Osiris); One (fem.).

uā — one; fem. ; , being one, or alone; to be one .

uā—ki one ... the other; one embraced the other; fem. ... ; one in one; one of one.

uā = indefinite article ,

uā neb any one, each one, every one.

uā uāu one alone, only one.

uāu alone. Also and .

uāuti solitude.

uā with at once, all at once; and compare , .

uāt in a piece of cloth.

Uāau the herald of the Third Ārit.

uār passage.

uār to depart.

uārt passage, the name of a place.

uārt , , thigh; the two thighs.

"thigh" of water.

"thigh" of the lake.

"thigh" surrounding.

"thigh" of iron whereon is the station of the gods.

that "thigh" of Kher-āḥa.

that "thigh" whereon is the House of the Moon.

uārt stream.

uu evil, evil one.

uu region, district; ,

ui sign of the dual. two very mighty gods.

Ui a proper name.

uit chamber.

uben to rise (of a luminary), to shine; rising and setting;

ubennu, *ubentu* rays of light.

ubennu to flow.

ubekh, *ubekht* to shine, light up, shining, blazing.

ubes water-flood.

ubesu beings of fire, sparks (?).

Ubes-ḥer-per-em-khetkhet "Fiery face, coming forward in retreating"; a proper name.

ubeṭ to be scalded, to set fire to, to burn up.

ufa to chance on, to light upon.

umet a garment.

umet the middle (?).

umet walls, fortifications, building.

un lightness, defect.

un, unen , to be, being, existence, to become, to exist; as an auxiliary verb see *passim*.

unt, *unent* being, existence; , , , , ; plur. , , ; those who are, things which are.

uniu human beings.

un maā , in very truth.

un , , , , , , , to open, opener, opening; , opened.

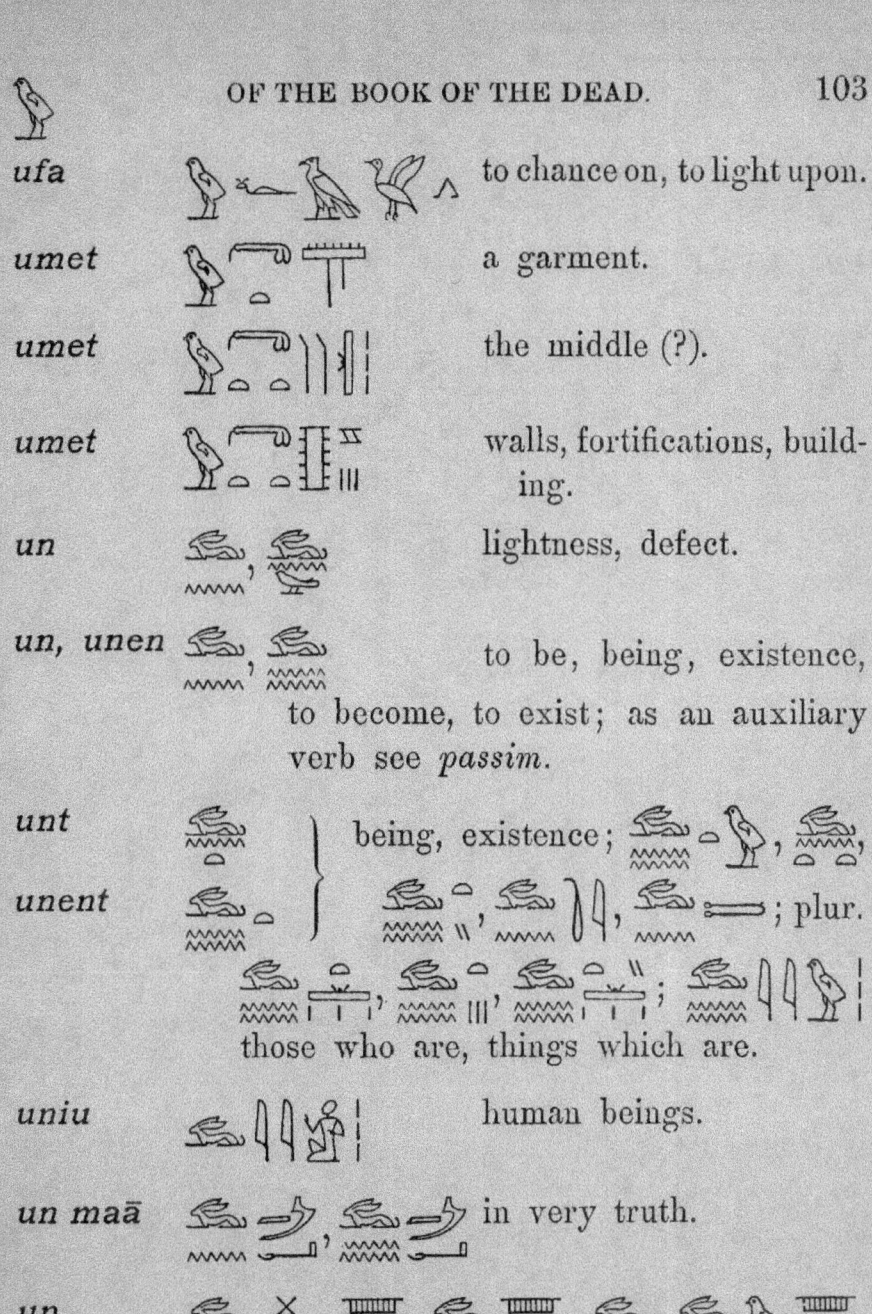

uniu / *uneniu* openers, scatterers.

un ḥer to open the face, *i. e.*, show the face, to appear; ; to open the mouth , .

un shrine.

un shaved.

un / *unnu* to pull out the hair.

un, uni, unt , , to walk, run, rise upright; runners.

unun , , / *unn-unn* to run, stand up.

unun to sow seed.

Unȧset name of a city.

unām unguent.

Uniu, or *Unniu* name of a city.

unini light.

uni light, defective.

Unen-em-ḥetep a division of the Sekhet-Àaru.

unb flower, bloom; plur.

unpet flowers, blossoms.

Unpepet ent Ḥet-Ḥeru "Flower of Hathor"; a proper name.

unef to remove, to uncover, to unloose.

unem
unemi
unemt the right side, the right as opposed to left.

unem to eat, see *Àm*.

unnu evil, wrong, defect.

Unnu Hermopolis, the city of Thoth.

unnuiti sacrificer.

unnut a brief space of time, a moment, an hour, a season, interval. Plur.

Unnut goddess of the hour.

Un-Nefer, *Unen-nefer*, *Unen-Neferu*, *Unen-Neferu* A title of Osiris, meaning something like "the well-doing Being". Coptic forms of the name are ⲟⲩⲉⲛⲉⲃⲣ̄ⲉ, ⲟⲩⲉⲛⲟⲃⲣ, ⲟⲩⲉⲛⲟⲃⲣⲓ, ⲱⲛⲟⲫⲣⲉ, etc.

Un-Nefer-Rā.

Un-Nefer, son of Nut.

Un-ḥāt a proper name.

unkh, *unkhu* to dress, to array oneself, to put on a garment.

unkh to tie, untie, set loose.

unkh a garment.

Unes — the metropolis of the XIXth Nome of Lower Egypt.

unshu — wolves.

Unt — a city of the Twelfth Àat.

Unti — the name of a god.

un tini — be ye.

unṭu — mankind, people, kinsfolk, relatives.

Unth — name of a district or country.

ur — to be great, great, mighty, supreme, powerful.

ur, uru — great one (God); plur.

urt — great one (fem.), goddess.

uru — dual masc. "two great".

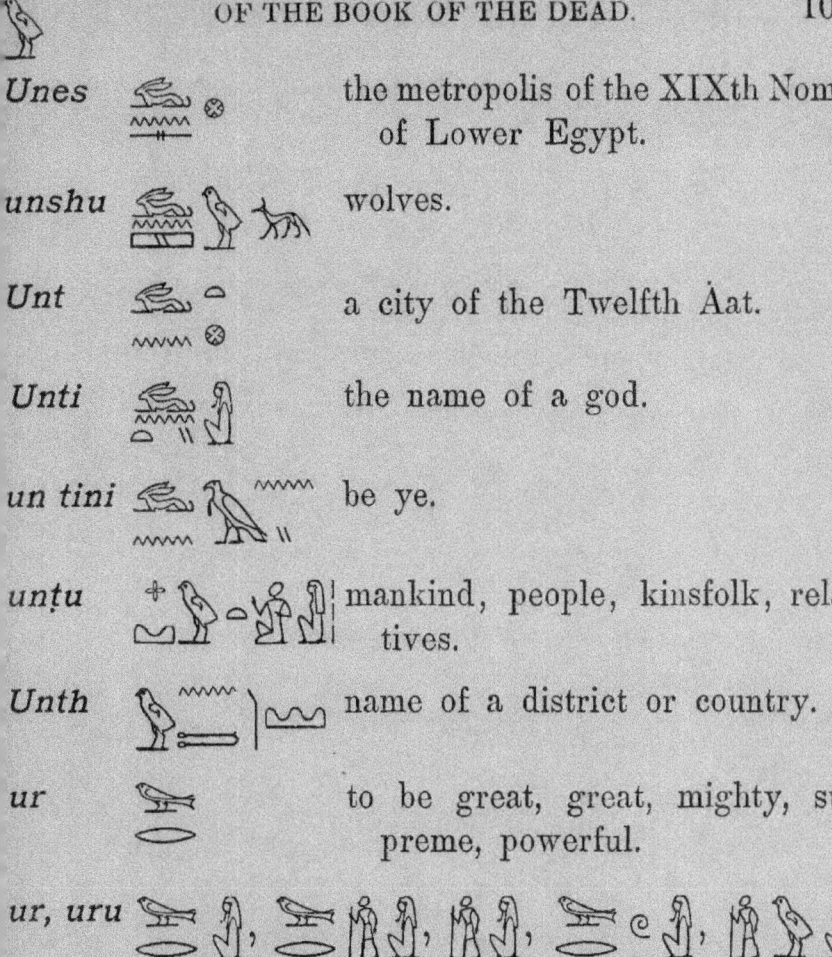

urti dual fem. "two great goddesses".

two very great goddesses.

ur , , , great man, chief, prince, nobleman, master; princess. Plur. masc. , , , , , ; plur. fem. .

ur sep sen X doubly great.

ur as comparative, ... greater than.

ur as superlative, greatest of 5 gods.

ur in titles etc.:

, , .

.

.

.

.

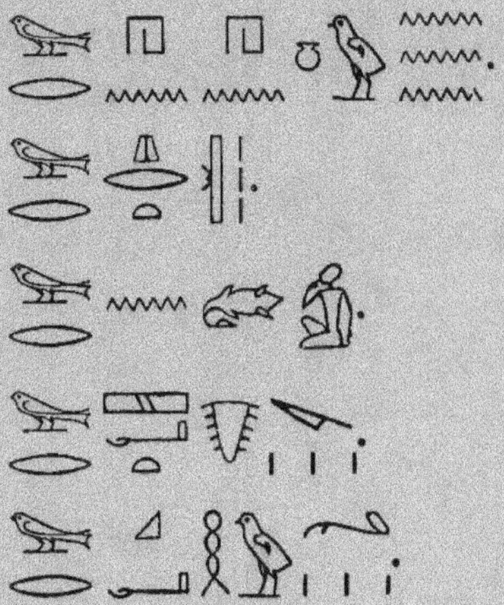

ur  a joint of meat, haunch, carcase; 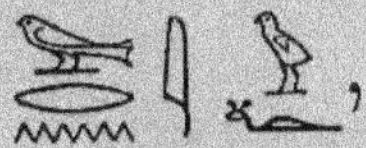, 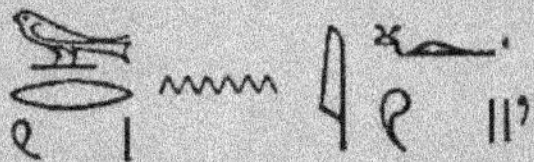 

Ur-at  "great of moment", a proper name.

Urit 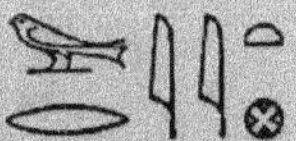 name of a city.

urit 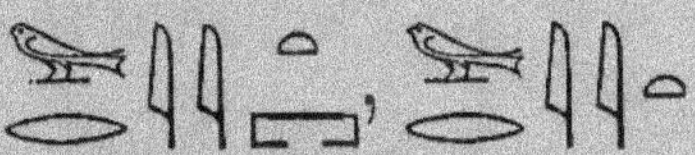 hall, house, room.

Ur-årit-s 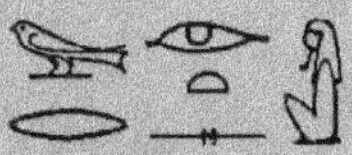 a proper name.

Ur-peḥui-f  a proper name.

Ur-ma 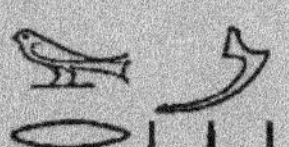 title of the high-priest of Heliopolis (?).

Ur-maat  a proper name.

Ur-mertus-ṭeshert-shenu 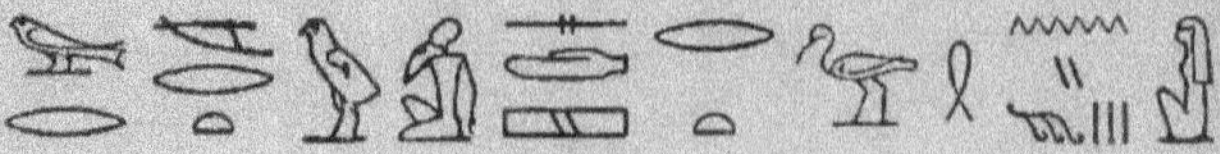

Ur-mertis-ṭeshert-shenu  "The red-haired one who is greatly beloved"; name of one of the Seven Cows.

Ur-ḥekau 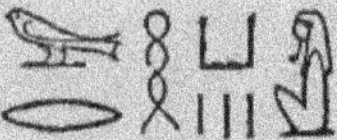   a deity who is mighty in words of power, a god or goddess of magic.

Ur-kherp-ḥem 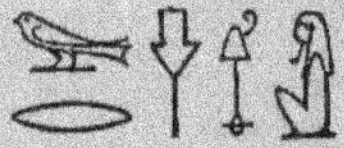 "chief master of the blacksmith's tool"; a title of the high-priest of Memphis.

Ur-senu 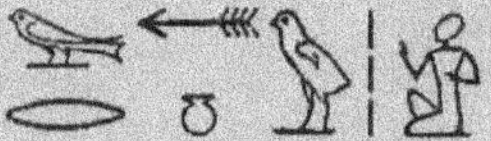 chief of the physicians.

urer 

urert  

urertu 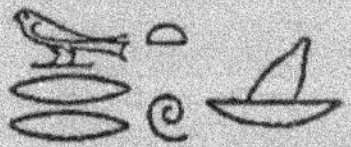

the name of a crown. 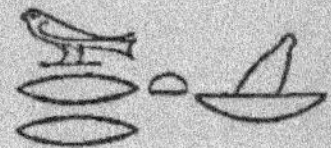  the gods who wear the *urert* Crown.

urḥ 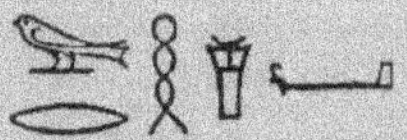

urḥu  to smear or rub with unguent, to anoint.

Urḥetchati  two goddesses of Heliopolis.

urs 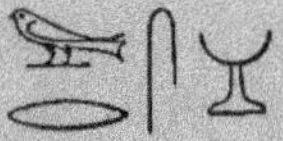 a pillow, head-rest.

ursh 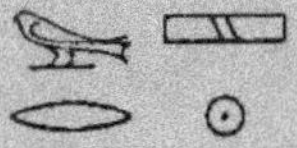 to pass the day, to watch;  watchers.

Urek 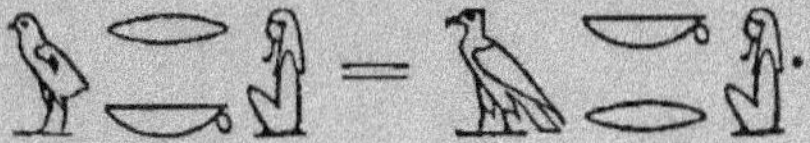

urt 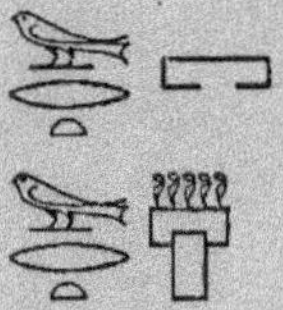 hall, palace.

urt 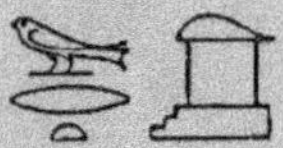 funeral chest, or coffer.

urt 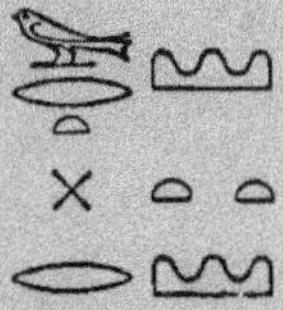 funerary mountain, cemetery.

urt 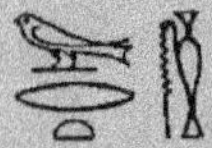 flood.

urt 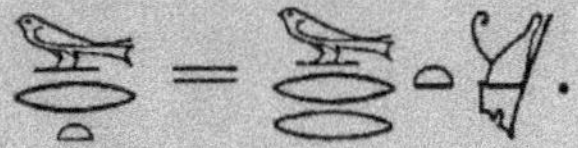

Urt-urt  a proper name.

urṭ, urṭu  to be inert, motionless, helpless, to rest.

Urṭ-àb  "He whose heart is still"; a title of Osiris.

urṭu , see .

uh  to be troubled?

uhau  to supplicate.

uhaȧu  to fail.

uhem
uhemu
uhemm  to repeat, to report, to narrate;  to repeat; .

 to speak again.

 to renew life, live again.

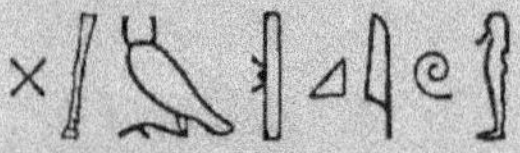 a new form.

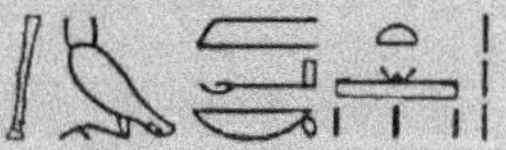 to renew protection.

, with , a second time, again.

uhem-ā 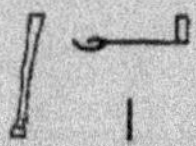 anew, afresh.

Uhem-ḥer  a proper name.

uhen  decay, failure.

uhen 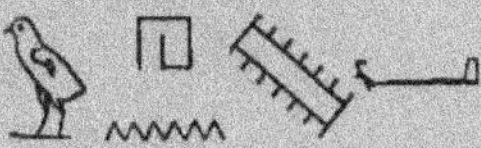 to overthrow; 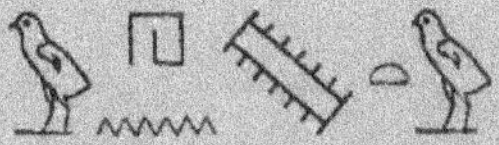 be overthrown.

uḥā 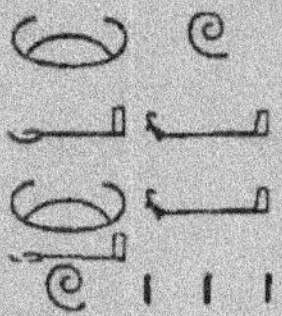 to unloose, be set free from, to return (in the evening).

uḥā  cord, rope.

uḥā  to catch fish, to snare game, fisherman, fowler.

uḥeset 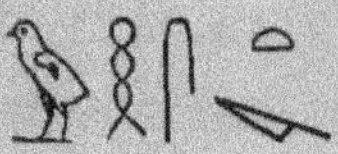 to beat down, to slay.

uḥet  baked meats, stew (?).

ukha  to lay down, set down, to seek after, search for.

ukha  darkness, night.

ukha  pillar.

ukhakh  to seek after.

ukheb  to shine.

ukhert  wooden implement.

ukheṭ  to be angry, be pained, disgusted.

ukheṭet 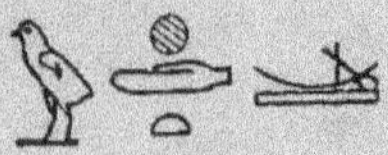 boat.

us 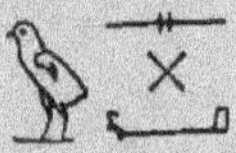 to do away with.

usfau  idle, lazy.

user 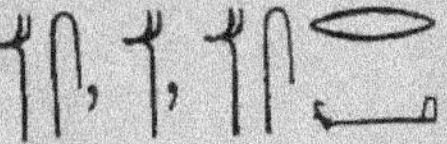 to be strong, mighty, strength, might, power, strong; .

useru  powers, mighty beings (human or divine).

usert 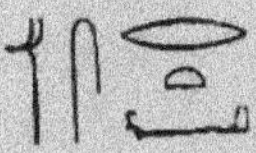 strength.

usert 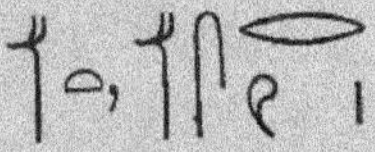 skull, top of the head; plur. 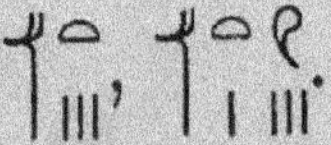.

User-àb  "Strong-heart"; a proper name.

User-ba  "Strong-soul"; a proper name.

useru 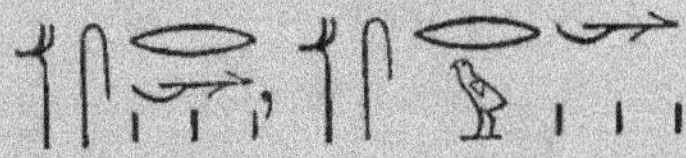 oars, rudders, steering poles.

useru  to steer a boat.

Usert  the name of a goddess.

useḥ to advance.

usekh collar, neck ornament, pectoral.

usekh to be in a wide space, to be wide or spacious, breadth, broad.

Usekh-nemmet "He of the long stride", the name of one of the Forty-two Judges in the Hall of Osiris.

Usekh-ḥer "Broad Face", a name of Rā.

usekht the wide space of the sky, a large hall or room; the great double hall.

Usekht Maāti the name of the double Hall wherein Osiris judged the dead.

Usekt Shuu the Hall of Shu, *i. e.*, heaven.

Usekht Ḳeb the Hall of Ḳeb, *i. e.*, earth.

usekhu plated (?).

usesht urine.

usesh to micturate.

usten, *ustennu* to walk, to follow.

Usṭ a proper name.

ush to cry out.

ush misery.

ushau night, darkness.

ushā te eat, to gnaw, crunch bones.

usheb to answer, to eat (?).

to make an answer at the right time.

usheb to beget, begotten.

ushen	to net, to snare.
ushenu	feathered fowl.
uḳ	to burn, be burned.
uḳa	name of a festival.
uḳaiu	wooden pegs or legs.
ut	the city of embalmment, the abode of Anubis.
utu	embalmment.
utu	the god of embalmment, *i.e.*, Anubis.
ut	coffin, mummy bier.
uta	to embalm, swathe a mummy.
Ut (*Uḥet* ?) *meḥt*	the Northern Oasis (Baḥrîyah).
Ut (*Uḥet*) *res*	the Southern Oasis (Khârgah).
Utau	a class of divine beings.

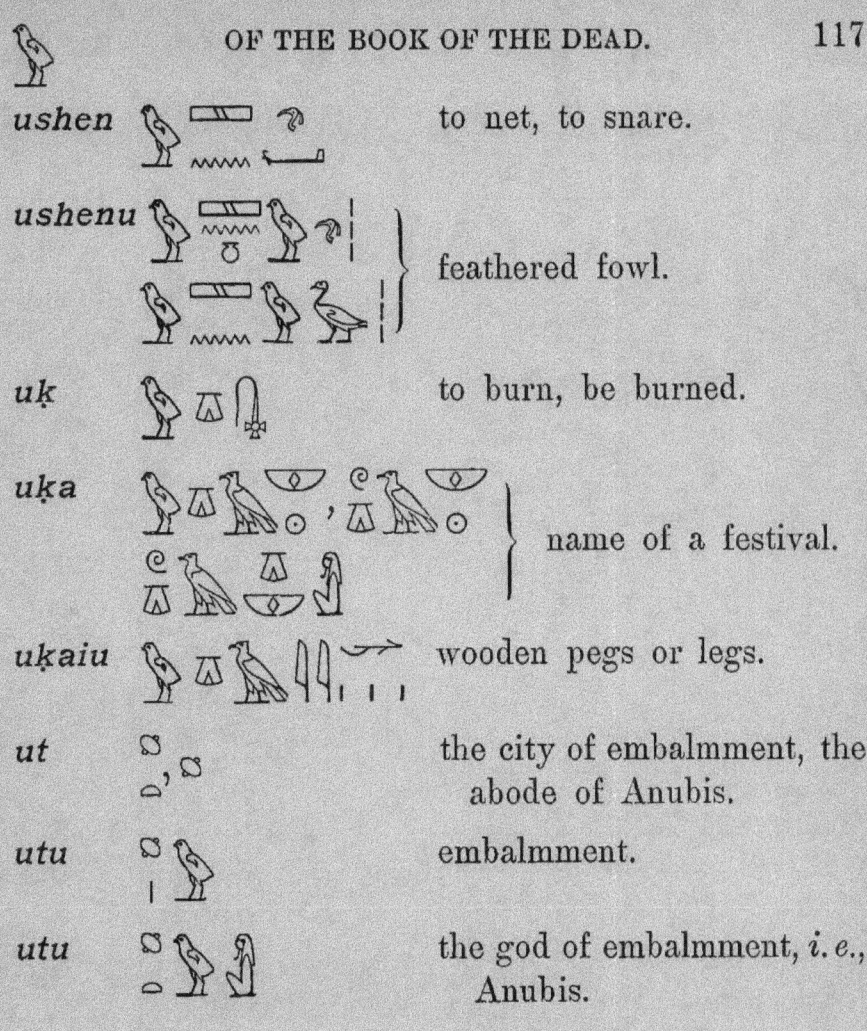

utu  to set out on a journey, to make an expedition.

utu 
uṭeṭ
to issue an order or command, to decree, to ordain.

utet 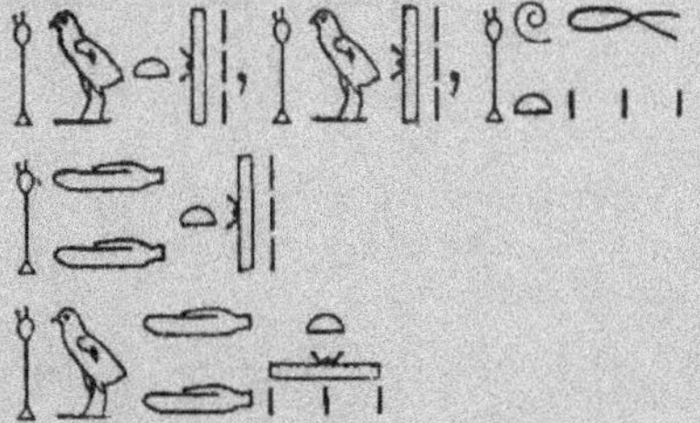
uṭeṭt
commands, behests, things ordered or decreed, records, documents, deeds, copies of deeds.

Utu-nesert 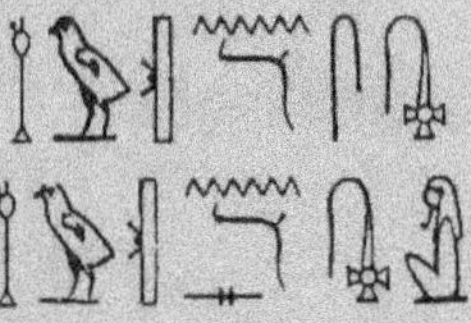 the name of one of the Forty-two Judges in the Hall of Osiris.

Utu-rekhit 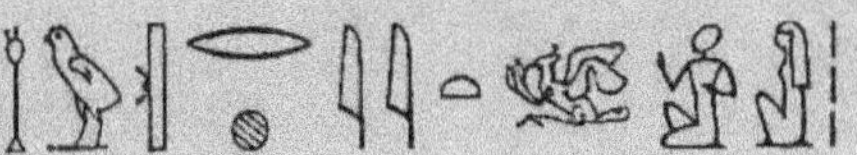 The name of one of the Forty-two Judges in the Hall of Osiris.

utu 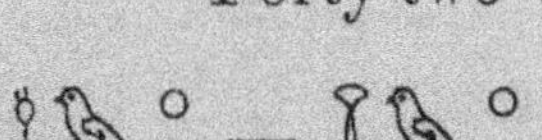

utu  flowers.

utuit 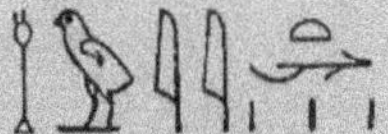 oar rest.

Utent 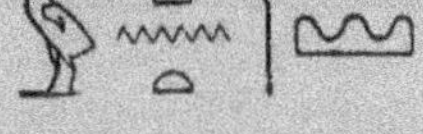 the name of a country.

utet 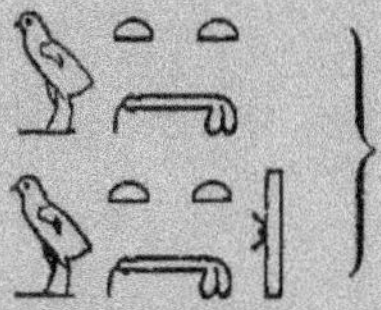 to beget.

 begetter.

Utet  "Begetter", a name of Osiris.

Utet-Ḥeḥ 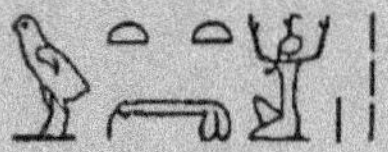 "Begetter of millions of years"; a proper name.

uṭ, *uṭet* 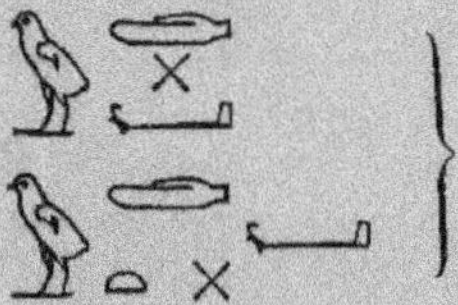 to cast down or out, to shoot out, dart forth, to utter a cry.

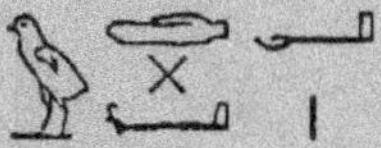 to lay violent hands on someone.

uṭaiu  strong ones.

uṭit 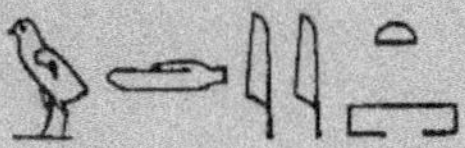 chamber.

uṭebu  mutable.

uṭeb 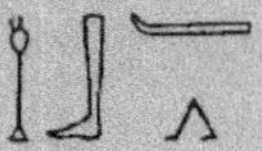 to go round, turn about.

uṭeb, *uṭebu*  furrow; plur. , .

uṭebtu 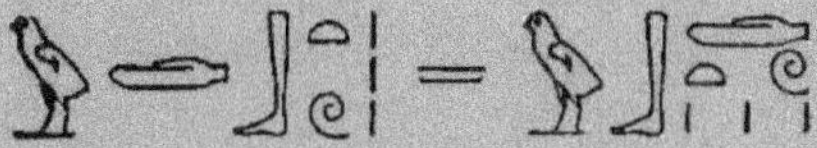 burned.

uṭen, *uṭenu*  to bring something as a gift, to make an offering; 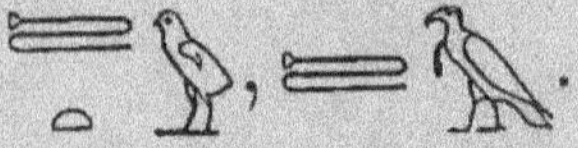.

uṭenu, *uṭent*  offerings, things given as offerings.

uṭeḥ 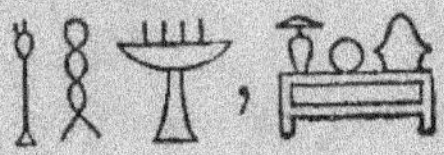 altar, table of offerings; plur. .

uṭeṭ 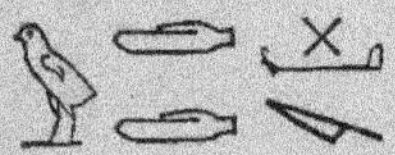 to void, shoot out.

uthes 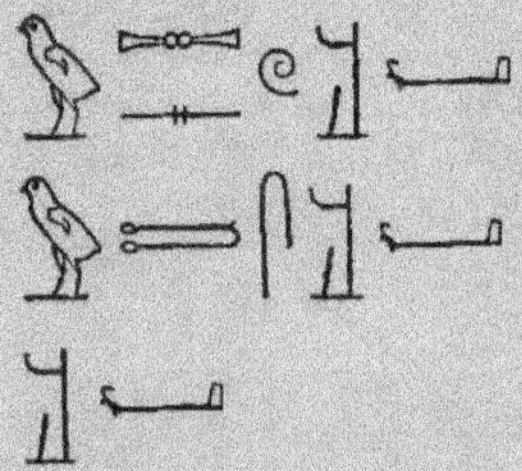 to raise up, to lift up, support.

utcha 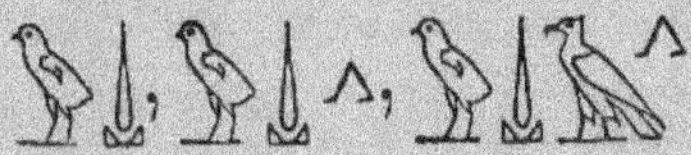 to go out, set out, to begin a journey.

utchat  a journey, a going forth.

utcha  to be in a good state or condition, sound, healthy, well.

utchau  strength, power.

utchau  amulet, object of power.

 magical powers.

Utcha-re 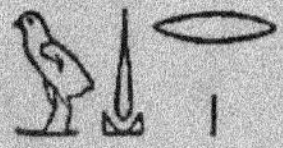 "Strong-mouth"; a proper name.

utcha sep  strong with good fortune.

utchat  the "strong", *i. e.*, the Eye of Rā, whence came all power, strength, health, protection, etc.

utchat 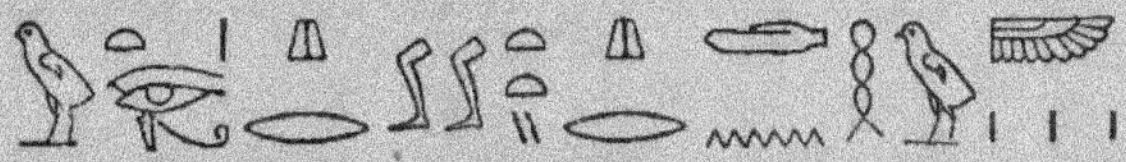 the Utchat with legs und wings.

utchat  the Utchat of Sekhet, the great lady, the mistress of the gods.

utchati  "the two Utchats", *i. e.*, the two Eyes of the sky, or the Sun and Moon.

utchā  to weigh, to estimate, to consider, to reckon up, to decide.

 to consider or weigh deeds or words.

utchā senemm  to weigh hair?

utchā 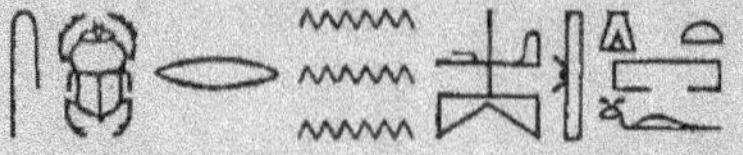 making the water to balance his throne, or making his throne to balance on the water.

utchāiu   to estimate the fields; weighers, those who try something in a balance.

utchāt 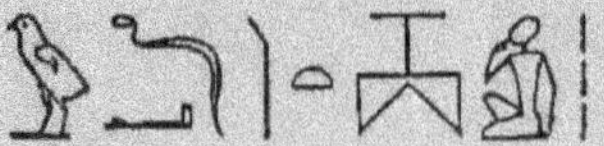 judges.

utchāti 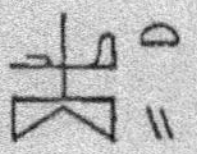 judgment, decision.

Utchā-aābet 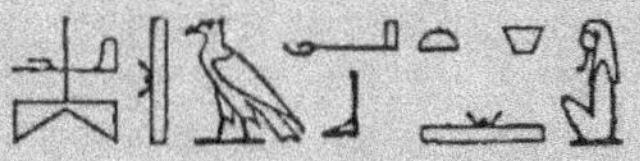 "computer of the offering", name of a god.

utchfau  to delay, to tarry.

utcheṭ  to walk.

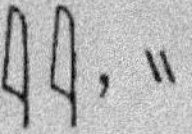 I.

i / *iu* 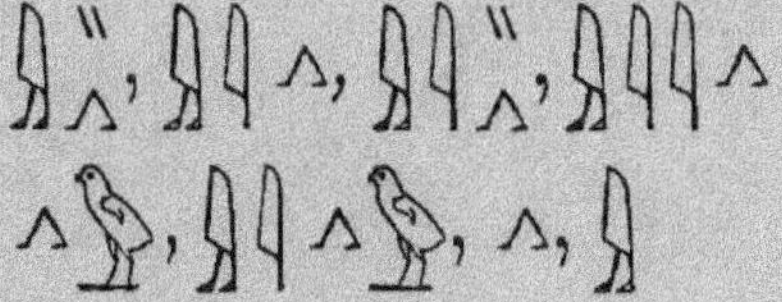 to come, 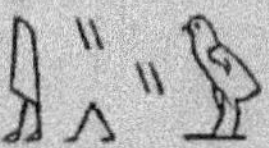 come, come!

i-tu / *iu-tu*  coming, a coming, advance.

it 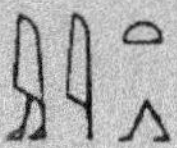 a coming. 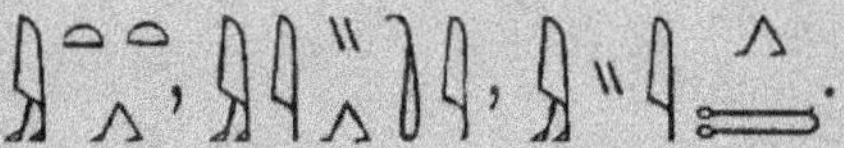

iu  comers;  comers with glad tidings.

iu  to end (of a book) 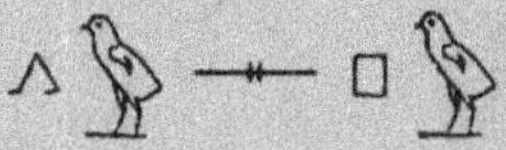  it has gone out in peace.

iu āq 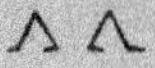 going in and coming out, entrance and exit.

Iu pastu  a class of divine beings.

i, it 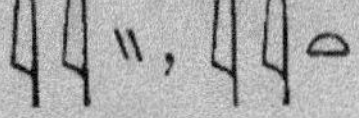 hail, O.

iu  O verily.

iumā  sea, lake, river, any large collection of water.

Ir-qai  a name of Ȧmen-Rā.

ikh  to stretch out the heavens.

isu  abodes, chambers.

 B.

ba  one of the two souls of man, the heart-soul, which was intimately connected with the *ka* and the heart, as opposed to the spirit-soul *khu* . Plur. , , , .

ba  mentioned with  and ; with , with , with  and .

 a perfect soul.

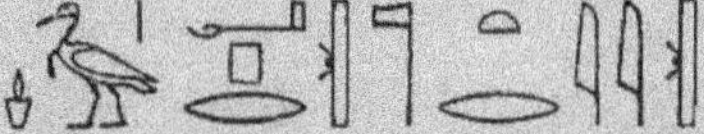 an equipped divine soul.

 a living soul.

 a living heart-soul and a perfect spirit-soul.

 soul of souls.

 my soul is the souls of the gods.

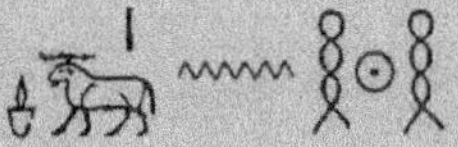 soul of eternity.

 soul in the body.

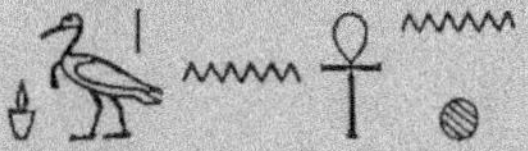 soul of life.

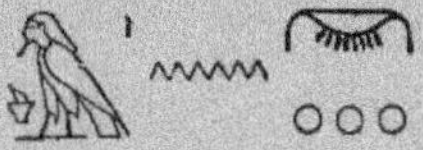 a soul [made] of gold, an amulet.

 thy soul is to heaven, thy body is under the ground.

ba  the divine Soul, or soul of God.

ba  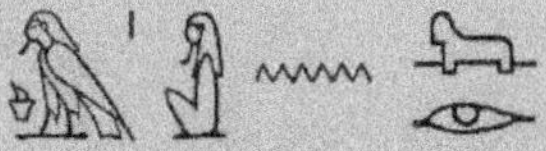 soul of Osiris;

 of Rā;

ba 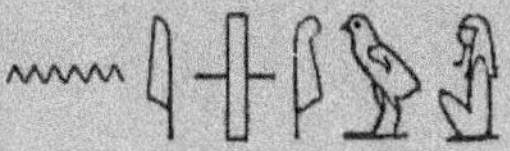 soul in Shu;

ba  soul in Ḳeb;

ba 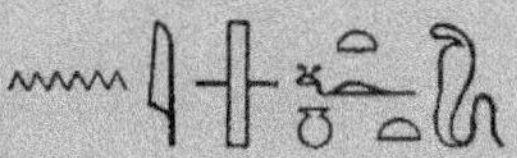 soul in Tefnut;

 Holy Soul, a name of Osiris.

 Holy Soul, a name of Osiris.

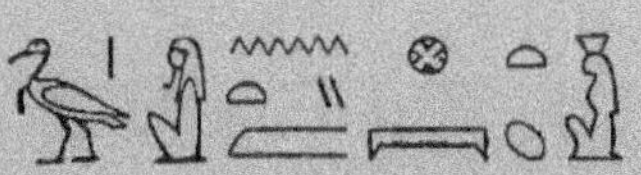 the Soul which is in Nut.

 the Soul of the gods who exist in the body of Osiris.

 the Soul of the Great Body which is in Saïs, Neith.

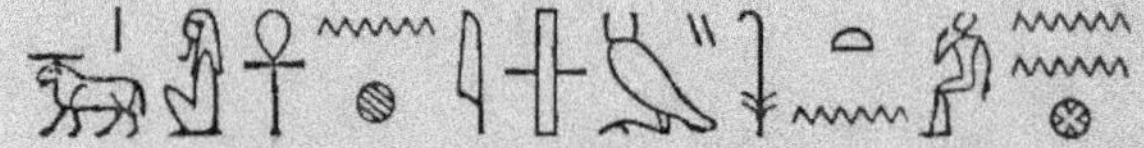 the Living Soul in Suten-ḥenen.

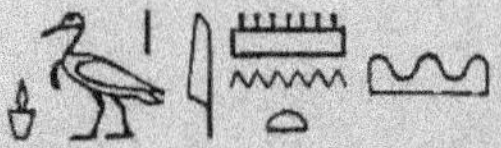 the Soul of Ȧmenti.

baiu  divine souls, souls of gods.

 the souls in the gods.

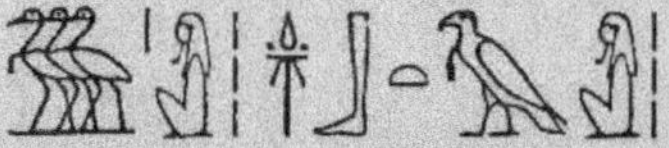 the souls of the gods of the East.

 the souls of the gods of the West.

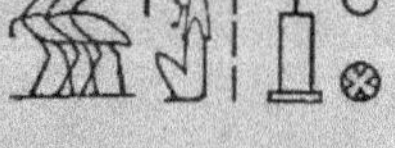 the souls of Heliopolis.

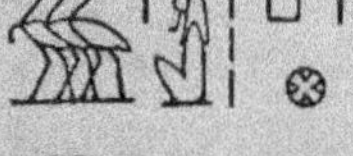 the souls of Pe-[Ṭep] (Buto).

 the souls of Nekhen.

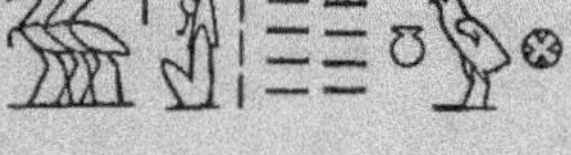 the souls of Hermopolis.

 living souls.

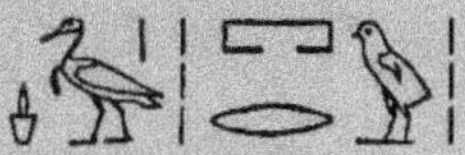 souls who have appeared.

 souls of the dead (*i. e.*, damned).

 souls of his father (Osiris).

baui  the double soul.

 the double soul in the Tcha-fui, *i. e.*, the souls of Osiris and Rā.

Bai  the Soul-god, or the Divine Soul, or the Ram-god;  the double-soul god.

Bati 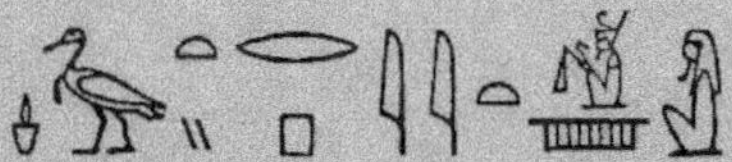 a name of Osiris.

Ba  divine soul with plumes .

Ba  the metal-god; a proper name (?).

ba  to be endowed with a soul.

ba  to cleave, make a way through something.

Bau  a proper name.

baba  to work.

babau  cavern, cave, den or lair; plur. .

Baba  the name of the first-born son of Osiris.

Ba-neb-Ṭeṭṭeṭ 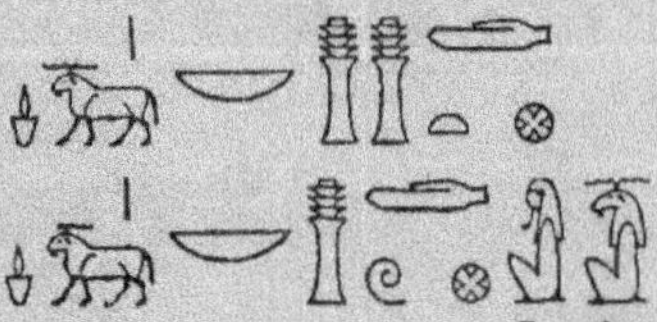 Soul-god, or Ram-god, lord of Ṭaṭṭu (Mendes), a title of Osiris.

Barekathȧ tchaua 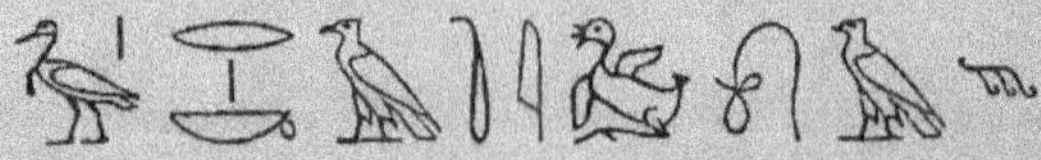 a proper name.

baḥ , or , with  before, in front of.

Bakhau  the Mountain of sunrise.

Bast  the city of Bubastis in the Eastern Delta, the modern Zaḳâziḳ.

Bast 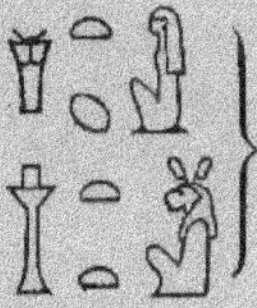 the goddess of Bubastis.

Bast  Bast dweller in Thebes.

Basti  the name of one of the Forty-two Judges in the Hall of Osiris.

bak  to work, to toil, to serve.

 works, labours.

baq  olive tree.

baḳ  to be weak, weary, feeble, helpless.

bak  weak one, the helpless one (*i. e.*, the mummy); plur. .

bat / *bȧat*  plants, boughs, branches.

Bati 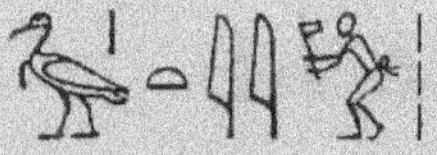 name of a fiend, or of a group of fiends.

bȧa 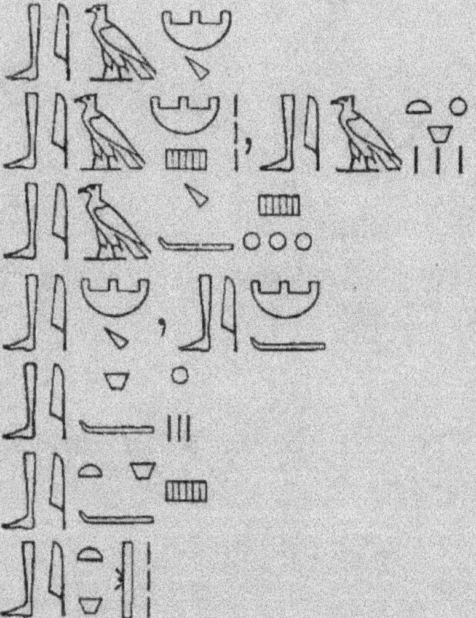 the ore of a metal, iron, copper, etc., a metal tool, a name of the sky or firmament.

bȧa en pet 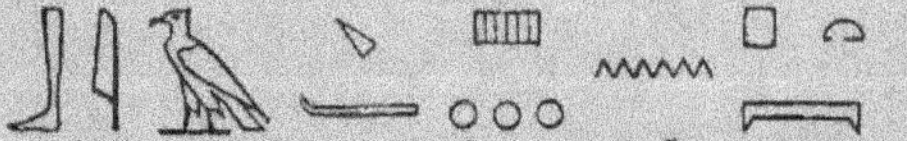 metal of the sky, meteoric iron (?).  that iron in the sky.

bȧat shemāu 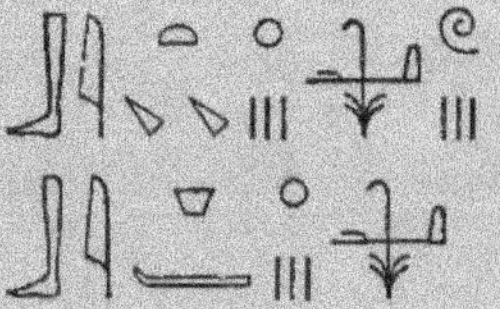 "the metal of the south", iron.

bȧat shemāu 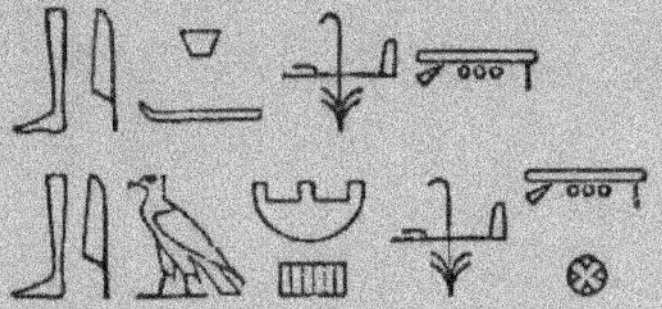 "the metal of the south", iron.

bȧau 
bȧat 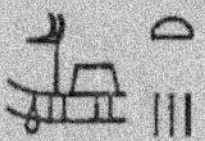 } wonders, wonderful things.

bȧaq  a kind of grain, or fruit.

Bȧbȧ 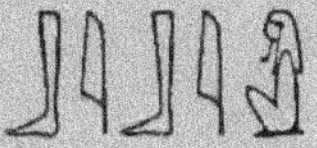 the name of a god, Baba (?).

bȧbȧ 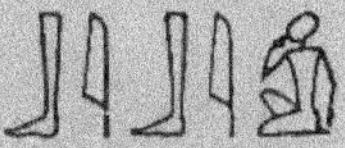 a cry of joy.

bȧn  evil, wickedness.

bȧk   } hawk; plur. .

 the double divine hawk.

Bȧket  the city of the divine hawk.

bȧt, bȧti  king of the north.

Bȧti  a proper name.

bābāt 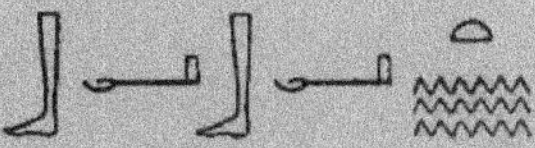 water-flood, stream.

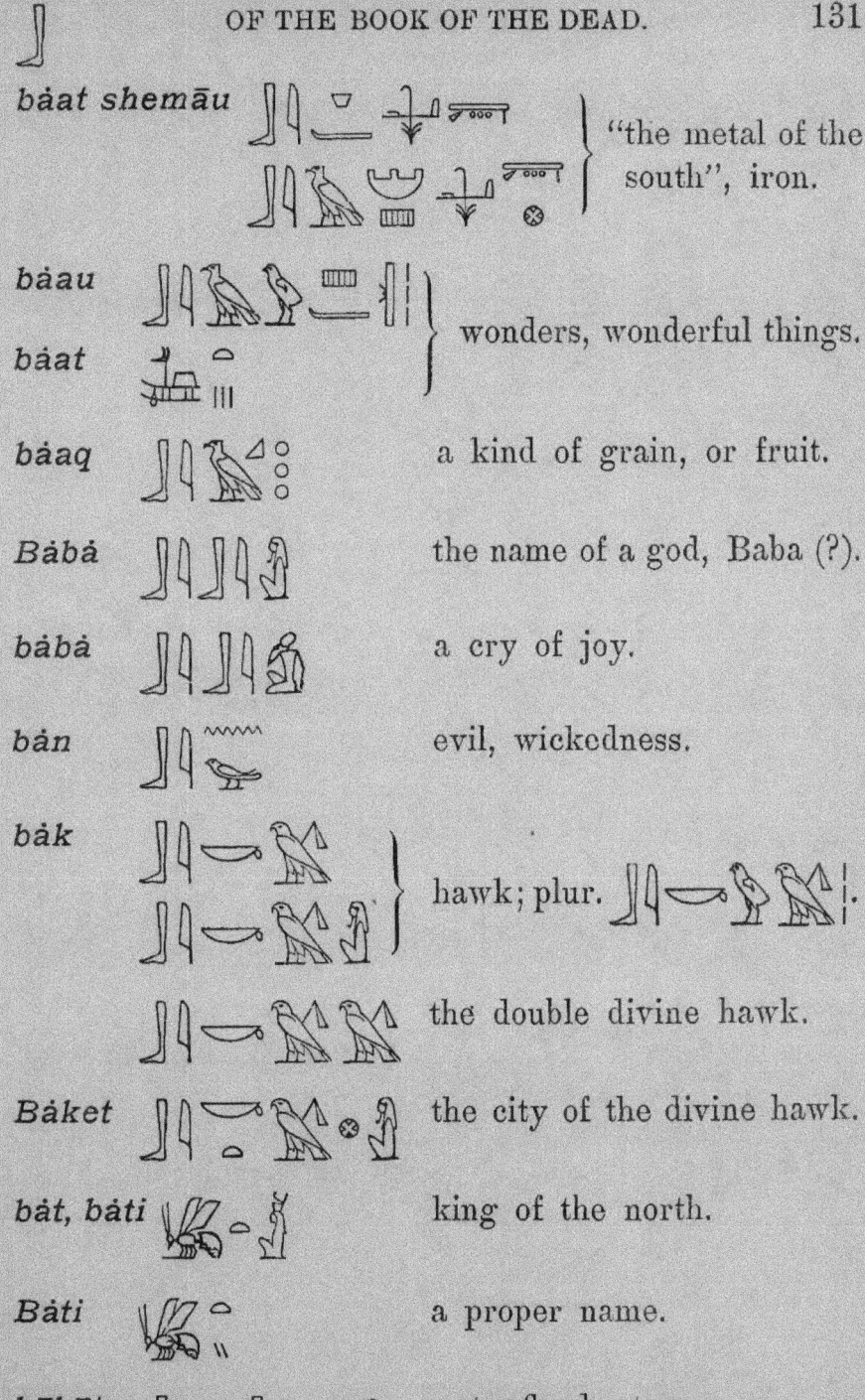

bāḥ  to be flooded, inundated.

Bāḥ  the god of the Inundation.

bi 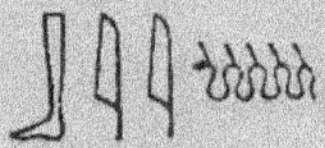 name of a fiend.

biu  strength.

bu 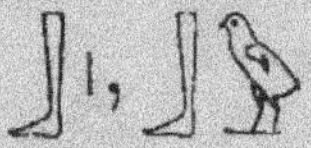  purity,  oneness (?), altogether,  lawfulness, legality, truth, 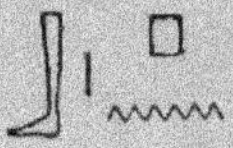 this place (?).

bu neb  everywhere, every place.

bu nebu  all men, all people, everyone, folk in general.

bu nefer  prosperity, happiness.

bu ṭu  evil thing, calamity.

bu		not, it is not; 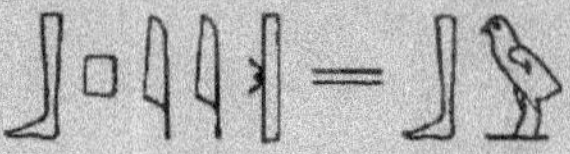  (?).
bu-pu		
but		evil thing, abomination.
buṭ		offering.
bebait		the mantis.
bebuu		strong.
Bebi	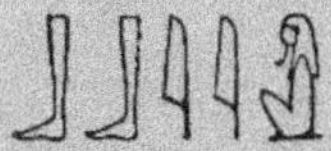	the name of a god.
bebet		flowers.
bebet		fountain head.
bebet	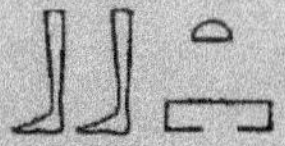	hollow place, cavity.
ben		not.
benānā	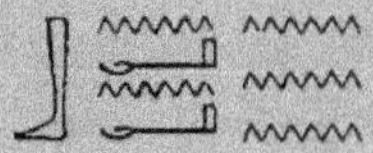	to bathe.
benben	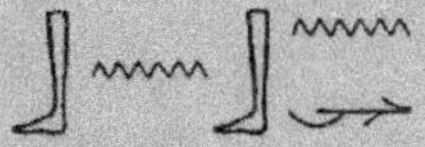	a kind of wood.
benben	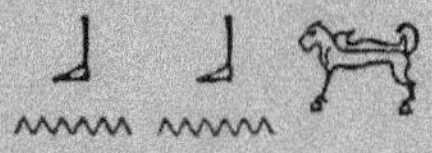	bier, funerary couch.

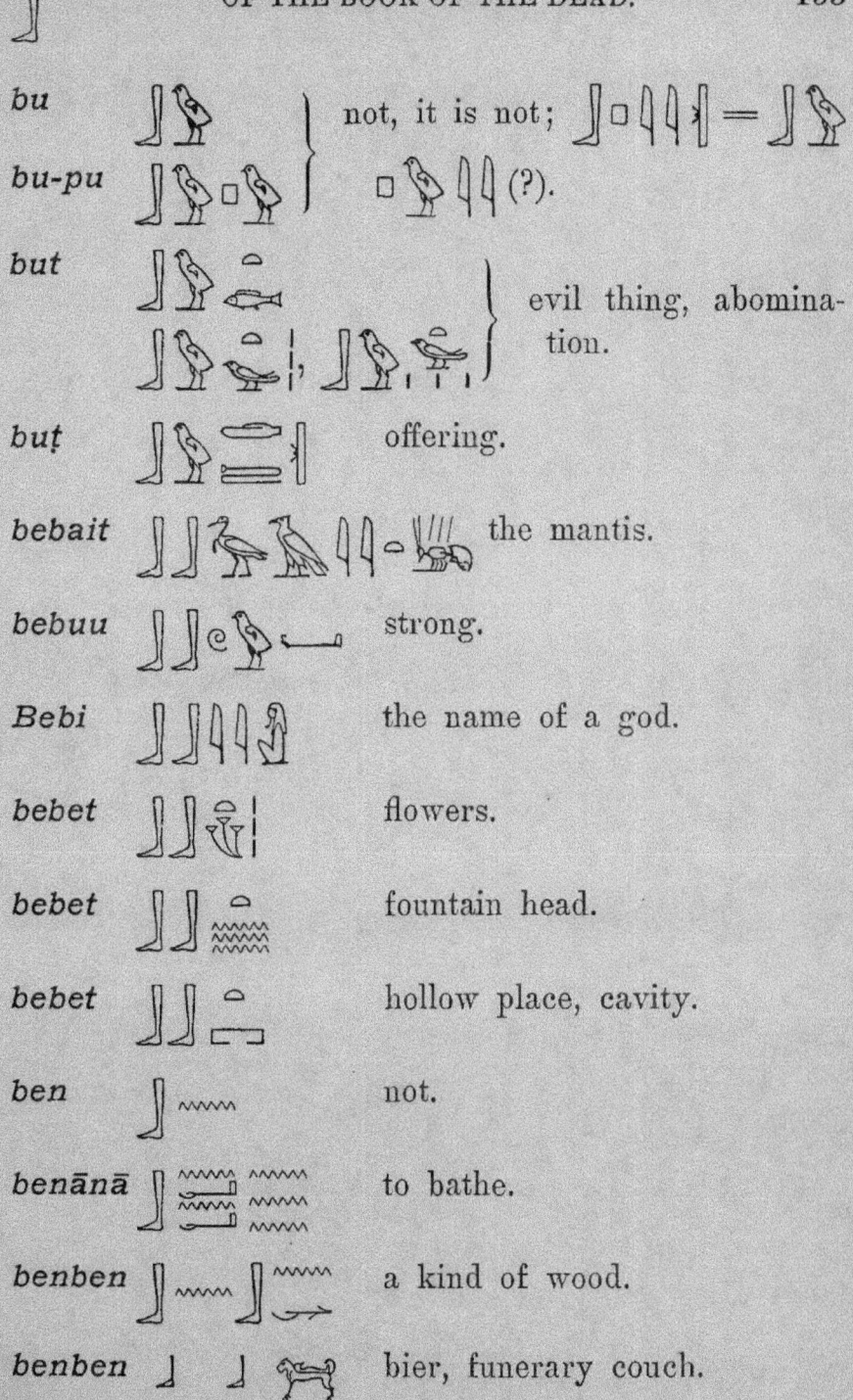

benbent — hall, pylon chamber.

ben — to pass away, to dissolve, to go on.

ben, *benen* — to beget, to be united with, union.

benen — ring.

benen — a kind of wood.

bennu — a bird commonly identified with the phoenix.

the Bennu, the Soul of Rā.

bennut — matter, pus.

bennu, *bennut* — cakes (?), bread.

Bener — the name of a city.

benrȧ — to be sweet, pleasant.

benrȧu  sweet things, dates, date wine, pleasant, nice.

benshu  bolts.

bent 

benti 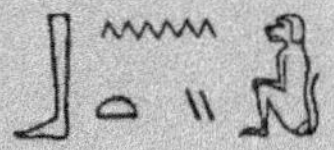 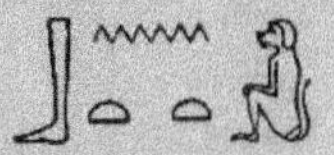 divine apes, incarnations of the spirits of morning.

beḥ 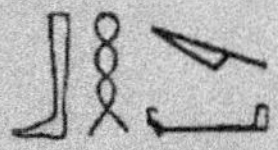 to cut, to split.

beḥen  baleful one.

beḥen 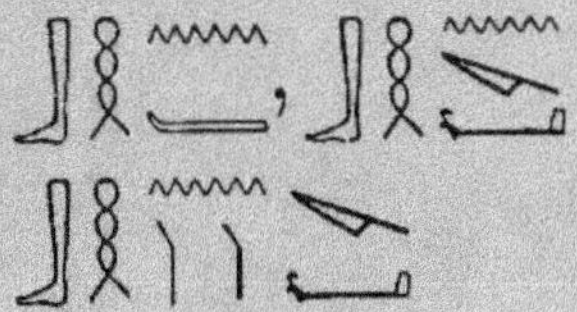 to cut, to pierce; 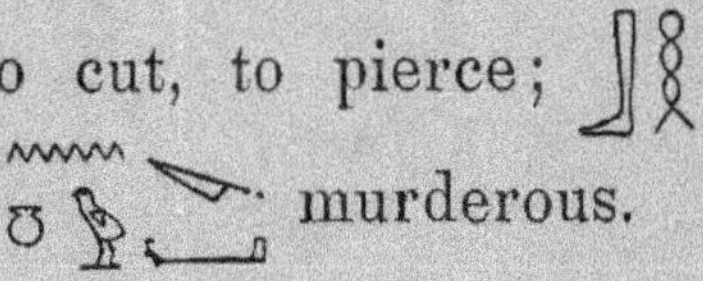 murderous.

beḥennu  animals of the wolf or dog species.

beḥes  calf.

Bekhennu  a proper name.

bekhekhu  fire.

bes  form (?).

bes to enter, to pass in, to rise (of the river).

increase.

bes, *besu* flame, fire, blaze.

Besu-Aḥu a proper name.

Besu Menu a proper name.

bessu humours, excretions, filth.

Besek = Sebek, the Crocodile-god.

besek internal organ of the body; plur.

besh to vomit.

beshu (?) (?) metal plates, scales.

beka pregnant.

beka to shine, the dawn, to-morrow.

bekau weakness.

beq — olive tree, olives; the olive tree in Heliopolis.

beq — a proper name.

beqsu — eyeball, skin (?).

beqsu — balance, scales.

Beqtui — a proper name (?).

beḳ — misery.

beḳi — helpless one, sinner.

beḳa — defect, sin, crime, evil, sinner; plur.

beḳa — evil man, sinner.

beḳai — evil man, sinner.

beḳasu — . . . .

beḳsu — part of a boat.

beḳset — . . . .

bet — place, every place, everywhere.

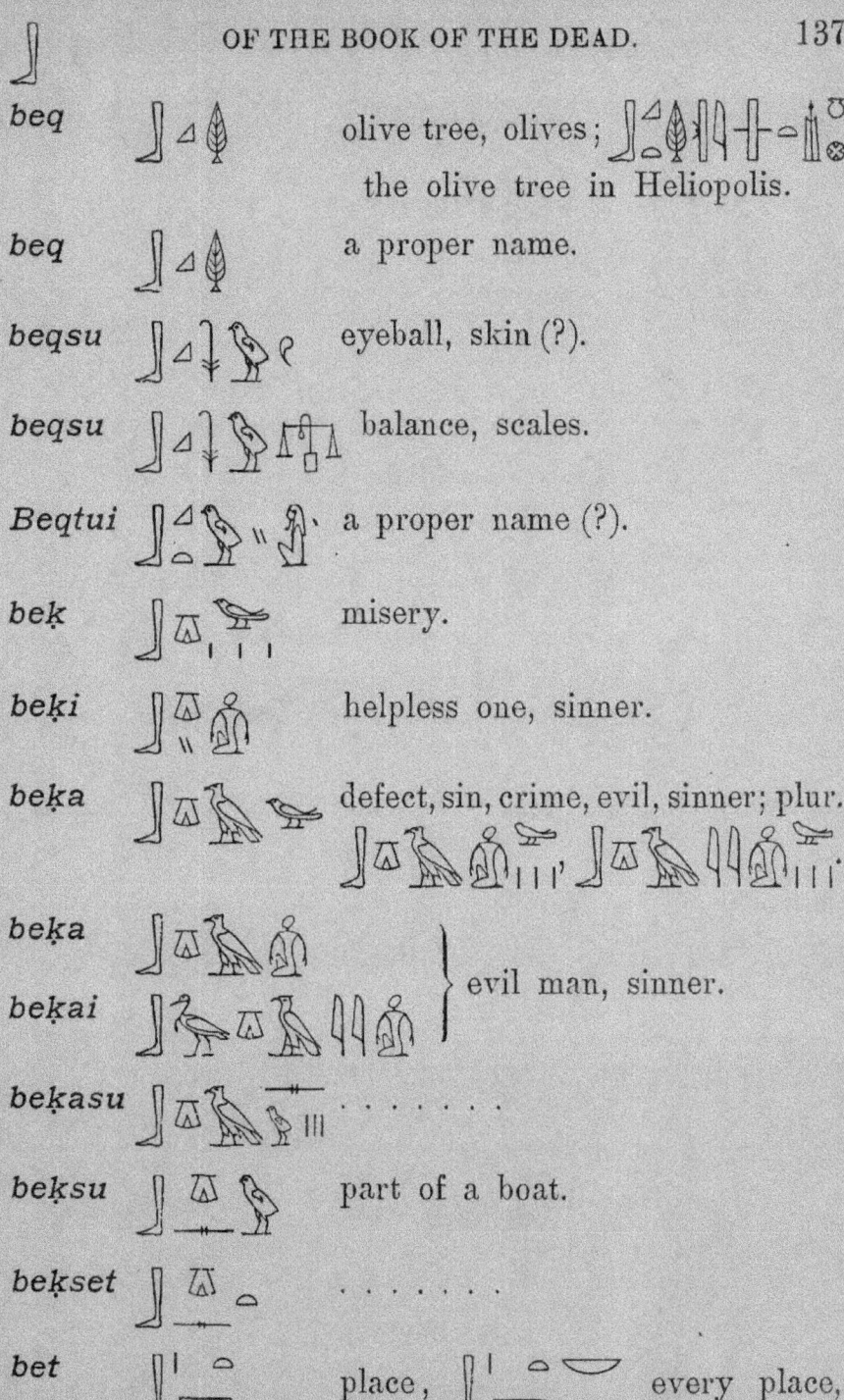

bet incense.

bet grains, seed.

bet flower.

beta to sin, commit a fault, do wrong.

betau, *betu* sin, wrong, abominable thing; plur.

Betȧ name of a city.

betennu, *betnu* swift.

beṭ incense.

beṭ, *beṭ-ti* barley.

white barley.

red barley.

beṭesh — to be weak, powerless, but disposed to do evil.

beṭesh, *beṭeshet* — impotent fiends; fem. sing.

Beṭshu — the name of a city.

Beṭ-ti — a proper name.

bethet (?) — brought.

betcha — a tool or instrument.

P.

Pe — One half of the city of Buto (Per-Uatchit).

Pe . . . . . — the little Pe (?).

p — the.

pa — the; the one who; the one who is between.

pai-à  my.

pai-f  his.

pa 

pai  to fly, flight.

pait  bolt hole.

paut  stuff, substance, matter, cakes, offerings in general.

paut  primeval matter, the material out of which the gods and the universe were formed.

pauti  the god of primeval matter, the chief Egyptian god of the Predynastic Period.

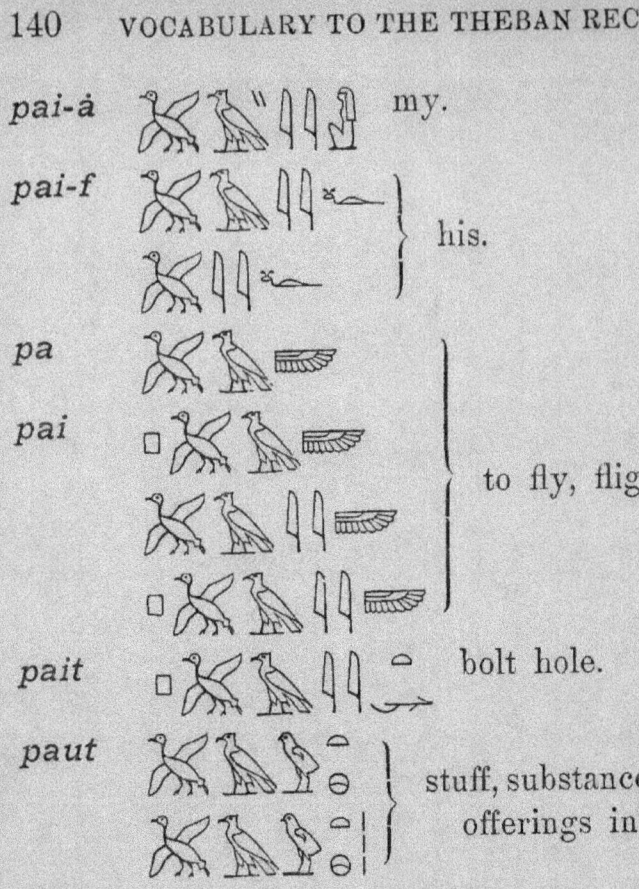

paut neteru  the whole company of the primeval gods, *i. e.*,  . The 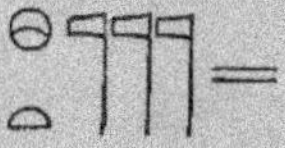 = the names  of Nu.

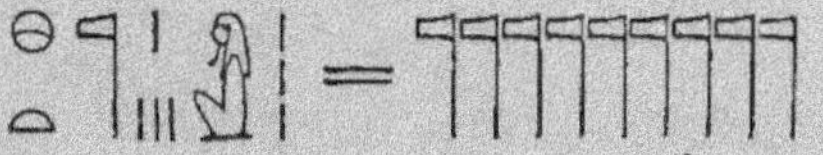 or 

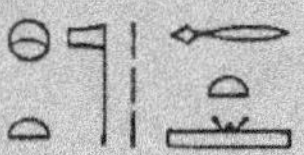 the Great Company of the gods.

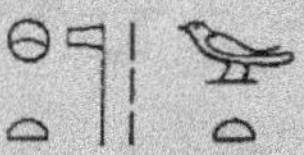 the Little Company of the gods.

 the complete Company of the gods.

paut-ti  the Great and Little Companies of the gods.

pan 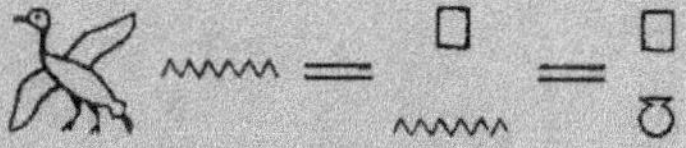 this.

Par, or *Pal*  a proper name.

Parehaqakheperu  a proper name.

pas an ink jar.

pasekh .

Pashakasa a proper name.

pat (?) light.

pā spark, flame, fire; plur. .

pāt men and women, people, a class of people.

pāit ḥer-f human-faced.

pu a mark of emphasis: ; .

puȧau cakes.

pui a demonstrative particle.

Punt
Punṭ the region whence came *ānti* (myrrh) and other aromatic gums and spices, a region in Africa near the southern end of the Red Sea. The district of Punt proper was probably situated some distance inland.

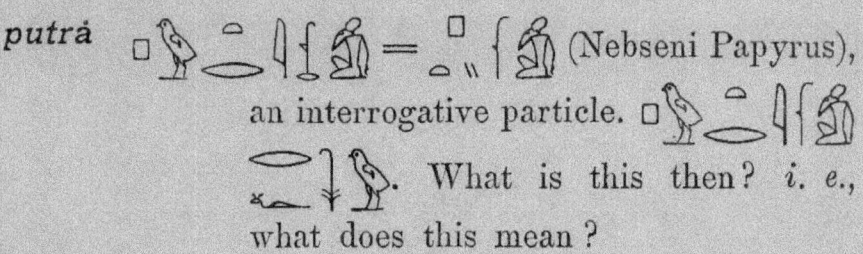

putrȧ (Nebseni Papyrus), an interrogative particle. What is this then? *i. e.*, what does this mean?

pef, *pefa*, *pefi*, *pefat* — a demonstrative particle.

pefes, *pefses* — to burn, be hot, fiery, a spark, to cook, bake.

pefsit — baked.

Pen, *Pen-ḥeseb* (?) — a proper name (?).

penā — to overturn, capsize (of a boat), to invert a matter.

peni — land (?).

penu — rat, mouse.

pens — . . . . .

penq 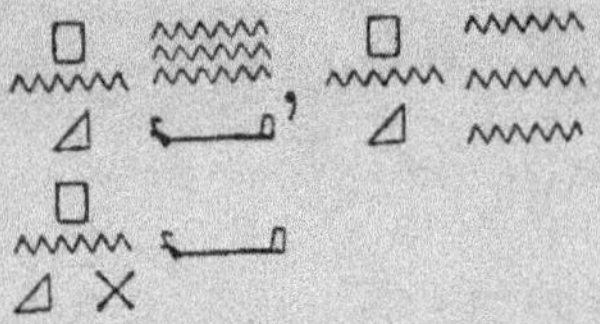 to beat to pieces, to macerate.

Penti 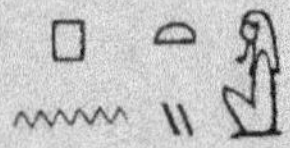 the name of a god.

pert 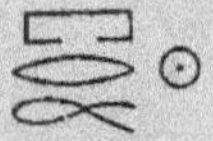 a season of the Egyptian year.

per 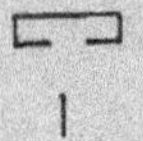 house, abode, temple, habitation; plur. 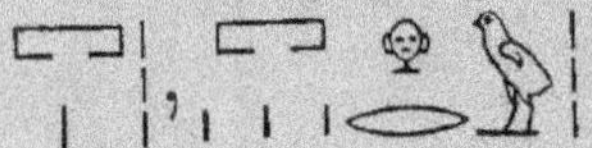 celestial mansions.

perui  double house.

per āa  "great house" פַּרְעֹה.

Per-àbu 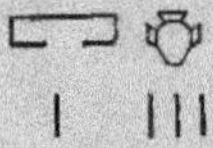 the temple of hearts, *i. e.*, the judgment hall.

per Àsàr 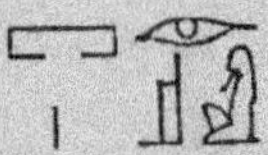 temple of Osiris.

Per-Àst 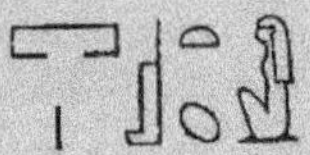 the temple of Isis.

Per-Àsṭes 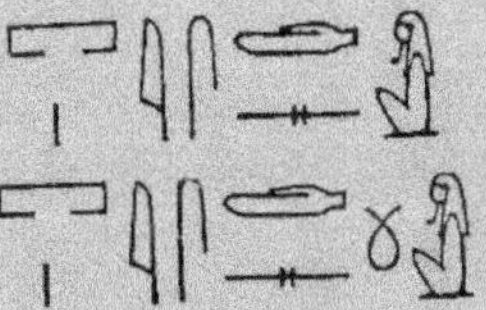 the temple of Àsṭes.

Per-Unnut  the temple of the Hour-goddess.

Per-ur 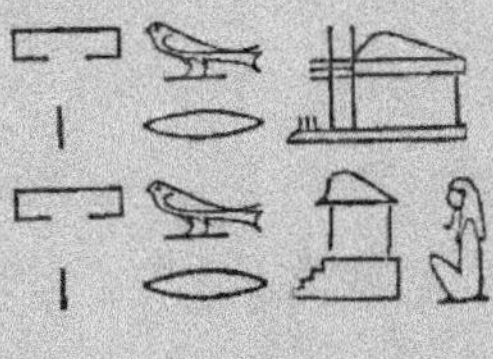 the "great House", *i. e.*, the tomb.

Per-Ptaḥ	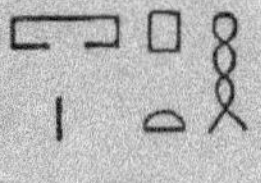	the temple of Ptaḥ at Memphis.
Per-Menȧ	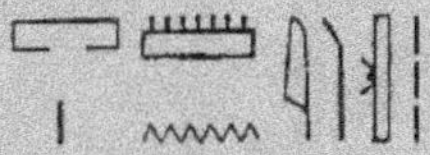	the house of coming into port, *i. e.*, the tomb.
Per-Menu	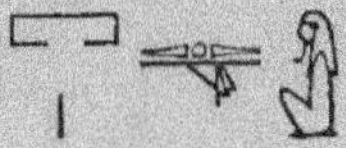	the temple of Menu.
Per-neḥeḥ	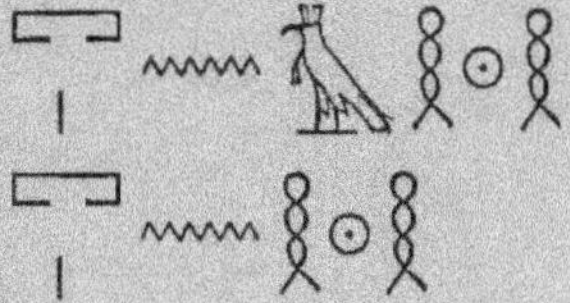	the house of eternity, *i.e.*, the tomb.
Per-neser	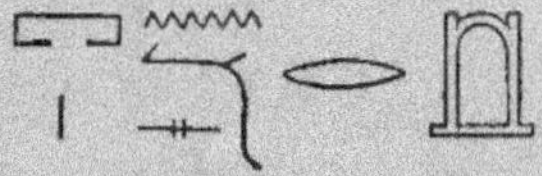	the house of fire.
Per-neter	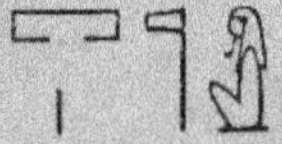	the temple of the god, *i. e.*, Osiris.
Per-neter-āa	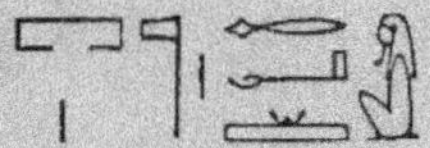	
Per-Rerti (?)	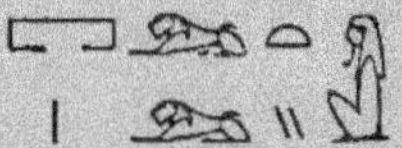	the temple of Shu and Tefnut.
Per-Ḥapṭ-re		the temple of Ḥapṭ-re.
Per-ḥāt		the temple of hearts, *i. e.*, the judgment hall.
Per-Ḥepṭ-ur		the temple of Ḥepṭ-ur.
Per-Ḥeru		the temple of Horus.
Per-Ḥetch		the "White House".

Per-Khenti-menȧtu-f 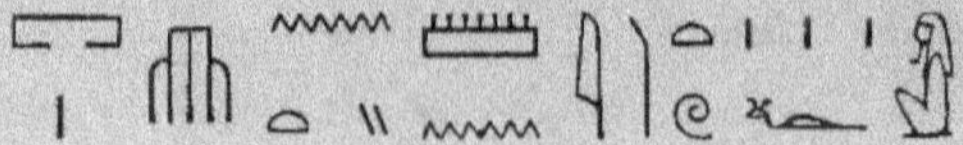 the temple of the "President of his dead".

Per-Sabut  the house of Sab (or Ḳeb), the earth (?).

Per-Sati 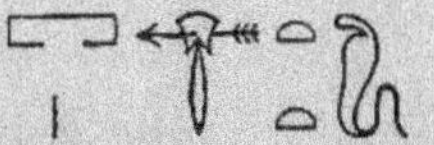 the temple of Sati.

Per-suten 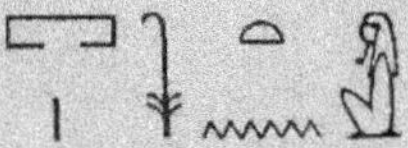 the house of the king, *i. e.*, palace.

Per-seḥeptet  the temple of Seḥeptet.

per-shāt (?) 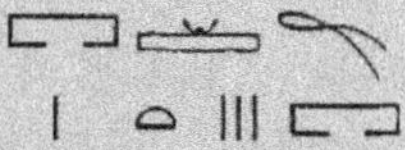 the house of books, *i. e.*, library.

Per-Kemkem  the temple of Kemkem.

Per-Keku  the temple of darkness.

per qebḥ 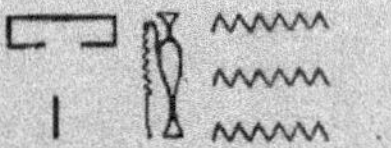 the house of coolness, *i. e.*, bath (?).

Per-tep-ṭu-f  the temple of him that is on his hill, *i. e.*, Anubis.

Per-Tem 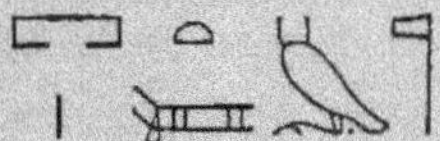 the temple of Tem.

Per-Ṭeḥuti  the temple of Thoth.

per, *peru*, *perr*, *perru* — to come forth, to rise up, to appear, to make oneself manifest; to come forth retreating; to appear in the presence. comer forth; plur. things which appear, manifestations; to come forth; appearance, exit.

per-ā — to come forth boldly, brave.

per ḥer ta — to be born on the earth.

pert em hru — to come forth by, or in, the day; the title of several groups and Chapters of the Theban Recension of the Book of the Dead.

pert — offspring.

pert, *pertu* — things which appear, *i. e.*, offerings.

pert er kheru  "things which appear at the words", *i. e.*, sepulchral offerings of bread, beer, oxen, geese, unguents, etc. Determinatives of these objects are usually added to 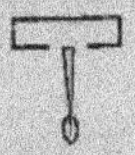 thus: 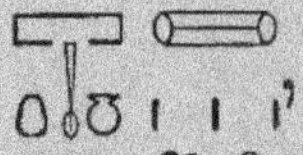 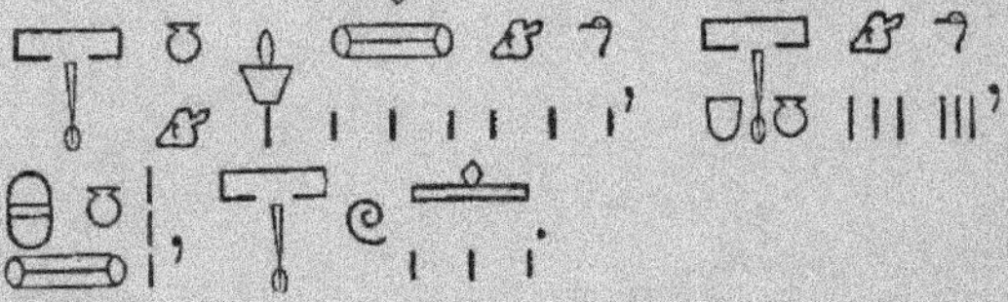

perit 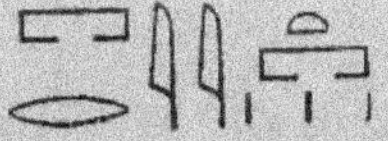 temples.

peri  strip of linen, bandage.

persen 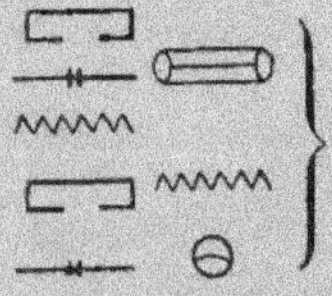 a kind of cake; plur. 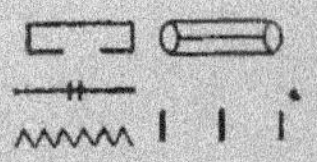

pert  corn, grain in general.

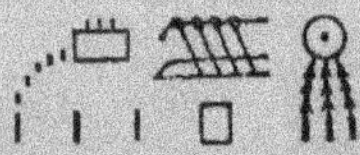 white grain.

1. Perhaps "measures of grain" *ḥeqat.*

black grain.

red grain.

peḥ
peḥu
peḥuut
peḥt
— to arrive at, attain to, to reach the end.

peḥu — the back part, the end.

peḥi
peḥui
peḥti
— the lower part of the back, the buttocks, thighs.

peḥuit — stern of a boat.

peḥu — swamp, marsh.

peḥrer — to run.

peḥreru runners, a class of beings.

Peḥreri "Runner", a name of Rā.

peḥti strength of the thighs originally, then strength, might, power, in general.

pekha to separate.

Pekhat the name of a goddess.

pekhes to cover over, fall on.

pes ink-jar.

pesaḳes a mistake for to spit.

peseḥ to eat, to bite (of an insect or animal), to sting.

Peskheti a divine envoy.

pesesh to divide, to cleave, to allot.

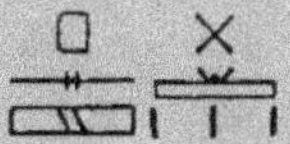 divisions.

pesk  to spit.

Pesk-re  a proper name.

pest (*pestch*) 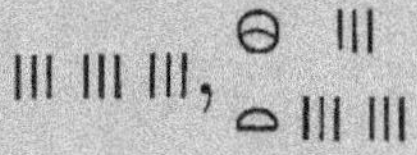 nine, 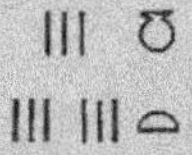 ninth.

pest 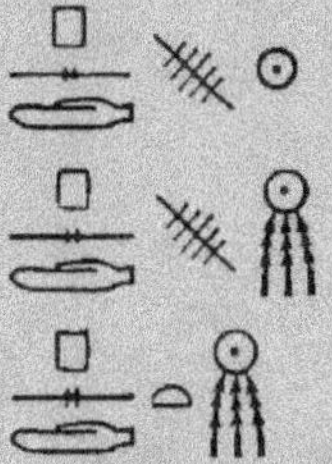 to shine, to illumine.

pest, *pesttu* 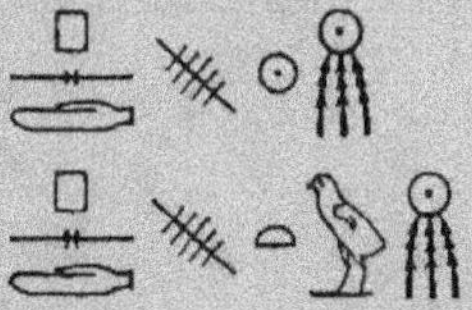 rays of light, radiance, brilliance.

Pestu 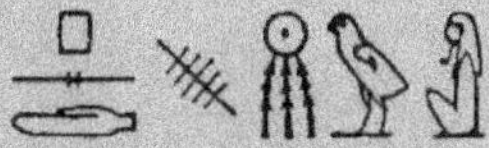 the god of light.

pest 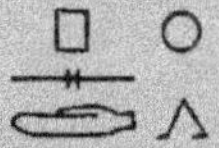 to spread out like light.

pest, *pestu*  back, backbone; 

pest tep  to move the head.

pesh  to spread out.

peshen	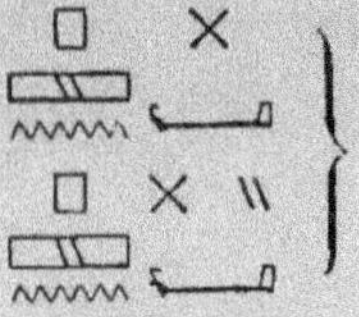	to divide, to cleave.
Peshennu		name of a city.
Peq	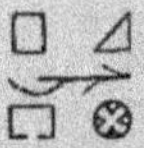	a region near Abydos.
pequ *peqt*		cakes, food.
peqt	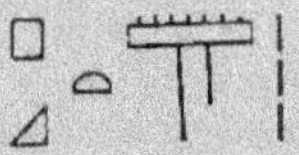	apparel of fine linen.
peḳ	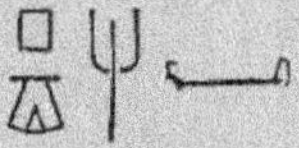	to explain.
peḳ	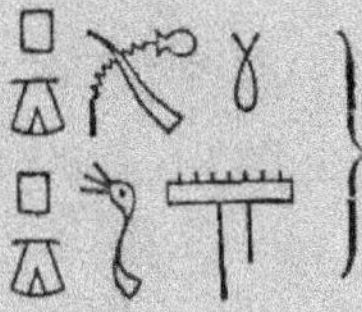	byssus, very fine, semi-transparent linen.
Peḳa		name of a city.
peḳes *peḳas*		to spit upon.
Peḳes	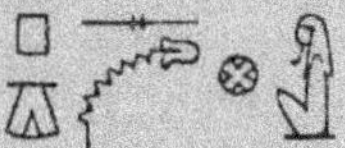	name of a city and a god.
pet		the sky, heaven; 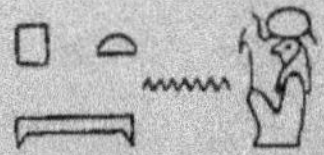 the heaven of Rā.

pet 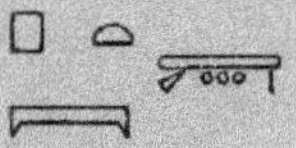 heaven and earth.

 heaven, earth and the Other World,

petti  heavenly beings, denizens of the sky.

pet  eastern heaven, or sky.

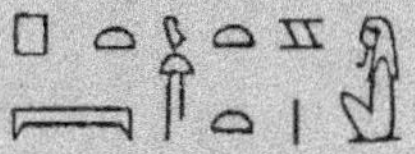 western heaven, or sky.

 northern heaven, or sky.

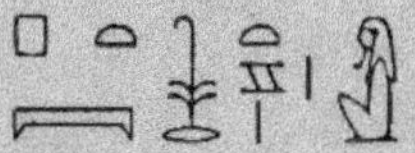 southern heaven, or sky.

petpet  to crush, break.

Peti  a proper name.

pet 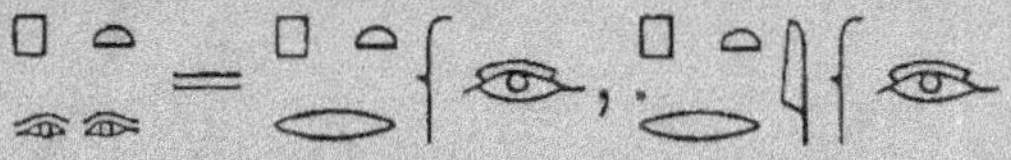 to see.

peti, *peter*  who? what? an interrogative particle.

 what then is it? *i. e.*, what does this mean?

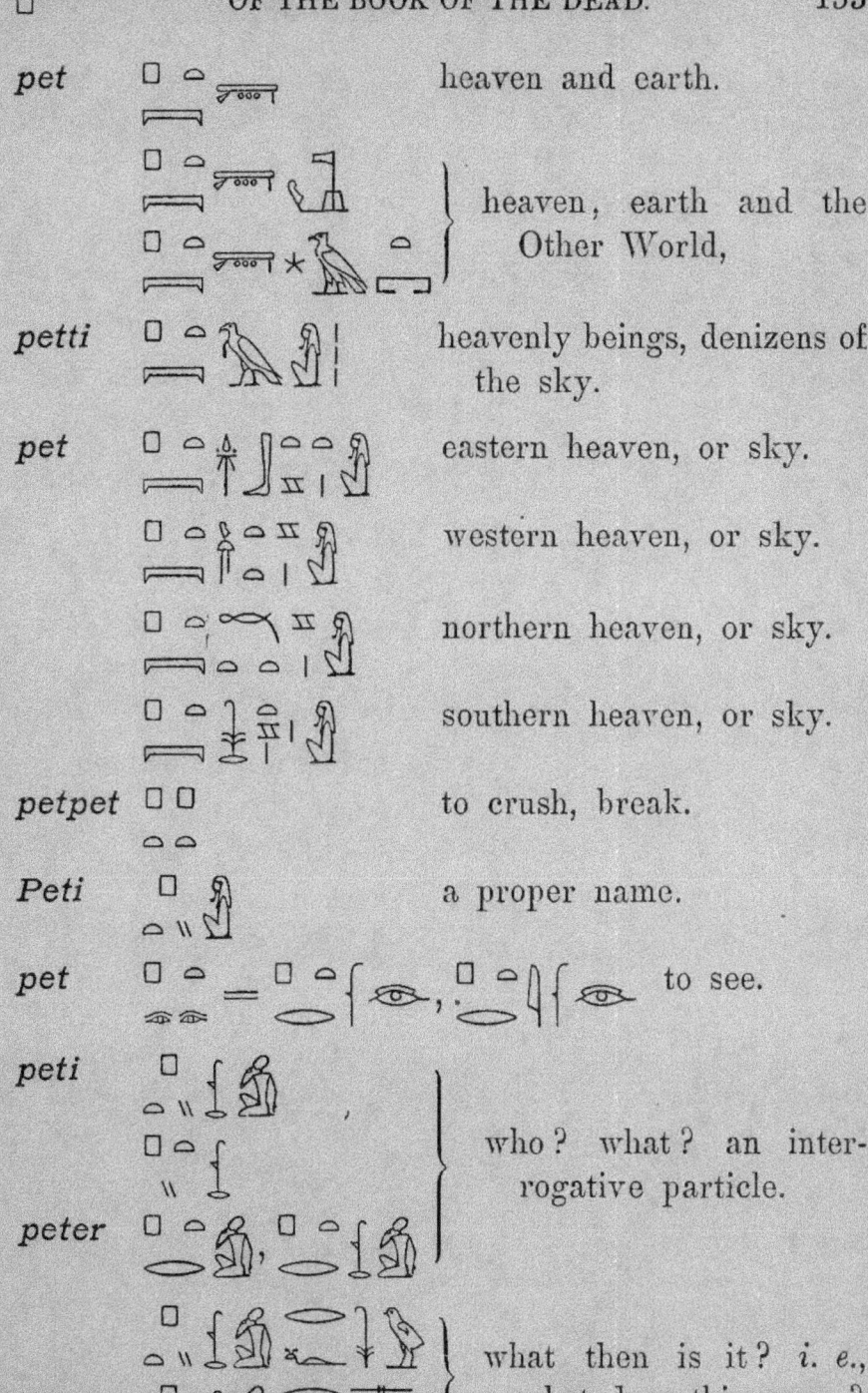

peter 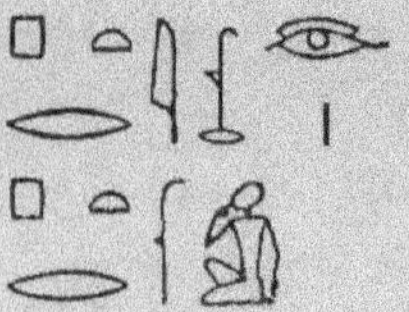 to see, look at, observe.
petrá

Petrá  the name of a god.

Petrá-sen  the name of a river.

Ptaḥ 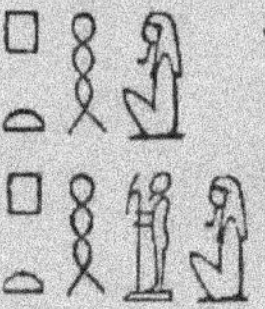 Ptaḥ, the blacksmith-god of Memphis. 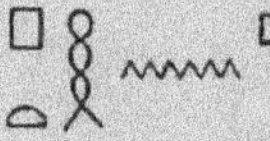,  the temple of Ptaḥ.

Ptaḥ-ḥet-ka 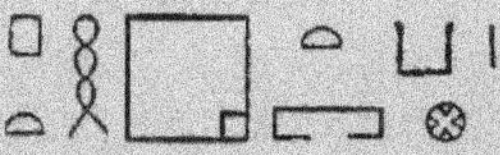, or Ḥet-ka-Ptaḥ, "House of the double of Ptaḥ", a name of Memphis. The common name of Egypt, Ἀἰγύπτος, appears to be derived from these words.

 Memphis of the Other World.

Ptaḥ res àneb-f 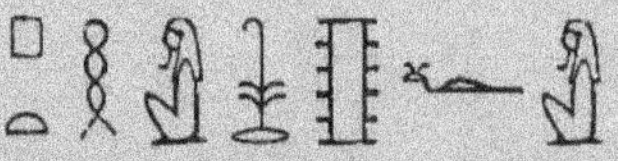 "Ptaḥ [to the] south [of] his Wall", Ptaḥ of Memphis.

Ptaḥ-Seker 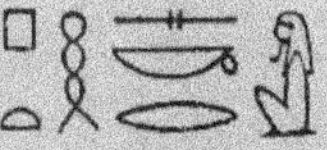
Ptaḥ-Sekri 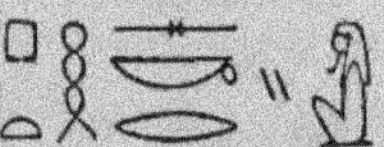 a dual god formed of Ptaḥ of Memphis and Seker, the old god of the Other World of the region of Memphis and Ṣaḳḳârah.

Ptaḥ-Sekri-Tem  a triad formed formed of Ptaḥ of Memphis, Seker, and Temu, an old god of Ȧnu, or Heliopolis.

Ptaḥ-Tanen 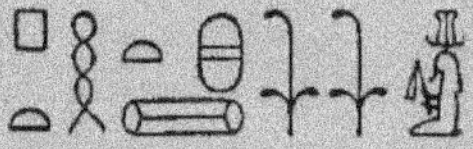 a dual god formed of Ptaḥ of Memphis and Tanen, an old cosmic god of the region.

Ptaḥ-mes  a proper name.

peṭ 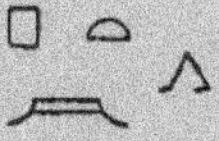 to open out, to extend, to stretch out.

peṭ 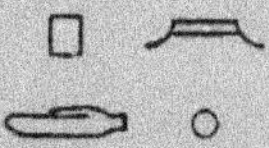 a kind of unguent.

Peṭeṭ  name of a god and city.

peṭsu  to break open, opener.

Peṭ-mer  "Broad Lake", the name of a shrine.

 F.

f  he, him, it, its, his.

fa, *fat*  to bear, to carry, be carried, to lift up, to diminish through decay.

 bearers, carriers.

Fa-ā  to raise the hand.

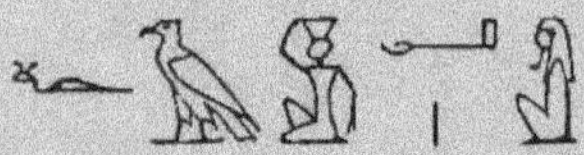 the god of the lifted hand.

Fa-ākhu  a proper name.

Fa-pet  "Supporter of the sky"; the name of the god of the Seventh Ȧat.

Fa-Ḥeru  "bearer of Horus"; a name of Osiris.

Fat-Ḥeru  "the city of the bearer of Horus".

Fau-ḥeru-sen 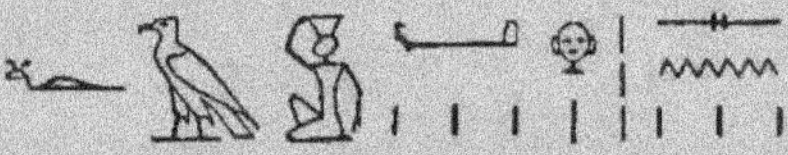 "those who lift up their faces"; a class of divine beings.

fau 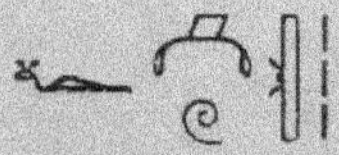 riches, wealth, abundance.

fenkhu  offerings.

Fenkhu  the name of certain dwellers in Syria.

fent 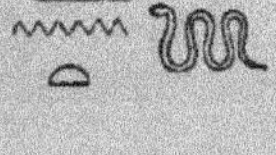 worm, serpent, reptile; plur. 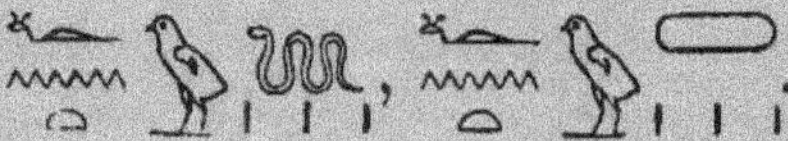

fenṭ 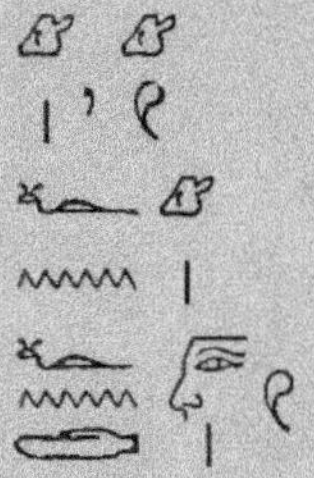 nose; plur. , .

Fenṭi  a form of the god Thoth; the name of one of the Forty-two Judges in the Hall of Osiris.

fekh 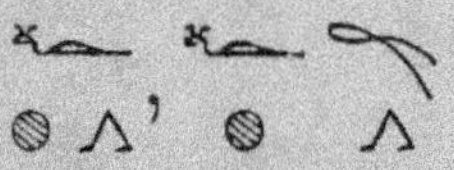 to untie, unloose, destroy.

fekhekh  to burst through.

feqat  a bread-cake, food in general.

feḳa  to make water.

fetu 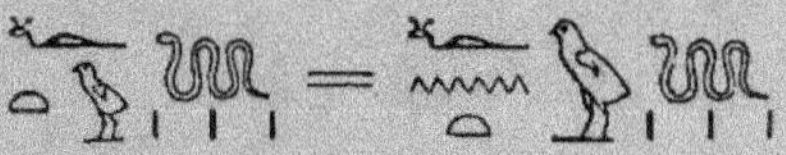 worms.

fettu  fish.

feṭ-ȧb  languor, disgust, weariness.

fṭu  four; 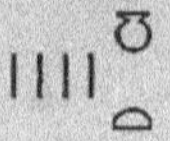 fourth.

feṭqu  destruction, damage.

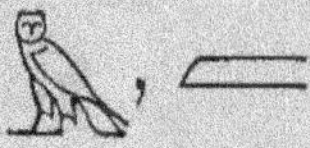 M.

em  sign of the present participle.

em  particle of negation, no, not; 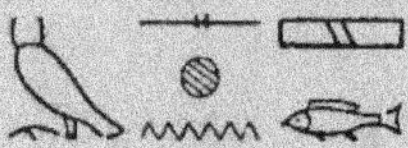 let not make to stink (my name).

em  in, into, from, on, at, with, out from, of, upon, as, like, according to, in the manner of, among.

em āb 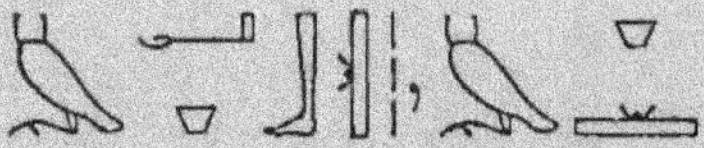

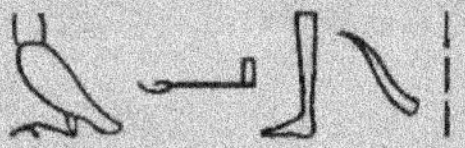 opposite, in front of, confronting.

em ābu 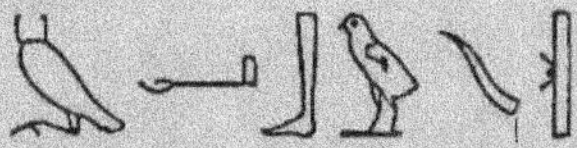

em āb sa 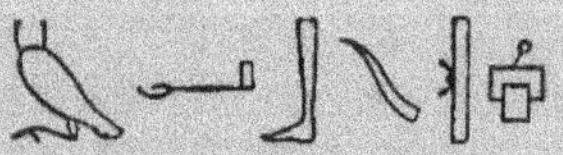

em baḥ  before, in the presence of; the old form is  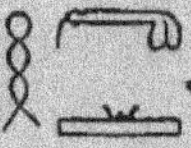.

em baḥ ā	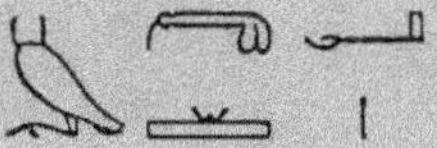	before, in the presence of.
em paitu		before, when not yet.
em nem (uhem)	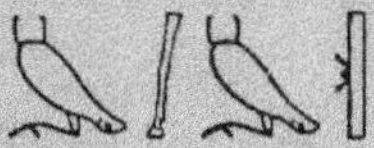	a second time.
em nem (uhem) ā		
em ruti		outside.
em ḥāt		before.
em ḥāti ā		
em ḥer		upon.
em khen	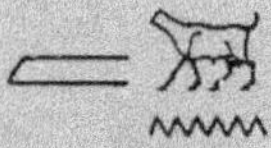	inside, within.
em khennu	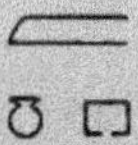	

em khennu ā		
em khert	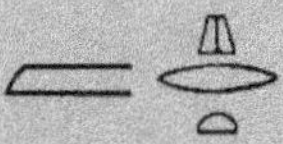	on behalf of.
em khet		behind, after, in the train of.
	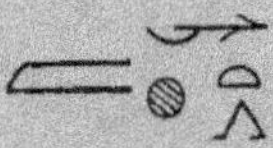	
em sa	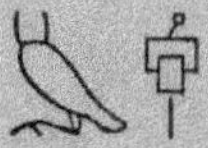	at the back of, behind, after.

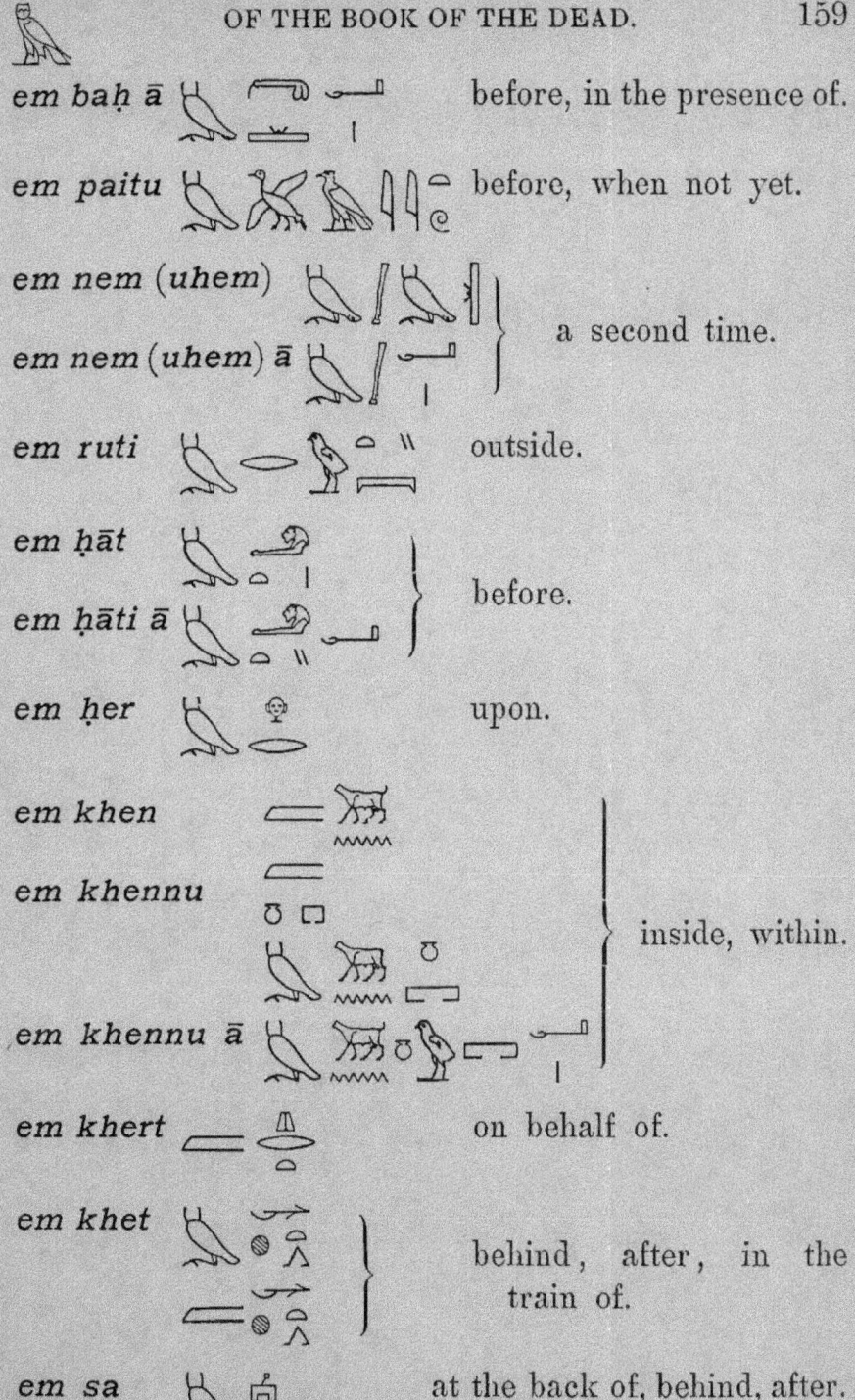

em qeṭ round about, throughout.

ma part of a boat.

ma, *maui*, *mat* to be new, to renew, made new, new.

maa, *maau*, *maat* to see, to look upon, to behold, observe, perceive; seen, observed; plur. part.

maa sight, view, glance.

maat (or *ȧrit*?) eye; eye to eye; an eye.

maati (or *àriui* ?) — the two eyes.

maat — eyes.

maat nebt — every eye, *i. e.*, every body, all people, folk, mankind.

maat Rā — eye of Rā.

right eye of Rā.

maat Ḥeru — eye of Horus, the name of offerings.

maat Shu — eye of Shu, *i. e.*, the sun.

maat Tem — eye of Tem, *i. e.*, the sun.

maa-ànt-f — the name of a plank, or peg, in the magic boat (Chap. XCIX).

maa-ànuf — the name of one of the Forty-two Judges in the Hall of Osiris.

Maa-ȧtef-f-kheri-beq-f   the name of one of the spirits who guard the bier of Osiris.

Maati-f-em-khet  "he whose two eyes are of fire"; the name of one of the Forty-two Judges in the Hall of Osiris.

Maati-f-em-ṭes  "he whose two eyes are like knives"; the name of one of the Forty-two Judges in the Hall of Osiris.

Maa-em-ḳerḥ-ȧnnef-em-hru   "he who seeth in the night what is brought to him in the day"; a proper name.

Maa-ḥa-f
Maa-ḥa  "seeing what is behind him"; a proper name.

Maa-ḥeḥ-en-renput  "seeing millions of years"; a proper name.

Maatuf-ḥer-ā  a proper name.

Maaiu-su (?)  a proper name.

Maa-thet-f 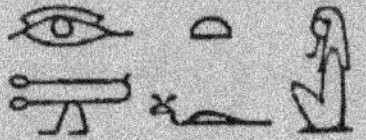 a proper name.

maar 

maȧr  } restraint, misery, affliction, wretched one, oppressed one.

maȧ 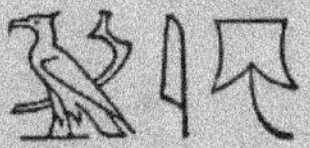 lion.

maȧuti 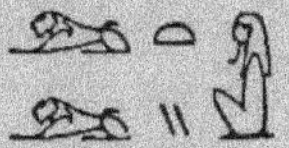 the lion-lioness god, *i. e.*, Shu and Tefnut.

maā 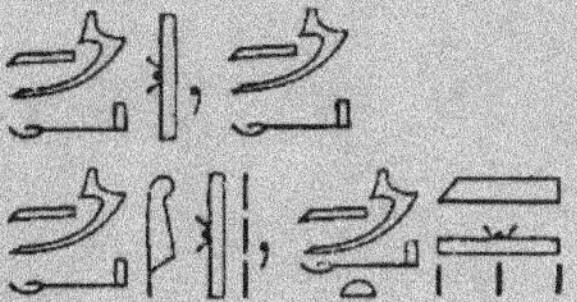

maāu  } to be right, straight, just, true, to pay which is legally due, or what it is right to pay, to give a statutory offering.

maā-kheru 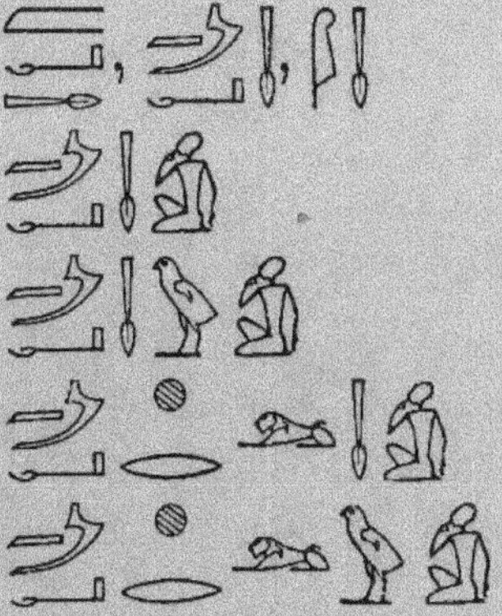

maāt-kheru 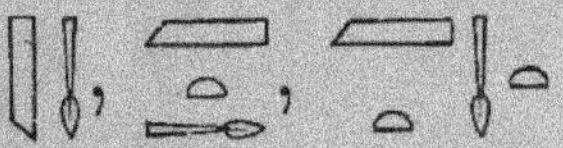 } "true word", or "true of word", or "true voice", or "true of voice", he whose word when spoken is followed unfailingly by the effect desired. These words are placed after the names of the dead, and appear to mean something like "triumphant",  a crown of triumph;  to be right.

maāt 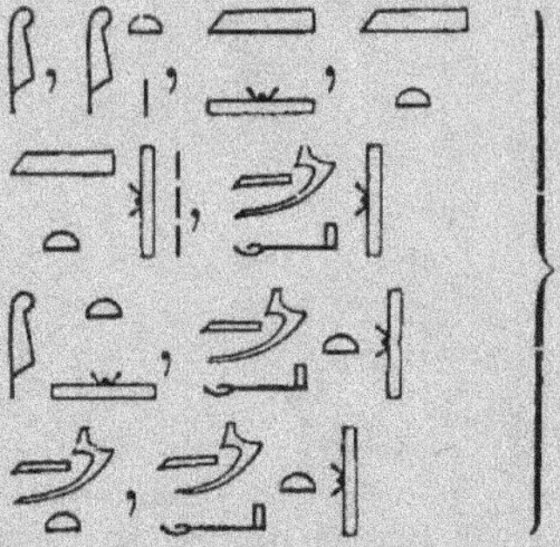 truth, what is right, true, straightness, law, order;  doubly true:   the scales balance exactly.  "[with] the cord of maāt", *i. e*, uniformly and regularly; 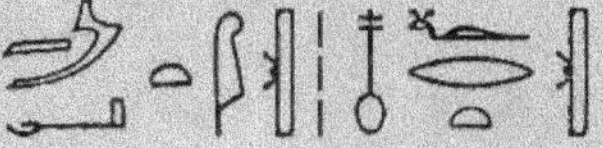 beautiful truth.

 a righteous judge.

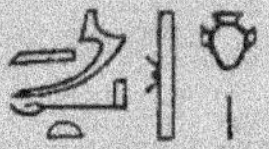 true, right of heart.

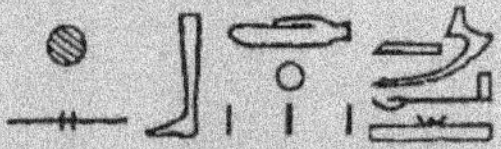 real lapis-lazuli.

 thy genuine friend.

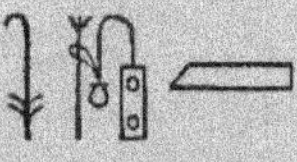 real royal scribe.

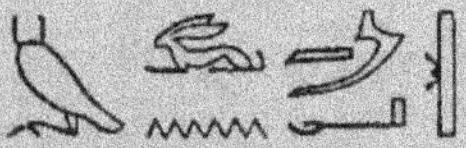 in very truth.

 really true.

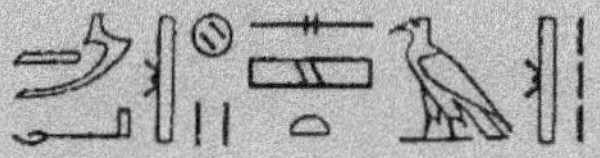 most truly a mystery.

Maāt 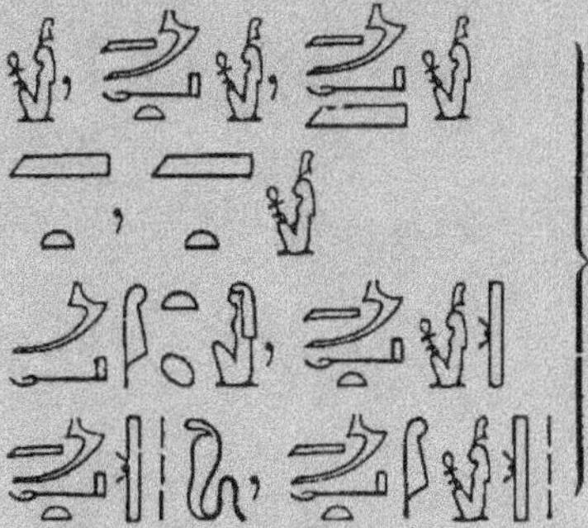 the goddess of truth, law, order, etc.

Maāti  the two goddesses of truth, law, order, etc.

maāti  truth, right.

Maātiu 

the gods of truth, law, order, etc.

maāt 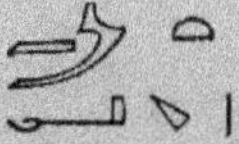 a district, or region.

Maāti 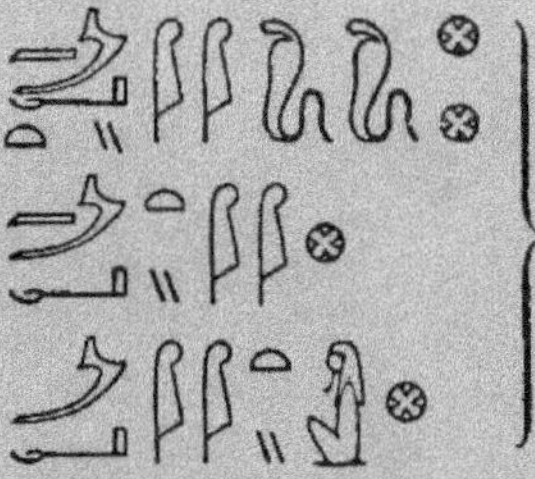 the cities or districts of the two Maāti goddesses.

maā  limb.

maā  windsail, wind, breeze; plur. 

maā	to stretch out (?).
maā	to journey.
maautu	stalk.
maftet	lynx.
mama	palm (?) tree.
Manu	the Mountain of Sunset.
maḥa	a part of the head.
maḥu	part of a boat.
maḥu	a crown, wreath.
mast	leg; dual .
Mastiu	a group of star-gods.
maqet	ladder; plur. .
maḳ	a precious stone.
maut / *matu*	incense.

Matchat the name of a city.

mȧ as, like, concerning, even as.

like that same one.

inasmuch as, even as.

like that which.

after the manner of.

mȧti a person or thing resembling another person or thing, type, copy.

divine image; his divine images.

mȧtet picture, likeness, similitude, like unto, copy of; likewise.

mȧn to-day.

mȧnt , , , with , daily.

mȧu to be like .

mȧu , cat, cat's skin.

mȧu lion; lions.

mȧu to knead, to mould, to fashion.

mā , give, grant, let there be! who? what? behold! be-hold thou! behold ye!

mā
māȧ
māȧi come! give! bring! .

Māau-taui name of a god.

māāt place.

māāat name of a place.

māb thirty.

mābiu the thirty great gods.

mābit 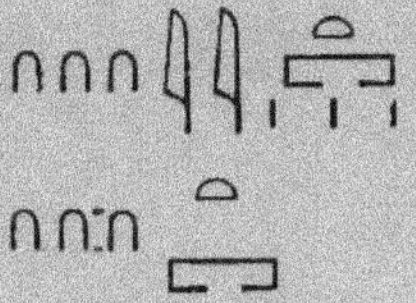 name of a place or building.

māfket 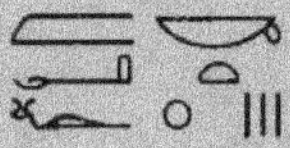 turquoise.

Mānāat 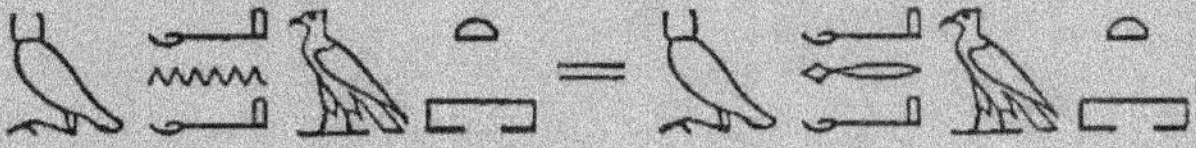 ?

Mārqathȧ 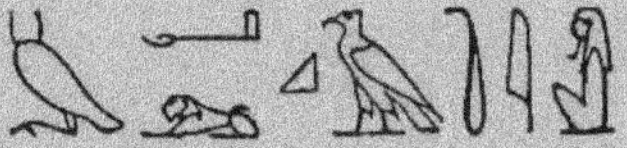 the name of a god.

māhaiu  people, tribe, generations (?).

māhaṭti  fire.

māhui  milk vessels, udders (?).

māhenȧ 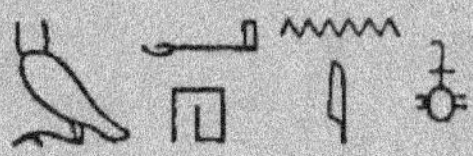 milk vessel.

māḥā 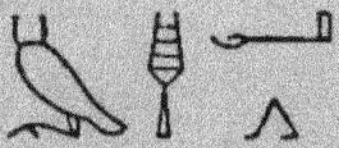 standard.

Māḥu 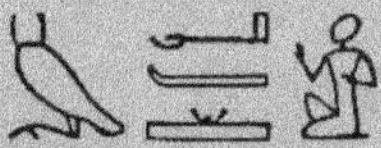 the name of a man.

mākha 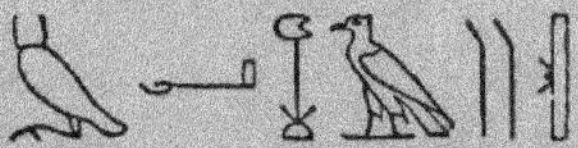 to weigh.

mākha 

mākhat 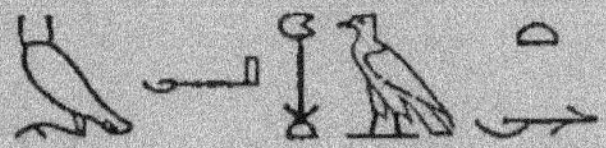

mākhaȧt 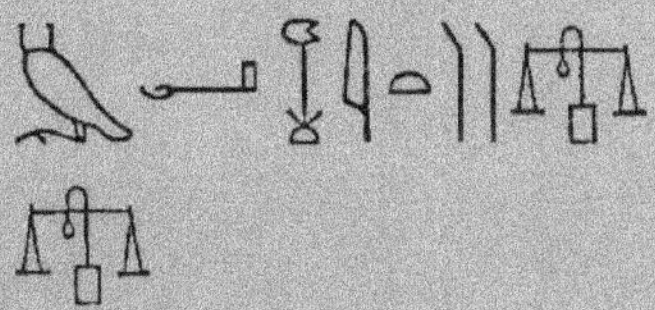

a pair of scales, a balance; 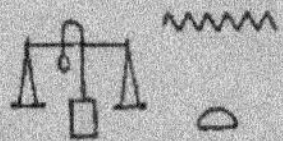 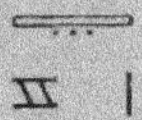 the balance of the earth.

mākhatu  intestines.

mākhait  sledge for a sacred boat or god.

mākhiu  altars with incense burning on them.

mākhent  a boat.

māsheru  evening, eventide.

mākat  place.

māku  to protect, protection.

māki  protector.

māket  a thing which protects, amulet.

mākefitiu 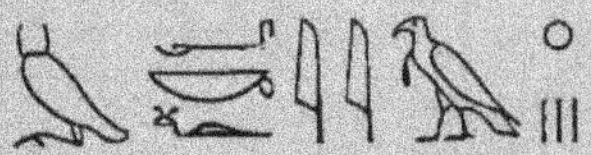 objects made of turquoise.

mākḥa 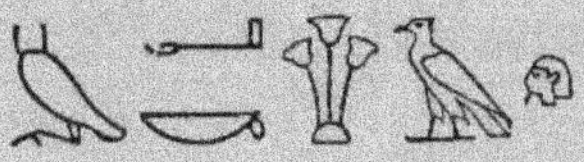 to turn round, or behind, back of the head.

māket  station, place.

māqet  ladder.

mātau  weapons, short spears, harpoons.

mātenu  ways, roads, paths.

Māṭes 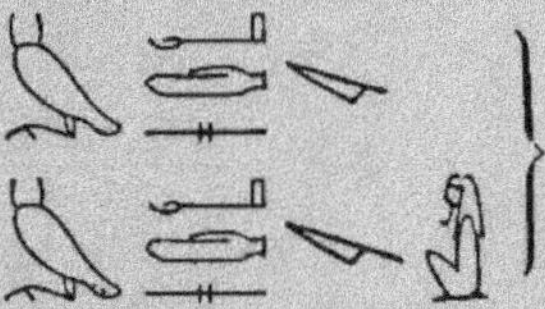 a proper name.

Māṭes-ȧrui (?)  the gods with knife-like eyes.

māṭet (*māntchet*) 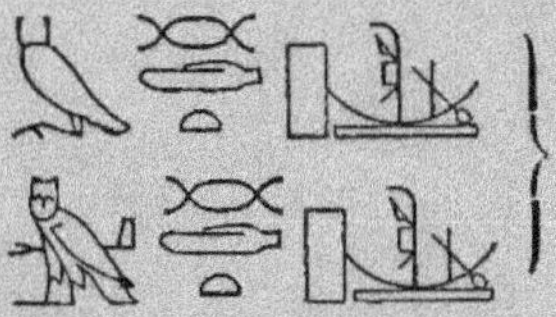 the boat in which the sun sailed from sunrise to noon.

māthennu  ways, roads, paths.

mātcha  phallus.

mātchabu
mātchabet 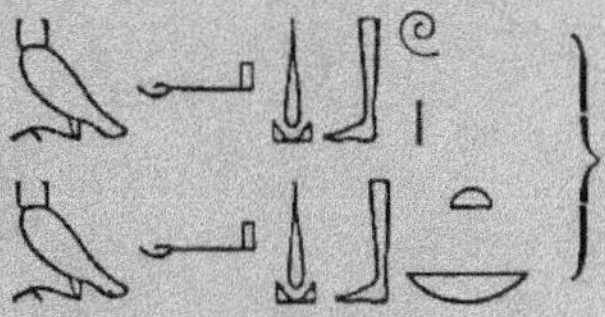 chain, fetter.

mātchabet  part of a ship.

Mātcheṭ 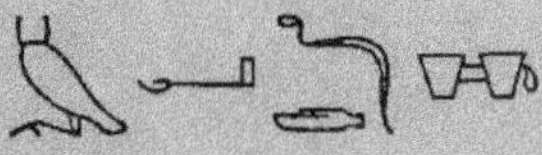 a proper name.

mātcheṭ to use force, to compel, to constrain.

Mi-sheps a proper name.

mu water, essence.

pool; the pool of the well of Àmenti; the pool of Kher-āḥa.

the god of the water, or divine essence; essence of Rā.

brow (surface?) of the water.

what is in the water.

m[u]it water.

mu a decoction, as in:—

ānkham flower water.

myrrh water.

saltpetre water.

incense water.

incense water.

dirty water.

mut mother.

muti parents.

Mut the Mother-goddess *par excellence* of Egypt; "Mut in the horizon of heaven". mother-deities.

mut weights for scales.

Mut-restȧ a proper name.

Mut-ḥetepth a proper name.

mut to die, death, the dead, the damned; plur.

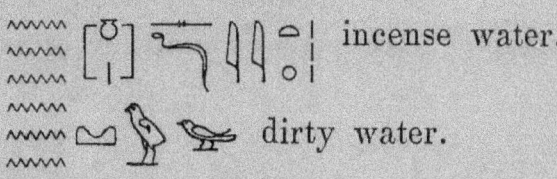

Menu  name of a god of generation and fertility.

Menu-Ḥeru  Menu + Horus.

Menu-suten-Ḥeru-nekht  a name of Osiris.

Menu-qeṭ  a proper name.

men, *ment* 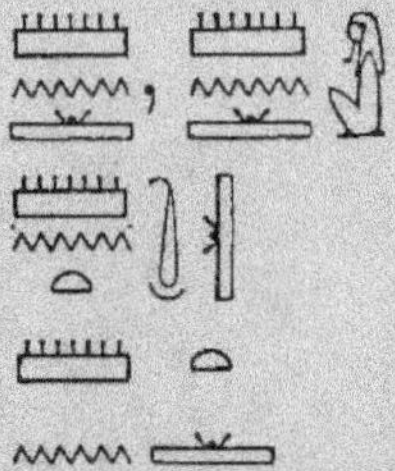 to be permanent, stable, firm, to be fixed, to remain; 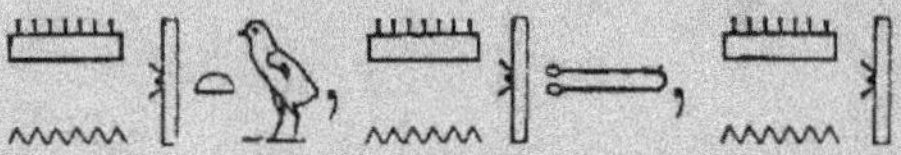 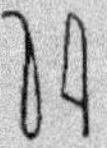 abiding, fixed.

menu  possessions, things which abide.

menu  chamber.

menu 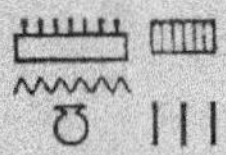 bases, pedestals.

Ment  name of a god.

menti 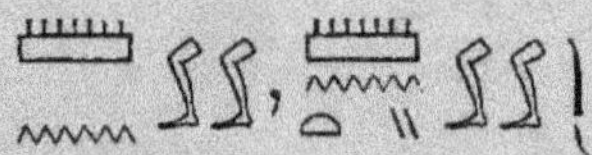, *mentiu*  the two thighs.

men  to be in pain, sick.

ment 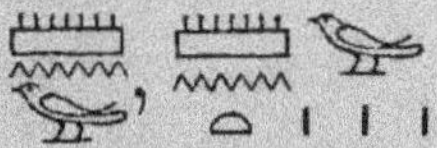, *menut*  pain, sickness, disease.

men — such and such an one.

Menȧ — name of a god or city.

menȧ — to tie up a boat to the mooring post, to come into port, to land, to die; arriving.

menȧ, *menȧt* — post to which boats are tied up or moored.

menȧu — mooring posts, stakes of death.

menȧ, *menȧt* — end, ending a happy ending, or death.

menȧ, *menȧ-tu* — the dead.

menȧt — funerary bed, bier, death.

meni — to slay, put to death.

menȧt 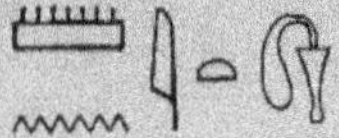 a musical instrument.

menāt 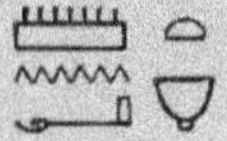 breast.

menu  ministrants.

menmen 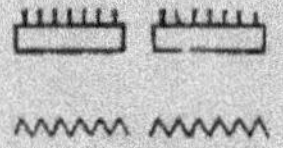 to go about.

menment 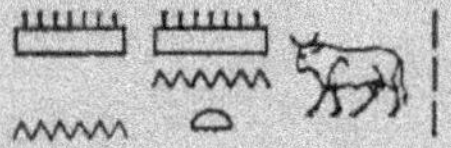 cattle, farm stock.

menḥ 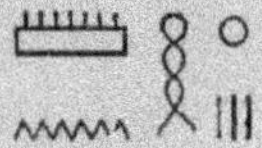 wax.

menḥu 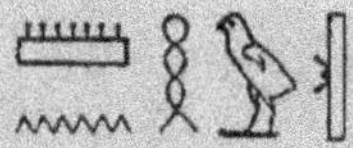 to offer up.

Menḥu 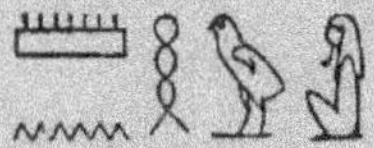 name of a god.

menkhu   to work, wrought, well finished, excellent, worked or inlaid, perfect, well disposed, well-doing; 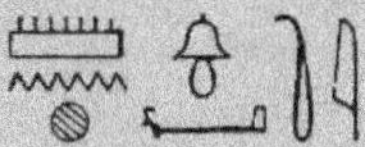 perfected;  valuable things.

Menkh 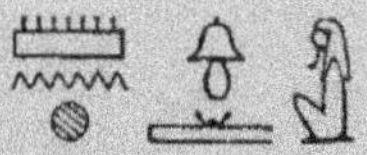 the beneficent god (?).

menkhet 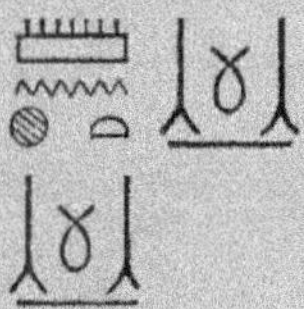 apparel, clothes, garments.

Menqet	the name of a goddess.
Ment	a proper name.
ment	swallow.
menṭ-t	apple of the eye.
menṭi	the two breasts.
Menthu	the War-god of Hermonthis, who was at a later period identified with Rā.
Mentchat	the name of a city.
mer	overseer, superintendent.
	major-domo, steward.
	officer of soldiers.
	overseer of the granaries.
mer	a water-course, canal.

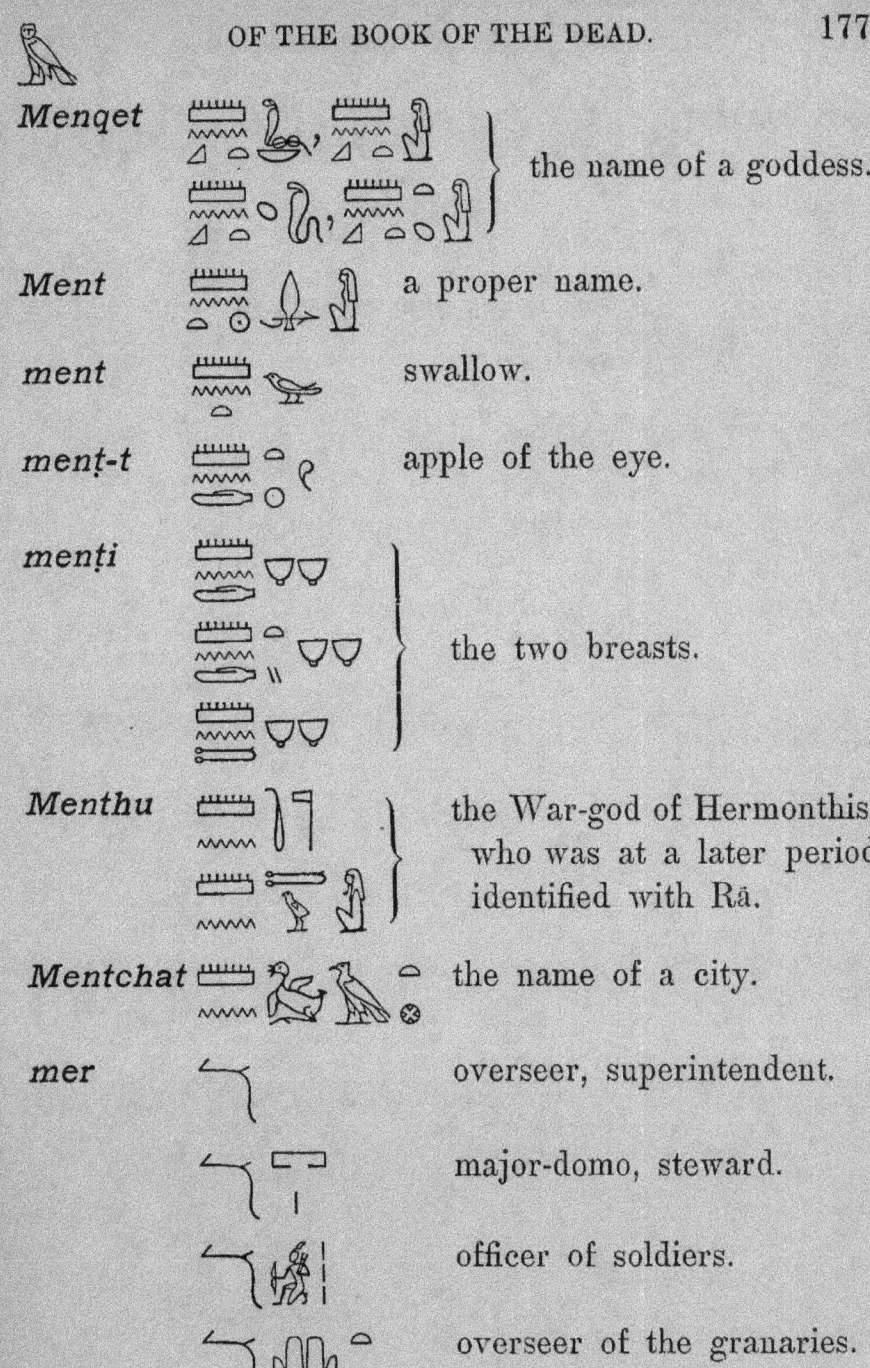

mer 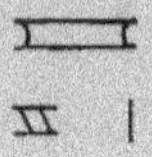 pool, tank, cistern; plur. 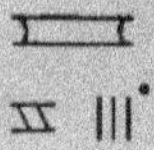

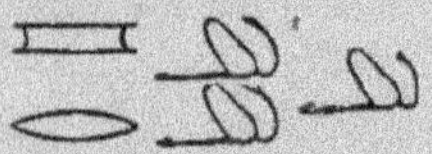 swamps, lakes.

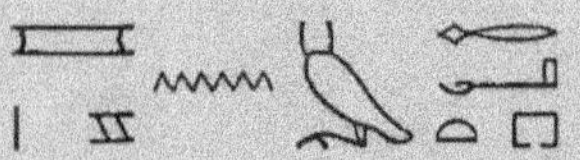 Lake of Maāt.

 Lake of the Maāti gods.

 Lake of the geese.

 Lake of the horizon-gods.

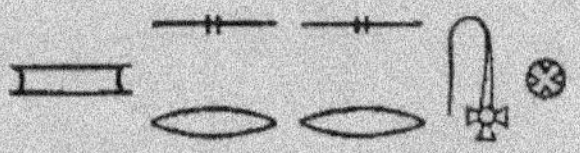 Lake of Fire.

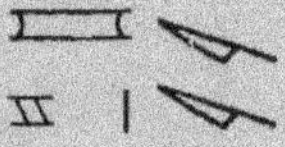 name of a mythological Lake.

meru  peasants, agricultural labourers.

mer  to be sick, ill;  sick; 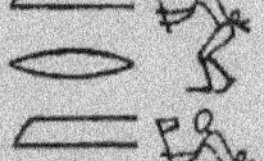 diseased, or perhaps =  the dead.

meru 
meràu 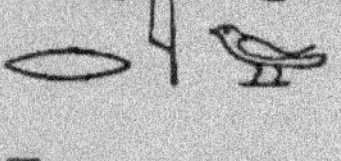 } pain, sickness, disease, decay.

Mer  a proper name.

mer — to love, to desire, to wish for, to will.

meru — loving, lover, beloved;

merr — lover, beloved;

merru — lovers.

mertu, *mert*, *merit*, *merrt* — love, desire, wish, will.

Mer — a proper name.

Mert — name of a goddess.

Meritti — a group of gods.

Merti — two goddesses.

mer — to bind, to tie.

meru swathing, bandage.

Mer-ur the Mnevis Bull.

merāḥāt tomb, sepulchre.

meruḥ oar, paddle.

meriut a kind of tree.

Meres
Meri-s } a proper name (?).

merḥ
merḥet } wax.

mert the name of a part of a boat.

Mert name of a city.

Mert a proper name.

mehait roof.

meḥ , } cubit, , , , , , , .

meḥ — to fill, be full; , full; filling, filler; the filling of the Utchat, *i. e.*, full moon; the filling of the Eye of Horus; a stream filled with flowers.

meḥ sa — to be complete.

meḥ — to be inundated, submerged, drowned.

meḥit — flood.

Meḥ-urt, *Meḥt-urt* — a very ancient sky goddess, afterwards identified with Nut.

meḥ — unguent (?).

meḥ 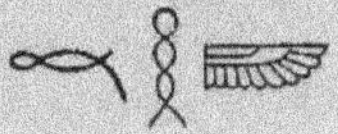 wing, pinion.

meḥ 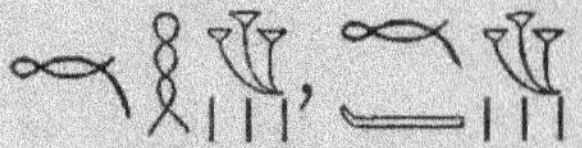 garland.

Meḥānuti-Rā  a proper name (?).

meḥut 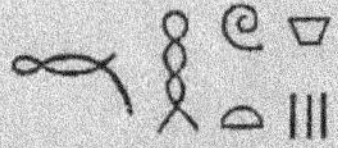 offerings.

meḥuti 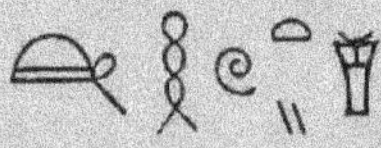 oil.

Meḥi 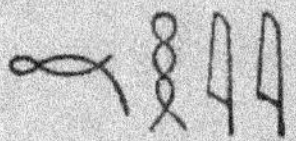

Meḥiu 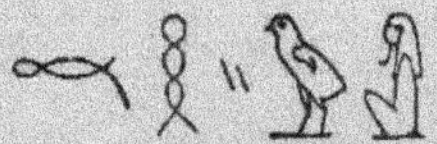

(Mehi and Mehiu) a proper name.

meḥit 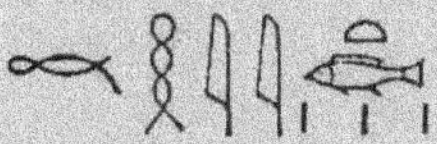 fish.

meḥef 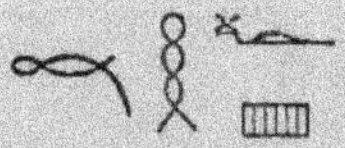 a kind of stone.

Meḥen 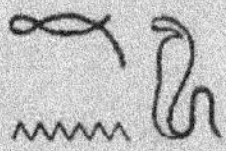

Meḥent 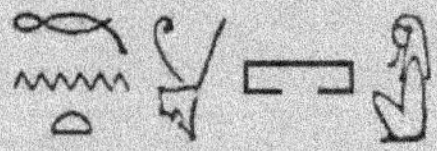

Meḥenit 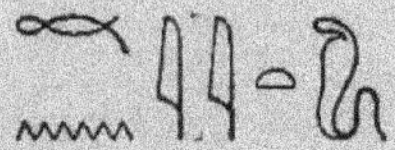

(Mehen, Mehent, Mehenit) name of a god and goddess.

Meḥenet  name of a city.

meḥenet 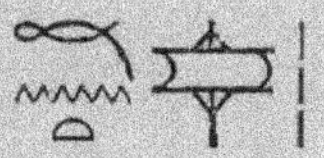 the north wind.

meḥt 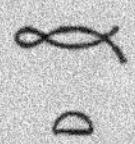 placed before numbers; 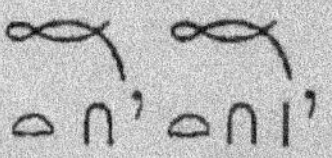 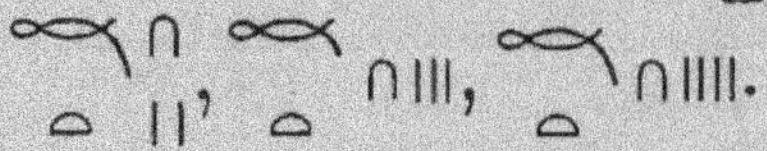

meḥt — vessel, plaque (?).

meḥt, *meḥti* — the north in general, the north of Egypt, *i. e.*, the Delta; north-west.

meḥtiu — northern beings, men or gods, lords of the north, *i. e.*, in late times, the Greeks; nest of the northerners.

Meḥt — the goddess of the North.

meḥt, *meḥit*, *meḥuiu*(?), *meḥu* — the north wind.

meḥti — oil.

Meḥti (?)-*sāḥ-neter* the name of one of the Seven Cows.

meḥṭet to bathe.

Em-khent-maati (?) (?).

em khennu within.

mekhsef name of a wooden instrument.

mes, *mesu* to bring; bringer, bringing.

mest to walk, approach.

to give birth to, to bring forth, to produce, to fashion; born of; born; giving birth a second time to mortals; ; .

mest genetrix.

mest  birth; plur. 

mestu  birthday.

mes  child, offspring.

mesu  children.

mesesiu

mesu nebu  all who are born, *i. e.*, the human race.

mesu beṭesh 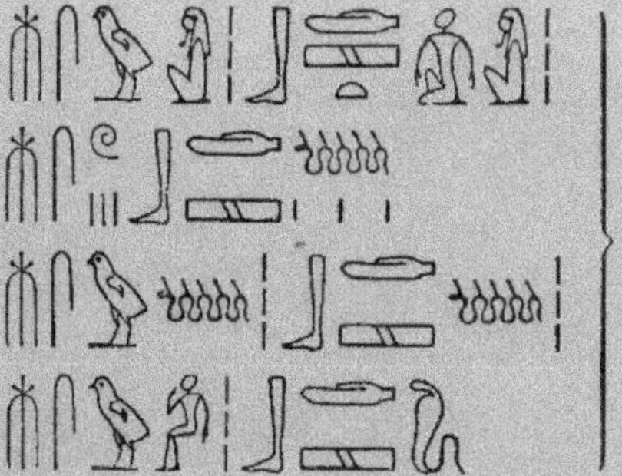 malicious but powerless fiends.

mesu ent Nu 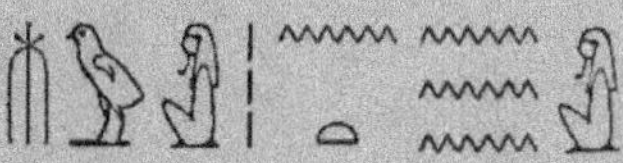 children of the divine water, *i. e.*, plants.

mesu Nut children of the Sky-goddess.

mesu Ḥeru children of Horus (Kesthȧ, Ḥāpi, Ṭuamut-f, Qebḥsennuf).

mesu Serȧt beqet ....

mesit cakes eaten in the evening.

mesbeb (?) banded (?).

Mes-peḥ a proper name.

Mes-Ptaḥ a proper name.

Mes-em-neter a proper name.

mesmes to count (?).

mesmes Vol. II, p. 251, l. 2.

mesnekht birthplace.

emseḥ
emseḥu crocodile; plur. , eight crocodiles .

emseḥu  to slay.

meskhen
meskhent  the birth-place of a god or goddess; a region in the Sekhet-Àaru where the gods were produced; 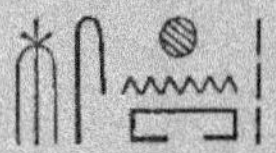 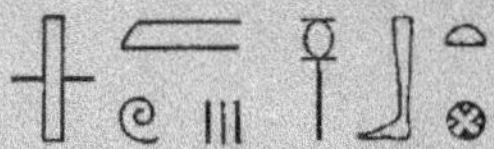 the four birth-places of Abydos.

Meskhen-āat 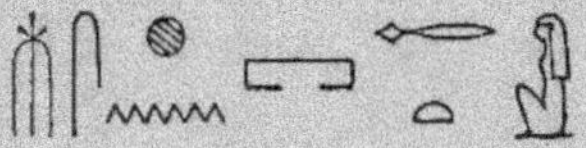 the name of a goddess of birth, or of a birth-place.

Meskhen-ment 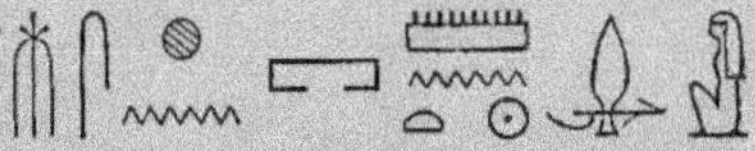 the name of a goddess of birth, or of a birth-place.

Meskhen-nefert  the name of a goddess of birth, or of a birth-place.

Meskhen-Seqebet 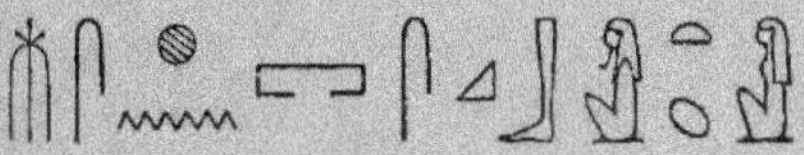 the name of a goddess of birth, or of a birth-place.

Mesespekh 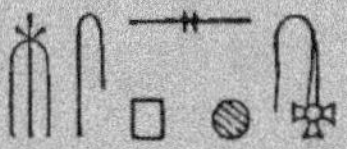 a proper name.

Messhenu 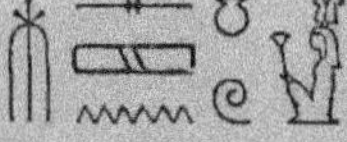 = Meskhenu.

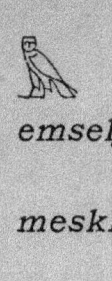

meska  skin.

Mesqen 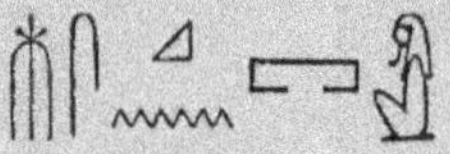

Mesqet 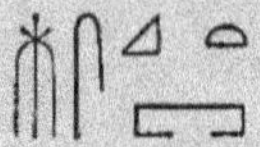

} a region of the Other World through which the deceased must pass before he could reach the Sekhet-Ȧaru.

mesqet 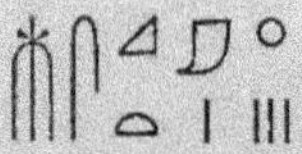 weapons.

mesṭemu  to paint the eyes with *koḥl.*

mesṭemet 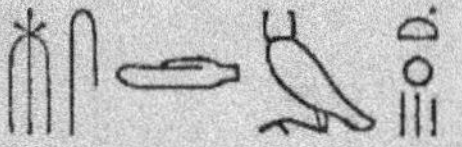 eye-paint, stibium, *koḥl.*

mesṭet  leg.

mesṭ 

mesṭeṭ 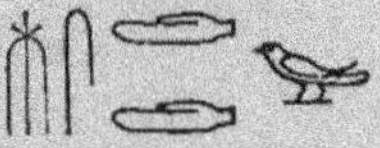 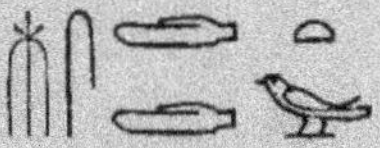

} to dislike, to hate.

mesthȧ 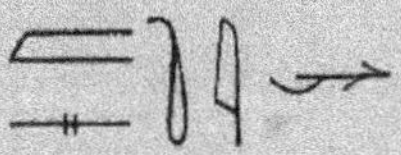 palette. The true reading is Ḳesthȧ, *q. v.*

Mesthȧ 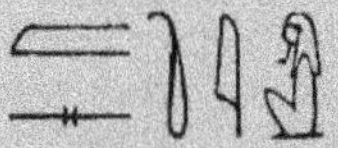 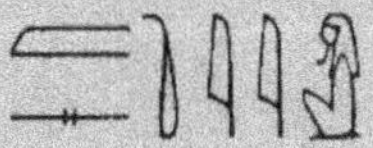 one of the four sons of Horus. The true reading is Ḳesthȧ, *q. v.*

mestcher  ear.

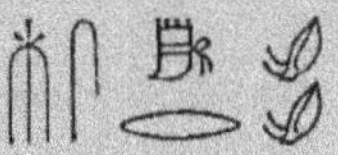  the two ears.

mestchetch — to hate.

meshā — bowmen, soldiers.

meshen — Chap. CX. B. 16.

Em-qeṭqeṭ — the name of a spirit, or god.

met (*mut*) — the dead, the damned.

met — ten.

tenth.

metu — venom, poison.

metut — seed, progeny;

metmet — to eavesdrop (?).

met
meti — to be right, what is right, the mean; the exact truth (?).

meter
metru — to bear witness, to testify, to give evidence.

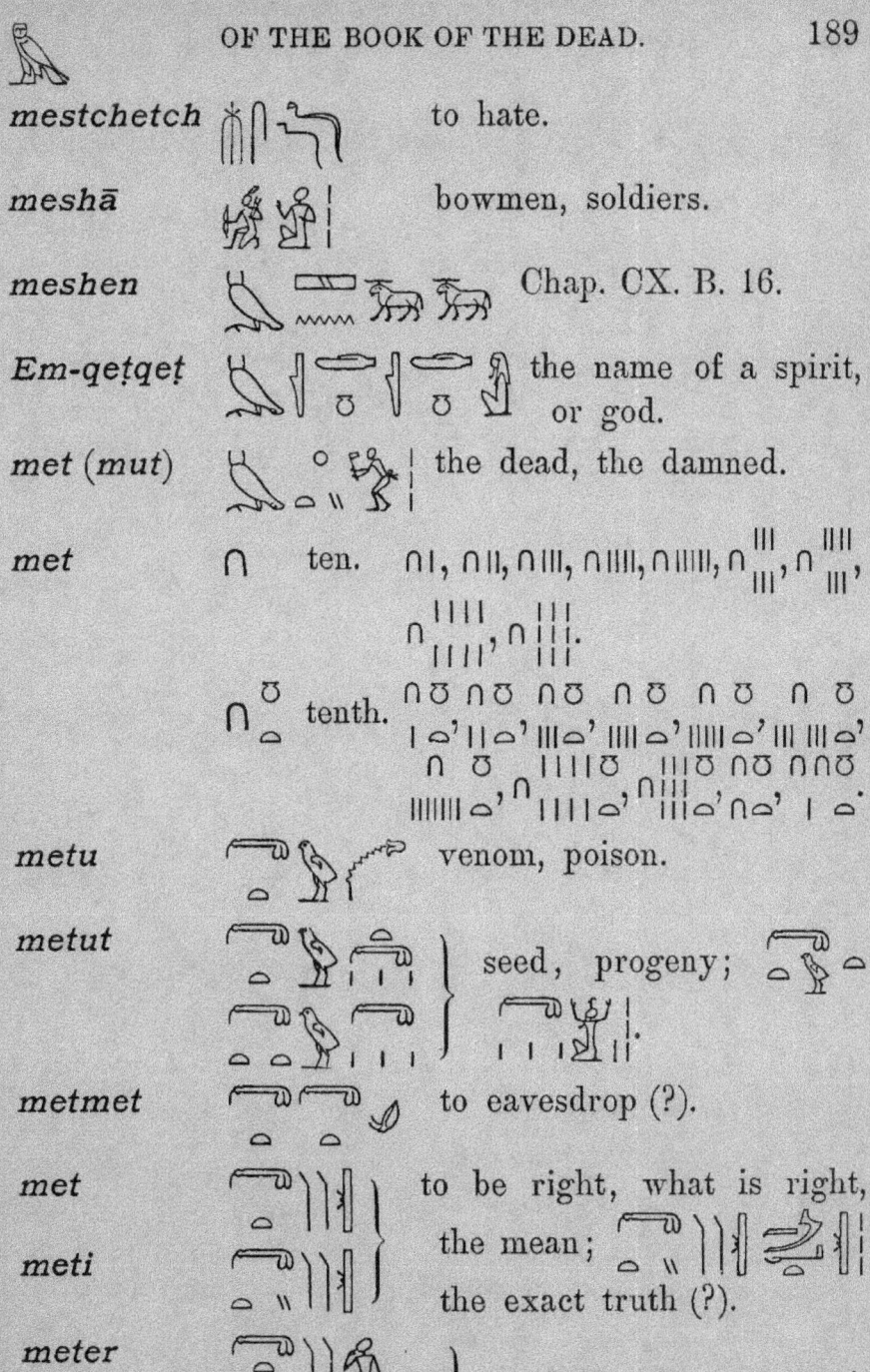

meṭu  to speak, to talk, tell, declare.

meṭ, meṭu, *meṭet* 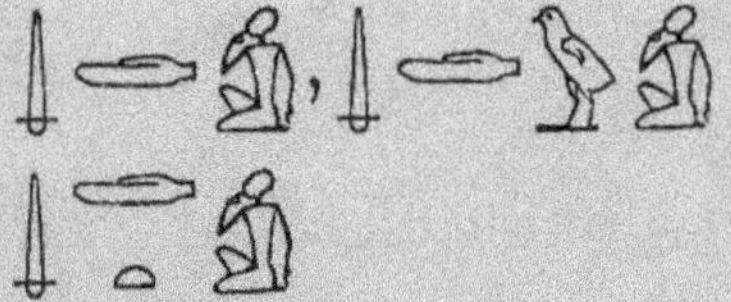 word, speech, talk, declaration; pronouncement.

meṭut  words, speech, things (like the Hebrew דָּבָר);  word of wisdom; 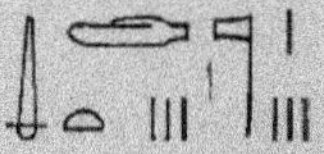 words of the gods; 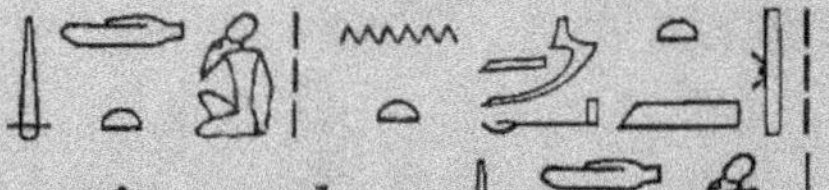 words of truth; 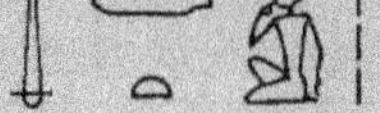  words of evil, blasphemy.

Meṭu-ta-f  a proper name.

Meṭes-ḥer-àri-mer 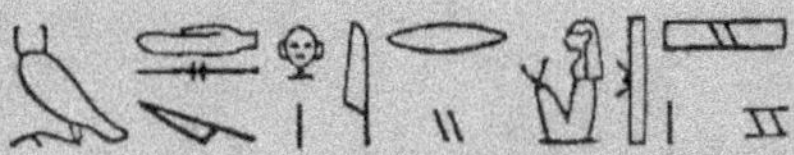 "Knife-face, guardian of the Lake"; the name of the doorkeeper of the Sixth Ārit.

Meṭes-sen — the name of the door-keeper of the Seventh Ārit.

metch — to be deep; deep; very deep.

metchtu — abyss.

deeps, depths.

metchaub — to fetter.

metchet — salve, ointment, oil.

N.

n — a preposition, in, to, for, because. With additions :—

n — of; with plural following,

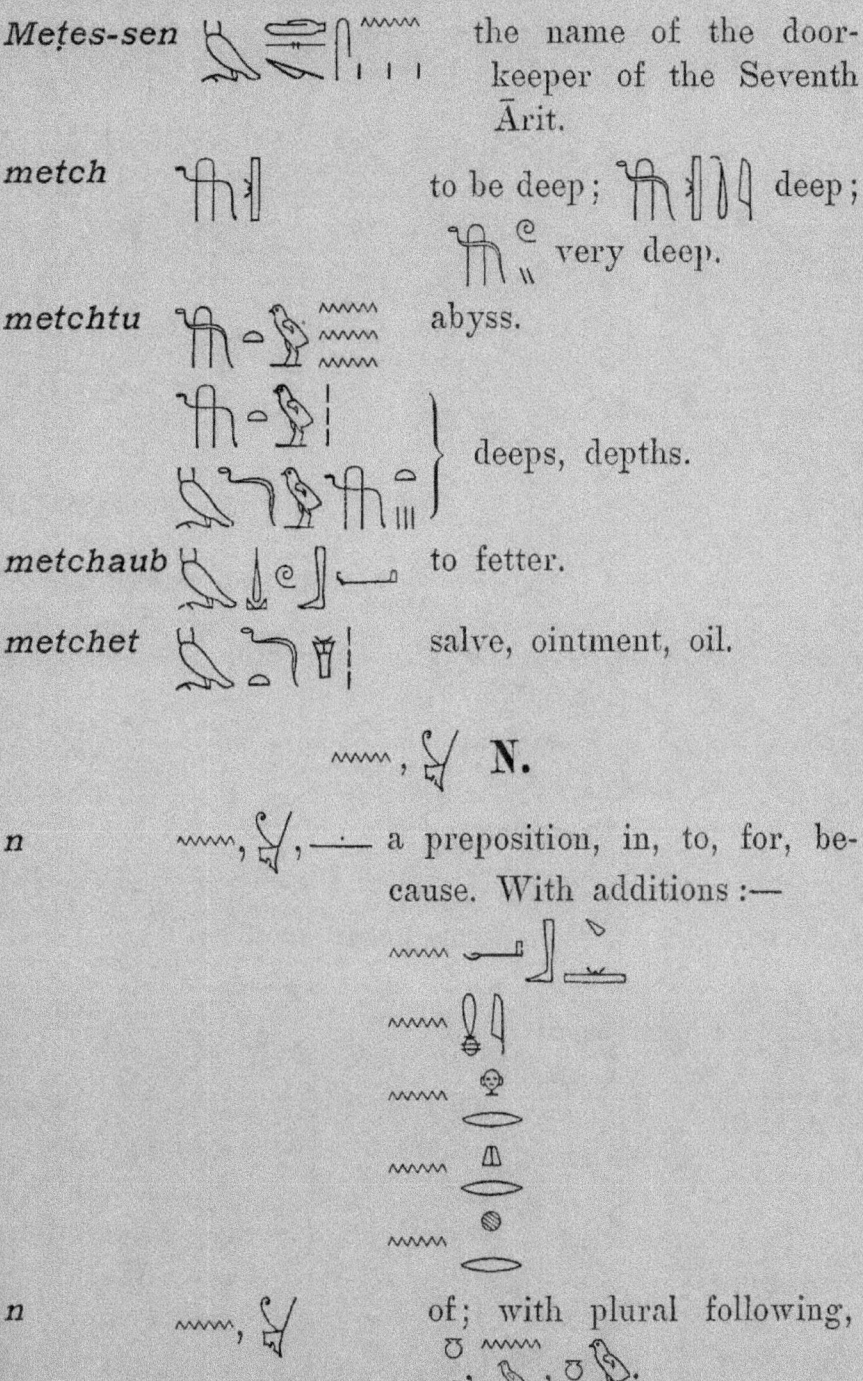

n 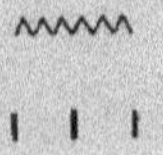 we, us.

n 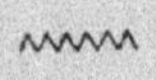 no, not = 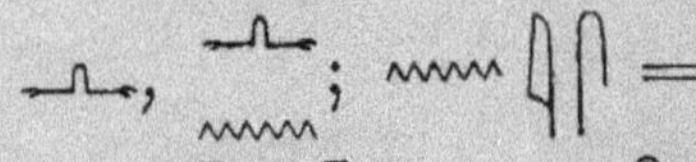

invisible.

na  those, the;  those who are after.

naiu 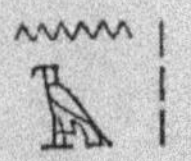 those of;  those of thine;  those belonging to.

na
nai
nȧu

air, wind.

Naȧrik  a proper name (?).

Naȧrruṭ
Naȧrruṭf
Nanȧaruṭf
Nȧareruṭ
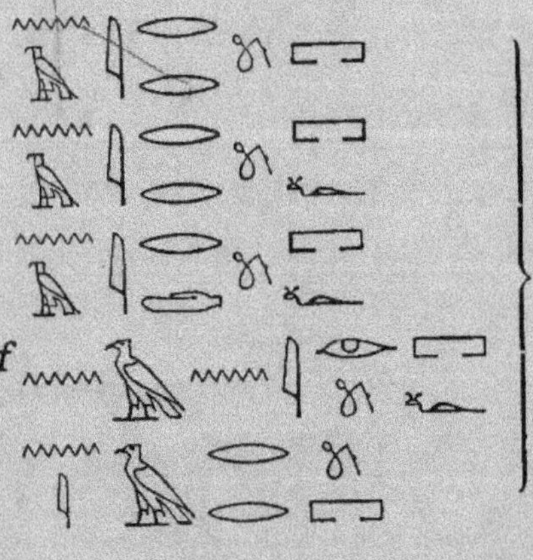
"the place where nothing grows", a name for a region of the Other World. See Ȧn-ruṭ-f.

Nasaqbubu  name of a god.

Nak (?)  = en Aker 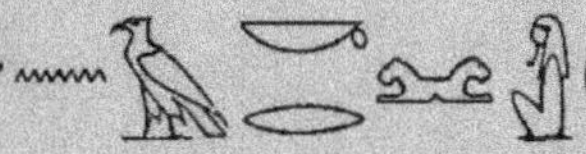 (?).

Nathkerthi  name of a god.

n-ȧ  I, me, my.

nȧh  injury.

nȧs, ***nȧsu*** 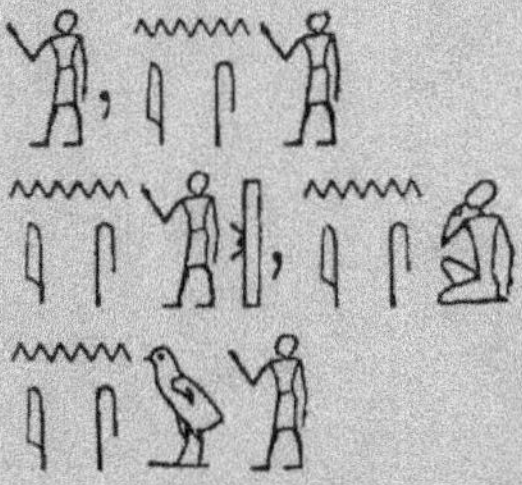 to call, cry out, invoke; 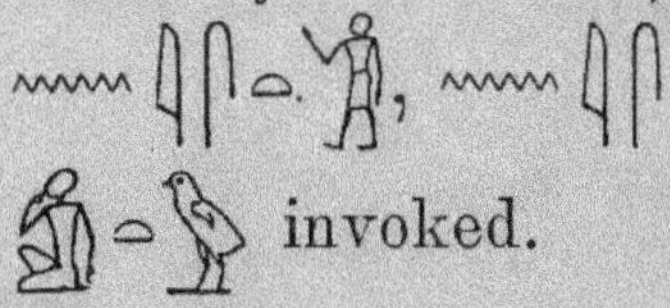 invoked.

Nȧk 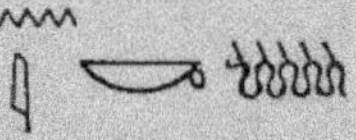 the name of a fiend and enemy of Rā.

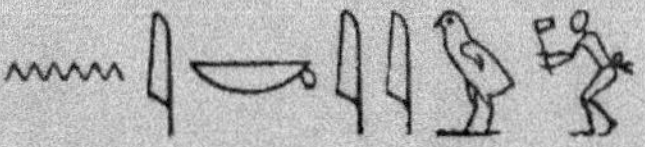 fiends, enemies.

nā, ***nāai***, ***nāt*** 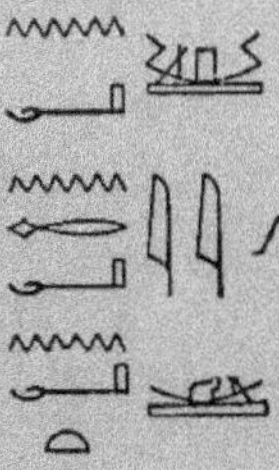 to journey, to travel, to come, to arrive, to advance.

Nāȧu 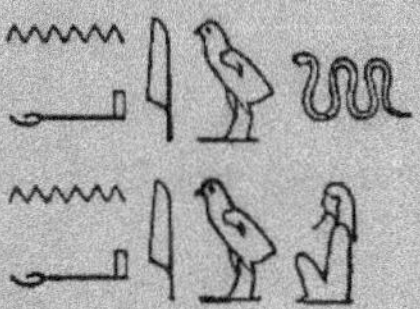 name of a god or devil.

nāu  fiend, devil; plur. .

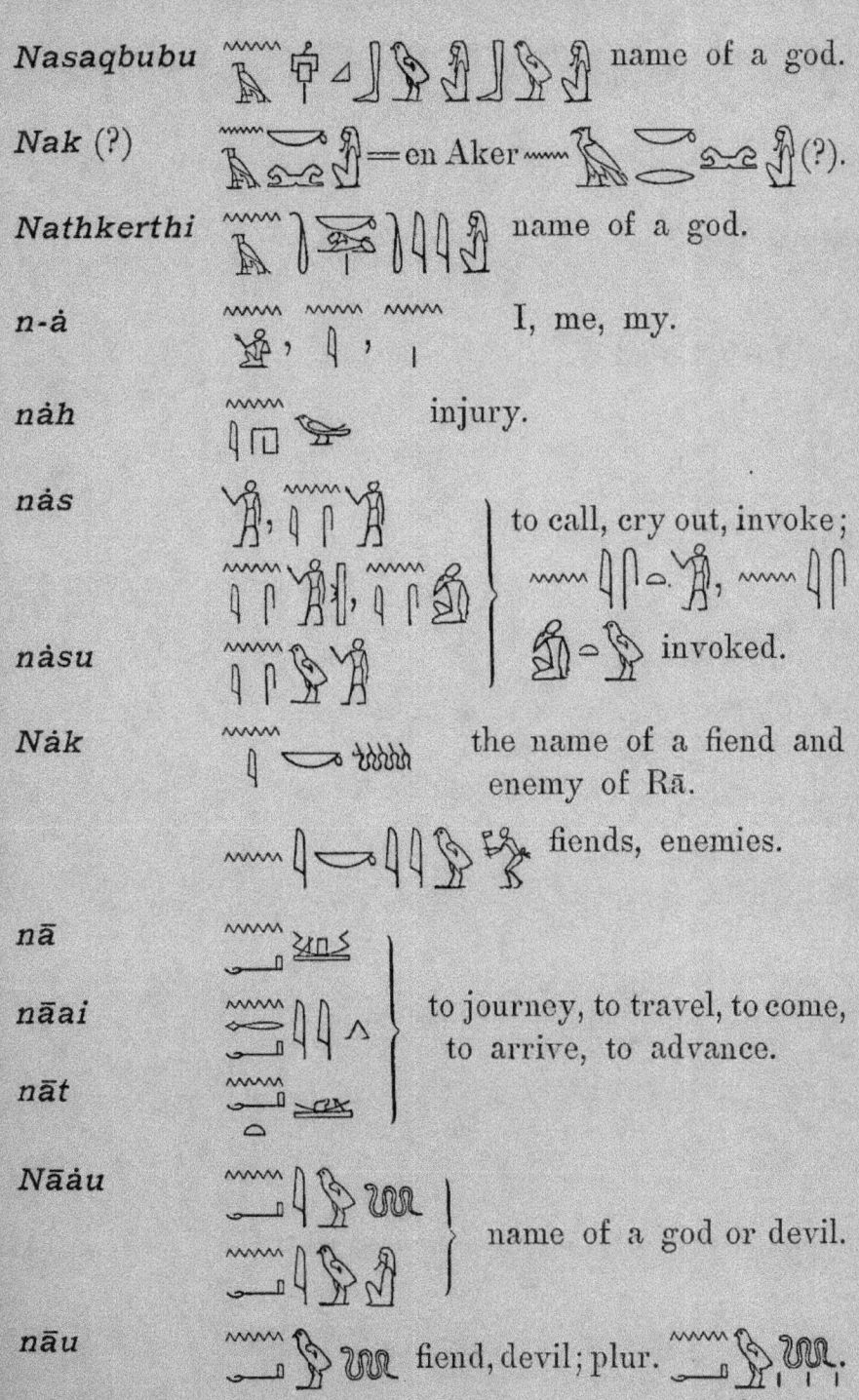

nāā 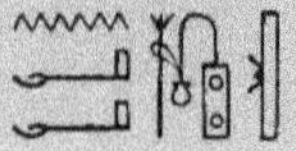 a decree (?), a design, picture.

nār  a reed pen, painting reed.

Nārt  a proper name.

Nārtiānkhemsenf 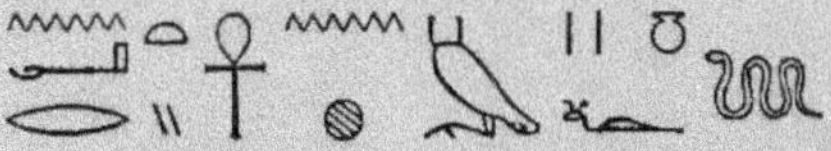 name of a fiend.

nāsh 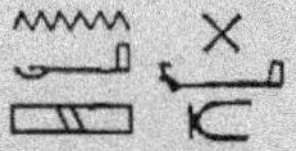 mighty one.

nāḳ  to break open, to split.

nāḳeḳa  to cackle.

ni (?) 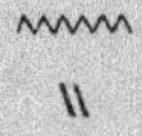 in 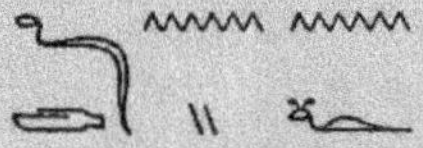 and .

nimā  who?

nini 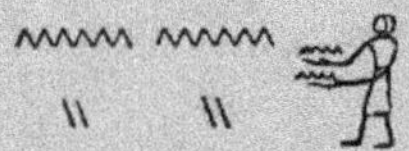 to salute, to acclaim.

nu  of. 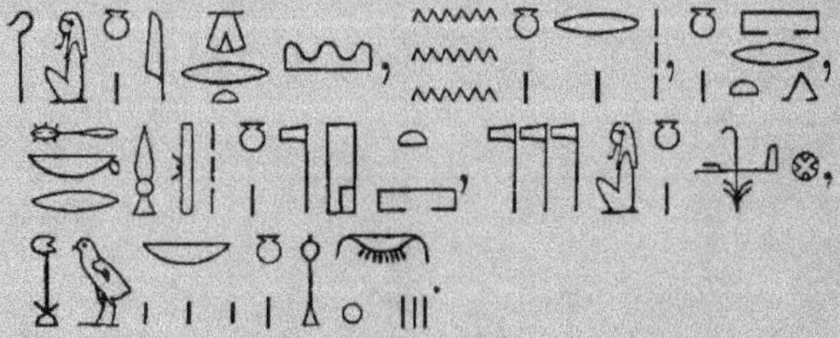

Nu  name of a scribe.

nu the watery abyss of the sky.

Nu the Sky-god.

nu these; these very ones; these; these who.

nu season, period, time.

nu to see, to watch, to observe

nu to go away, go about.

nu to be strong, to strengthen.

nu hours.

nu (?) adorations, praise, worship.

nuit weapon, knife, short dagger.

nub gold; fine gold; golden light.

Nub-ḥeḥ "Eternal gold"; a name of Osiris.

nub, *nubȧu* 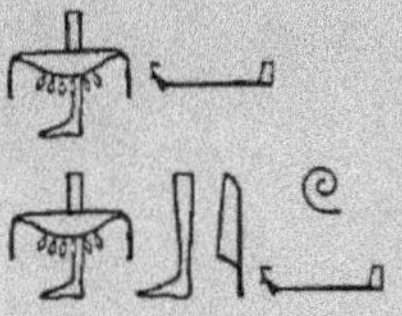 to mould, to shape, to fashion, to form; 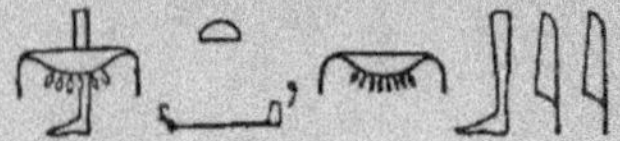  fashioned, inlaid.

nubḥeḥ 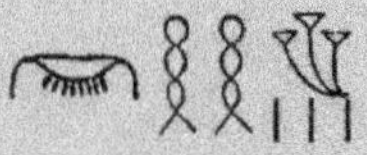 blossom, flower.

Nubti  name of the god of Ombos, *i. e.*, Set.

nun  to pay homage.

nur 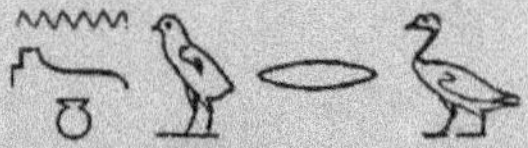 a kind of bird.

nuḥ  to masturbate.

nuḥ  to bind, to tie, to fetter.

 cords, cordage, rigging, tackle.

nuḥu 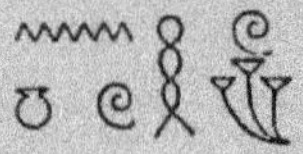 flower, blossom.

nuḥti  pair of horns.

nukh  to be burnt.

nuk  I.  I; even I.

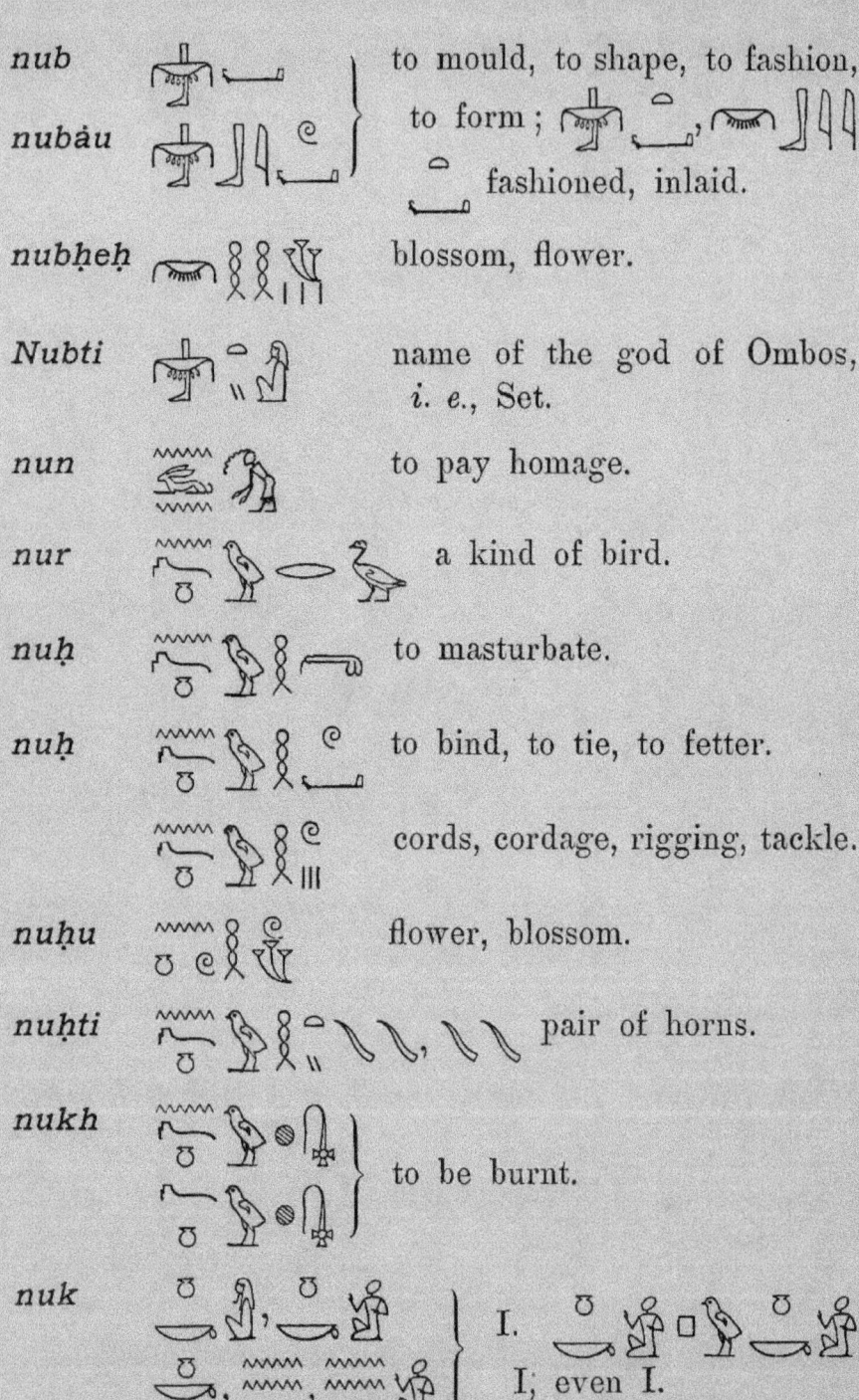

nut  the sky, heaven.

Nut 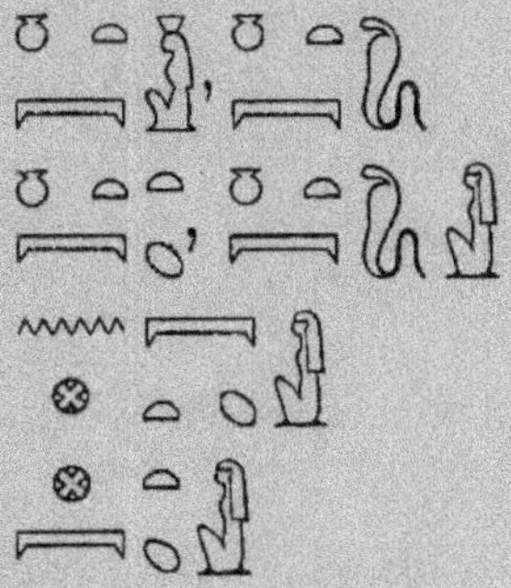 the Sky-goddess, the wife of Seb, or Ḳeb; the name of a sail in the magic boat.

Nut 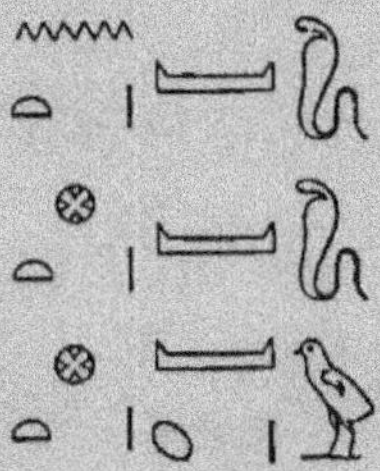 the night sky.

nut  cords, ropes.

nut 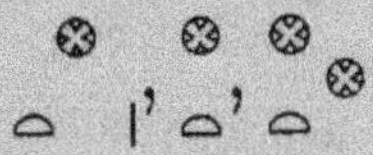 city; plur. 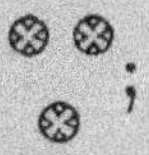; 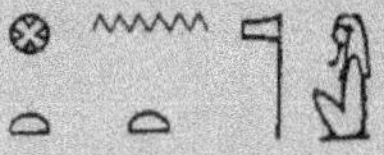 city of god.

nuti  citizens.

nui
nut  canal, stream, river, flood, any large collection of water.

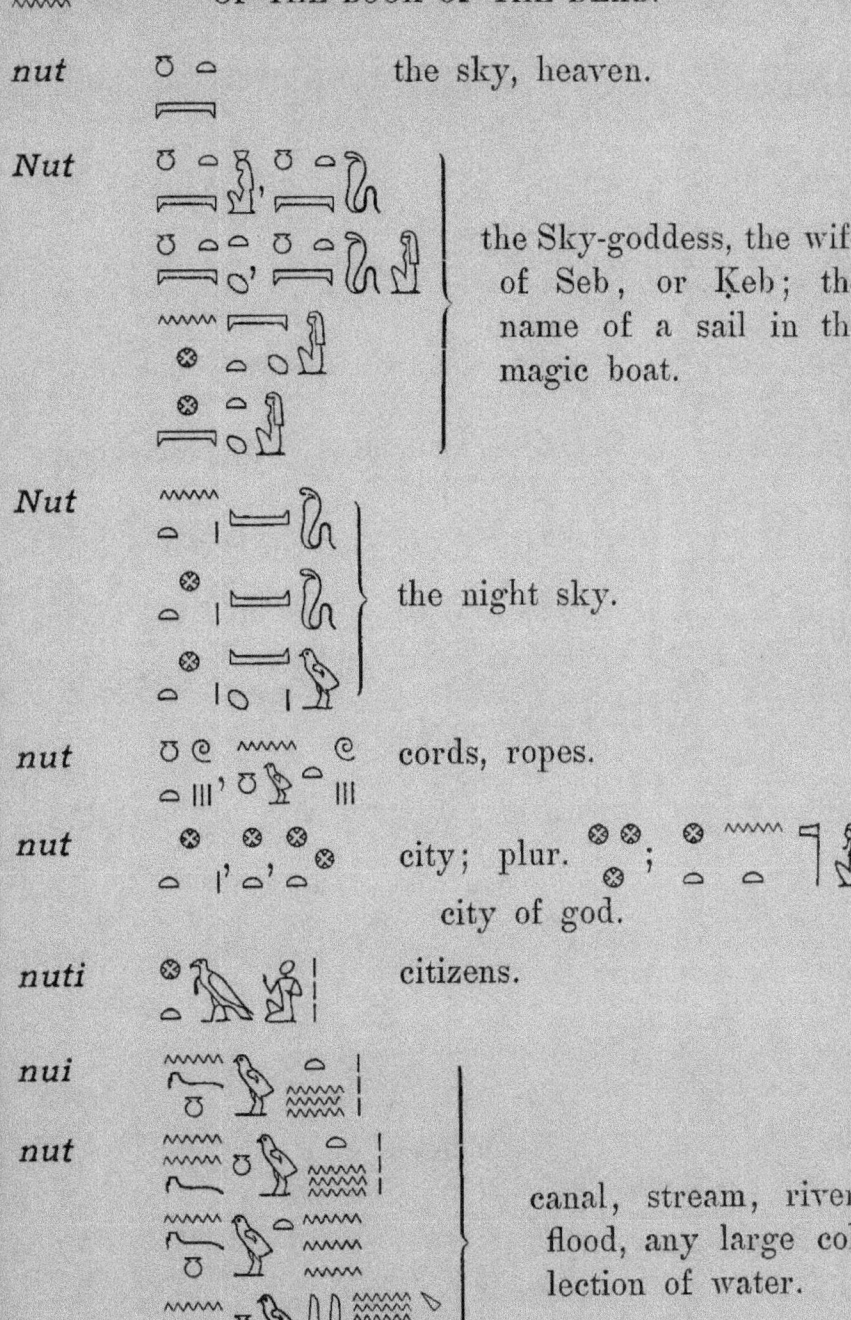

Nut-urt "great city"; the name of a lake in Sekhet-Åaru.

Nutu-hru a proper name.

nuti sweet air (?).

nuṭ to bear, to carry, to journey.

Nuṭiu a class of divine beings.

neb
nebt (in late times or), each, every, any, all; plur. , ; ; every kind of evil thing.

neb with *bu*, , every-where. See also under .

neb , , , lord, master, sovereign; plur. , , .

nebt lady, mistress; in late times "lord".

neb lord of, possessor of, owner of, *e. g.*, , ; compare the use of בַּעַל.

neb àbu "lord of hearts"; a name of Àḥi.

neb Àbti "lord of the East"; a title of Rā.

neb àmakh "lord of veneration", *i. e.*, one to whom service is rendered and homage paid; .

neb Àmenti "lord of Àmenti"; a name of Osiris; the lords of the Other World; "lady of Àmenti", a title of Hathor.

neb āāui "lord of the two hands".

neb ābui "lord of the two horns"; a title of Àmen; the name of one of the Forty-two Judges in the Hall of Osiris.

neb ānkh "lord of life"; a title of Osiris.

the title of the sarcophagus and the bier; late form .

nebt ānkh 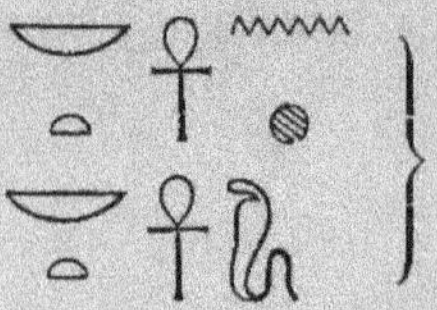 "lady of life"; a title of Isis.

nebt unnut  "lady of the hour"; a proper name.

neb urert 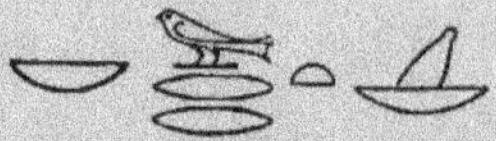 "lord of the *urert* crown"; a title of Osiris and of Horus.

neb useru  "lord of strength, or powers"; a title of the Sun-god.

neb baiu  "lord of souls"; a title of several gods.

neb pāt 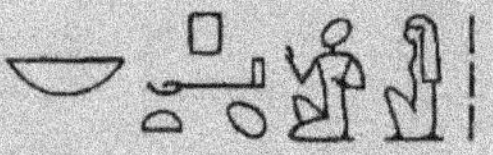 "lord of mankind"; a title of Horus.

nebt per 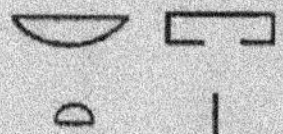 "lady of the house", *i. e.*, a married woman, house-wife. It is possible that  is not intended to be read, and is only a determinative. The Egyptian to-day speaks of his "house", meaning his wife, or his wife and family.

neb mau  possessor of many eyes, or good sight.

neb maāt 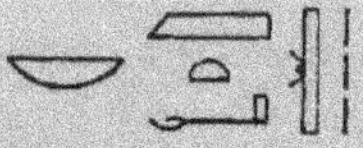 possessor of truth or law,  .

neb Maāti  lord of the double City of Truth.

nebt māket 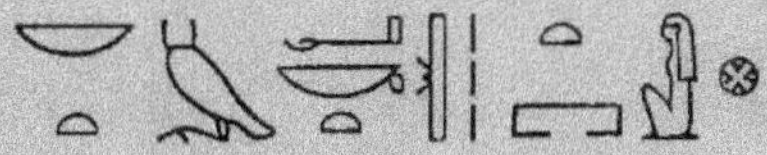

nebu en meḥt 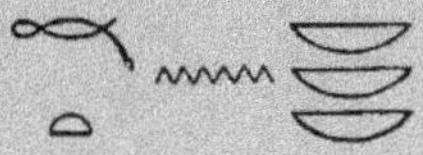 "lords of the north"; the peoples of the Delta; in late times the Greeks.

Neb nebu 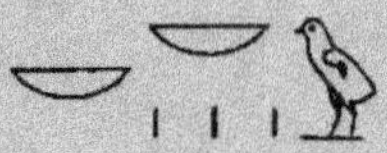 "Lord of lords"; the name of one of the Forty-two Judges in the Hall of Osiris.

neb nefu  "lord of winds"; a title of Osiris.

neb nemt 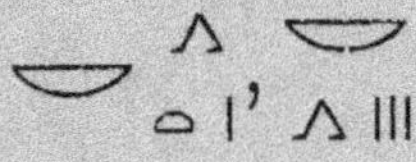 "lord of steps", *i. e.*, one who has the power to walk.

neb neru  "lord of victories"; a title of the heart of Osiris.

neb neter meṭut 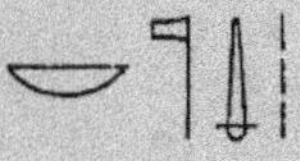 "lord of the words of the god", *i. e.*, one who understands the hieroglyphic language.

neb renput 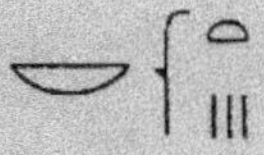 "lord of years", *i. e.*, aged one.

neb rekhit  "lord of the *rekhit*", a class of men.

neb Re-stau  "lord of Re-stau", *q. v.*, a title of Osiris.

neb henu  "lord of praises", *i. e.*, he who is praised.

neb ḥeru 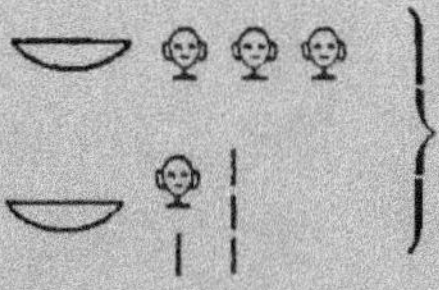 "lord of faces"; the name of one of the Forty-two Judges in the Hall of Osiris.

neb ḥeḥ "lord of eternity"; a title of Osiris; plur. .

Neb khat the goddess Nephthys (?)

nebu khaut "lords of altars", *i. e.*, gods to whom altars have been dedicated.

neb khāu "lord of crowns, or risings"; a title of Rā.

neb khut "lord of the horizon"; a title of Rā.

neb kheperu "lord of transformations", *i. e.*, he of many changes.

neb khet "lord of things", *i. e.*, lord of creation; plur. .

nebu Kher-Āḥa "lords of Kher-āḥa", *i. e.*, Temu and his fellow deities.

nebt Sau the "lady of Saïs", *i. e.*, Neith.

neb setut "lord of light", *i. e.*, giver of light.

neb senṭ "lord of fear", *i. e.*, he who inspires fear.

neb sekhti 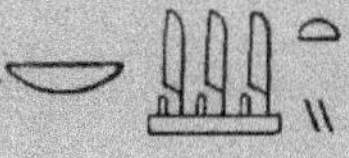 "lord of the field", *i. e.*, master of the field, a title of the Bull-god.

nebt Seḳer  "lady of silence"; a name of the Other World.

nebu kau  "lords of food", *i. e.*, gods to whom food offerings are given.

neb kesu  "lord of bowings", *i. e.*, he to whom homage is paid.

neb qerset 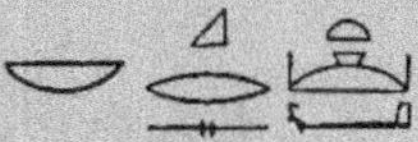 "lord of the bier"; a title of Osiris.

neb taui 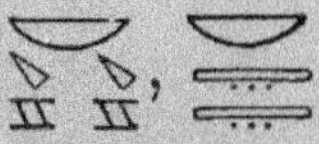 "lord of the Two Lands", *i. e.*, of Upper and Lower Egypt.

neb taiu 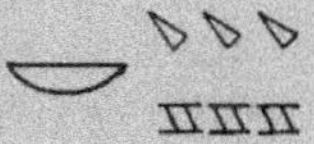 "lord of the lands", *i. e.*, of the world, a title of Osiris.

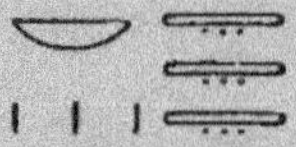 "lords of lands".

Nebt-taui 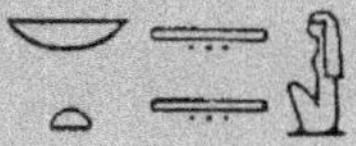 the name of a lake in the Sekhet Ȧaru.

Nebt-taui em karȧ  the name of the mooring post for the magic boat.

Neb ta ānkhtet 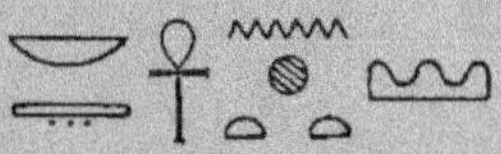 "lord of the Land of Life", *i. e.*, the Other World.

Neb ta tchesert 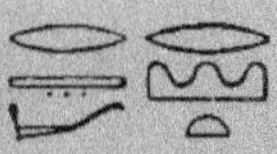 "lord of the Holy Land"; a title of Osiris.

neb tau 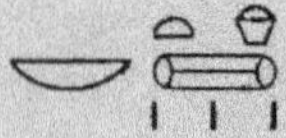 "lord of cakes".

neb temu  "lord of mankind".

nebu ṭuat 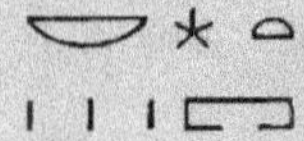 "lords of the Other World".

neb ṭeshert 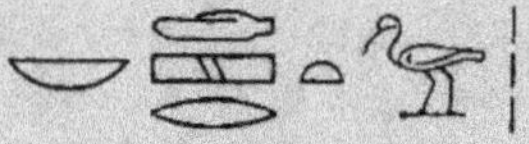 "lord of the red things", red clouds, or desert (?).

neb tchefau  "lord of divine food".

neb tchetta  "lord of eternity", *i. e.*, Osiris.

Neb-peḥti-petpet-sebȧu 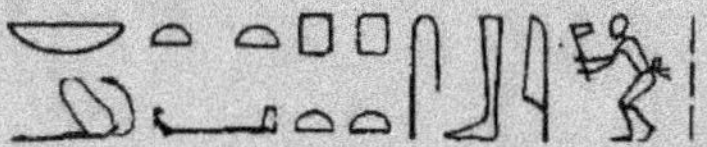 "lord of might, crusher of fiends"; a proper name.

Neb-peḥti-thes-menment 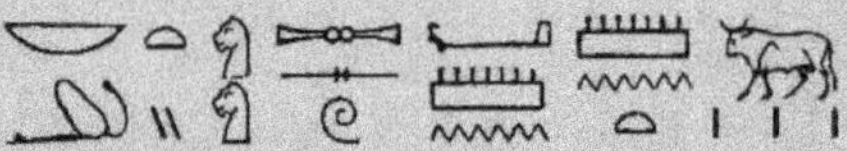 "lord of might, roper in of cattle"; a proper name.

Neb-maā̄t-ḥeri-reṭui-f  a proper name.

Neb-er-tcher 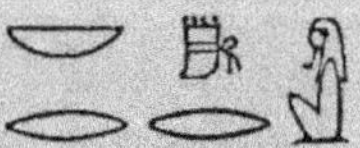 "lord to the boundary", *i. e.*, the Lord of the Universe, a title of Osiris.

Nebt-er-tchert 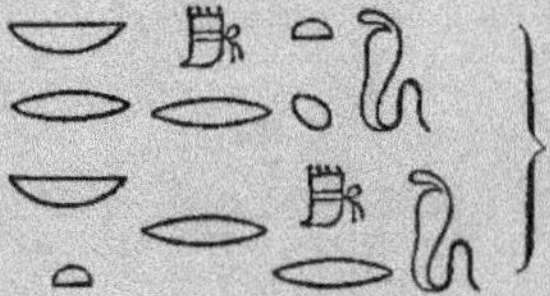 fem. of preceding.

Nebt-ḥet 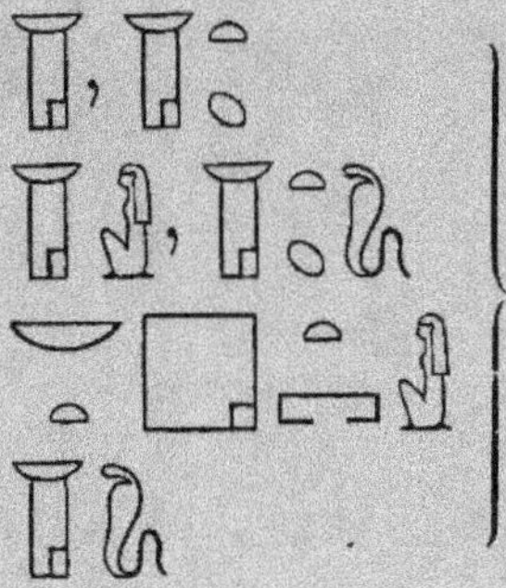 the goddess Nephthys, sister of Isis.

Neb-s  a proper name.

Neb-seni 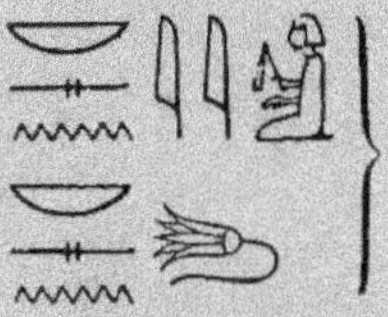 the name of a famous scribe.

Neb-qeṭ 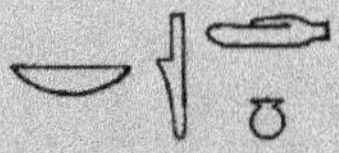 the name of a scribe.

neba  a weapon or tool, a pole.

Nebȧ  the name of one of the Forty-two Judges in the Hall of Osiris.

nebȧu 
nebȧnȧu 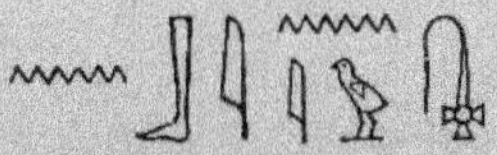 flame, fire, a burning.
nebȧt 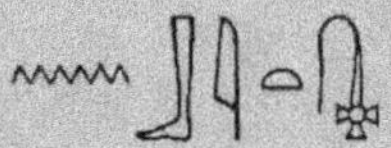

nebȧu 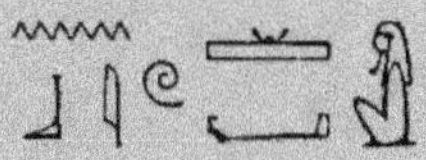 fashioner, moulder.

nebeḥ 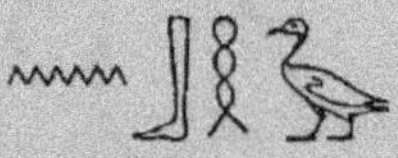 a kind of bird.

nebti  (= 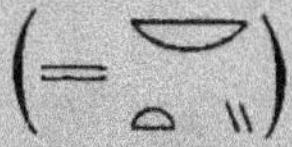), the two goddesses Nekhebit and Uatchit.

nebṭ — lock of hair, tress; the name of a storm cloud; the name of a fiend.

nebṭet

nepu — a part of the body.

neper — grain, wheat, barley, dhura.

Neprȧ — the Grain-god.

nepert — corn-land.

Nepert — the name of a city.

nef — he, him.

nefa — a sign of the demonstrative, this, that; plur.

nefu — air, wind, breath; breath of life.

nefu — sailor.

Nef-ur — the name of a city or district.

nefer 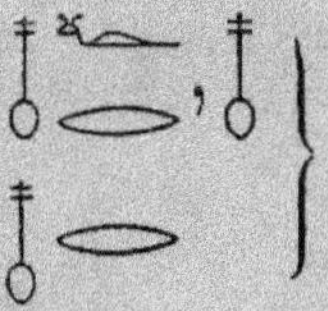 to be good, to be happy, to be beautiful, good, pretty, gracious, well-doing; 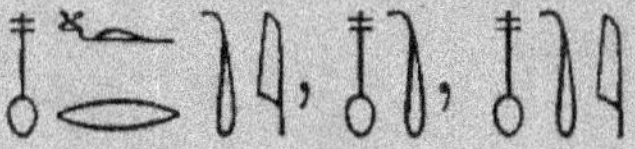 beautiful, good; 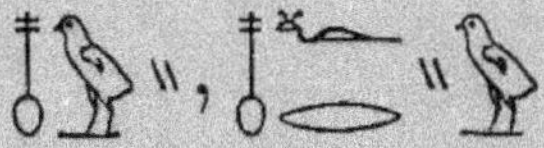 twice good, very good; 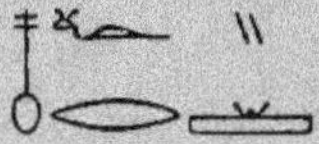 good one or thing; 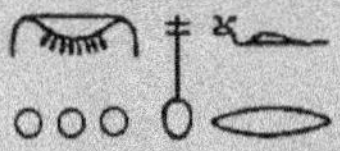 fine gold; 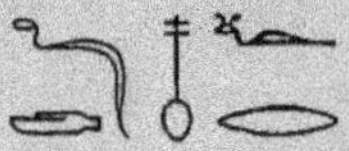 gracious speech.

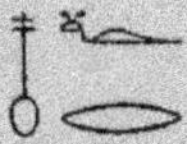 with 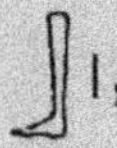, happiness, joy, gladness,

neferu 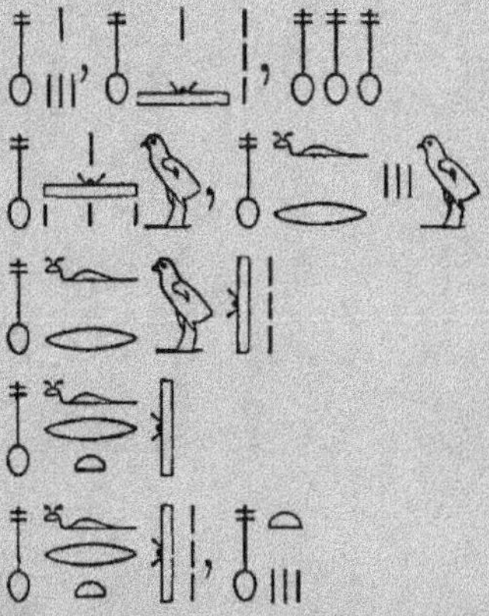

nefert beauties, splendours, fair things, good things.

Nefer-ḥer  "fair face", a title of Rā and of Ptaḥ.

Nefer (?) 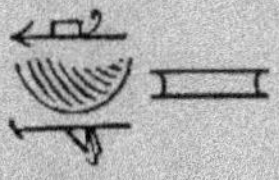 the name of a lake.

neferu  to be glad (?).

Nefert  girl, maiden; a proper name.

nefert name of a tree.

Nefer-uben-f , a proper name.

Nefer-sent name of a city.

Nefer-Tem , name of a god, the son of Ptaḥ and Sekhet.

nem to defraud = (?).

Nem a proper name.

nem ,

nemȧ

nemnem

nememti

to walk, to stride, go about, wander about.

nemt , step, stride; plur. , , ,

nemā who? who then? who then art thou?

nemm  to lie dead.

nemmȧt  bier.

nemmȧ  pygmy, dwarf.

nemeḥ  to understate the reading of the tongue of the balance, to be young, lowly, poor, humble.

nemes 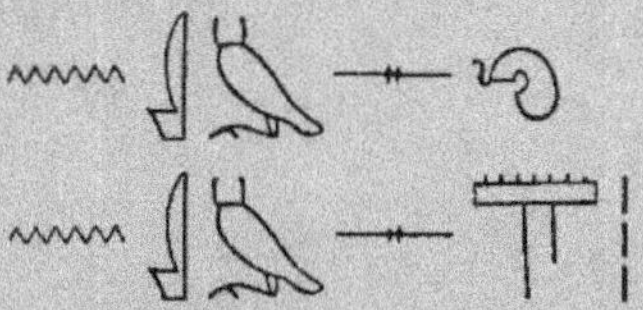 the name of a crown, tiara, or fillet for the head.

nemt 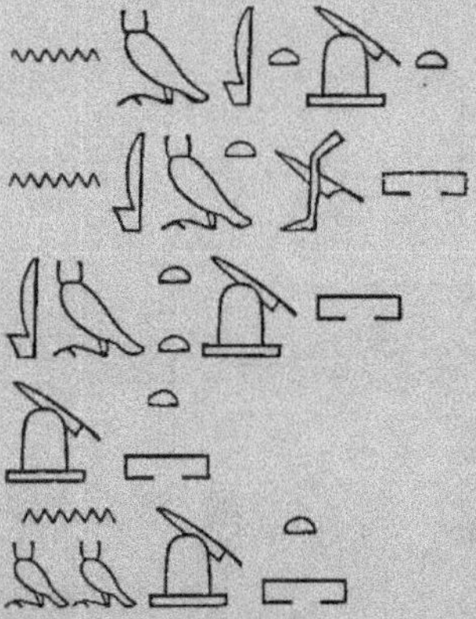 block for slaughter, the chamber in which the damned suffered decapitation and mutilation; plur. .

nemtchet 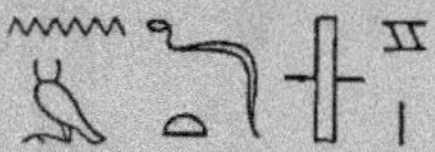 a place of slaughter.

nen 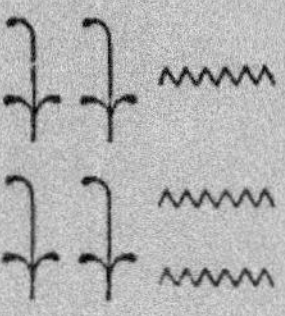 a sign of the demonstrative;  this is he who; 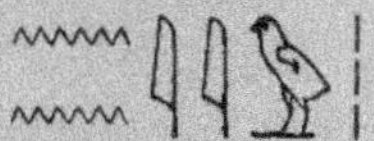 these who; 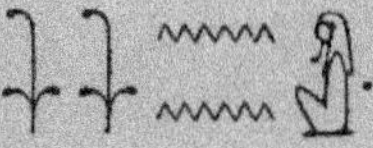.

nen 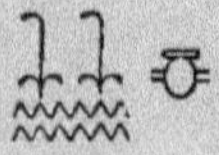 unguent.

nen 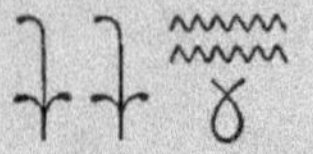 a kind of stuff, linen.

nen 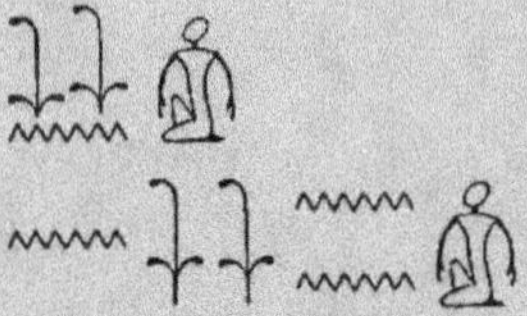 to be weak, helpless, exhausted.

neni
neniu  weak or helpless folk, fiends, etc.

nenaiu  winds.

Nin-årruṭ-f (?)
Nen-aårruṭ-f  see Ån-ruṭ-f.

Nenunser  name of a Cow-goddess.

nenmet  (a late form) bier.

Nentchā 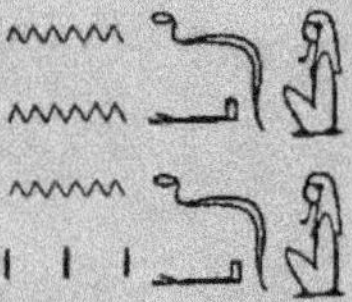 the name of a god.

Ner  name of the Herd-god; a proper name.

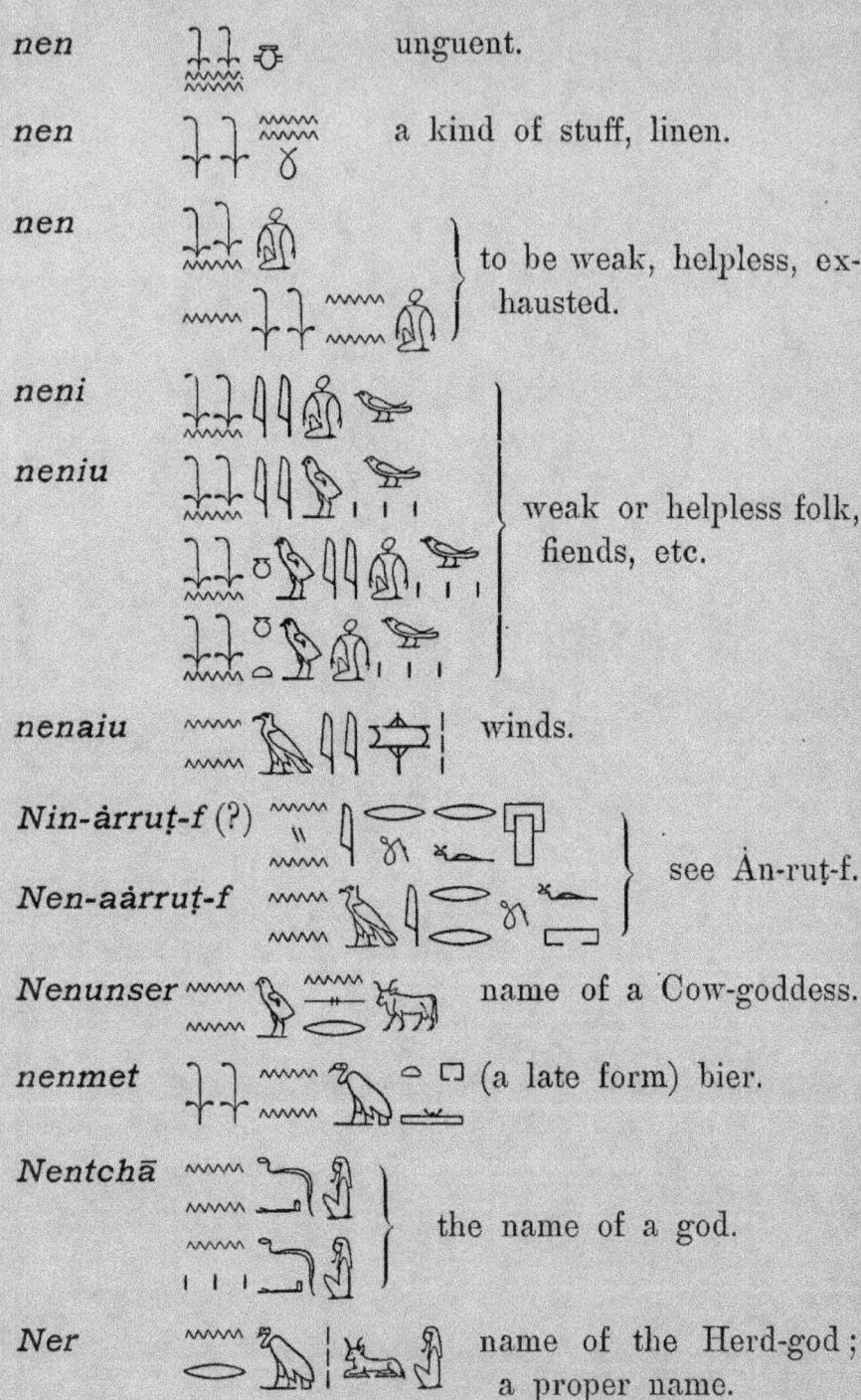

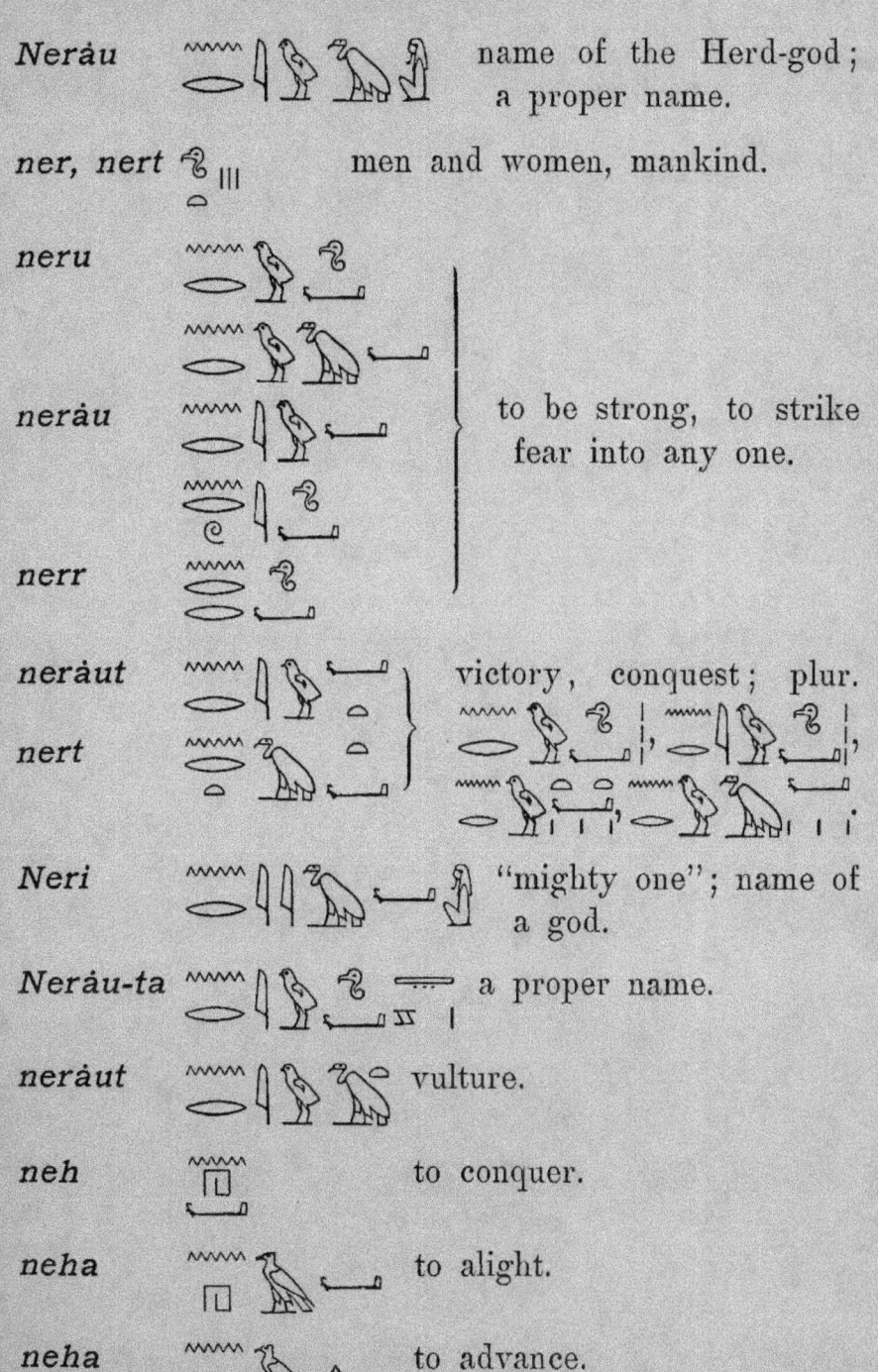

Neràu name of the Herd-god; a proper name.

ner, nert men and women, mankind.

neru

neràu to be strong, to strike fear into any one.

nerr

neràut victory, conquest; plur.

nert

Neri "mighty one"; name of a god.

Neràu-ta a proper name.

neràut vulture.

neh to conquer.

neha to alight.

neha to advance.

nehaȧs	to awake.
nehapu	to shine, give light.
nehat	sycamore, fig-tree; the two sycamores, fig-trees.
Nehatu	the name of a city.
nehep	to copulate.
nehep	to have power over.
nehpu	strength.
nehpu	light, fire, to shine.
nehem	to rejoice.
	rejoicings.
nehemnehem	to destroy (?).
neheh	fire.
nehhu	needy one.

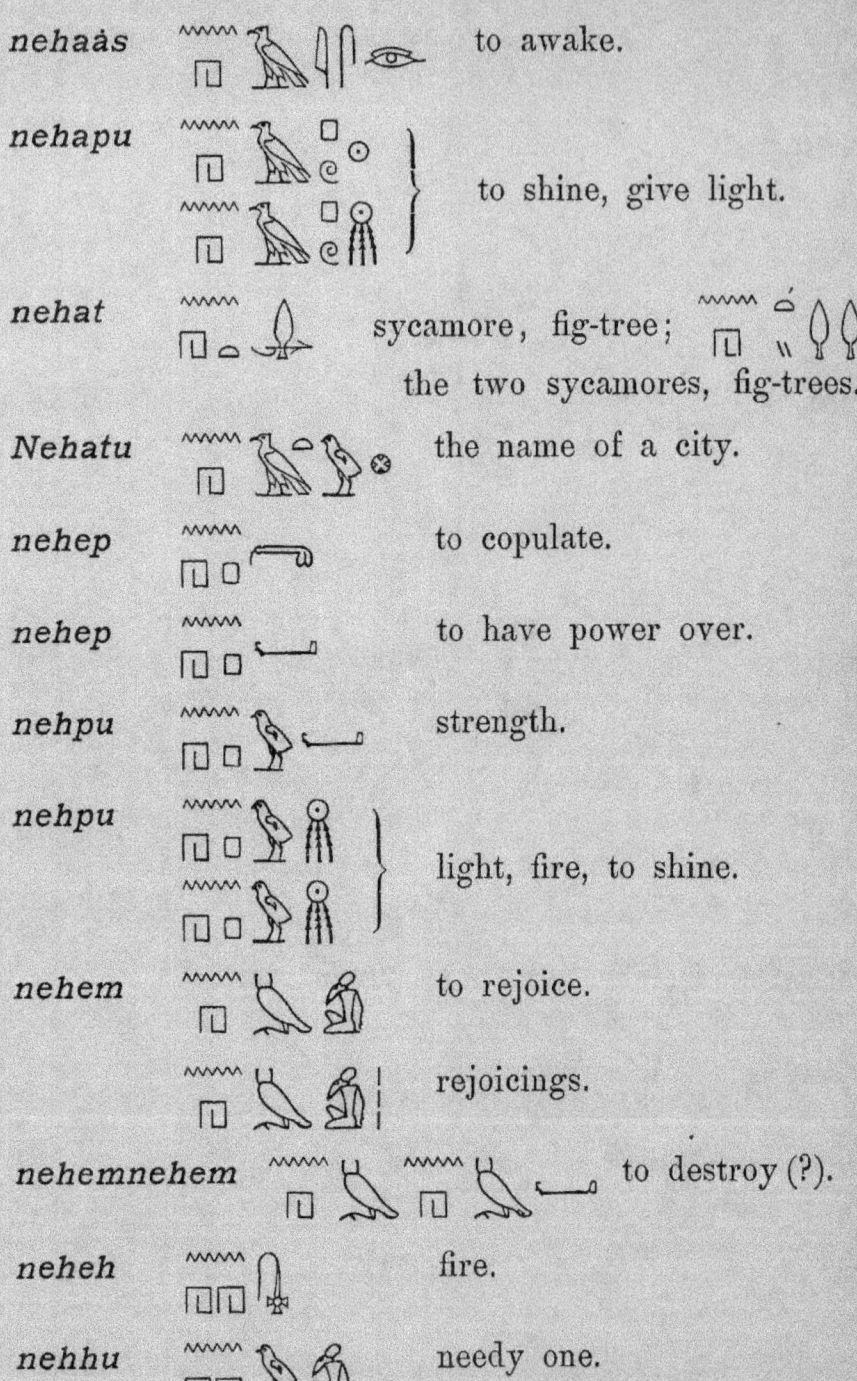

nehes  to wake up, rouse up.

Nehesu  a group of divine beings.

Nehes-ui  a proper name.

Neḥ  the name of a god.

neḥ 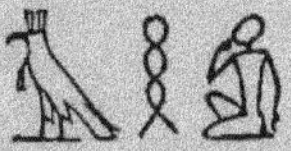 to beseech, pray, entreat.

neḥa  to be bad, stinking.

Neḥa-ḥāu  "stinking limbs"; a proper name.

Neḥa-ḥer  the name of one of the Forty-two Judges in the Hall of Osiris.

neḥait 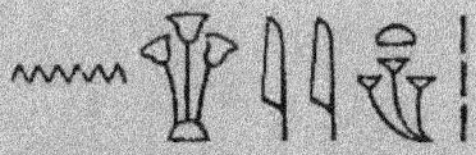 flowers.

neḥit 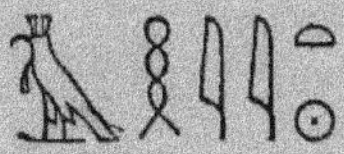 time, eternity (?).

neḥeb 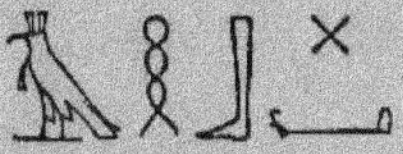 to coerce, put the yoke on some one.

neḥebet 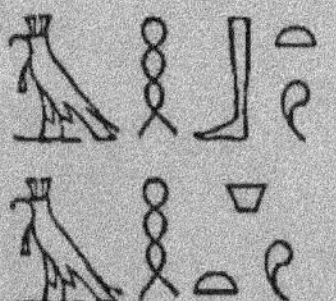 neck; plur. 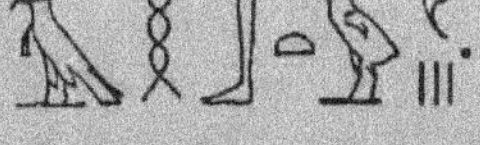

Neḥeb-nefert the name of one of the Forty-two Judges in the Hall of Osiris.

Neḥeb-ka, *Neḥeb-kau* "he who yokes together the Kau"; a proper name.

neḥep the divine potter's table.

neḥem to carry off, to plunder, to deliver, release; deliverers; delivered.

neḥeḥ eternity, for ever; with time without beginning or end.

neḥeḥ to invoke, entreat.

neḥes negro, a Sûdânî man in general.

neḥṭ-t jaw teeth (?).

neḥṭ-ui the two jaws (?).

. . . . . .

nekh to cry out, complain.

nekha a sharp knife.

nekhakhat , humours (?), variant .

nekhȧu protector.

Nekhebet the goddess of the city of Nekheb (Al-Kâb).

nekhebet flowers.

Nekhen , a city of Upper Egypt, the god of Nekhen.

nekhen babe, child.

nekhenu , children.

Nekhenu the name of one of the Forty-two Judges in the Hall of Osiris.

nekhenit girls (?).

nekhekh old man.

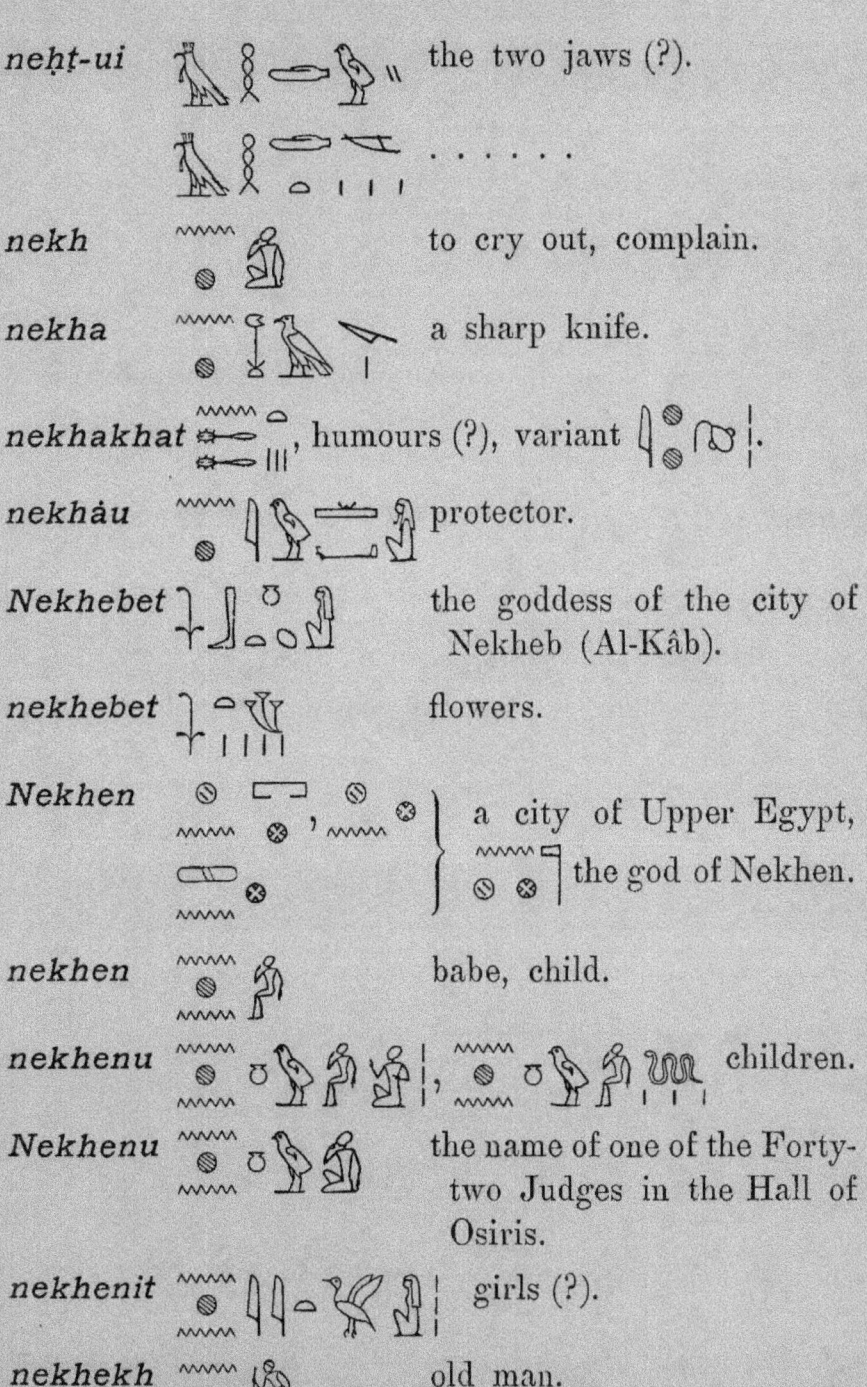

nekhekh 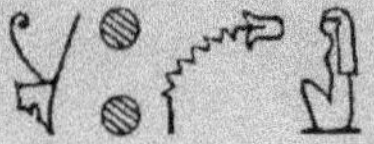 Vol. II, p. 251, l. 10.

nekhekh   whip, flail.

nekht 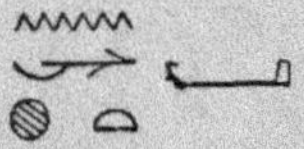  to be strong, strength, powerful.

nekhtu  valour, bravery, conquest.

Nekht 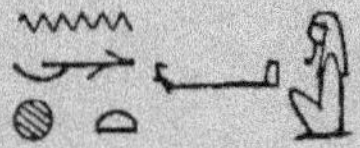 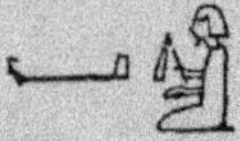 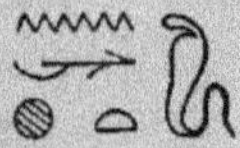 a proper name.

nekht  strong (in a bad sense).

Nekhtu-Ȧmen 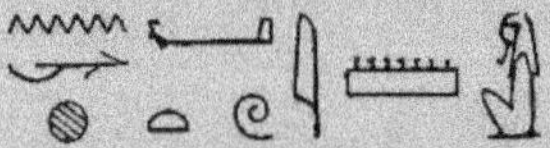 a proper name.

nes 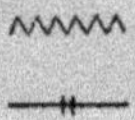, 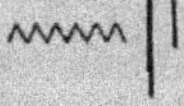 she, her, it.

nes 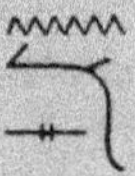 to belong to.

 belonging to him.

nesu  . . . . . . 

nes / *nesau*  tongue; ; plur. .

nes  to eat, devour, consume.

nes  to arrange (?), order (?).

nes / *nesnes* 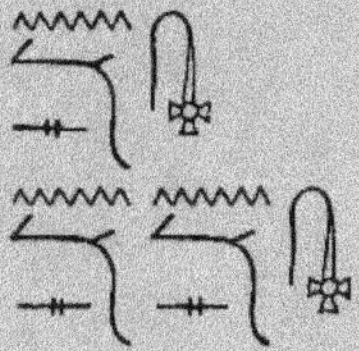 flame.

nes 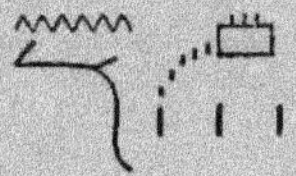 grain (?).

nesut  weapons of war.

nesb 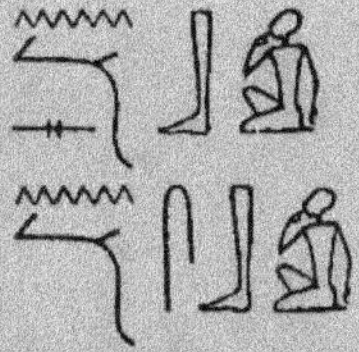 to eat; .

nesbit 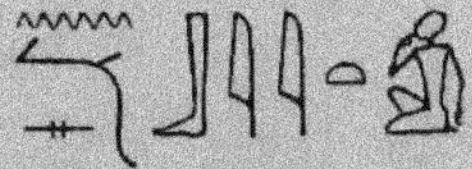 to eat, devour.

Nesbu  devouring gods.

nespu  slaughter, wound, knives.

nesert 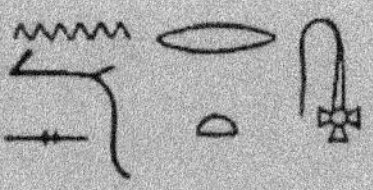 flame, fire.

Nesert 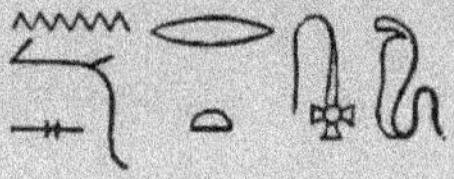 a fire-goddess.

Nesersert 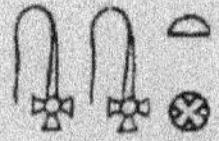 the Fire-city.

nest  throne; plur. 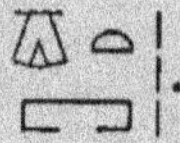.

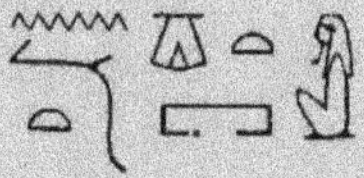 Throne.

nesti  a class of divine beings.

nest 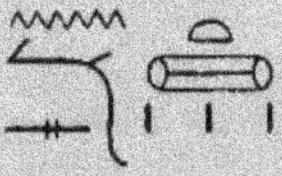 cakes (?).

nesh  to walk (?).

neshau  plates of metal.

neshu  a weapon (?).

neshi 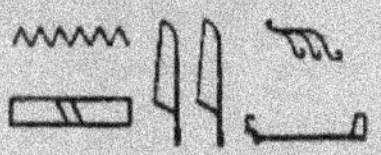 —  to make the hair bristle.

neshep  to snuff the air.

neshem 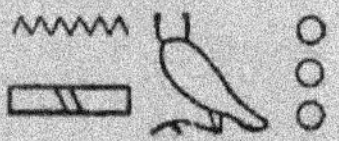
neshmet  } a precious stone.

neshmet 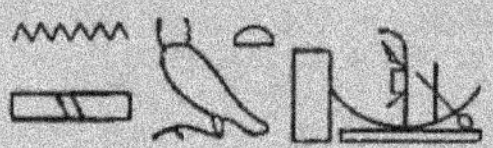 the name of a sacred boat.

neshni 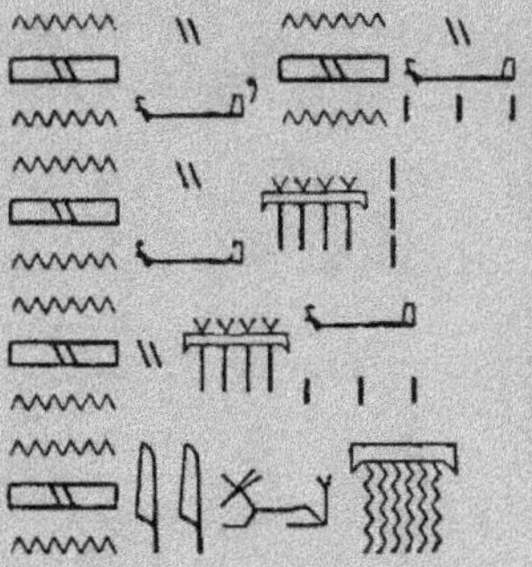

neshen 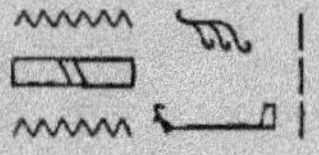

neshenu 

to be stormy, to revolt, a thunder-storm, destructive winds, whirlwind, tempest in general, revolt; 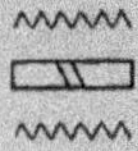 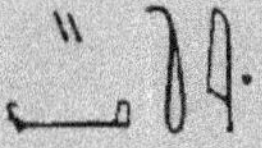.

nek  thou, thy.

nek  to copulate;  to have union with himself.

nekek 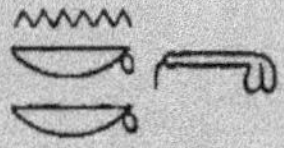 to commit sodomy.

nek nekek  to have union with a sodomite.

nekau  . . . . .

nekai  injury.

 ill-doing fiends.

Nekȧ 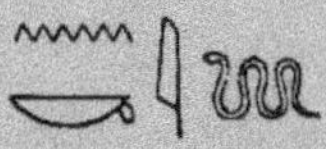

Nekȧu 

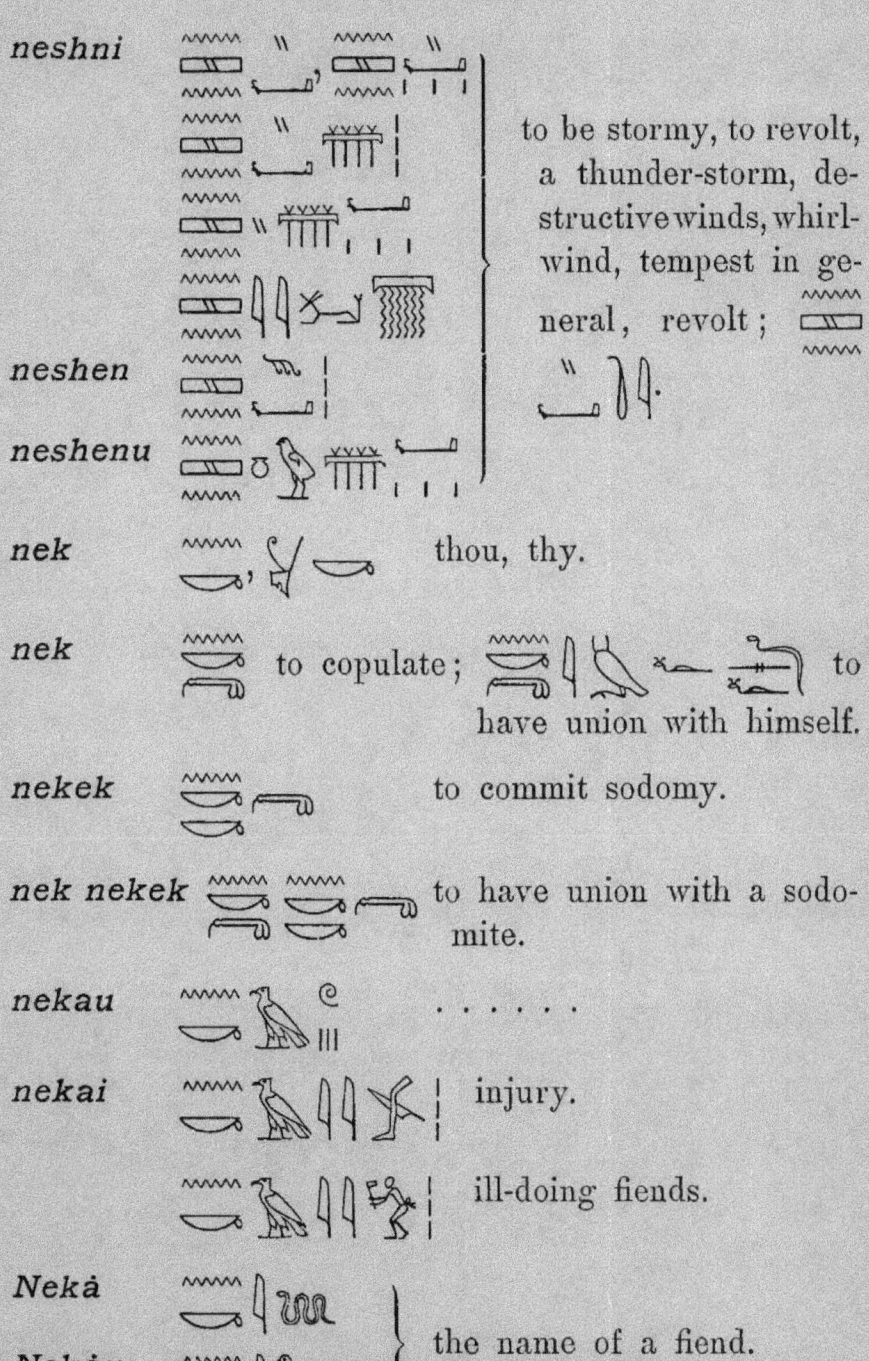

the name of a fiend.

neken  to do harm or injury to anyone.

nekent  injury; plur. , .

nekenu  injury, evil, harm.

neqāut  shackles.

neqāiut  those who steal away.

neḳa  to chew.

Neḳau  a Bull-god.

neḳeḳ  to cackle.

Neḳeḳ-ur  "Great Cackler"; name of the Goose-god.

Net  Neith, the great goddess of Saïs.

ent  of.

net 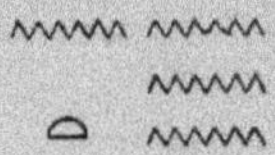 water, stream.

ent-ā — to ordain, order, ordinance, decree, customary rite;

enti — who, which, that which; plur.

entiu, *entet* — things which exist, persons or beings who are.

enti — sign of the negative, no, not, without.

neti — to vanquish, conquer.

Enti-mer-f — a proper name.

Enti-ḥer-f-emm-mast-f — a proper name.

entu

netu — fastenings, cords.

entuten — ye, you.

entef — he.

netnet — that which flows.

neter  god, Copt. ноʏтє  great god; 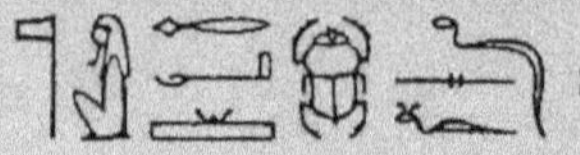 self-created, great god;  god One;  the City-god; 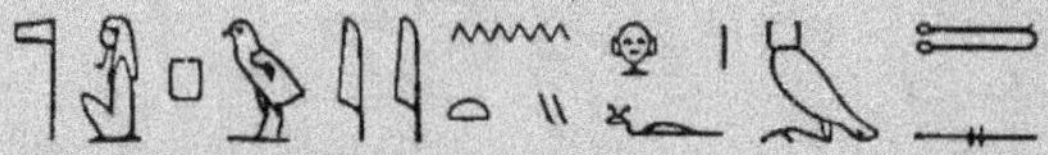  god with a dog's face.

neteru  gods, all the gods of the Three Companies, *i.e.*, Heaven, Earth, and the Ṭuat; 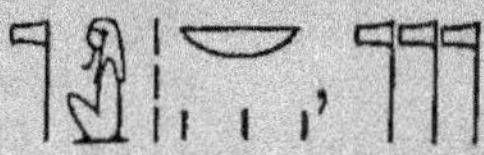  all the gods.

 the father-gods.

 the mother-goddesses.

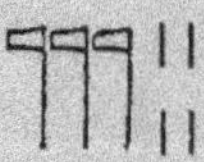 the Four gods.

 the Forty-two gods.

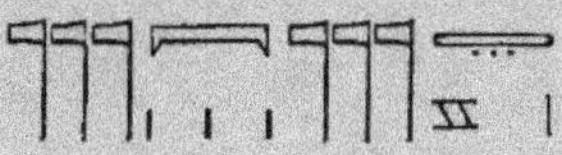 gods celestial and gods terrestrial.

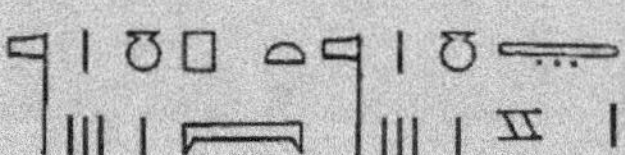 gods of heaven and gods of earth.

gods of the Ṭuat.

gods of the Qerti.

gods guides of the Ṭuat.

gods of the East.

gods of the North.

gods of the West.

gods of the South.

neter-ui the two gods Horus and Set; ; the two divine eyes, *i. e.*, Sun and Moon.

netert goddess, late form ; plur. , , .

netri to be a god or like unto a god, divine , , , divine.

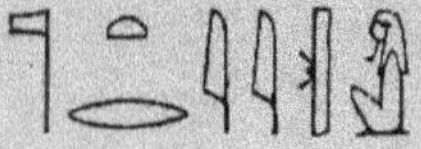 he who is divine ; 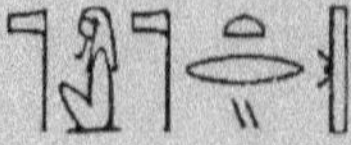,  "divine god".

neter àtfui  the two divine fathers.

neter meṭu 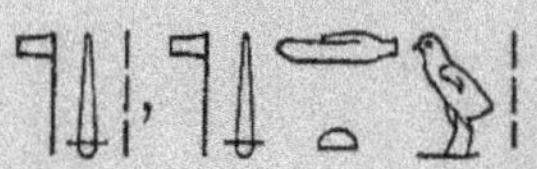 "the words of the god", *i.e.*, hieroglyphic writing.

neter nemt  the block or execution chamber of the god (Osiris).

neter ḥāu 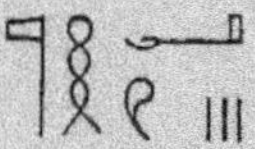 the body, or limbs, of the god.

neter ḥet  "god-house", *i. e.*, temple.

neter ḥetepu 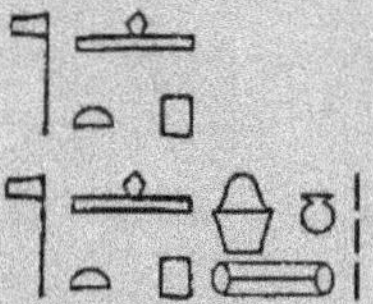 "god-offerings", holy offerings, sepulchral meals.

neter khert 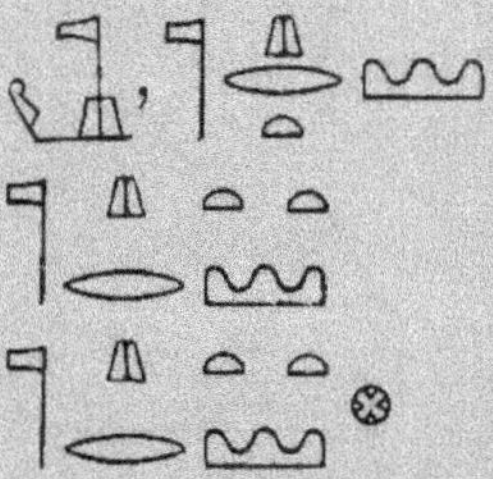 "underworld of the god"; a name for the grave and for the place of departed spirits.

neter khet  "god-property", *i. e.*, things dedicated to the service of the god.

neter shems 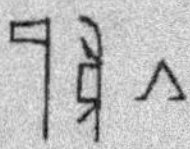 "god-follower", a member of the god's "body-guard".

neter ṭuai  "god-star", the morning star, Venus.

neter ṭuau  "god-adoration", to give thanks to God.

neter ṭept 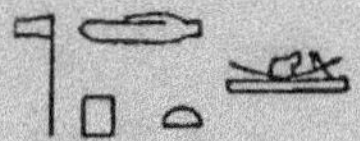 "god-boat", divine barque.

neter tcheṭ  "god-word", sacred speech.

Neter 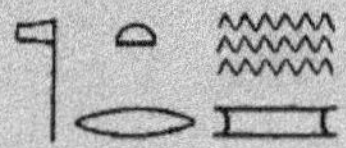 name of a lake in the Other World.

Neteru, *Netri*  name of a town or city.

Netert-utchat  name of a place.

entes 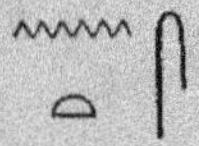 she.

ent-sen 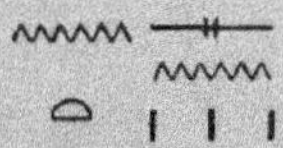 them, they.

entek  thou (masc.).

Netqa-ḥer-khesef-àtu  the name of the herald of the Fourth Ārit.

ent  thou (fem.).

netet  cattle for sacrifice.

entet 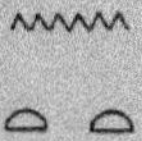 which, that which is.

neṭ 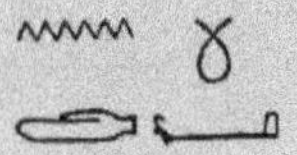 to bandage, to tie.

Neṭit 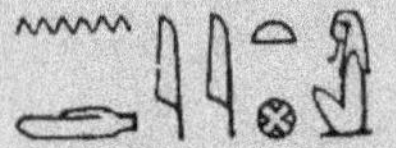 a proper name.

Neṭbit 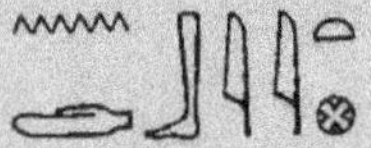 name of a town or city.

Neṭet  name of a town or city.

netch 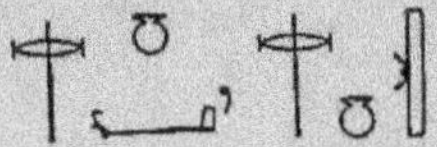
netchet  } to protect, guard, avenge.

netch ḥer 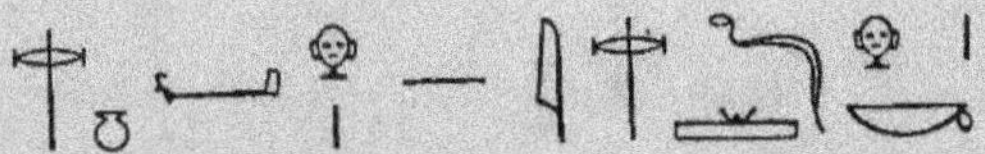 "homage to thee", a form of salutation to gods.

netchti 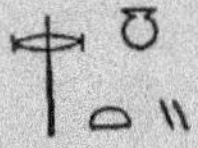 protector, advocate, avenger.

netch meṭu 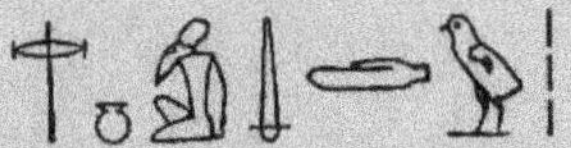
netchtu re  } to discuss a matter with someone, to converse, to take counsel.

netchnetch  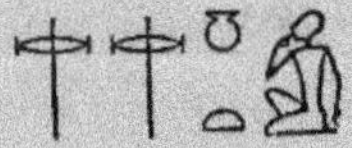 } to take counsel with someone, to discuss a matter.

Netcheb-ȧb-f  a proper name.

Netchfet   } name of a town and its god.

netchem, *netchemu*, *netchemet* — to be sweet, pleasant, to rejoice, be glad; very pleasant; pleasant things.

netchemmit — love-making, the delights of sexual love.

Netchem — the god of love.

netcher — to grasp, hold fast.

netcheriu, *netcherit* — clinchers, grapplers.

netcherȧ — to hew, to carve.

netchḥet — to strengthen.

Netcheḥ-netcheḥ, *Netcheḥ-tcheḥ* — the name of one of the Seven Spirits who guard Osiris and his bier.

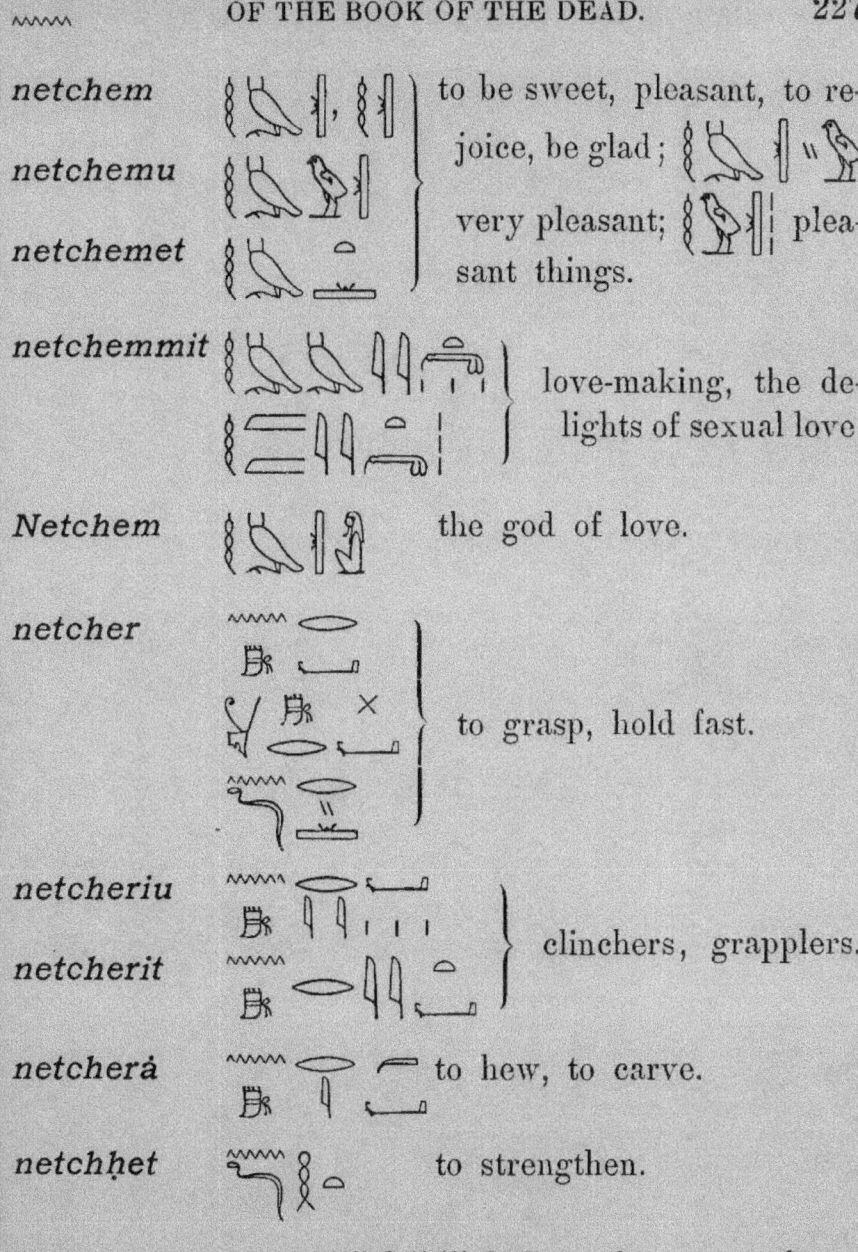

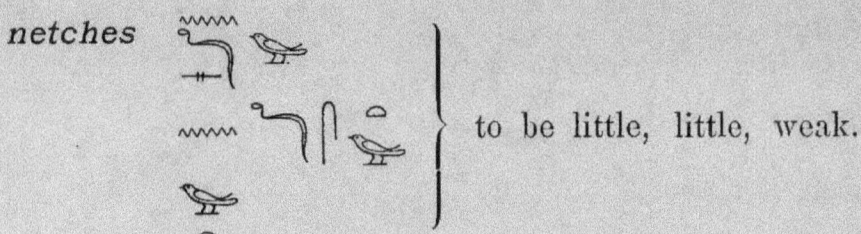

netches — to be little, little, weak.

netcheset — lesser gods, perhaps "false gods".

Netchesti — a name of Osiris.

Netchses — a name of a god.

Netchet — a name of a town or city.

R or L.

er — at, to, with, into, among, against, from, according to, near, by, towards, upon, concerning. With compounds :—

er ȧmi — among.

er ȧmi tu, *er ȧmi thu* — among, between.

er ȧsu — in return for, as reward or recompense for.

er mā — with, near.

er men	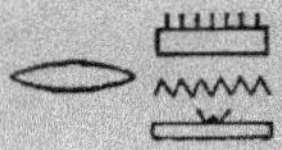	as far as.
er entet	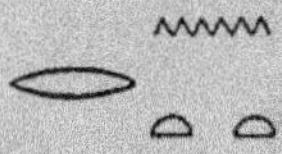	because.
er ruti		outside.
er ḥāt	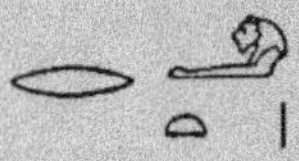	before.
er ḥenā	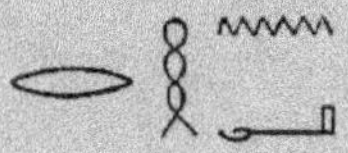	with.
er ḥer		away from.
er ḥeru		above.
er kheft ḥer		in the face of.
er kher		under.
er kherth	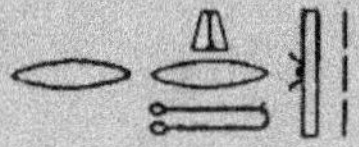	on behalf of.
er sa		by the back of.
er ḳes	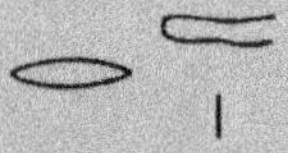	near, by the side of, in the track of.
er		sign of the comparative: more than, *e. g.*,

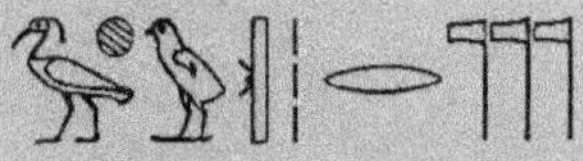 glorious more than the gods.

 divine more than the gods.

 swift more than greyhounds.

 swift more than the shadow.

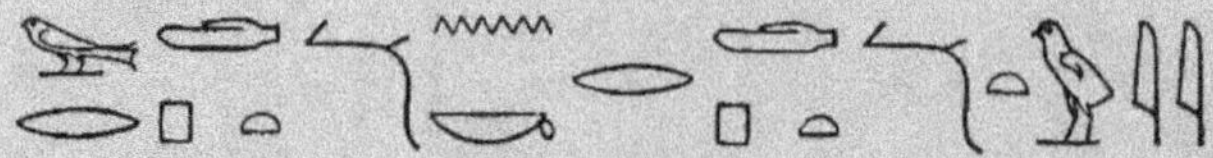
great is the taste to thee more than that taste.

Horus is bolder than all the gods.

 provided more than the gods.

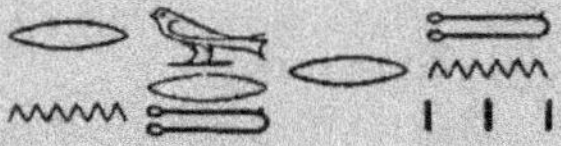 a name greater than yours.

 stronger than the gods.

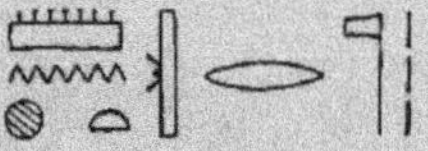 more gracious than the gods.

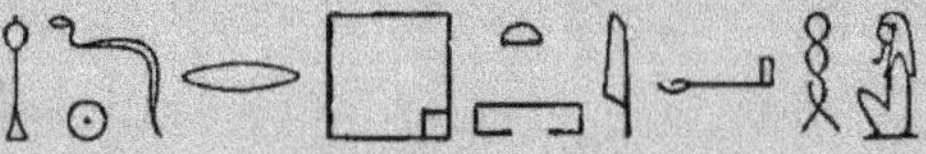 brighter than the House of the Moon.

thy speech is more piercing than the [cry of] the *tcheru* bird.

er 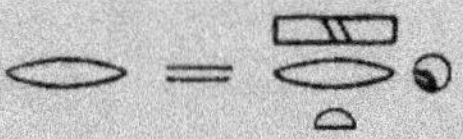 cake, offering.

re  goose.

re 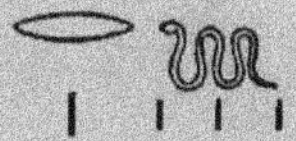 worms (?),

re  door, opening, entrance, mouth, speech, chapter; plur. ;   opening of the mouth, appearance;  strong of mouth; 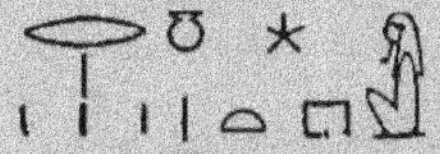 doors of the Ṭuat; 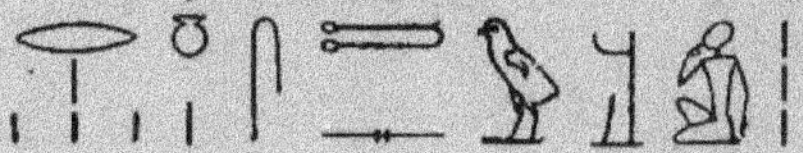 chapters of commemorations; 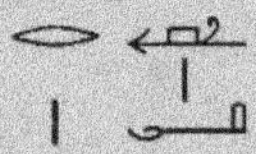 a single chapter; 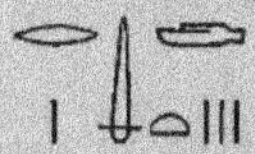 a chapter of words;  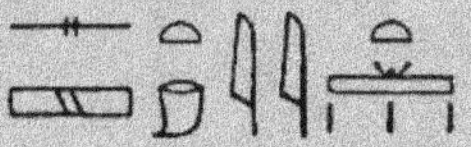 a chapter of mysteries;  to set the mouth in motion against any one, *i. e.*, to slander.

re ȧpt (?) 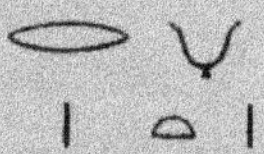 brow.

Re-āa-urt 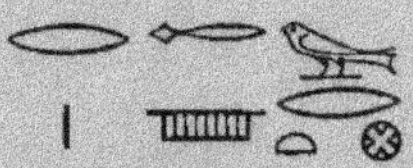 "opening of the great door"; the name of a town.

re-uat 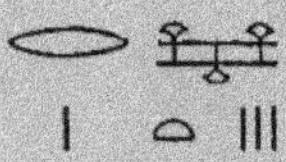 entrance to the roads.

re Ḥāp 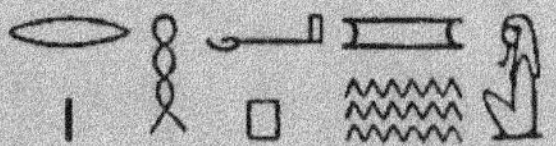 mouth of the Nile.

re Khemenu 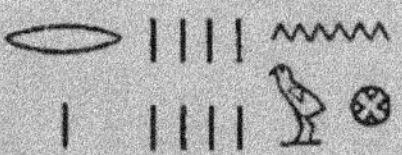 the entrance to the city of Hermopolis.

re Sekhait 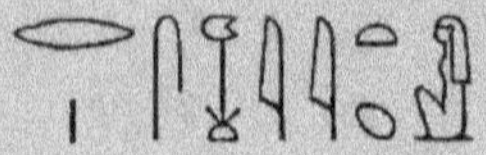 mouth of the goddess Sekhait.

Re-stau 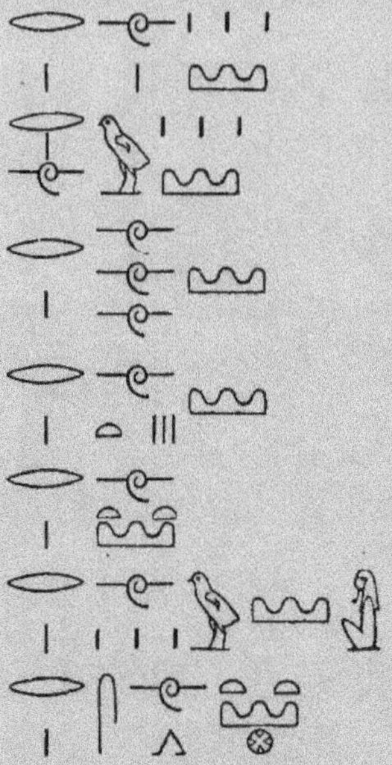 the "entrance to the corridors" in the Other World of Seker at Ṣaḳḳârah.

re-pu  or.

re-per 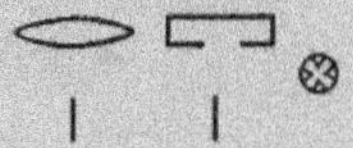 temple.

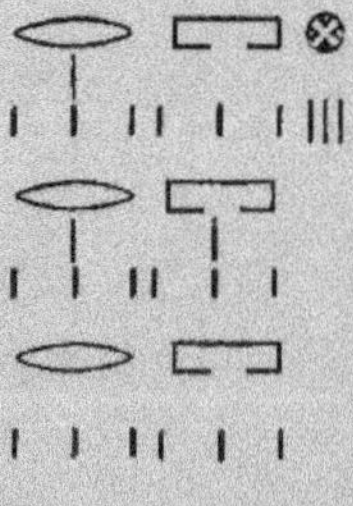 temples; 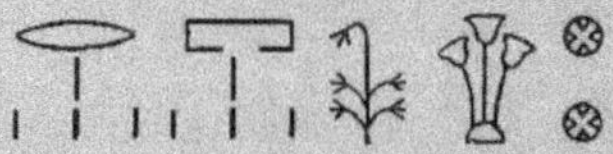 temples of the South and North.

Re (Maȧu ?)  the Lion-god.

Re (?)-Iukasa  the name of a god.

Re (?)-Rā  the Lion-god Rā.

rā 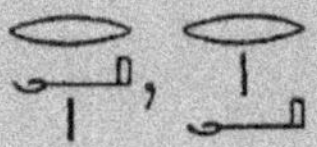 work.

Rā  the Sun-god *par excellence*;  like Rā.

rā  day. 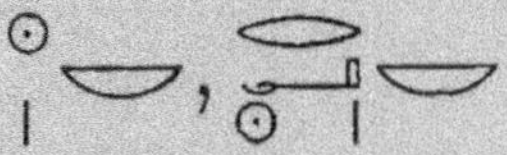 daily, every day.

Rā-Ȧsȧr  Rā-Osiris, the Sun-god of day and night.

Rā-Ḥeru-khuti  "Rā-Horus of the two horizons", Rā-Harmachis.

Rā-Tem  Rā-Tem, the Sun-god of day and night.

Rā-Maāt-men  the prenomen of Seti I.

Rā-men-kau 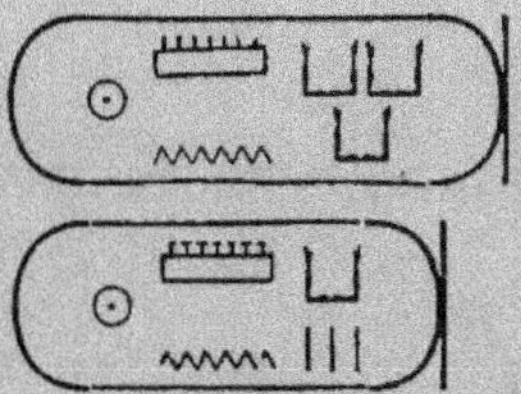 the Mykerinos of the Greeks.

Rā-mes-meri-Ȧmen-meri-Maāti  Rameses IV.

Rā-er-neḥeḥ 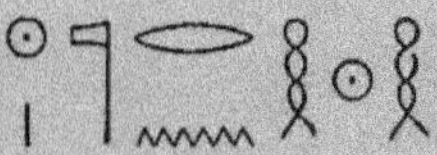 a proper name.

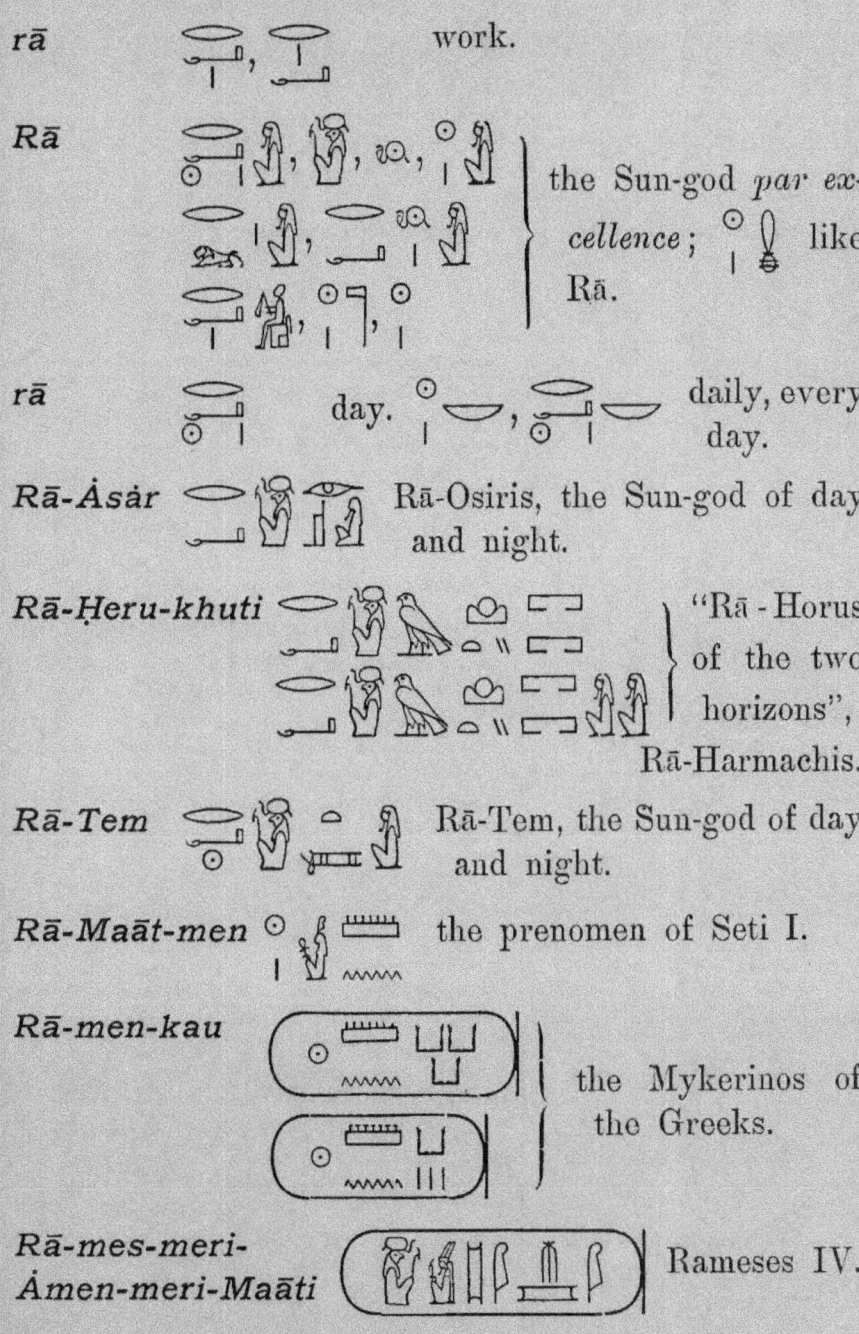

ri 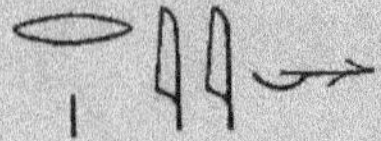 door.

ri  bandage, swathing.

riu  emanations.

ru  . . . . . .

ru  . . . . . .

ru  to fall, drop (of the wind).

ruȧ 

ruȧa 
to separate from, move away from, depart.

rui  journey, departure.

ruti 

the two leaves of a door.

ruṭ  to grow, flourish, to be firm and healthy, to be taut (of ropes and sails); 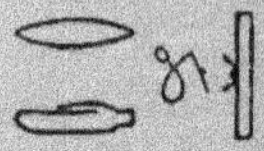 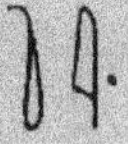.

ruṭi  strong, vigorous.

ruṭ, *ruṭu* — plants, things which grow.

Ruṭ-en-Ȧst — a proper name.

Ruṭu-nu-Tem — a proper name.

Ruṭu-neb-rekhit — a proper name.

ruṭu — superintendent, overseer.

ruṭ — staircase.

eref — an intensive particle, then, therefore.

erpā, *erpāt* — hereditary tribal chief.

erpit — image, statue, august person.

erpti — the two august goddesses, *i. e.*, Isis and Nephthys.

remu — fish.

Remu — the "town of fish"; a proper name.

Remi — the Fish-god.

rem
remu — to weep.

remt — tear; plur.

rem-tȧ — studded (?).

ermen — arm, shoulder, one side of the body.

ermenui — the two arms, shoulders.

— the two sides of a ladder.

ermenu — shoulders, arms, supporters, the branches of a tree.

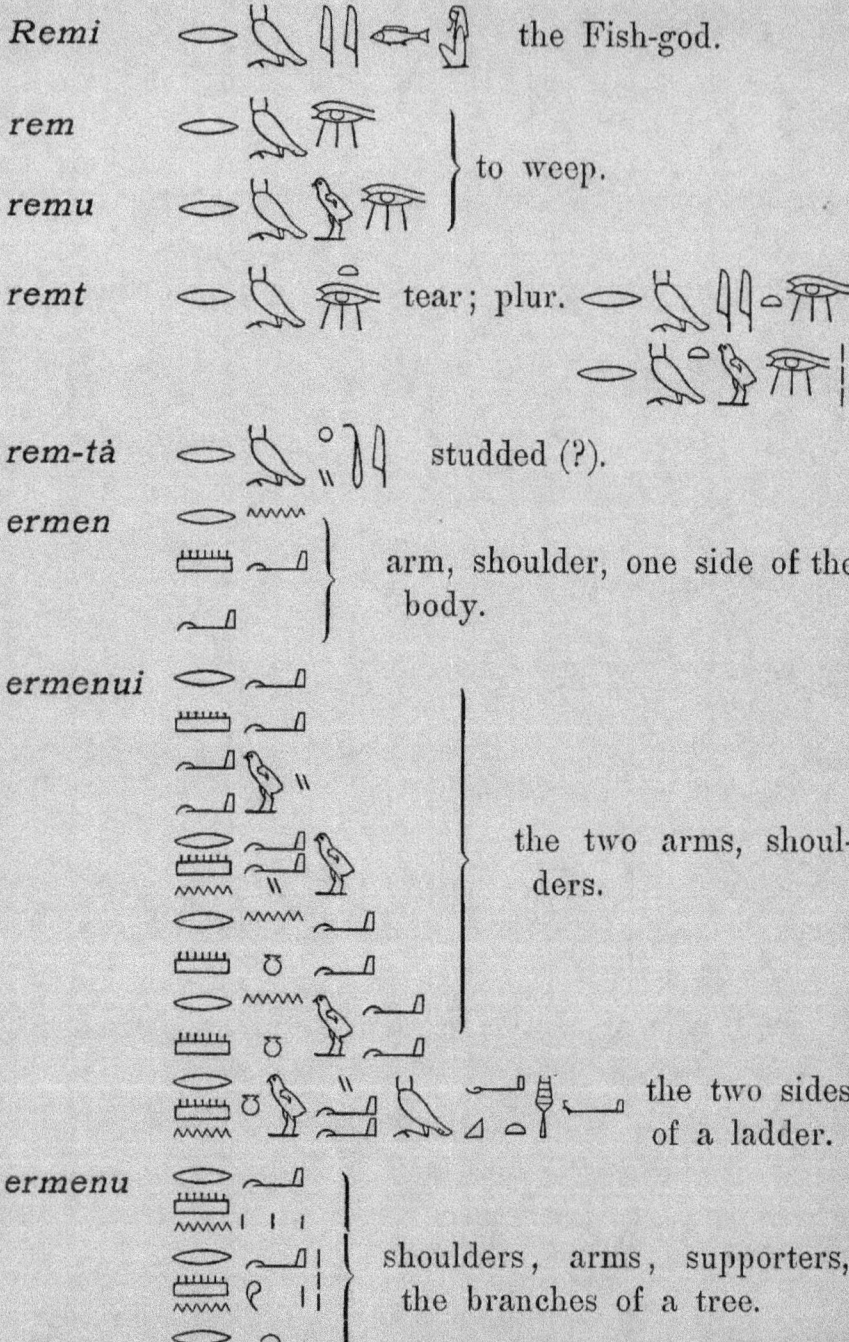

ermen 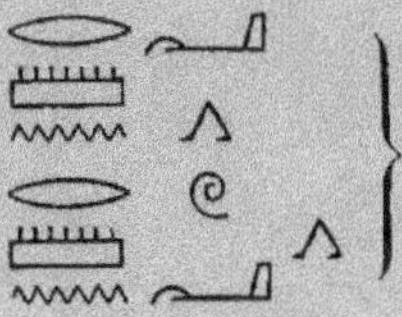 to carry away, to bear, to remove something, to shoulder.

Remrem  the name of a god.

ren  name; plur.  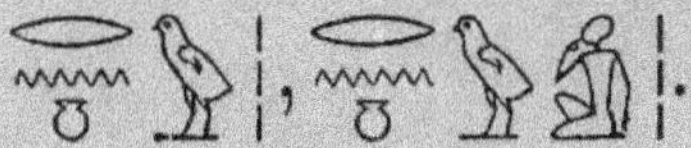

ren  to nurse (see *renen*).

renp  to be young or youthful, renewal of youth, to become young; 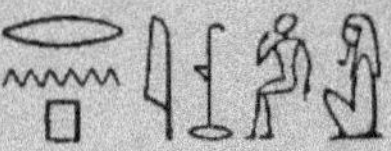 youthful one.

renp-tȧ 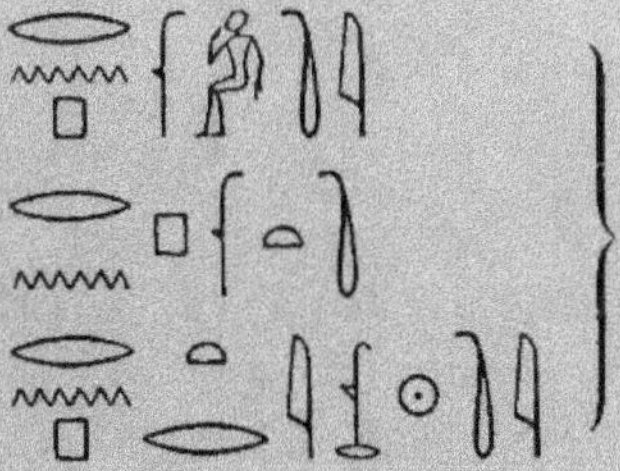 youthful, made young; 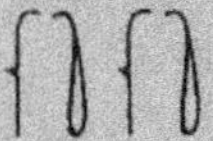 very young.

renpit  year; plur. *renput* 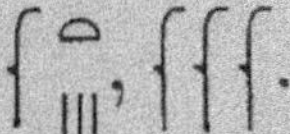

renpit 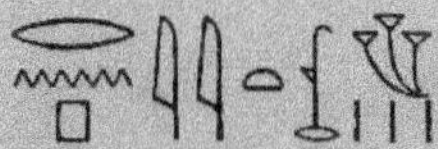 plants, vegetables, fruits.

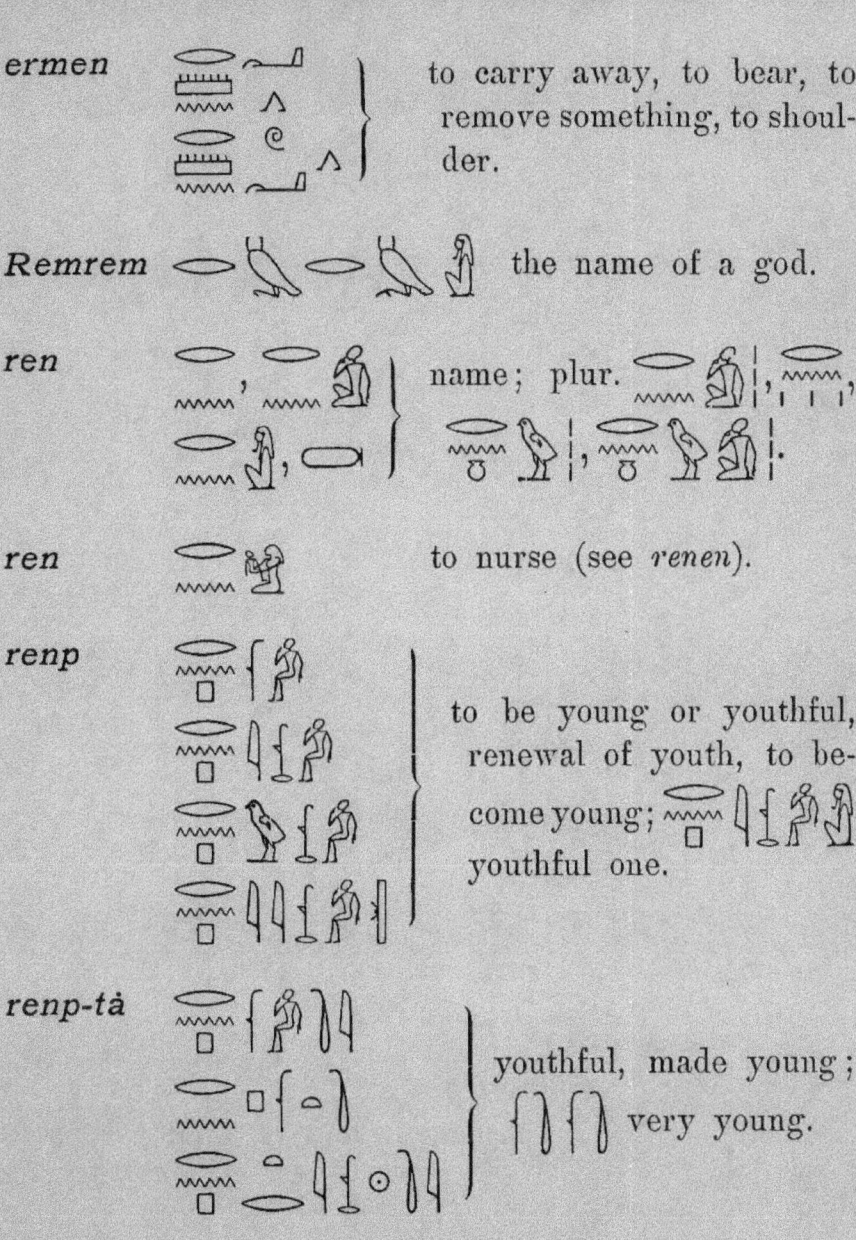

Renen — the name of a god.

renen — to nurse, to suckle.

Renenet, *Renutet* — the goddess of grain crops and the harvest.

rer (*peḥer* ?) — territory, a place for walking about.

rer, *reru* — to walk about, to go round about, to revolve, to encircle; *thes rer* again, repetition, conversely.

rertȧ — encircled.

reri — those who revolve, or go about.

rer khet — going about retreating.

rert — circle.

rert — drugs, medicine.

rer — pig.

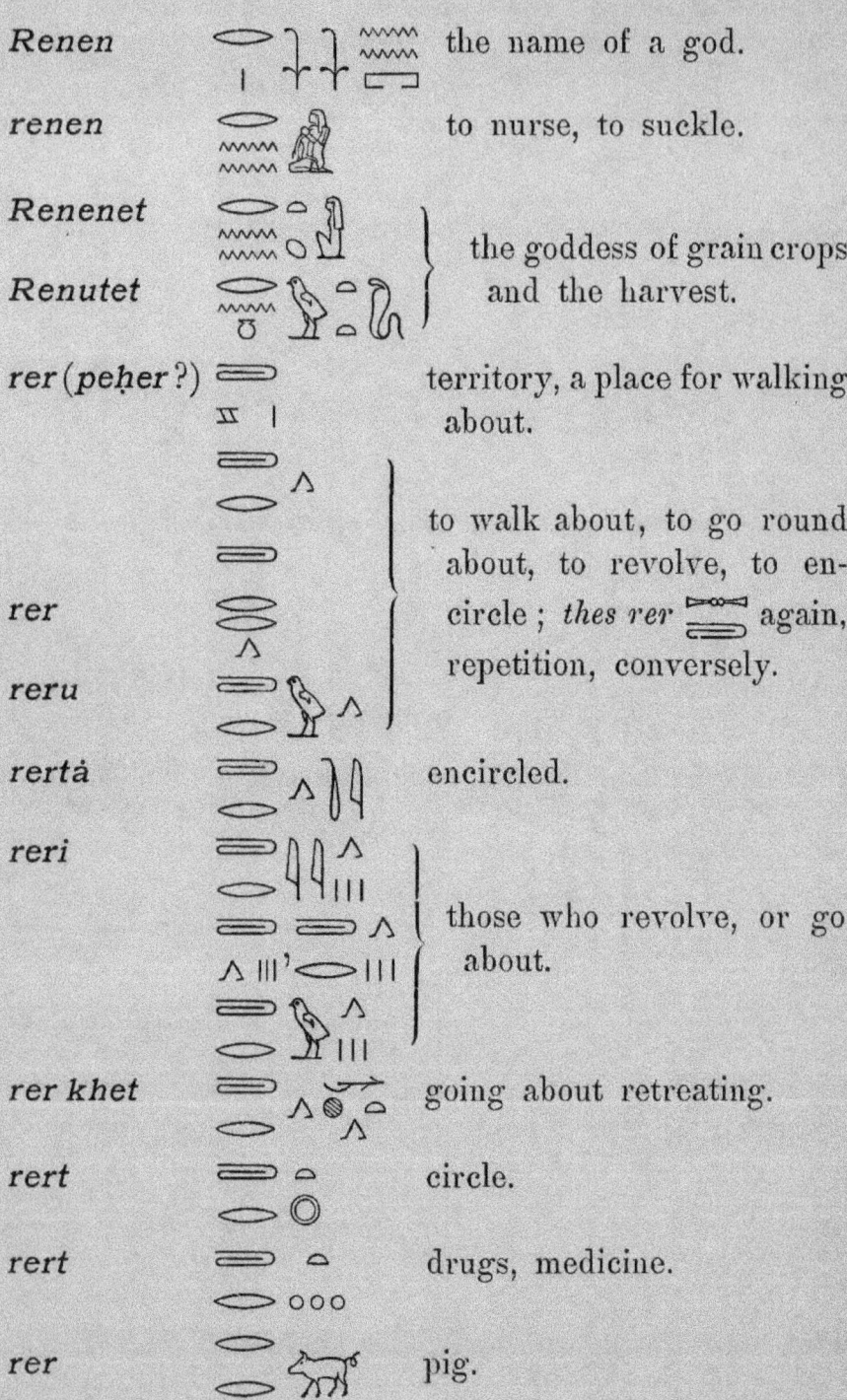

reru  . . . .

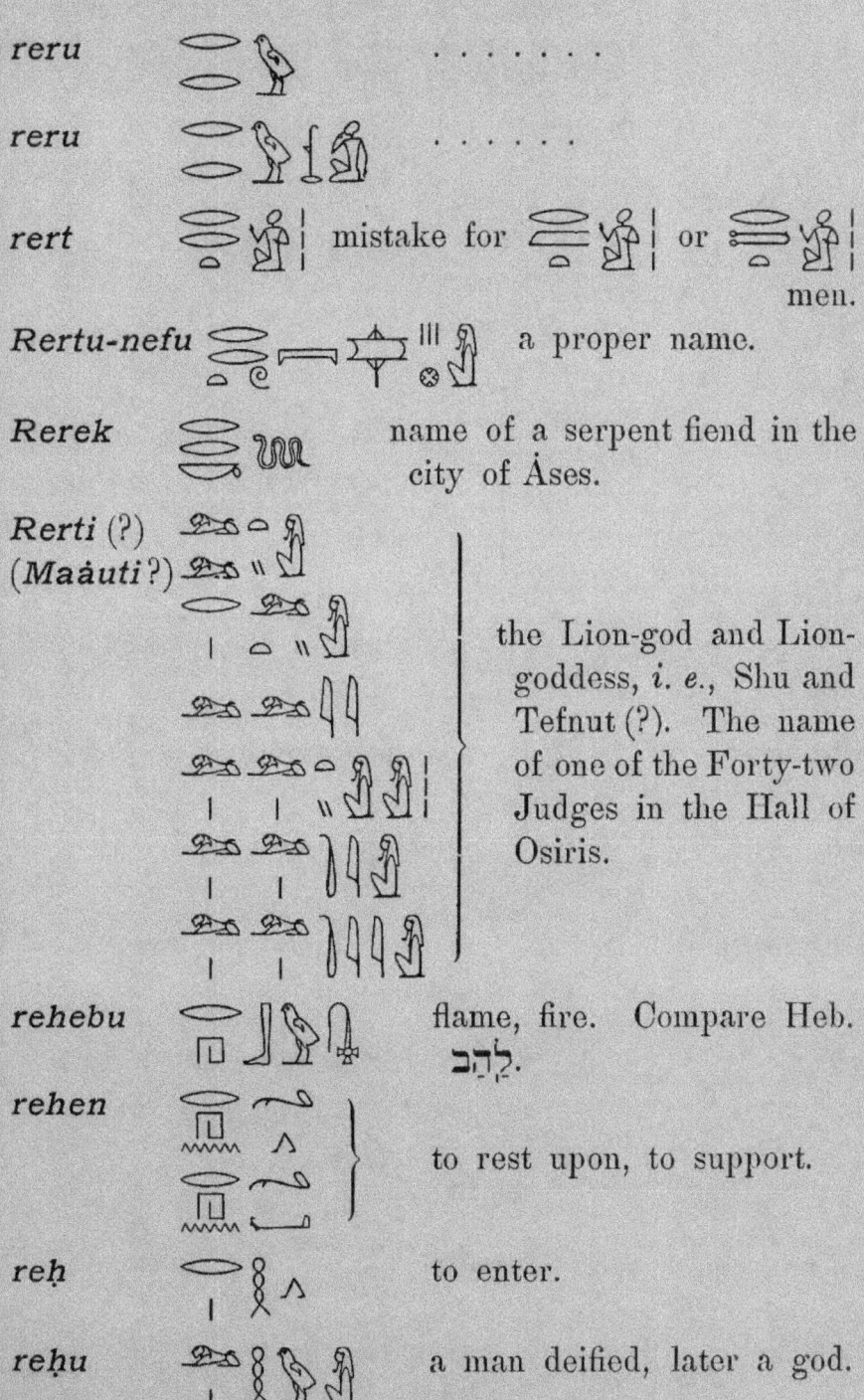

reru  . . . . . .

rert  mistake for  or 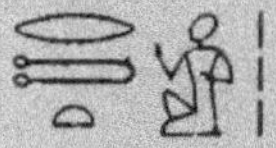 men.

Rertu-nefu 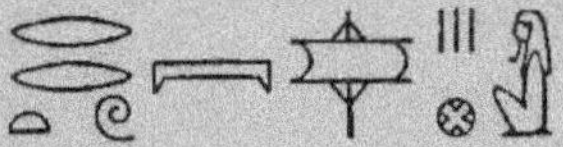 a proper name.

Rerek 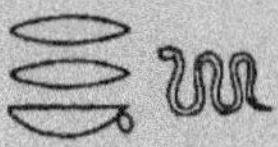 name of a serpent fiend in the city of Ȧses.

Rerti (?) (*Maȧuti* ?) 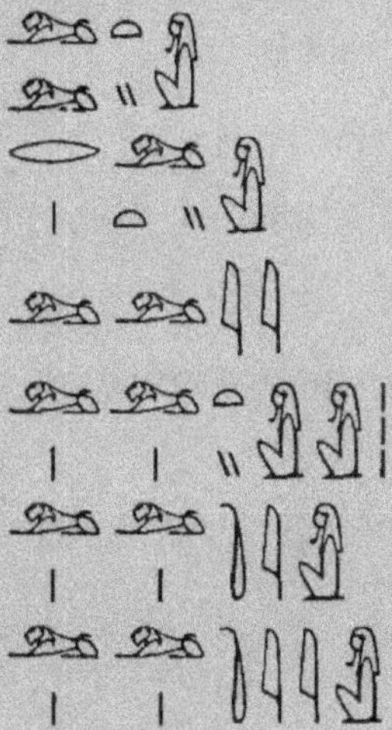 the Lion-god and Lion-goddess, *i. e.*, Shu and Tefnut (?). The name of one of the Forty-two Judges in the Hall of Osiris.

rehebu  flame, fire. Compare Heb. לַהַב.

rehen 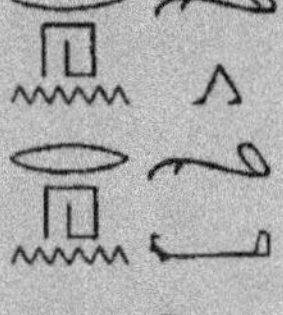 to rest upon, to support.

reḥ 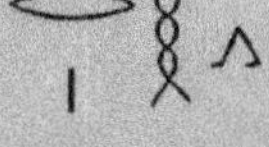 to enter.

reḥu  a man deified, later a god.

reḥui 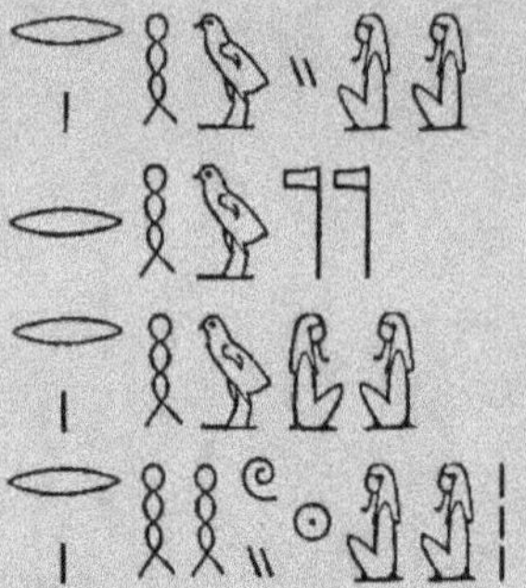 the two combatant gods, Horus and Set.

reḥti 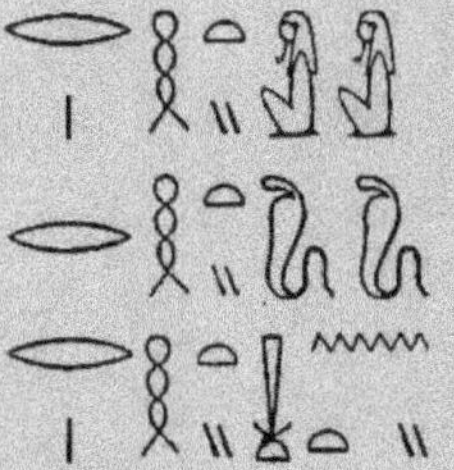 the two combatant sister goddesses, Isis and Nephthys.

Reḥui 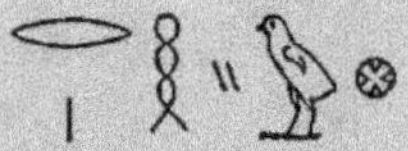 the town of the two combatant gods.

Re-ḥent 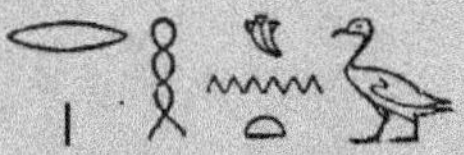 a proper name.

Re-ḥenent 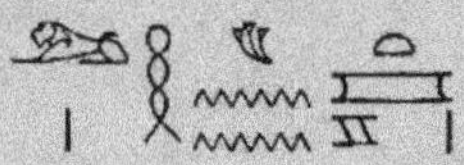 name of a lake or canal.

Re-ḥenent 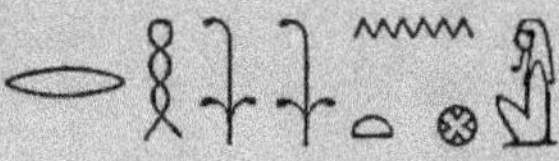 the name of a town or its god.

rekh 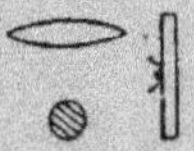 to be wise, to have knowledge;  knowingly, with intent;  known; 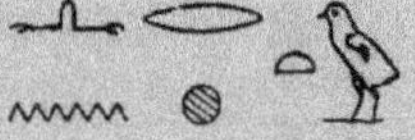 unknown.

rekht  knowledge, a list, inventory, total.

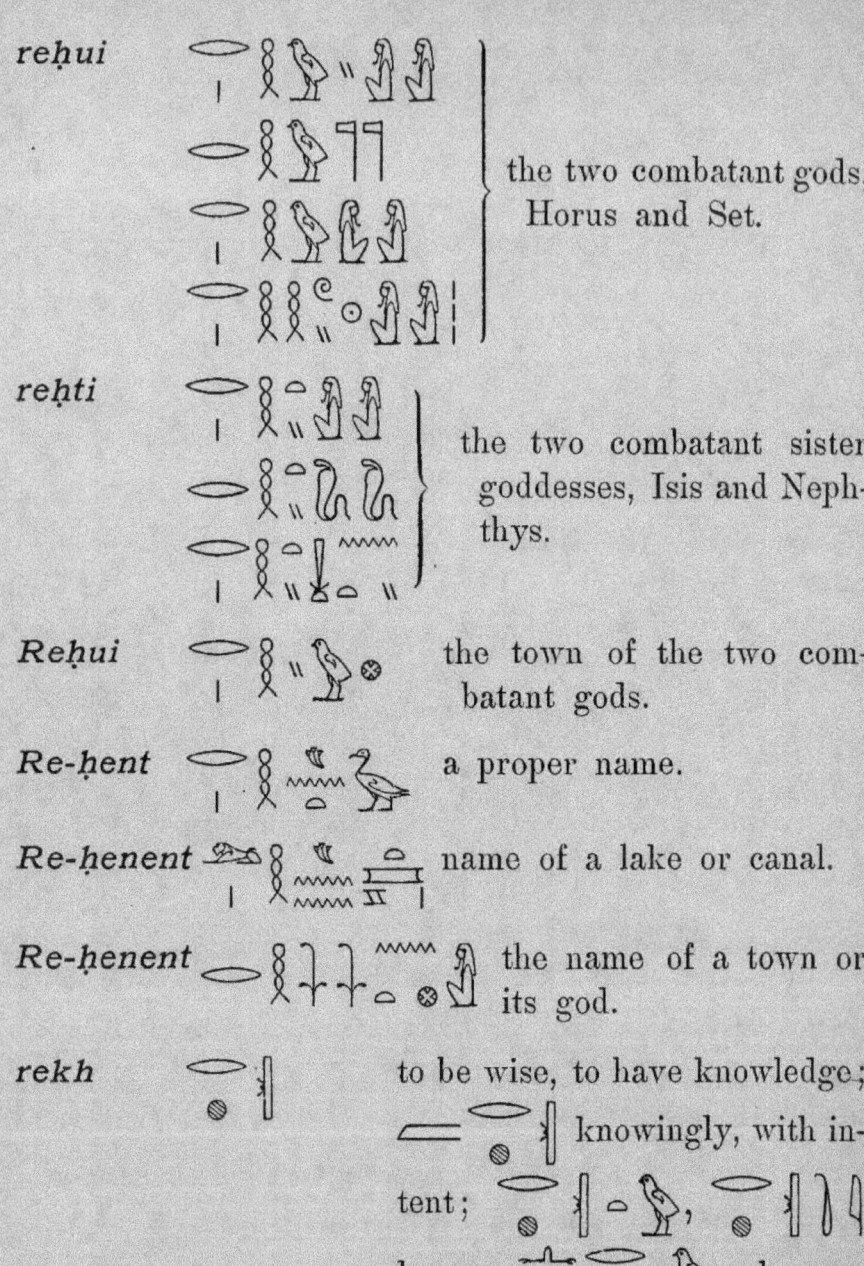

rekh àb 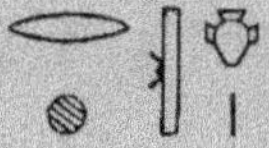 to understand.

rekhu khet 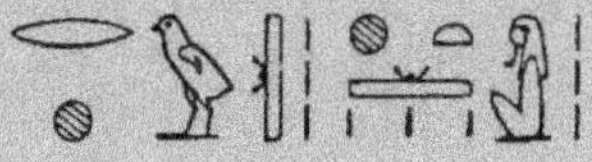 "knowers of things", *i. e.*, the wise gods.

rekhit  beings of knowledge, rational beings, men and women, people, mankind.

rekhes 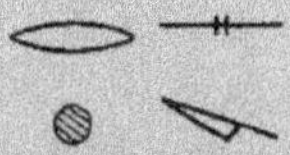 to sacrifice, to slaughter.

Rekhti  the two goddesses Isis and Nephthys.

Rekhti-Merti-neb[ti]-Maāti 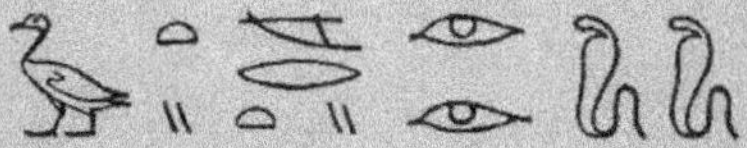 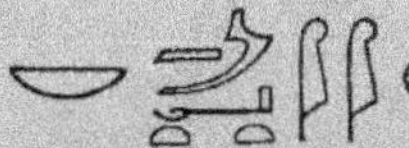 the two goddesses who were the ladies of the city of Maāt.

res 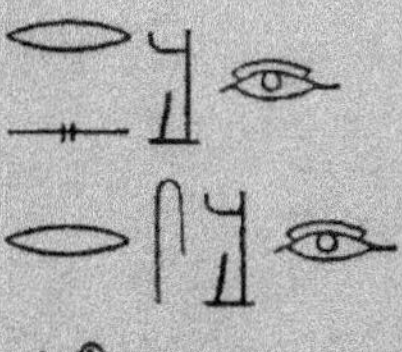 to watch, be awake;  awake; 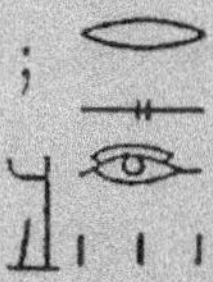 rouse up! wake up!

resu 

resit  the nine watchers.

restu  night watchers.

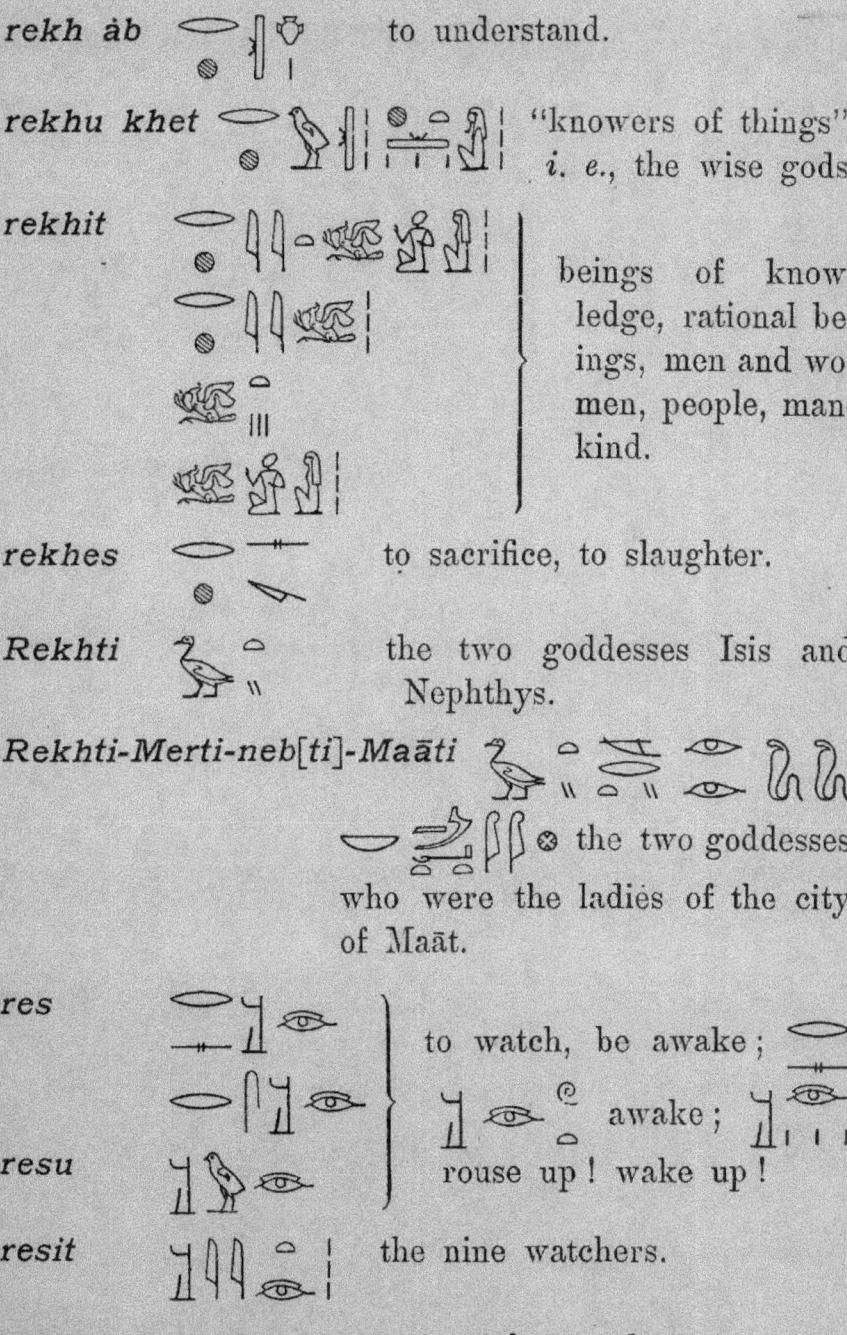

Res-âb 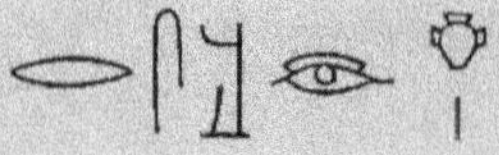 the warder of the Fourth Ārit.

Res-ḥer 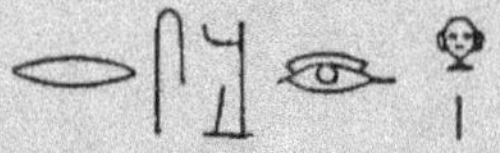 the warder of the Third Ārit.

res 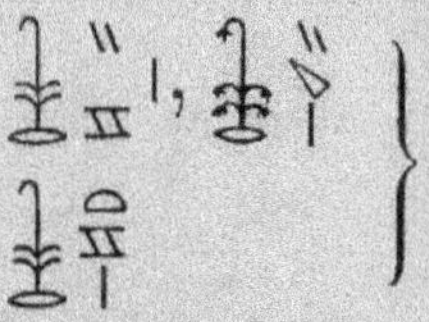 south, southern;  South and North, all Egypt.

resiu  southerners, southern gods.

Resu  a proper name; fem. .

resu 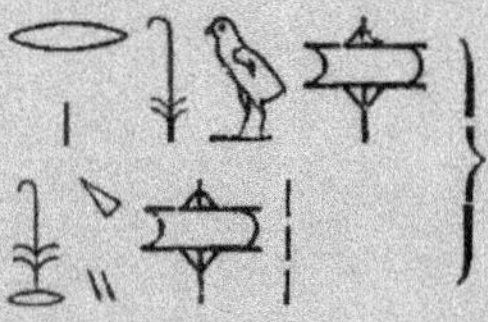 south wind.

Resenet (?) 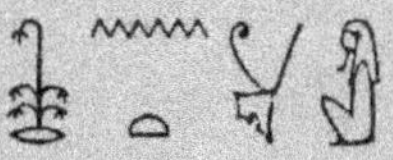 a proper name.

resh 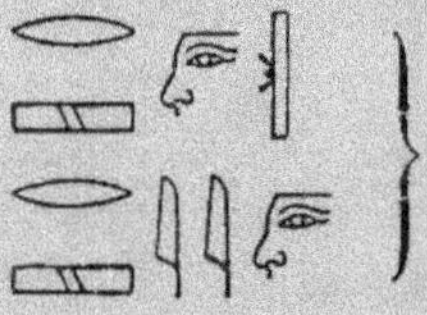 to breathe with joy, to rejoice.

resht  gladness, joy, to snuff, to inhale.

reshui  the two nostrils.

rek  then, an emphatic particle.

rek  time.

rekḥ 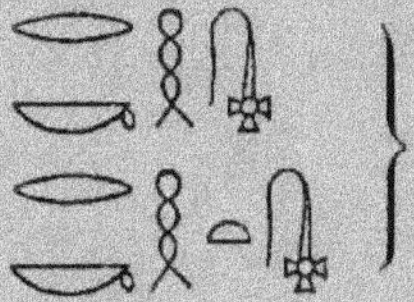 to burn, to be hot.

rekḥu  fire, flames.

Rekes 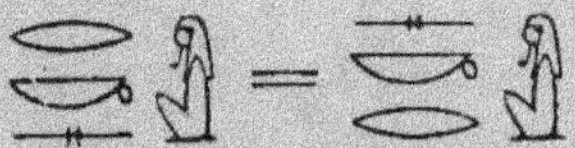

req, *reqa*  to incline away, fall away from; .

reqi  fiend, enemy.

reqau  (or ) fiends, enemies.

ret 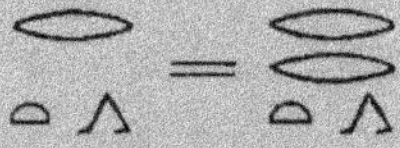 *i. e., reret*, or *peḥrert.*

ret (*remt*)  men and women, people, mankind.

 everybody.

Retasashaka  a name of Ȧmen.

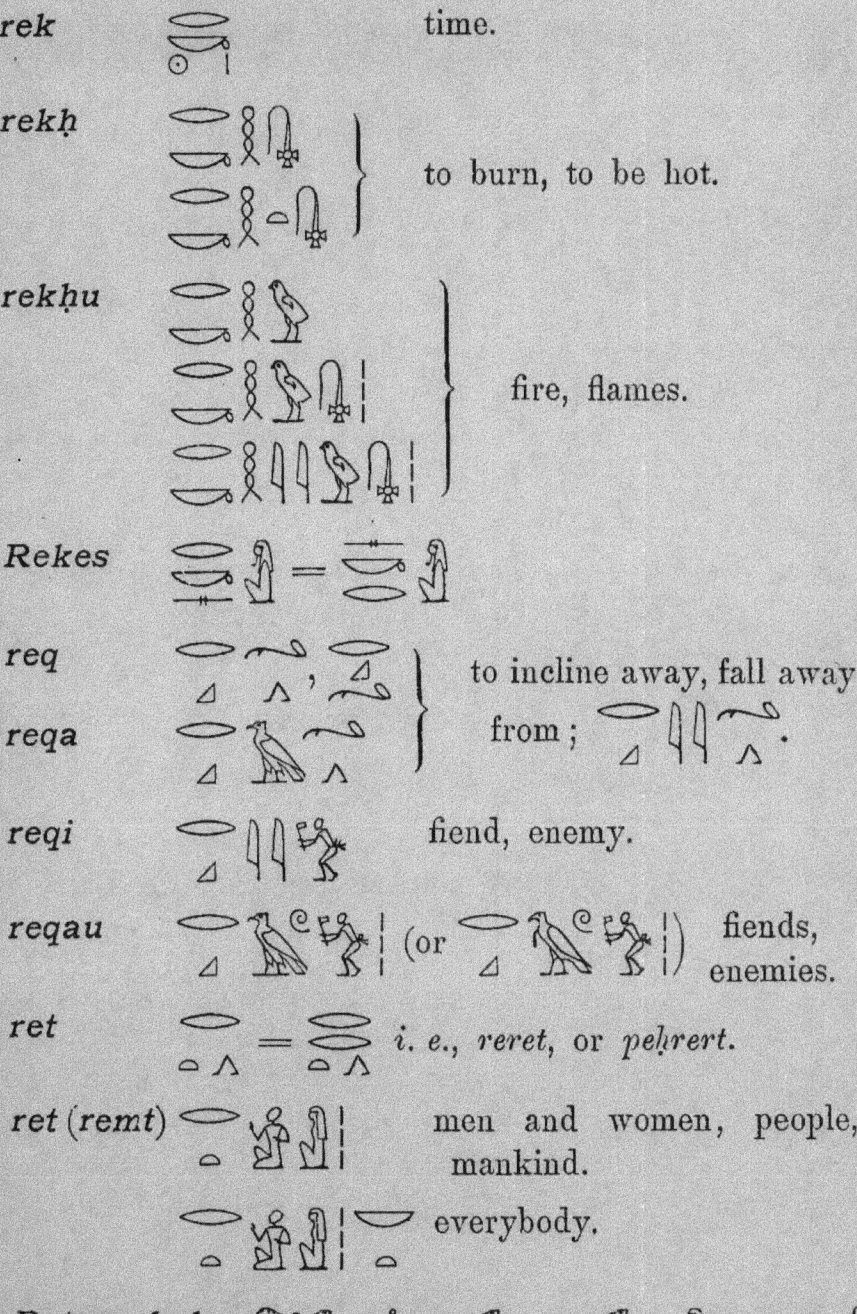

reti the two leaves of a door.

reṭ leg, foot.

reṭui
reṭi the two feet.

reṭȧu feet.

reṭ (*remt*) men and women, people, folk, mankind.

reṭ steps, staircase.

erṭā
erṭāt to give, to set, to place, to put, to cause or make to happen;

As an auxiliary verb:

and see *passim*.

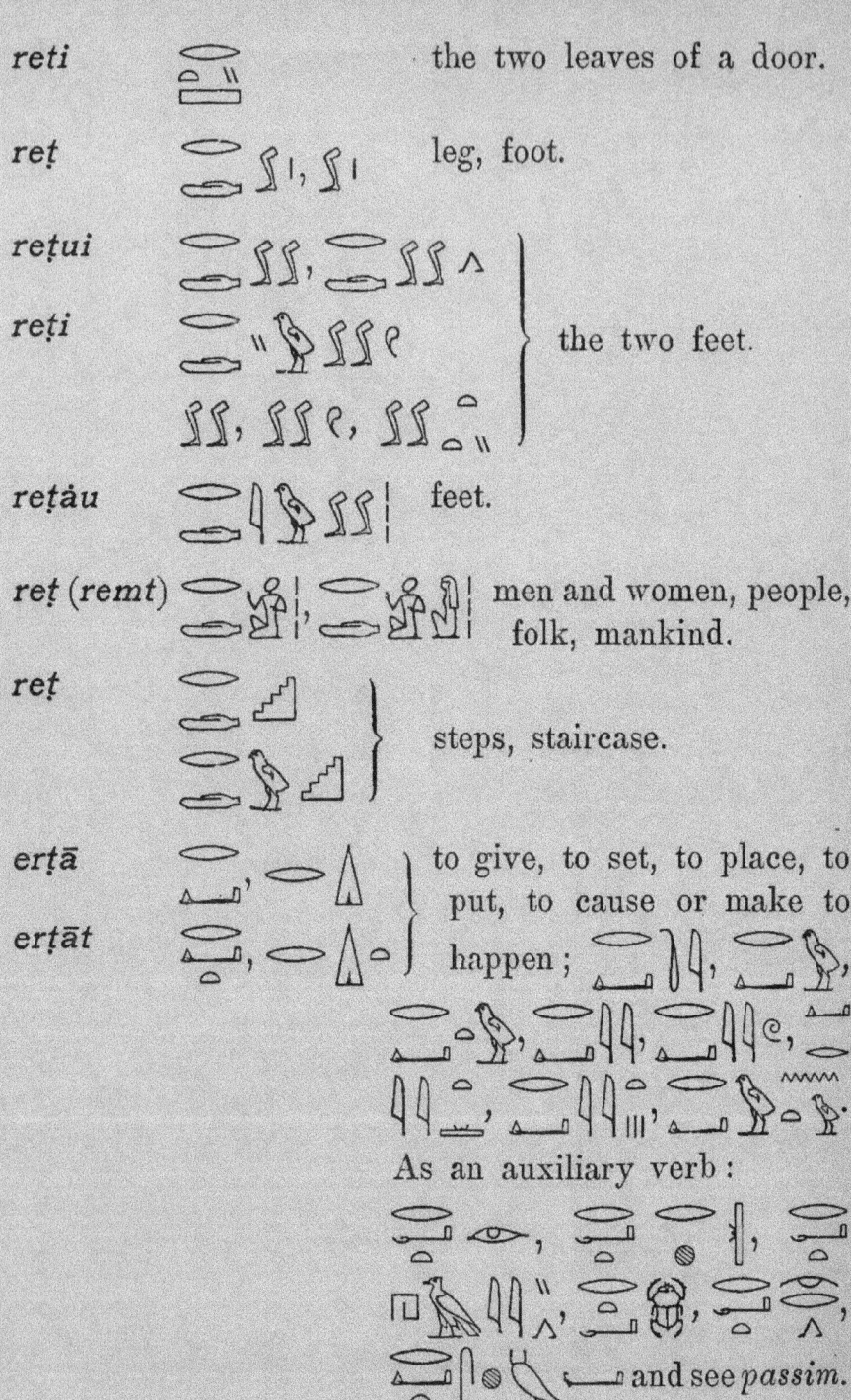

Erṭā-nefu a proper name.

Erṭā-ḥen-er-reqa a proper name.

reṭut places, abodes.

reṭu . . . .

reṭu emanations, effluxes, droppings.

reth men and women, people, folk, mankind.

everybody.

H.

ha interjection, O! Hail!

ha to be strong; strength.

ha *hai* *hait*		to descend, to go down into a place, to embark on a ship, to fall, to go in, enter, advance into  those who enter.
hau		time, period, reign.
Haåker	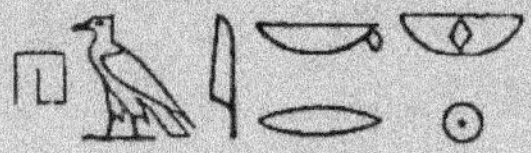	name of a festival.
Hai		"phallus"; the name of one of the Forty-two Judges in the Hall of Osiris.
hai		interjection, O! Hail!
hai		to shout with joy, rejoice.
haiu	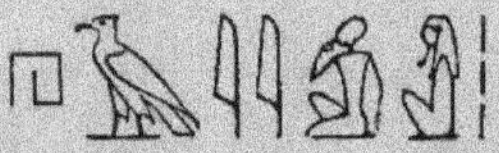	the gods who rejoice.
hait		a large chamber, heaven (?).
hab		to send, to send forth, to go forward.

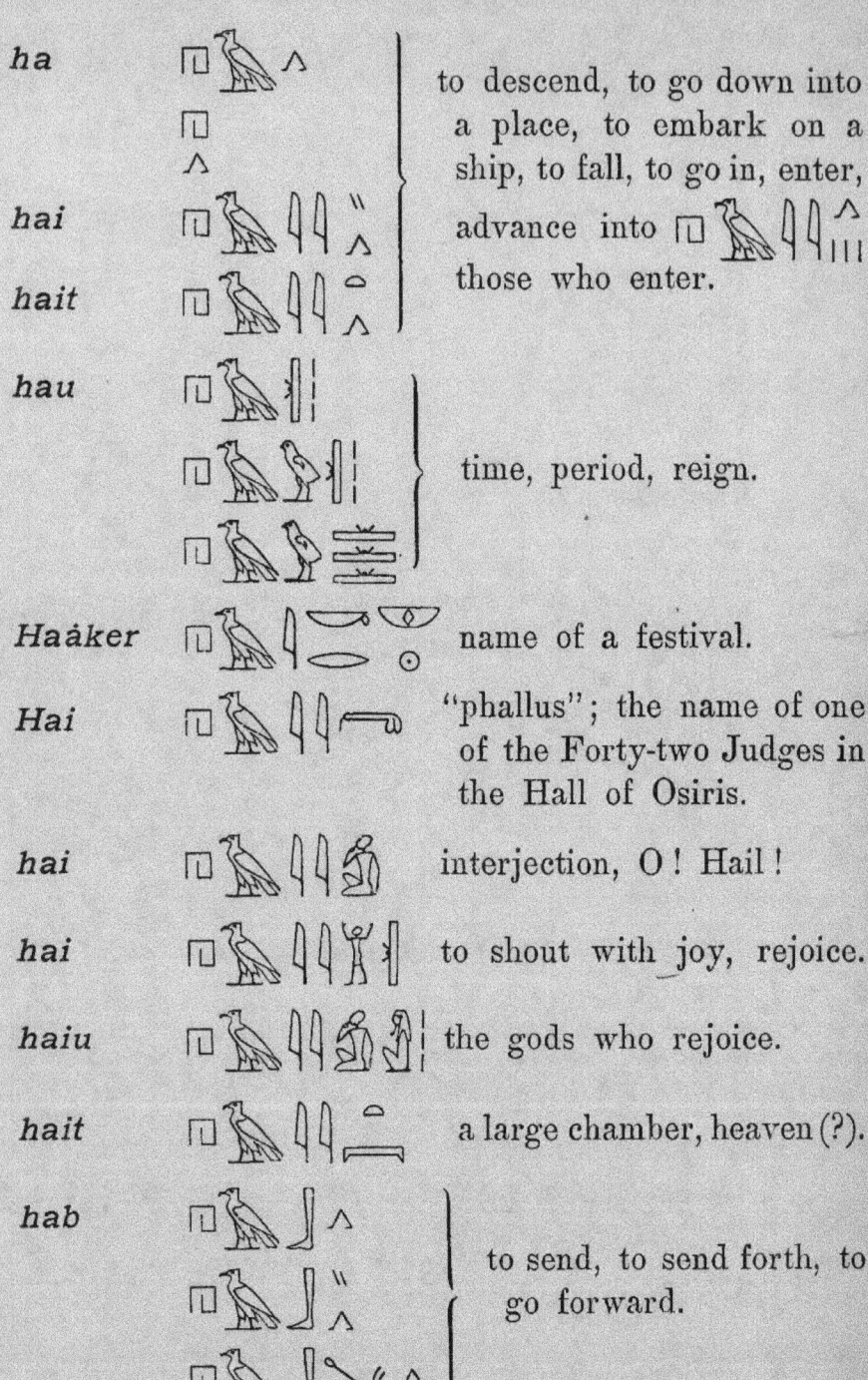

habu  those who fall down.

Hab-em-atu  "advancing at the moment"; a proper name.

habeq  to fail.

hamu  blemish, defect, sin.

Hart-ȧb  to please.

Hahuti-ȧm- . . . . .  the name of a fiend.

Haḥetep  a proper name.

Hakheru 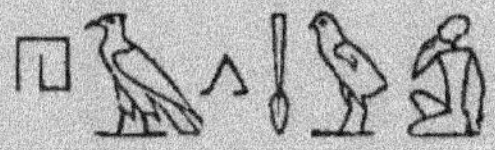 a proper name.

Hasert  a city in the Seventh Ȧat.

haker  the name of a god and of a festival.

haq 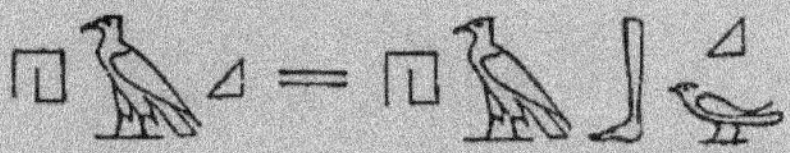

Haqahakaḥer  a proper name.

hat  interjection, O!

hat  descent, entrance, embarcation.

hatu  brow (?).

haṭ  to suppress, to beat down, subdue.

hi 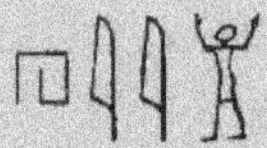 to rejoice.

hu  to enter, descend, fall.

Hunefer  the name of a scribe.

Hu-kheru  the name of the herald of the first Àat.

heb  ibis, the bird sacred to Thoth.

heb, *hebt* 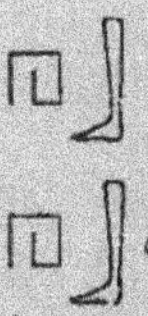 to send out, to go forward.

hepu  laws, ordinances, regulations.

hem  fire.

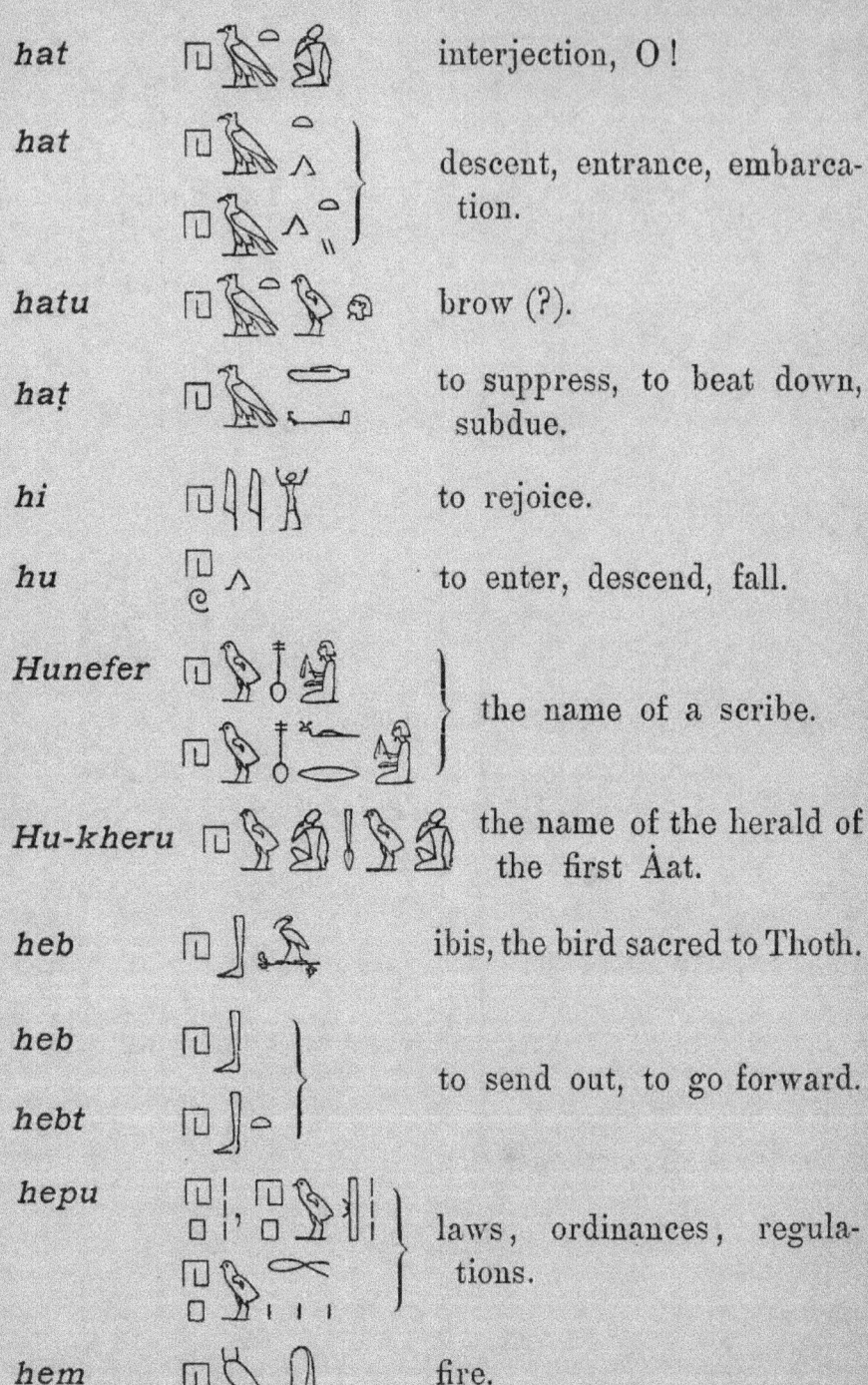

hemu		men and women, folk, people: see also ***ḥenmemet***.
hemhem	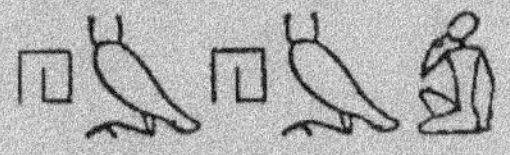	to roar, cry out, bellow (of a bull).
hemhemet	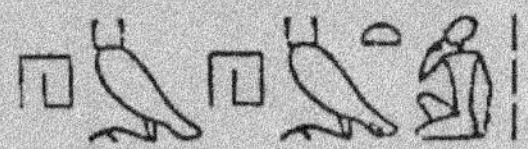	outcries, roarings.
Hemti		runner.
hen	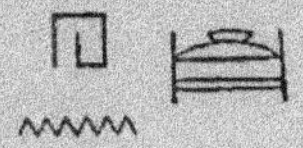	funeral chest, coffin.
Henȧ	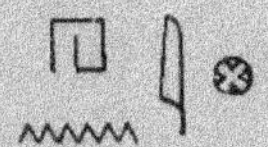	the name of a city.
henȧnȧu	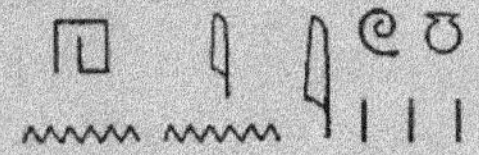	pleasant things.
henu		to sing songs of joy, to praise.
henu		praises, shouts of joy, singers.
henhenu	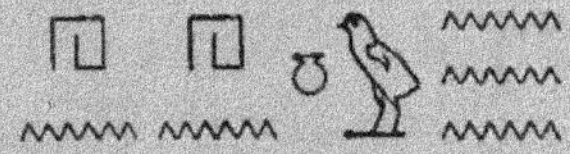	the watery abyss of heaven, flood.
henhenit	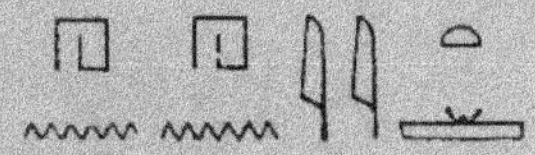	the watery abyss of heaven, flood.
hensheses	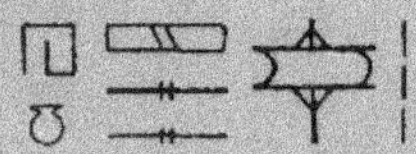	the east wind.
her		to be content, pleased.

her-àb, *hert-àb*	pleased in heart, content, pleasure.
herà	a vessel.
heru	day; plur.
	this day, to-day.
	judgment day.
	birthday.
	birthday of Osiris.
	day of the funeral.
	every day, daily.
	a happy day.
	daily, course of each day.
heriu	those who are content (?).
herret	things which please.
heh	flame.

heker 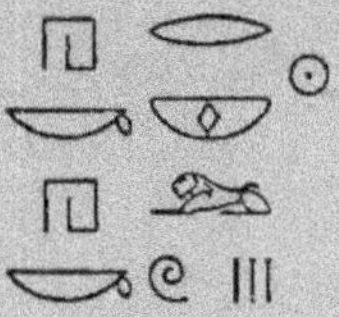 name of a festival.
hekeru

heq 

hetu  to be addressed.

hethet 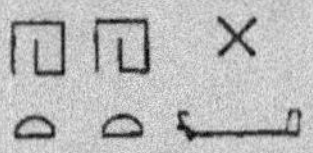 to go round about.

heṭ  to subdue. 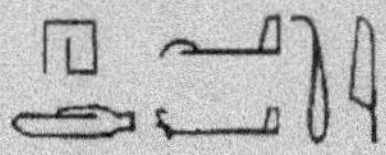 subdued.

 Ḥ.

. . . . . .  with  . . . . . .

ḥa  behind, get back! back thou! (in addresses to fiends).

ḥa  back of the head and neck.

ḥa  a cry, a precative particle.

Ḥaȧs  a proper name.

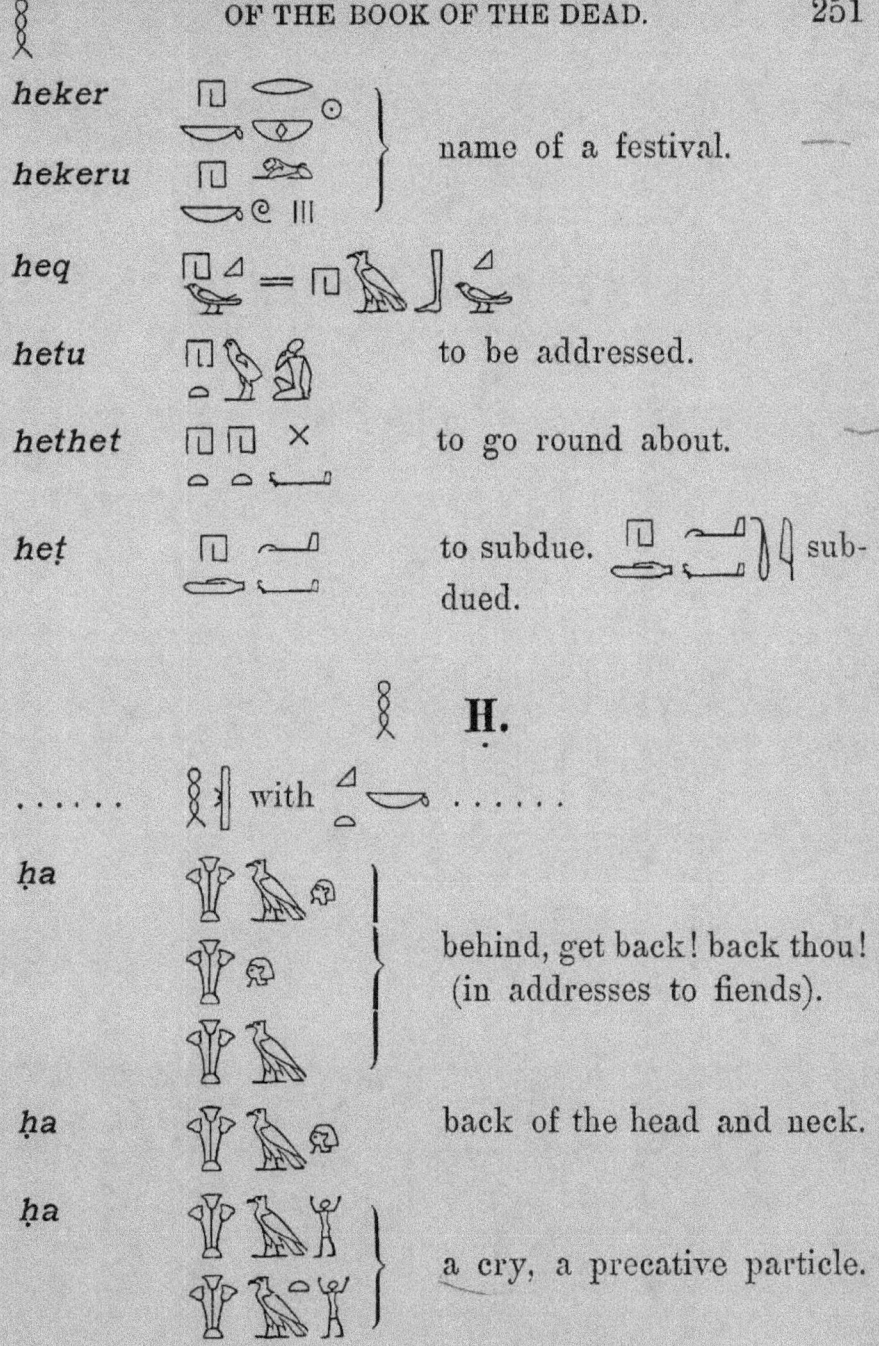

ḥaȧu 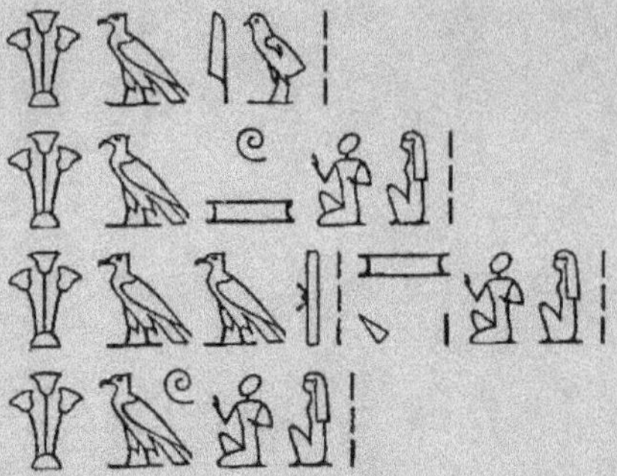 the dwellers in the Delta and in the marshes near the sea-coast.

ḥai 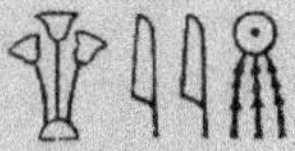 to be bright, to shine.

 light.

Ḥai, *Ḥait*  a proper name.

ḥait  to grasp.

ḥau, *ḥauu* 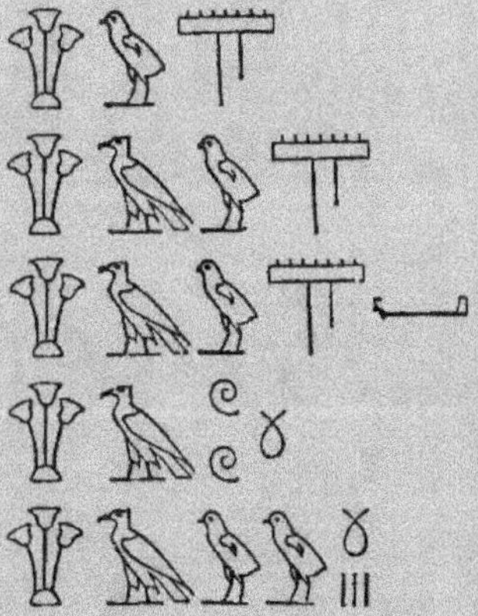 to be unclothed, to strip off apparel.

ḥaui  naked man.

ḥau  addition, increase, things added.

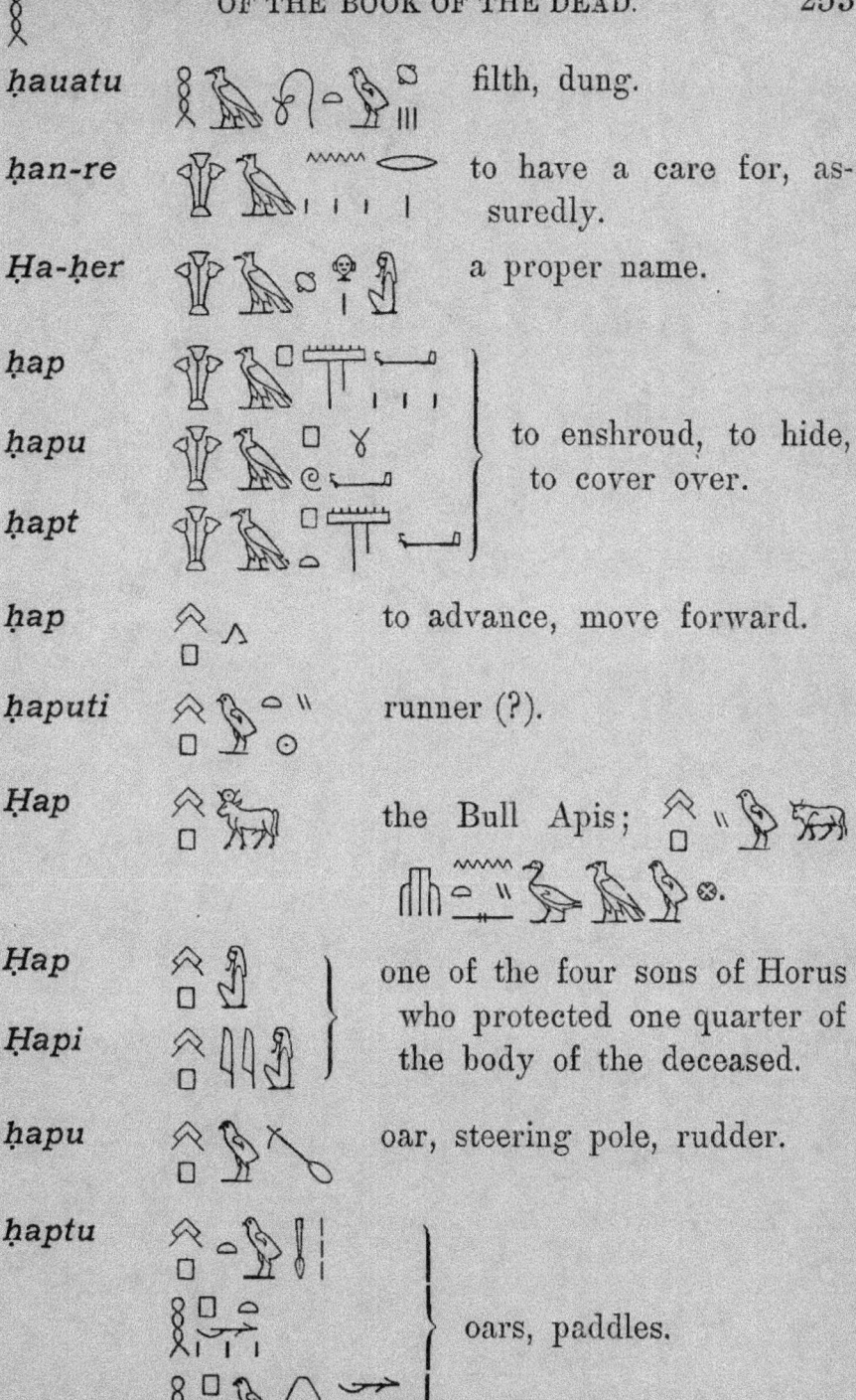

ḥauatu — filth, dung.

ḥan-re — to have a care for, assuredly.

Ḥa-ḥer — a proper name.

ḥap
ḥapu
ḥapt — to enshroud, to hide, to cover over.

ḥap — to advance, move forward.

ḥaputi — runner (?).

Ḥap — the Bull Apis; .

Ḥap
Ḥapi — one of the four sons of Horus who protected one quarter of the body of the deceased.

ḥapu — oar, steering pole, rudder.

ḥaptu — oars, paddles.

Ḥapu-en-neb-sett 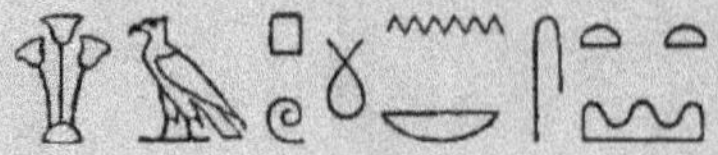 a name for the cemetery.

Ḥapṭ-re 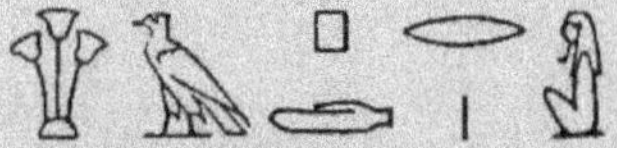 a proper name.

ḥam 

ḥamt  } to net birds and fish.

ḥamiu 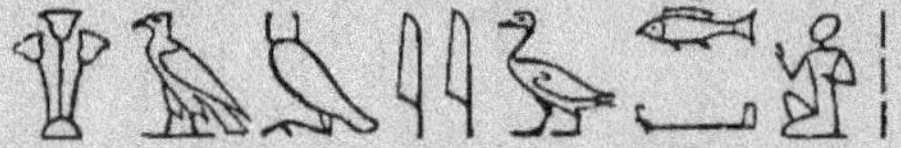 fishermen, fowlers.

Ḥarpuḳakashareshabaiu  a proper name.

Ḥareti  a proper name.

ḥaqet  to capture, make prisoners, captives.

ḥaqet  fetters.

ḥaqu  name of a plank or peg in the magic boat.

ḥat  pit.

ḥaṭ  tomb.

ḥaṭ 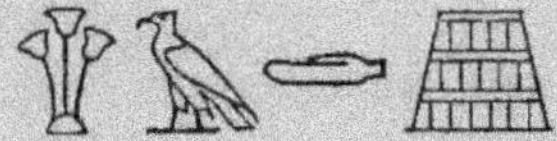

ḥaṭu  } net.

ḥatȧ, *ḥatȧtu*, *ḥattui* 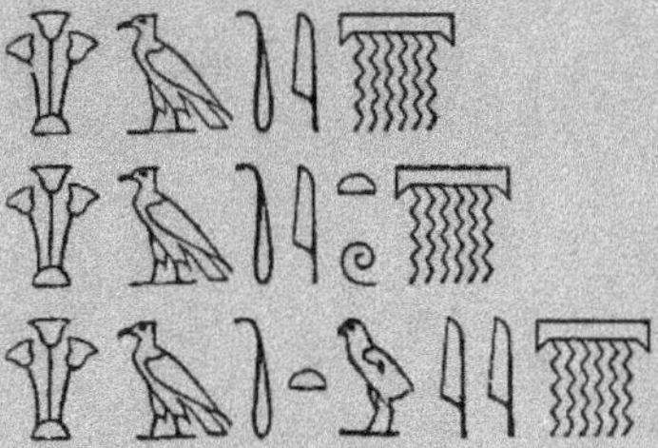 storm, whirlwind.

ḥā, *ḥāa*  to rejoice, be glad; 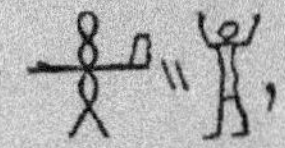, 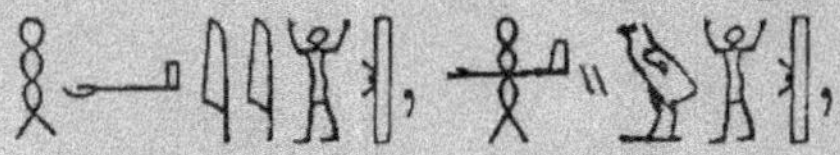, rejoicing;  glad.

ḥāiu 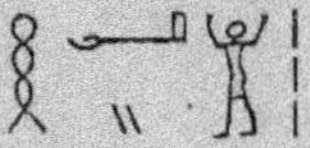 rejoicings.

ḥāā 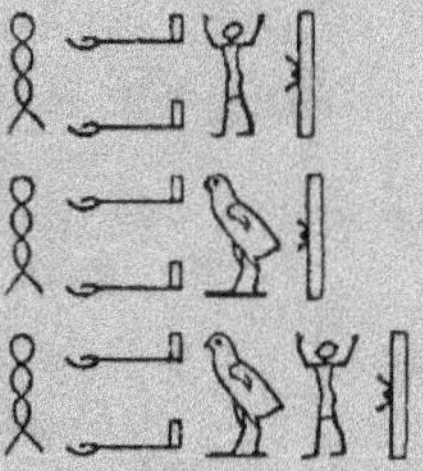 to rejoice.

ḥāāiu, *ḥāātu* 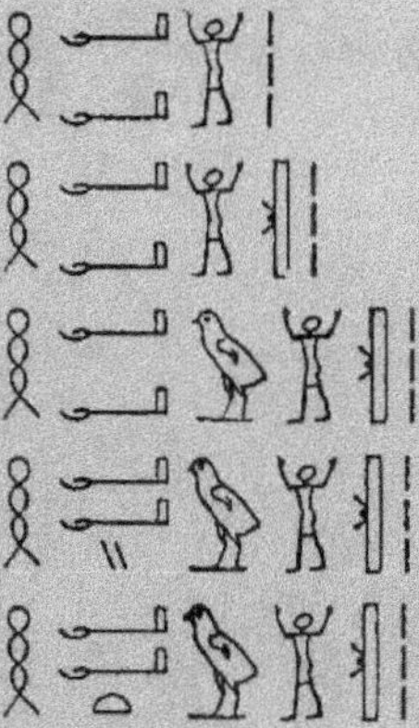 rejoicings, those who rejoice.

[*ḥā* 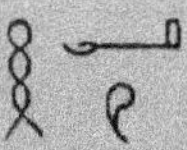 limb, member of the body, the body itself.]

ḥāu, *ḥāt* — limbs, members of the body; one body; thy own self.

Ḥāp, *Ḥāpi* — the Nile.

Ḥāp-ur — the Great Nile.

ḥā[t]-ā — the beginning or front of anything; the opening words of a book.

ḥāt — the beginning or front of anything, bows of a boat, the breast; before.

[*ḥāt-ā* — prince, chief] the two divine princes.

ḥāti — the heart; plur.

ḥātet — a rope in the bows of a boat.

ḥāti 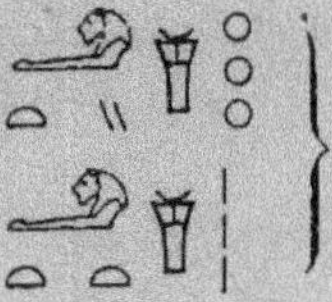 unguent of the best kind.

Ḥi-mu (?)  the name of one of the Forty-two Judges in the Hall of Osiris.

Ḥit 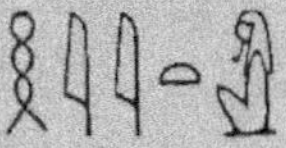 a proper name.

ḥu  a mistake for .

ḥu  hair, tresses.

Ḥu

Ḥui 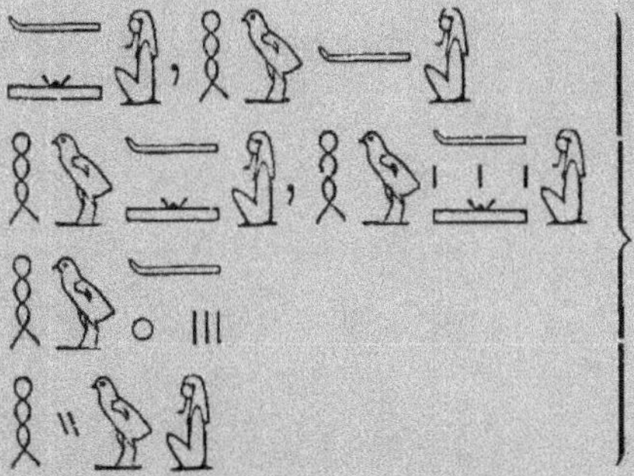 the god of food, divine food.

ḥu  to smite, to strike; 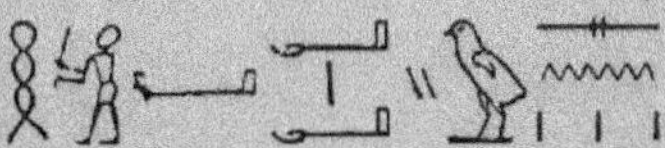 smiting (*i.e.*, clapping) their hands;  smiting.

ḥut 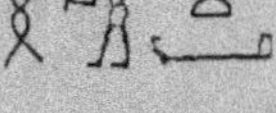 a smiting.

ḥuit-Rā  smiters of Rā.

Ḥu-tepa  a proper name.

ḥua  to be filthy, in a stinking, corrupt, or rotten state.

ḥuaat  filth, dung, offal; 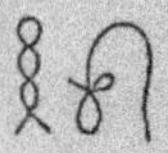 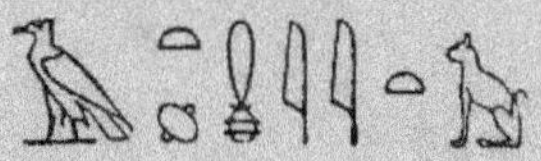 "filthy cat".

ḥui 
ḥuia  to decree, issue a command.

ḥun  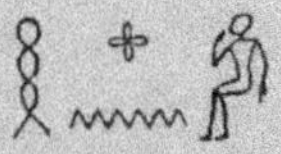
ḥunu 
ḥunen 
to be in the state of a child; boy, child, young man; plur.   

ḥunt  maiden, girl.

Ḥunt-Pe-...  . . . .

ḥuḥu  waterflood, a large mass of water.

ḥeb 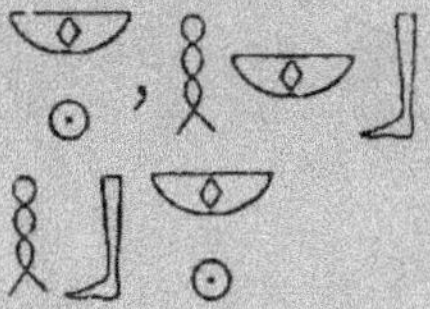 festival.

ḥebu / *ḥebit* 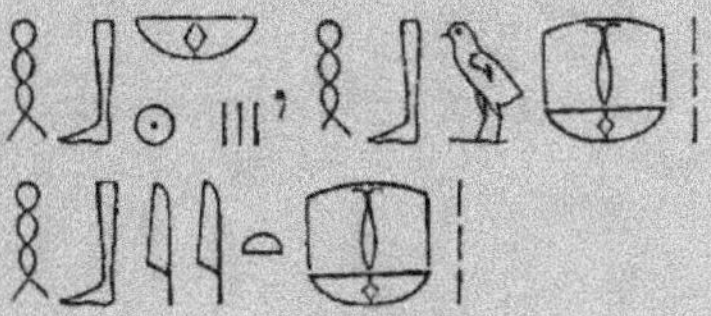 festivals.

ḥebt  the book containing the words of the festival service.

ḥeb  fowls and fish for the festival.

ḥebā  to play (at draughts).

ḥebt / *ḥebbet* 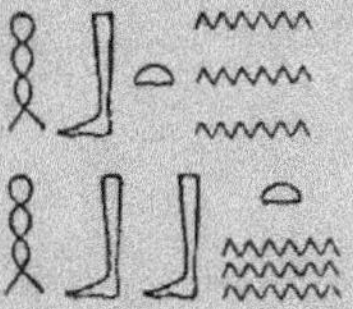 stream, flood.

ḥebenut 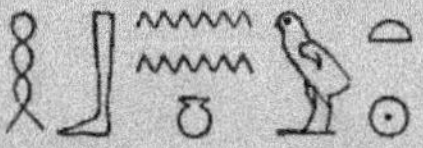 a cake, confectionery.

ḥebs 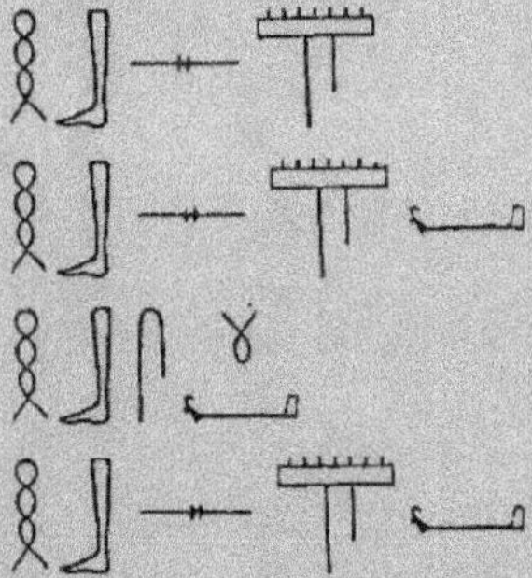 to be clothed;   clothed, a garment.

ḥebs 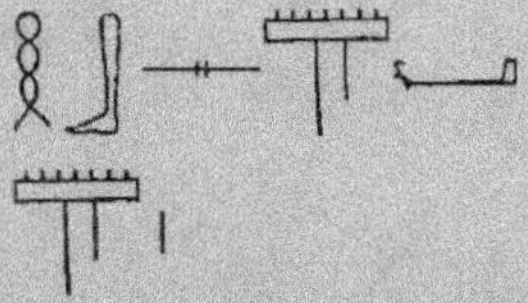 garment, clothing, a swathing; plur. 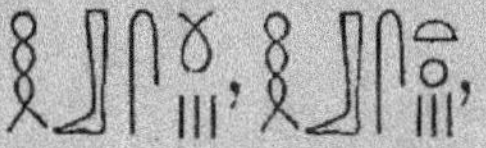, 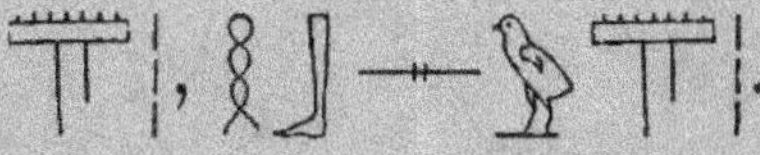.

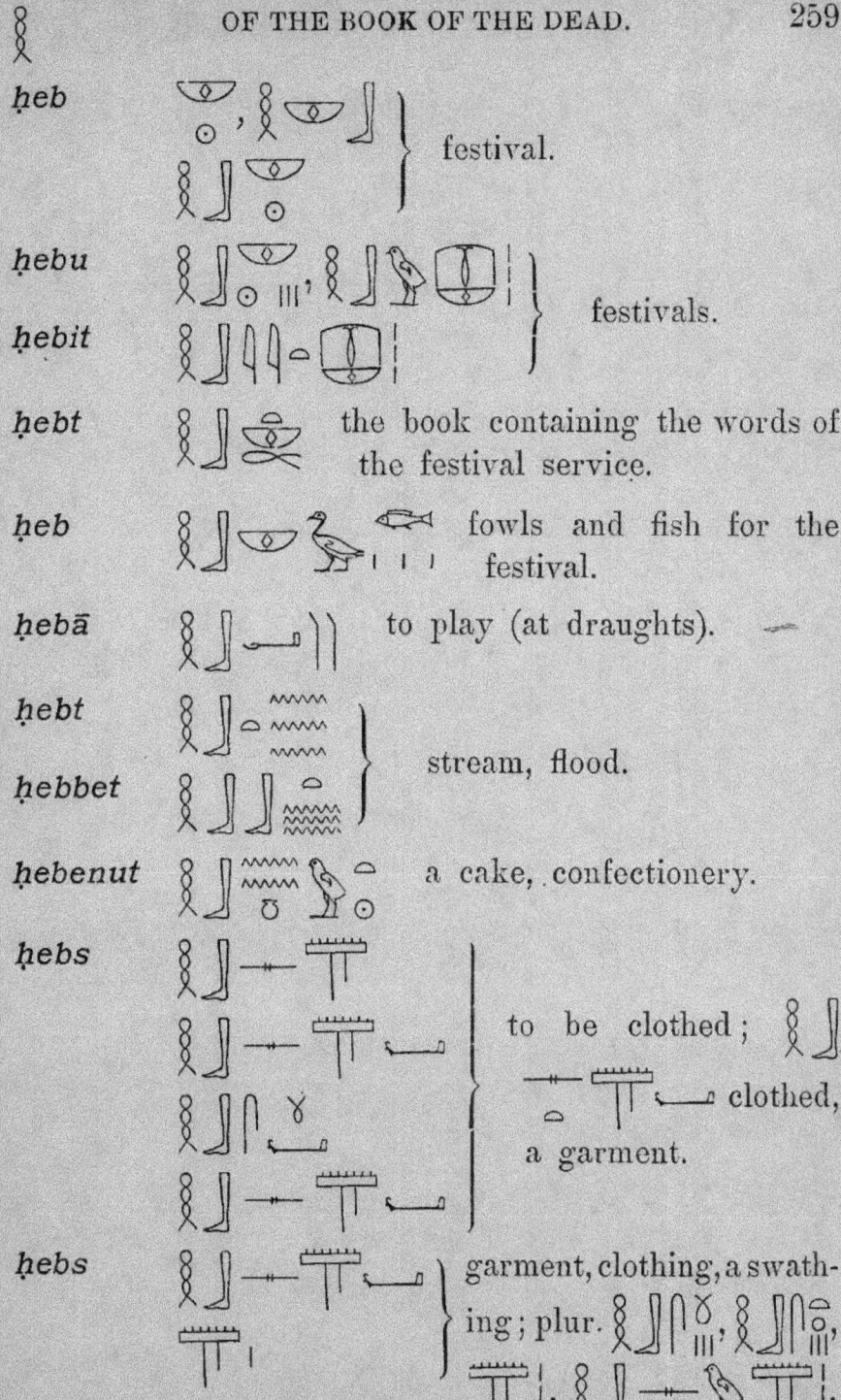

17*

Ḥebṭ-re-f 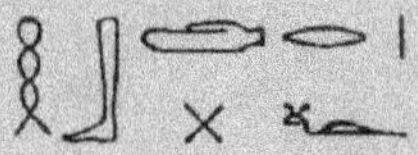 a proper name.

ḥept 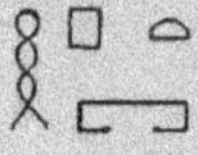 for 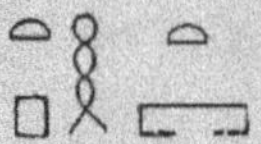 *q. v.*

ḥept 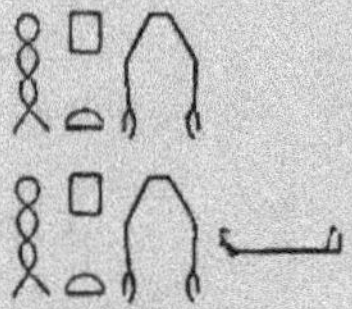 to embrace, embrace; 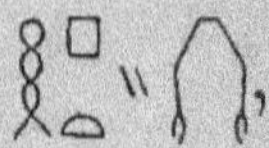, 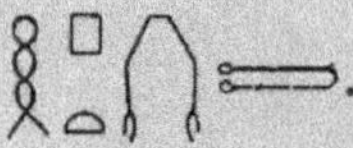.

ḥept 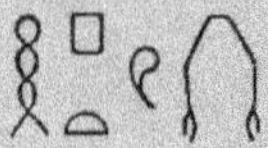 breast (?), embrace.

Ḥept-ur 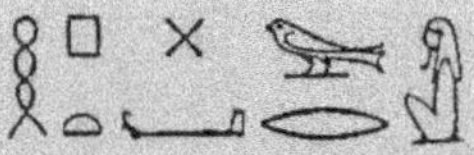 a proper name.

Ḥept-shet 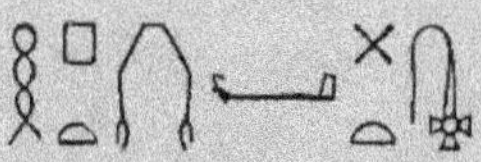 the name of one of the Forty-two Judges in the Hall of Osiris.

ḥeptu  oars of a boat, doorposts.

ḥept 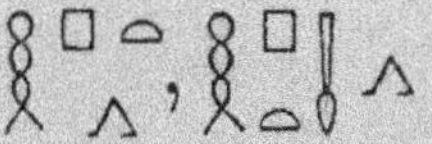 to move forward, advance; see  advancing.

ḥeptet 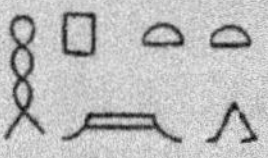 a course, a place for walking.

Ḥepṭ-ur 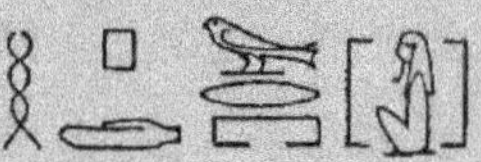 a proper name.

Ḥepṭ-re  a proper name.

ḥepṭ-re 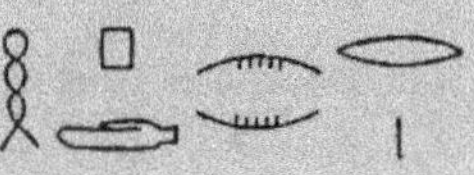 to shut the mouth, to gnaw (?).

ḥefau  serpent, snake.

ḥefi 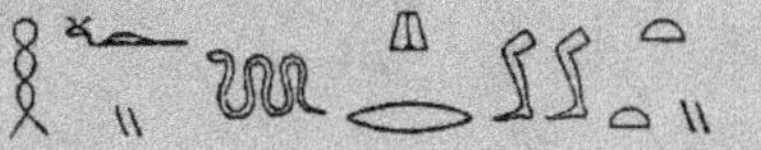 a serpent with two legs.

ḥefait
ḥefiu  . . . .

ḥefen 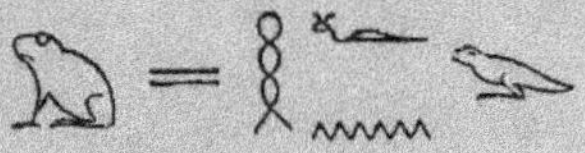 one hundred thousand.

ḥefṭ  to sit down, to rest.

ḥem  a particle.

ḥem  to retreat, make to go back.

ḥem  to steer, or paddle a boat.

ḥemu
ḥemi  paddle, oar, rudder, steering pole.

ḥemu
ḥemit  paddles.

ḥemaḳa  to grasp.

Ḥemaḳa  the name of a town and of a god.

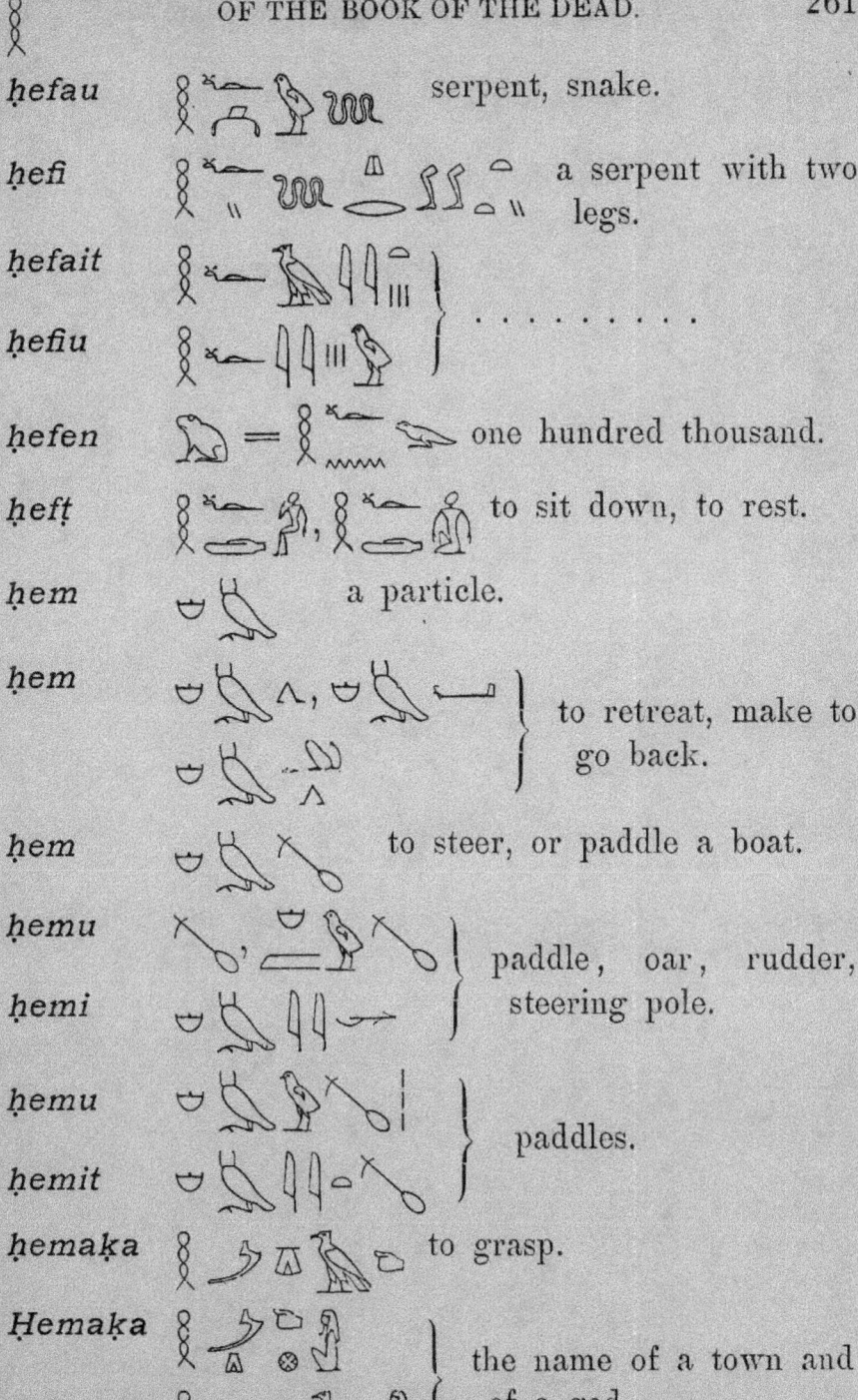

ḥematet name of a chamber.

ḥemu artificer, workman.

ḥemt work, handicraft.

ḥemt a mineral.

ḥemt copper, bronze.

ḥemen slaughter.

Ḥemen the name of a god.

ḥement forty.

ḥems to sit, be seated, to dwell; sitting, sitting ones; seated.

ḥemset a sitting, seat.

ḥemt woman, wife; plur.

woman belonging to a man, wife.

king's woman, *i. e.*, queen.

 god's woman, *i. e.*, priestess.

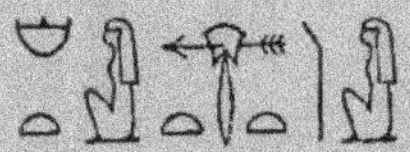 Asiatic woman.

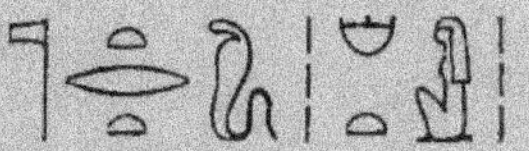 women goddesses.

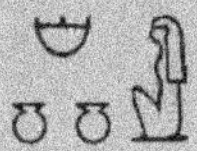 a proper name (?).

ḥemt  cow, cow-goddess; plur. .

ḥen  servant, slave; plur. .

ḥent  servant (fem.), slave.

ḥen neter 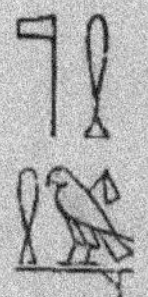 god's servant, *i. e.*, priest.

ḥen ka  priest of the *Ka*, or double.

ḥen 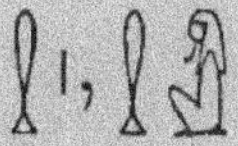 majesty; .

ḥen 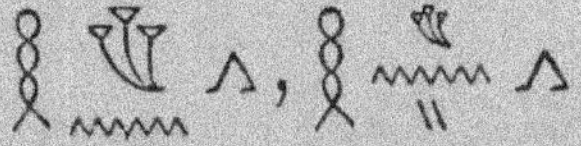
ḥenen 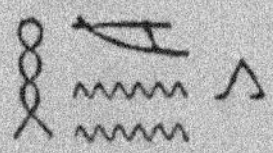
ḥenḥen 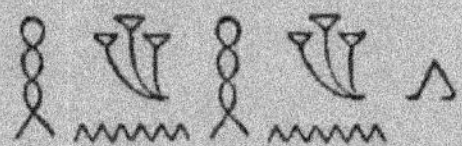
} to go forward, to run.

ḥen 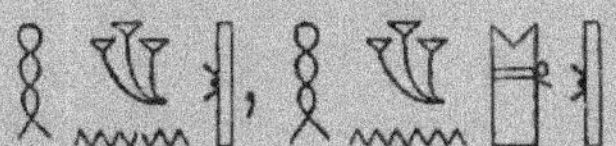

ḥenu 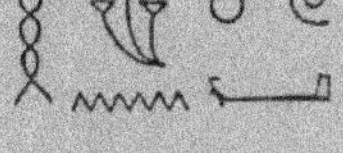
} to bestow, to be given or provided with, ordered, arranged.

ḥen, ḥeni 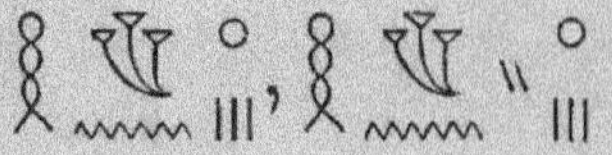 flowers, plants, blossoms.

ḥen 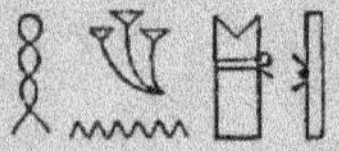 to praise; 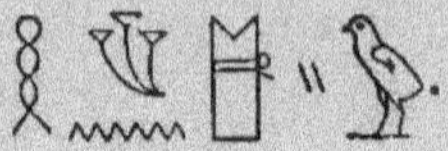.

ḥenā  with, along with, and; 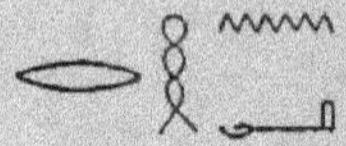 with;  triumphant with you;  god spake with god.

ḥenu 

ḥeniu  } offerings, gifts.

ḥenu  pillars.

ḥenu 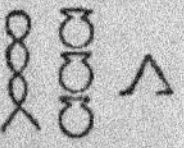 to draw to oneself.

ḥenbet 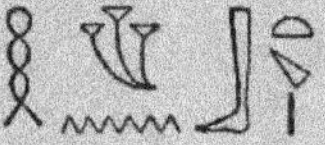 corn-land.

ḥeneb 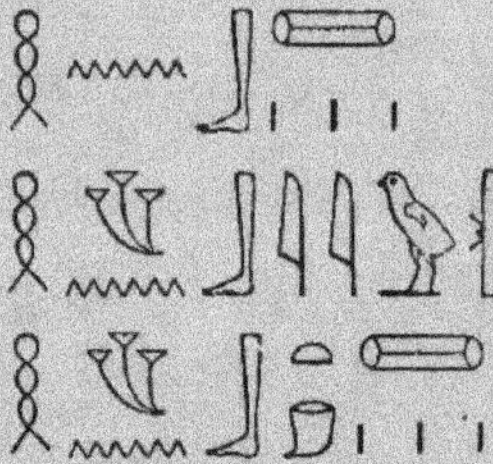 } offerings of grain produce.

Ḥenbi 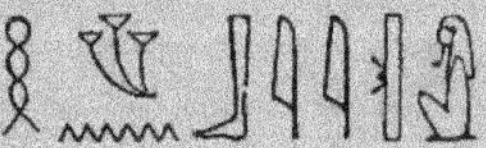 the god of the cultivated lands.

ḥenmemet  } also  men and women, folk, people, mankind.

ḥenemnemu  devourers (?).

ḥenen  to labour, toil.

ḥenen 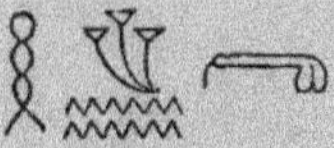
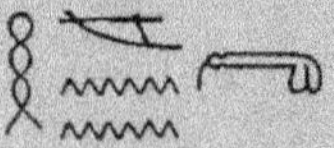

ḥenu (or *ḥennu*) 
} phallus  phallus of Rā.

Ḥenu 
Ḥennu 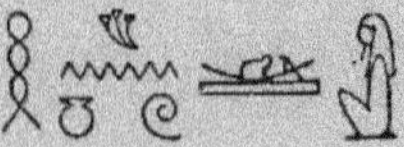
} name of a sacred boat which was drawn round the sanctuary at dawn at Memphis.

ḥennui 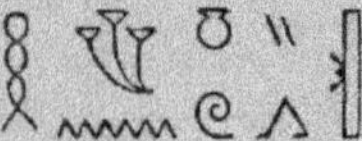 to go about, to wander, move forward.

ḥennui 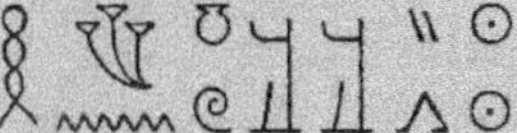 the beginning and end of time or of eternity.

ḥennuti 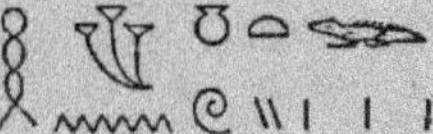 crocodiles.

ḥennuit 
ḥennut 
} fraud, deceit.

ḥennuti 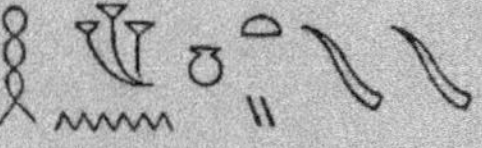

} two horns, a pair of horns.

ḥens 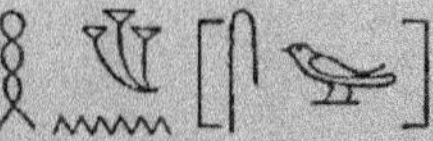 to block the way.

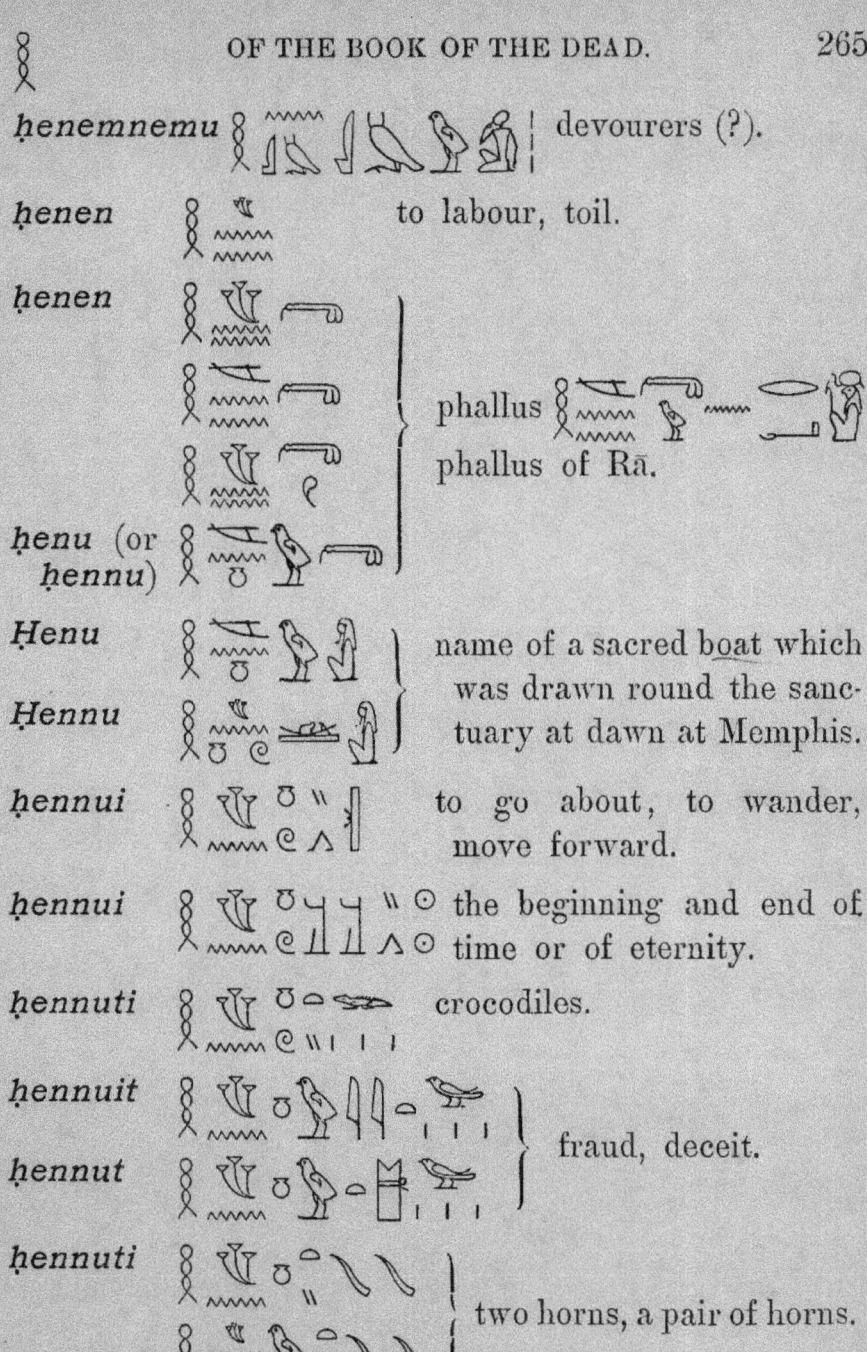

ḥenseki
ḥensekit
ḥensekt — hair, lock of hair, tress.
ḥensekti
ḥenkesti (sic)

Ḥensek — a god with much hair.

Ḥensektiu — the gods with much hair, *i. e.*, the gods with long hair and beards.

Ḥenseket-menȧt-Ȧnpu-em-kat-en-utu — name of a rope.

ḥenk — to give, present, offer; offered, given.

ḥenket — offerings.

Ḥenku-en-Ȧrp — a proper name.

Ḥenku-en-fat-Maāt — a proper name.

ḥenku  balance.

ḥenket 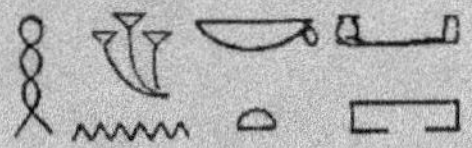
ḥenkit 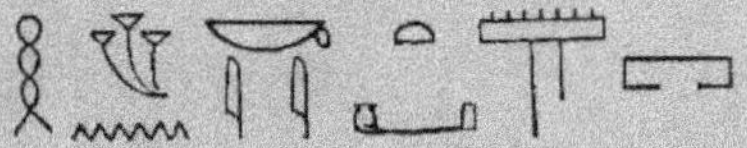 } the funerary bed, or chamber.

Ḥenket 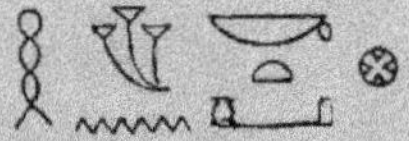 the name of a town.

ḥent 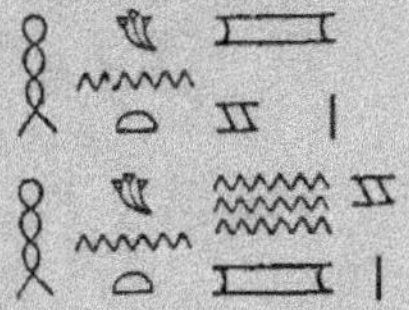 lake, canal, stream, pool.

ḥent 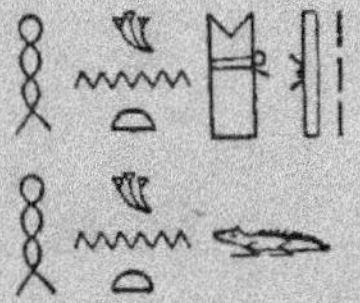 to be hostile.

ḥent 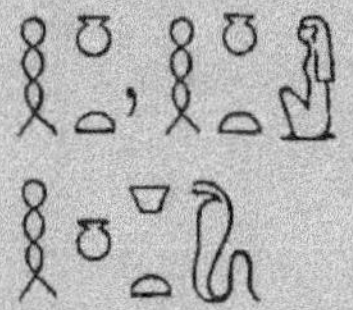 mistress, lady, sovereign, queen.

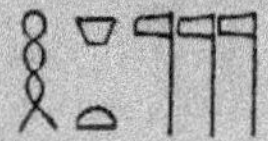 queen of the gods.

 lady of the crowns of the South and North.

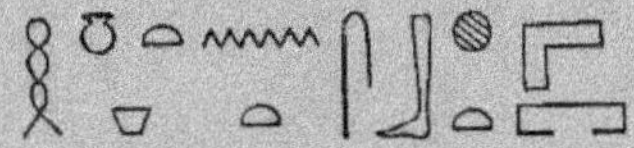 mistress of the pylons.

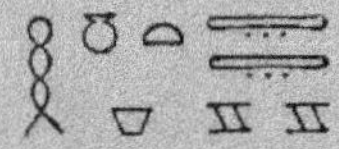 queen of the Two Lands.

Ḥent 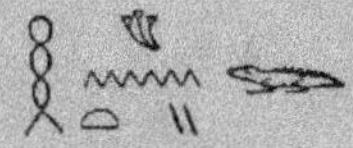 crocodile.

ḥenta 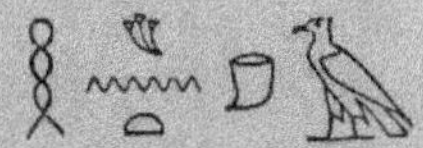 to fall into oblivion, or decay.

Ḥenti  god of the two crocodiles, a name of Osiris.

ḥenti 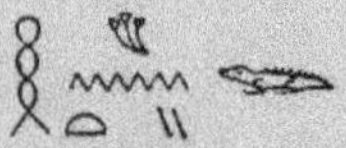 crocodile.

ḥenti 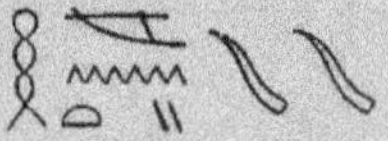 a pair of horns.

 the two-horned gods, or the two two-horned gods.

ḥenti 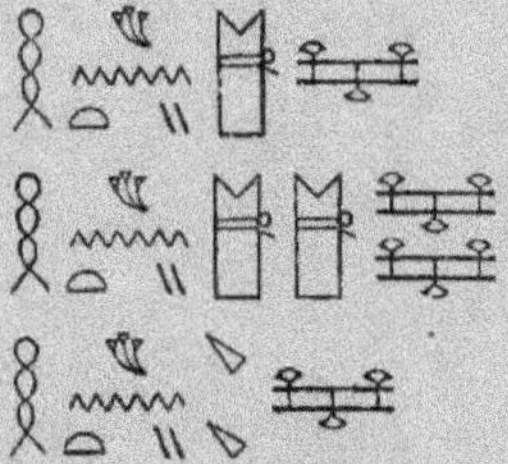 the beginning and end of time, or of eternity.

ḥenti pet 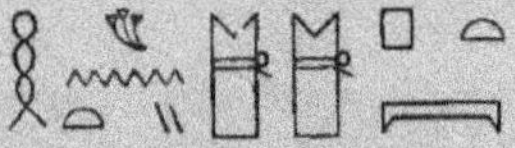 the two ends of heaven.

Ḥenti-requ  a proper name.

Ḥent-khent-ta-meru 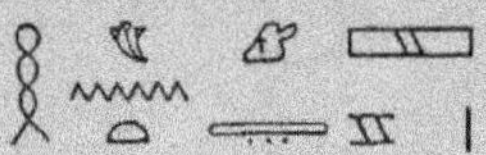 a proper name.

ḥer  in, at, upon, on, by, etc.; 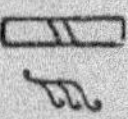 *en ḥer* upon.

ḥer-ā  on the hand, *i. e.*, straightway, immediately.

ḥer-ȧb 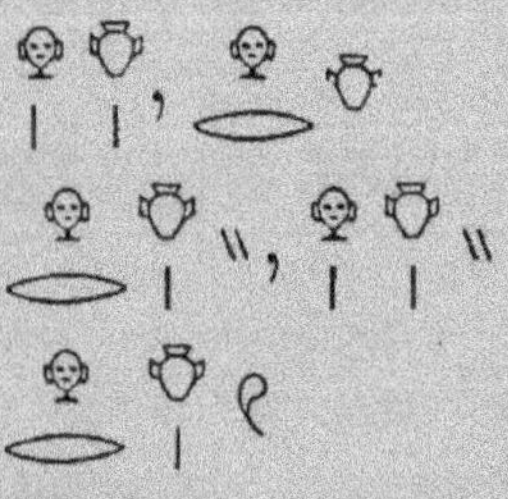 in the middle of, dweller in; plur. .

ḥer-ȧbt 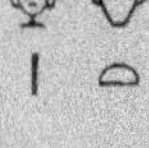

Ḥer-àb-uàa-f  "within his boat"; a proper name.

Ḥer-àb-àrit-f 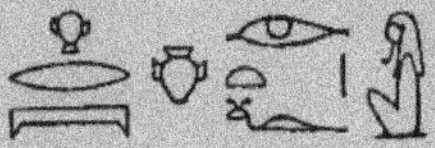 "within his eye; a proper name.

Ḥer-àb-karà-f 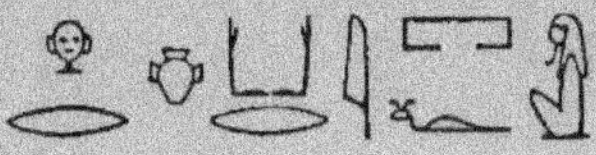 "within his shrine"; a proper name.

ḥer mā  straightway, forthwith.

ḥer entet 
ḥer enti sa 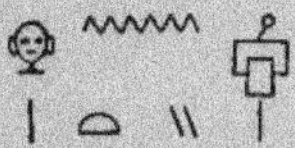 } because.

ḥer sa  besides, in addition to.

ḥeri  he who is above, or over, chief of, principal of.

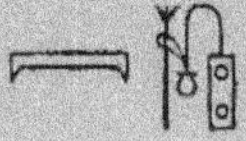 chief scribe; 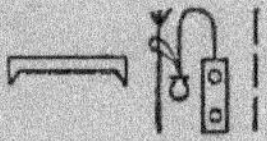 chief of the writings;  chief of the altar;  chief of the altars.

ḥeriu  those who are over, those who are above, celestial beings; chiefs.

ḥeriu

ḥertu  those who are over, those who are above, celestial beings; chiefs.

ḥeru  the upper regions, what is above; 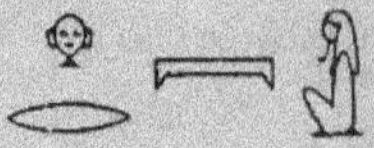 heaven, 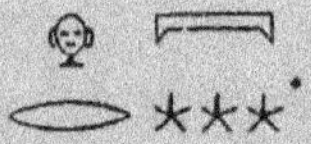.

ḥeri tchatcha  chief, governor, president.

 chieftainess, goddess.

ḥert 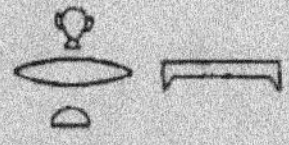 the upper regions, the sky, heaven.

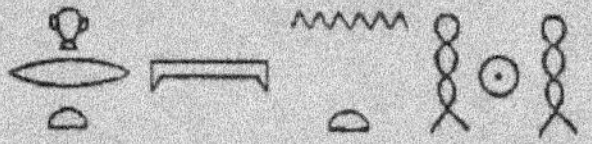 the heaven of eternity, *i. e.*, the everlasting heaven.

Ḥeri-aḳebȧ-f  "chief of his ocean"; a proper name.

Ḥeri-uatch-f  "chief of his sceptre"; a name of Horus.

Ḥeri-uru 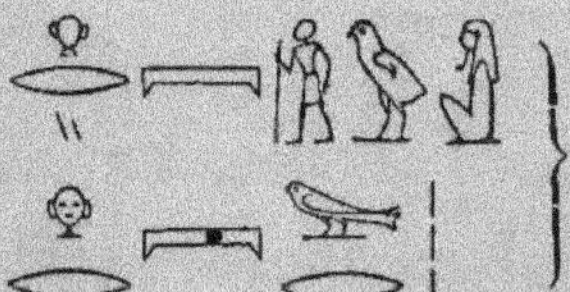 "chief of the great ones"; the name of one of the Forty-two Judges in the Hall of Osiris.

Ḥeri-sesh "chief of the writings"; a proper name.

Ḥeri-sep-f "chief of his time"; a proper name.

Ḥeri-sesh[*eta*] "he who is over the secrets"; *i. e.*, secretary.

Ḥeri-shā-f "he who is on his sand"; a title of Osiris.

"those who are on [their] sand"; a name of the dwellers in the desert.

Ḥeri-ta "governor of the land".

Ḥeri-tchatcha-taui "governor of the Two Lands"; *i. e.*, Egypt.

ḥer and.

ḥer face; plur. , ; two faces ; the divine face.

ḥer em ḥer face to face.

ḥer neb every one.

ḥeru nebu , folk, all men, mankind, all the people.

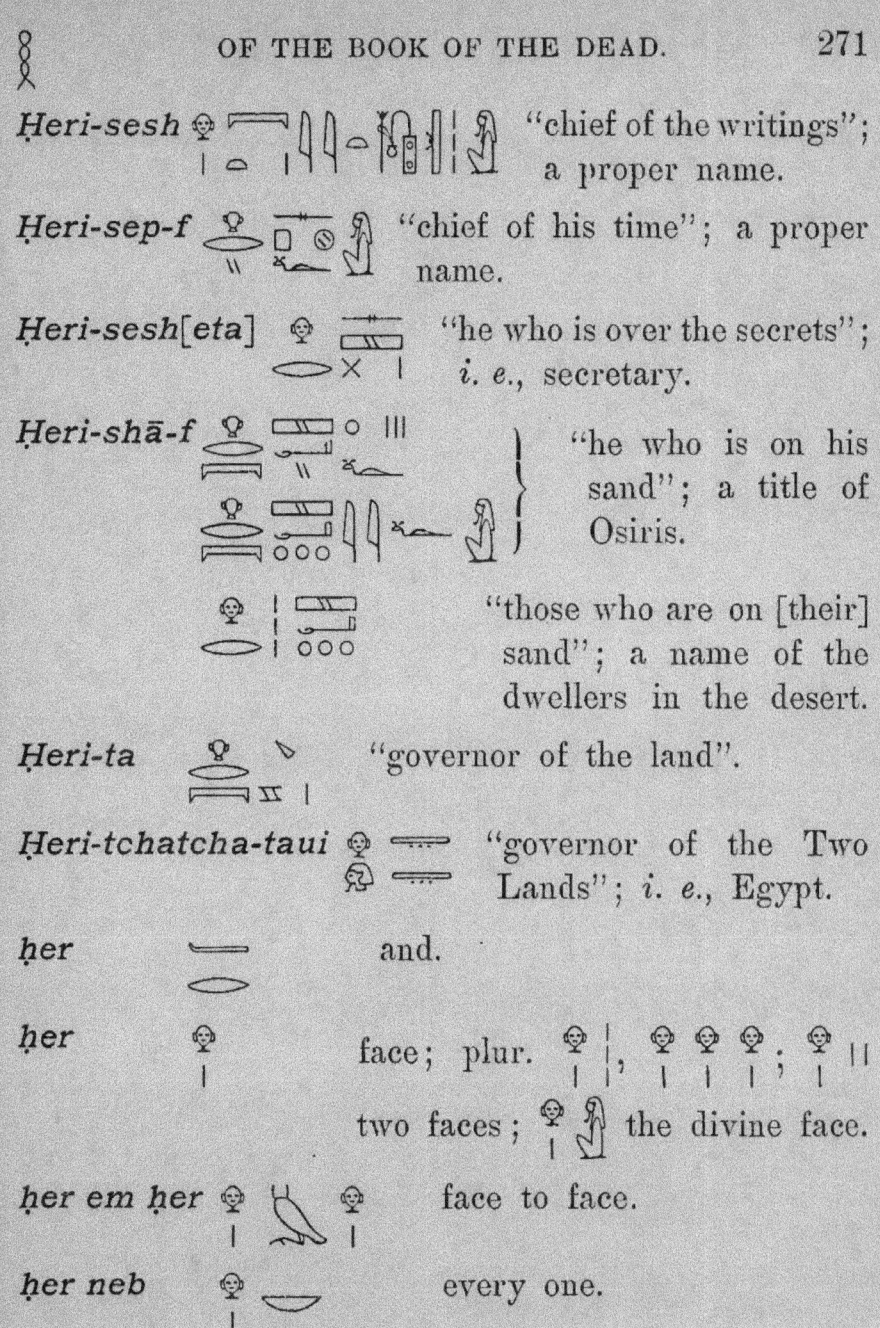

Ḥerui  the god of the two faces.

Ḥerui-f  he of the two faces.

Ḥer-uā 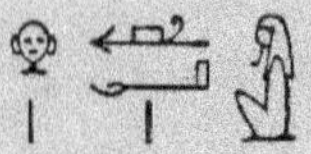 a proper name.

Ḥer-f-em-qeb 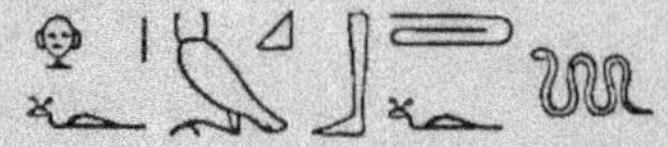 the name of a fiend.

Ḥer-nefer 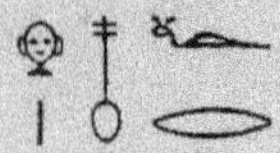 "beautiful Face"; a name of Rā and Ptaḥ;  

Ḥer-f-ḥa-f  "he with his face behind him"; the name of one of the Forty-two Judges in the Hall of Osiris.

Ḥer-k-en-Maāt 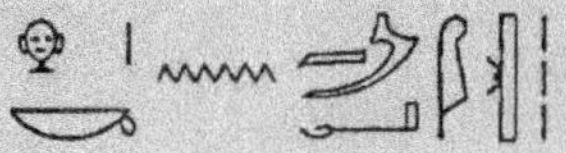 a proper name.

ḥer 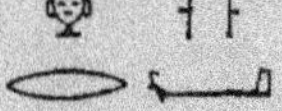

ḥeru   to terrify, be frightened.

ḥerit 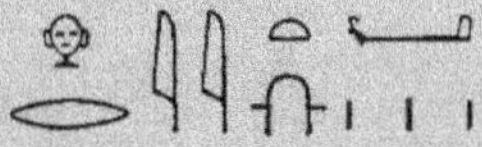 terror, fright.

ḥeri 

ḥeru  to go away, depart, be away, be afar off; 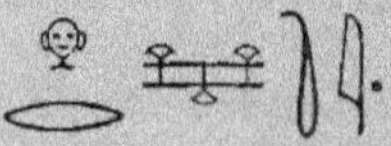.

Ḥer — the ancient name of the Sun-god; applied to the king as the representative of the Sun-god on earth.

Ḥerui — the pair of Horus gods, *i. e.*, Horus and Set.

Ḥerui-senui — the two Horus brethren.

Ḥeru-āa-àbu — "Horus, great one of hearts".

Ḥeru-àmi-àbu-ḥer-àb-àmi-khat — "Horus, dweller in hearts, he who is in the intestines".

Ḥeru-àmi-àthen — "Horus, dweller in the Disk".

Ḥeru-àrit (?) — the "Eye of Horus".

Ḥeru-āḥāi — Horus the Fighter (?).

Ḥeru-Un-nefer — "King of the South and North, Horus Un-nefer".

Ḥeru-ur 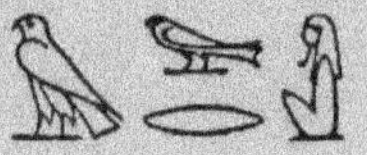 The elder Horus as opposed to Horus the son of Isis.

Ḥeru-merti  Horus of the two Eyes, *i. e.*, Sun and Moon.

Ḥeru-em-khebit  Horus of the North.

Ḥeru-em-khenṭ-en-merti 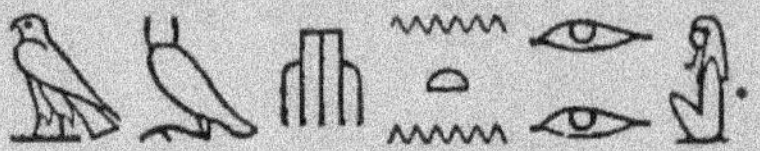

Ḥeru-neb-urert  "Horus, lord of the Urert-crown".

Ḥeru-netch-ḥer-âtef-f  "Horus, the advocate of his father".

Ḥeru-ḥer-neferu  "Horus on the pilot's place [in the Boat of Rā]".

Ḥeru-khuti  Horus of the horizons of sunrise and sunset.

Ḥeru-Khuti-Kheperȧ 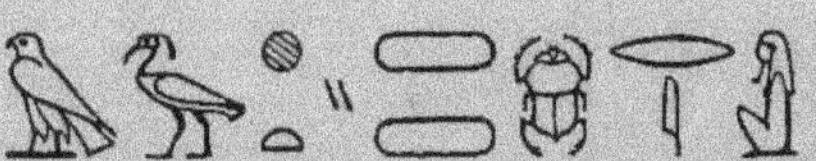 Harmachis Kheperȧ.

Ḥeru-khenti-ȧn-Merti (?) 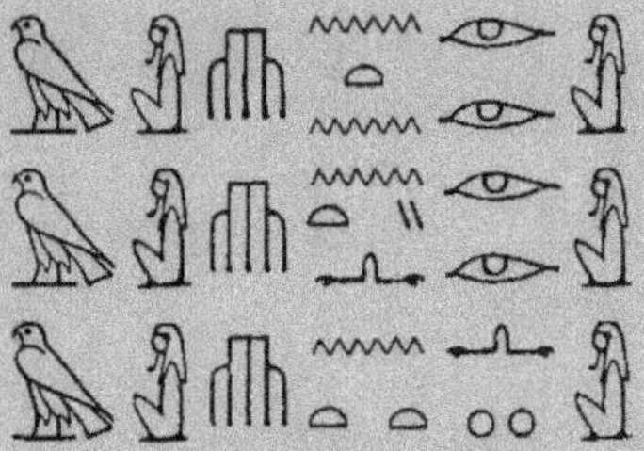 "Horus dwelling in blindness", *i. e.*, Horus (the sky) when neither the sun nor moon is visible.

Ḥeru-khent-Ḳhaṭti 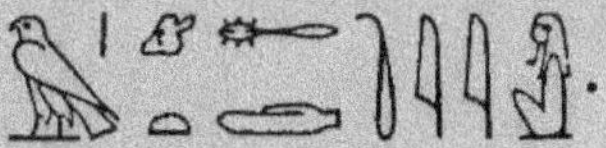.

Ḥeru-khenti-ḥeḥ  "Horus, governor of eternity".

Ḥeru-khenṭ-ḥeḥ  "Horus, traveller of eternity".

Ḥeru-khenti-Sekhem 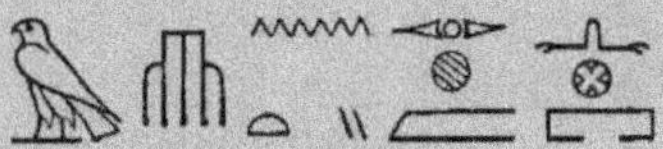 "Horus, governor of Sekhem" (Letopolis).

Ḥeru-khesbeṭ-merti  "Horus with eyes of lapis-lazuli", *i. e.*, blue-eyed Horus.

Ḥeru-sa-Ȧst  "Horus, son of Isis".

Ḥeru-sa-Ȧsȧr  "Horus, son of Osiris'.

Ḥeru-sa-Ḥet-Ḥeru  "Horus, son of Hathor".

Ḥeru-sekhai 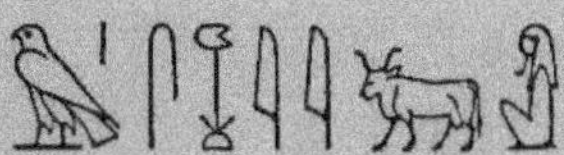

Ḥeru-sheṭ-ḥer an obscure form of Horus.

Ḥeru-Ṭeḥuti "Horus-Thoth".

Ḥeru-ṭesher-merti "Red-eyed Horus".

Ḥeru-shemsu "followers of Horus", or "body-guard of Horus"; a class of mythical beings.

Ḥeru ṭāṭāf a son of King Khufu who "found" certain Chapters of the Book of the Dead.

ḥerset crystal.

ḥeḥ million, a number past counting; plur. , . Two millions (?) .

ḥeḥui . . . .

ḥeḥ en sep a million times, millions of times.

millions of festivals.

ḥeḥ . . . .  the land of millions of years.

ḥeḥ 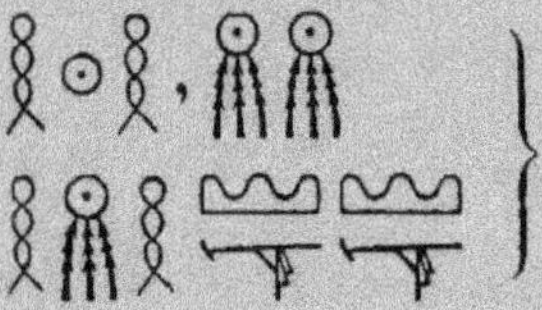 eternity, everlastingness.

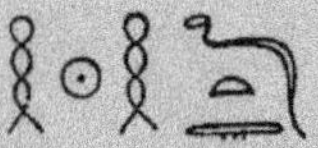 for ever and ever.

Ḥeḥi 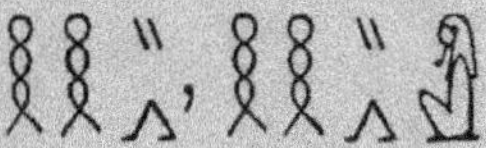 the name of a god.

ḥeḥi 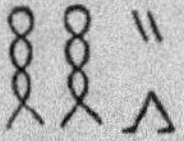 to hasten after, search for; 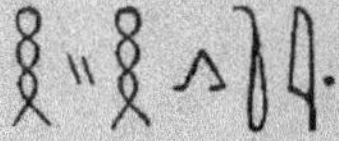.

ḥes 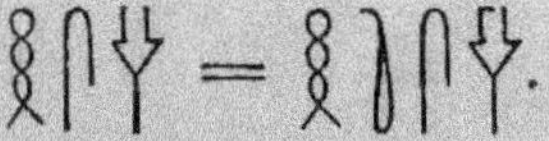.

ḥes 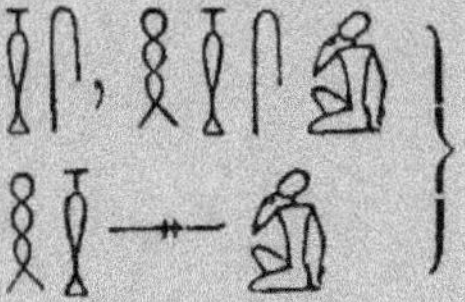 to praise, be praised, to give a reward as a sign of praise;  praised.

ḥesu

ḥeset  favour, act of grace, the gift of praise.

 favours, praises.

ḥesi  he to whom favour has been shewn by the king or god.

ḥesiu — plur. of preceding.

ḥesuiu

ḥesu — a hymn of praise; the 70 hymns of praise of Rā.

Ḥest — name of a very ancient goddess.

Ḥes-ḥer
Ḥesi-ḥer — "savage face"; a proper name.

Ḥes-tchefetch — "savage eye"; a proper name.

ḥesu — dirt, filth.

ḥeseb — faïence (?).

. . . .

ḥeseb  to count up, reckon, estimate, calculate;   reckoned up.

ḥesbet  a reckoning, an account.

 computer of holy offerings.

ḥeseb qeṭu 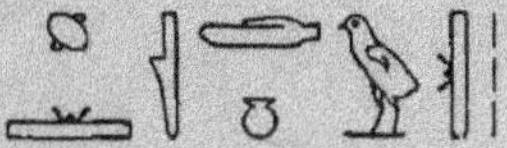 he who estimates characters or dispositions.

ḥeseb ..... 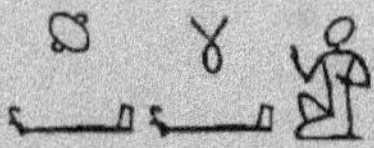 accountant of the linen cloths.

ḥesbet 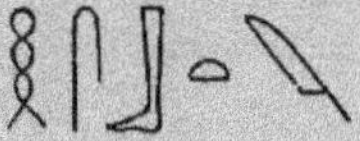 knife (in the passage 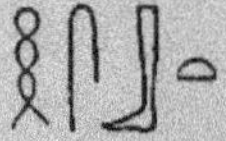 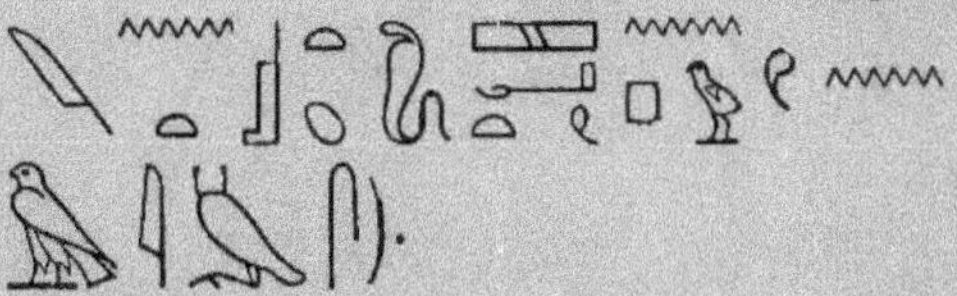).

ḥesepu 
ḥespu  nomes.

ḥespet 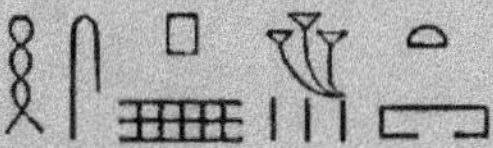 gardens.

Ḥesepti 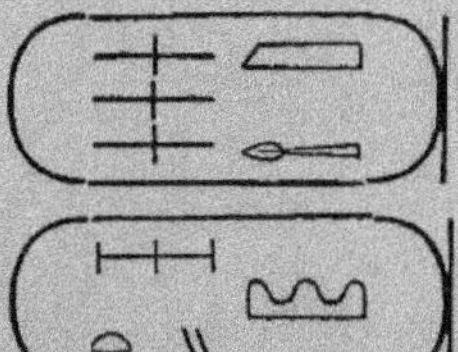 a king of the 1st dynasty. The true reading of this name is Semti, *q. v.*

ḥesmen — natron.

Ḥesert — the name of a town sacred to Thoth.

ḥesq — to cut, be cut, cut off, to wound, to mow. — cut.

ḥesqet — knife.

Ḥest — the name of a city.

ḥest — libation vase.

ḥekau — incantations, enchantments, magical formulae, charms, amulets.

ḥekat

[*ḥeken*] — to praise.

ḥekennu — a hymn of praise, praise.

— praises, songs of praise.

 those who praise, singers.

ḥekennu  an unguent or salve.

Ḥekennut  the name of a city.

ḥeq  to rule, give commands.

ḥeq  ruler, governor; plur. .

ḥeqet 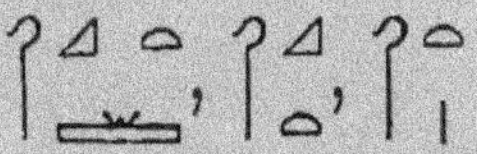 rule, sovereignty, dominion.

ḥeq 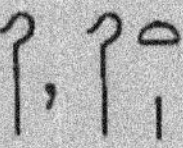 sceptre, emblem of rule.

 ruler of Ȧmenti.

 governor of towns.

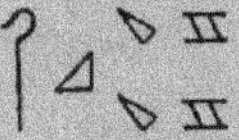 governor of the Two Lands.

 governor of the world.

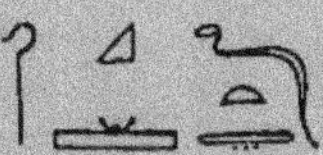 governor of eternity.

Ḥeq-ānṭ — the XIIIth nome of Lower Egypt (capital Heliopolis).

Ḥeq-Maāt-Rā setep-en-Åmen — prenomen of Rameses IV.

ḥeq, *ḥeqt* — ale, beer.

ḥeqr — to be hungry.

ḥeqr — hunger.

ḥeqr, *ḥeqråu* — hungry man.

Ḥeqtit — a goddess.

ḥet — to rejoice.

ḥet — house, section of a book, chapter. Compare the Arabic بيت *bêt*, couplet, stanza, portion of a poem. first section, , etc.

ḥet		house, temple; plur. 
Ḥet-ȧāḥ		House of the Moon-god.
Ḥet-Ȧsȧr	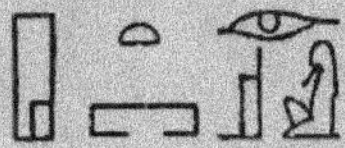	House of Osiris.
Ḥet-Ȧmen	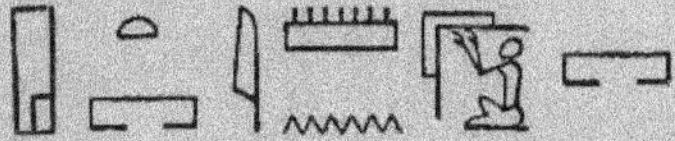	the Hidden House.
Ḥet-Ȧnes		House of the Ȧnes garment.
Ḥet-āshemu	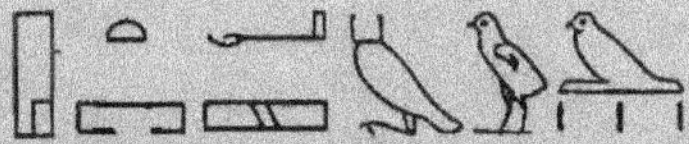	House of the statues of the gods.
Ḥet-ur		House of the Prince.
	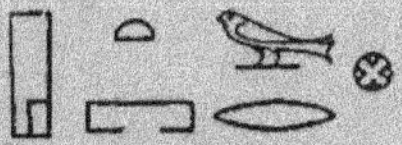	city of the Prince.
Ḥet-uhem-ḥer		House of the Face Renewer.
Ḥet-Usekh-ḥer	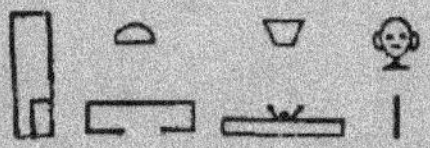	House of Broad-face, *i. e.*, Rā.
Ḥet-Ba		House of the Soul.
Ḥet-Bȧti		House of the king of the North.
Ḥet-Benbent	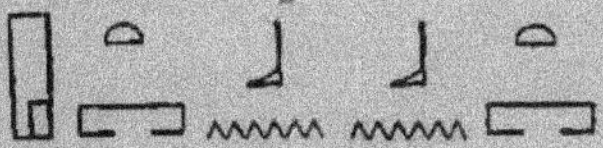	House of the Obelisk.

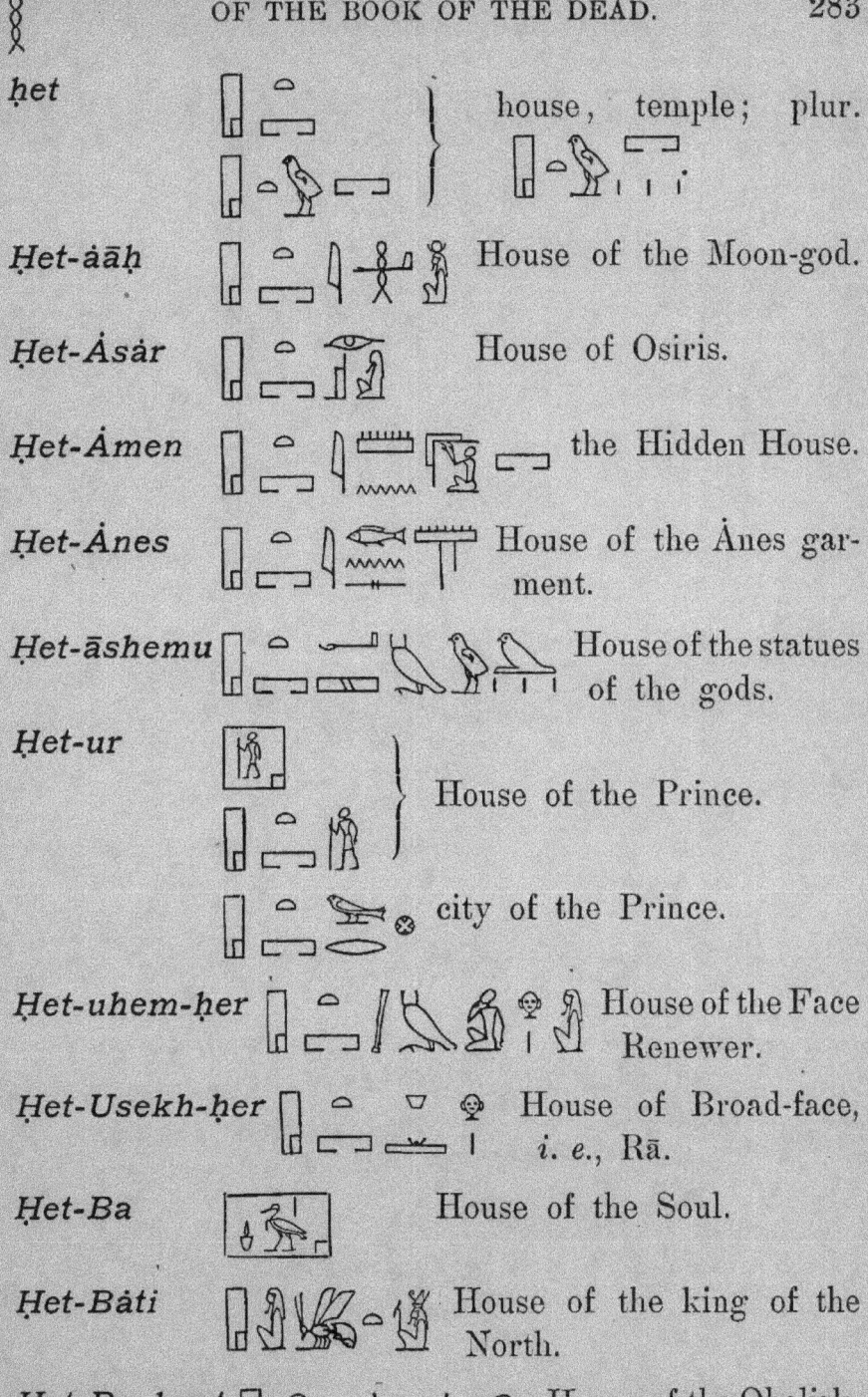

Ḥet-ka-Ptaḥ  House of the Ka of Ptaḥ, *i. e.*, Memphis.

Ḥet-nemt 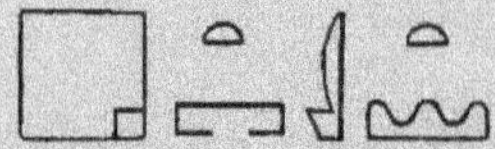 House of the . . . . .

Ḥet ent Ȧnpu  House of Ȧnpu.

Ḥet ent ḳem-ḥeru 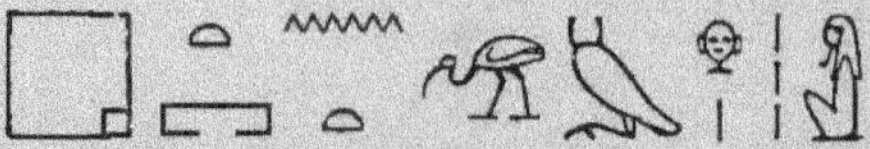 House of the gods who have . . . . their faces.

Ḥet-nub  House of gold, *i. e.*, sarcophagus.

Ḥet-nemes 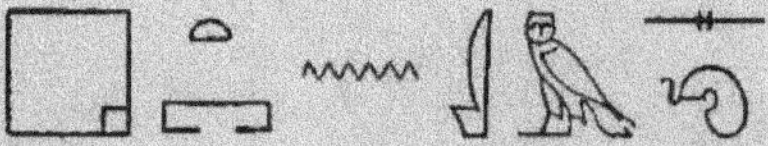 House of the Nemes tiara, or headcloth.

Ḥet-Ḥeru  House of Horus, *i. e.*, the goddess Hathor.

Ḥet-Kheperȧ  House of Kheperȧ.

Ḥet-seru  House of the Ram-gods.

Ḥet-kau-Nebt-er-tcher 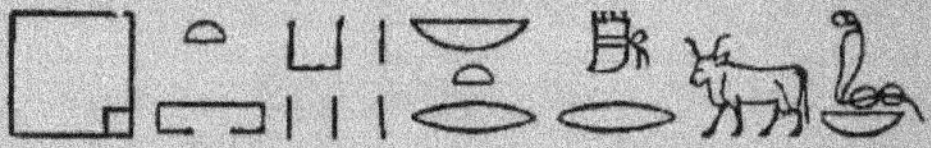 House of the Kau of the Universal Lady.

Ḥet-ṭesheru 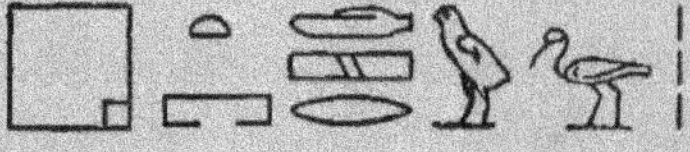 House of the red-gods.

ḥeti 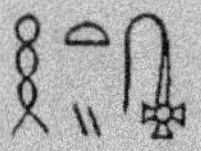 smoke.

ḥeti 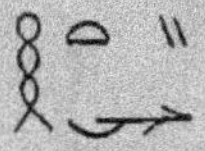 a wooden pole.

ḥeti  heart.

ḥeti 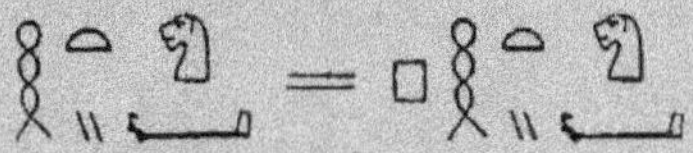 strength.

ḥeti  throat, gorge.

ḥetit  throat, gorge.

ḥetep 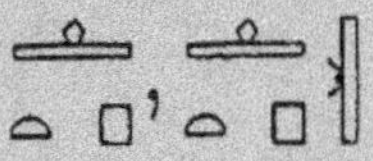 to be at peace, to rest, be satisfied or content, to be at peace with anyone, to remain in one place, to set (of the sun);  satisfied, content;  setting in life, *i. e.*, alive when setting; 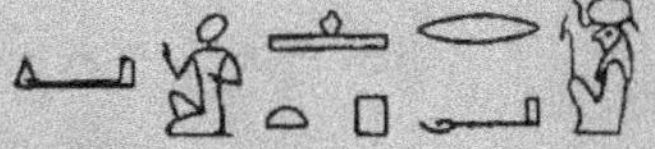   "I make Rā to set like Osiris, and Osiris to set as Rā sets".

ḥetep
ḥetepu  peace, content;  peace of heart;  at peace on truth, or resting on truth.

in peace;

ḥetep — a table of offerings.

ḥetep, *ḥetepet* — food which is offered to the gods and the dead.

ḥetep neter — offerings, sacrifices, temple property in general.

ḥetep, *ḥetepet* — offerings of cakes, ale, oxen, fowl, etc., offerings of propitiation.

Ḥetep — the god of offerings; plur.

Ḥeteptiu  gods who are regularly provided with offerings.

Ḥetep  the town of the god Ḥetep.

ḥetepu  geese.

Ḥetep-mes  a proper name.

Ḥetep-Ḥeru-ḥems-uāu  a proper name.

Ḥetep-sekhus 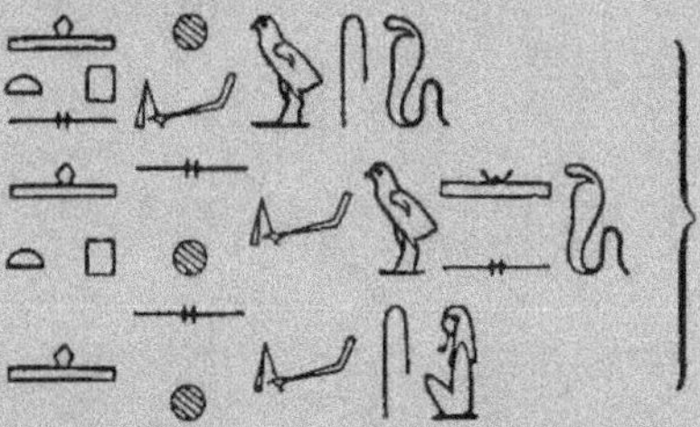 the name of a goddess.

Ḥetep-ka 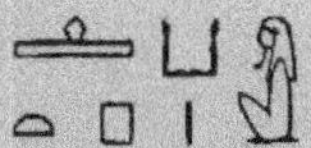 a proper name.

Ḥetep-taui  a proper name.

ḥetem  to destroy, be destroyed.

ḥetemu  destroyers.

ḥetem	to be filled with, provided with; provided.
Ḥetem-ur	"great destroyer"; name of a god.
Ḥetemt-ḥer	"destroying face"; name of a god.
ḥeter	to pay something which is obligatory, legal due, something like tithe.
ḥetru	impost, tax.
ḥetes	to be lord of.
ḥeṭeṭ	scorpion.
Ḥeṭeṭ-t	Scorpion-god.
ḥetch	to do evil, to plunder, steal, waste, destroy, filch away.
ḥetchet	theft, wickedness.
ḥetch	white metal, silver.
ḥetch	to be bright, to shine.

ḥetch ta 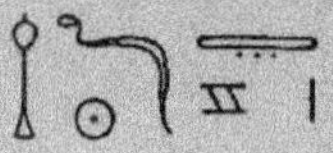 dawn, daybreak.

ḥetchu  light.

Ḥetch-ȧbeḥu 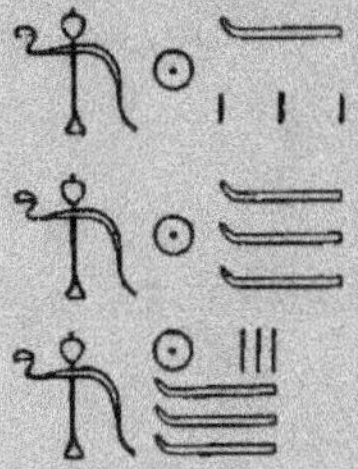 "White teeth"; the name of one of the Forty-two Judges in the Hall of Osiris.

Ḥetch-re 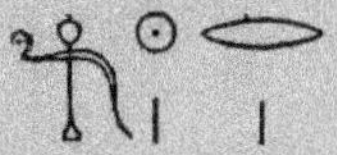
Ḥetch-re-pesṭ-tchatcha  a proper name.

ḥetch-ḥetch  light.

ḥetchet 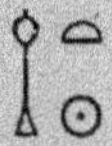 white.

ḥetchet  the White Crown, or Crown of the South.

ḥetchti 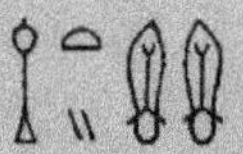 white sandals.

ḥeṭṭ  light.

ḥetchu  loaves.

ḥetchas  . . . .

KH.

kha one thousand; two thousand; plur.

kha chamber.

kha, ***khat*** the material body, dead body; divine corpse; plur.

khaā to set aside, cast away, to throw.

khāā emissions.

khaām to hasten.

khaāmt throat.

khaibit shade, shadow; plur.

khaitiu slaughterers.

khau  fire.

khaut  fire-altar, altars for burnt offerings.

khaut  festival of burnt offerings.

khau  evil, sin.

khau  basins, bowls.

khau  to be plentiful, abundant.

khaui  darkness, night.

khaut  fiends, the dead.

Khau-tchet-f  a proper name.

khabesu 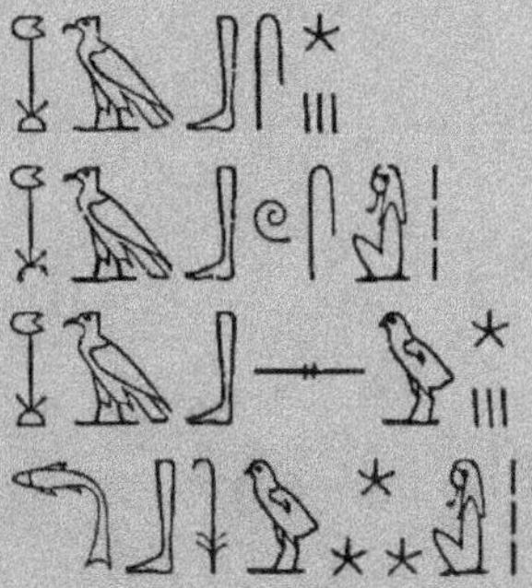 the stars, the thirty-six dekans; the sing. is .

khabet fraud, deceit.

khapa a portion of the body, the navel; plur. buttocks (?) *pudenda muliebris* (?) thighs (?).

Khap-khap a part of the sky, the god of the Ecliptic (?).

kham to subdue, be submissive.

khamesu ears of corn.

khart, ***kharu*** a kind of bird with a piercing cry.

Kharsatȧ a proper name.

khakh to seek, run after.

swift.

khasu the lower eyelids.

khasi 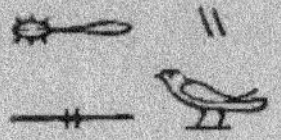 bad, evil, wicked, cowardly.

khast  territory, country. Perhaps the reading of 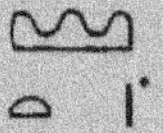.

khak-ȧbu  the timid-hearted, enemies.

khaker  to be decorated, pretty.

 ornaments, decorations.

Khatiu 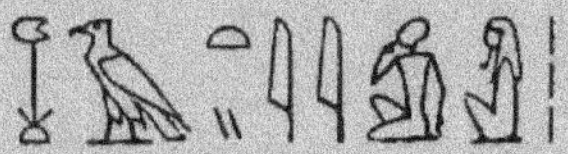 a class of divine beings.

khat 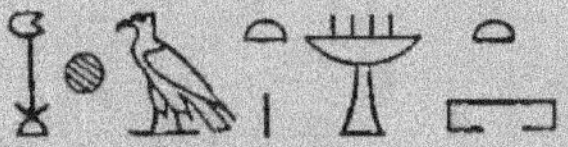 fire altar.

khat 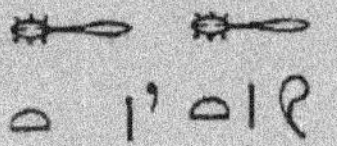 body, belly, womb; 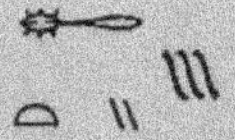  core of the sycamore; plur. 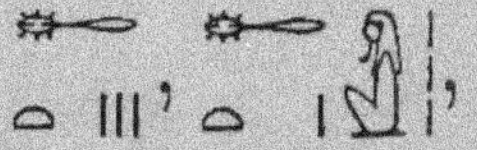 .

khat  the XVIth nome of Lower Egypt (?).

khat  a kind of ground.

khatu  dead body.

 dead bodies.

khatememti  nostrils.

khā, *khāu* 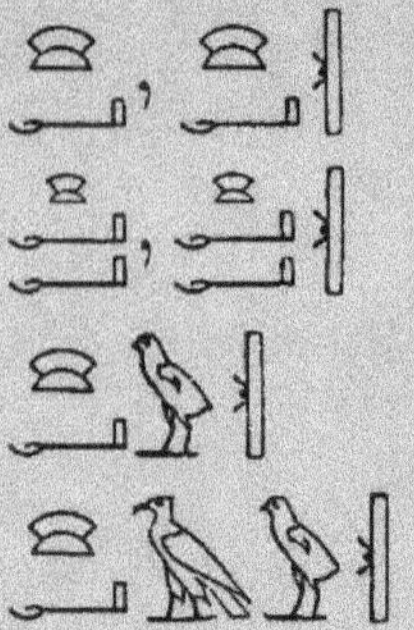 to rise like the sun, to ascend the throne, to be crowned, to appear (of the king or god).  he who rises;  one who rises; 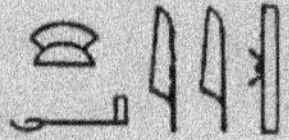 rising;  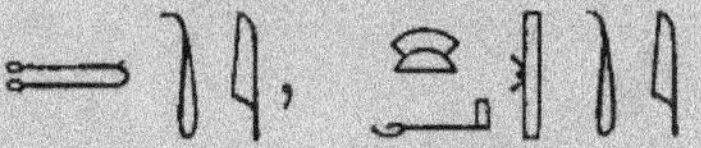 risen, crowned; 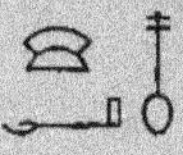 beautiful appearance.

khāu 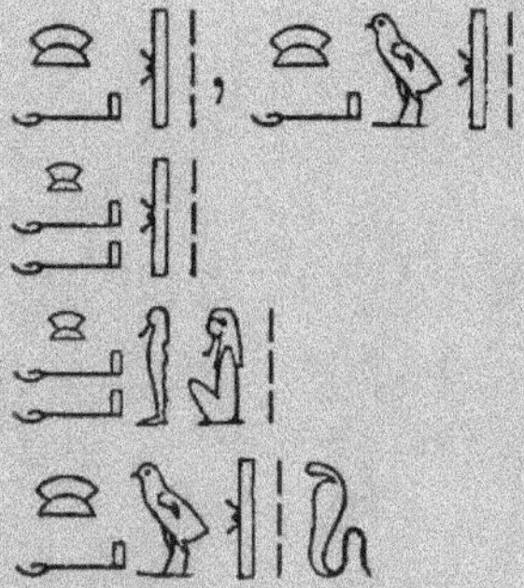 risings, splendours, coronations.

khāu  crowns, diadems.

khāi  crown.

khi 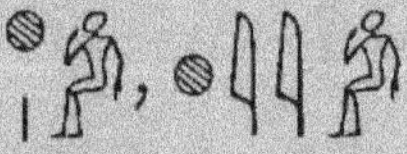 babe, child.

Khiu  the name of a god.

khiuaut  perfume.

khu  to dress.

khu
khui
khaui

to protect, strengthen, to do good to.

khu
khut

protection.

khu

the spirit soul of man which was immortal, as opposed to the  or heart soul which fed upon offerings and lived with the Ka.

the equipped soul.

the perfect soul.

khu

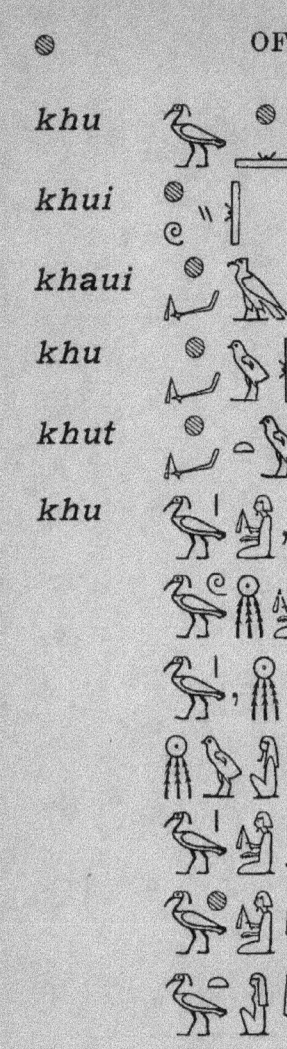

plur. of preceding. Four Khu and Seven Khu are mentioned, and certain of the Khu were nine cubits high.

khu  the spirit soul of Osiris, or Rā.   is a title of Osiris.

khu  to shine, be glorious.

khu / ***khut*** 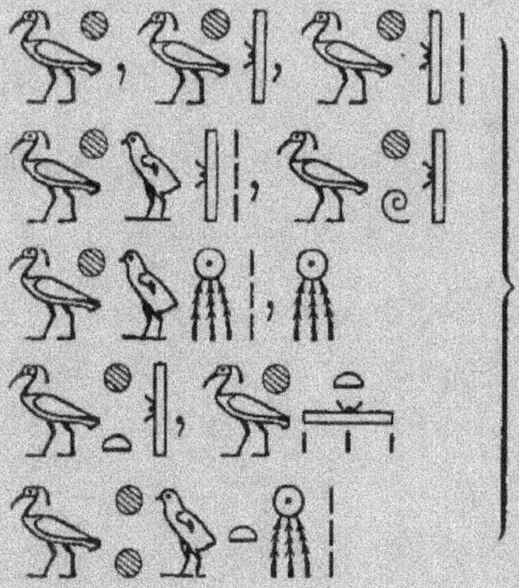 glory, splendour, radiance, brilliant things, light.

khu  words of power.

khut  the name of a light-goddess.

Khu-kheper-ur  a proper name.

Khu-tchet-f 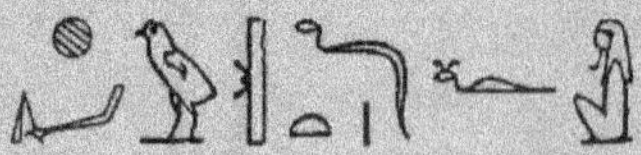 a proper name.

khunt 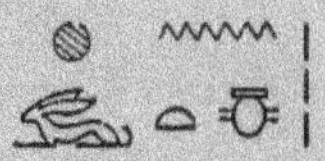 drink offerings.

khus  to construct a building, make a cistern.

khut  fire.

khut  the place in the sky where the sun appears on the horizon in rising or setting, the horizon.

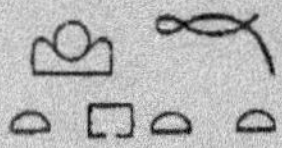 northern horizon.

 western horizon.

 eastern horizon.

 the horizon of the mountain of sunset.

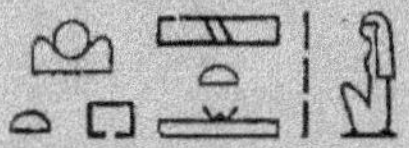 the hidden horizon.

khuti  the gods or beings of the horizon.

khui  words of power.

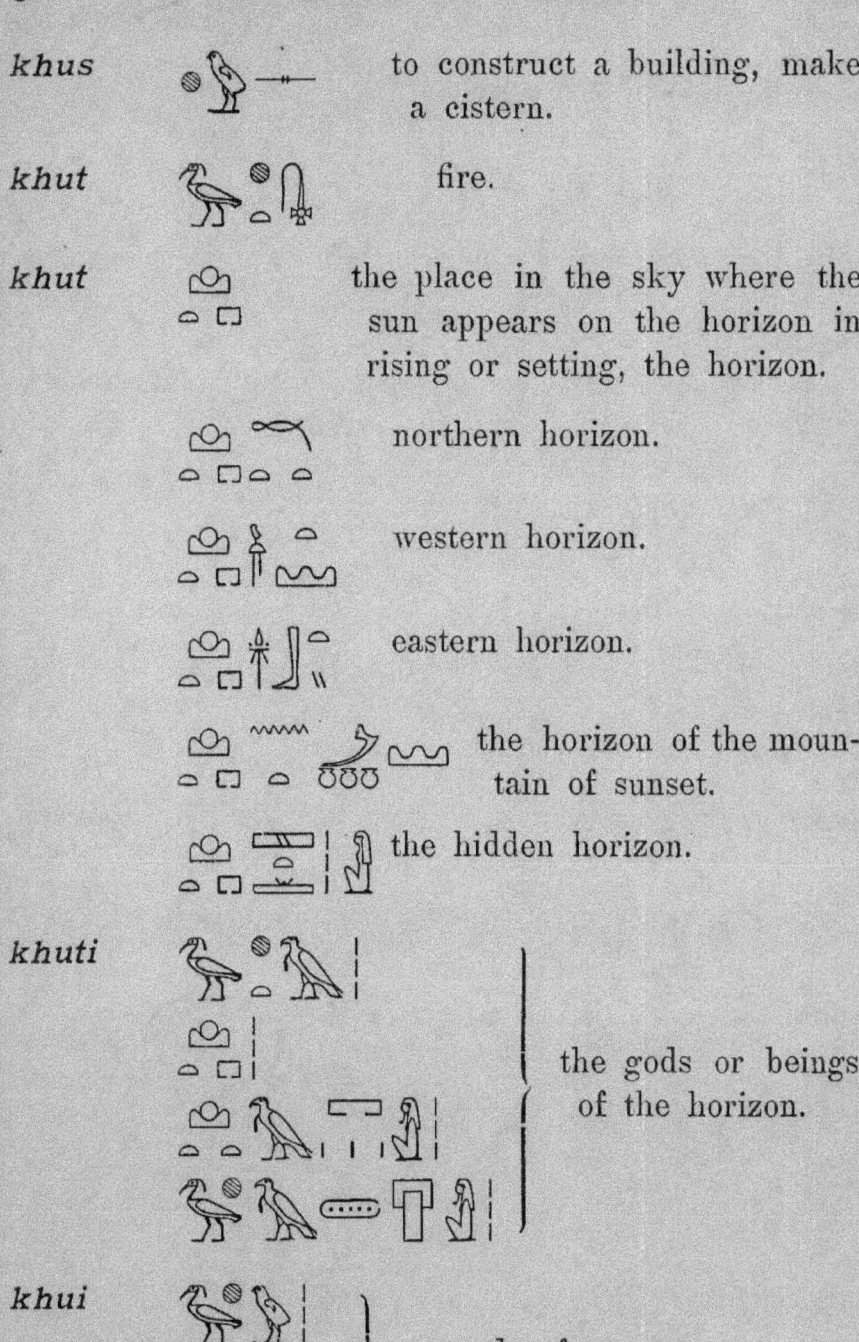

kheb 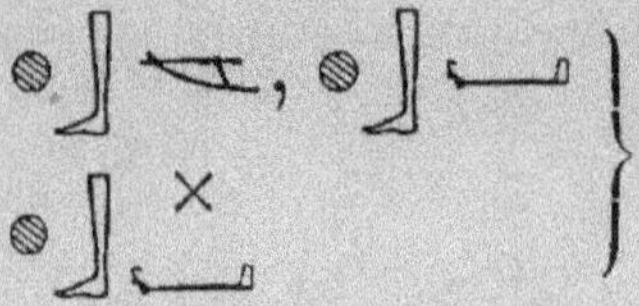 to defraud, pilfer, steal.

kheb  slaughter.

kheb 
khebȧ  to be defeated, overthrown.

khebu  defeat, defeated ones.

kheba  to destroy.

khebu  to be dipped into some liquid, steeped.

Khebent  a proper name.

khebent  evil, wickedness.

khebenti  evil doers.

khebkheb  to destroy.

khebkhebt  destruction.

khebkheb  torture chamber.

khebs 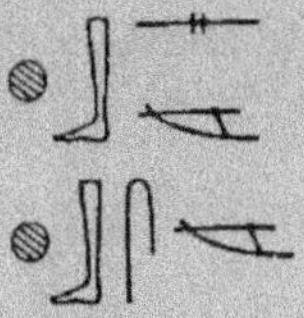 to plough;  plougher.

khebs ta  the ceremony or festival of ploughing the earth.

khebsu  devourer (?).

khebs 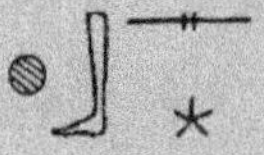 star, lamp.

 stars, the Thirty-six dekans.

khebt  loss, injury, damage; 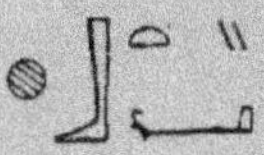 destroyer.

khebt 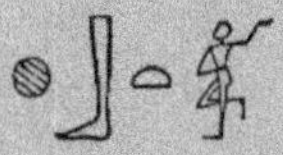 dance.

khebt 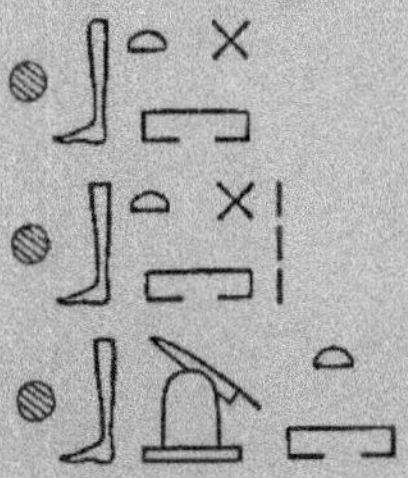 torture chamber, slaughter house.

khep 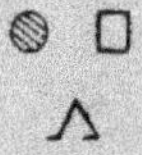 to travel, journey.

khept  journey.

khep  a part of the body, navel (?).

khepu 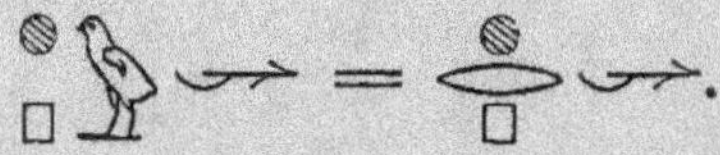

Khepiu 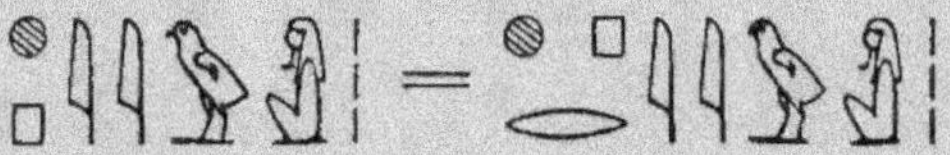 the gods who are.

kheper, *kheperu* 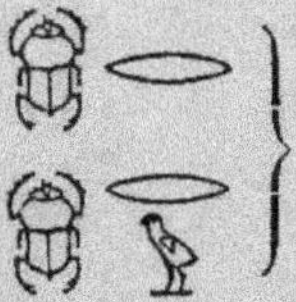 to come into being, become, exist, subsist, to turn into something, to create, to form, fashion; 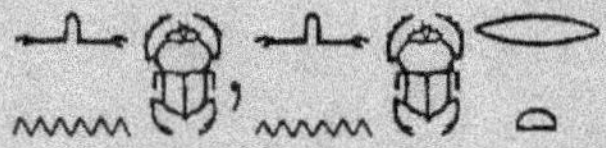 non-existent; 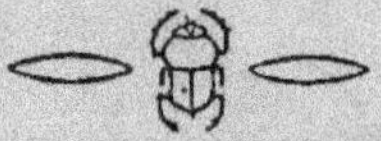 when takes place, when it happens;  to be or become satisfied;  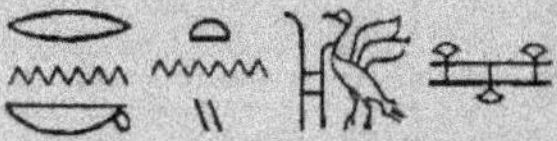 is thy name what?  those who become.

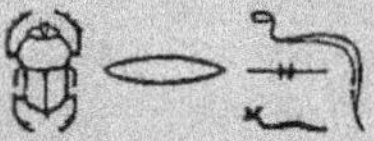 self-created.

khepert 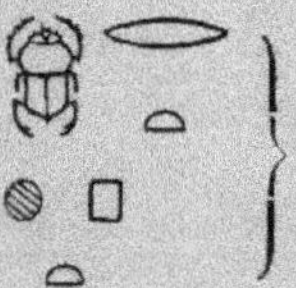 that which is, what exists, thing.

kheperu — form, phase of being, something evolved, transformation, change.

kheperu — forms, transformations.

kheperut

kheper — scarab, beetle.

kheprer

Kheperȧ / *Kheperrȧ* (?) — the Beetle-god, a form of the Sun-god.

khepesh — thigh; plur.

Khepesh — the constellation of the Thigh.

khept

kheptet buttock; plur. …,

khept …

khefa food.

khefā to grasp, to seize with the hand; …

khefā
khefāt fist, grasp.

khefit quay, river bank.

kheft in front of, according to, conformably to, when.

kheft her opposite to, before the face of.

khefti enemy, fiend.

kheftiu enemies.

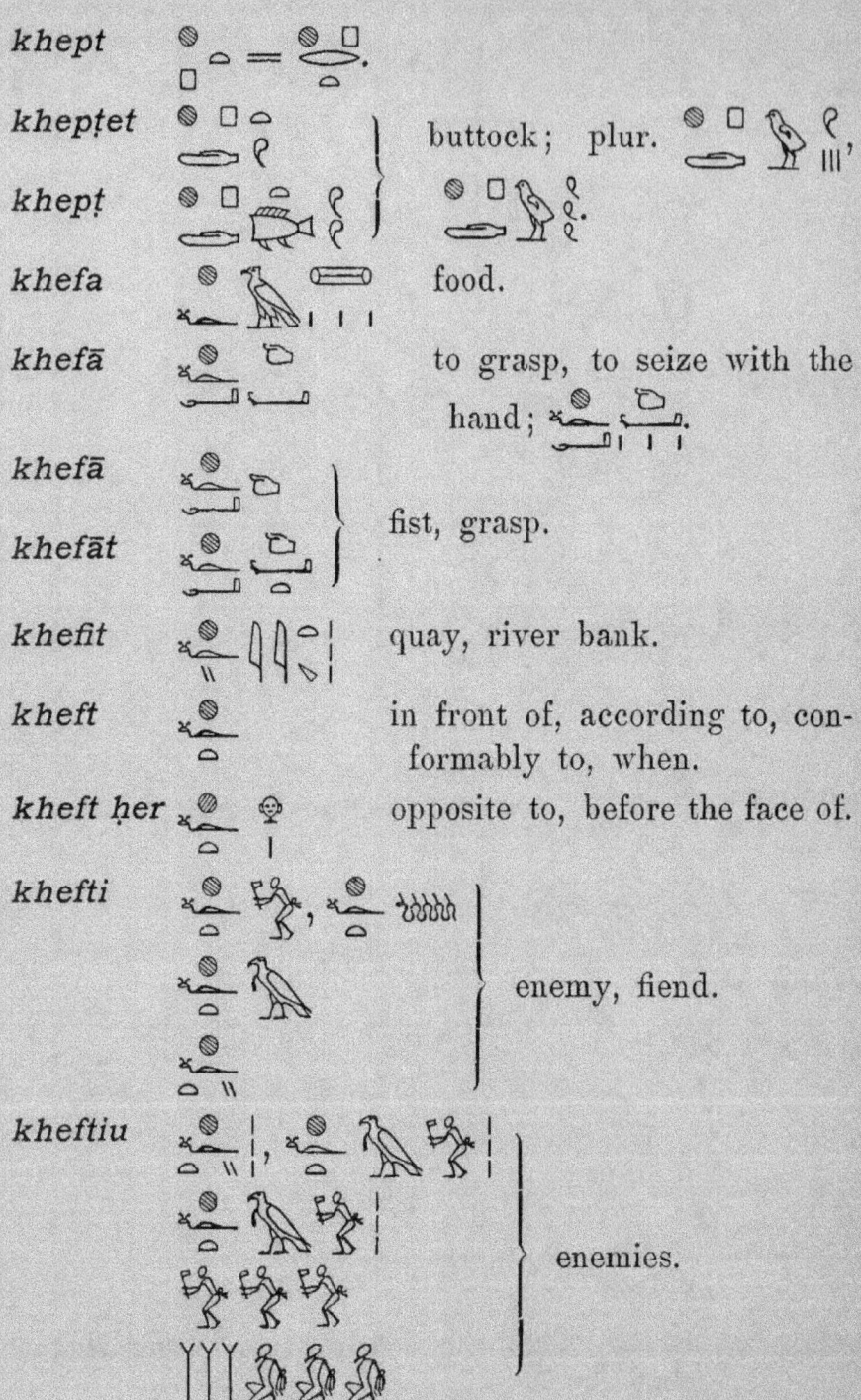

khem  to burn.

khem  shrine.

khem  to be ignorant, to put an end to (?); 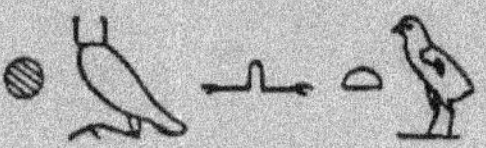 ignorant, helpless; 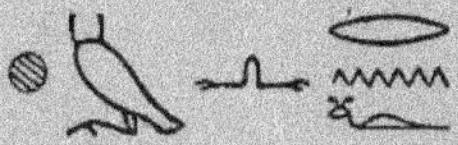 unknown is his name.

khem 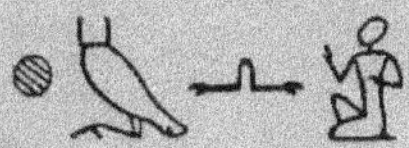 an ignorant man.

khem 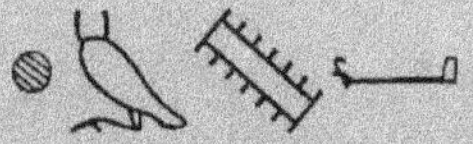  to overthrow, destroy.

khemiu 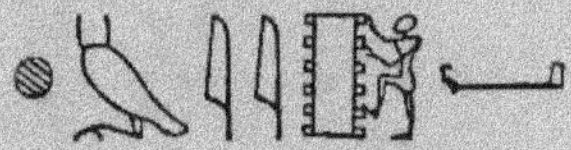  *khemit* 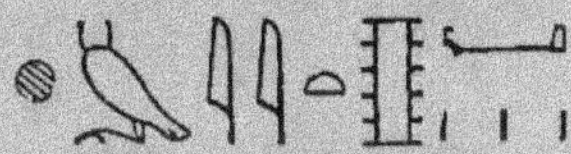 overthrower, those who overthrow, destructions.

Khemi  the name of one of the Forty-two Judges in the Hall of Osiris.

khemā  to lay hold of, to seize and carry off.

khemāu  snatchers, seizers.

khemu  wind, air.

khemenu eight; eighth.

Khemenu the eight gods of the Company of Thoth who dwelt at Hermopolis.

Khemenu the city of the Eight gods, Hermopolis.

khemt three; third.

khemt to think, to know, to intend. is sometimes written by mistake for .

khemt the god of thought.

khen

khenn to hover over, to flutter like a bird when alighting on a tree, to perch on something.

khennu

Khenit the goddesses who fly or dance.

khen 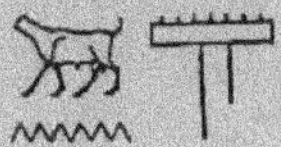 to be dressed, garment.

khen  the inner part of a house, house.

 within.

Khennu  the name of a city in the Sekhet-ḥetep.

khen, *khenn* 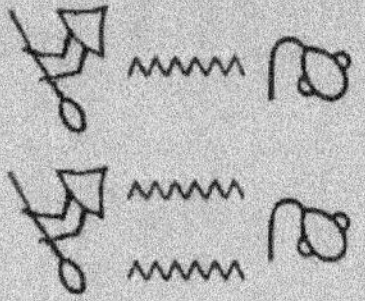 to decay, to rot, to wither.

khen 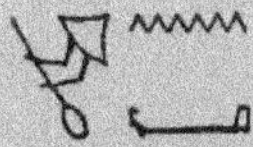 to break, smash, destroy, stir up strife, disturb, trouble.

khennu 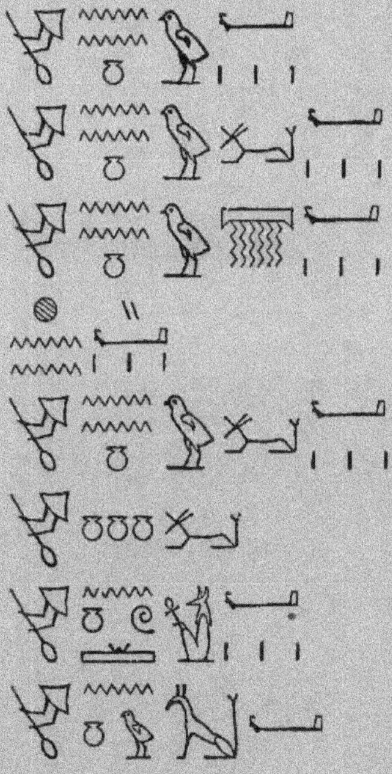 trouble, revolt, destruction, storm, opposition.

khenui  rebels.

khen 

khenen 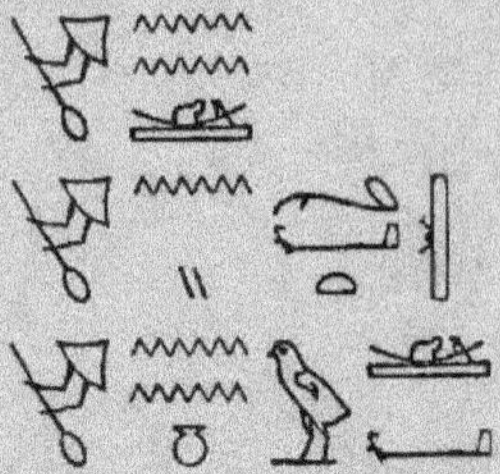 to ferry across a stream, to transport by water, to row, to paddle.

khent  a passage, a journey.

khenen 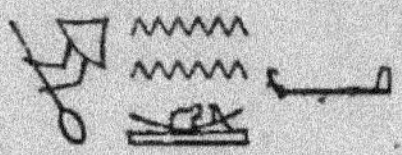 sailor.

khenȧ 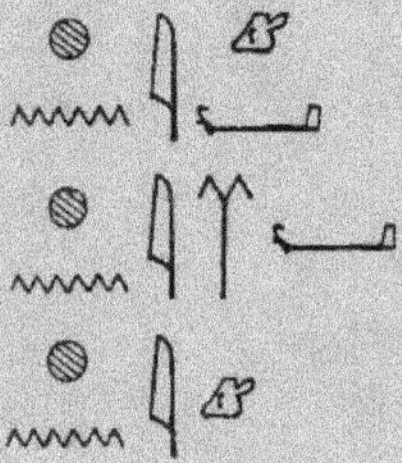 to lock up, shut up, keep in captivity.

khenp 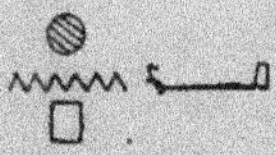 to draw out, pluck out.

 a tearing; 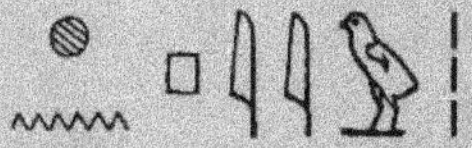 tearers, renders.

khenf  a bread-cake.

khenem  jasper, carnelian.

khnem  to form, join up or together.

Khnem  the god Khnemu, the Potter-god.

Khnemu-Ḥeru-Ḥetep  the name of a god.

khnem 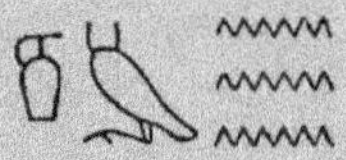 well;  a proper name (?).

Khnemet-urt  a proper name.

Khemet-em-ānkh-ȧnnuit 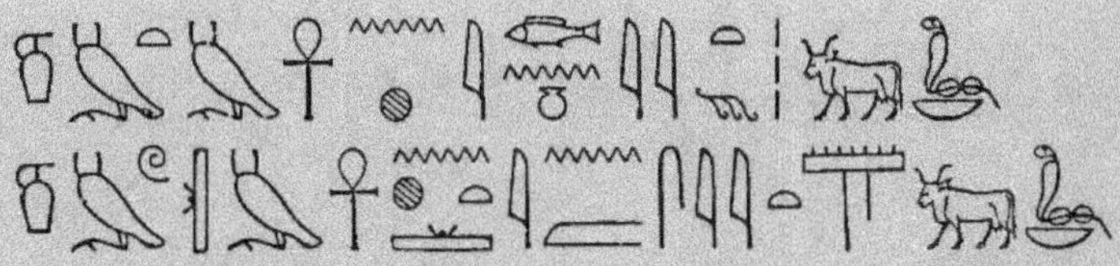 the name of one of the Seven Cows.

khenem 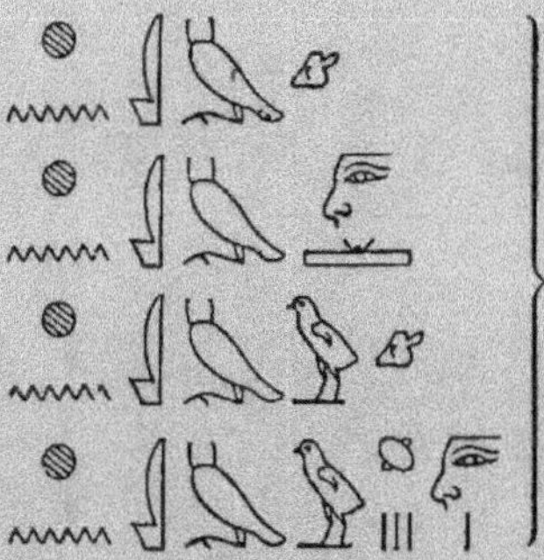 to snuff the air, to smell, scent out.

khenemti  nurse, servant, companion.

khenemu  . . . .

Khenem-nefer 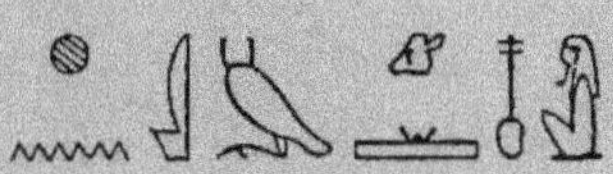 a proper name?

khenemem  to smell, feed upon (?).

Khenememti 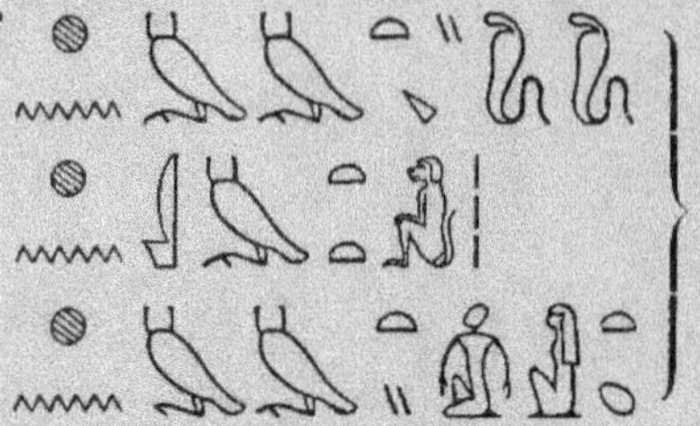 the two ministering goddesses, Isis and Nephthys.

khenemes  protector, friend.

khennu  those who cry out.

khennu 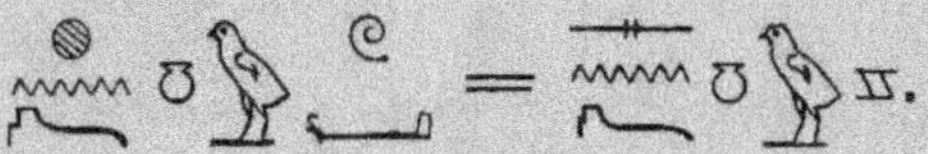

khennu 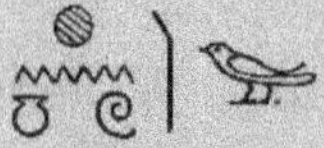 injury, evil hap.

khenrȧ 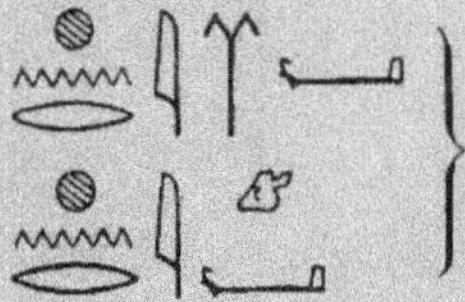 to shut in, imprison.

khenrȧ  fiends.

khenrit 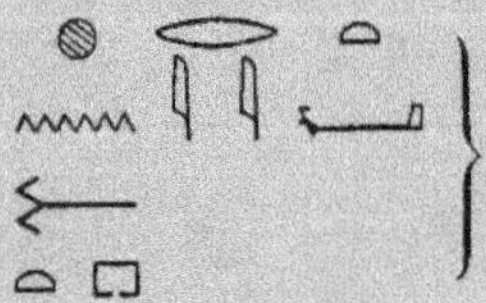 prison.

khens 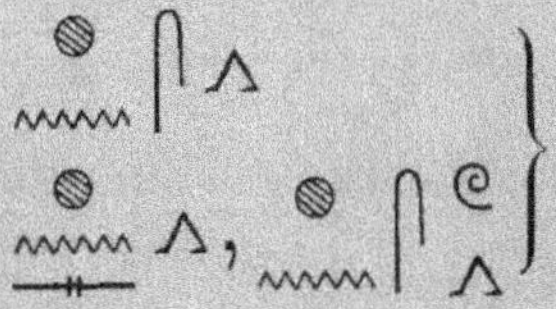 to stride about, to journey, travel.

Khensu  "traveller", a name of the Moon-god.

Khensu-p-àru-sekheru em Uast 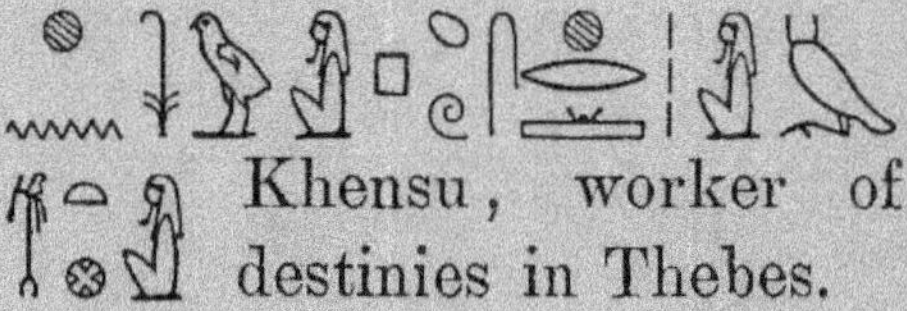 Khensu, worker of destinies in Thebes.

Khensu em Uast Nefer-ḥetepi  Khensu in Thebes, Nefer-ḥetep.

khent 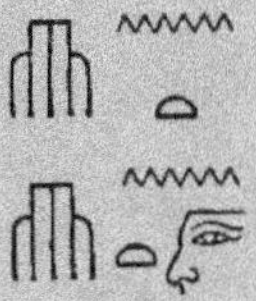 the nose.

khent 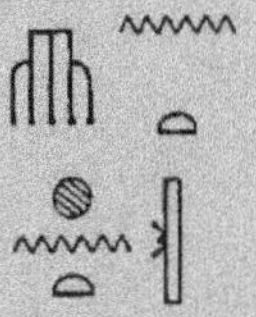 the fore part of anything, the front, in front of, before.

khenti  he who is in front, or at the head, chief, governor.

Khenti Àmenti  He who is at the head of Àmenti and of those who are therein; a title of Osiris.

Khenti Āḥa 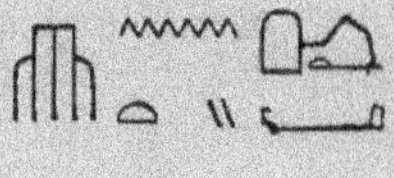 he who is chief of the fighting.

Khenti-aḥāt 

Khenti-āt-àment 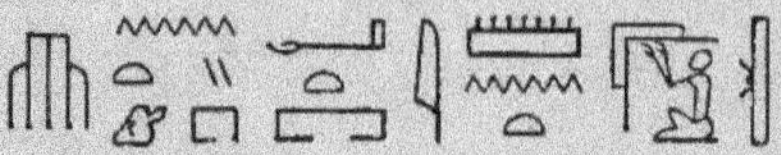 a title of Osiris.

Khenti-Un  a title of Osiris.

Khenti-Peḳu 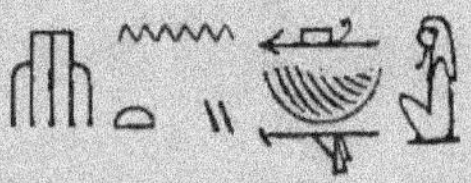 a title of Osiris.

Khenti-menàtuf 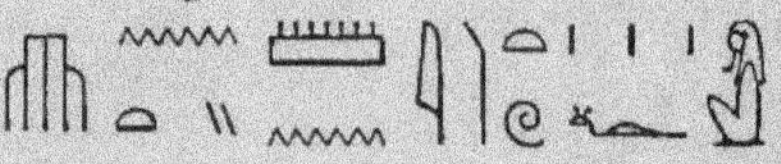 a title of Osiris.

Khenti-Naàreṭ-f 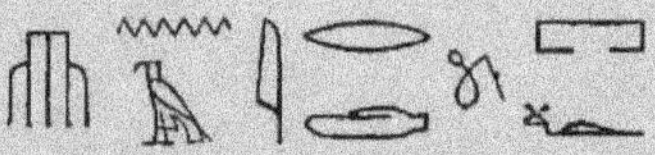 a title of Osiris.

Khenti-nut-f  a title of Osiris.

Khenti-nep  a title of Osiris.

Khenti-n-merti (?) 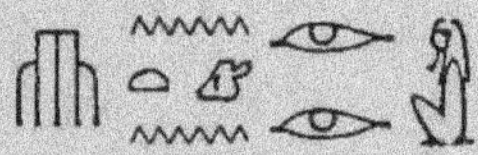 a title of Horus.

Khenti neter ḥet 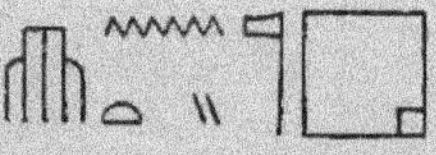 "Chief of the god-house".

Khenti neter seḥ 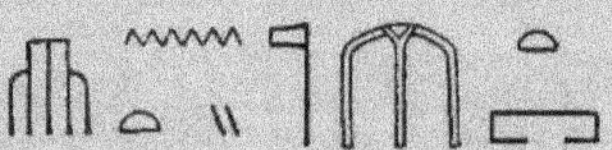 "Chief of the god-hall".

Khenti Re-stau  "Chief of the funerary corridors"; a title of Osiris.

Khenti-hetut-f  "Chief of his fire".

Khentiu ḥensekti 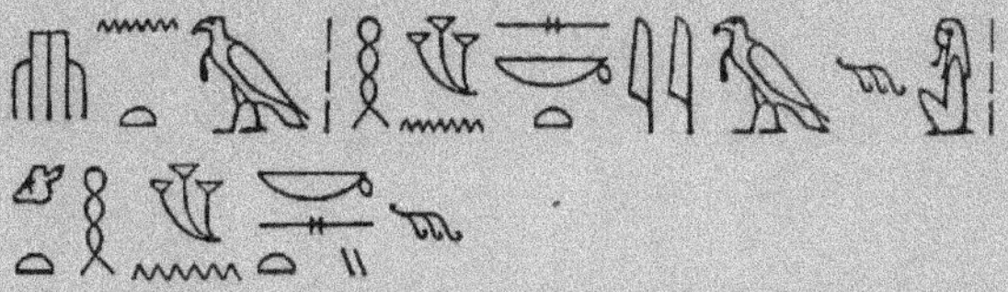 "Chiefs of long hair and beards".

Khent ḥeḥ  a title of Osiris.

Khenti Ḥeq-ȧnṭ 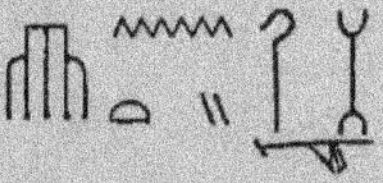 a title of Osiris.

Khenti ḥespu 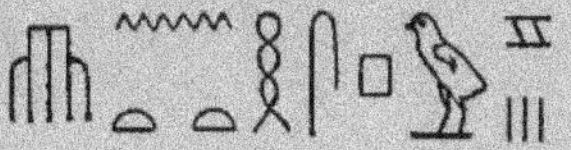 the name of the bows of the magic boat.

Khenti-khas  a name of a god.

Khenti-Khati

Khent-Khaṭti  "the dweller in the belly"; a title of Horus.

Khenti-Suten-ḥenen 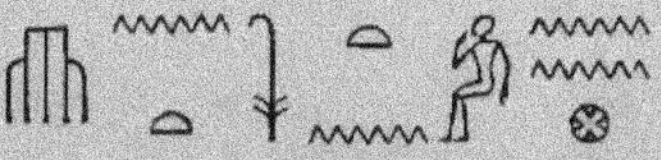 a title of Osiris.

Khenti-Sekhem  a title of Horus of Letopolis.

Khenti-seḥ-ḥemt 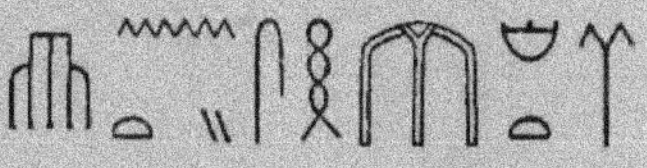 "chief of the house of the wife"; a title of Osiris.

Khenti-seḥt-kaut-f  "chief of the house of his cows"; a title of Osiris,

Khent-she (or *mer*)-*Āa-perti* "chief of the Lake of Pharaoh"; a title of Osiris.

Khenti-Tenent a title of Osiris.

khent abode, the private portion of a palace or temple; plur. , .

khent, *khenti* to sail upstream, usually to the south; .

khentiu sailors.

khenti a mineral colour.

khenṭ to travel, journey.

khenṭi traveller.

khenṭi to ascend.

khenṭ thigh, haunch.

Khenṭ-Ḥepiu name of the steering pole.

khentch to travel.

kher a preposition, with, before, etc.; under the Majesty of, in the reign of.

khert the things of, the affairs of, property of; the affairs of the country; the business of the Two Lands.

kher under, beneath; things or beings who are below.

under the favour of.

before.

kheri low-lying land, the earth as opposed to the sky; plur.

kheru  men and women in subjection, serfs, vassals, or perhaps the tillers of low-lying lands.

kher 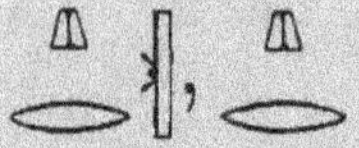 to have, hold, possess. 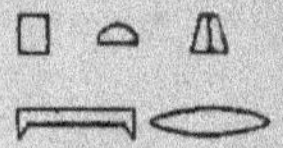
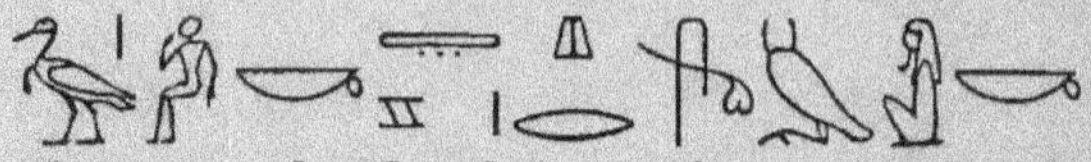
"heaven hath thy soul, earth hath thy form".

khert 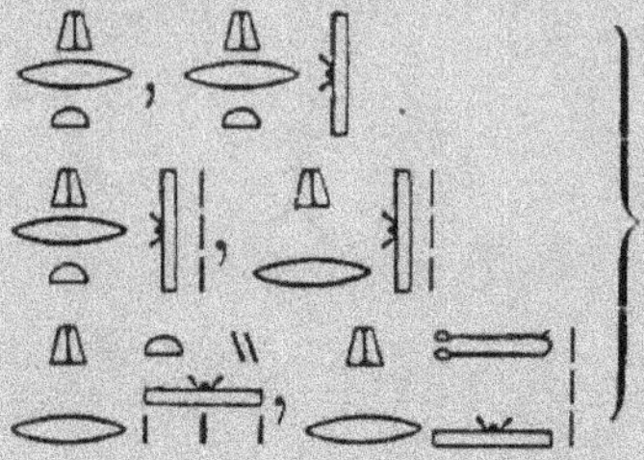 goods, possessions, share, portion, lot, what belongs to someone, property, wealth, products of.

khert hru  the things of the day, what belongs to the day, daily round or routine.

 every-day matters.

kher
kherui 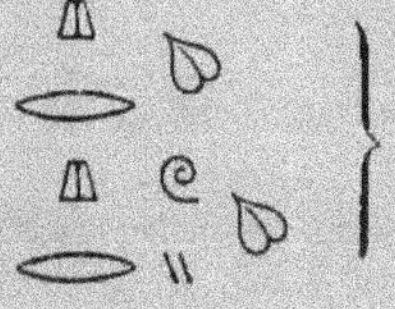 testicles.

kher 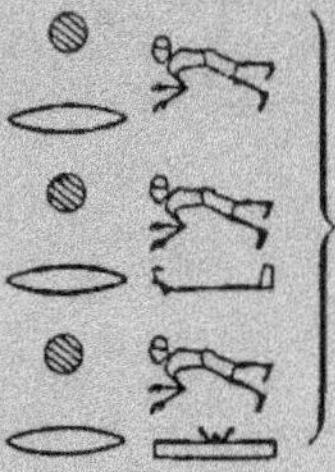 to fall down, to happen.

kheri 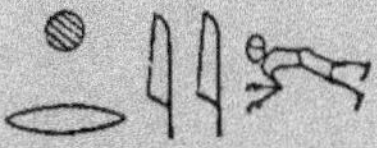 fallen one, foe.

kherit 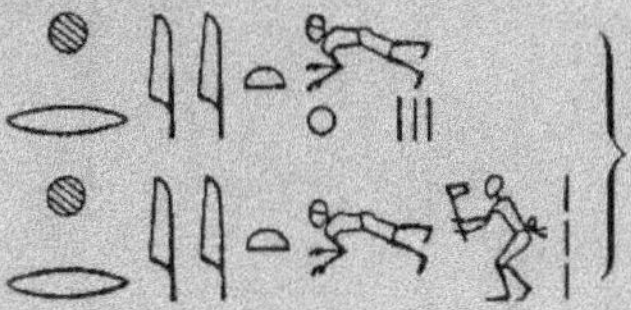 the dead, the damned.

kherit 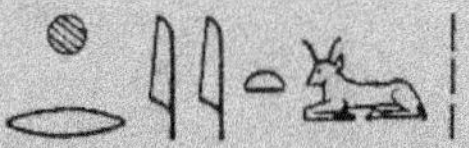 victims for sacrifice.

Kher  the name of a god.

Kherȧ  a proper name.

kheru 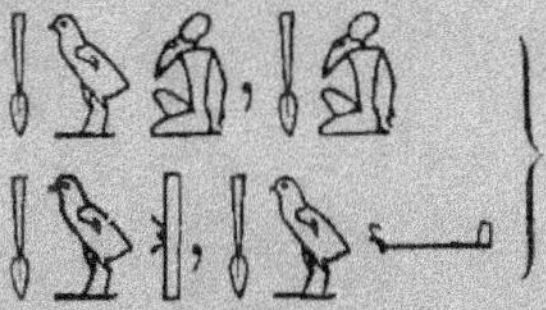 voice, word, speech, sound; plur. 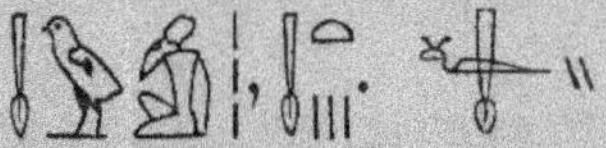 reading unknown.

 loud-voiced.

 a man's voice.

 multiplying the sound of words, *i. e.*, talking overmuch.

kheriu  enemies, hostile attacks.

Kher-āḥa  a city near the site of the modern Fusṭâṭ, or Old Cairo.

kherp  to be chief or master, to direct, be in command, to present an offering.

Kherp  Prince, Chief; plur. .

Kherp-nest  title of a priest.

kherpu  steering pole.

kherefu  two Lion-gods.

kher ḥeb 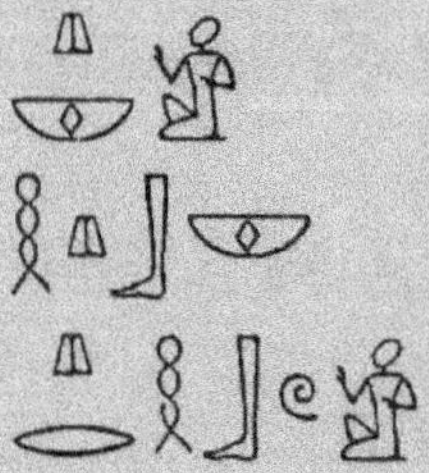 the priest who recited religious compositions and the Liturgy.

Kherserȧu  a proper name.

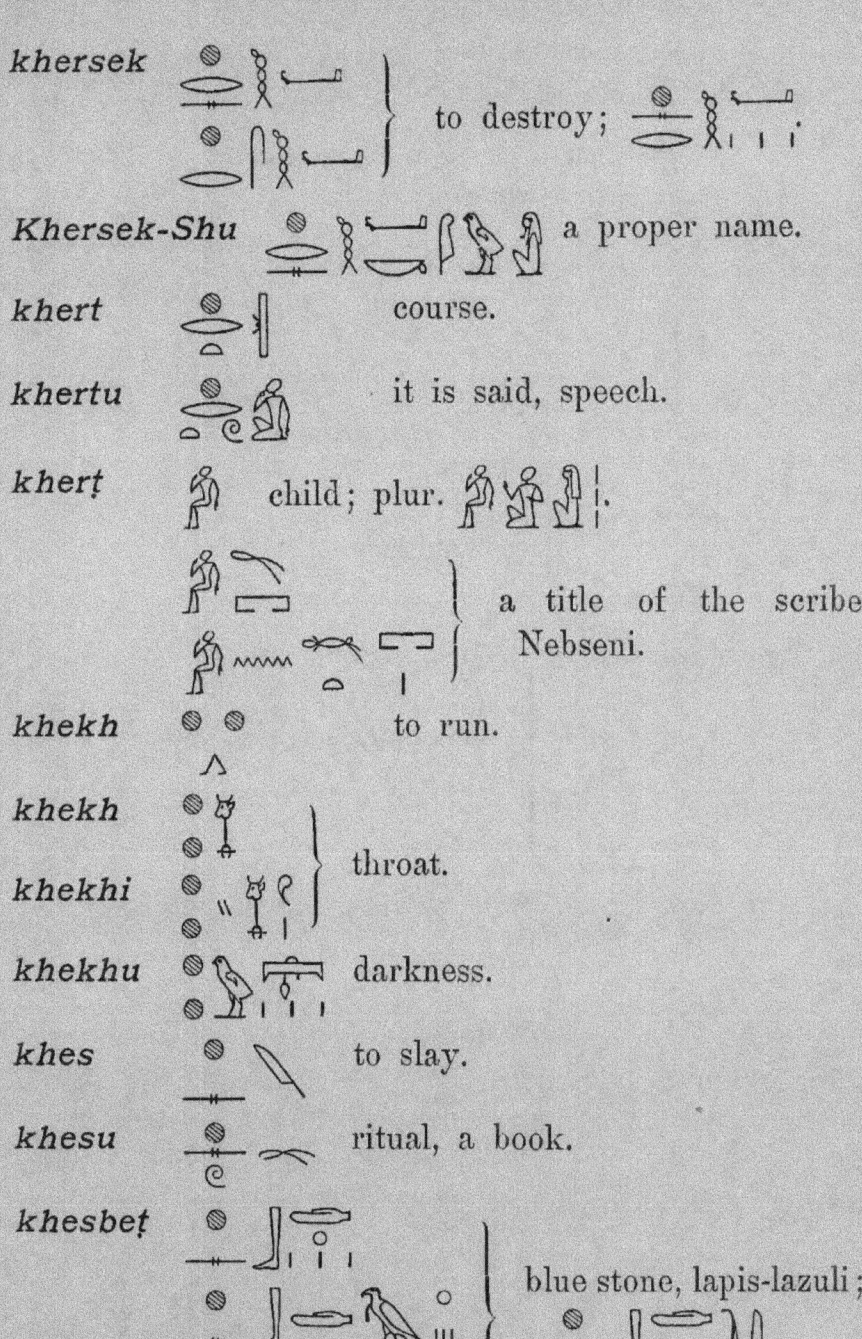

khersek to destroy;

Khersek-Shu a proper name.

khert course.

khertu it is said, speech.

khert̩ child; plur.

a title of the scribe Nebseni.

khekh to run.

khekh
khekhi throat.

khekhu darkness.

khes to slay.

khesu ritual, a book.

khesbet̩ blue stone, lapis-lazuli;

real lapis-lazuli as opposed to blue paste.

blue-eyed.

khesef to meet, to oppose, to drive back, repulse; repulse; irresistible.

khesef-ā

kheseft repulse.

khesefu adversaries, foes; hostile faces.

bowings down before.

Khesef-aṭ a proper name.

Khesef-ḥer-āsh-kheru a proper name.

Khesef-ḥer-khemiu the name of the herald of the Seventh Ārit.

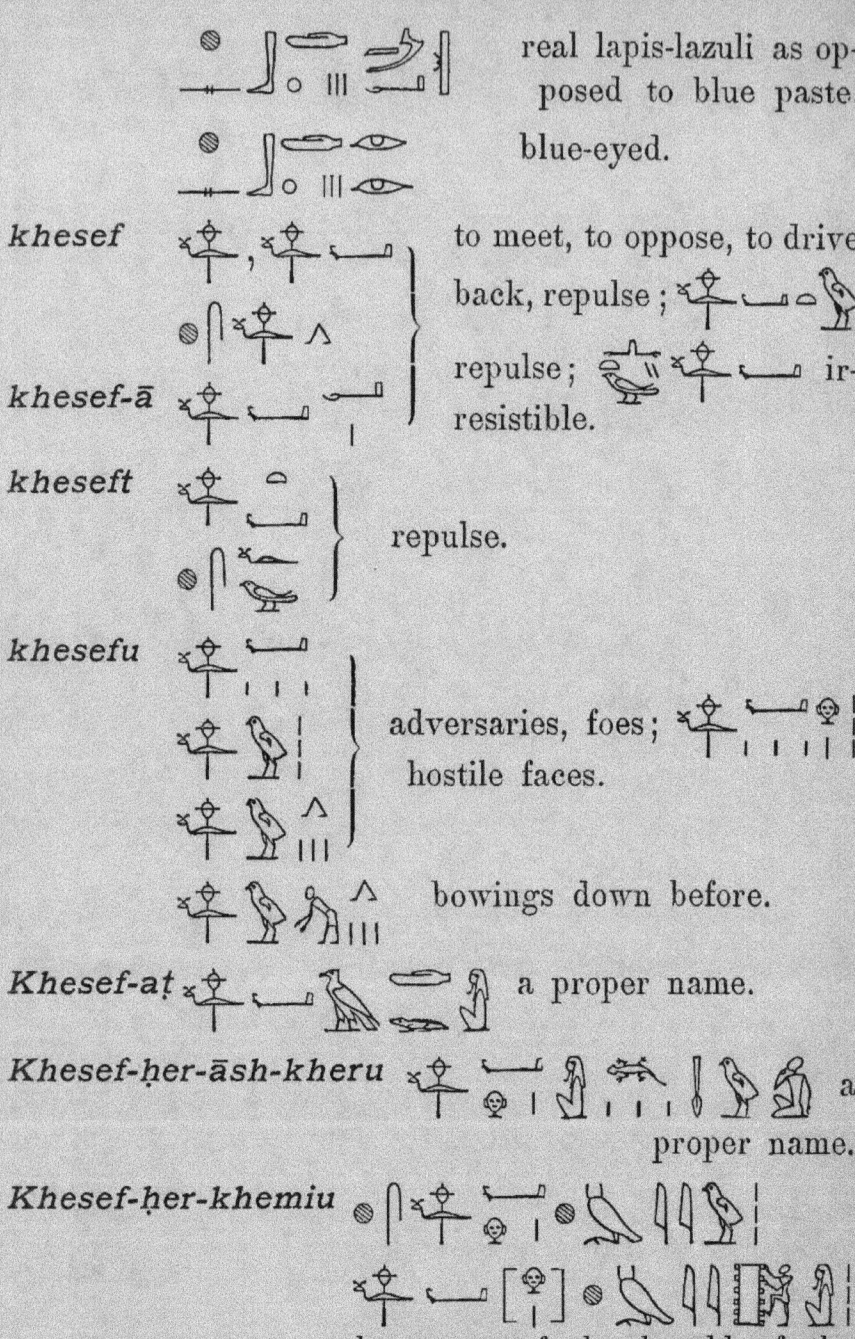

Khesem 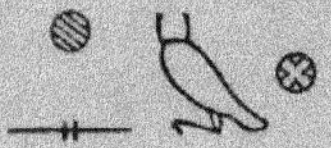 Letopolis.

khesṭeḥ 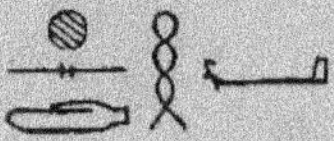 to destroy.

khet  steps, throne.

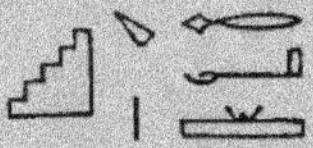 great stairs of Osiris.

khet 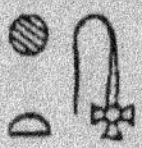 fire, flame.

khet  wood, tree, stick, staff, sceptre, board; 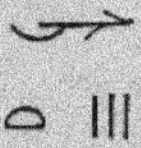 planks of a ship; 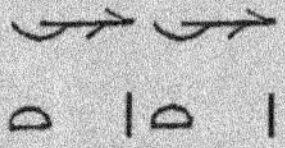 rod.

khet 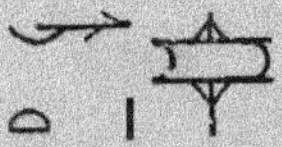 mast.

khet 
khetkhet 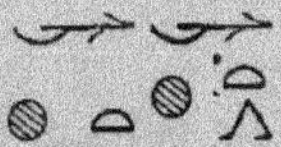 } to retreat, go back.

khet 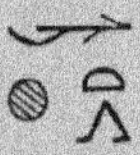 back, behind.

 behind, in the following of.

 followers.

khet 
khetu 
 } to write, to cut on wood or stone; ,  cut, engraved.

khet  things, affairs, cases, goods, property.

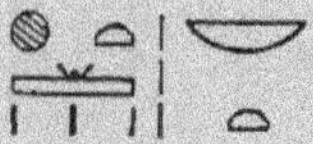 everything.

 all sorts of bad things.

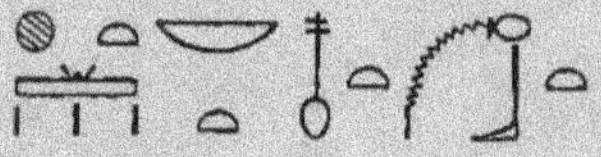 everything beautiful and pure.

 all most beautiful things.

 sweet things.

 everything bad and evil.

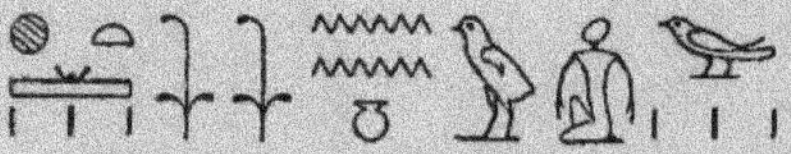 weak things.

 things about Osiris.

 things on the altars.

 things of Horus (*i. e.*, offerings, property of).

 things (offerings) of the night.

 things of the festal altars.

 things of his father Osiris.

 things of the Eye of Horus.

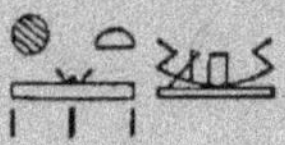 things of the Boat.

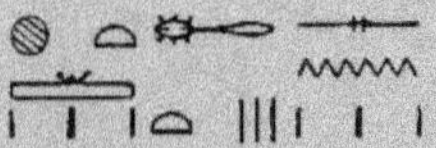 their personal things.

khetu 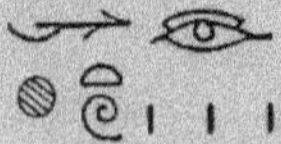 . . . .

khetita  fiends, devils.

khetem  to shut in, to seal, close the door on; 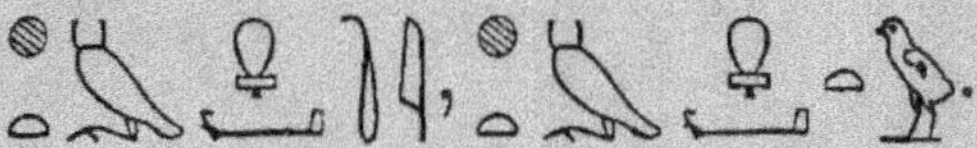

khetemiu  those shut in.

khetemit  closed place, prison.

kheṭ 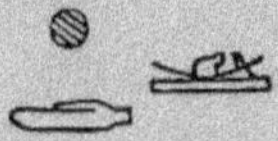 to float down stream.

kheṭebet 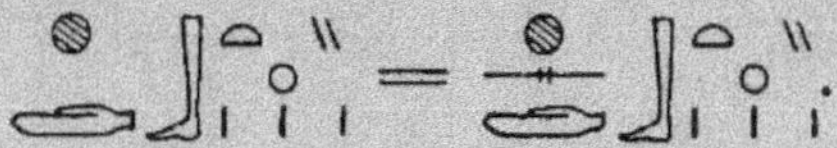

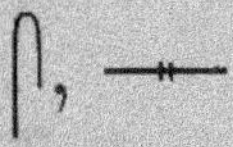 S.

s 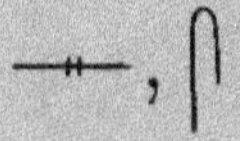 her, she, its; 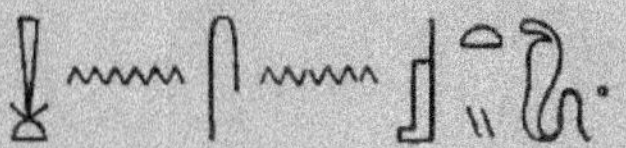

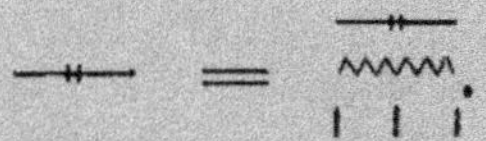

sa  person, man, one.

 everyone, everybody.

set  woman.

sa  son.

 son of Rā.

 firstborn son.

sat  daughter.

 daughter of Rā.

sati  the two divine daughters, *i. e.*, Isis and Nephthys.

Sa-mer-f 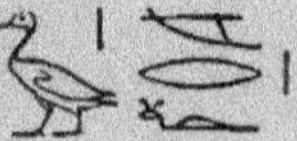 "Son loving him"; title of a priest.

Sa-pa-nemmȧ  a proper name.

Sa-ta 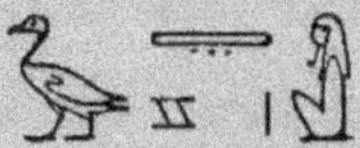 "son of the earth"; the name of a serpent.

sa  side, back.

 in the side.

 afterwards.

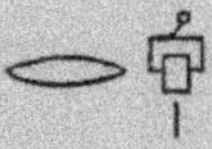 behind.

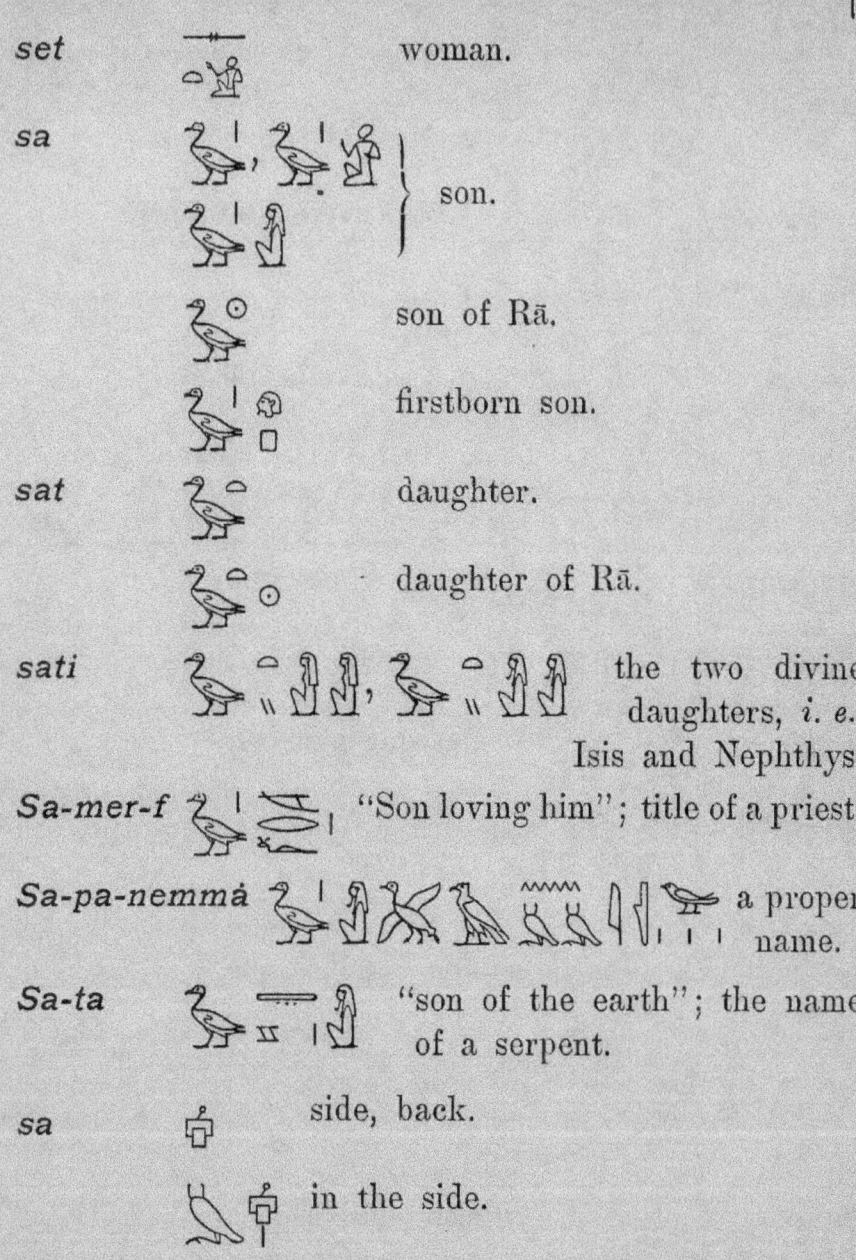

 after.

 by the back.

sa 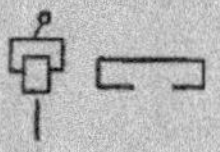 chamber (?).

sa  to protect, a thing which protects, amulet; plur.  as a protection. See .

sa  to perceive, know, recognize.

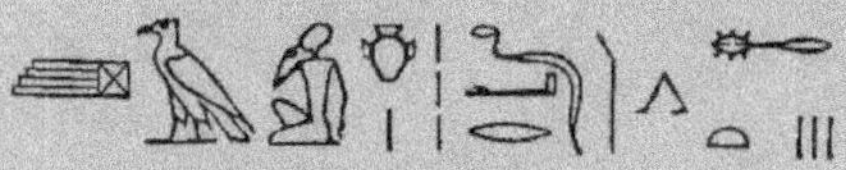 knower of hearts, trier of reins.

sauu  wise man.

Sa, *Sau*  the god of knowledge.

Sa-Åmenti-Rā  a proper name.

Saau-ur  a proper name.

Saa  "shepherd"; a name of Osiris.

sau 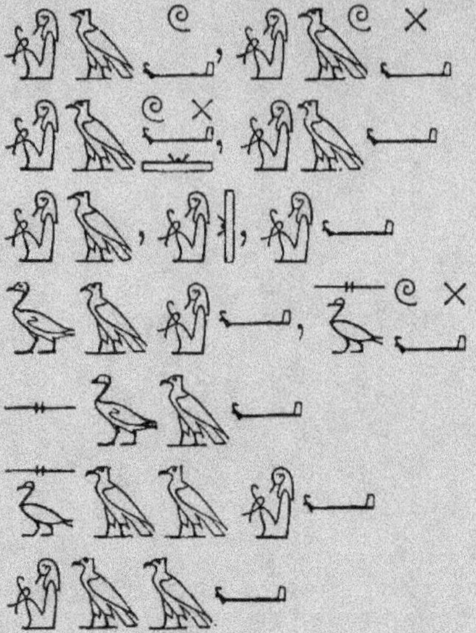 to watch, keep guard over, protect, keep in restraint; to tend sheep.

sau, sai  watcher, guardian, shepherd.

 plur. of preceding.

 people in fetters.

 watchers, warders, fetterers, fetters.

sait restraint, ward.

sau corruption.

Sau the city of Saïs.

Upper Saïs.

Lower Saïs.

saāiu evil ones (?).

s-au to make glad, to provision.

wide goings, journeyings.

sauṭ to transfer.

sab making to cease.

sab jackal; plur.

Sab (?)
Sabȧ the name of a god.

Sabes the herald of the Second Ārit.

sam to consume, burn up.

Samiu a group of gods or fiends.

samiu the gods with hair.

samut hair.

samit tresses, hair.

Saneḥem the city of grasshoppers.

saneḥemu grasshoppers.

Sar Osiris.

saru order of dismissal (?).

sariu evilly disposed persons.

saḥ to journey, to travel.

saḥt journey.

saḥ an estate, farm, homestead.

saḥ fingers, toes, claws.

Saḥ  Orion.

Saḥ-en-mut-f 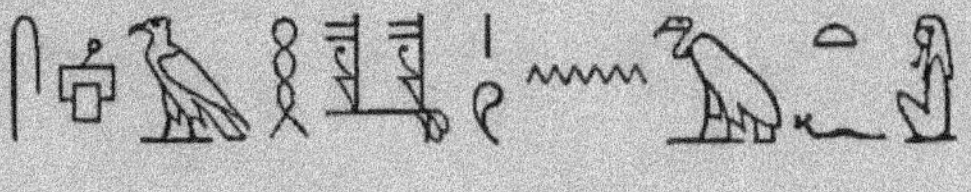 a proper name.

saq  to collect, gather together.

Saq-baiu  "collector of souls"; the name of a boat.

Saqnaqat  a proper name.

sat 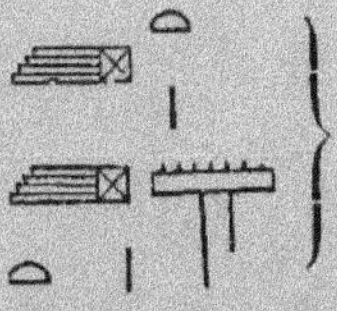 apparel, garment, robe, dress.

sat  to think scorn of the god.

sat  evil, evil one.

satu  wall, building.

sat  earth, ground, floor of a chamber.

sati  threshold.

Satiu	the city of Siut, the modern Asyûṭ.
saṭu	terrors.
Sȧ	the name of a town and of a god.
Sȧa	the god Sa.
Sȧa	the name of a town and of a god.
Sȧu	to cry out.
sȧat	to encroach, attack.
Sȧatiu	slaughterers. ; plur.
sȧu	to drink water.
sȧbit	animals for sacrifice.
sȧb-kui	to make to weep.
sȧp	to judge, decide, compute, reckon up, examine, inspect, inquire into; , judged, computed.

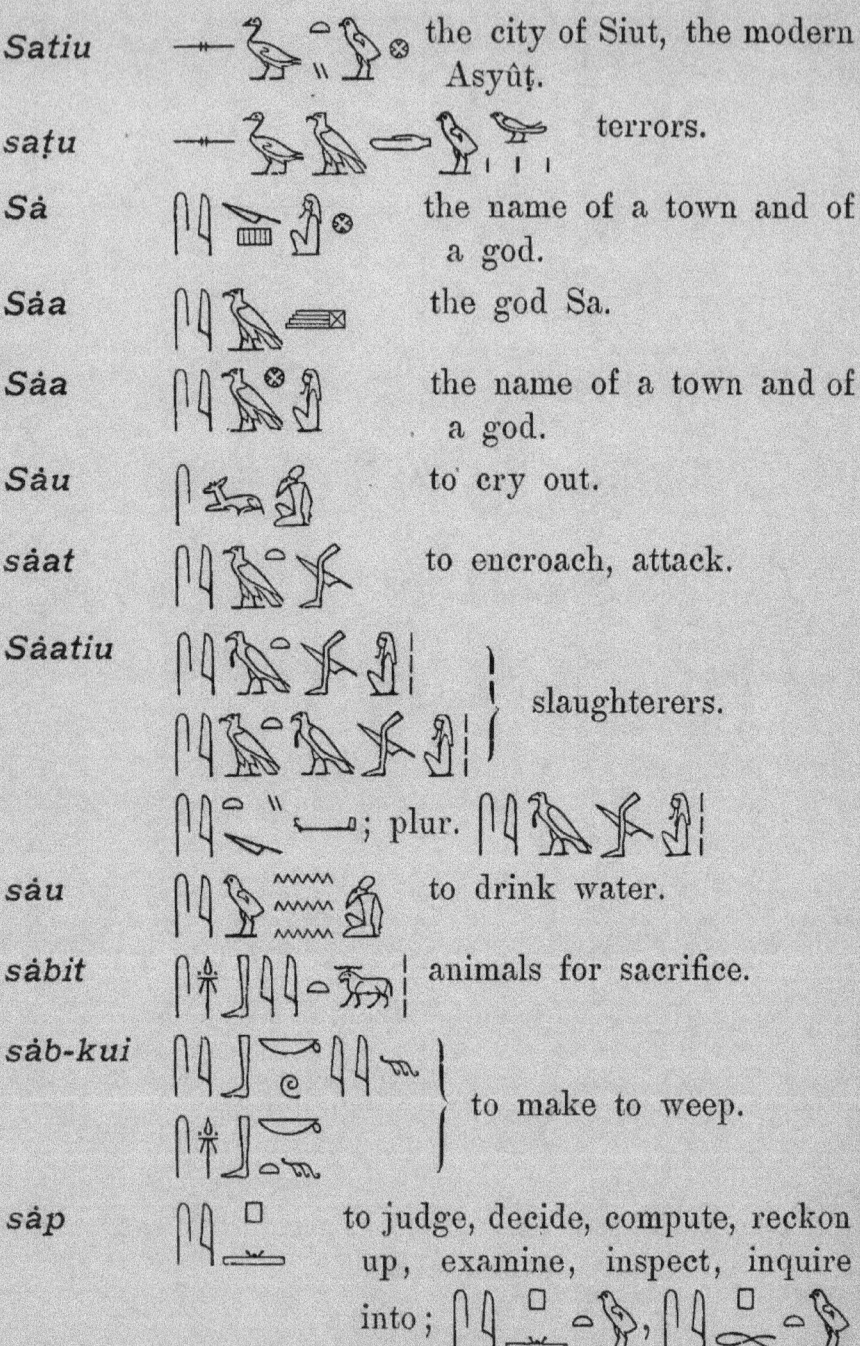

sȧpu judge, judgment; plur.

sȧp account, reckoning, a list of goods, property.

sȧpti

Sȧp the name of a god.

sȧpt abode of the god Sȧp.

sȧm (sȧam) to shew kindness.

sȧn length, extent.

sȧn to be kind, do good to, benefit, nourish; things which benefit.

sȧn clay.

sȧn to walk, march, pass along.

sȧn to pull, draw.

sȧn to be in good case.

sȧs six; sixth; = $^1/_6$; the festival held on the sixth day of each month.

Sȧsȧ		the name of a city =
sȧka		to afford relief.
sȧqer		to make strong, or perfect.
Sȧti		the name of a city.
sȧtti (?)		executioners.
sȧṭi		headsman, executioner.
sȧṭen		to transfer.
sāa		to magnify.
sāam		to slay.
sāb (*suāb*)		to wash, purify, cleanse.
		washed, plated.
sāba		to make to enter, force an entrance.

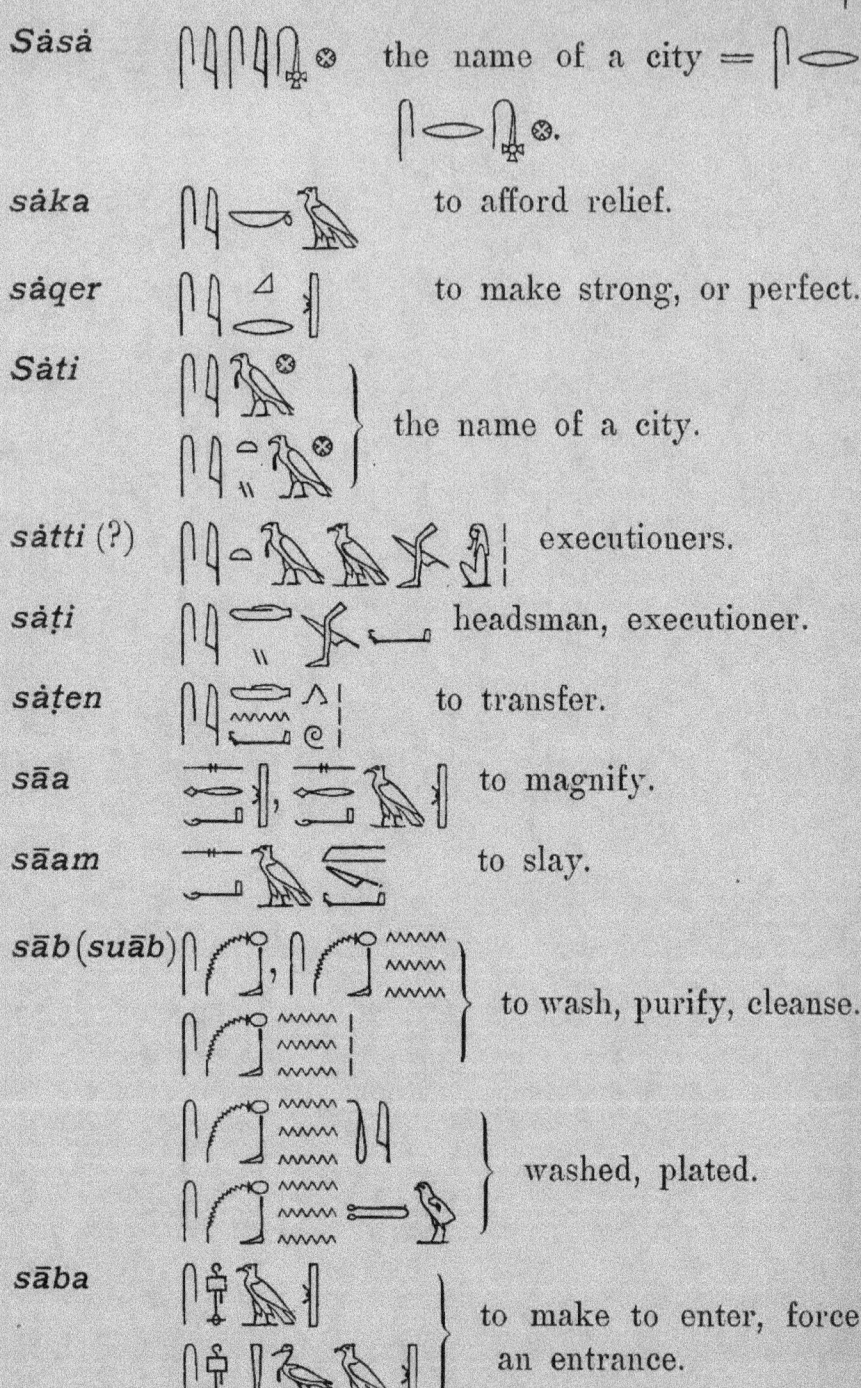

sām  to make to eat or drink, to swallow.

sāmiu  eaters, devourers.

Sām-em-senf 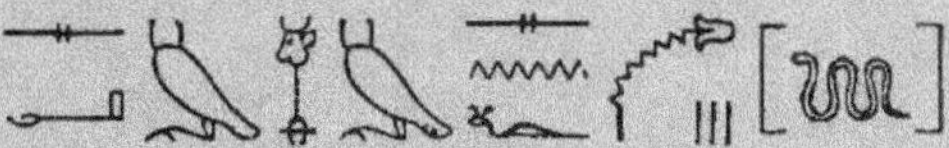 "drinker of blood"; a proper name.

Sām-em-ḳesu  "eater of bones"; a proper name.

sām  flowers, plants.

sāma  . . . .

sānkh 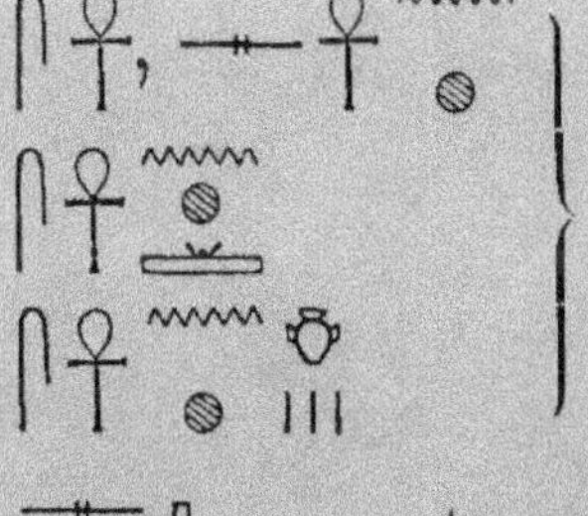 to vivify, keep alive. to support life, to feed, give sustenance to, "vivifier of hearts"; a title of Osiris.

sānṭ 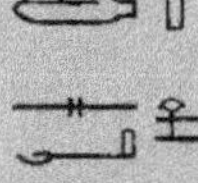 to make strong.

sār 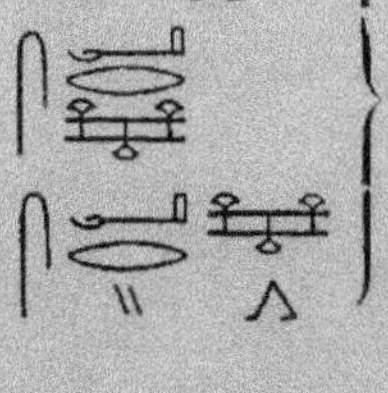 to make to come, to introduce.

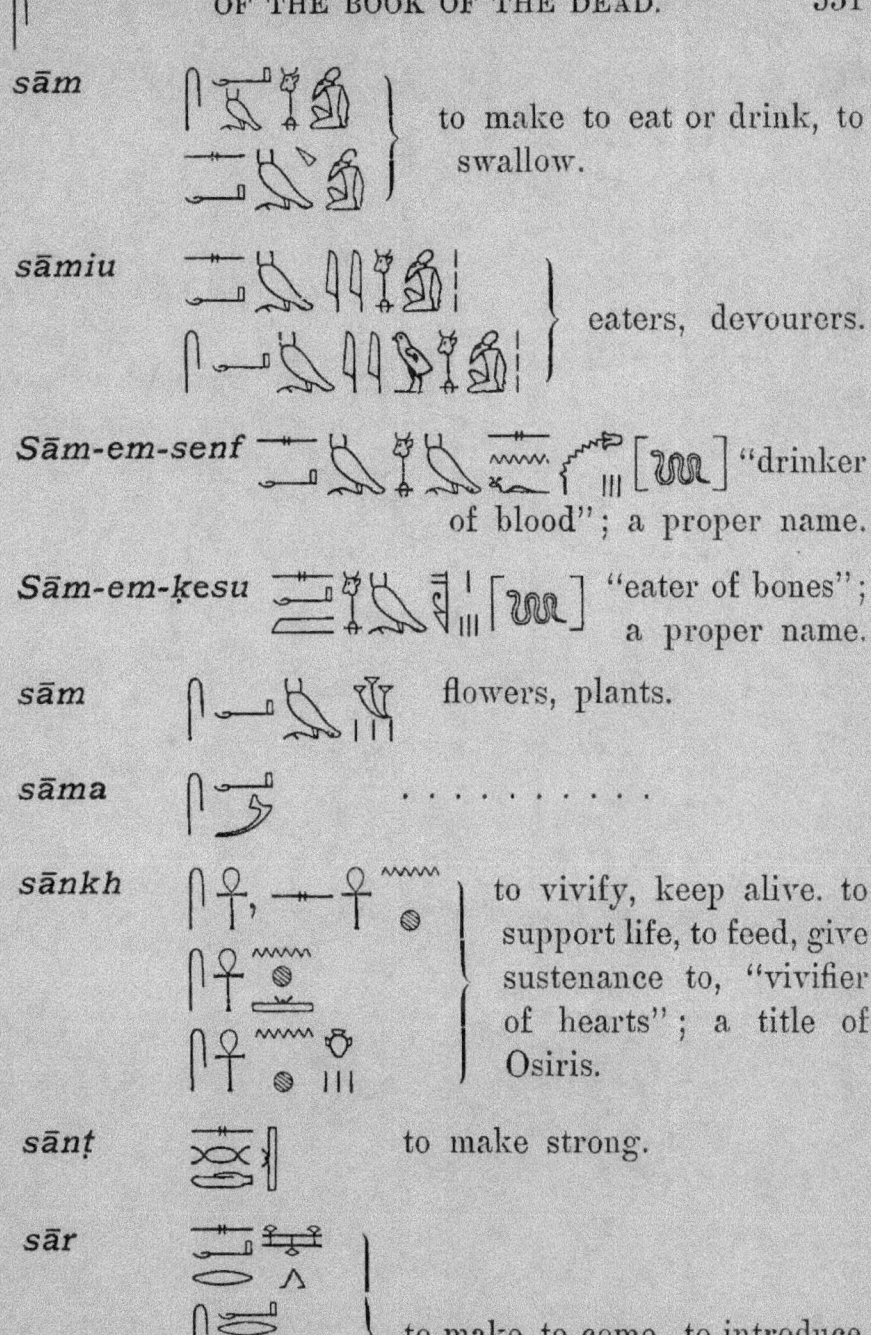

sārt 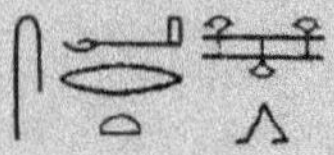 approach, introduction.

sāriu  introducers.

sāḥ, *sāḥu* 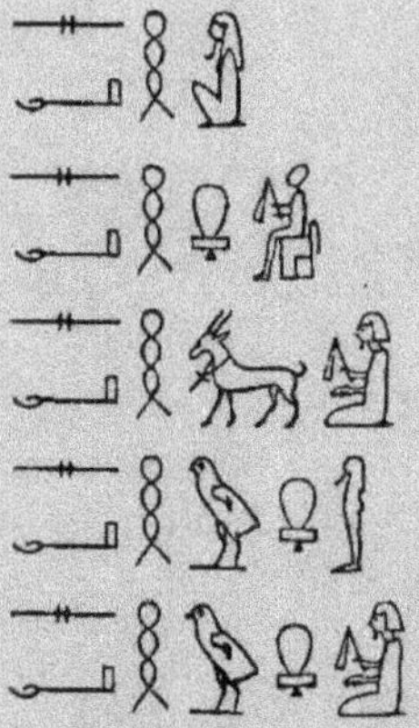 the spiritual body of a man, later the mummy; plur. . Mentioned with the  and the .

sāḥ 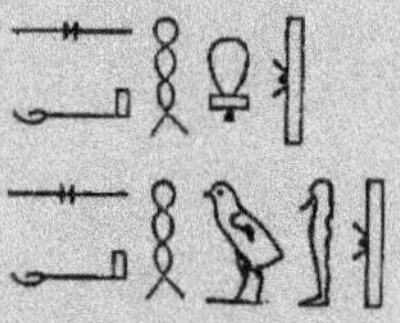 to become a *sāḥ*, 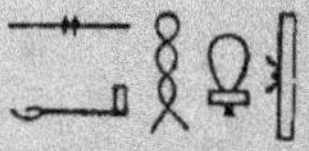 endowed with a *sāḥ*.

sāḥ 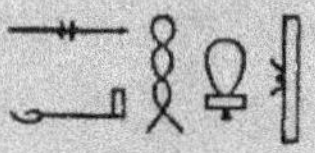 honour.

sāḥā 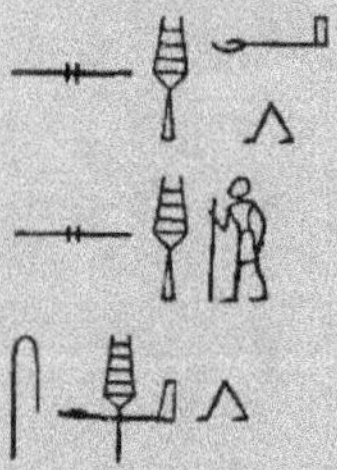 to set up, make to stand up.

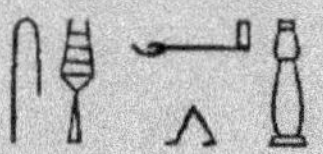 set up a pillar.

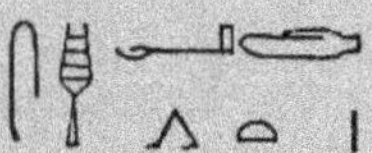 set up the Ṭeṭ.

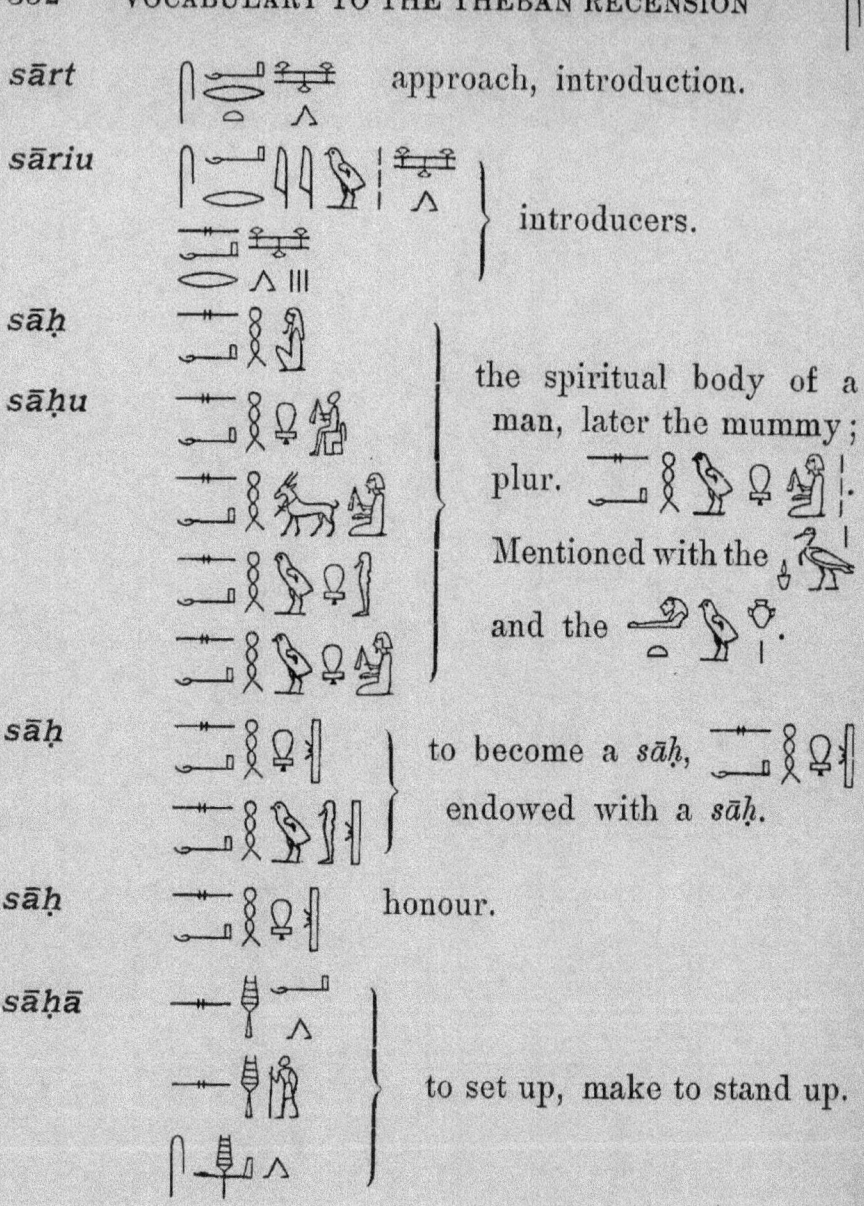

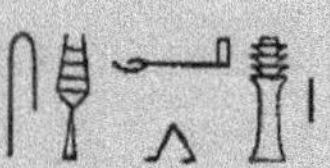

su  he, him; 

su tchesef  he himself.

sua  to pass by.

suash 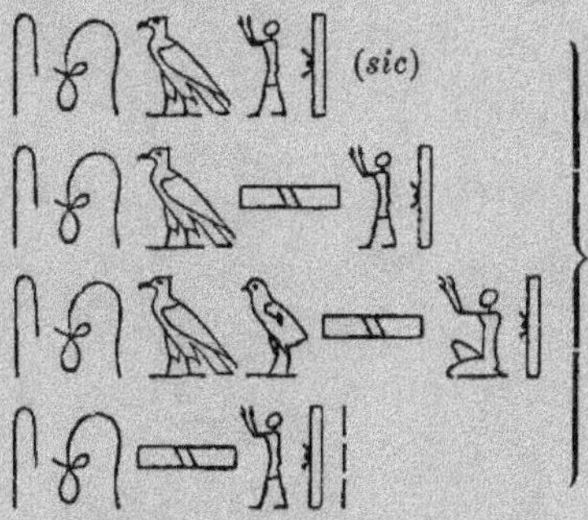

suatch 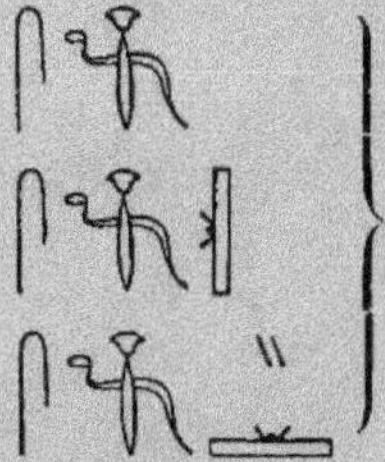 to be green, vigorous, flourishing.

suȧs  decay.

sui  crocodile.

sun 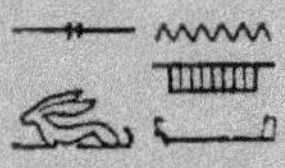 to open.

sun  to be destroyed.

sun, *sunen* — pool, lake, any large collection of water.

sunȧt — unguent.

Sunnu — the city called by the Greek Syene. Heb. סְוֵנֵה.

surȧ — to give to drink, to drink.

suriu — drinkers.

surṭ — =

suha — to supplicate.

suḥ — a garment.

suḥt — egg; testicles (?).

sukha — evil recollection.

sukheṭ — to embalm, mummify.

suser — to strengthen.

susekh — to make broad, to make wide (*i. e.*, long) the steps.

Suḳaṭi  the name of a god.

sut  he, it, himself, they, them.

sut  hair.

Sut 
Suti  } the god of darkness and night, and of physical and moral evil.

Suti-mes  a proper name.

suten  } king; 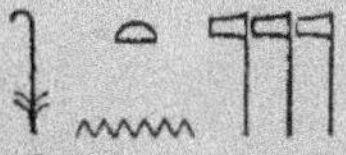 king of the gods.

 the reigning king.

 kings.

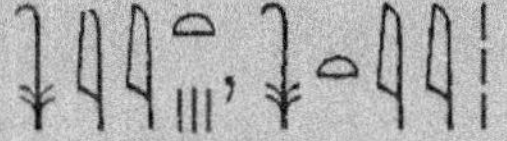 sovereignty, kingship, reign.

sutenit  to reign, sovereignty.

suten bȧti  } King of the South and North.

suteniu bȧtiu  } plur. of preceding.

suten bȧt Ȧsȧr  Osiris, king of the Two Egypts.

suten ḥeḥ  "king of eternity"; a title of Osiris.

suten Ṭuat  "king of the Ṭuat"; a title of Osiris.

suten ḥemt 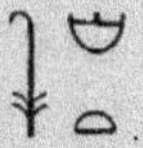 "king's woman", *i. e.*, queen.

suten sesh  "king's scribe", *i. e.*, royal scribe.

suten . . . . 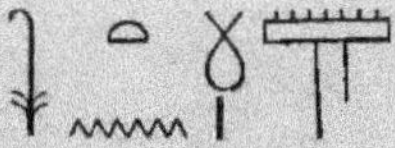 byssus; plur. .

suten ṭā ḥetep  an ancient formula meaning "may the king give an offering", dating from the time when the king sent gifts for the funeral feasts of his loyal servants. At a later period its use was purely conventional in funerary texts.

***Suten-ḥenen* (or *Ḥenensu*)**  Herakleopolis, the חָנֵס of Isaiah XXX. 4. The Copts called it ϩⲛⲉⲥ, or ϩⲛⲏⲥ, or ⲉϩⲛⲏⲥ, and its Arabic name is اهناس.

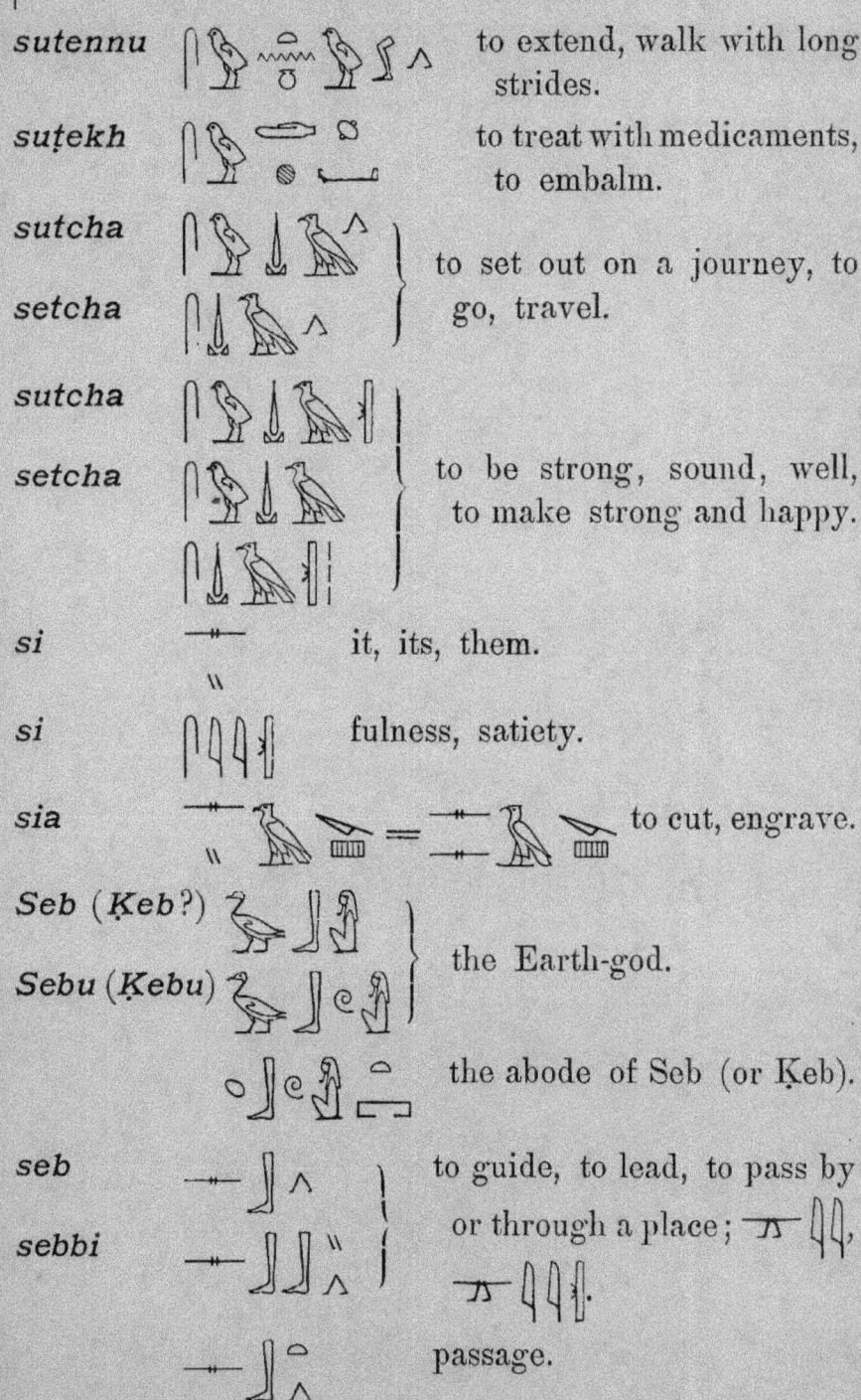

sutennu — to extend, walk with long strides.

suṭekh — to treat with medicaments, to embalm.

sutcha, *setcha* — to set out on a journey, to go, travel.

sutcha, *setcha* — to be strong, sound, well, to make strong and happy.

si — it, its, them.

si — fulness, satiety.

sia — to cut, engrave.

Seb (*Ḳeb*?), *Sebu* (*Ḳebu*) — the Earth-god.

the abode of Seb (or Ḳeb).

seb, *sebbi* — to guide, to lead, to pass by or through a place;

passage.

sba  star, Star-god; plur. .

sbaiu  stars.

sba 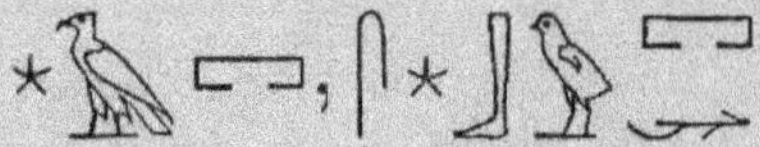

sbau 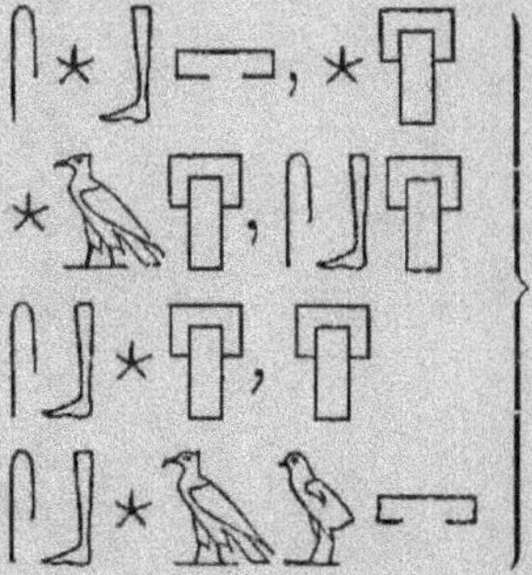 door, gate, pylon; the forms ,  also occur.

sbau 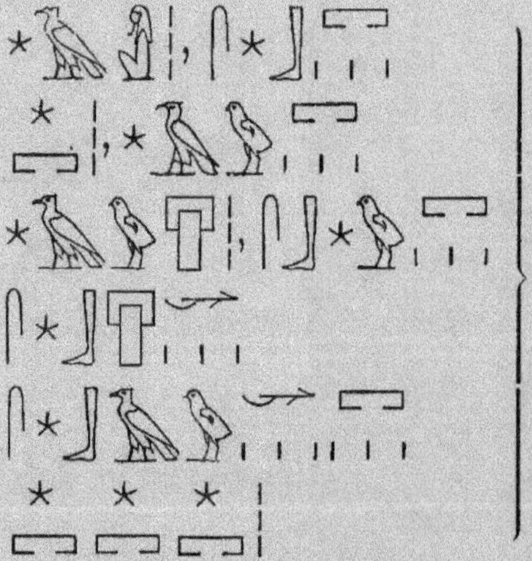 plur. of preceding.

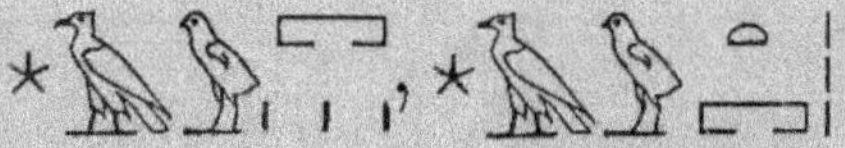 doors of the Other World.

sba  to instruct.

sbaut  to rebel.

sebaḳi  helpless one, inert, weak.

Sebȧ 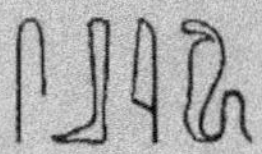 the name of a goddess.

sebȧ 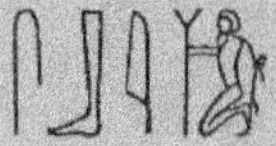 to be an enemy of some one.

sebȧ  enemy, fiend.

sebȧu  plur. of preceding.

seben  to retreat, depart.

sebeḥ 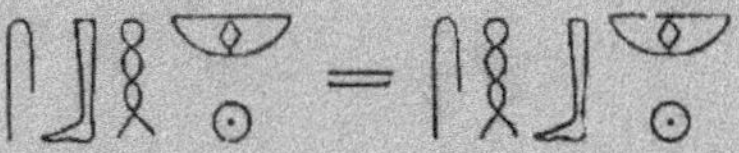 to keep a festival.

sebeḥ  to call upon someone, to invoke.

sebḥet 
sebḥit  invocation, praise.

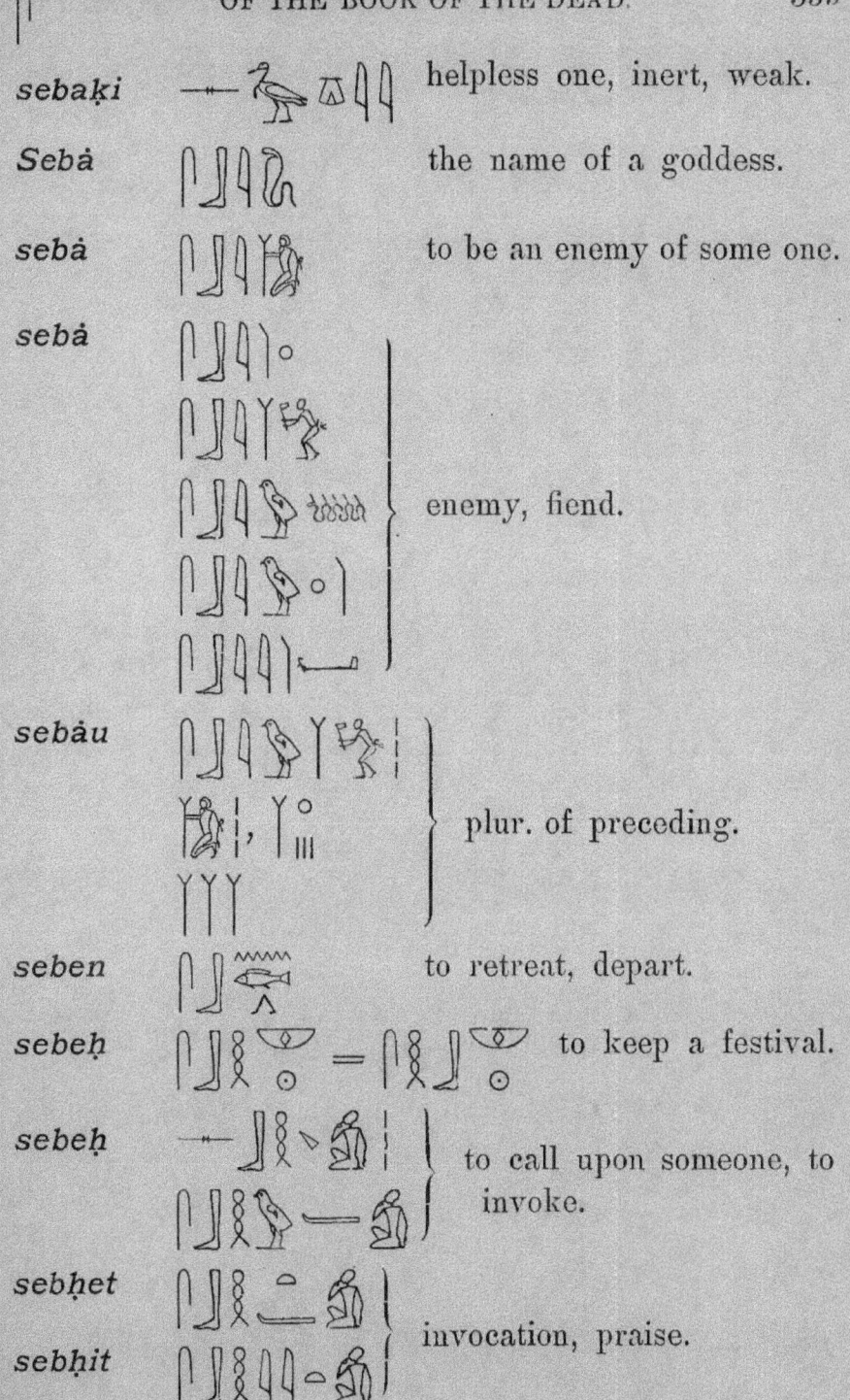

sebekh  be master of, have power over (?).

sebkhet 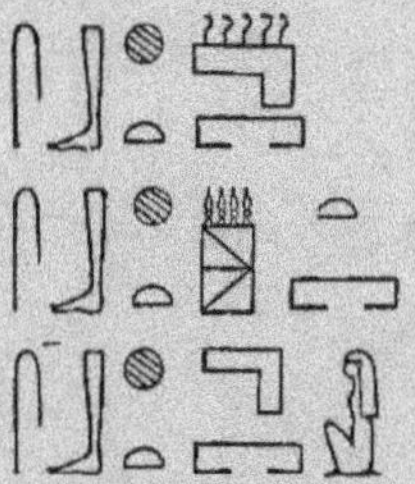 gate, pylon.

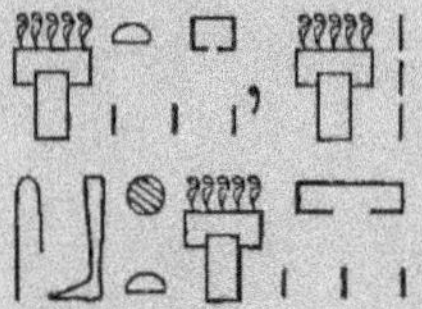 plur. of preceding.

sebekhbekht  to scatter (?).

Sebek  the Crocodile-god, who was a form of the Sun-god.

Sebeku  the Crocodile-gods.

sebeq  leg, thigh.

Sebeq-en-Shesmu  a proper name.

Sebeq-en-Tem  a proper name.

Sebeḳ 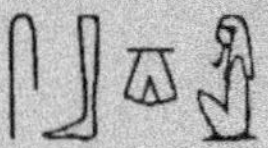

Sebḳa  the name of a god.

Sebaḳu 

sebt  to be pleased (?), laugh, laughter.

sebt 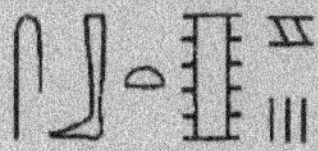 walls.

sep 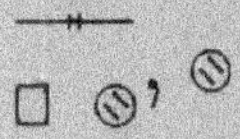 season, luck, fate, occasion, opportunity, circumstance, case, etc.; plur.  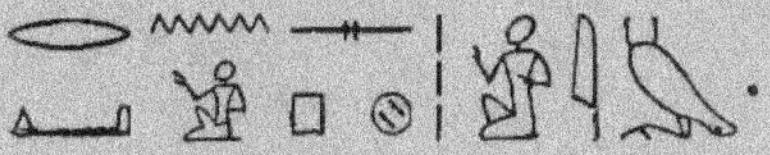.

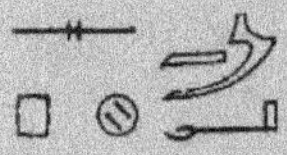 a right case, a just trial.

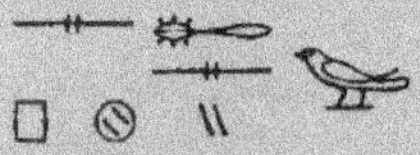 ill luck, a bad time.

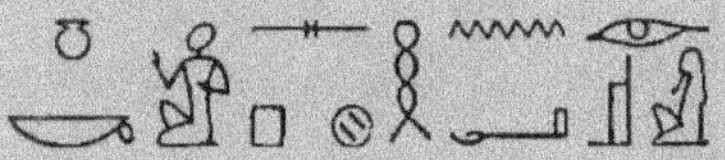 I am Fate and Osiris.

 a prosperous time.

 the occasion of the night.

 likewise, at the same time.

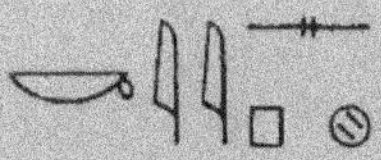 another time or opportunity.

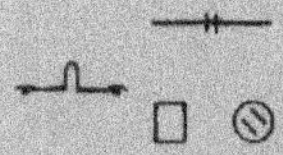 at no time, never.

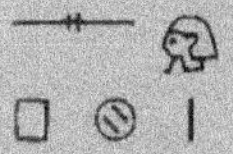 primeval time, when the world began.

sep 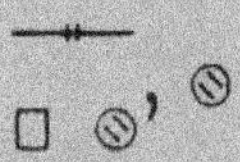 time;  twice;  four times;  millions of times.

sep sen 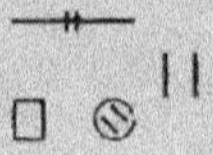 duplicity.

sep  to pass sentence.

sep 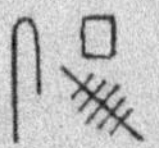 crown (?).

Sep 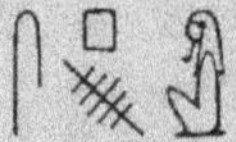 the name of a god.

Sepa 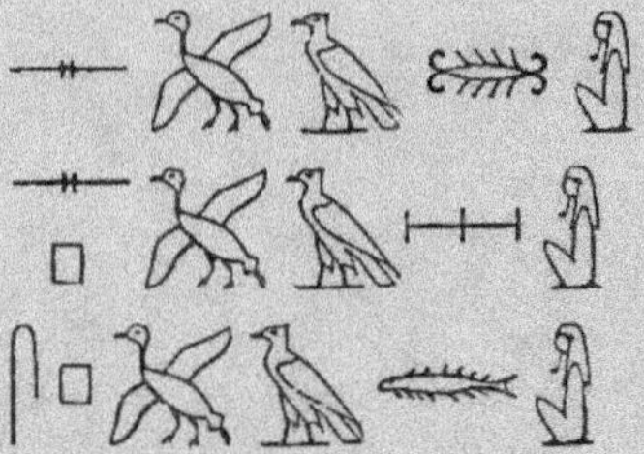 the name of a god.

seppi 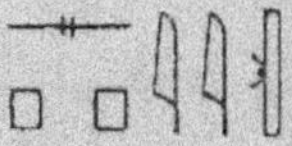 remainder.
sepi 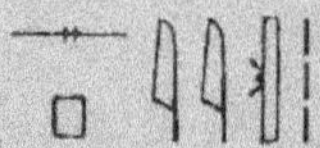

seppu 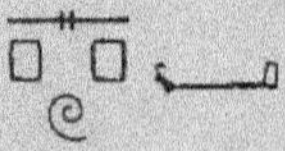 omission.

sper  to come to a place, to arrive at;  comers.

sper  to speak to, address.

speḥ 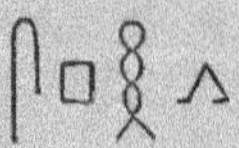 to make to arrive at.

sepeḥ 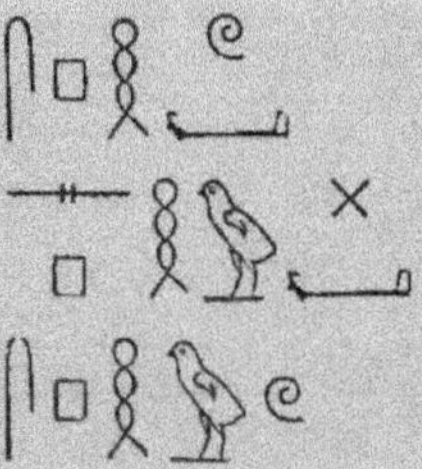 to tie with a rope, to fetter.

sepḥer to design, make a plan, draw, write.

sepḥer to make to revolve.

Sepes a proper name.

sept lip; edge of the water.

the two lips.

sept nome; plur. .

the nome of Maāti.

Sepṭu a god of the Eastern Delta; a form of Horus.

Sepṭ the star Sirius.

sepṭ to be ready to do or use something, prepared; to be provided with. provided.

prepared for the moment.

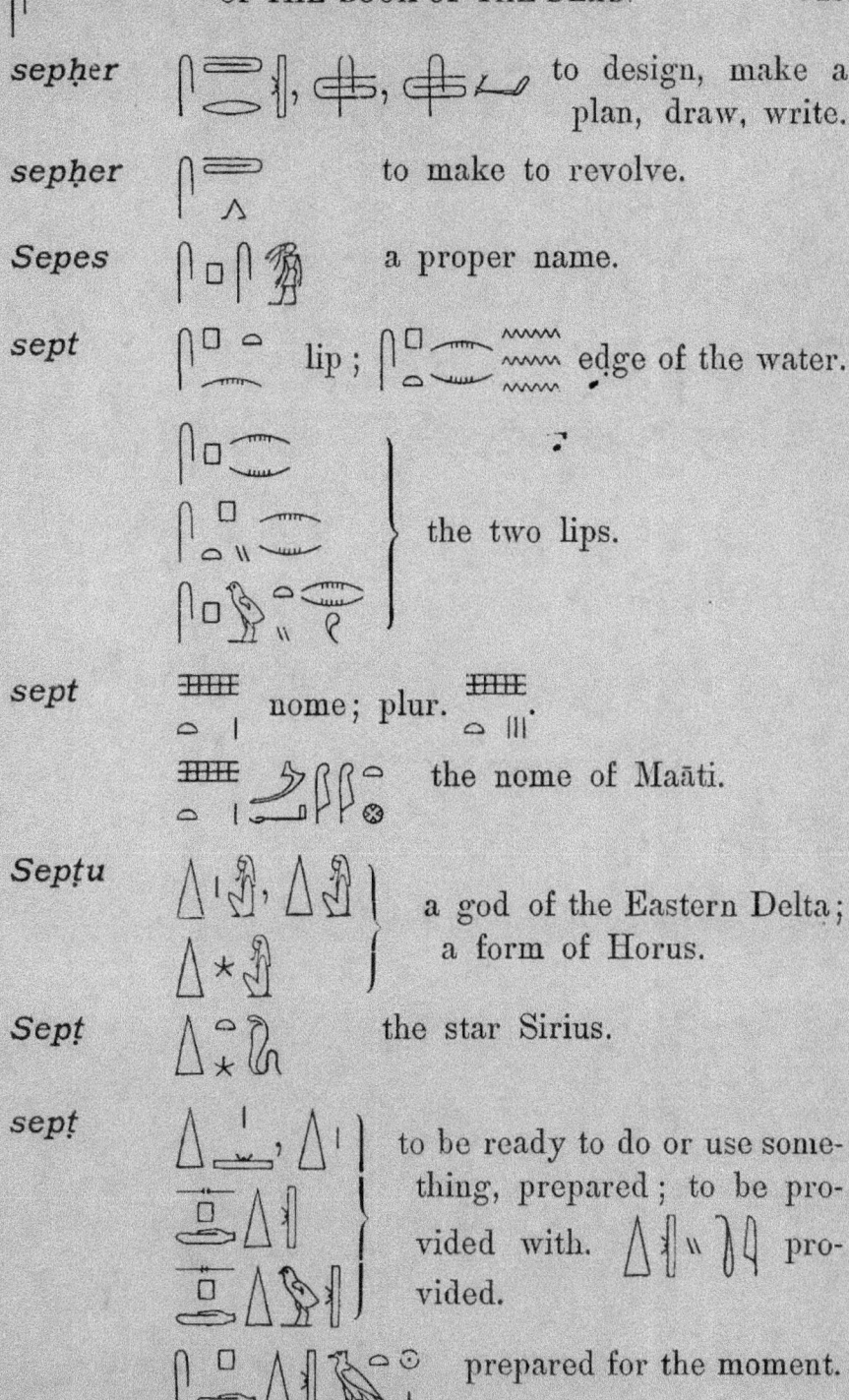

having horns ready to strike.

ready of face, keen, alert (?).

sepṭ a kind of wood.

sepṭ leg.

Sepṭ-kheri-neḥait-ȧmi-beq a proper name.

Sepṭ-mast-ent-Reruti a proper name.

sef yesterday; .

sef maāt . . . . .

sef ḥer to be gracious, longsuffering.

sefi babe, child.

sefekh seven.

sefekh to untie, undress, set free; , .

Sefekh-neb-s a proper name.

seft 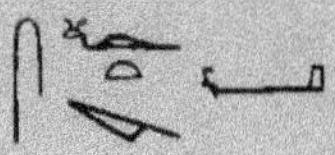 to slay.

seft 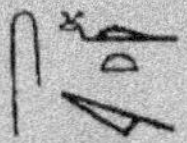 knife, sword.

seft 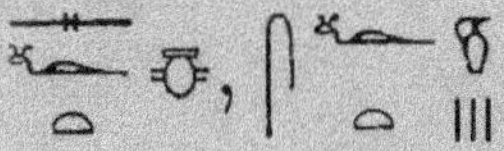 pitch, unguent.

sem  a priest (also setem ).

sma 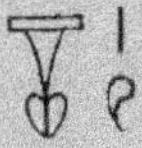 loin.

sma 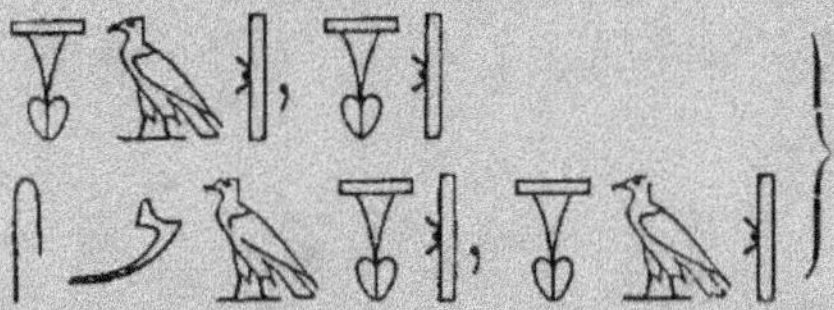 to join together, to unite with.

 union, assembly.

smat (?)  a burial place.

sma ta  union with the earth, *i. e.*, burial.

 day of burial.

 to unite the Two Lands, *i. e.*, Egypt.

sma 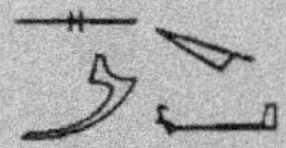 to kill, slaughter.

 slaughterer, butcher.

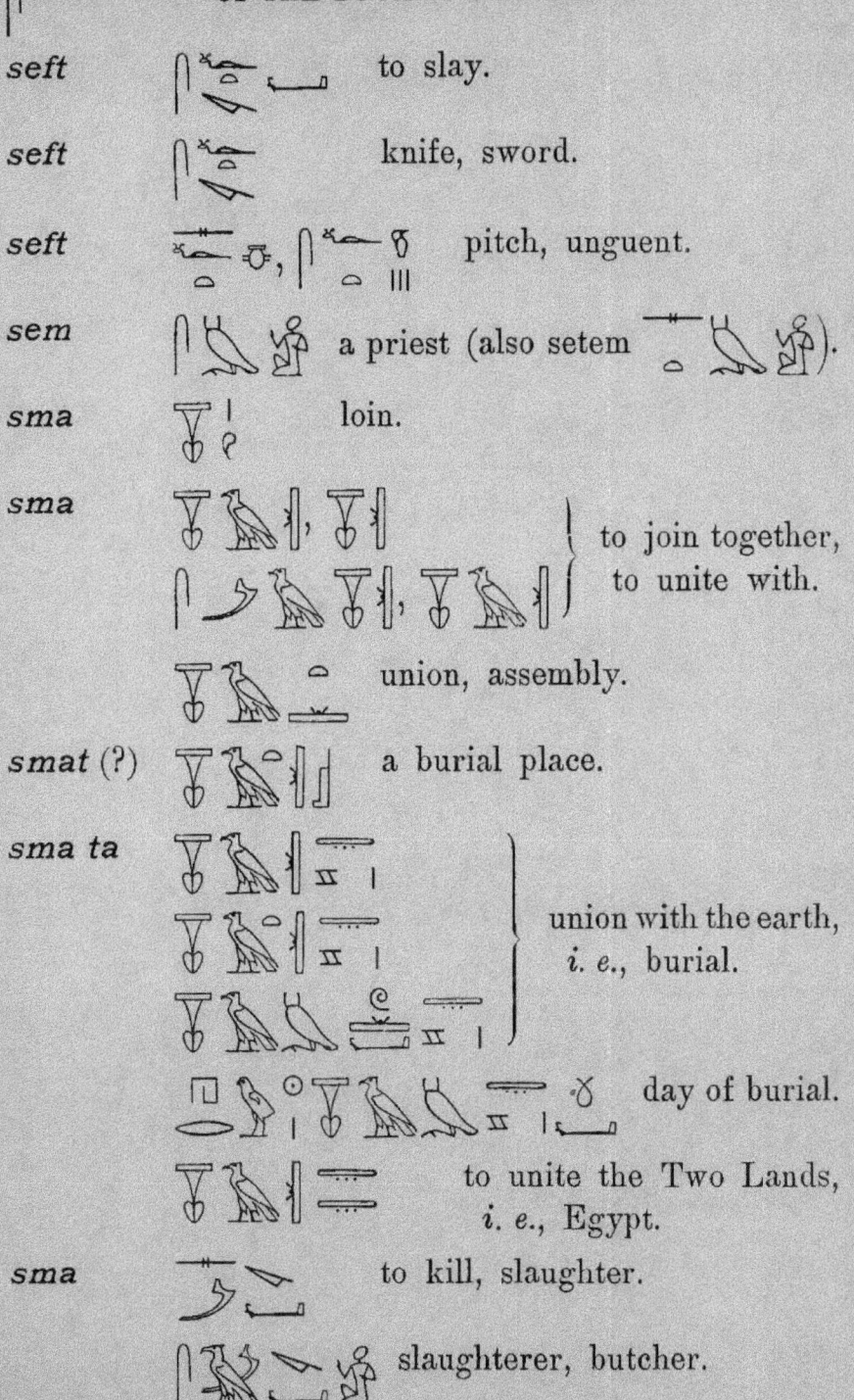

sma  cow or bull bound for sacrifice.

smaui 
 to renew, remake.

smaȧr  to oppress.

smau  branches.

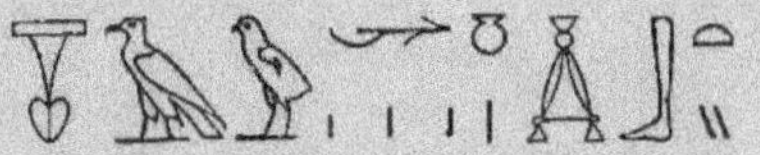 poles of a bier.

smaiu  branches.

smaiu  slaughterers, fiends.

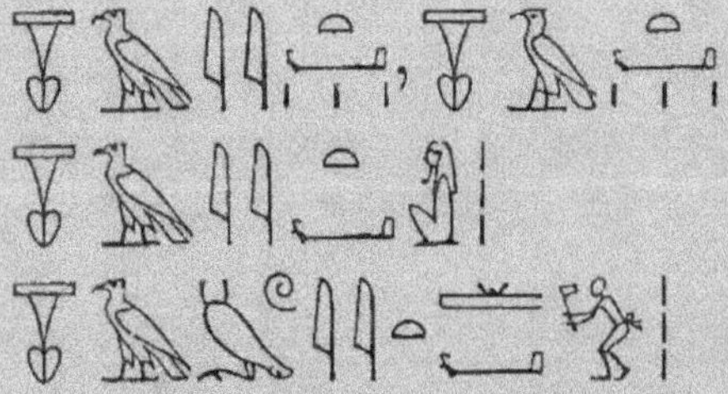 plur. of preceding.

 butchers of Set.

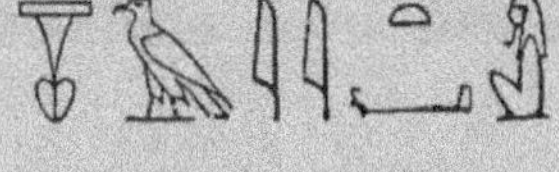 god of slaughter.

Smait two goddesses of slaughter.

smaā to pay what is due, make an offering.

smaāiu slayers.

smaā-kheru to justify, to make triumphant, to proclaim blessed.

smam to slay, sacrifice.

smam butcher.

smamiu slaughterers, fiends.

smam a bull for sacrifice.

smamu cattle for sacrifice, victims.

Smam the name of a god.

Smam-ur the name of the Soul of Seb (Ḳeb).

Smam the name of a lake.

smamu foliage or branches of a tree.

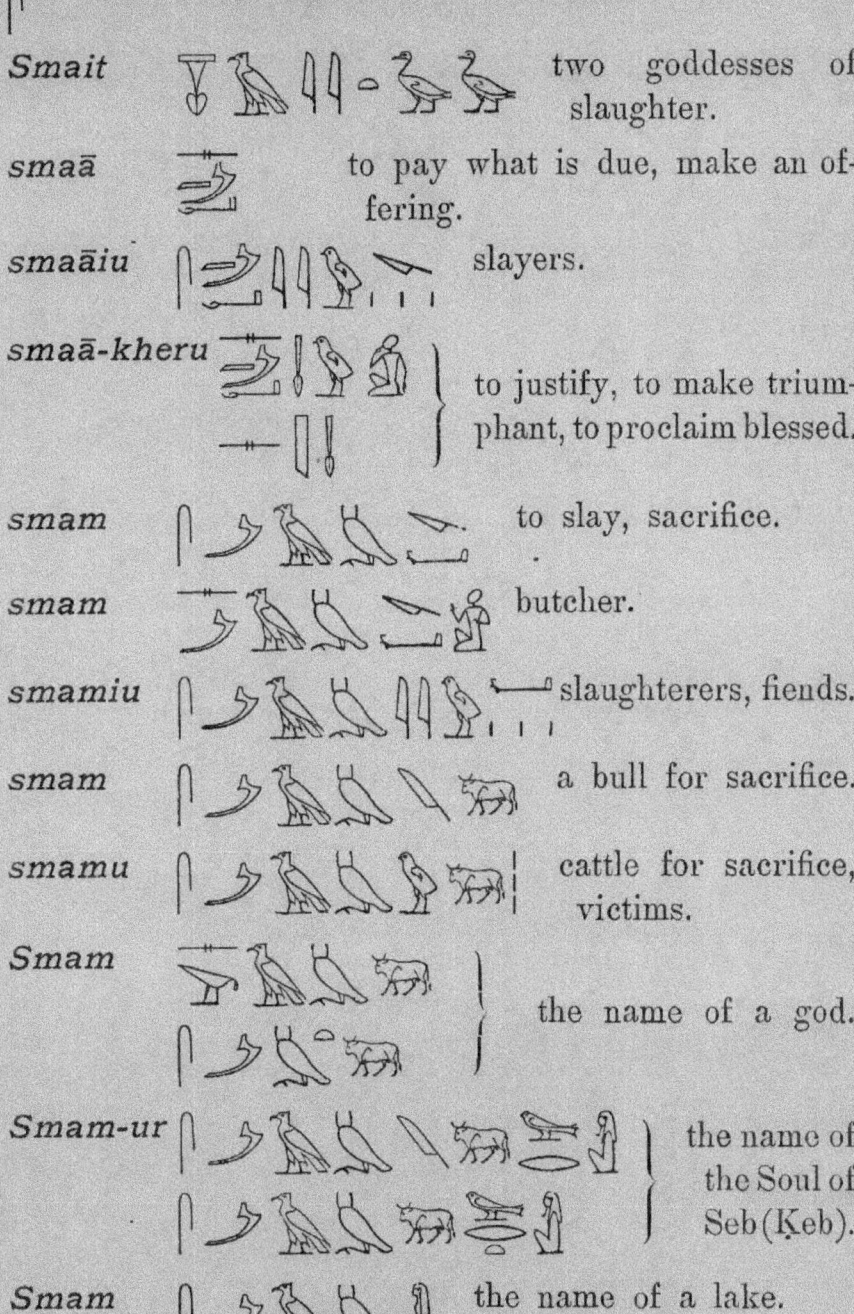

smamu 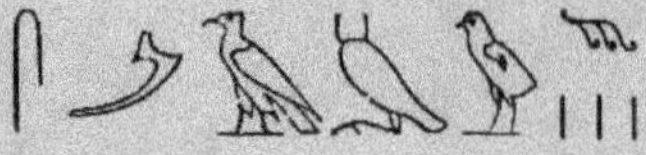 clouds.

smat  bows of a boat (?).

smatu  torture chambers, shambles.

Smati 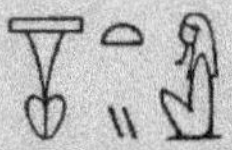 a proper name.

Smamti  a proper name.

smaṭ 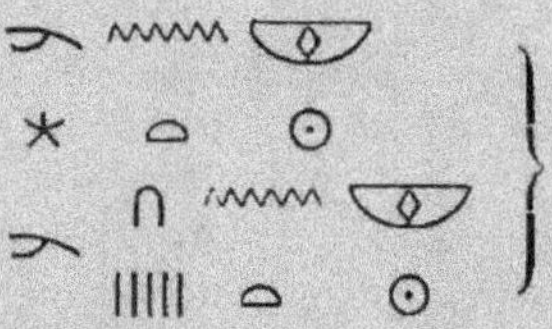 festival of the half month.

smȧ 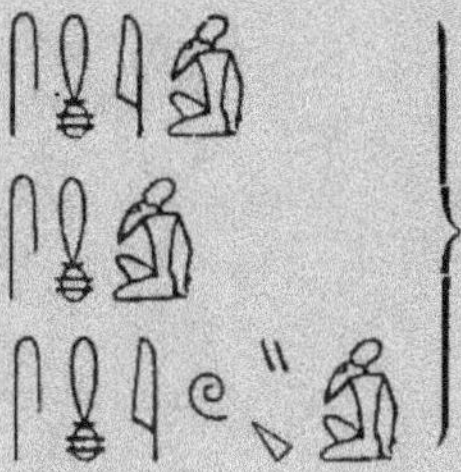 to report, announce, bear a message;  reporting; 

smȧ 
smȧiu  herald, announcer.

smȧ 
smȧt  report.

smȧ  leather.

smȧu  pieces of leather.

semu		herbs, pasturage.
semiu		devourers.
semi		to entreat.
smemā		to burn up.
smen		to stablish, be stablished, fixed, made firm.
		fixed head.
smen		a kind of goose.
smenkh		to repair, re-establish, beautify, make perfect.
smert		eyelids.
smer		to inflict or cause pain.
smeḥ		to flood, to submerge, water fields.

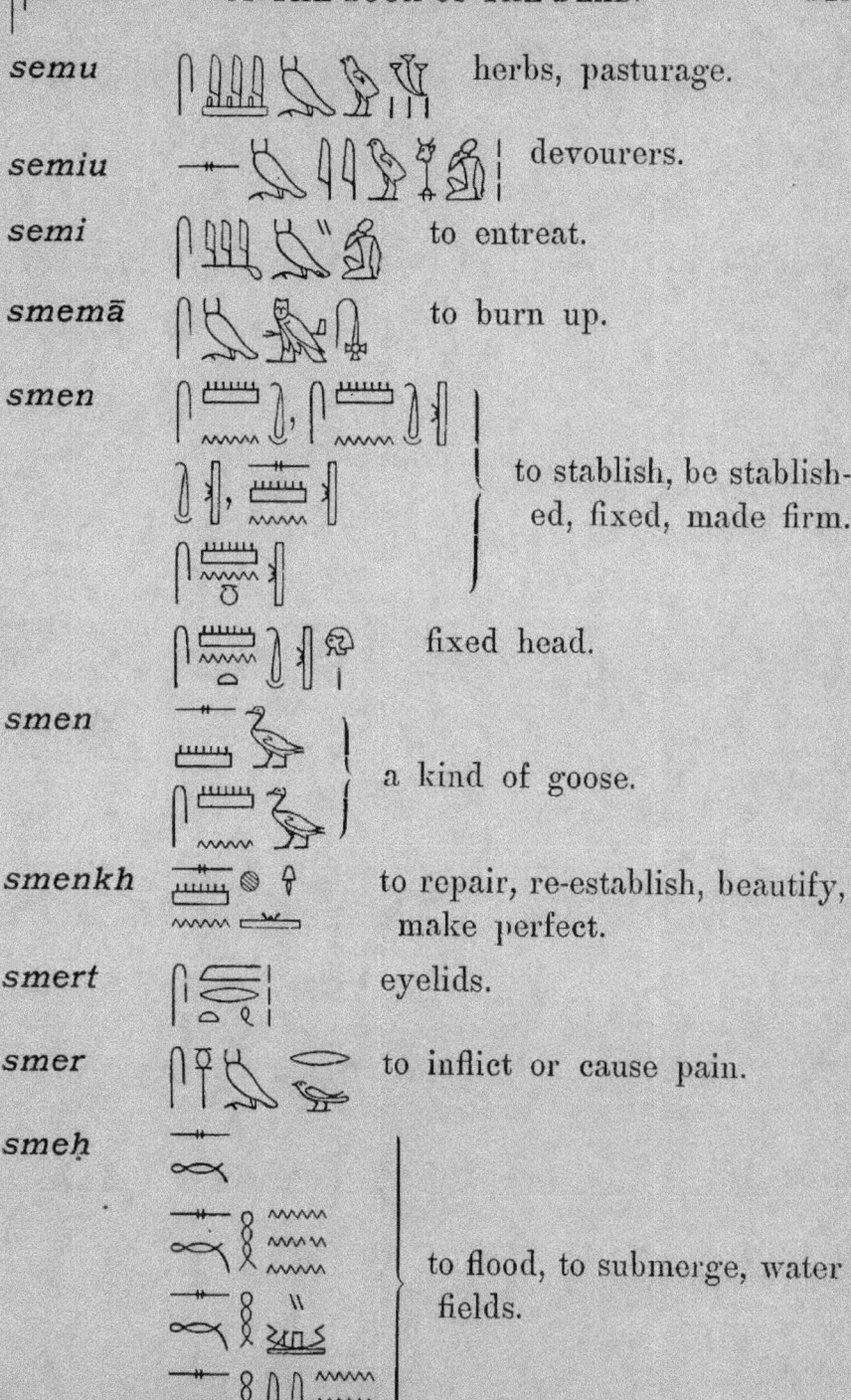

smeḥit  flood.

semkheṭ  . . . .

semes 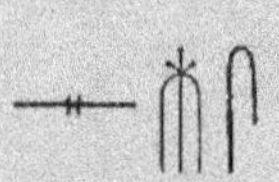 to make to be born, produce.

semsu  eldest, firstborn.

Semti (?) 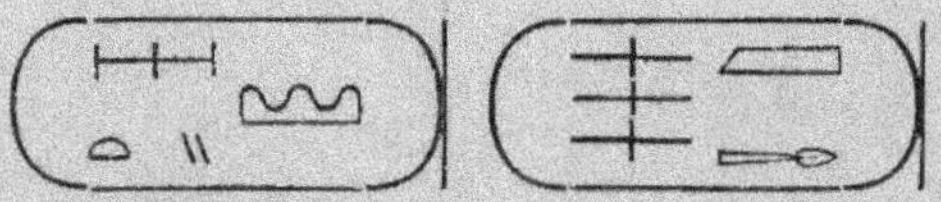 a king of the 1st dynasty. This name was formerly read Ḥesepti.

smet 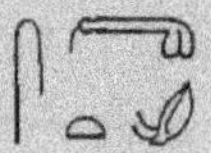 to listen.

smetmet (?) 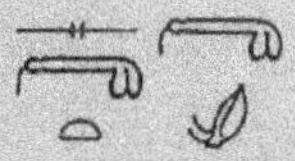 to pry into.

Smetu  the warder of the First Ārit.

smet 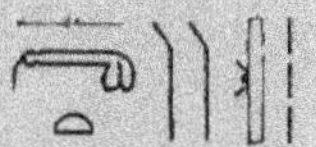 woven with, or shot with (of cloth).

Smet-āqa 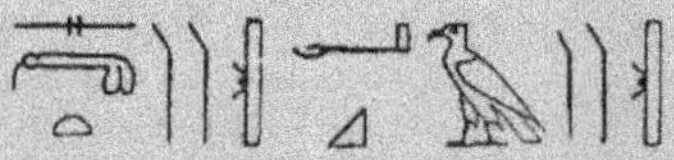 the name of a rudder.

Smeti-āqa  name of a part of the magic boat.

Smetti 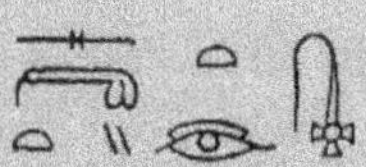 a proper name.

smetru  to investigate, search out, find the truth.

semṭet 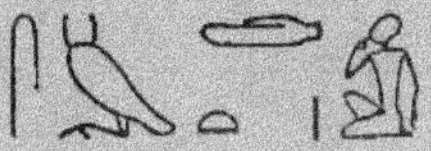 servant, serf.

sen 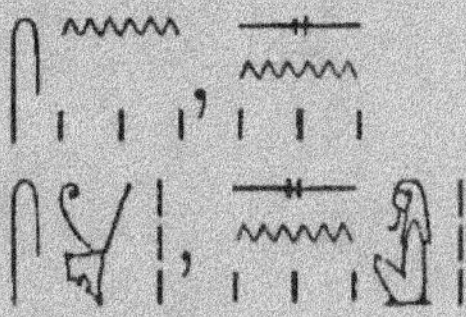 they, their, them.

sen 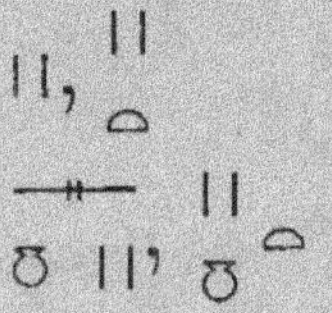 two; second, fellow, equal, companion, like, equal; 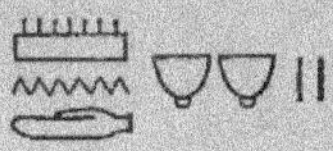 two breasts.

sen 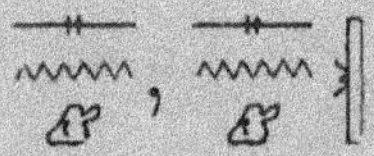 to smell, breathe.

sen ta 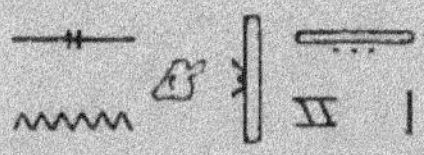 to smell the earth, to pay homage.

sen 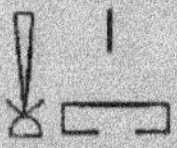 house, abode (?).

sen 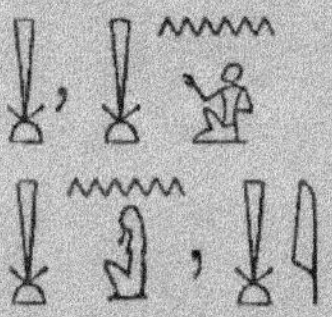 brother; dual  ; plur. 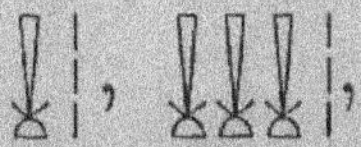 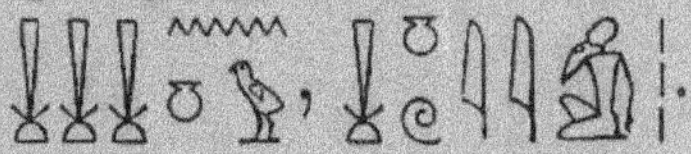.

sent  sister.

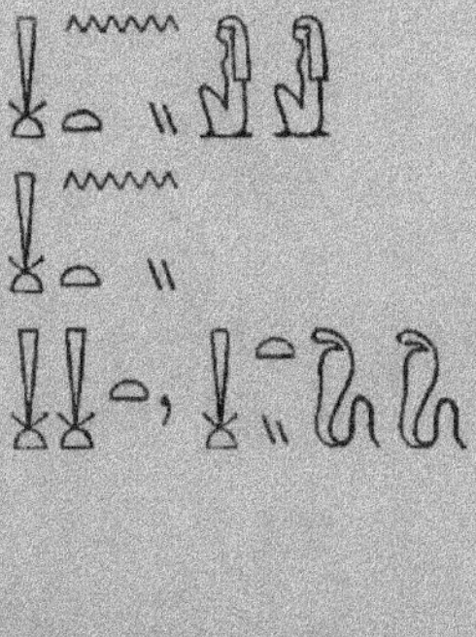 two sisters, pair of sisters.

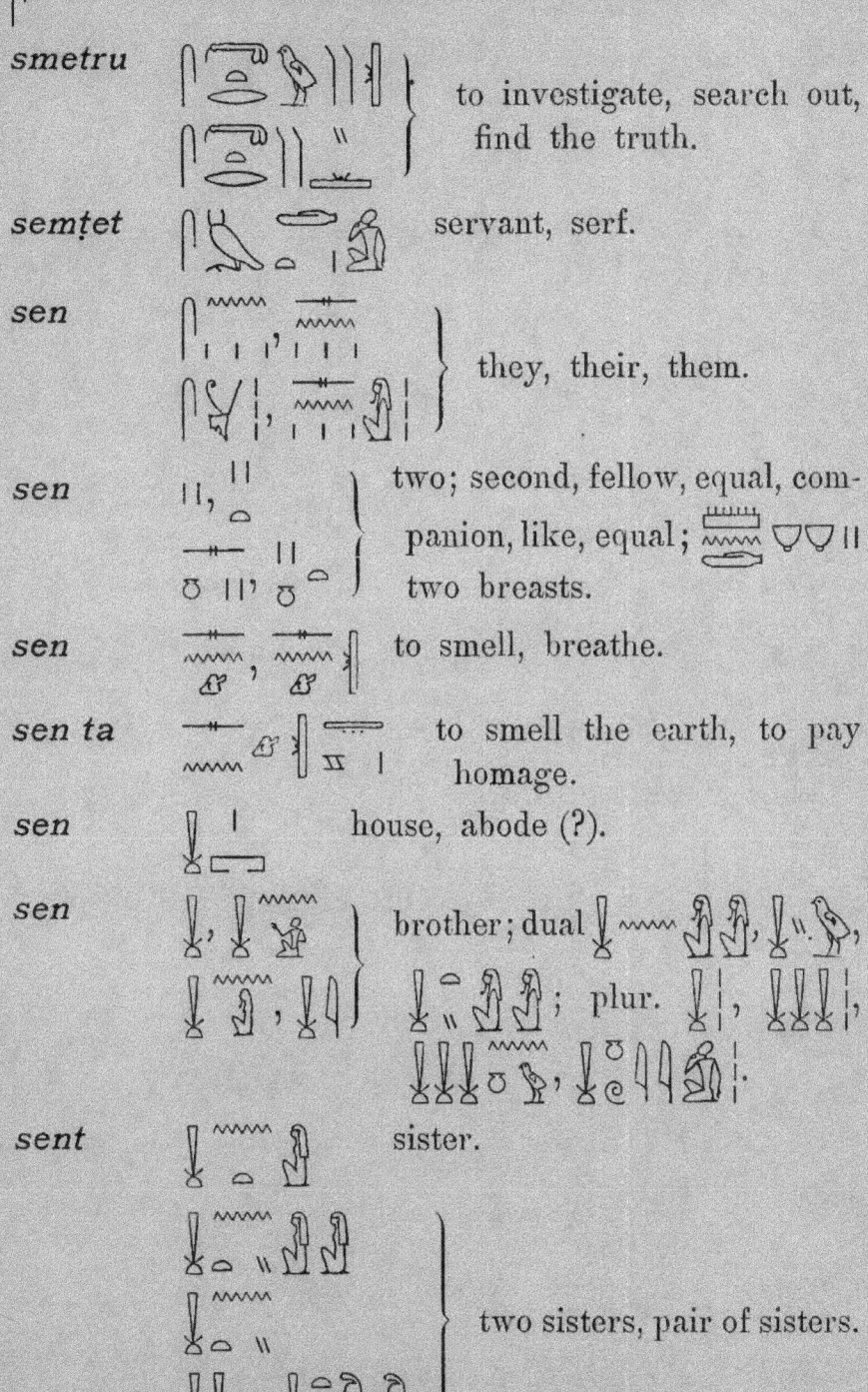

seni companion, fellow.

sen to pass away, depart, to walk.

sen to slit, to cut.

Senu a city near Panopolis.

senȧ adoration.

senȧha injury, misery.

senā restraint.

senāāt to beautify (?).

senb to be well, strong, healthy.

senbȧ health, soundness.

senb wall; plur.

senbet libation vessel.

senpu slaughterings.

senf 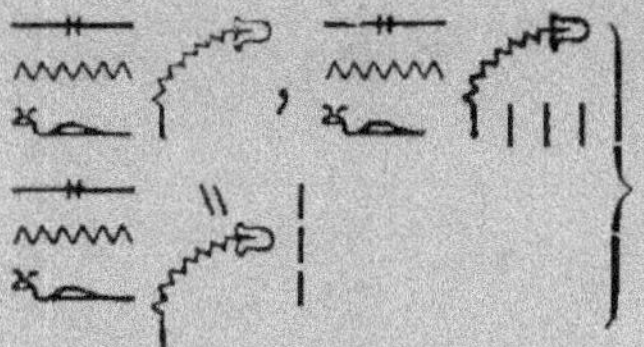 blood.

senfekhfekh 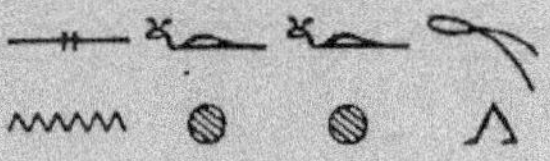 to be untied, set loose.

senem  abundance.

senem 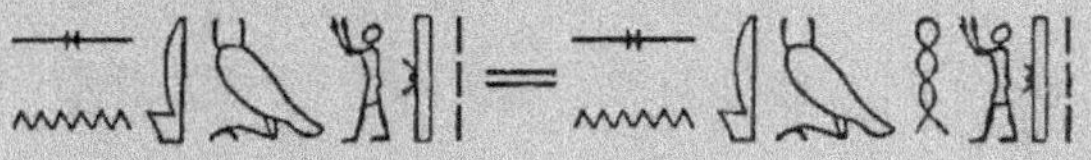 to pray, to adore.

senemȧi 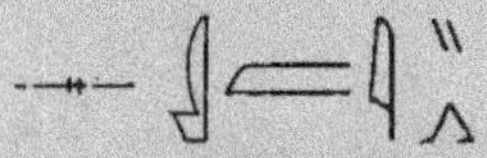 to make advance.

Senemti  a proper name.

senemem 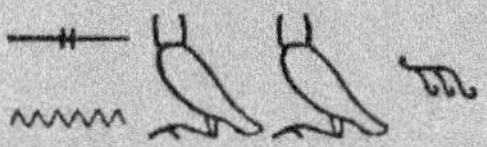 hair.

senen 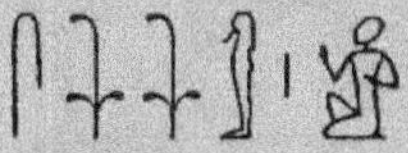 image, statue.

sennu  to cut, to sever; 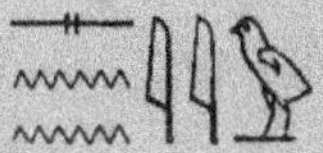 those who cut.

sennit 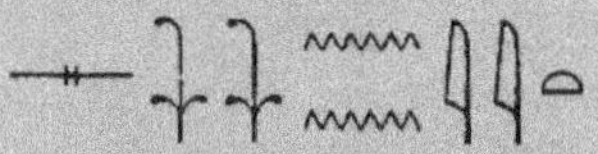 . . . . . .

sennu  to gather (?).

sennu  cakes, bread-offerings.

sennȧu  to fail.

sennuṭ  carrier.

senni 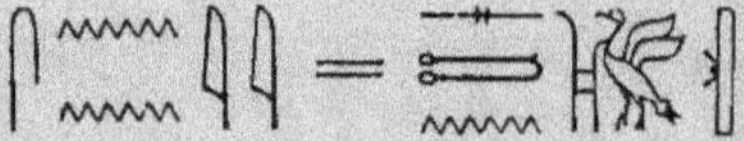

Sen-nefer  a proper name.

senneshni  storm.

seneh  to be in servitude.

senehep 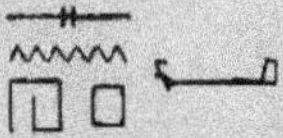 to be strong.

Seneh-paqarha  the name of a city.

Senehaparḳana 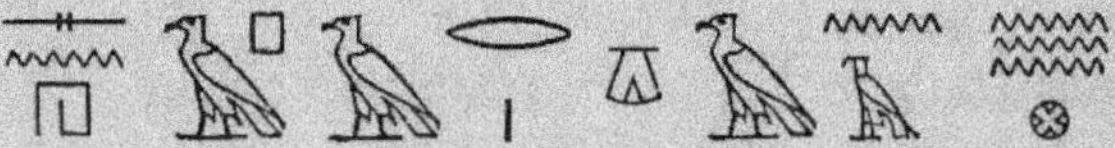 the name of a city.

seneḥem  to deliver.

senkha  to disembark (?).

senekhekh 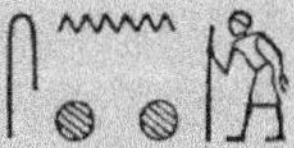 to grow old.

senes 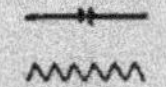 } to praise.
sensi 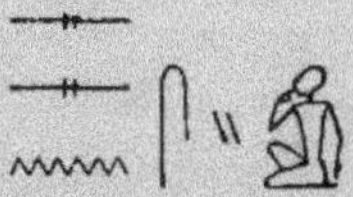 }

sensu  to cry out, invoke.

Senseneb  the name of the mother of Nu.

sensenni 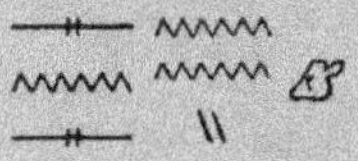 to breathe, snuff the air.

sensen 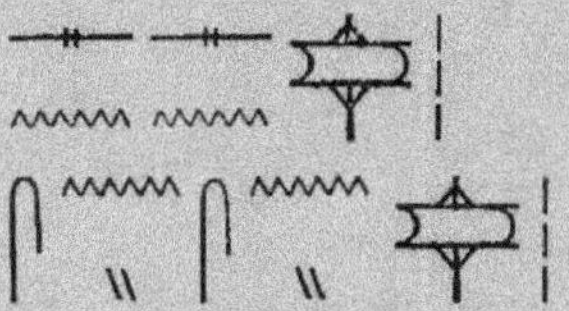 breathings, breaths.

sensen 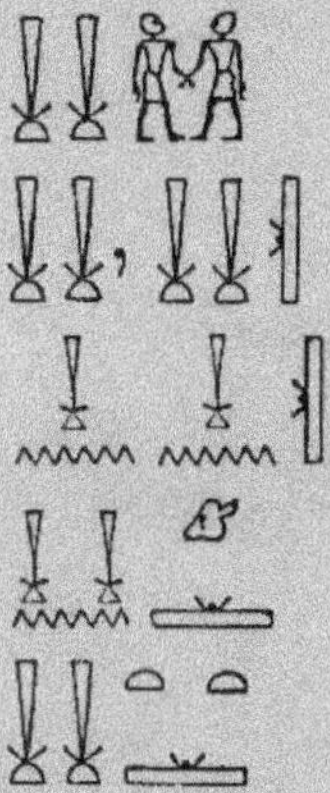 to become friendly with some one, to fraternize; to smell.

sensen 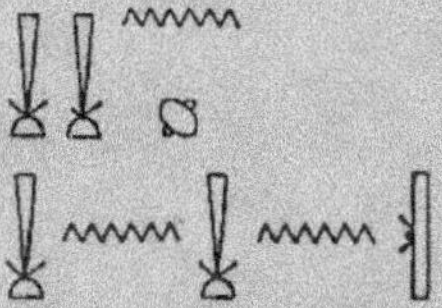 to have a bad smell, to become corrupt, to decay.

senesh 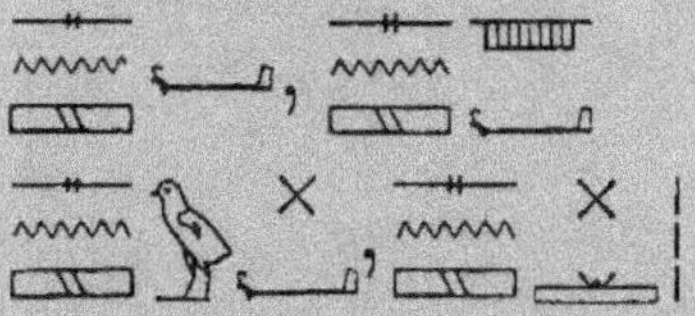 to unbolt, unbar, open.

senshu  bolts (?).

seneshni 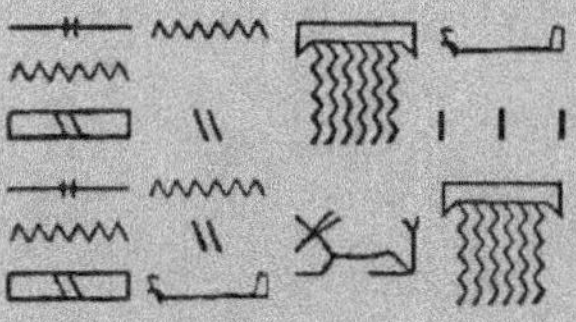 storm, hurricane.

Senk 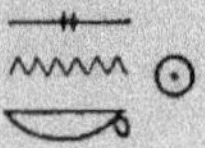 a proper name.

senket 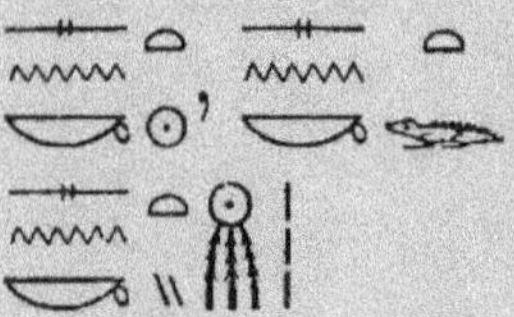 light.

Senket 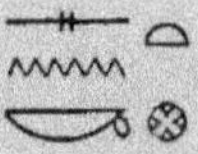 the name of a city.

senk-àb 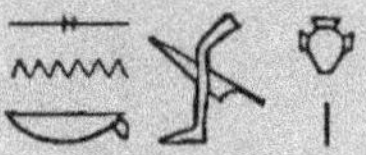 strong-willed.

senq (?) 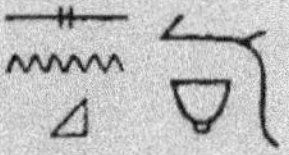
senqet 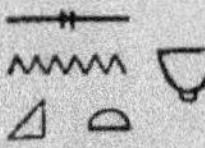 to suckle.

sent  labourers, builders.

sent 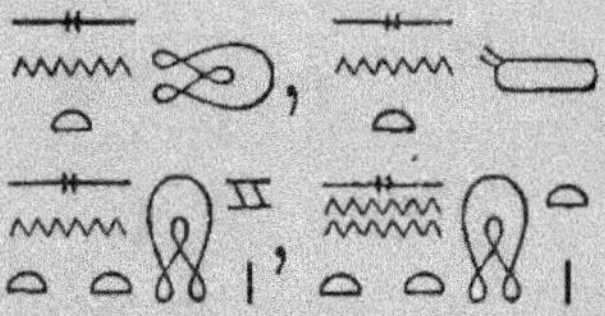 foundation.

sent 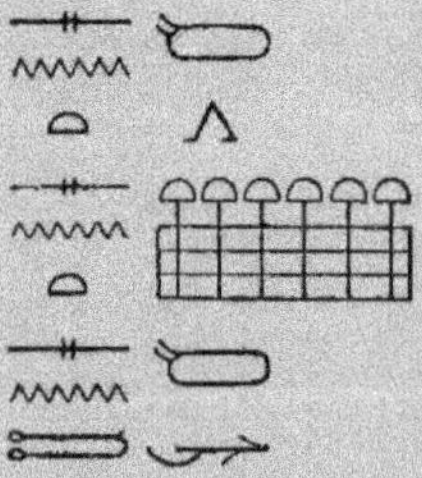 draughtboard, game of draughts.

sent 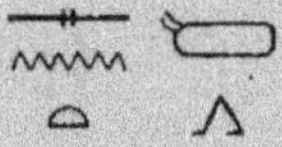 to pass away.

sent 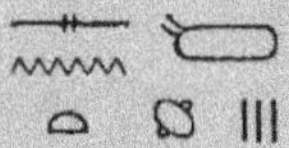 decay.

sentu  enemies.

Sent-Rā 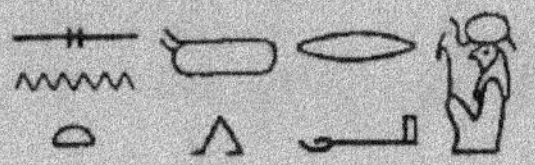 a proper name.

senter
senther 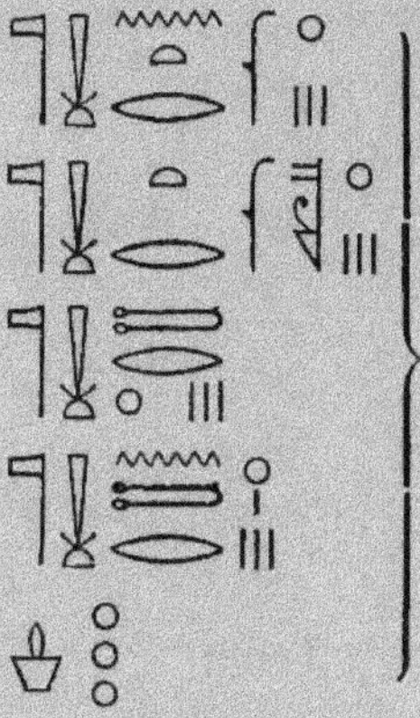 incense offered to the god; 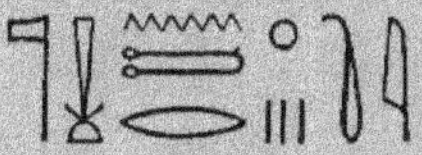 censed; 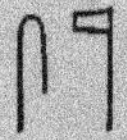 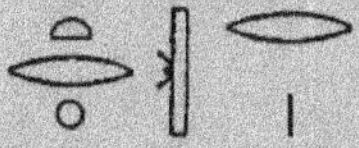 to cense the mouth.

senteḥ  to have power over.

Sent.....  the brother-gods Horus and Set.

sentˌ  to fear, be afraid.

sentˌ àb  timid.

sentˌ 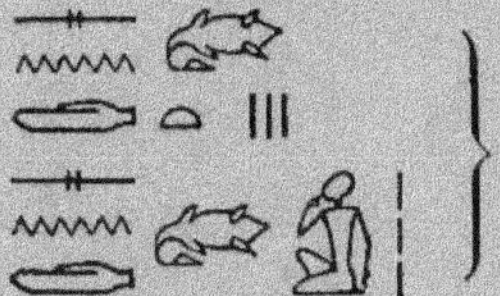 fear.

senetchem  to make glad or happy.

 pleasure.

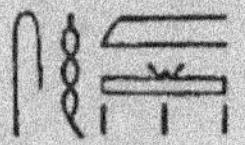 ease.

senetchem 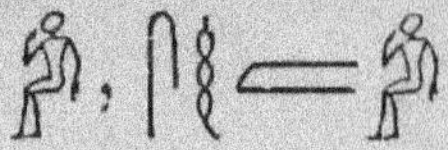 to sit.

sentchert  restraint.

ser 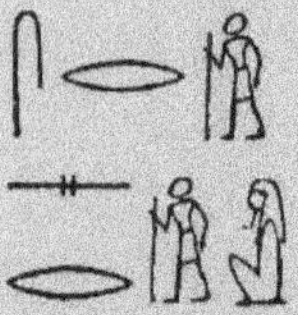 prince, chief;  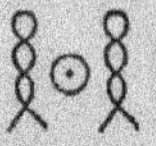 everlasting prince;  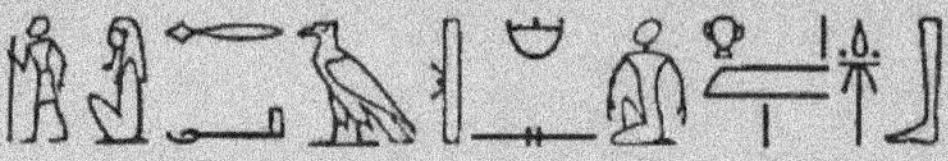 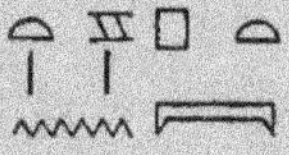 a proper name.

 plur. of preceding.

ser  to give orders or directions, to announce, give tidings; .

sert  order, announcement.

Ser-kheru 
Serȧ-kheru  the name of one of the Forty-two Judges in the Hall of Osiris.

Serȧt-beqet  the name of a sacred cow.

seru  grain, barley.

seru  geese of a special kind.

serui (?) 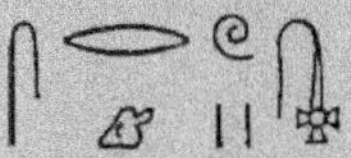 flame.

serukheṭ  to treat with medicaments, embalm.

seruṭ 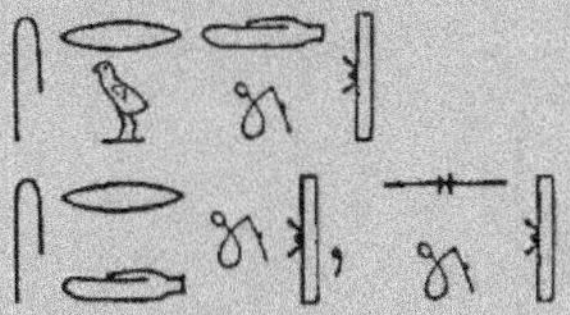 to make to grow, to flourish, to perpetuate.

seref 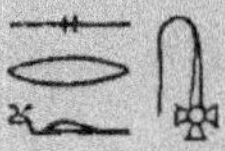 to be hot, flame, fire.

serem  to make to weep.

serenp 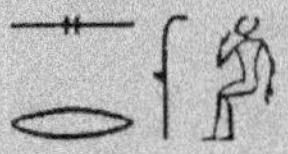 to make young.

serḥu (?)  to overthrow.

serekh 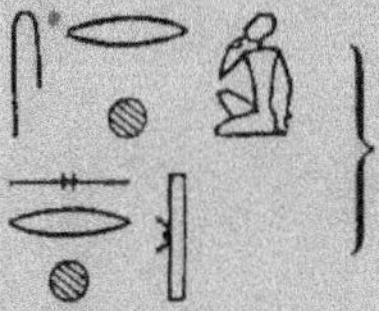 to make to know, to inform.

serekh 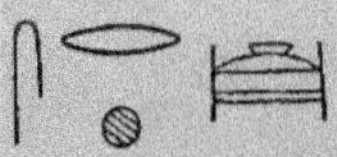 a funerary building, a cognizance.

Serekhi 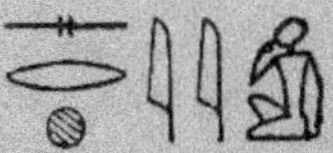 the name of one of the Forty-two Judges in the Hall of Osiris.

seres 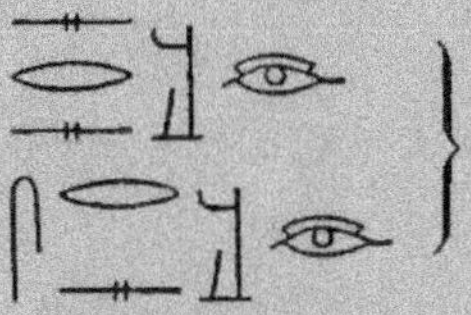 to be awake, to watch.

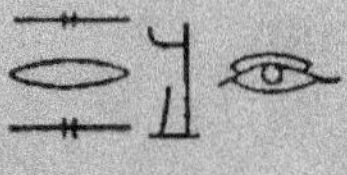 watch, watching, watcher.

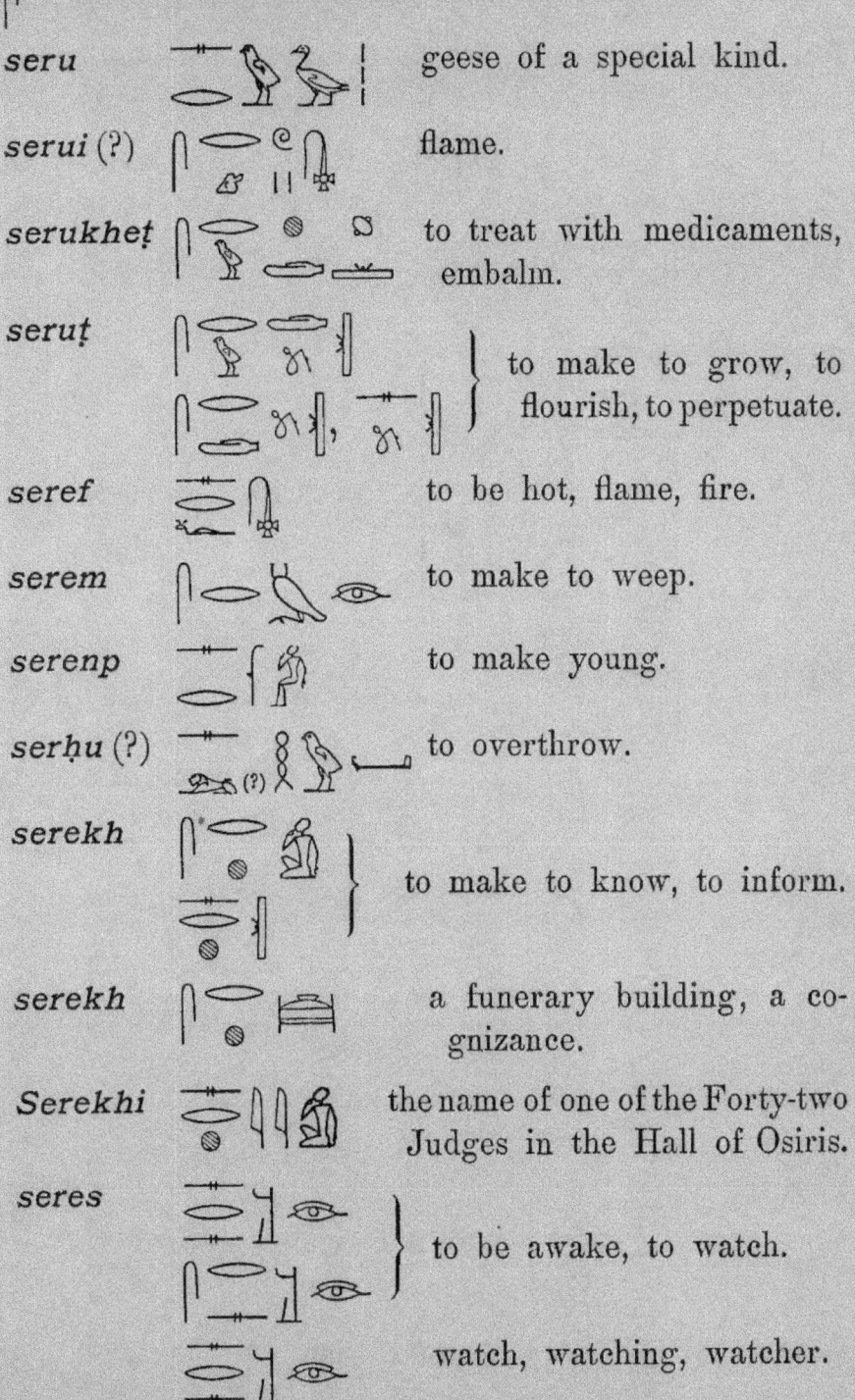

Seres-ḥer 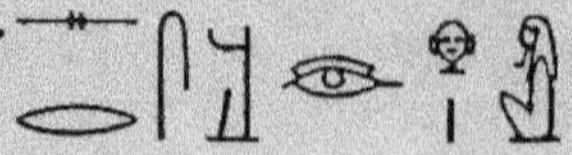 "watching face"; the name of a god.

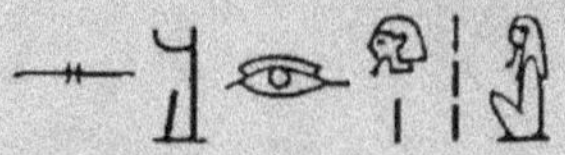 "watching faces"; a class of divine beings.

serqaȧu  to be refreshed, to breathe.

Serqet 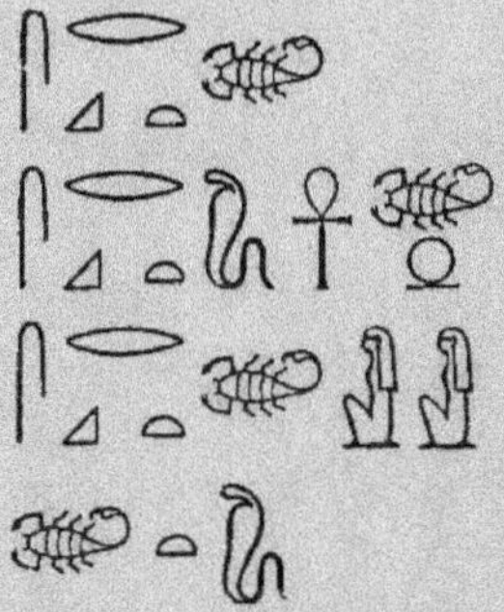 the goddess Serqet.

Sert 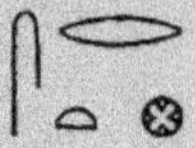 a city in the Seventh Ȧat.

sert 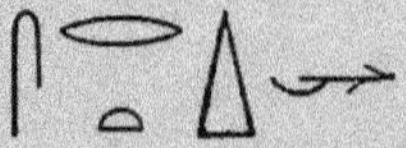 "goad"; the name of a part of the magic boat.

serṭ 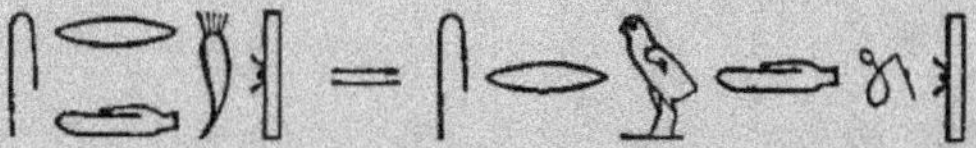

Serṭiu  the name of one of the Forty-two Judges in the Hall of Osiris.

sehep 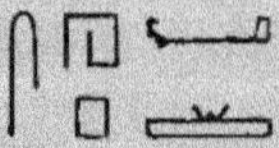 lawgiver.

seher, ***seherr*** 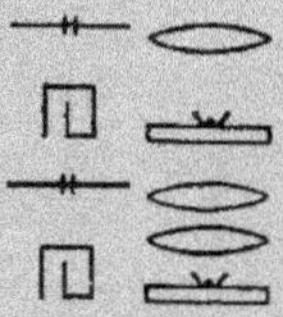 to make quiet, subdue.

sehert  carnelian.

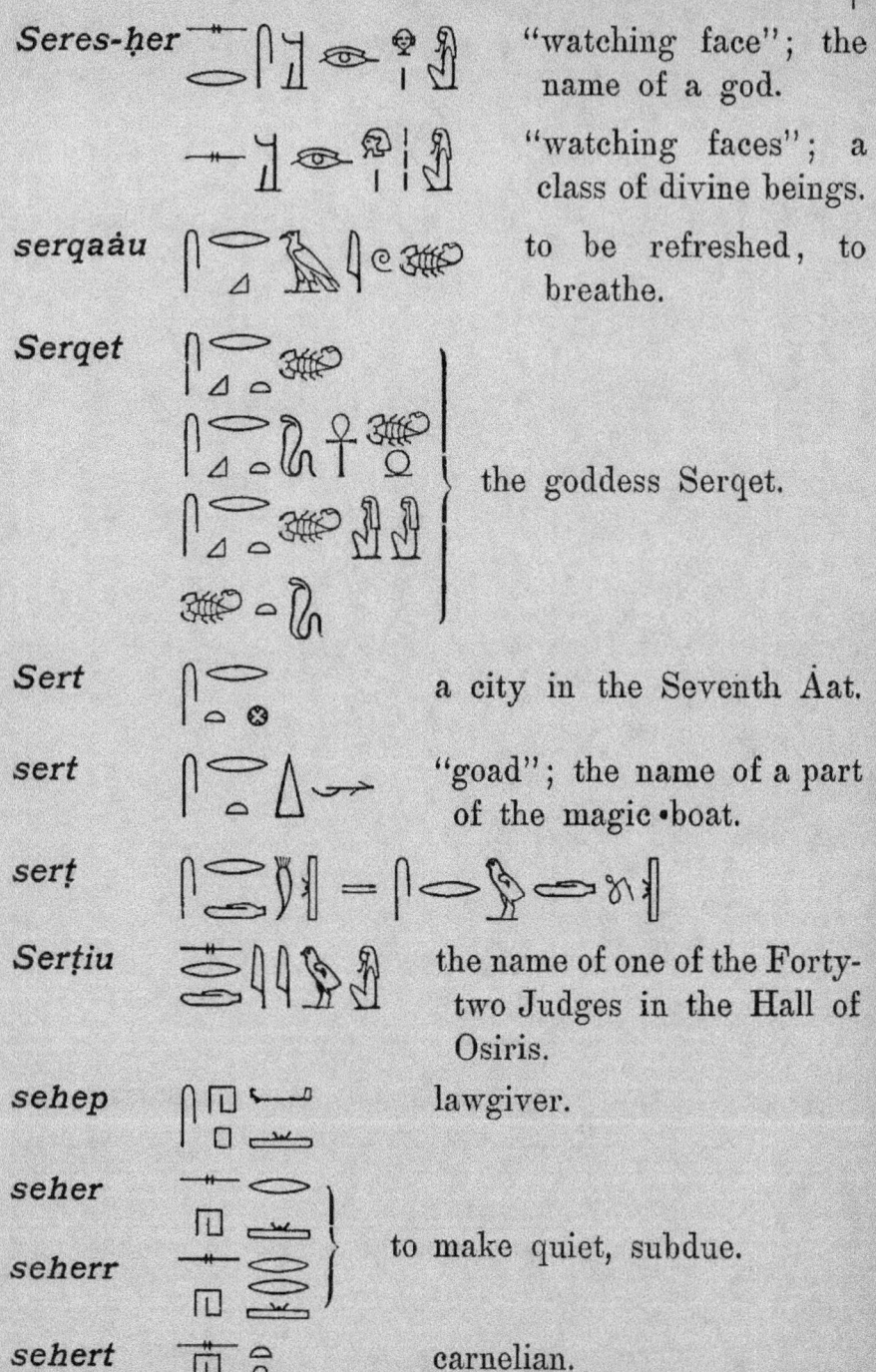

seḥ  hall; 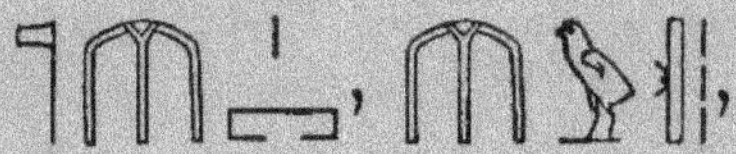 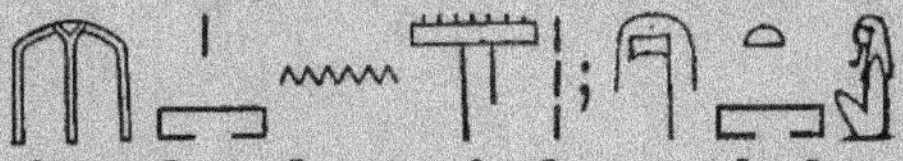 the chamber of the embalmment of Osiris.

seḥap  to hide.

seḥuā  to confuse, disarrange.

seḥui  to gather together, collect.

seḥurȧ 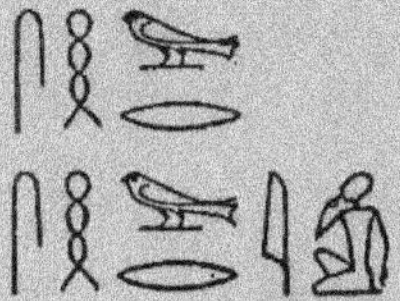 to curse.

seḥeb 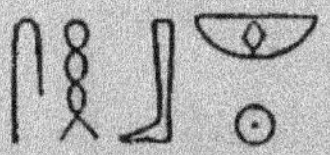 to keep a feast, to make festival.

seḥem 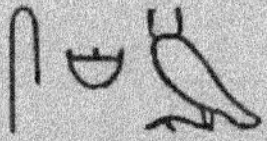 to turn back.

seḥeptet 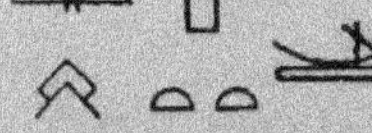 name of a boat (?).

seḥen  to order, arrange (?).

seḥer  to drive away.

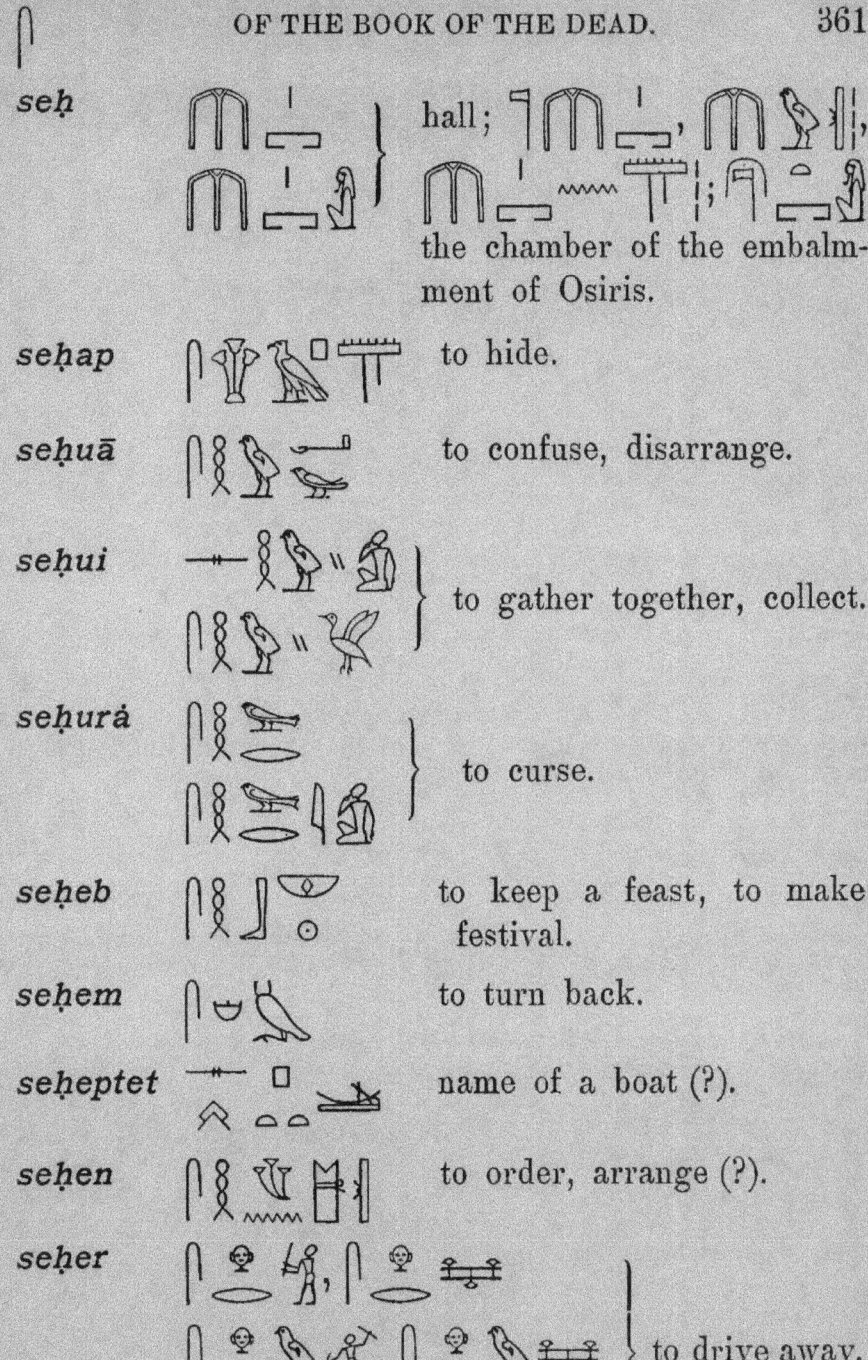

 driver away; plur. 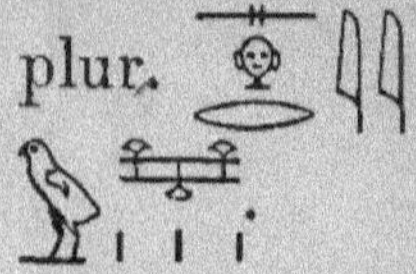

seḥes 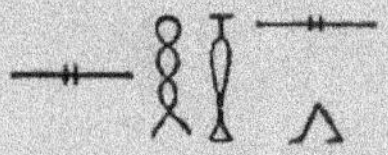 to make to meet.

seḥset 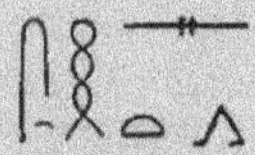 a meeting.

seḥeq  to cut off, hack in pieces.

seḥeq  to appoint to some office.

seḥeqer  to cause to hunger, to keep hungry.

seḥetep 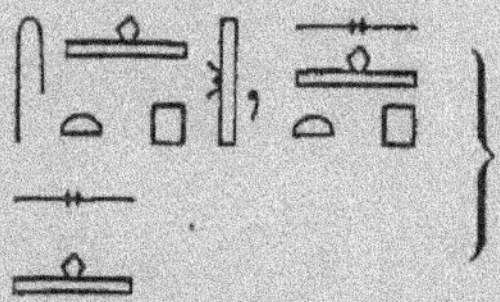 to make to be at peace, to propitiate, to pacify.

 to quiet the heart.

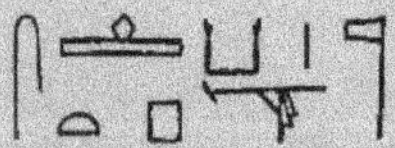 to propitiate the divine Ka.

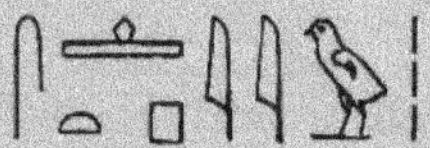 peacemakers.

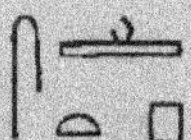 pacification.

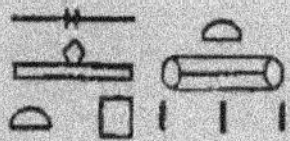 offerings which bring peace.

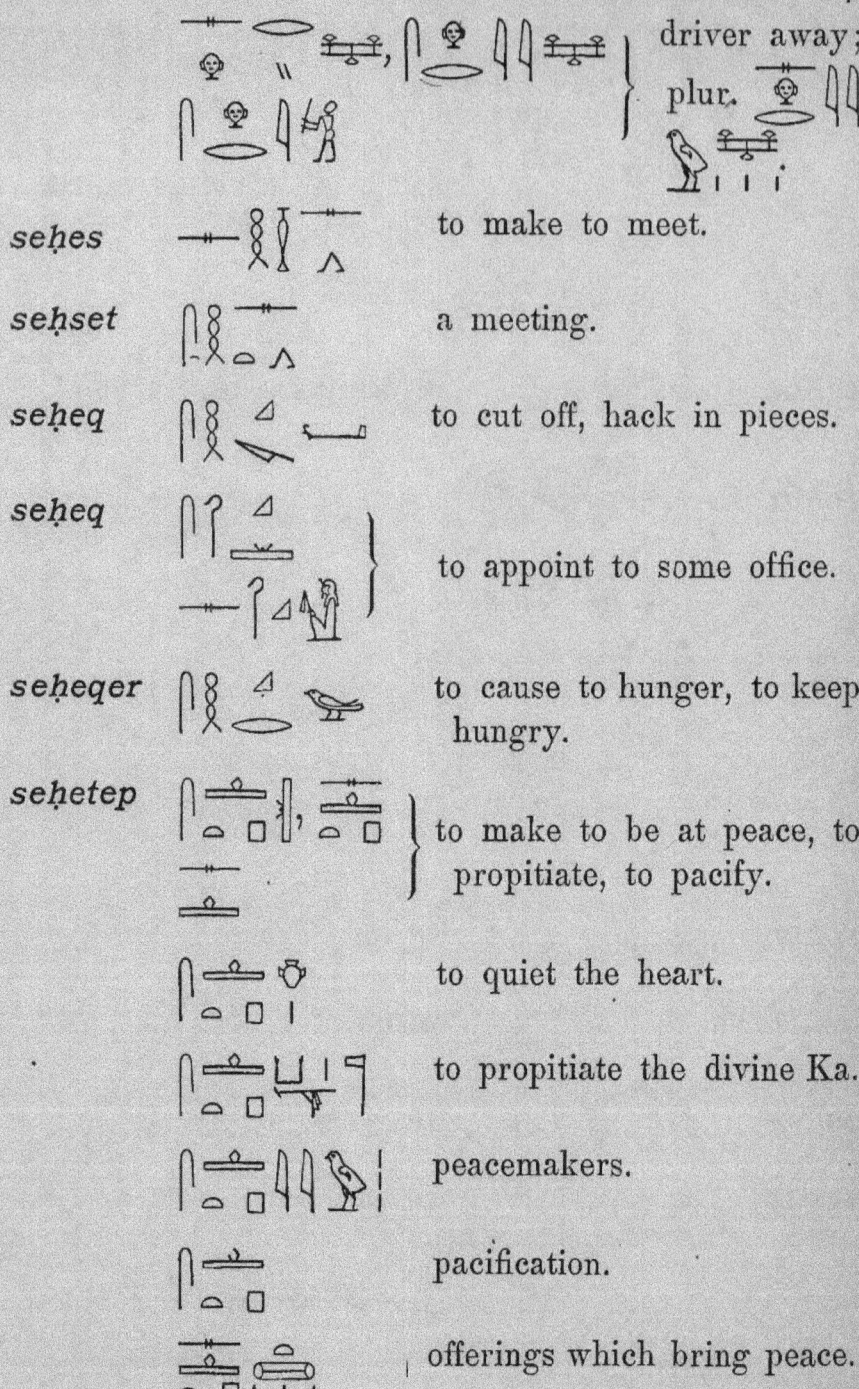

Seḥetep-taui "pacifier of the Two Lands"; a proper name.

seḥetem to destroy.

Seḥetemet-Au-ā-em-ābet the name of the banks of a river.

Seḥtet a proper name.

seḥetch to emit light, illumine, to shine.

light, radiance, brilliance.

Seḥetch-ur "Great Light", *i. e.*, Rā.

sekh

sekh to break, strike, cut, wound.

sekha to have in mind, to commemorate, to remember.

remembrance for good.

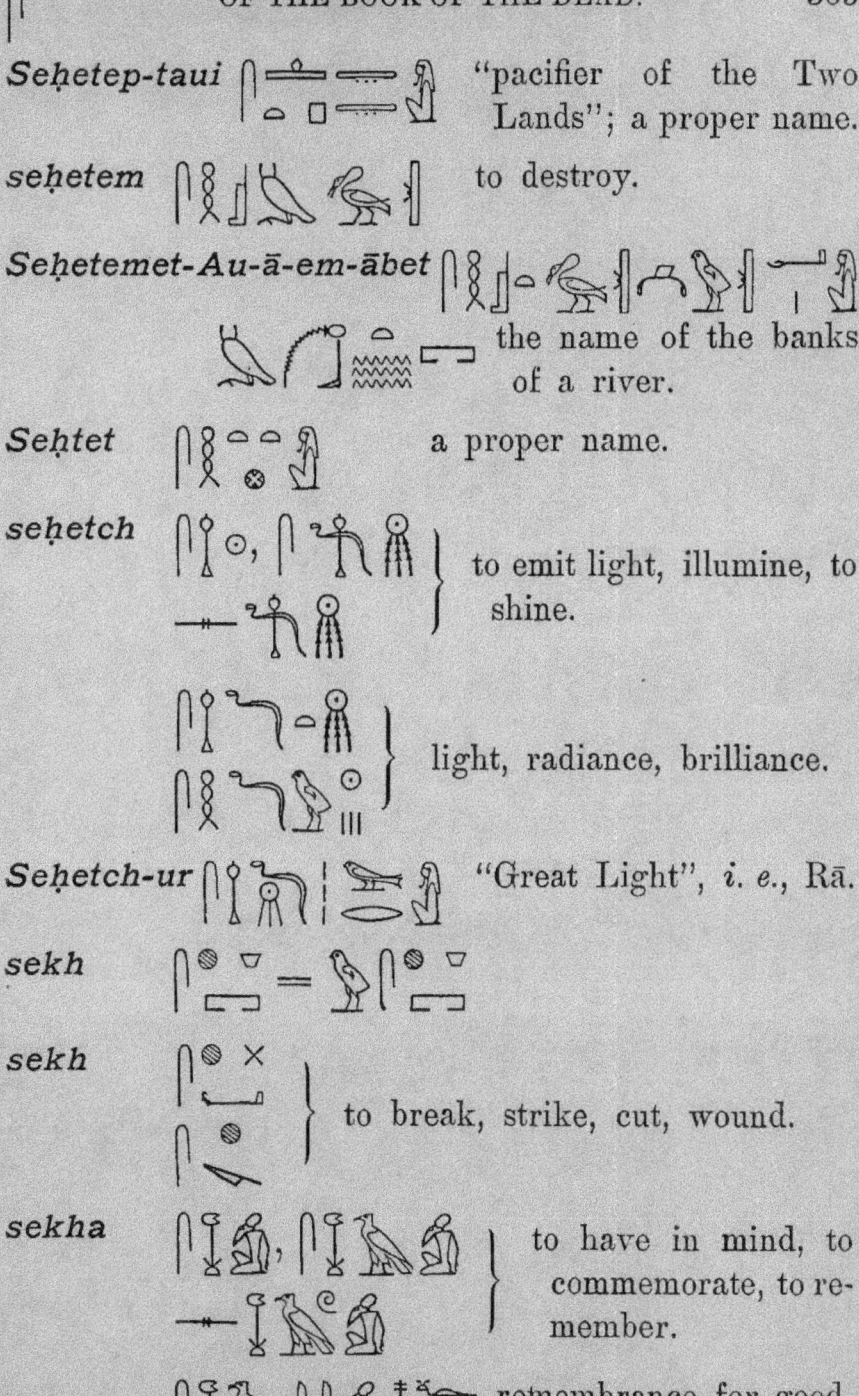

 memorial services.

 remembrance of evil.

sekha 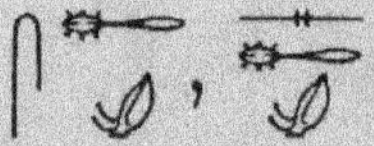 to be deaf.

Sekhai  a Cow-goddess.

sekhabui  eaters (?).

sekhap 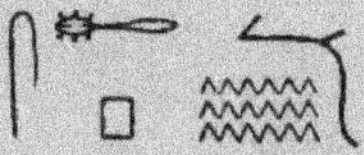 to swallow.

sekhar 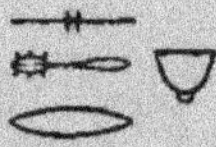 to milk.

sekharu  to plate, to mould.

sekhakeru  to ornament.

Sekhat-Ḥeru  a Cow-goddess.

Sekhāi 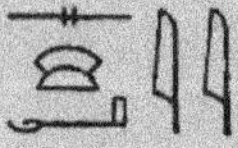 to make to rise or appear, to crown.

Sekhiu  the name of a double serpent god or fiend.

sekhu  to praise, glorify.

sekhu  praise.

sekhun  to revile, curse.

sekhuṭ  to fortify.

sekheb  see 

sekhep 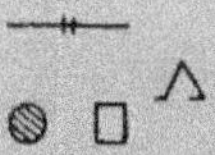 to make advance.

Sekhepti 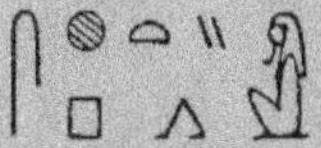 a proper name.

sekheper  to make to become, to create, fashion, form.

sekheperu 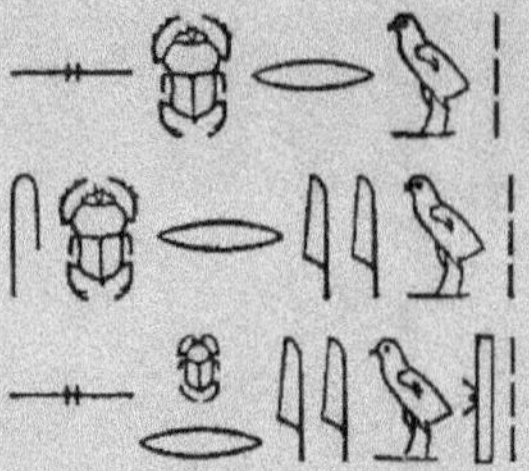 those who cause things to be.

sekhef 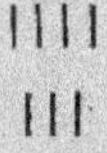 seven; 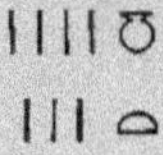 seventh.

sekhem 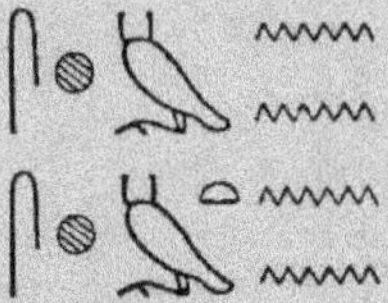 to forget, forgetfulness.

Sekhem  shrine, sanctuary.

 gods of the shrine.

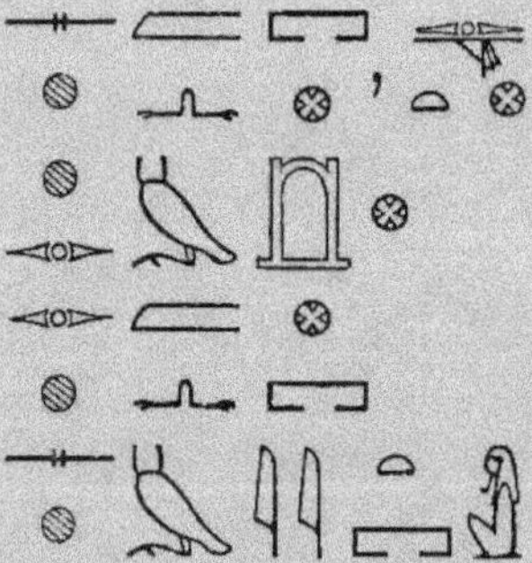 the city of Letopolis.

sekhem  to recite, to read.

sekhem  to be strong, mighty, to prevail over, to gain the mastery, show oneself strong, might, power.

 bold man, victor.

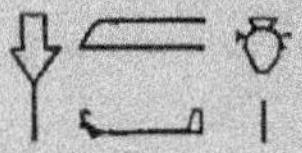 brave in heart.

 weak.

 mighty one, strong.

Sekhem  the natural power, vital power of a man, any power spiritual or physical.

Sekhemu 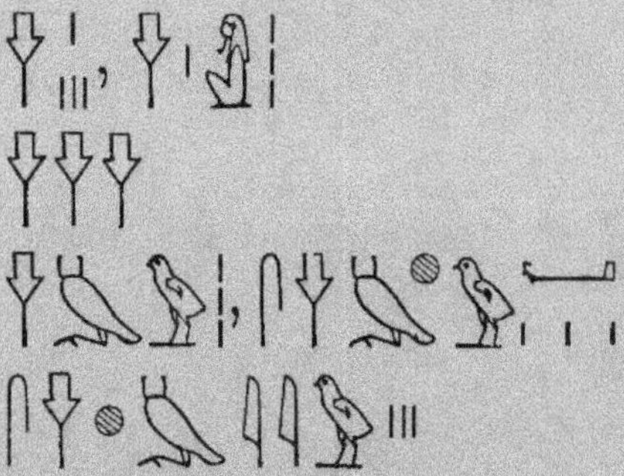 the Powers;  the Double Power.

Sekhem-ur 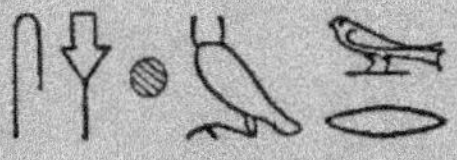 "great Power"; a proper name.

Sekhem-em-àb-f  "strong in his heart"; a proper name.

Sekhem-nefer "good Power"; a proper name.

Sekhmet-ren-s-em-ḥemut-s the name of a sacred cow.

Sekhmet (Sekhet) name of a goddess.

Sekhmet-Bast-Rā a solar triad.

sekhen to direct (?).

sekhen to embrace.

"great embracer"; a proper name.

sekhni to make to alight.

sekhenen to become rotten, to decay.

sekhensh to make to stink, to calumniate.

sekhent to make to advance.

sekhent 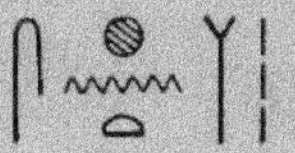 pillars.

sekher 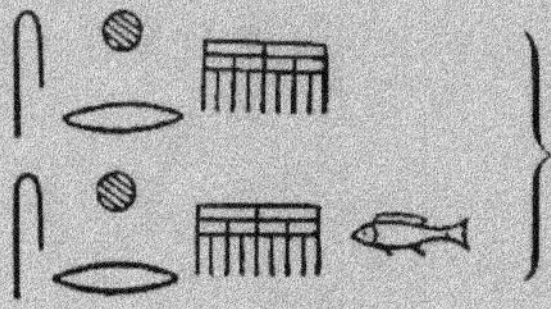 to offend.

[*sekher*  plan, device, counsel, arrangement.]

 plur. of preceding.

 a plan of triumph, or blessedness.

 celestial designs, ordinances of heaven.

sekher 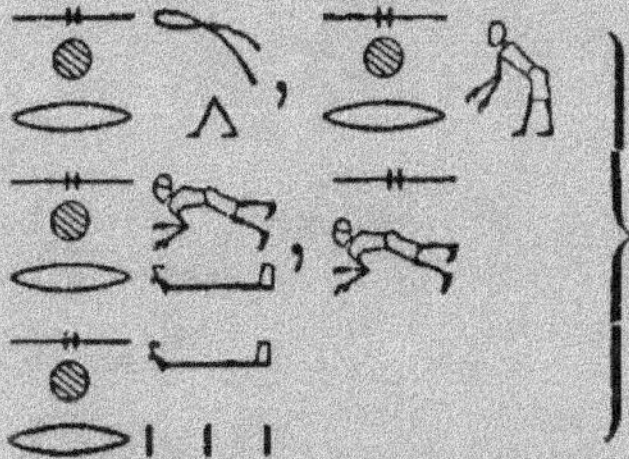 to overthrow.

 fallen.

 overthrow.

Sekher-āṭ 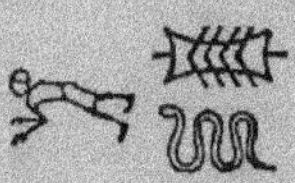 the god of the Sixth Ārit.

Sekheriu  the name of one of the Forty-two Judges in the Hall of Osiris.

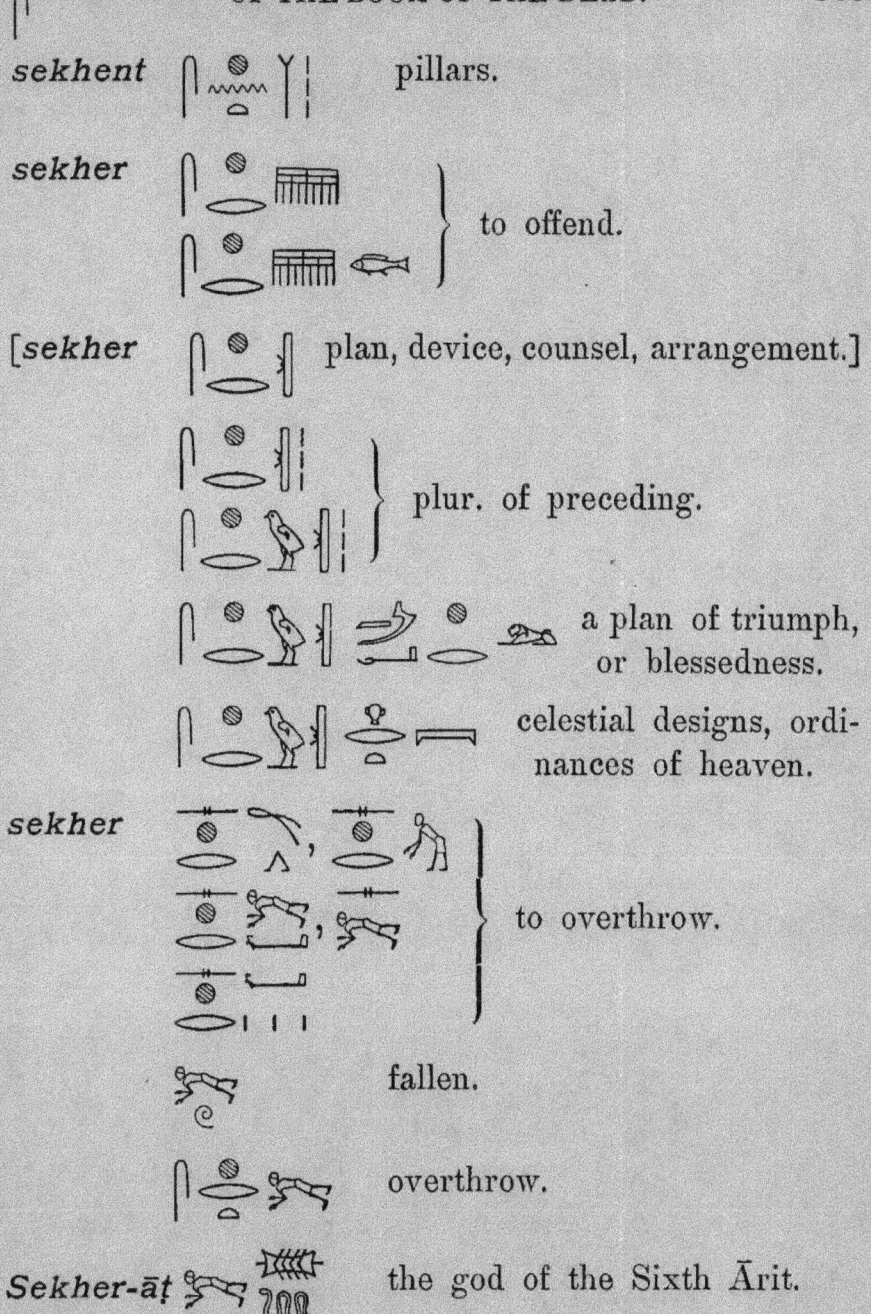

Sekher-remu  a proper name.

sekhekh 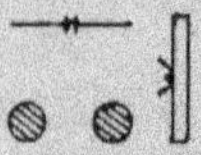 to straighten.

sekhes 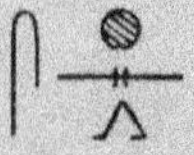 to run.

sekhes 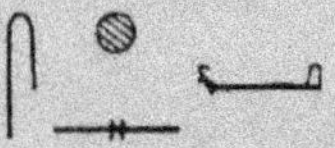
sekhsekh 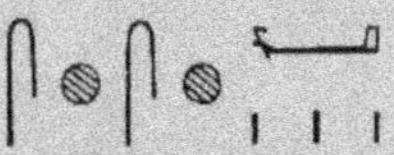 } to fasten, make firm.

sekhesef   } to meet with hostility, to repulse, to contradict, give evidence against.

sekhet 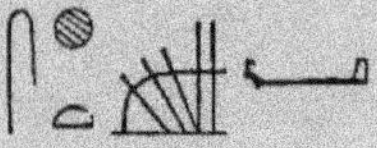 to net, to snare, spread out a net.

sekhtu 
sekhtiu 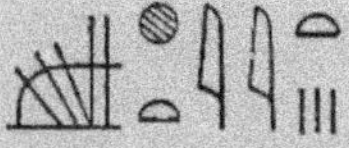   } snarers, hunters, fowlers, fishermen.

sekhet 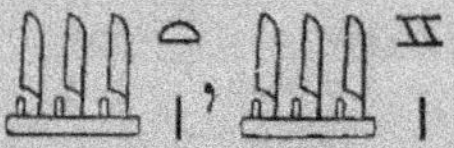 field, meadow; plur. .

sekhtiu  the divine field labourers.

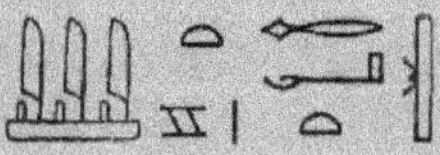 "Great Field", *i. e.*, heaven.

Sekhet-Åanru (or *Åaru*) 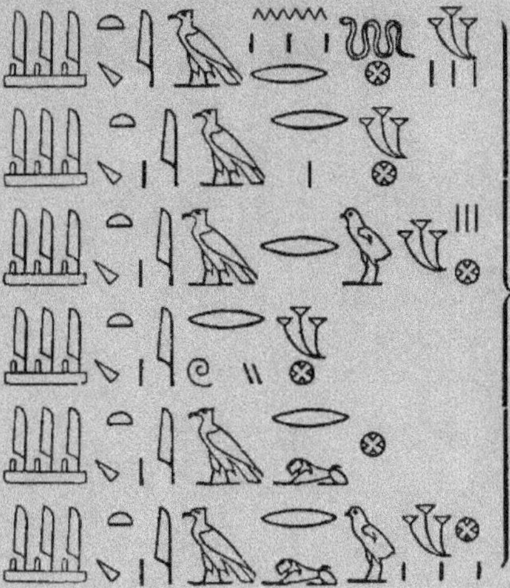 the "Field of reeds", *i. e.*, the Elysian Fields.

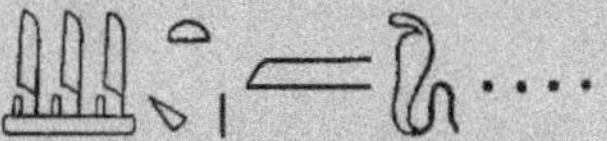 a proper name?

Sekhet-neḥeḥ  "Field of Eternity".

Sekhet-neteru 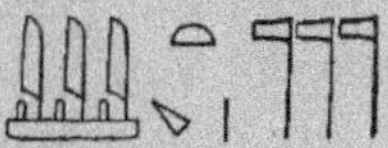 "Field of the gods".

Sekhet-Rā 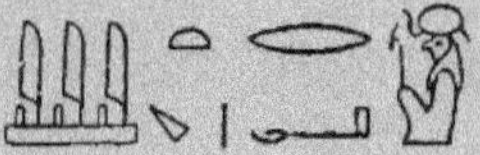 "Field of Rā".

Sekhet-ḥetep 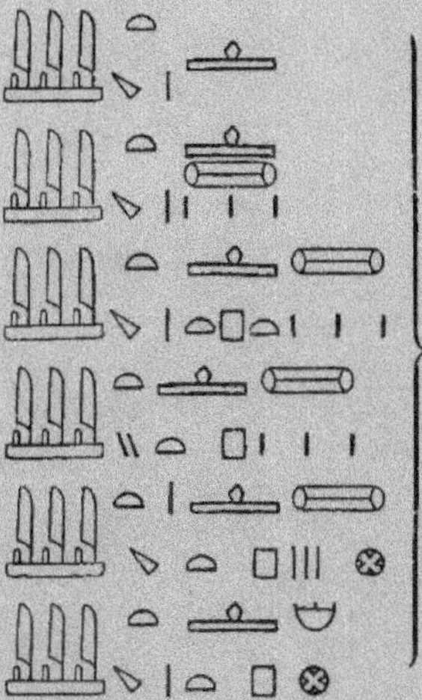 the "Field of Peace", or "Field of Offerings"; a name of the Elysian Fields.

Sekhti-ḥetep 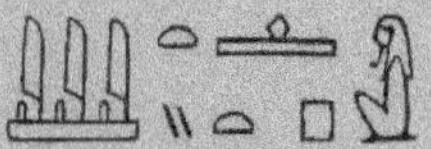 the god of the Field of Peace.

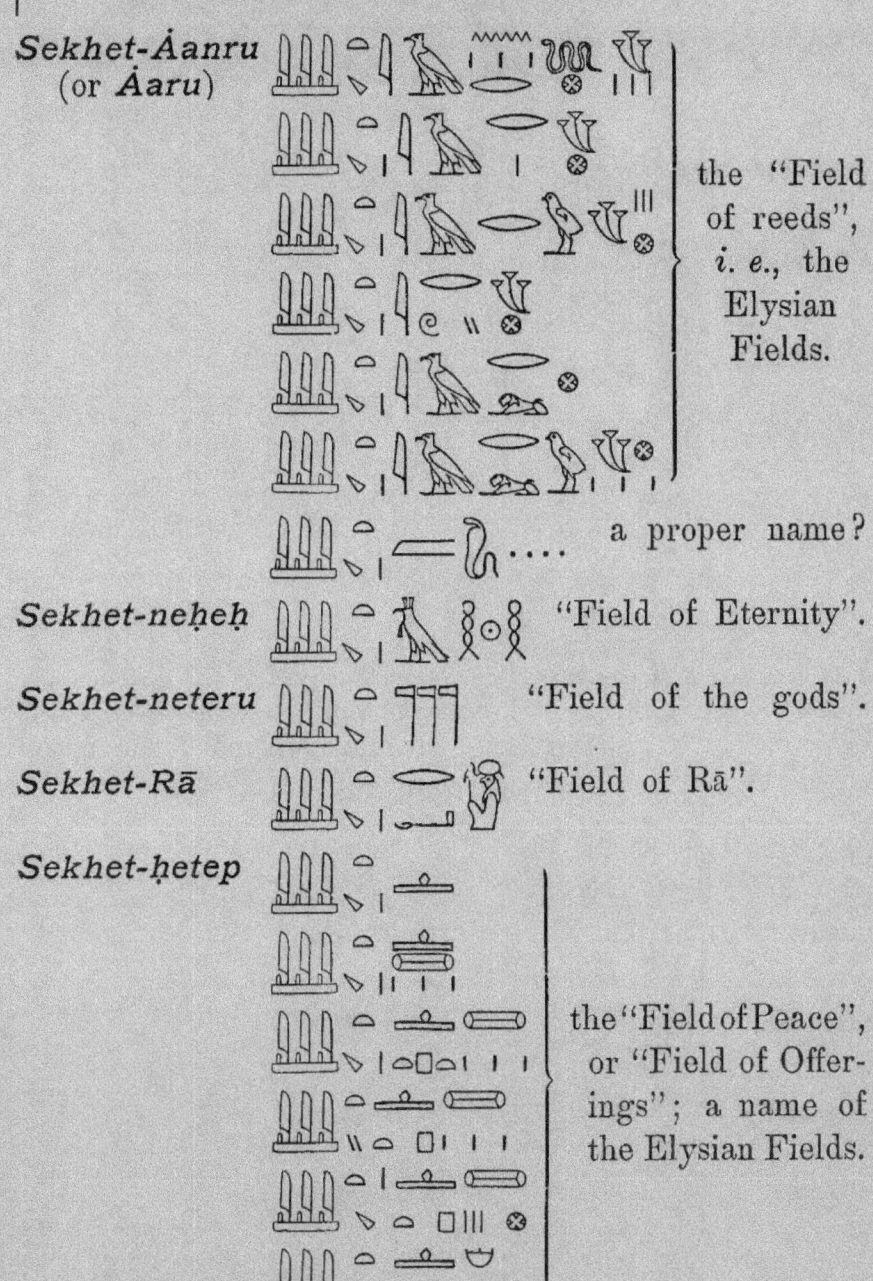

Sekhet-sanehemu "Field of the Grasshoppers".

Sekhet-Sȧsȧ "Field of Fire".

sekhettu plants.

sekhet

sekheṭ to turn upside down, invert, stand on the head;.

Sekheṭ-ḥer-āsh-ȧru "inverted face, of many forms"; the name of the porter of the First Ārit.

sekhṭu to hunger.

sesu times, days.

sesun to destroy.

sesunṭ to destroy.

seseb to slay.

sesen to snuff the air.

seska  body.

seset 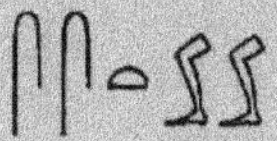 legs.

seset 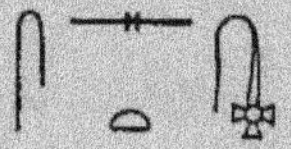 to burn up.

sesh 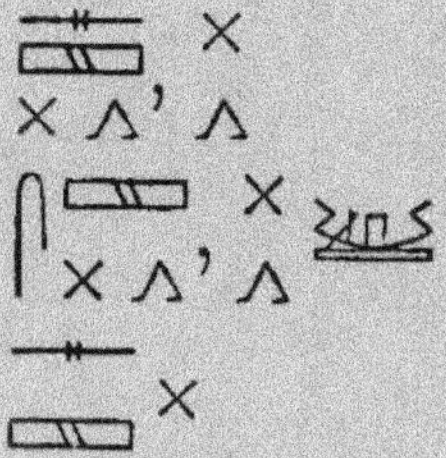 to pass, journey, travel.

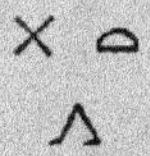 passage.

 impassable.

sesh 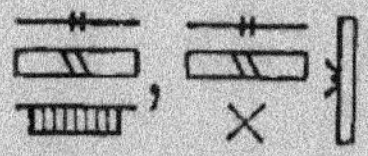 to open, unbolt.

sesh  to be wise, skilful, knowledge.

sesh 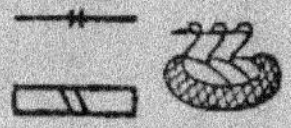 nest; plur. .

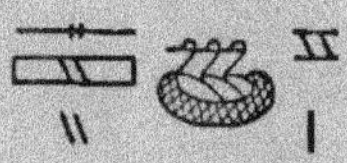 birth-place.

 two nests.

Seshet  name of a town and its god.

sesh 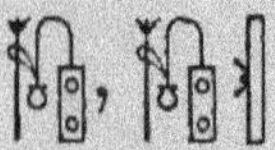 to write, draw, copy, make a plan.

seshu 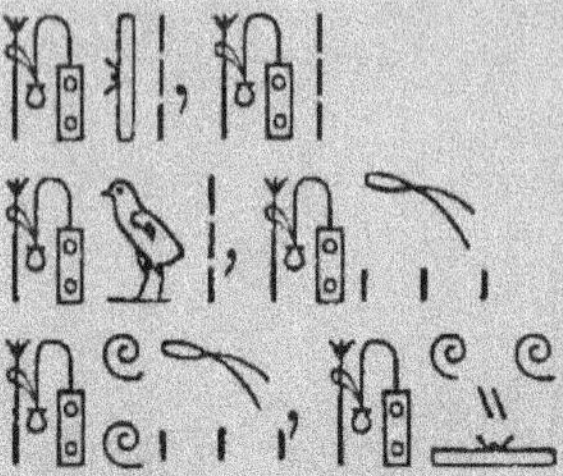 writings, decrees, documents, archives, books, copies of books, etc.

sesh 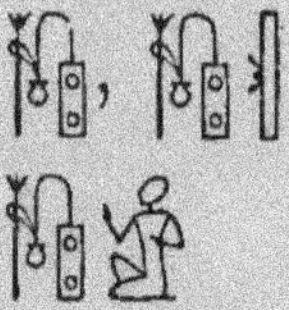 scribe, copyist.

 accomplished scribe.

 veritable scribe (as opposed to a titular scribe).

 scribe of the temple property.

 scribe and draughtsman.

 scribe and draughtsman of the house of gold.

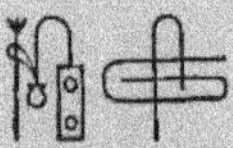 scribe and designer.

seshai  skilled, able, competent.

seshu  to be empty.

seshep 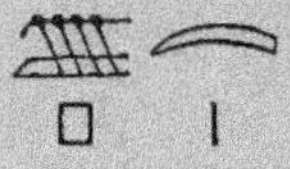 the measure of a palm.

seshepu 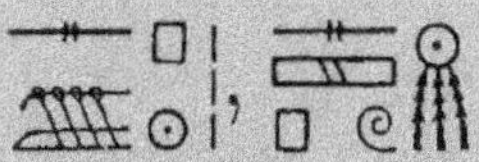 light, radiance; see SHESEP.

seshem 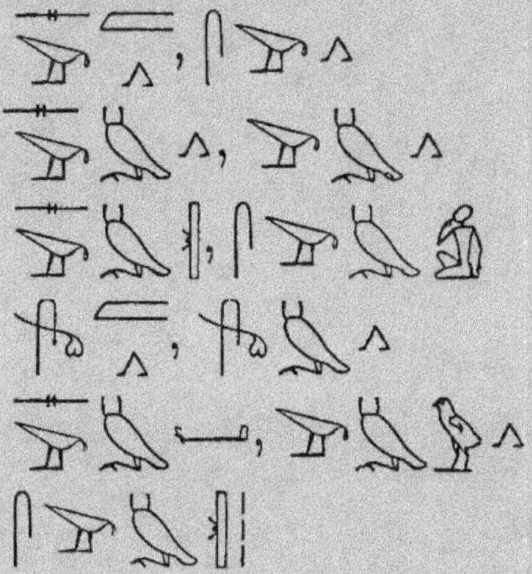 to lead, guide, conduct, guidance.

seshem  guide, leader.

 plur. of preceding.

seshmet  advance, guiding, guidance.

gratification (?).

Seshemit "conductress"; the name of a goddess.

Seshmu-ḥeḥ "guide of eternity"; a proper name.

Seshmu-ta "guide of the earth"; a proper name.

Seshmu-taui "guide of the Two Lands"; a proper name.

Seshem divine image, statue.

seshem figure, design, image, form, similitude.

seshen to scatter, destroy.

seshen . . . . . .

seshen, ***seshennu***, ***senshen***, ***seshesh*** lily.

seshru garments, apparel.

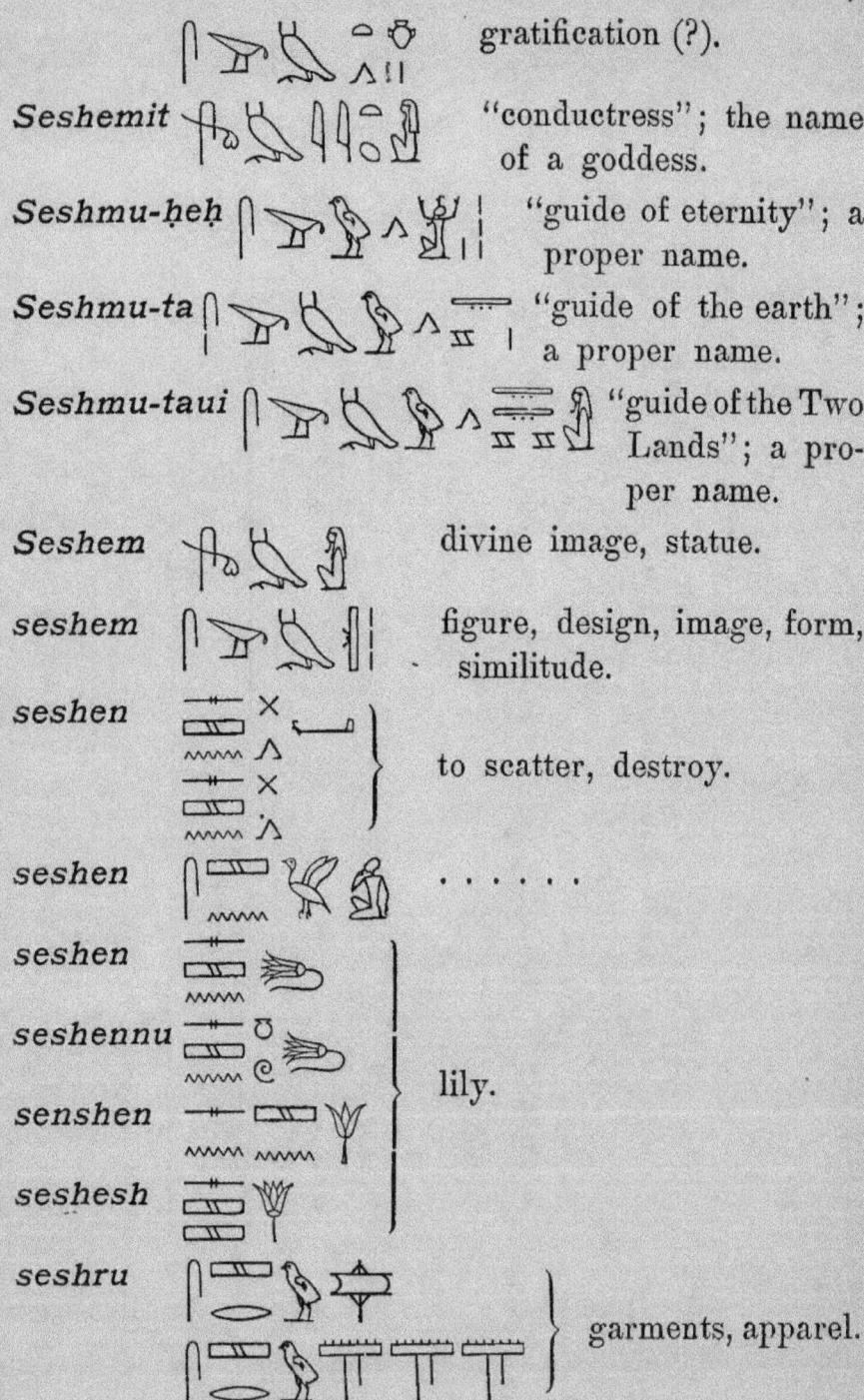

seshert a cake, loaf.

seshet (?) fire; plur. ; gods of fire .

Sesheta the goddess of architecture.

sesheta to be hidden, mysterious, incomprehensible.

sesheta hidden things, mysteries, secrets.

of invisible forms and shapes.

hidden of name.

very great mysteries indeed.

great secrets of Àmenti.

seshetu fiends (?).

sesheṭ bandage, bandlet, tiara, girdle, fillet for the head.

seshet-t — a chamber with a window or opening in it.

sek — to decay, perish; incorruptible.

sek — to break through, fight a way, to fight, destroy; to advance.

seksek

sek-re — to direct.

Sek-ḥer — a proper name.

Seku — (with *ákhemu*) a class of gods.

seka — to plough.

sekemiu — grey or white hair.

Seker
Sekri — the ancient god of the Other World of Ṣaḳḳârah.

Seker in his secret place.

Seker 

Sekri 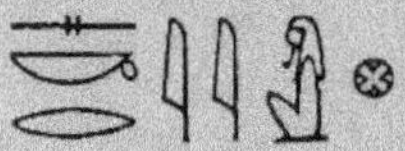 } the town of Seker.

Sekri 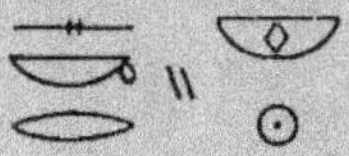 the festival of Seker.

Seker  the sacred bark of Seker.

Seksek  the name of a fiend.

sektiu  to fetter.

Sektet 

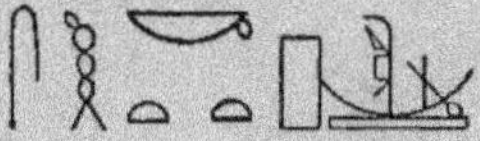

 } the boat in which the sun travelled from noon to midnight.

seq 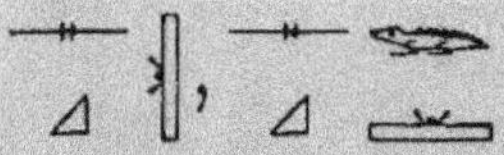

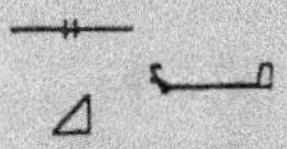 } to collect, gather together.

seqa 

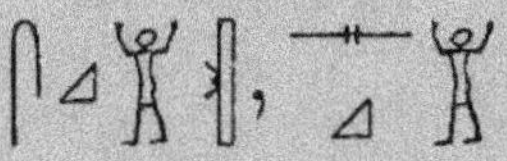 } to exalt, to lift up.

seqai  exalted one.

 } plur. of preceding.

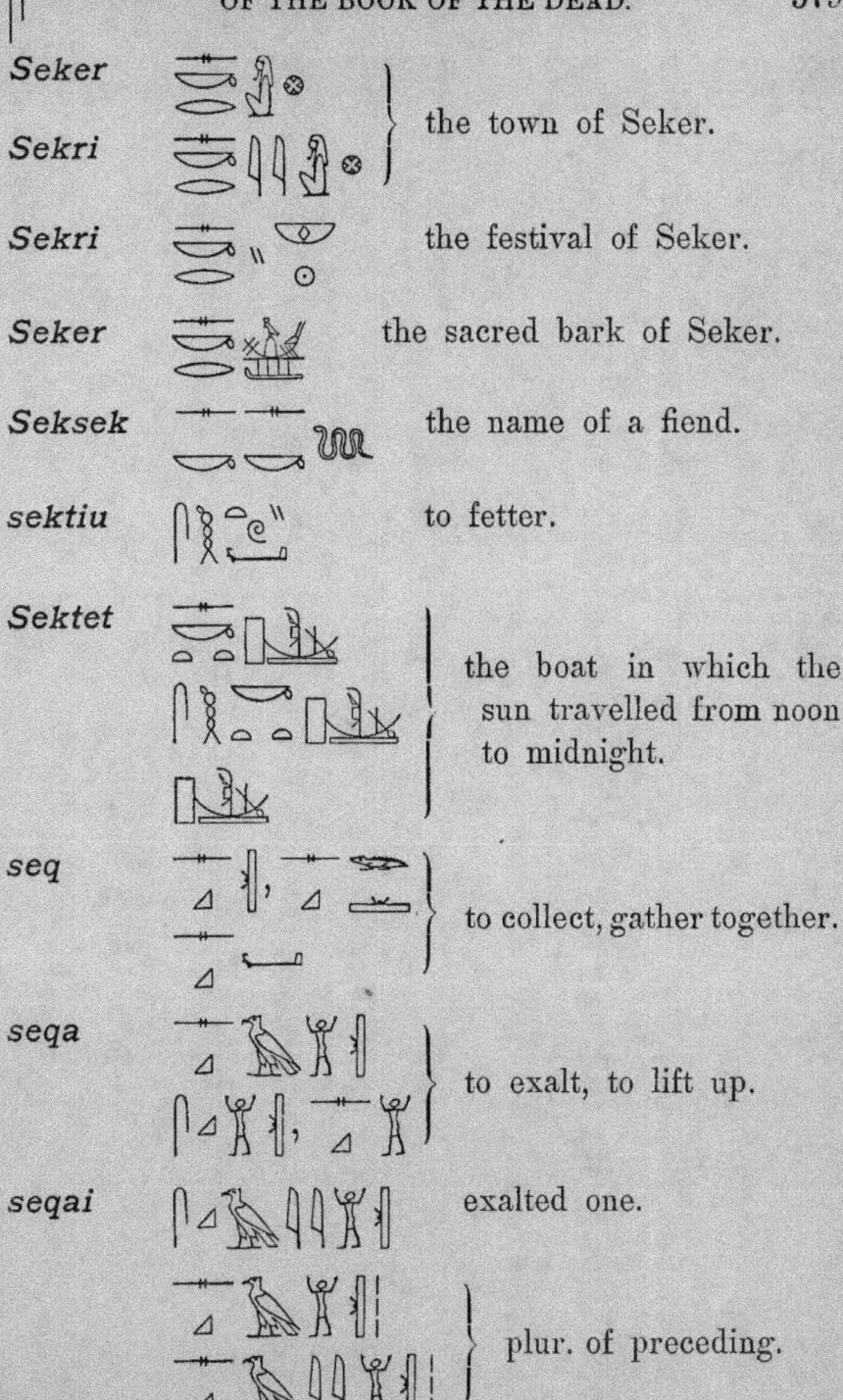

seqeb image (?).

seqebb to cool, refresh oneself.

Seqebit name of a goddess.

seqer to smite, take prisoner.

smiter.

seqeṭ to sail in a boat, to journey, make a voyage; encircled.

voyages, sailings.

sailors, boatmen.

seqeṭ 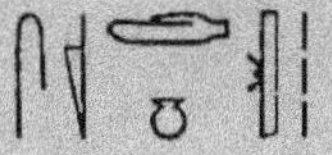 dispositions.

Seqeṭ-ḥer 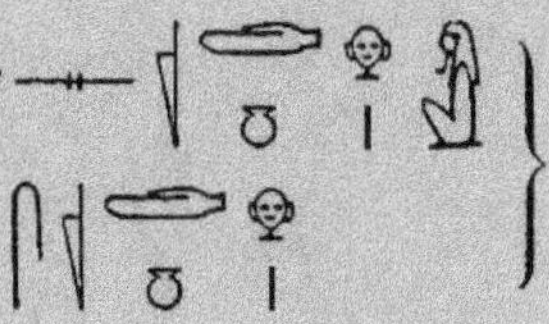 warder of the Second Ārit.

seḳenniu  helpless ones, weak.

seḳer  to put to silence, make quiet.

seḳert 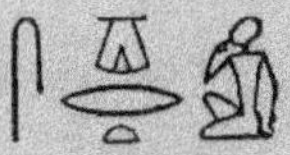 silence.

set 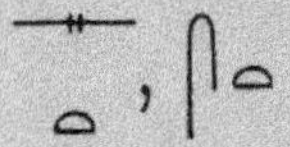 she, it, its.

set 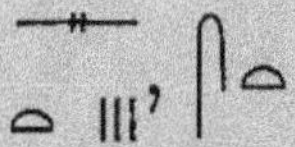 they, them, their.

set (?) 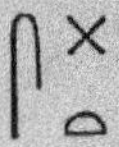 to break.

set 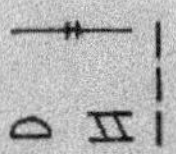 ground.

Set  the god of physical and moral evil; see Suti.

set (*semt*) 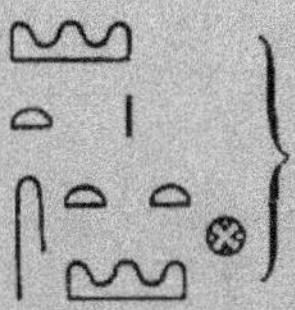 mountain; plur. 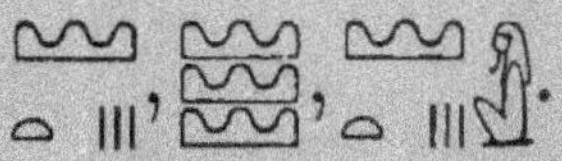.

set  to shoot arrows, to hurl stones.

set  to sow seed.

setit 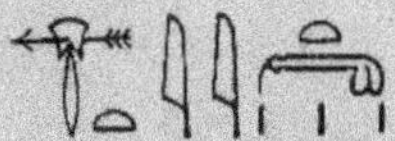 seed, progeny.

setut  arrows or beams of light, rays, radiance.

setau  to light a fire, to burn, flame.

seti  burning, burner.

setit  adversaries (?).

Sett 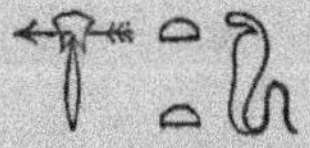 the name of a goddess of the First Cataract.

Sett  an Asiatic woman.

Set-ṭemui  a proper name (var.  ).

Sta 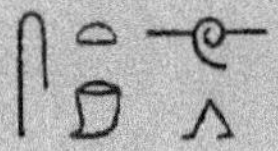 a proper name.

sta, stat
stau 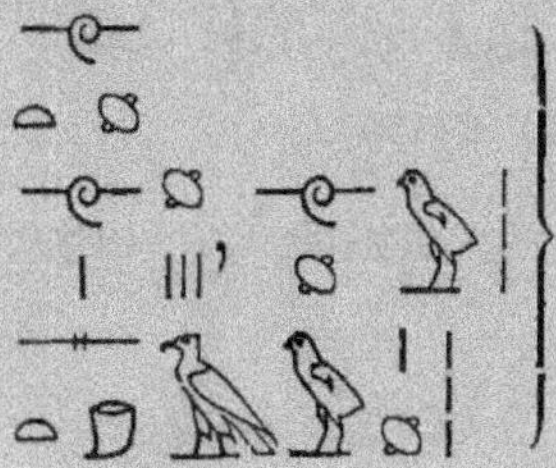 filth, dung.

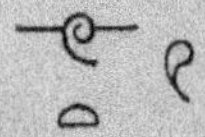 a portion of the body.

stat  filthy ones, fiends.

sta  to tow a boat, drag along, bring carry.

stau 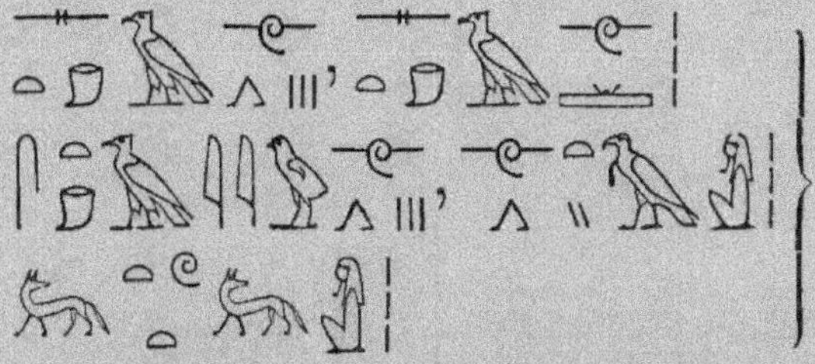 those who tow, bearers, carriers.

stau 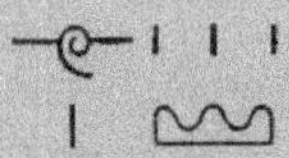 see 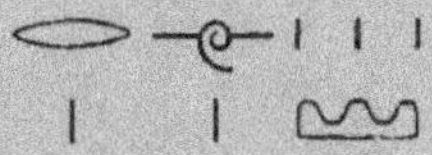 RE-STAU.

stat 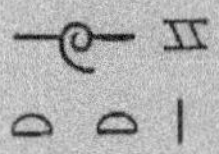 a measure of land.

sti 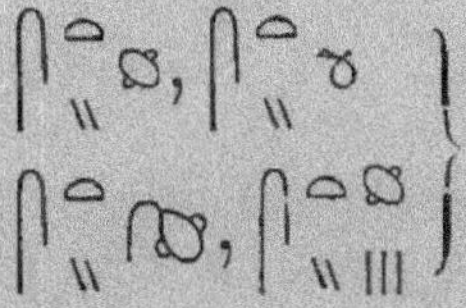 smell, odour.

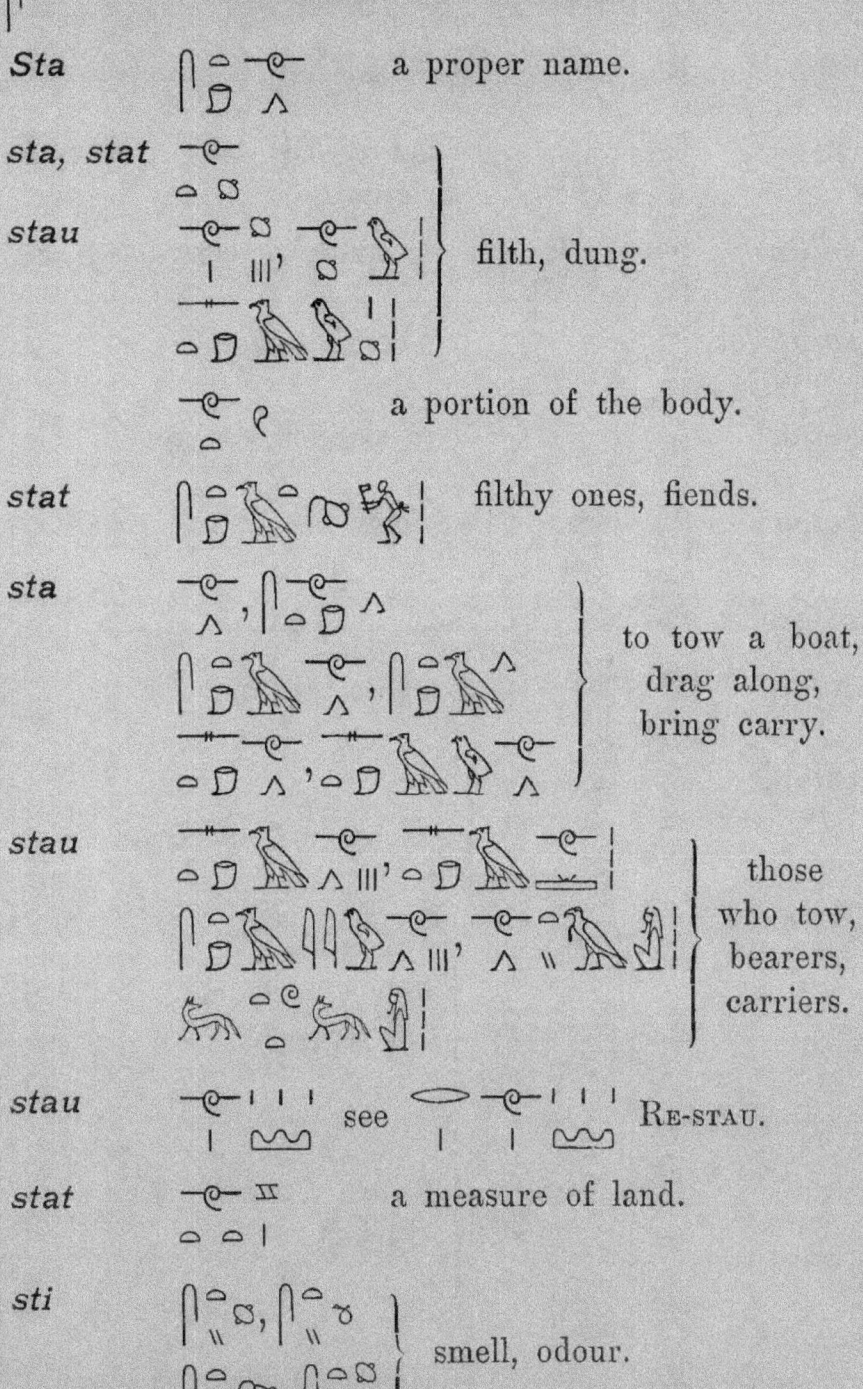

sti 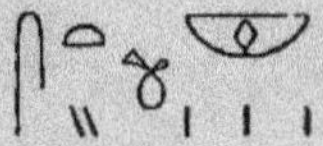 festal perfume.

Sti  "land of the bow"; a name of Nubia.

setua  to make or ascribe praise.

setut (or *sutet*)  to walk about.

setut  to symbolize, typify.

seteb  captives.

setep 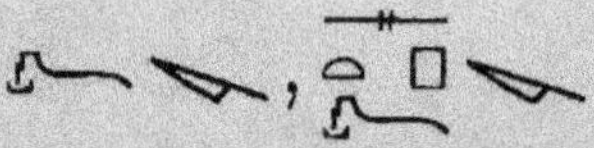 to cut.

setep  to chose, chosen.

setepu  choice cuts of meats.

setep sa  to work protection on behalf of someone.

setem  to hear; obey;  hearer.

 what is heard, listener.

setemiu listeners.

Setem-ḥeri the name of the upper hinge.

Setem-kheri the name of the lower hinge.

Setem-ȧnsi a proper name.

setennu to be distinguished.

setentit distinctions.

setenem to make to walk.

seter wooden tablet (?).

setḥu to open.

set-ḥemt woman, wife.

seteken to make to enter.

invaders, those who make to enter.

seṭ hair, foliage.

seṭ 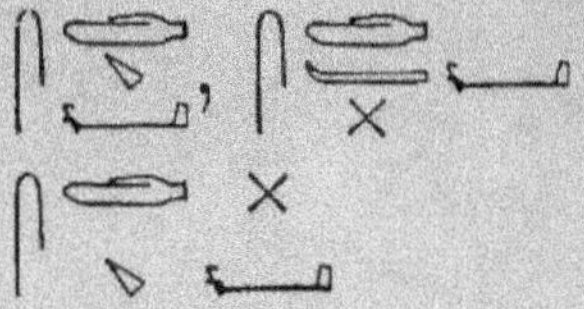 to break, split.

Seṭ-qesu (or, *Seṭ-qersu*) 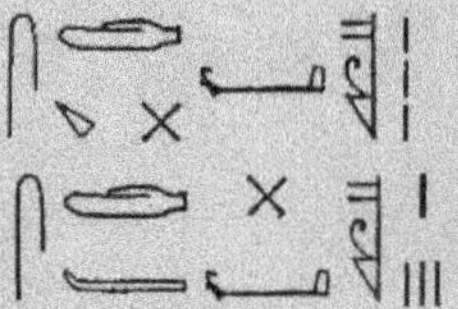 "bone - breaker"; the name of one of the Forty-two Judges in the Hall of Osiris.

seṭ 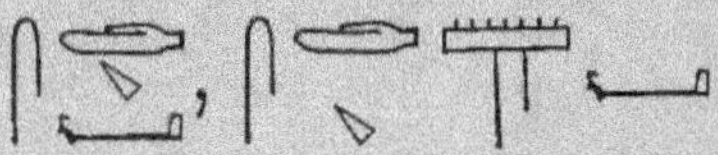 to clothe, to dress.

 a garment.

 those who clothe.

seṭa  to tremble, quake, trembling, terror.

seṭui  to defame.

seṭu  . . . . . .

seṭeb 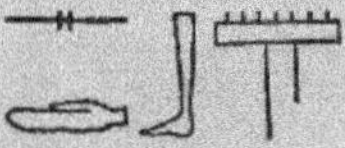 garment, hangings of a shrine.

seṭeb  obstacle, disaster, calamity, misfortune.

		plur. of preceding.
seṭebḥ	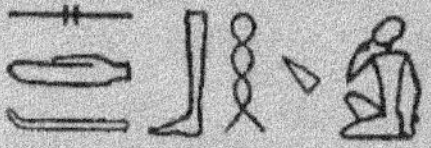	to be ready, equipped.
seṭemu		edicts for slaughter.
seṭen		distinguished.
Seṭeḳ		a proper name.
seṭeḳa		to cover.
seṭeḳaut		sleep.
seṭet	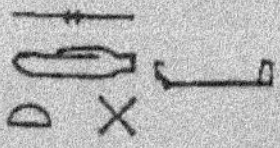	to break.
seṭeṭ	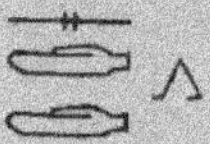	to travel.
seth	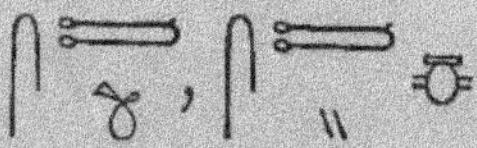	scent, unguent.
sethen	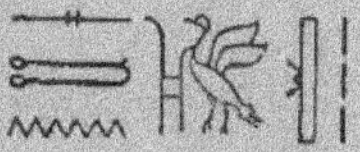	distinctions.
sethenem	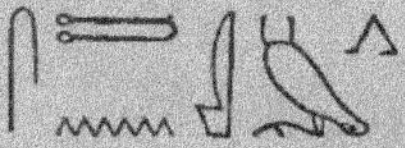	to make to walk.
sethes	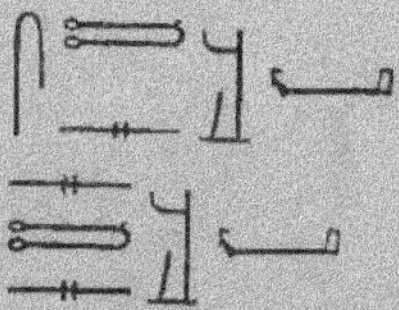	to raise up, lift up.

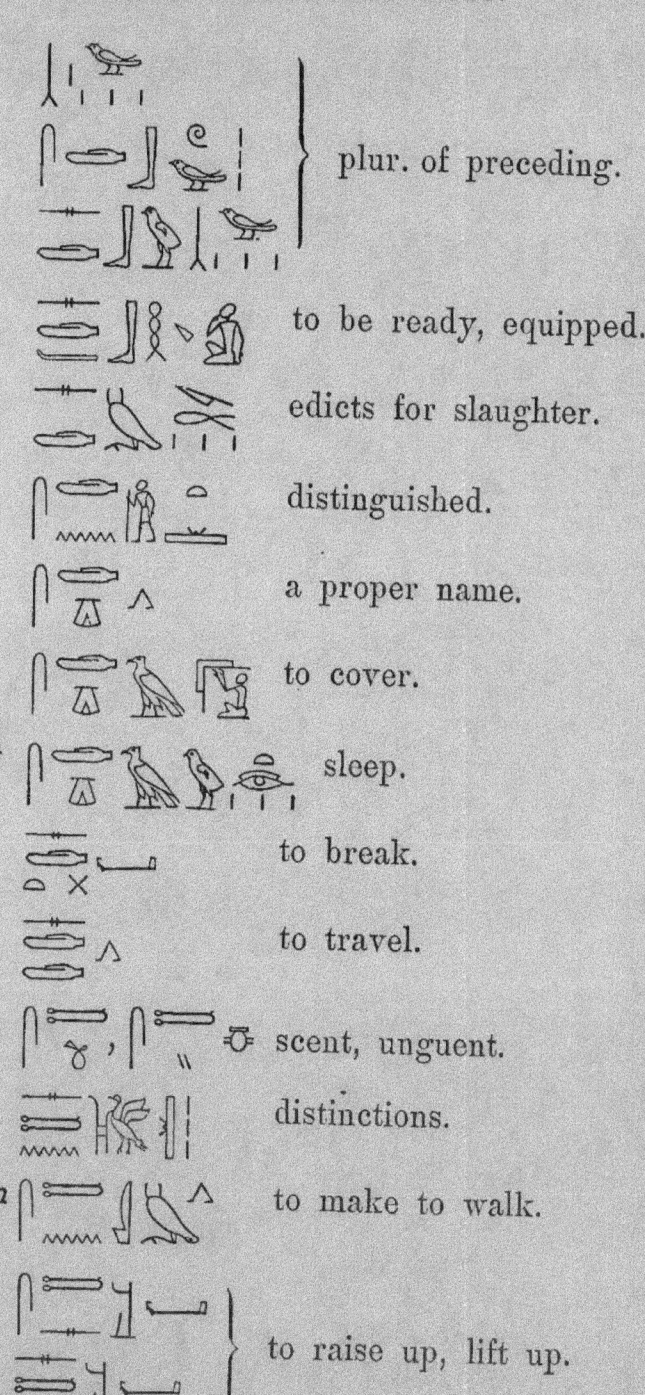

sethes  to praise, extol, "lift up", or "raise", a song or hymn, praisings.

sethesu  props, supports.

sethesu  supporters.

sethes Shu 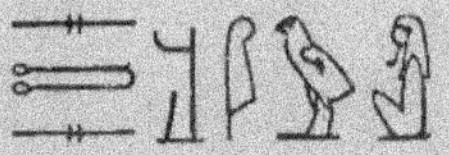 what Shu raises up, *i. e.*, the sky.

sethesu Shu  the supports of Shu, *i. e.*, the four cardinal points.

sethes 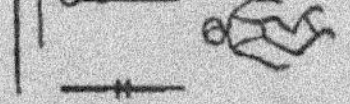 to be laid out.

sethes  to knit together.

sethesu  libations.

setheken  to have sexual union.

setcha  to make to set out, travel.

setchami  to protect (?).

setchit 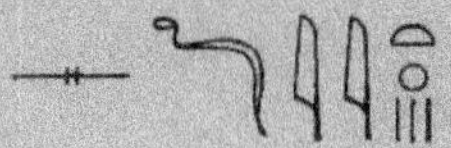 seeds of a plant (?).

setcheb 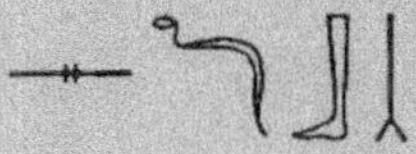 to oppose, be in the way of, obstruct.

setchefa  to feed with food celestial or terrestrial.

setcher  to lie down in sleep or death; dead, dead one;  the dead.

 bier.

setcheser 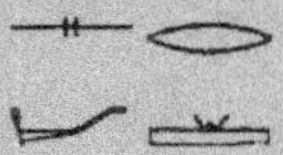 to sanctify.

setcheṭfu  to wound.

SH.

she pool, lake, laver; plur.

She asbiu Lake of flames.

She Aḳeb Lake of Aḳeb, *i. e.*, celestial ocean.

She Åqer Lake of Åqer, *i. e.*, the perfect lake (?).

She ur Great Lake.

She Maāti Lake of Maāti.

She em Māfket Lakes of Turquoise.

She Nu Lake of Nu.

She en Amu Lake of Fire.

She en Åsår Lake of Osiris.

She en Māat Lake of Māat.

She en Nesersert Lake of Fire.

	Lake of Fire.
She neter	Lake of the god, *i. e.*, Osiris.
She en Ḥeru	Lake of Horus.
She ḥeru	Lake of the celestial ones.
She ḥeḥ	Lake of Millions of years.
She en ḥesmen	Lake of Natron.
She Ḥetep	Lake of the god Ḥetep.
She ent ḥetch	Lake of Light.
She en khebentiu	Lake of the wicked.
She en kharu	Lake of the geese.
She en seḥetep	Lake of propitiation.
She en seshet	Lake of Fire.
Shet Ṭemui	Lake of the two knives.
She Tchesert	Lakes of the goddess Tchesert.
sha	field.

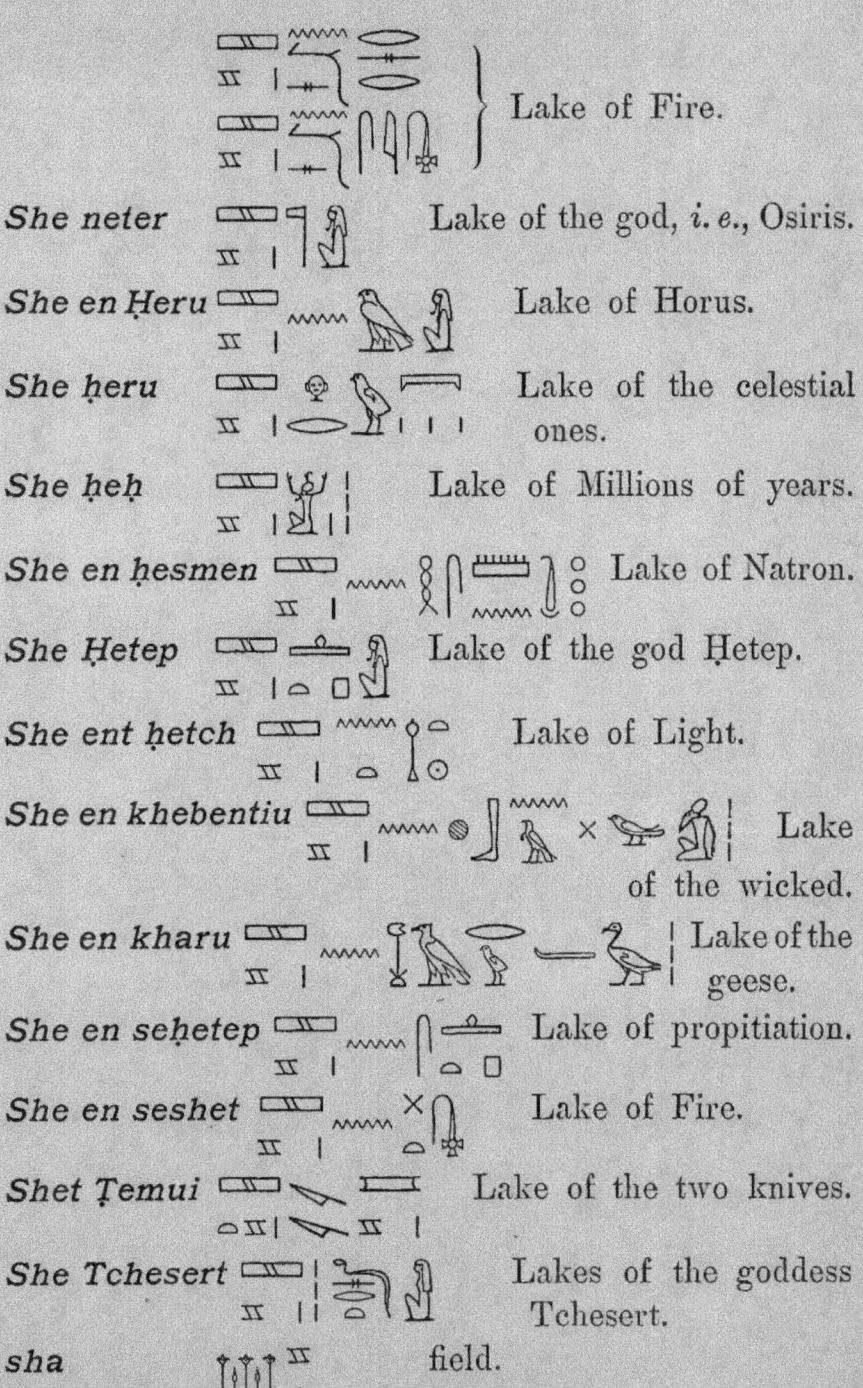

sha  bread-cakes, food.

sha  plants.

sha  to destine, predestine, fore-ordain.

shaȧ  pig.

shaȧs  to travel, journey, go forward.

shaā  one hundred.

shaā  to begin, beginning.

 unto,  unto all eternity.

Shau  the name of a city or town.

shauabti  the name of the figure inscribed with the VIth Chapter of the Book of the Dead.

shauā  book, writing.

Shai 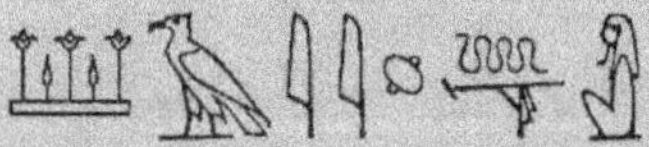 the god of Luck or Destiny.

Shabu  the name of a god.

shabu  water plants.

shabti  See SHAUABTI.

shabu  cakes, food.

Shapuneterȧrka  name of an Utchat.

shamu  damned (?).

Sharshar... 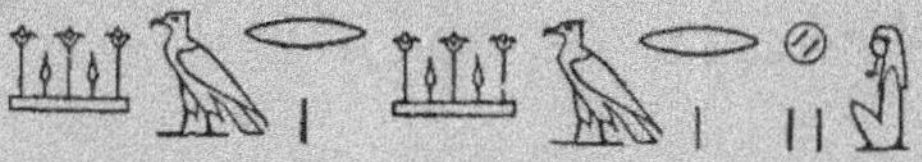 a proper name.

Sharsharkhet 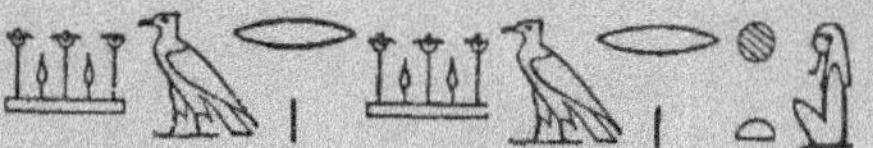 name of an Utchat.

Sharshatȧkatȧ  a proper name.

shaheb 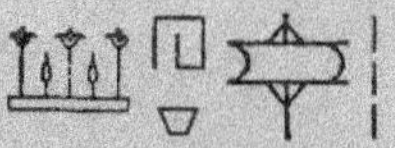 south wind.

shas  to journey, travel.

Shakanasa  a proper name.

Shaka  a name of Ȧmen.

shā 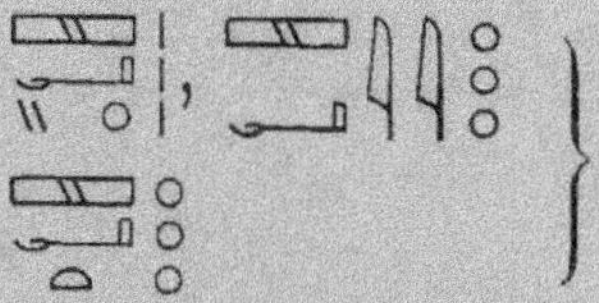 sand.

shā (?), *shāt*  book, writing, document.

 Book of praise.

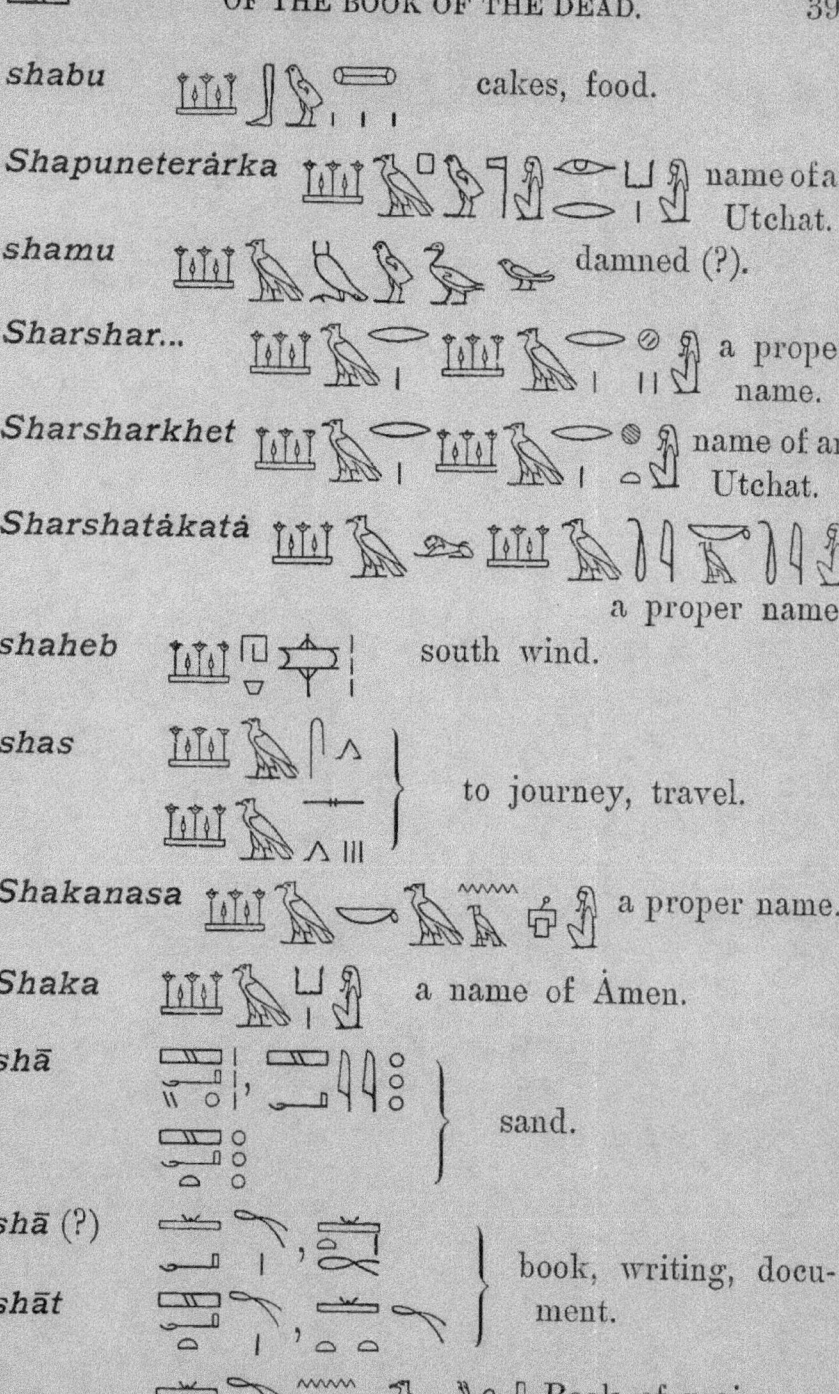

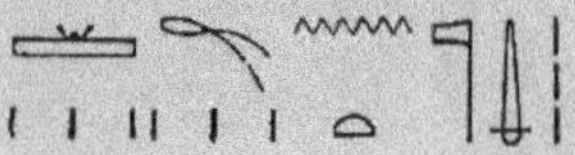 Books of holy words.

 Book of Thoth.

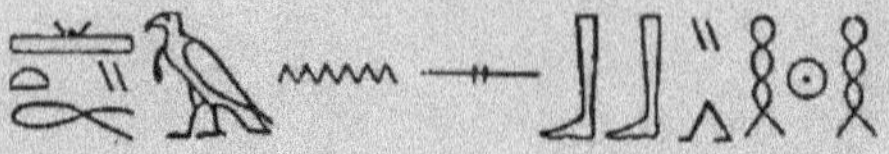 Book of traversing Eternity.

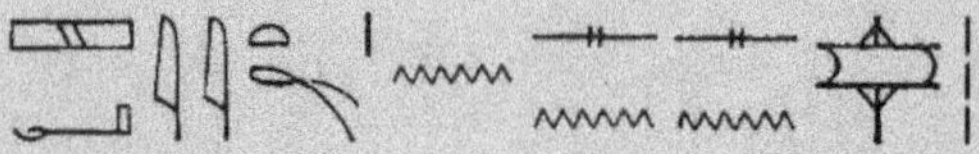 Book of Breathings.

shā 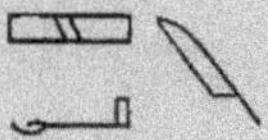 to cut, cut away, cut off.

shāit  knife.

shāmu  decorated (?).

shāt  knife, knives.

shāṭ 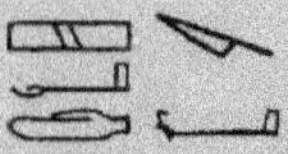 to cut, to wound, hack off.

shāṭ
shāṭet 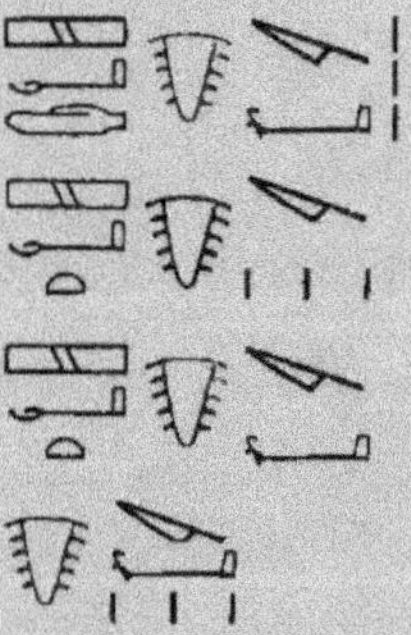 woundings, cuttings, slaughter, knives (?).

 slaughter-blocks (?).

shu  to be dry, hot.

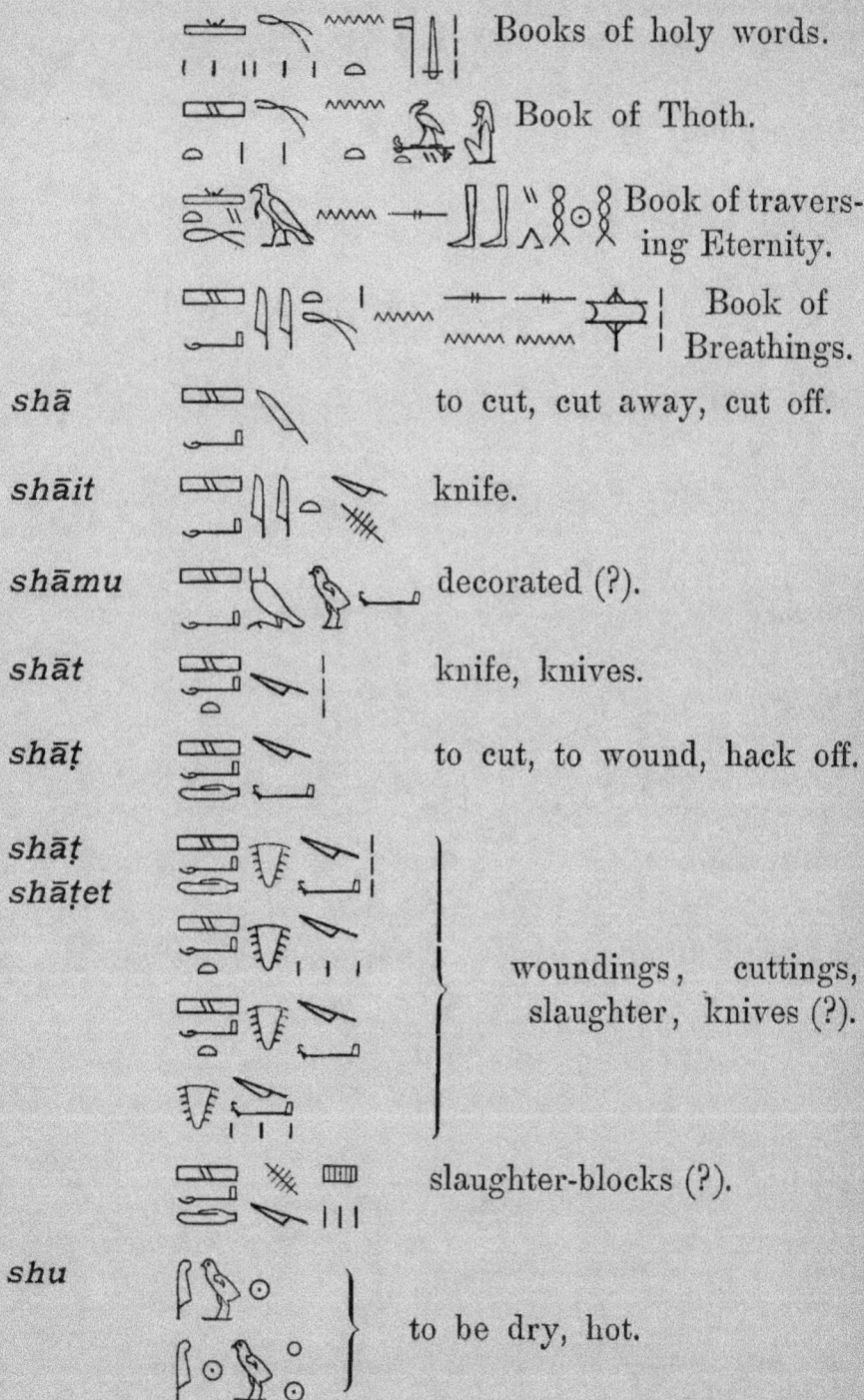

Shu  the god of the air, dryness, light, etc.; the counterpart of Tefnut.

Shut 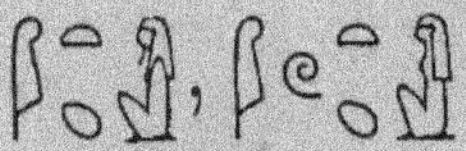 fem. of preceding.

Shuu  the Sun-god.

shuit  light.

shuit  the abode of light (?) sky (?).

shu  to lack, be needy, in want of.

shu  plants, papyrus.

shut 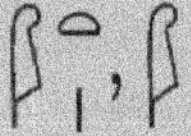 feather.

shuti 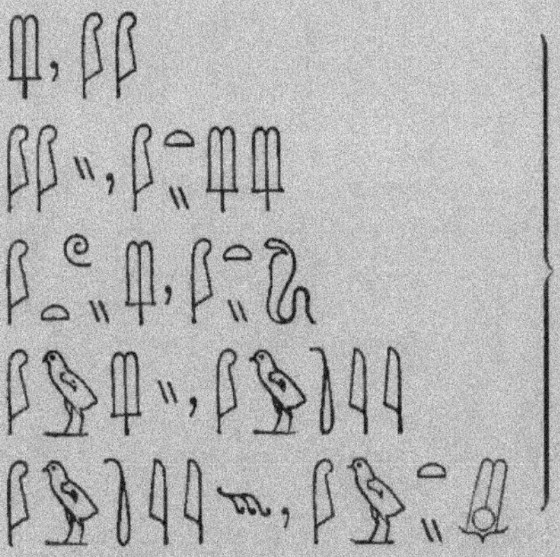 the two-feather crown, *e.g.*, that worn by Ȧmen.

shut  feathers, plumage.

shuti  merchant.

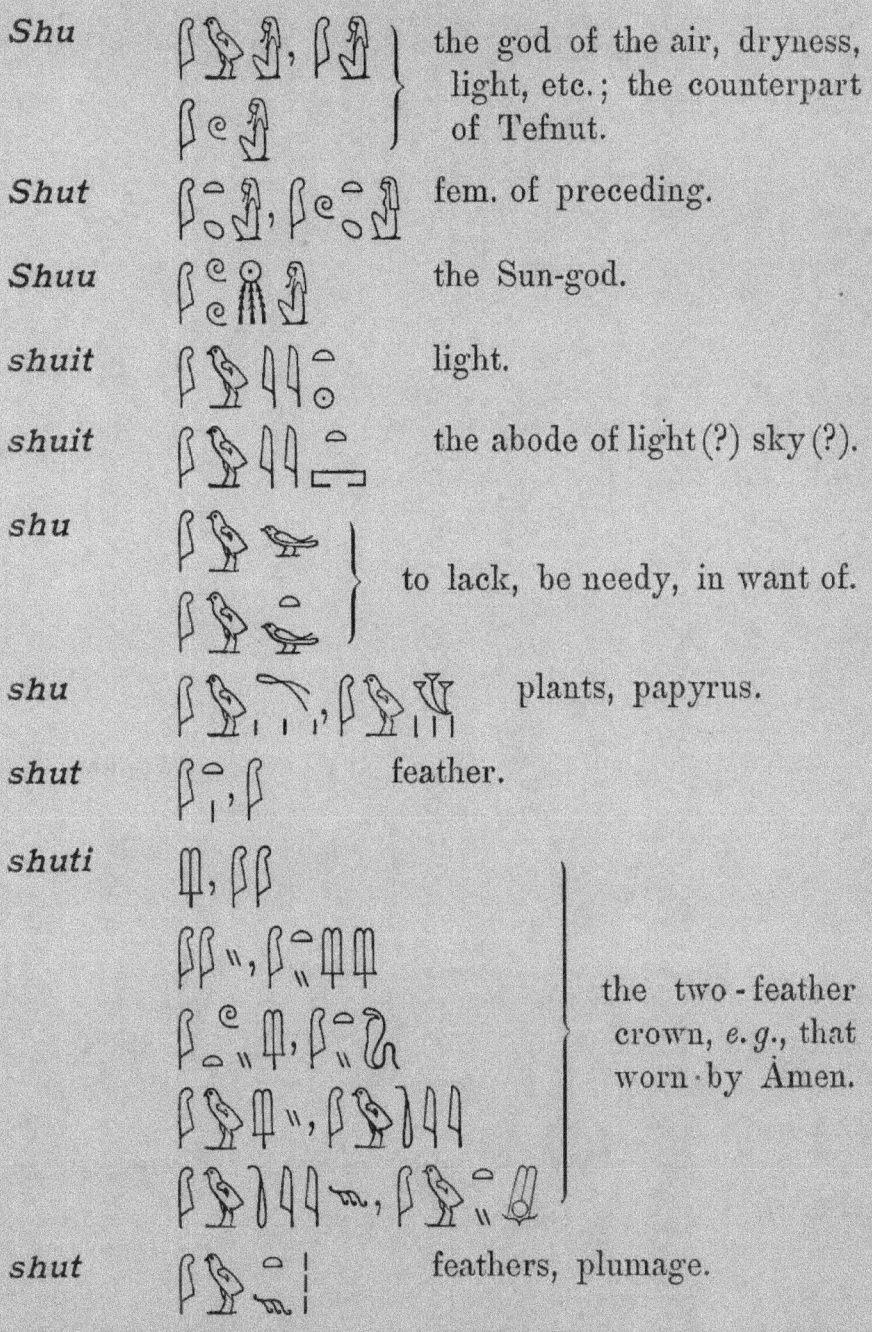

shutet . . . .

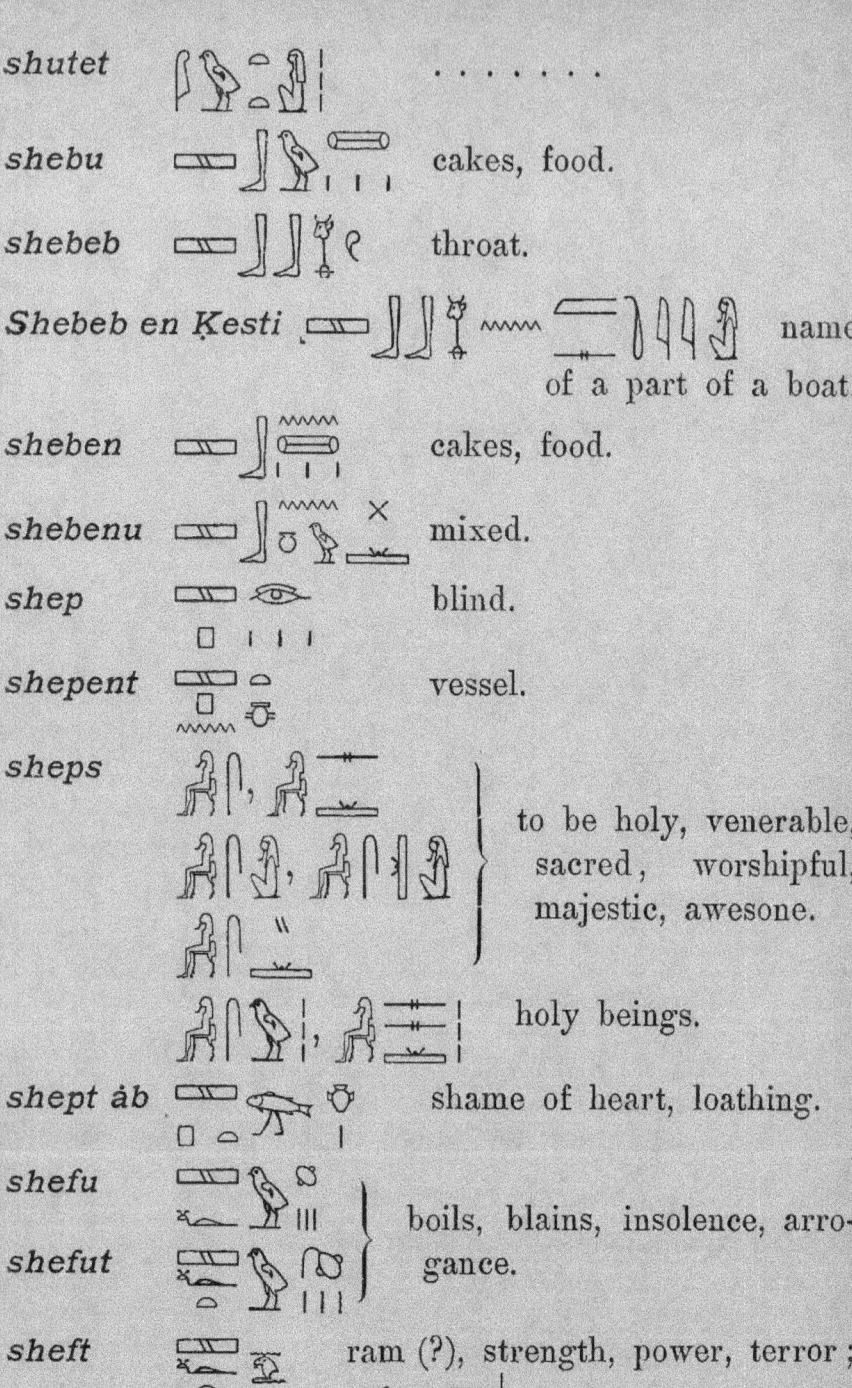

shebu cakes, food.

shebeb throat.

Shebeb en Ḳesti name of a part of a boat.

sheben cakes, food.

shebenu mixed.

shep blind.

shepent vessel.

sheps to be holy, venerable, sacred, worshipful, majestic, awesone.

holy beings.

shept ȧb shame of heart, loathing.

shefu, *shefut* boils, blains, insolence, arrogance.

sheft ram (?), strength, power, terror; plur.

	terrible of face.
sheft / *shefit*	strength, power, terror.
Shefit / *Shefiti*	the Ram-god, symbol of strength.
Shefshefit	strength, power, might.
shem / *seshem*	to walk, go, travel.
	to calumniate, set the mouth in motion against a man.
shemiu / *shemt*	journeys, goings about, travellers.
shemu	the season of summer.
shemem	to be hot.
shemmet	fire, flames.
shemmet	poison.

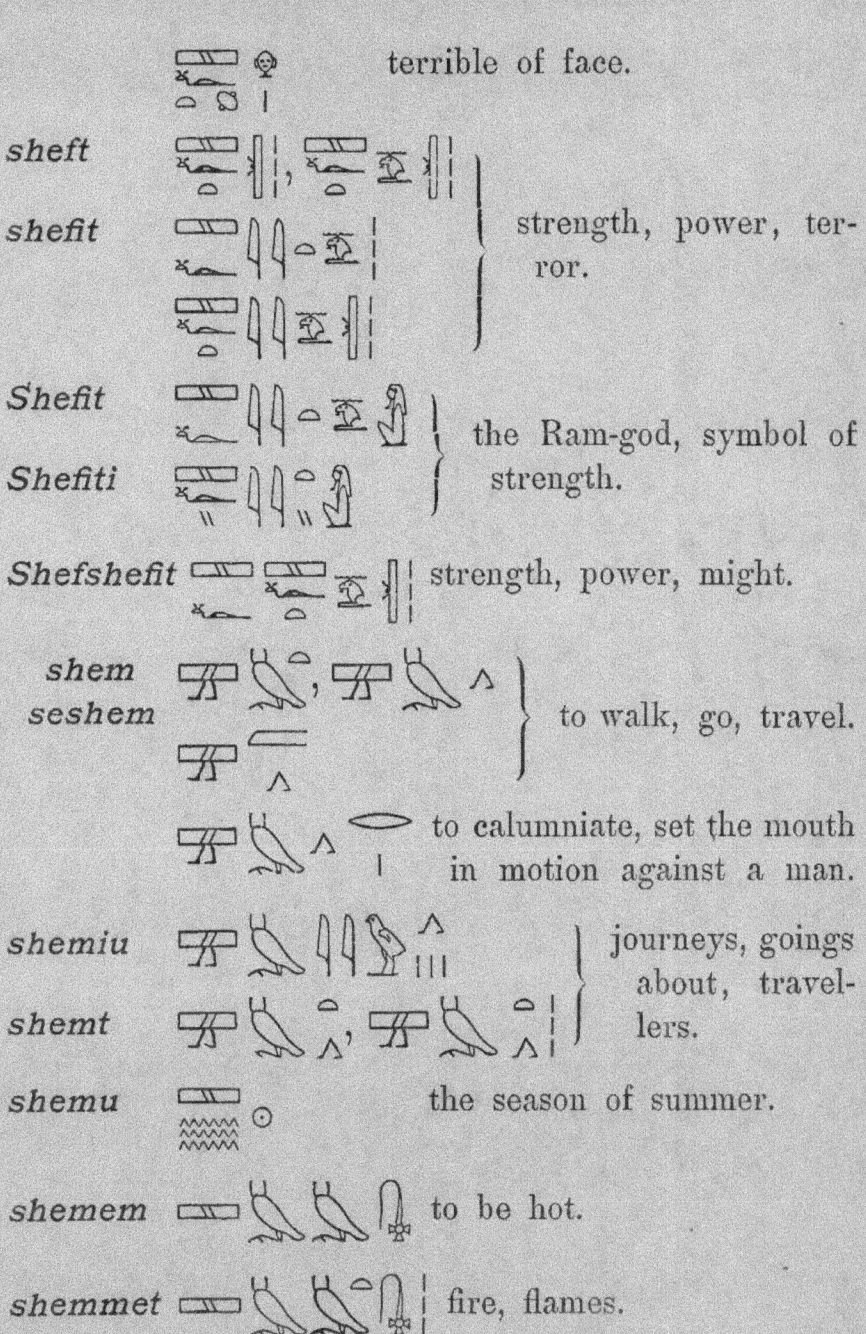

shemā — to sing, or play a musical instrument.

shemāit — a singer.

shemā — the south; — stones of the south.

Shemāit — the goddess of the South, *i. e.*, Nekhebit.

shems — to follow, to accompany, be the member of a bodyguard.

shemsi — follower, body-servant.

— plur. of preceding.

— chief servants of Osiris.

— servants of His Majesty.

shen — to revolve.

shen
shenit
shenu
shenn — circuit, circle, orbit; circuit of the earth.

shen — hair.

shenȧ — hair.

Shenȧt-pet-utheset-neter — the name of a sacred cow.

Shenȧt-sheps-neteru — the name of a sacred cow.

shenā — granary.

shenā — breast, body.

shenā — to turn back, repulse.

shenā — repulse, violence (?).

shenāāu — wayfarers (?).

shenā  to turn back, repulse.

shenstet  wickedness.

sheni 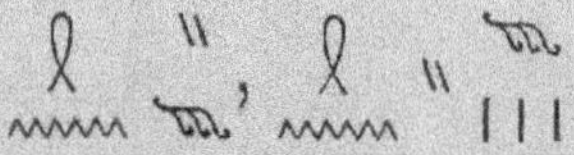 hair, locks.

shenit 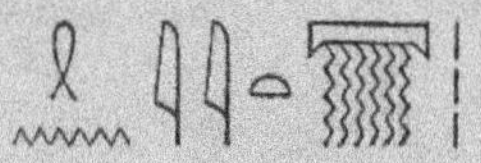 storm.

sheniu  chamber.

shenit 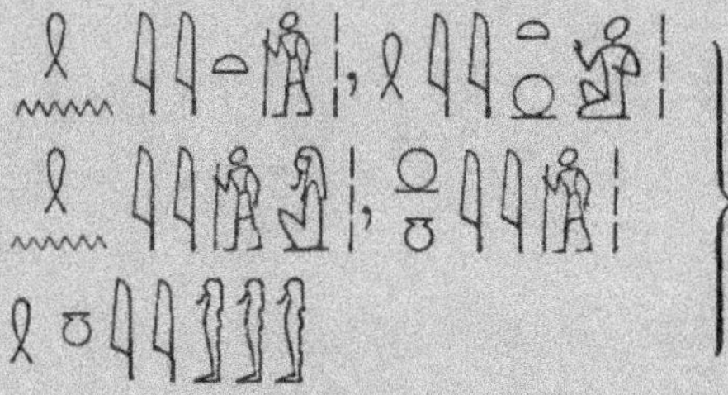 chiefs, princes.

shenbet 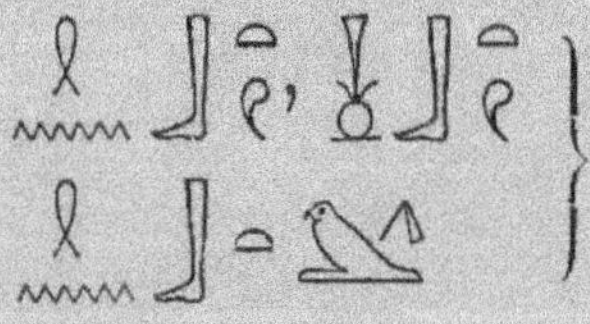 body.

shnemi 

Shenmu  the name of a town.

shennu  a powder of some sort (?).

shennu  snares (?).

shennu  acacia trees.

Shennu  the name of a town.

shens 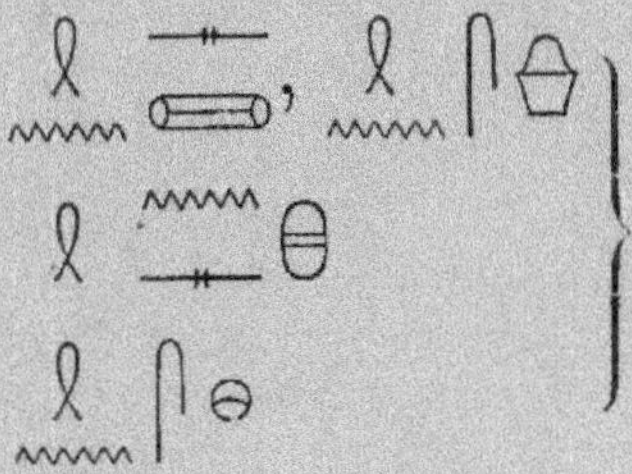 cakes, with 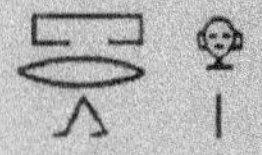 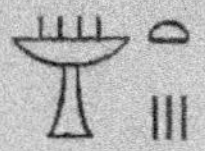 shewbread.

shent  flesh, skin (?).

shentu  to curse, blaspheme.

shenti 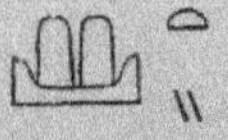 granary.

shenti 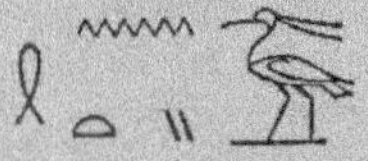 heron.

shenti 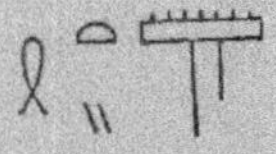 garment.

shentetu  curse.

shenṭet 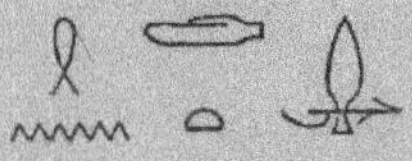 a tree, the acacia.

shen-tȧ 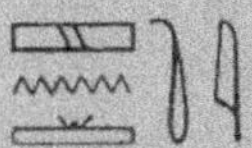 read .

Shentit 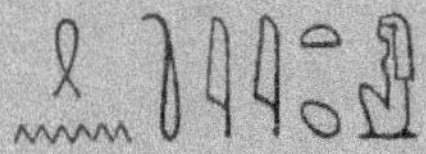 the name of a goddess.

sher  =  and .

[*sherr*  to be little.]

sherràu 

sherriu 

little ones, feeble men or gods.

sherȧt 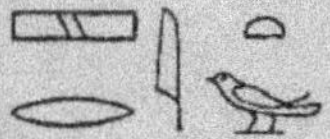

shert 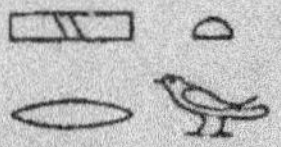

shertet 

little one or thing, something of no value.

Sherem 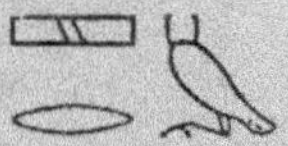 a proper name.

shersher 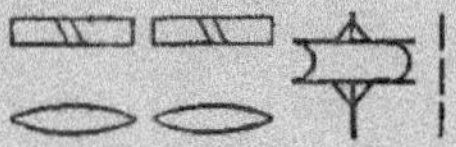 winds, breath.

shert 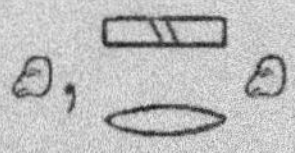

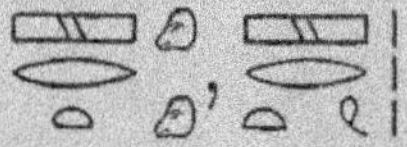

nose, nostrils.

shert  grain.

shert 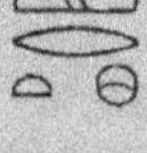 cake, bread.

shes (?)  linen weavers (?).

shes 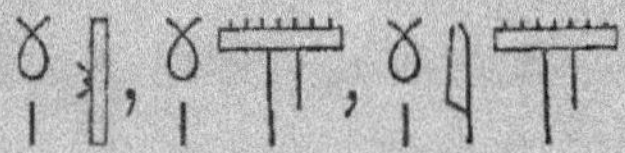 linen, a linen garment.

shes  linen of the finest quality.

shes maāt 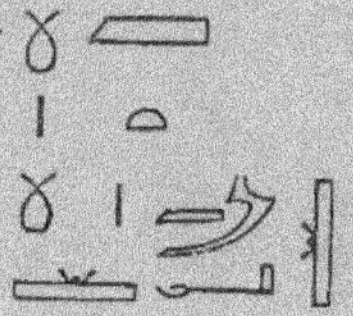 "cord of law", *i. e.*, with unfailing correctness and regularity.

shes 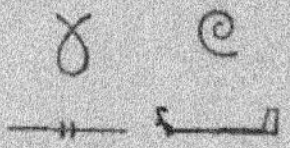 to be tied up, fettered.

shesui (?)  the two eyes (?).

shesep  palm, a measure.

shesep 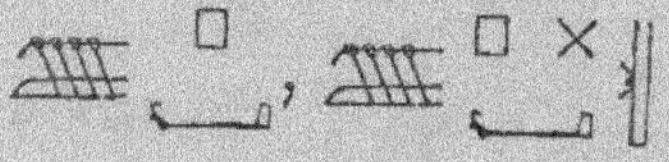 to take, undertake, accept, receive.

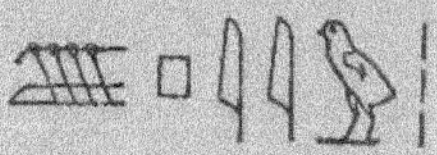 receivers.

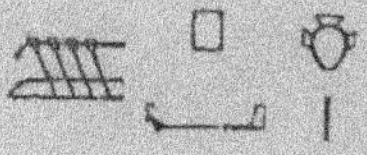 heart's desire.

shesep 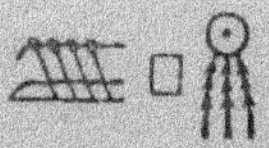 to shine, be bright.

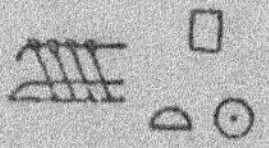 light. Note the forms 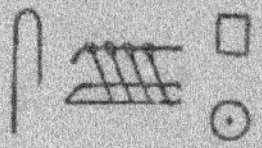 and 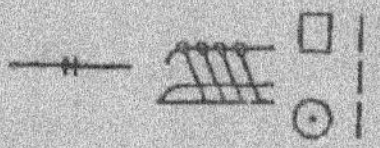 and SESHEP.

Shesep-temesu  name of a fiend (?).

shesau  skilled, able, intelligent, wise.

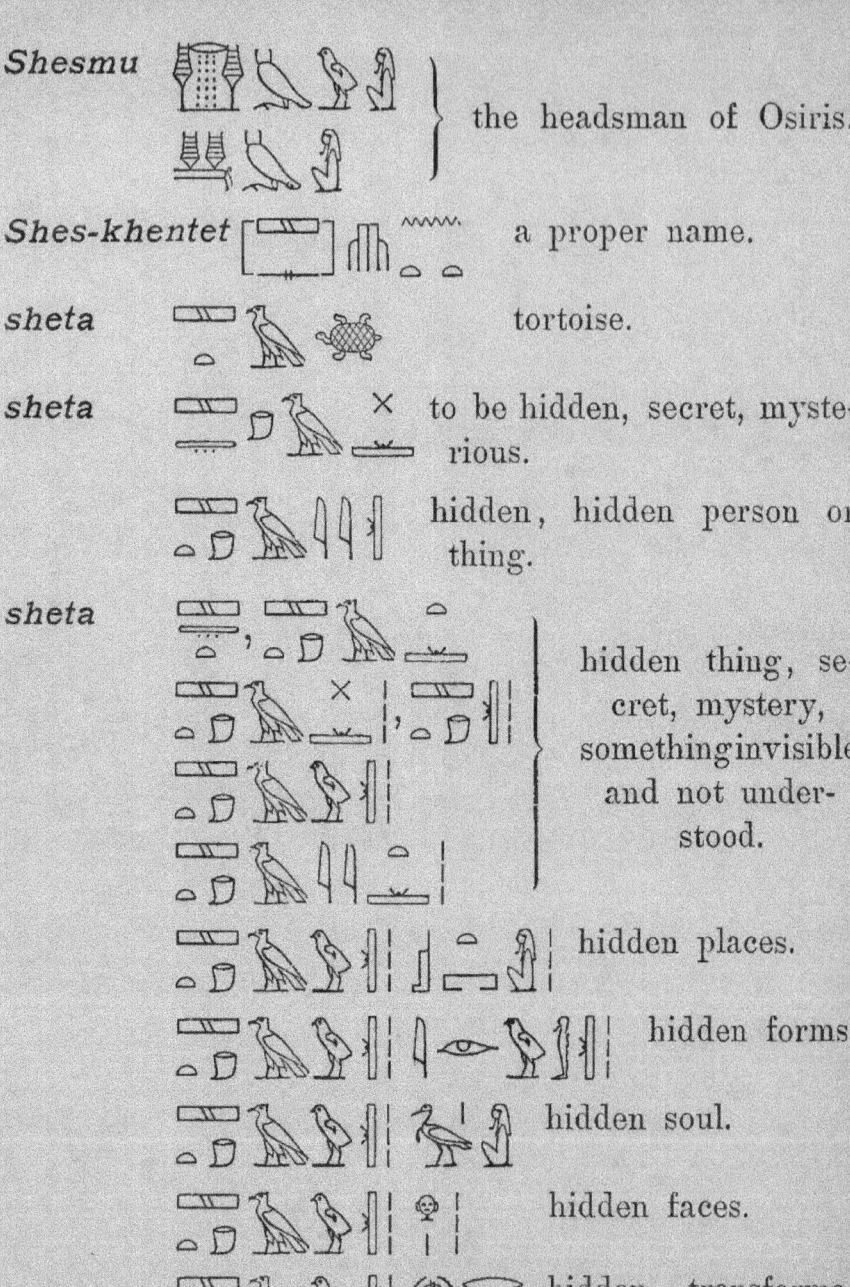

Shesmu the headsman of Osiris.

Shes-khentet a proper name.

sheta tortoise.

sheta to be hidden, secret, mysterious.

hidden, hidden person or thing.

sheta hidden thing, secret, mystery, something invisible and not understood.

hidden places.

hidden forms.

hidden soul.

hidden faces.

hidden transformations.

hidden things.

Shetait  the "hidden place"; a name of the Other World of Seker at Ṣaḳḳârah.

Shetat

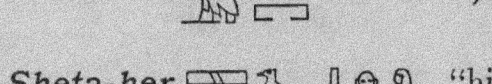

Sheta-ḥer  "hidden face"; a proper name.

Shetau-ā  "hidden of arm"; a proper name.

Shetet-pet 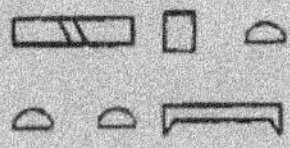 a proper name.

sheṭ 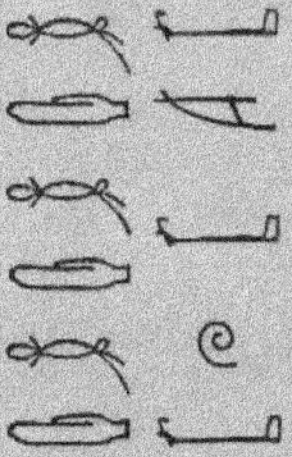 to break up the ground, dig out, tear open, to deliver, strengthen, tie, bind up. 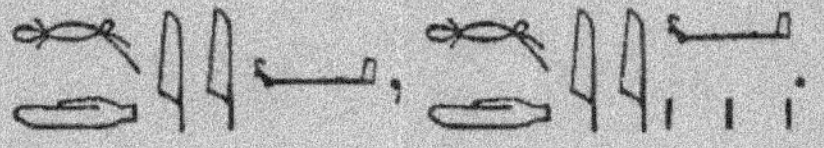.

sheṭet 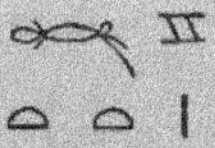 lake, pool; plur. .

sheṭit  tank, cistern.

sheṭ 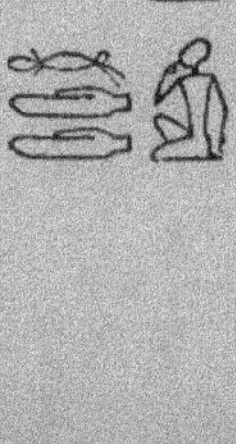 to read, recite a book or prayer.

sheṭ 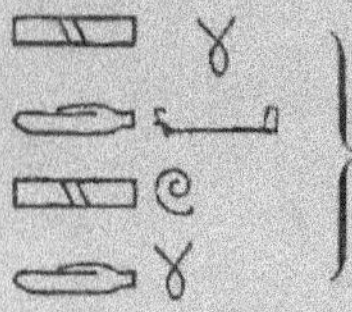 to swathe, to clothe.

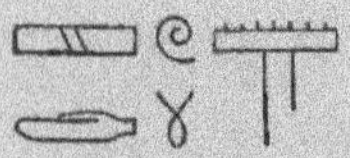 a garment.

 clothed, or covered, of arms.

sheṭu  leather straps.

sheṭḥu 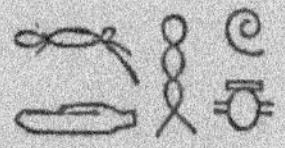 crushed grapes (?).

Sheṭ-kheru 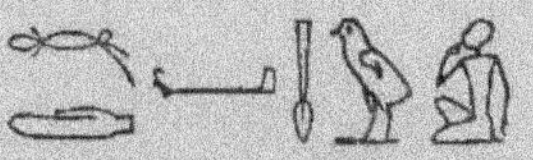 the name of one of the Forty-two Judges in the Hall of Osiris.

 K.

k  thee, thou, thy; with sign of the dual 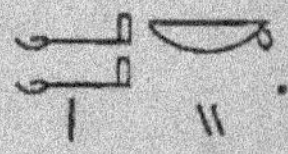.

ka 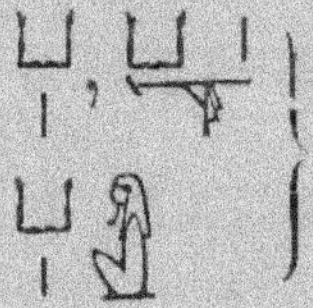 the double of a man or god, the personality of a man or god, self, the being of a man which is associated with the heart-soul , and is independent of the spirit-soul ; plur. 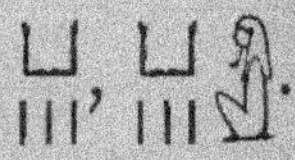.

Ka-ḥetep 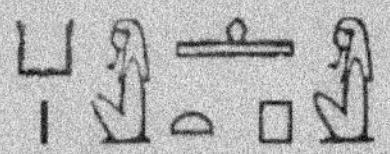 a proper name.

kau 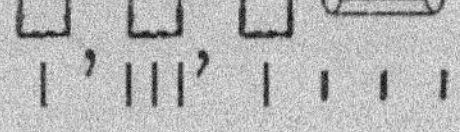 food.

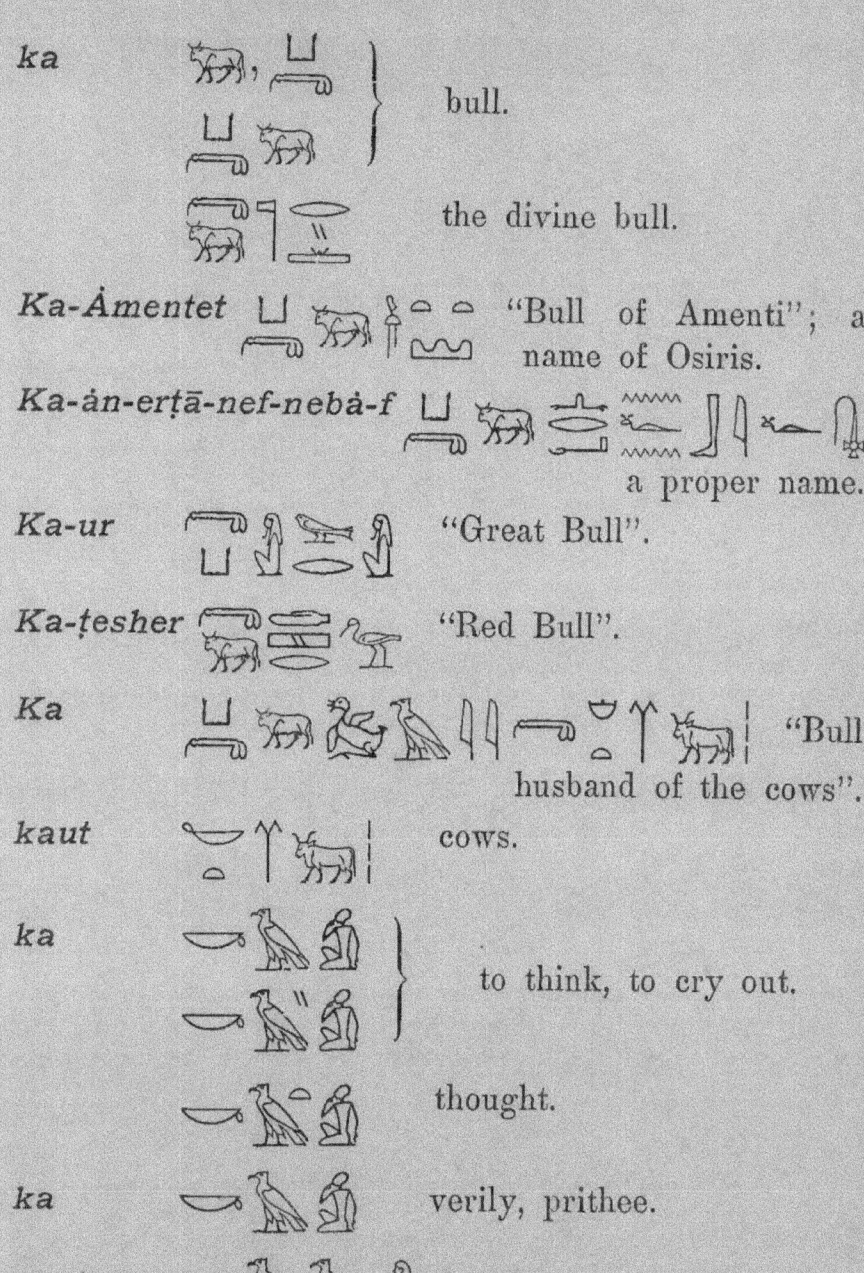

ka bull.

the divine bull.

Ka-Ȧmentet "Bull of Amenti"; a name of Osiris.

Ka-ȧn-erṭā-nef-nebȧ-f a proper name.

Ka-ur "Great Bull".

Ka-ṭesher "Red Bull".

Ka "Bull husband of the cows".

kaut cows.

ka to think, to cry out.

thought.

ka verily, prithee.

Kaa the name of a god.

kaiu cries (?), criers (?).

Ka-àri-k  a proper name.

kaui  a class of beings.

kabit  lamentations.

karà 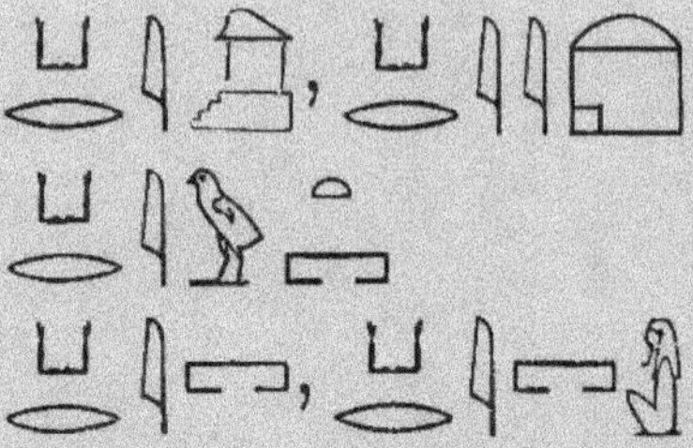 shrine, chapel, sanctuary;   gods of the shrine.

Kaharsapusar-em-ka-ḥerremt   a proper name.

Kasaika  a proper name.

kat  work, works, labours.

ki  verily.

ki  another.  ... 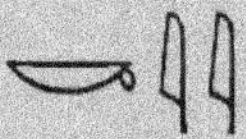 the one ... the other.

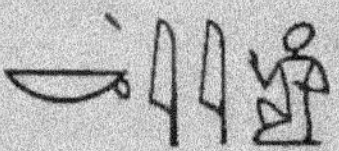 another man.

 another chapter.

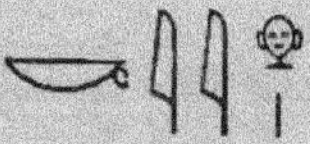 another person.

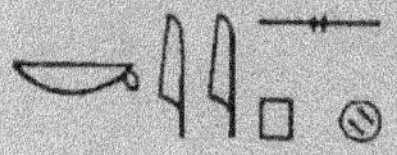 another time.

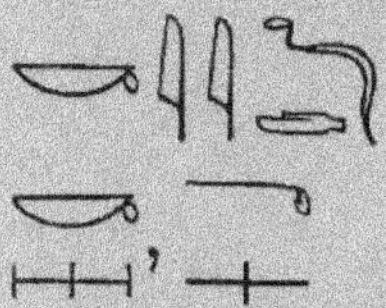 another reading, a variant.

kuȧ  I.

kep 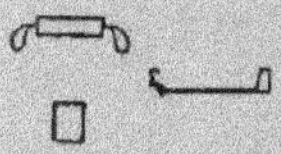 to hide.

 hidden place.

Kep-ḥer 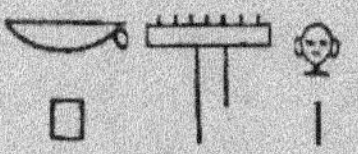 a proper name.

kefa 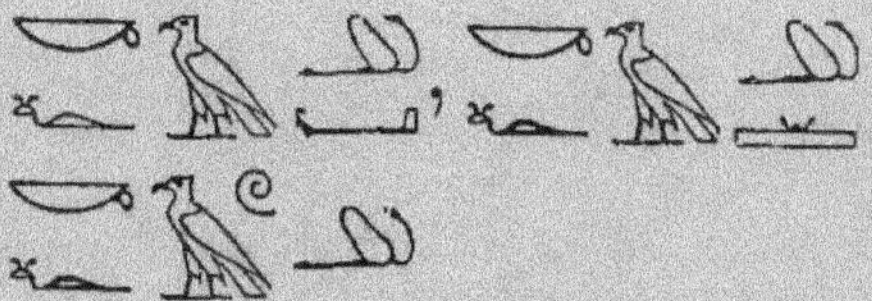 to act with violence, expel, drive away.

kefa  to remove the clothes, strip, undress.  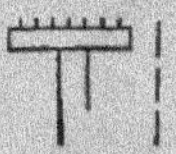 uncover.

kem 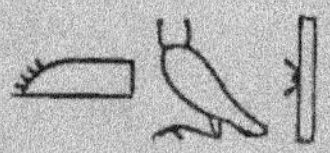 to make an end of, to finish.

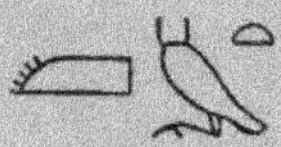 the end.

kem 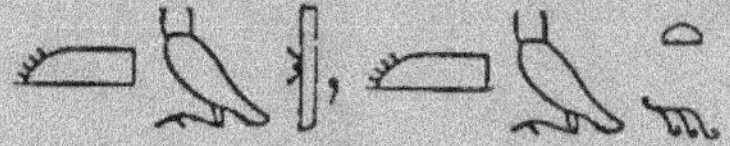 black.

Kem-ur  the name of a town and of a lake.

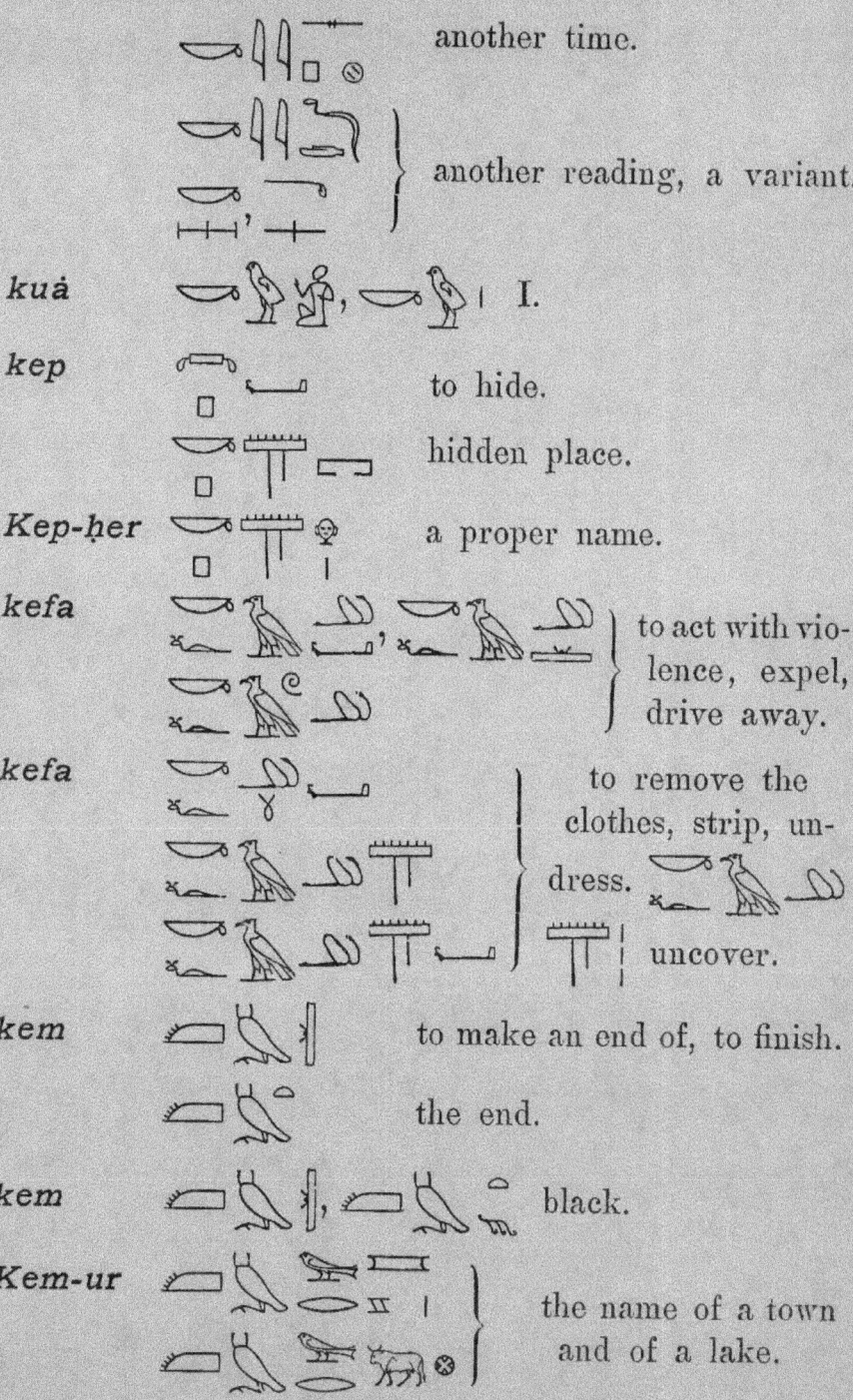

Kemt		the "black" land, *i. e.*, Egypt.
Kemkem		the name of a god.
kenȧ		to speak.
Kenemet		the name of a town.
kenemet	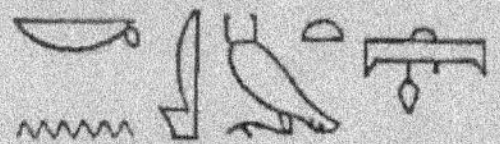	night, darkness.
Kenemti		the name of one of the Forty-two Judges in the Hall of Osiris.
kenḥu (?)		night.
Kenset		Nubia. The correct reading appears to be Sᴛɪ, *i. e.*, the "land of the bow".
Ker	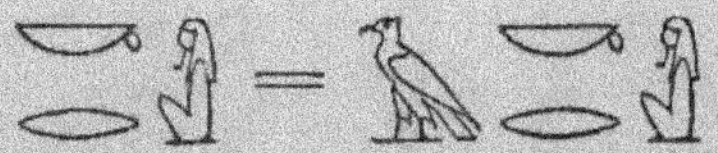 (?).	
kerit	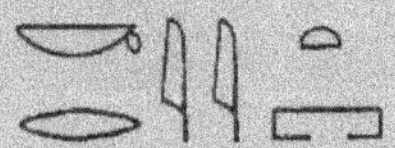	habitation, abode.
Keḥkeḥet		a proper name.
kes		to bow in homage.

kesu  homage, bowings.

Kesemu-enent  a class of divine beings.

kek, kekui  darkness, night.

ket  another.

ketuit  abode, habitation.

ketut 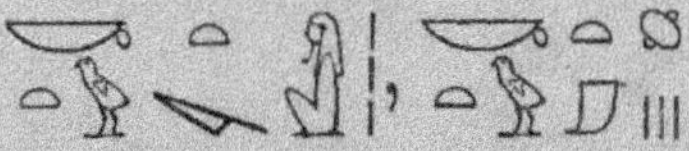 weapons, knives.

ket khu  other things.

ketet  little, bad.

⊿ Q.

qa  to be high, exalted, height.

 High God.

 Exalted one.

 doubly high, very high.

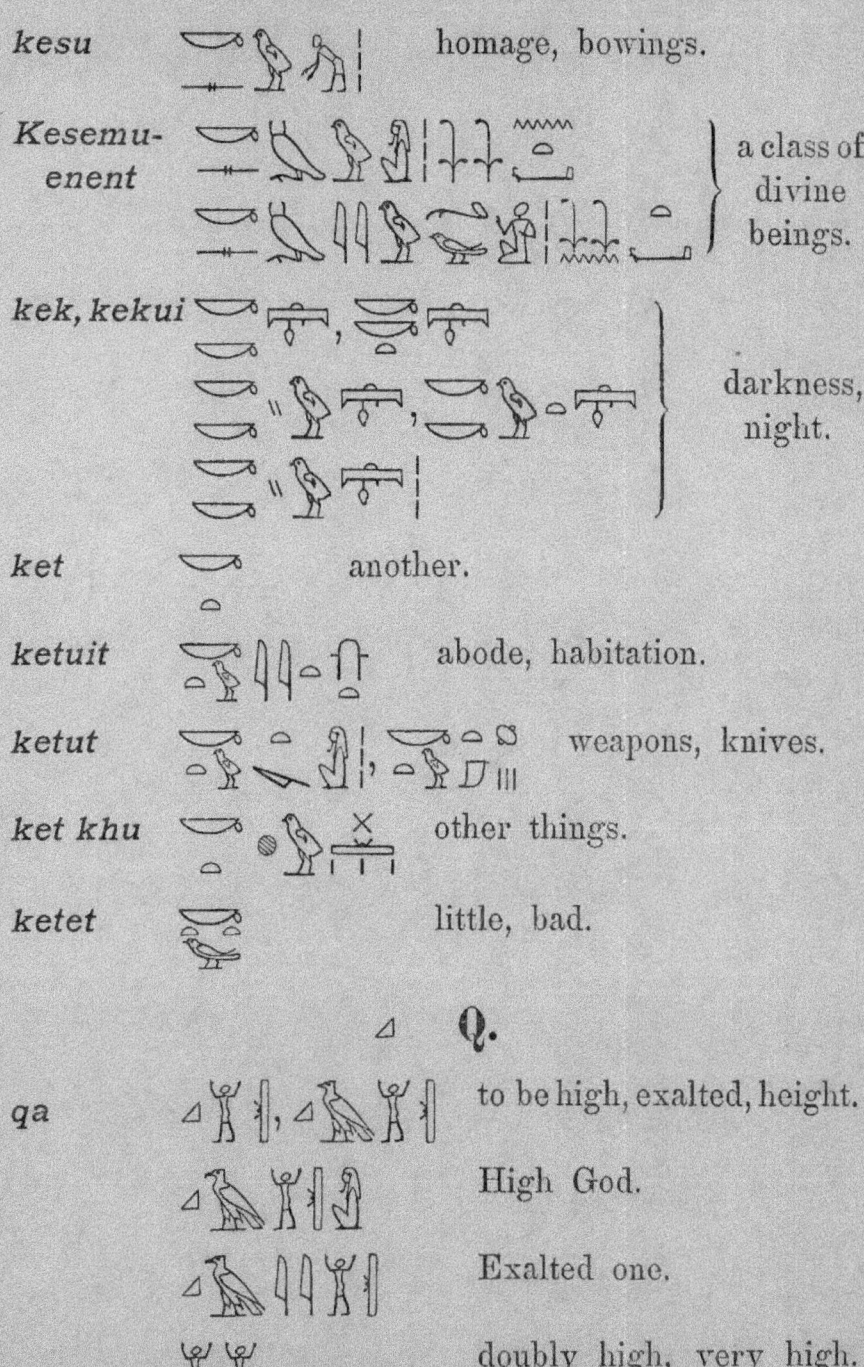

exceedingly high.

height of heaven.

high, *i. e.*, loud-voiced.

most terrible.

high up on the standard.

the god of the very high plumes.

Qa-ha-ḥetep a proper name.

Qa-ḥer a proper name.

qa high ground, hill, staircase.

qa to be rotten, putrefy.

qa form.

qaat bolts, fastenings.

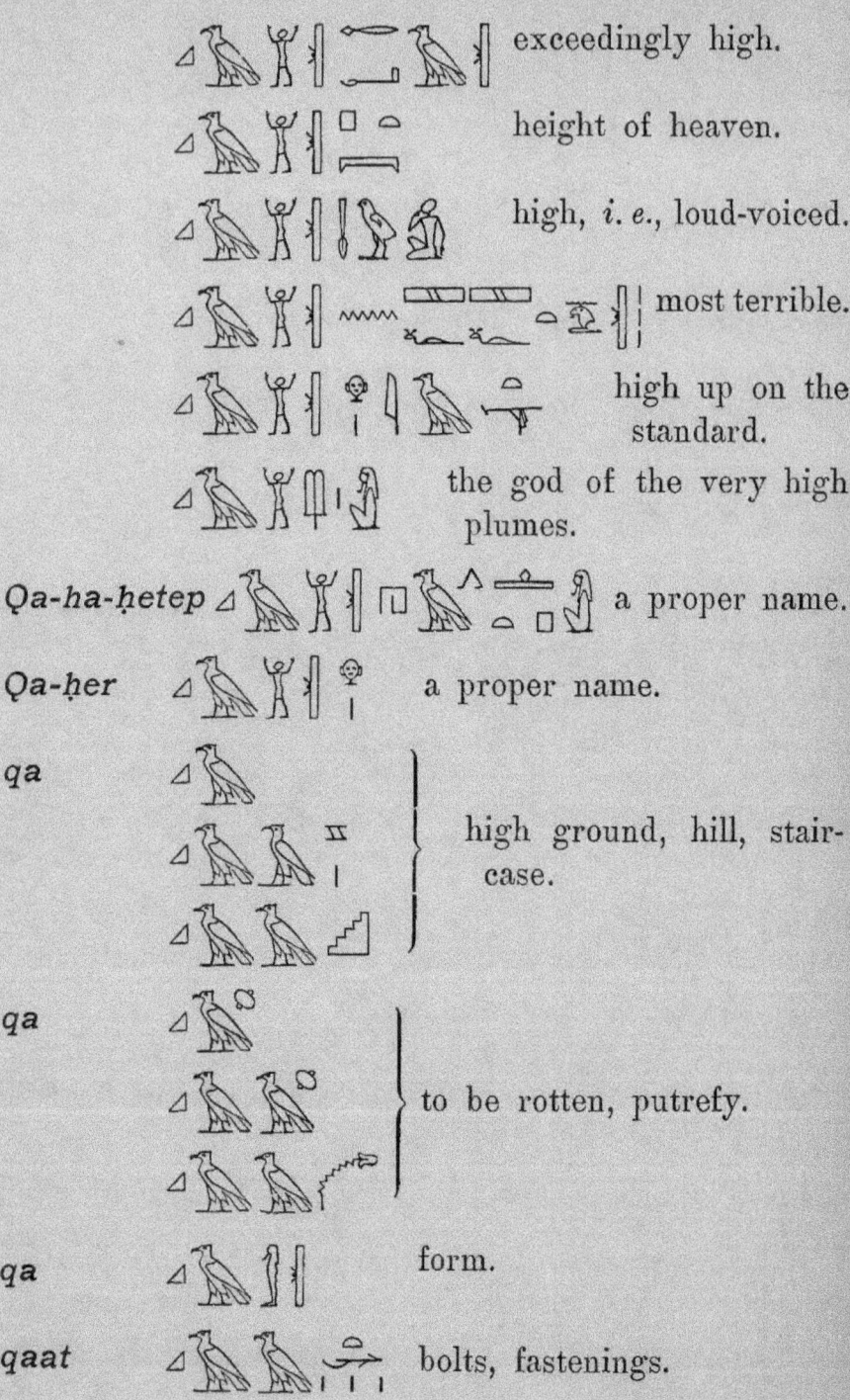

qaȧ  form, image.

Qai  the name of a god.

qab  the innermost part.

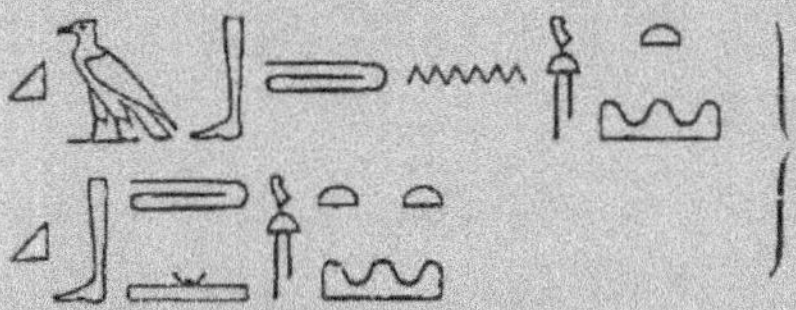 the centre of Ȧmenti.

qabt  a part of the body.

Qabt-ent-Shu-erṭā-nef-em-sau-Ȧsȧr 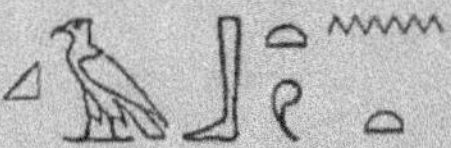 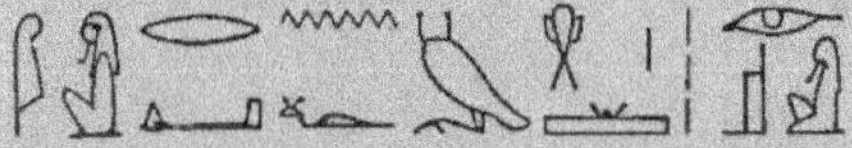 a proper name.

qamȧi  incense, unguent.

qamemt  to weep (?).

qart  a part of the Other World.

qart  bolts, fastenings.

Qaḥu 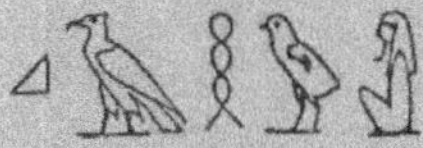 a proper name.

qaḥit  fire (?).

qasu, qass  to tie, bind, fetter.

 fetter.

 fetters.

qaqa  hill.

qā 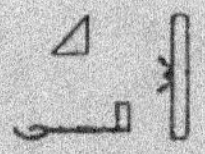 be provided with (?).

qāḥu  arm and shoulder; dual 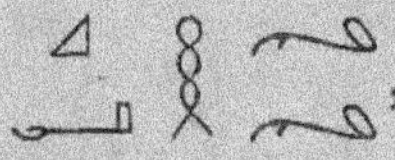, plur.  

qāḥ  side of (?).

qu  limbs, flesh.

qeb 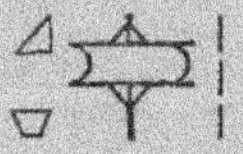 north wind.

qebbi, qebti 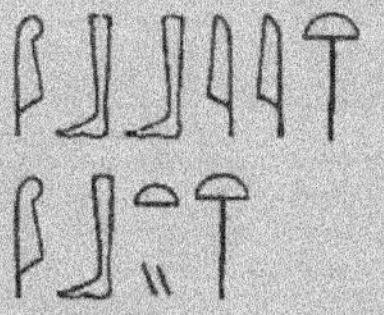 shade, shadow.

qeb 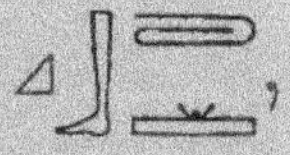, 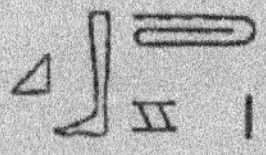 see .

qebḥ  to cool, refresh, be cooled, refreshed.

 place of cooling, the bath (?).

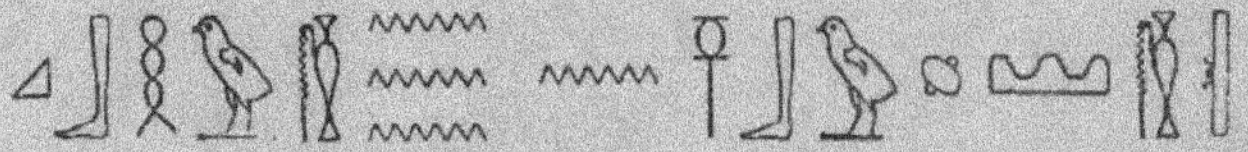 the cool water of the First Cataract.

Qebḥ 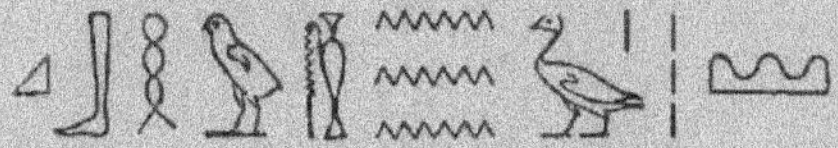 the marsh of water-fowl.

Qebḥ-senu-f  one of the four sons of Horus.

Qebti  Coptos.

qefen  baked cake.

Qefenu 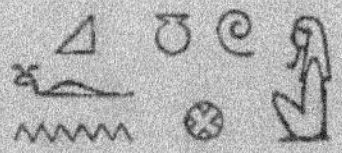 the name of a town.

qefṭenu 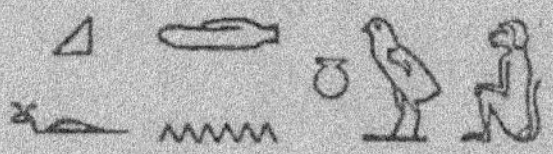 ape.

qema 

qemama  to create, to fashion, to form.

qemam  to create, to fashion, to form.

qemamu

 creatress.

 god of creation.

qemḥ 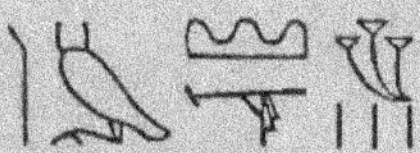 leaves of a tree.

qem-tu 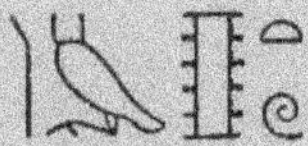 to overturn.

qemṭu 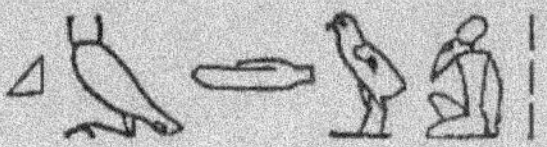 to say, repeat.

Qen  a proper name (?).

qen 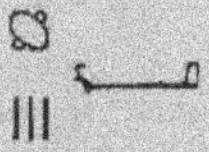 fat.

qen  to do evil, be evil.

qen  to be strong, bold, brave.

qenȧ 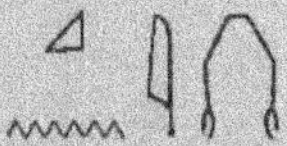 to embrace, embrace.

qenȧt 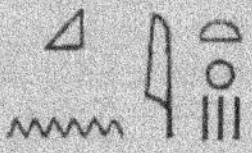 a kind of incense.

qeni a kind of linen.

qenu strong.

qenbet, *qenbit* a class of officials, human or divine.

Qenna a proper name.

qenert grain (?) fruit (?).

qenqen to beat, to strike.

qenqen to feed, eat.

Qenqentet the name of a lake in Sekhet-Ȧaru.

qer the north wind.

qerȧ storm, thunder, a proper name.

qerȧs sepulture, burial.

qerfi to tie, be tied.

Qernet the name of a town.

qert, qerrt cave, cavern.

qerti 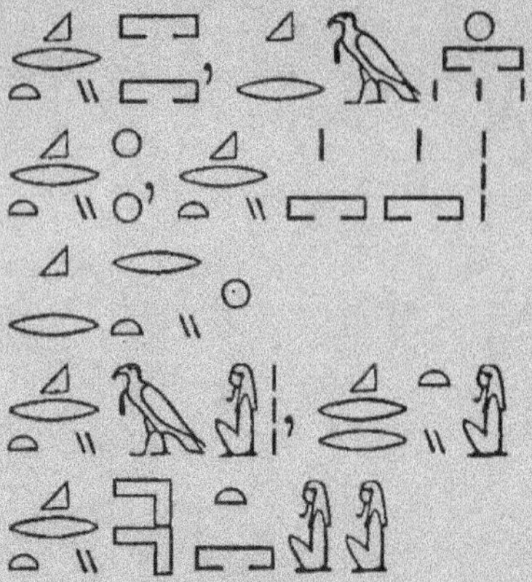 the name of the two caves near Philae wherein the Nile rose; the name of one of the Forty-two Judges in the Hall of Osiris.

qeres 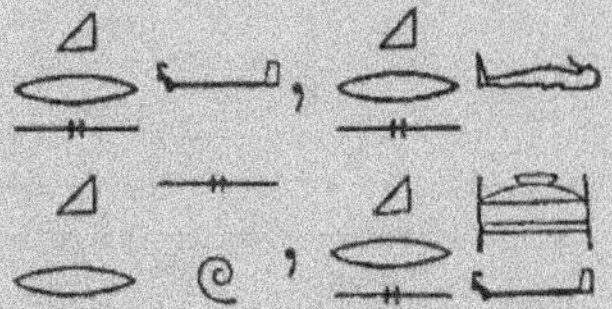 to bury; dead body.

qersu, *qerset*  coffin, sarcophagus.

qerset 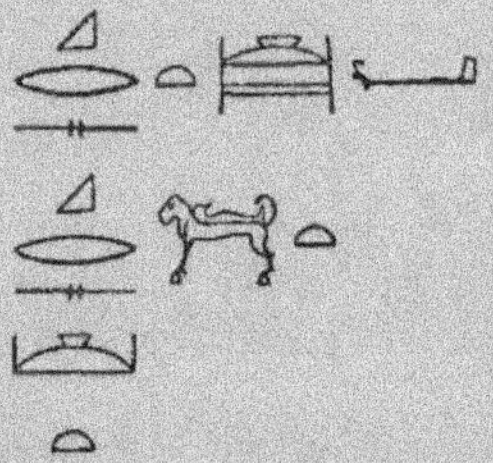 burial.

qerqer 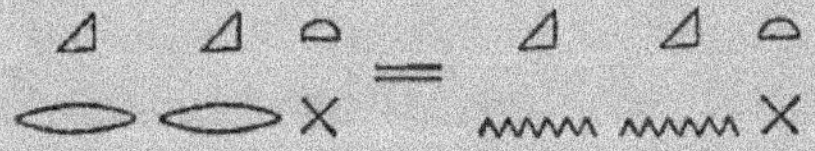

qert  bolt, fastening; .

qeḥḥtum (?)  castrated animals for sacrifice (?).

qes  burial (?).

qesu (for *qersu*) 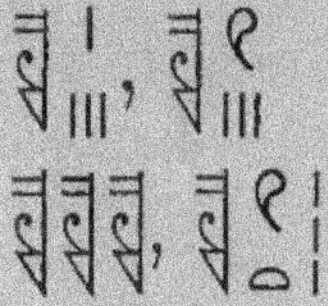 bones.

qesu (*qersu*) 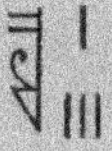 preserves (of birds).

Qesi  Cusae, the capital of the XIVth nome of Upper Egypt.

qesen  to be evil, bad.

qeq  see Ȧm to eat.

Qetetbu  a proper name.

qeṭ 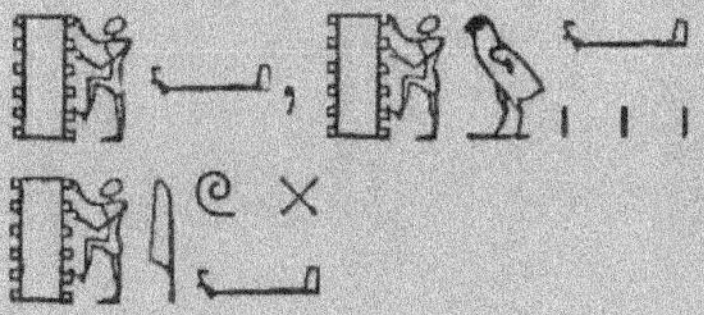 to build.

qeṭ, *qeṭu*  to draw, sketch, make a plan or design; work of the artist.

qeṭu  sailors, mariners, crew of a boat.

Qeṭu  a fiend.

qeṭ — orbit, circle, like, similitude, character, dispositions.

likewise, also, totality.

qeṭt — slumber.

K̦.

ḳa — to besiege.

ḳa — filth, dung.

ḳa — to stink.

ḳaut, *ḳau* — calamity, calamities, misery, to suffer want, to lack something or anything.

ḳai — lake.

ḳau — a substance offered to the gods.

ḳauasha — to break.

ḳab — to depart (?).

ḳabti — the hair of some portion of the body.

ḳaf  ape; plur. .

ḳas  chamber.

ḳast (?)  . . . .

ḳat  claw, limb.

ḳatu  thoughts, meditations.

ḳuat  to besiege.

Ḳeb  (?)

ḳeb 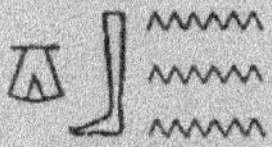 the celestial ocean.

ḳeba  to suffer, be in misery.

ḳeba  to cast an evil glance (?).

ḳeba  some wooden object.

ḳem  to find, discover.

 something found.

ḳemḳem to discover, find out.

Ḳem-ḥeru a class of divine beings.

ḳemut weak, evil beings.

ḳemḥ to see.

ḳemḥet eye.

Ḳemḥu the name of a god.

Ḳemḥusu a proper name.

ḳemḥut hair (?).

ḳen
ḳenn } weak, feeble, helpless.

ḳenu cattle.

Ḳem-ur
Ḳen-ur } a proper name.
Ḳer-ur

ḳenut deeds, documents, records.

Ḳenḳenur the name of a god.

ḳent 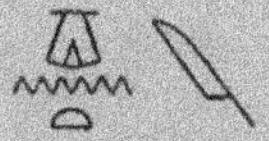 slit.

ḳer 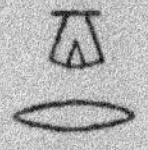 moreover.

ḳert 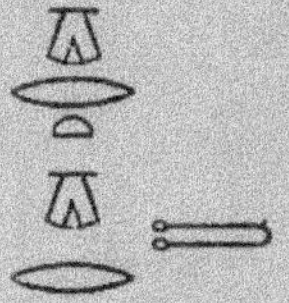 but.

ḳer  to be silent.

ḳerḥ 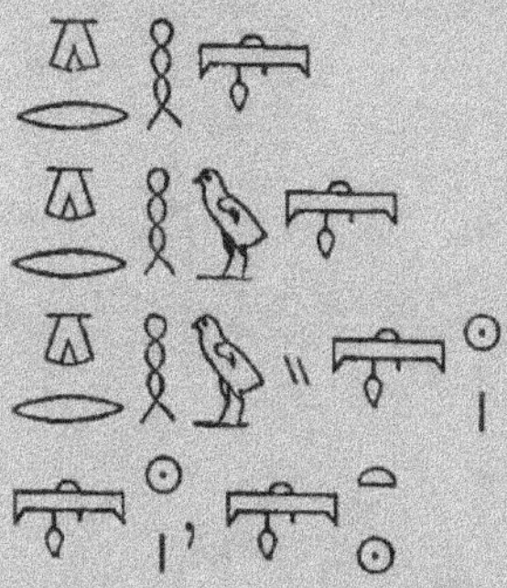 night, darkness.

Ḳersher 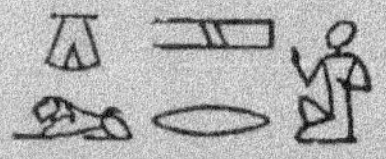 a proper name.

ḳer[ḳ] 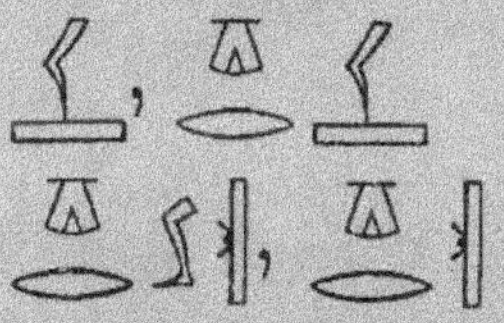 to have, to hold, possess.

 possessor.

 possessions.

ḳer[ḳ]  lie, falsehood, deceit.

 lie, falsehood, deceit.

Ḳer[ḳ]et  the name of a town.

ḳeḥ  weak, helpless, wretched.

ḳes 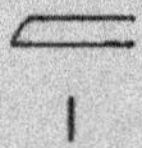 one half.

ḳes  side; dual 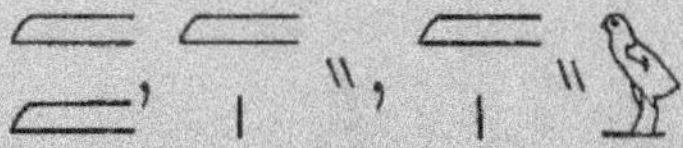 both sides; plur. 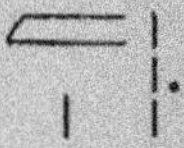.

 left side.

 right side.

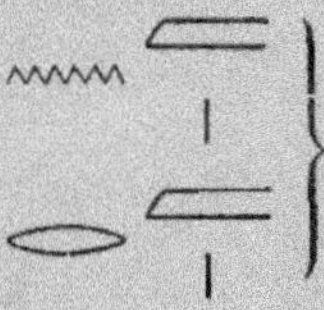 near, by the side of.

ḳesu  to anoint, ointment.

Ḳesui 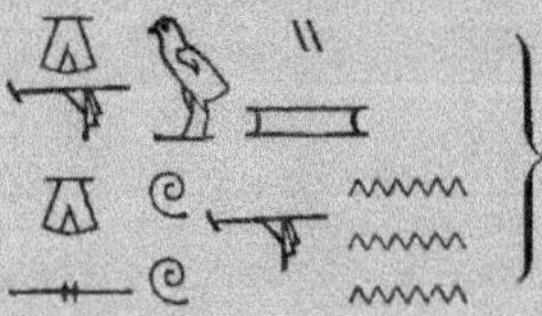 the name of a canal (?).

Ḳestȧ  one of the Four Sons of Horus.

ḳestȧ 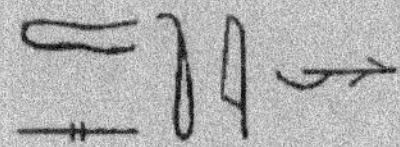 scribe's palette.

ḳesh 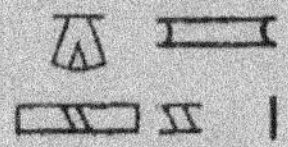 pool, lake.

T.

t 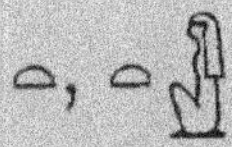 thy.

ta  the;  what is his, his.

ta  to be hot, to burn.

tau  flame, fire, hot, angry.

Ta-reṭ 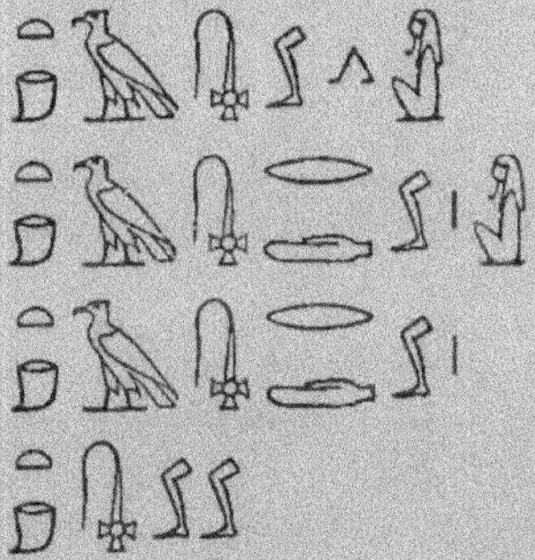 the name of one of the Forty-two Judges in the Hall of Osiris.

ta 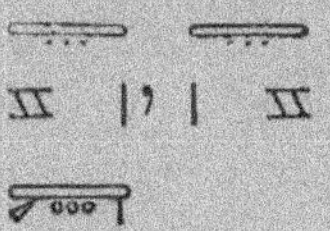 land, ground, country, the earth, the world.

taui  the "Two Lands", *i. e.*, Upper and Lower Egypt.

taiu 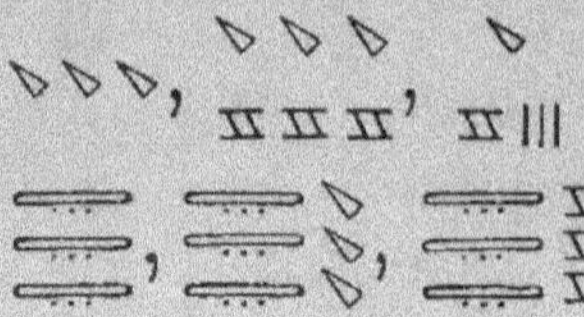 lands, countries, the world, all lands.

 the regions of the Other World.

 earth-gods.

Ta āb 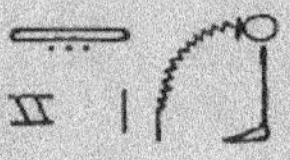 "pure land", *i. e.*, the Other World.

Ta ānkhtet  "land of life", *i. e.*, the grave.

Ta ur  "great land"; a part of Abydos.

Ta en Manu  "land of Manu", *i. e.*, the West.

Ta en Maāt 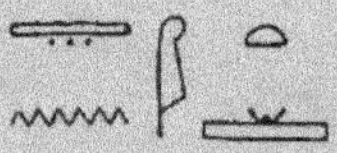 "land of Law", *i. e.*, the Other World.

Ta en maākheru 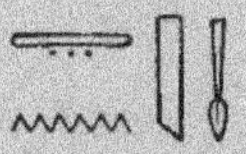 "land of triumph", *i. e.*, the Other World.

Ta Merȧ 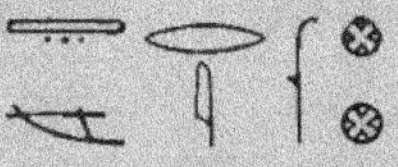 "land of Merȧ", *i. e.*, Upper and Lower Egypt.

Ta Meḥ 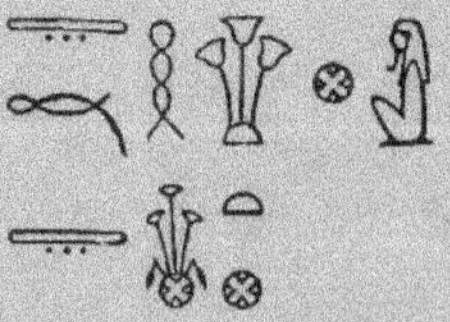 "land of the North", the Delta.

Ta mes tchetta 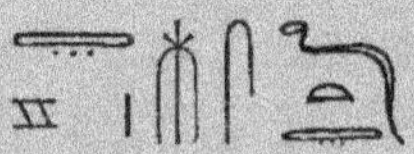 "land of eternity", *i. e.*, the Other World.

Ta Nefer 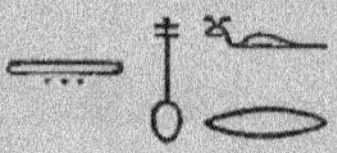 "beautiful land", *i. e.*, the grave.

Ta Nent — a portion of the Other World.

Ta neḥeḥ — "land of eternity", *i. e.*, the Other World.

Taiu nu neteru — "lands of the gods", *i. e.*, heaven.

Ta remu — "land of fish".

Taui Rekhti
Taiu Rekhti — "lands of the Rekhti", *i. e.*, Isis and Nephthys.

Ta kharu — "land of the *kharu* geese".

Ta Sekri — "land of Seker", *i. e.*, the Other World of Memphis.

Ta She — "land of the Lake", *i. e.*, the Fayyûm.

Ta shemā — "land of the South".

Ta sheta — "land of mystery", *i. e.*, the Other World.

Ta Sti — "land of the bow", *i. e.*, Nubia.

Ta qebḥ — "land of cool water", *i. e.*, the Cataract region.

Ta Ṭuat 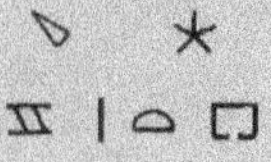 "land of the Ṭuat", *i. e.*, the Other World.

Ta Tchesert  "holy land", *i. e.*, the Other World.

Ta en tchetta 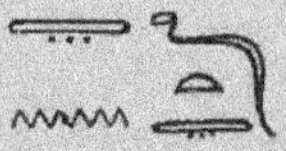 "land of eternity", *i. e.*, the Other World.

ta  bread, cakes.

 cakes made of fine flour.

 white bread.

 celestial bread.

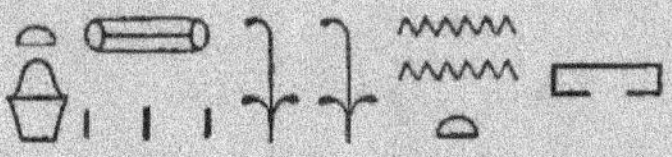 bread of Nenet (?).

 . . . . . .

Tait 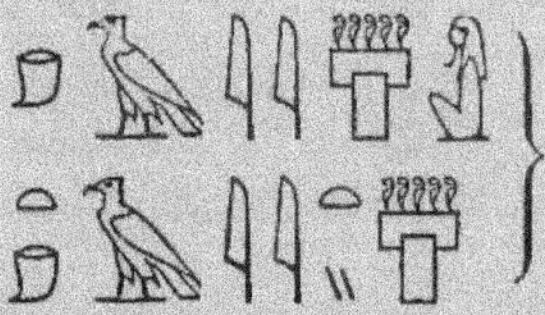 a proper name.

tait  sail.

Tait 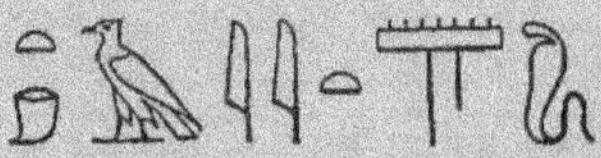 the name of a goddess.

Tar  the name of a fiend.

taḥenen 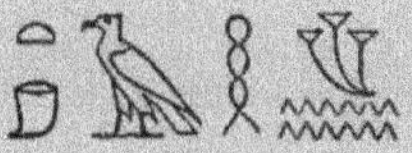 to dip in water (?).

Ta-ḥer-sta-nef 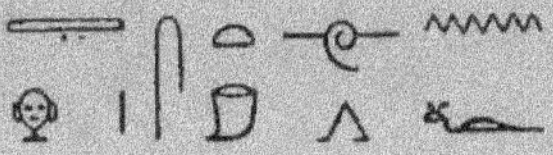 a proper name.

Tatunen 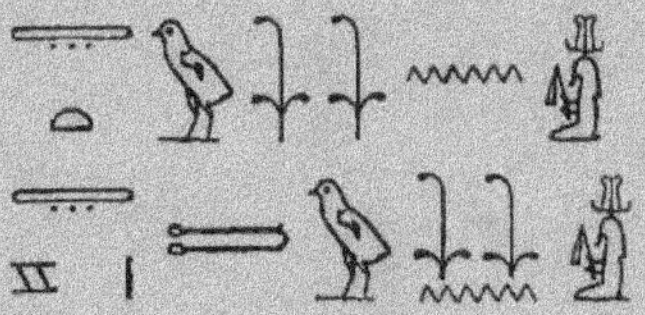 the name of a god.

tȧt  emanation; plur. 

tiu 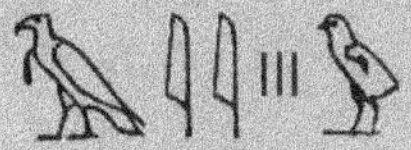 adorers.

tini 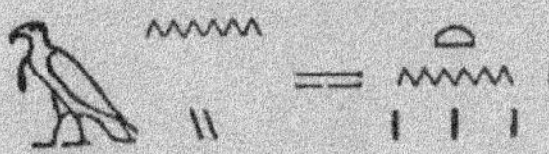 (?).

tu  a demonstrative particle.

tua  to adore.

tuȧ  I.

tui  a demonstrative particle.

tui  . . . . . .

tui 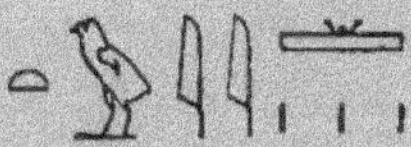 . . . . .

tuf  his.

tuni  . . . . . .

tur 

turȧ  to cleanse, purify, be pure, clean.

tuk thou.

tuḳ apparel.

tut to be like, similar.

tut type, form, image, statue, portrait figure.

as, like, similar.

tut to arrange, group together.

tebu to be shod, sandal (?).

teb sandal.

tebi, tebt pair of sandals.

Tebu, *Tebti* the name of a city.

tebteb to walk.

tebtebti the soles of the feet (?).

tep head, the tip, point, or top of anything.

tep upon.

tepi  he who is on, the first, best, or finest of anything.

 the best of the offerings.

 the finest linen.

 the choicest flowers.

 the earliest hour of every day.

 the earliest dawn.

 the earliest twilight hour.

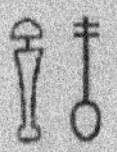 the greatest happiness.

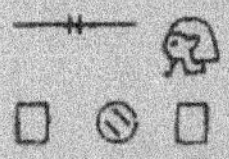 primeval time.

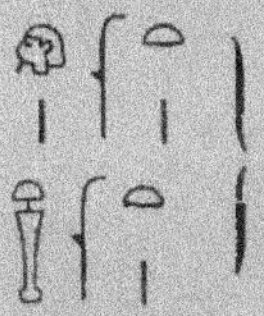 New Year's Day.

 the best water in the lake.

 the original state of anything.

tep ā 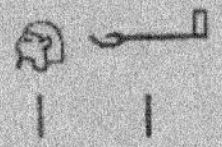 straightway.

tep ā 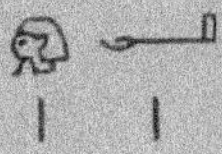 he of olden time, ancestor.

 she of olden time, ancestress. plur.  ancestors, forebears.

ṭep re / *tepi re*  mouth, then what comes from the mouth, speech, voice, utterance; plur. .

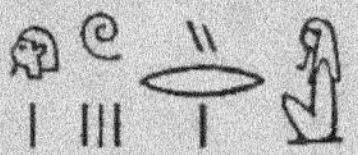

tep reṭui 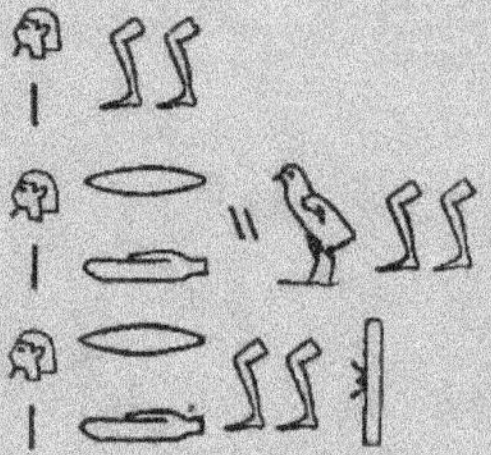 prescription, precept, command, chapter.

tep  unguent of finest quality.

tep  a kind of goose.

tept 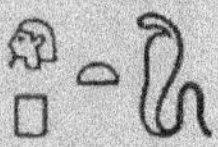 uraeus crown.

Tep-ṭu / *Tep-ṭu-f* 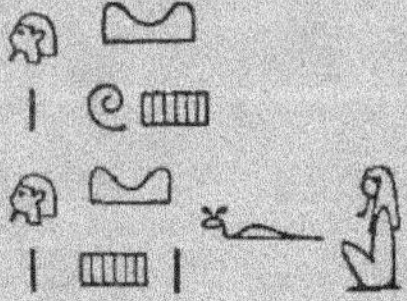 "he on the hill, or his hill"; a name of Anubis.

Tepa  the name of a cow.

tepȧ 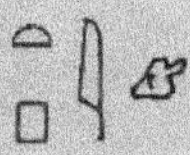 to snuff the air, breathe.

tephet 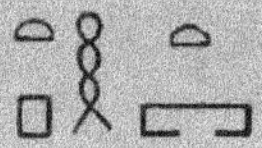 cavern, cave, den, hole in the ground; plur. 

tef  father.

tefa  that.

Tefnut 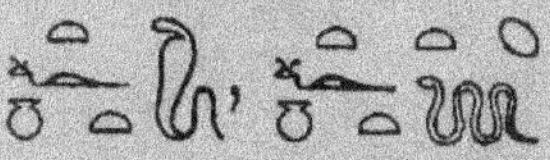 the name of a Water-goddess.

tem  to come to an end.

temt, *temtu*, *temti*  all, entirely;  wholly and entirely.

tem, *temem* 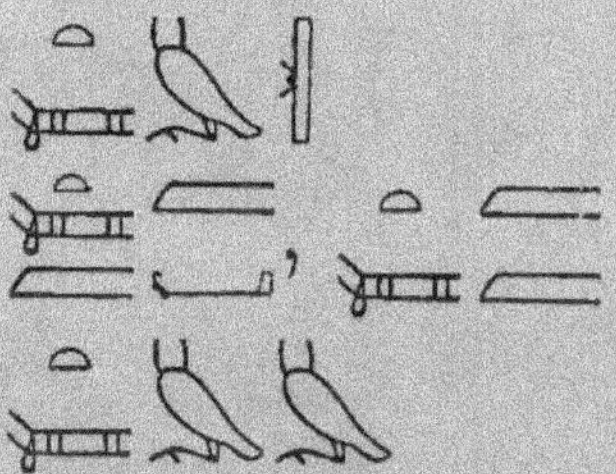 to be complete, whole, entire.

tem 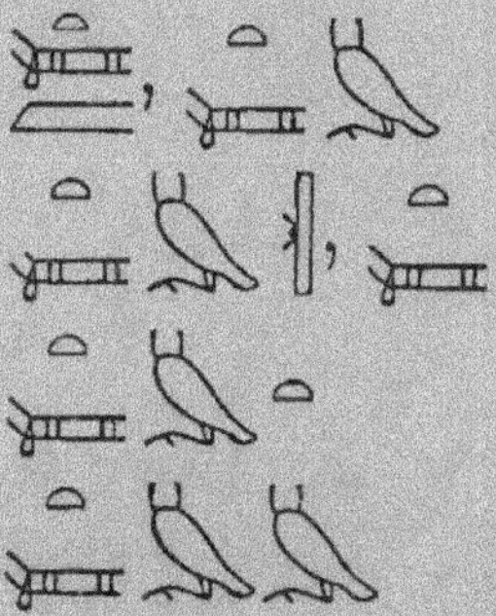 a particle of negation, no, not, without.

Tem / *Temu*  Tem, the "father of the gods".

 Tem Harmakhis.

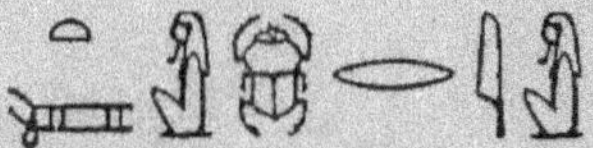 Tem Kheperȧ.

temam  basket (?).

temamu  stations (?).

temaāu(?)  winds.

temu / *tememu*  all people, mortals, mankind.

temem  part of a sledge.

tememu 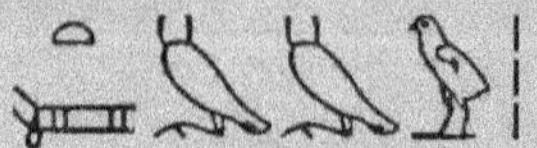 parts of a net.

Temem-re  a proper name.

Tem-sep  the name of one of the Forty-two Judges in the Hall of Osiris.

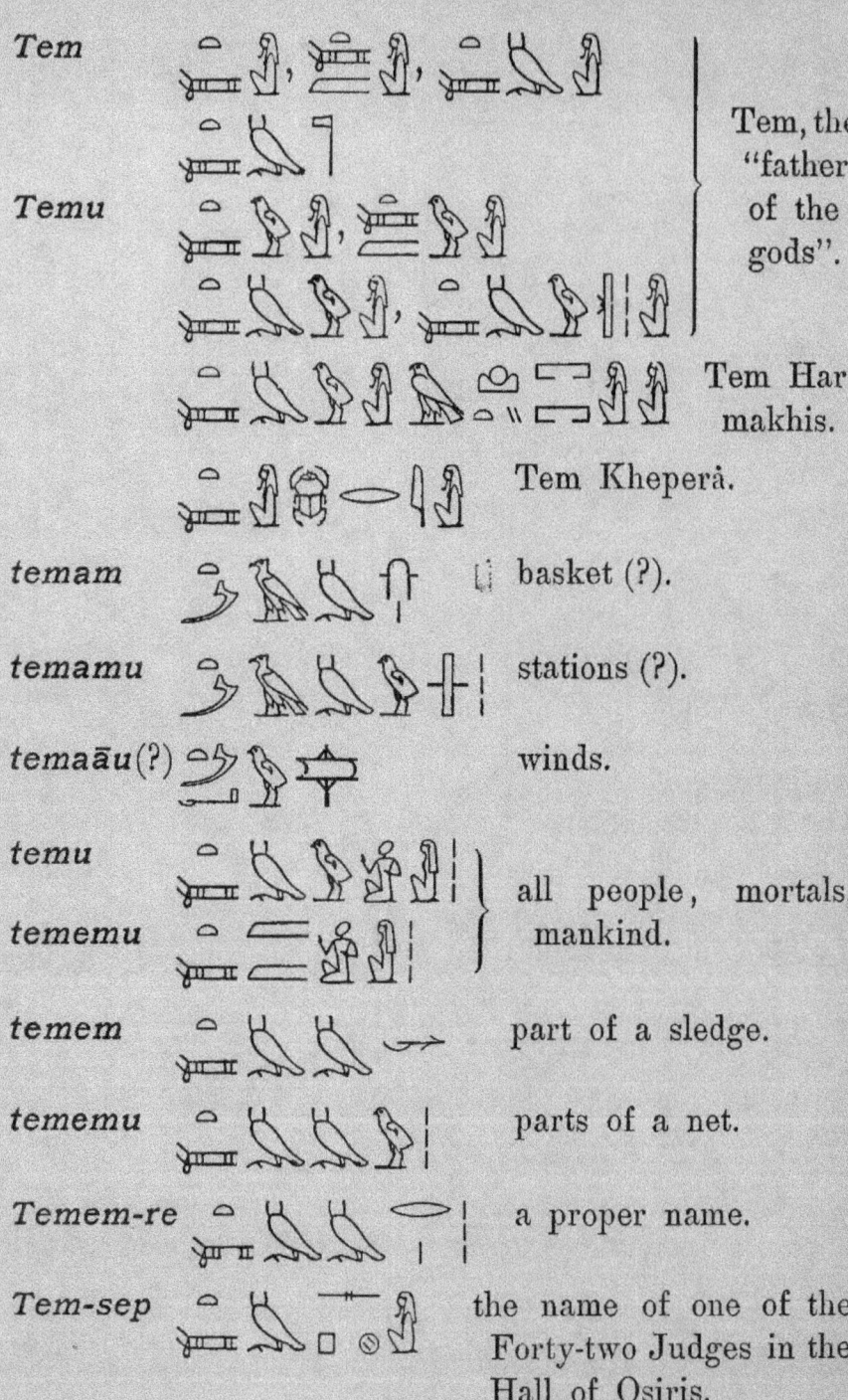

temt 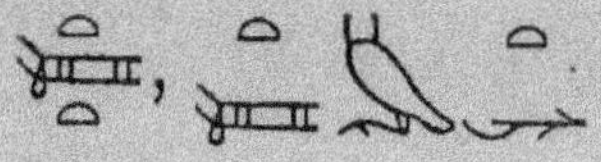 sledge.

ten 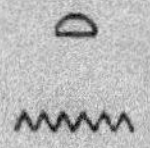 this.

ten 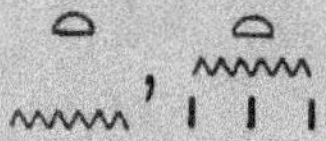 ye, you.

Teni  an ancient city near Abydos.

ten
teni
tenu 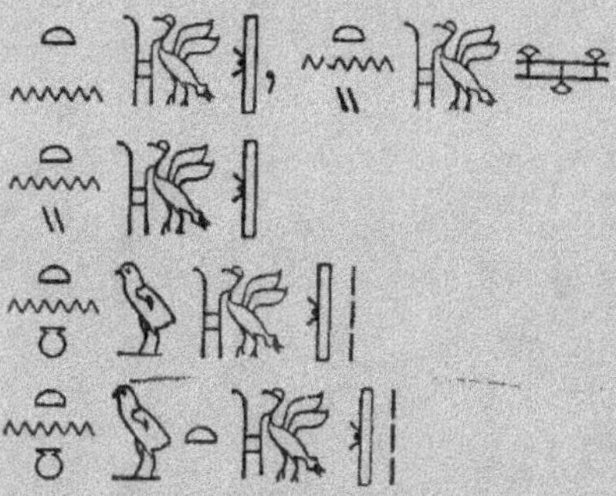 what kind of? what manner of? whence? where?

ten  to be or become great, great, distinguished.

tenait  light.

tenu 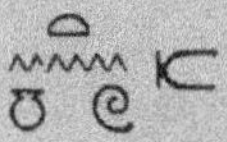 to divide, separate.

tenem 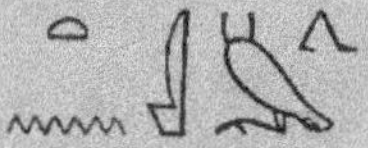 to turn back.

Tenemit  a proper name.

ter 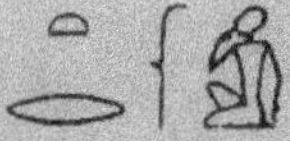 a particle, then, etc.

ter time, season; plur.

terui the two seasons, *i. e.*, morning and evening, or sunrise and sunset;

teriti the northern and southern halves of the sky.

teru stream.

teh
teha to march against, attack.

tehami strider.

tehenen to appoint, raise up.

tiḥṭut prayers, offerings.

tekh the pointer or tongue of a balance; "the pointer of the place of truth".

tekhni hidden.

tekhtekh to shake out the hair.

tesh to depart, to go.

Teshtesh	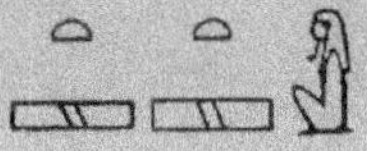	an image which was dressed up as Osiris.
teka	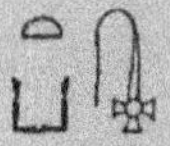	fire, flame, lamp.
tekau		fire, flame, lamp.
tekat	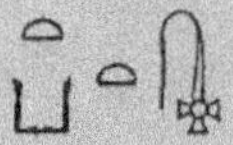	fire, flame, lamp.
Tekem		the name of a god.
tekem		to approach.
teken	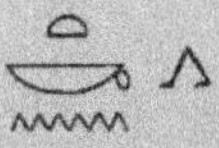	to enter, go in.
		those who enter.
tektek	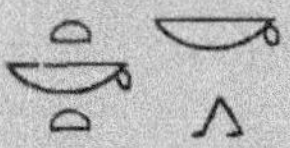	to pass, walk, go.
teḳa		to be hot, to kindle.
teḳas		to walk, march.
tetbu		to smear.

 T.

ṭa  to pass away.

ṭa  emission.

ṭaṭa  to pollute oneself.

ṭaȧu  the name of a garment.

ṭaȧr  restraint.

ṭā
ṭāṭā
ṭāṭāu
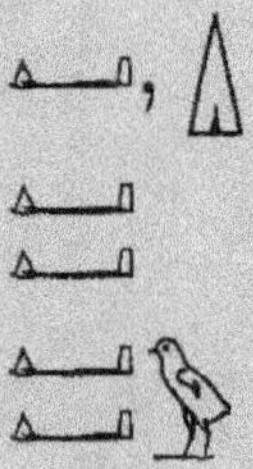 to give, grant, set, place, ascribe.

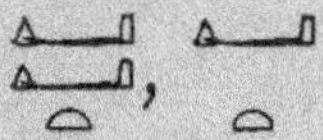 gift.

 giver, giving, placing.

 givers.

ṭāt ȧb 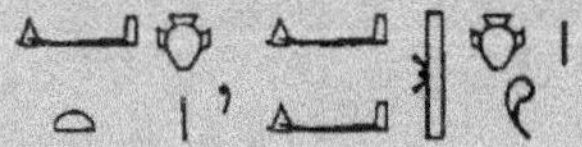 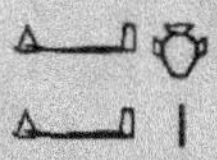 heart's desire.

ṭā  as auxiliary:

 make to fear.

cause to do.

cause to be.

cause to become, etc.

Ṭāṭāu — the city of Busiris or Mendes.

ṭit — gifts.

ṭu, *ṭut* — evil, evil thing, sin, fault, wickedness, sinner.

sin, evil.

ṭuu, *Ṭut* — wickedness.

Ṭuṭu — the name of one of the Forty-two Judges in the Hall of Osiris.

Ṭuis (?) — the name of the rudder in the magic boat.

ṭuȧu — ale (?), drink.

ṭu — mountain; plur.

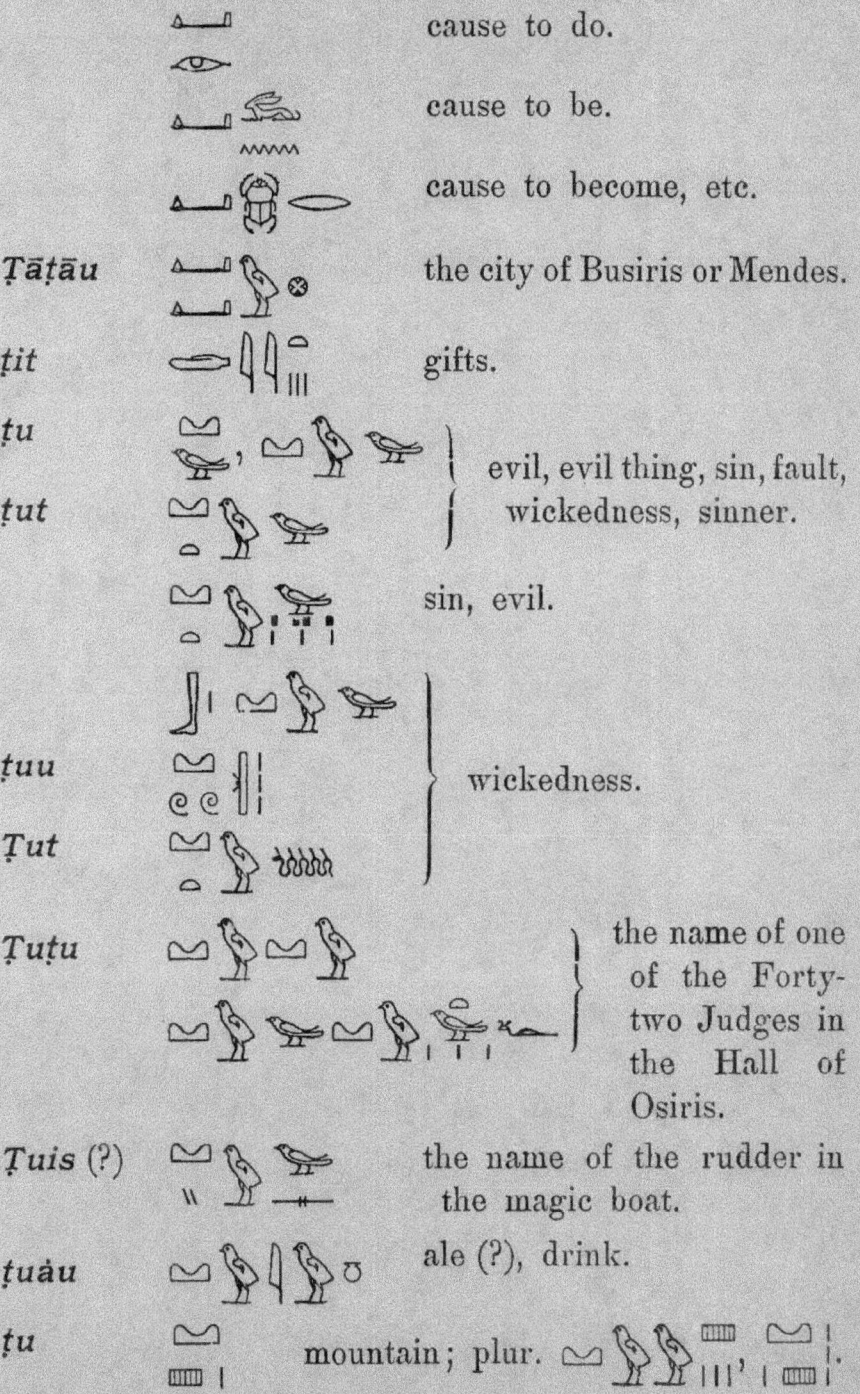

the two mountains.

two great high mountains.

Ṭu-en-Bakha Mount Bakha, the Mountain of Sunrise.

Ṭu-en-Neter-khert Mountain of the Other World.

Ṭut-f (?).

Ṭu-menkh-rerek a proper name.

ṭu-ā to put forth the hand (?).

ṭua five; fifth.

ṭuau to do something early in the day.

ṭuat, ***ṭuait*** dawn, daybreak, to-morrow.

ṭua to praise, worship, adore; praise.

praisers.

neter ṭua  to offer up thanksgiving.

Ṭuamutef  one of the Four Sons of Horus.

Ṭuat  The Other World.

 the everlasting Ṭuat.

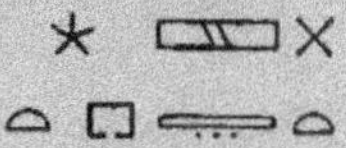 the hidden Ṭuat.

 the god of the Ṭuat.

 the beings of the Ṭuat.

ṭun 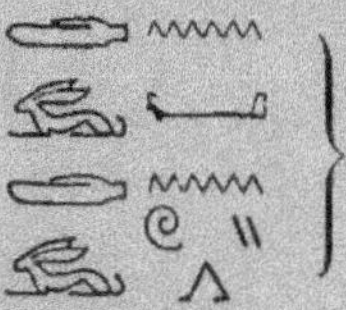 to lift up or stretch out the legs.

Ṭun-peḥti 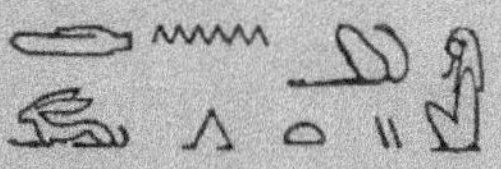 the porter of the Second Ārit.

ṭur 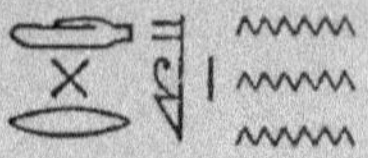 to be clean.

ṭurt  . . . . . .

ṭeb  horn; dual 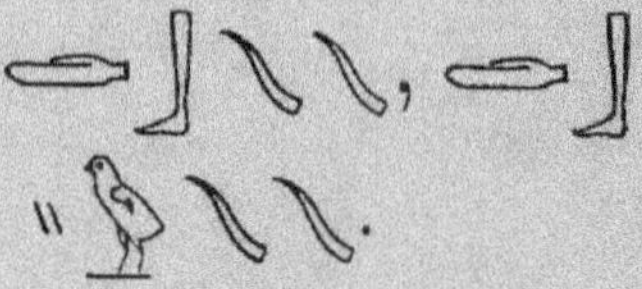.

ṭeb 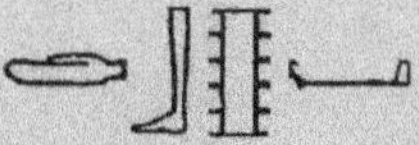 tomb (?).

ṭeb  to be furnished or equipped.

ṭeb  to wall up, to box in.

ṭebt 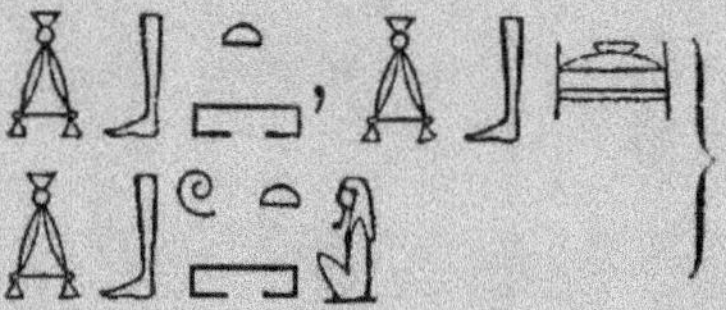 box, coffer, coffin, chest, tomb; plur. 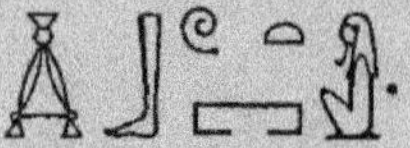.

ṭebu  frame, framework of a net.

Ṭeb-ḥer-kehaat  the herald of the Fifth Ārit.

ṭeben, *ṭebenu* 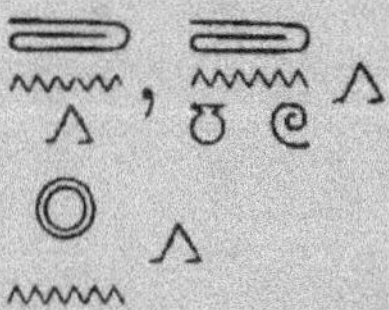 to revolve.

ṭebḥ  to pray, make supplication.

ṭebḥu (?) *ṭebḥet* 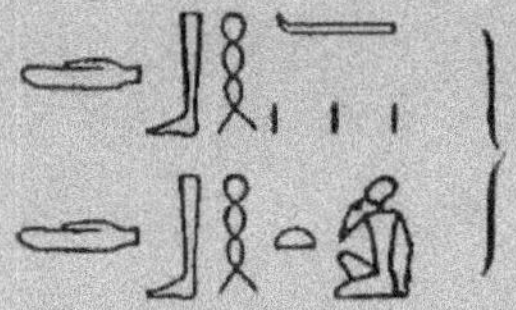 prayer, petition, supplication.

ṭebḥu 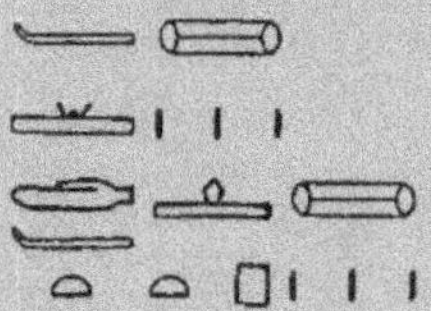 offerings, cakes, bread, etc.

ṭebḥu 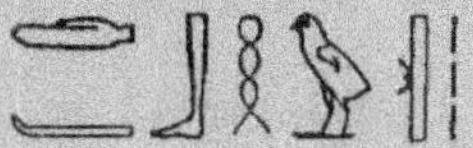 funerary furniture.

ṭebḥ 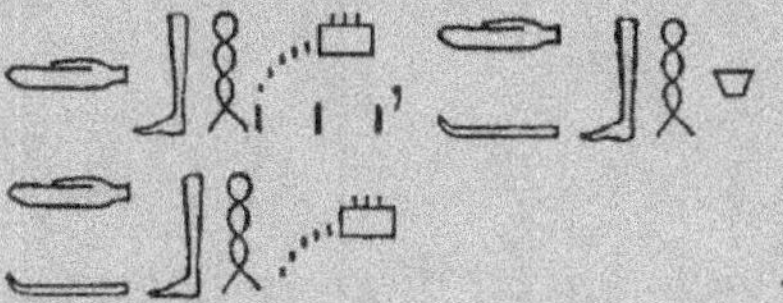 a grain measure.

ṭebt  block, slab, brick.

Ṭep 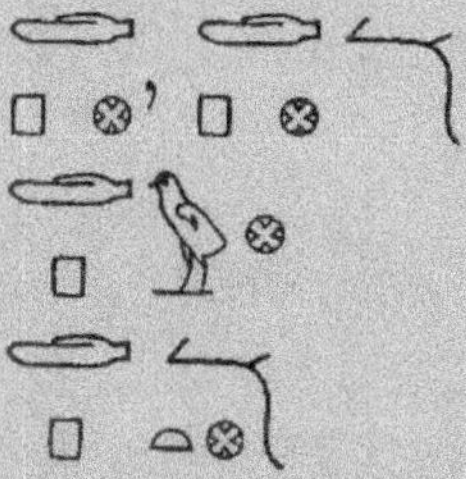 one half of the city of Buto,

ṭept 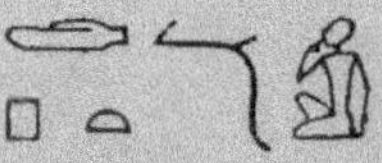 taste.

ṭepu 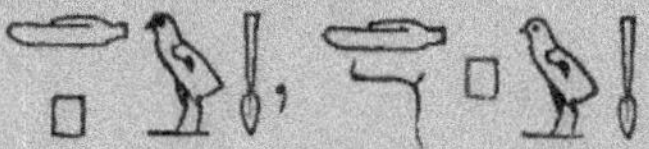 oar, paddle.

ṭept 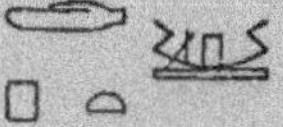 boat.

ṭem  to cut, stab.

 with  a piercing voice.

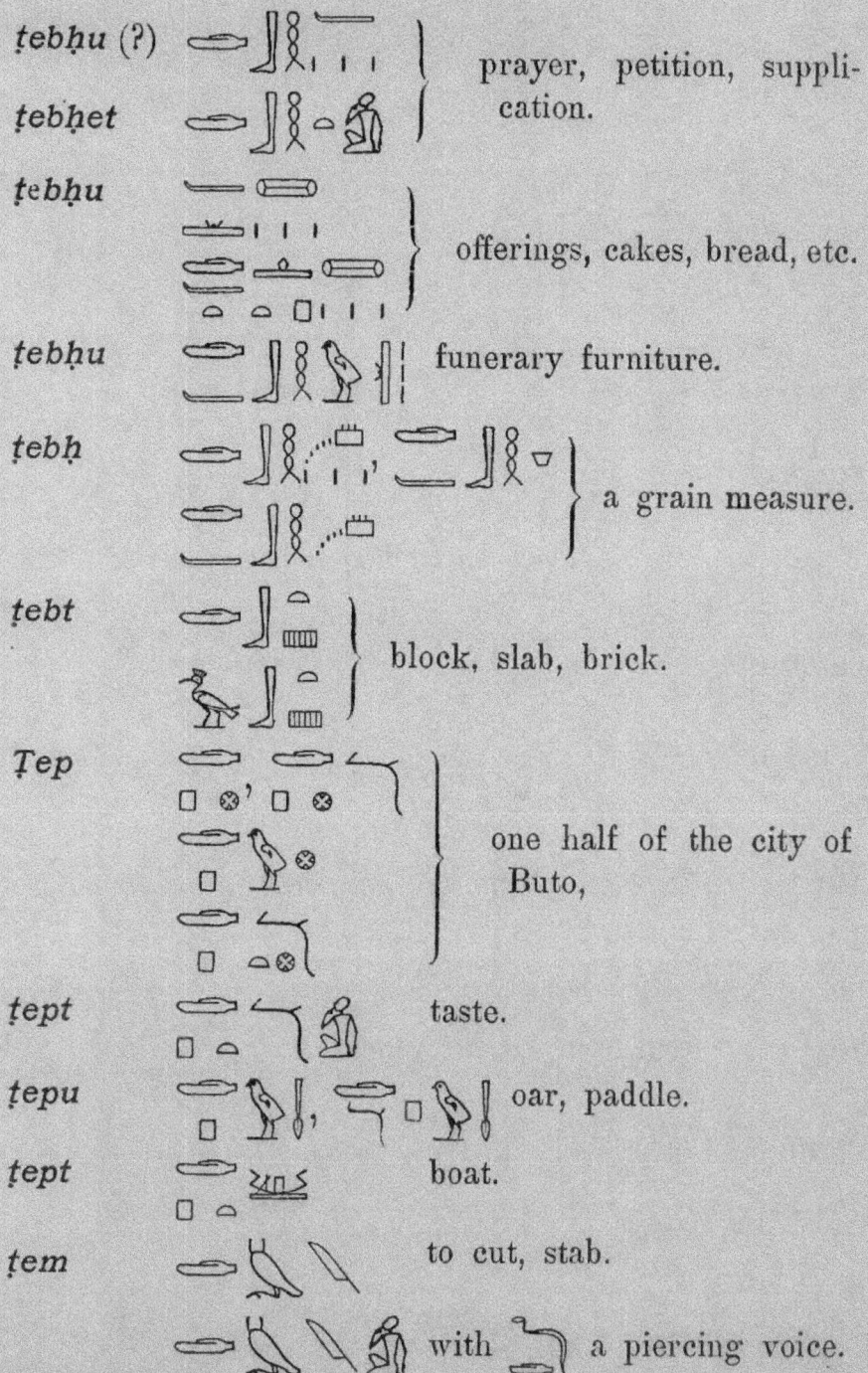

ṭem 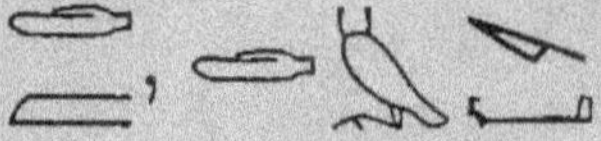
ṭemt 
knife, sword; plur. 

 two-edged knife, or sword (?).

Ṭem-r (?)-*khut-pet*  . . . . . .

Ṭem-ur  a name of Osiris.

ṭemamt  a hairy covering, two locks.

ṭemam  to make an end of.

ṭemam  (*sic*)

ṭemȧ
ṭemȧi 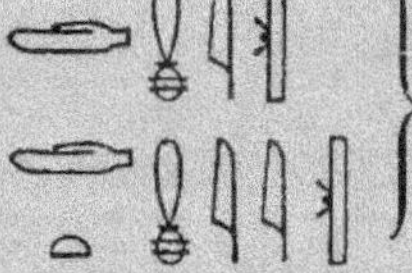 to unite, be united, touch, join.

ṭemȧ  city; plur. .

ṭemi 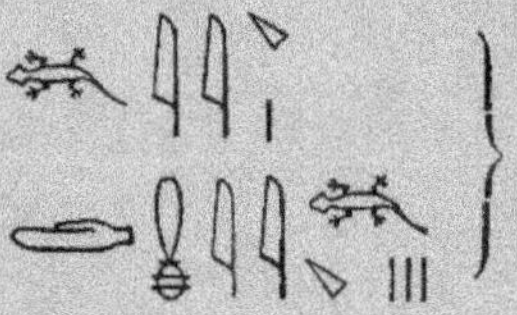 shore, bank.

ṭemem  entire, totality.

ṭemṭ *ṭemtch*		to collect, gather together, unite, all, entire.
	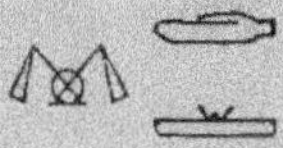	all, totality.
Ṭemṭiu		a class of divine beings.
ṭen	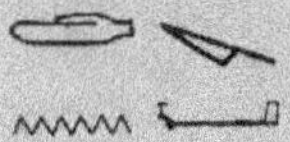	to cut off, or away.
ṭen	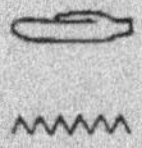	to place.
Ṭenȧ	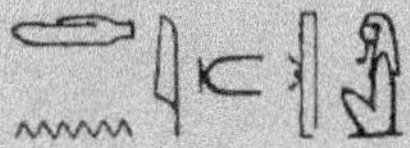	the name of a god.
ṭenȧ	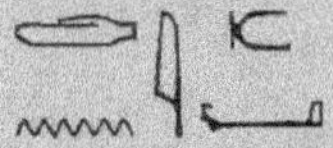	to separate.
ṭenȧt	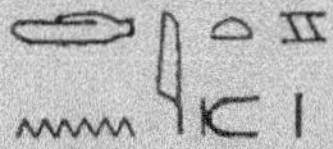	bank of a canal, piece of land.
ṭenȧt	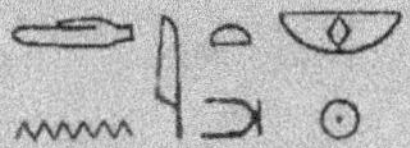	the weekly festival.
ṭenȧ	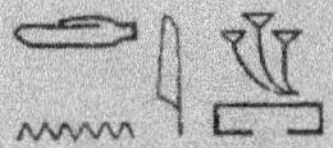	the name of a chamber.
ṭenȧ *ṭenȧt*	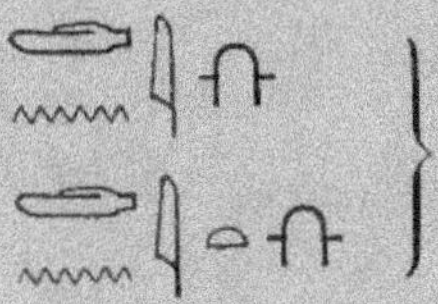	basket.
ṭenȧu		lot, share, division.
ṭeni	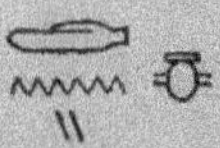	vessel.

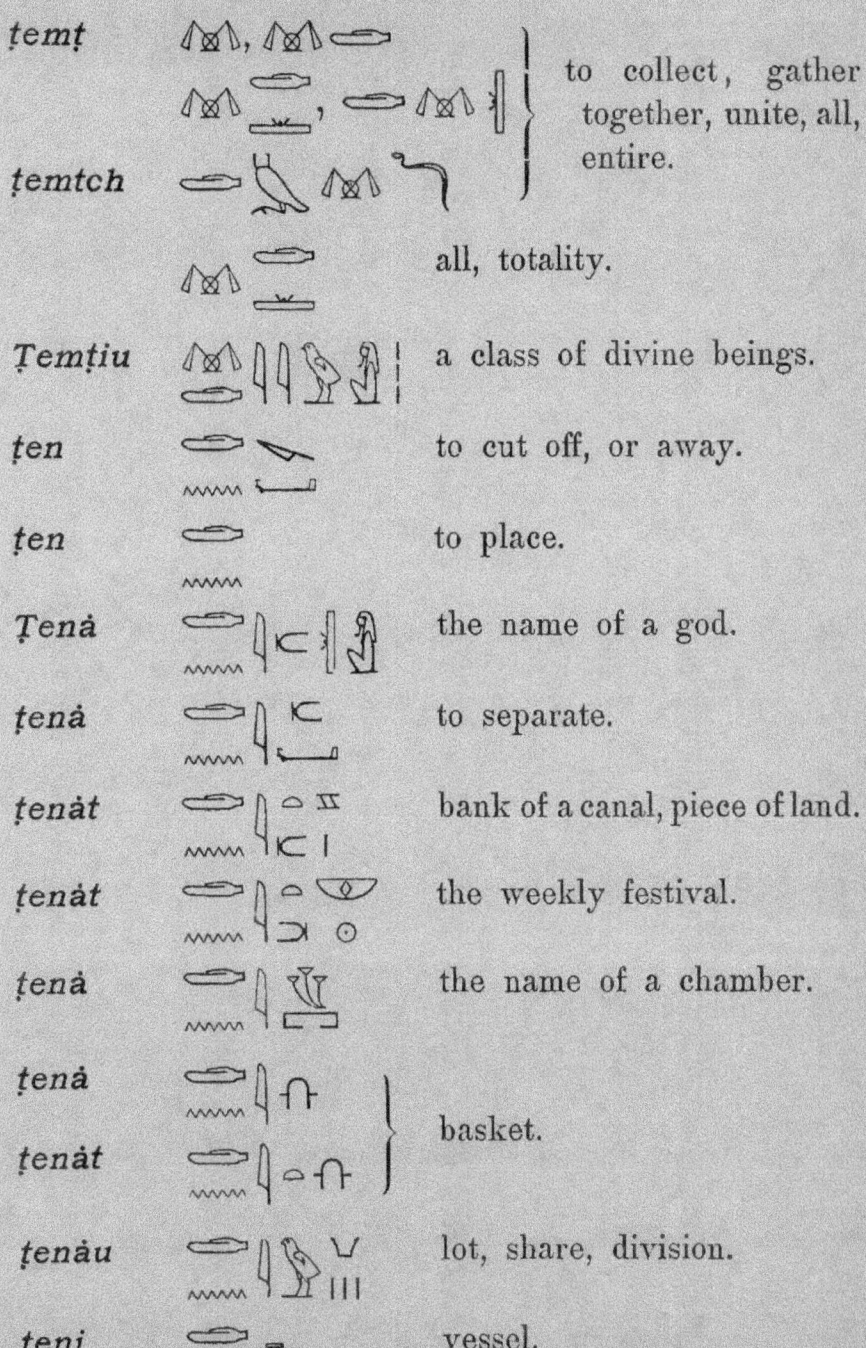

Ṭeni the name of one of the Forty-two Judges in the Hall of Osiris.

Ṭeniu the god of old age.

ṭenu to be distinguished.

ṭenb to gnaw.

Ṭenpu a proper name.

ṭenem worms.

ṭenḥ wing.

ṭenḥui pair of wings.

ṭenḥṭenḥ to fly.

ṭens weights.

ṭent abode.

ṭenṭ slaughter.

ṭenṭen might, violence, valour.

ṭer to destroy.

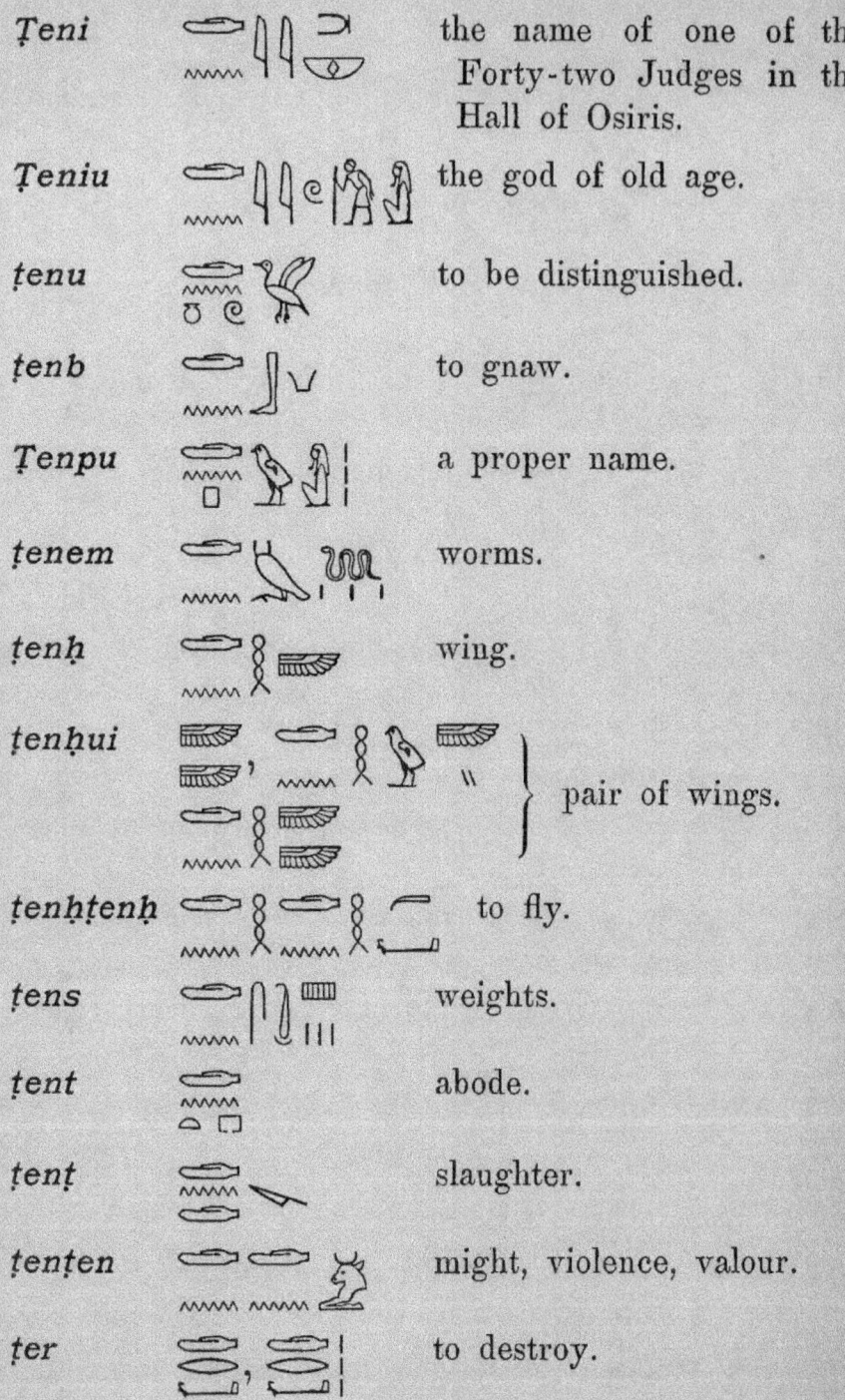

ṭerp	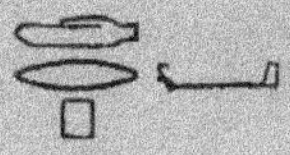	to offer.
ṭeref	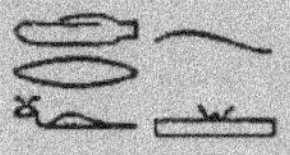	wisdom, skill, book of wisdom.
ṭehant		forehead.
ṭehen		to salute humbly.
ṭehen *ṭehen ta*	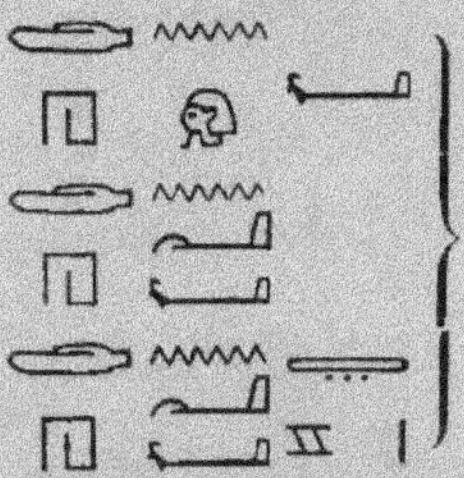	to place the forehead on the ground in token of homage.
Ṭehent	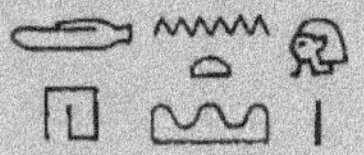	"brow of a hill"; a proper name.
Ṭeḥuti		the god Thoth, scribe of the gods, dweller in Khemenu 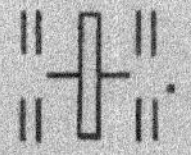.
Ṭeḥuti-Ḥāpi		Thoth-Ḥāpi.
Ṭeḥutit		the Thoth festival.
ṭeḥer	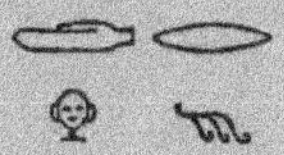	hair, feathers, foliage.
ṭeḥerȧu		injury, harmful person, sickness (?).
ṭes	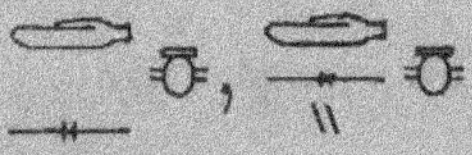	vase.

ṭes 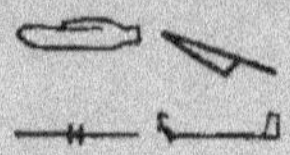 to cut, smite.

ṭes 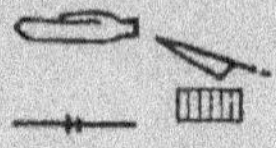 flint knife; plur. , 

ṭeser 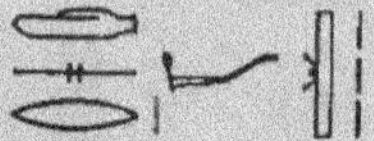 sacred, holy.

Ṭesert-tep  a proper name.

Ṭesher  the name of a town and of its god.

ṭesher  to be red, become red, red, ruddy.

 red ones, men or devils.

ṭesheru  gore, blood, redness (of clouds).

ṭesher  blood.

Ṭesher  the red land, *i. e.*, the desert.

ṭeshert 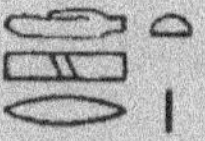 red flame.

ṭeshert 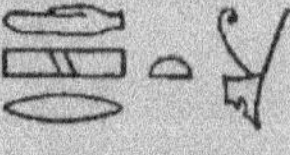 the Red Crown, *i. e.*, the Crown of Lower Egypt.

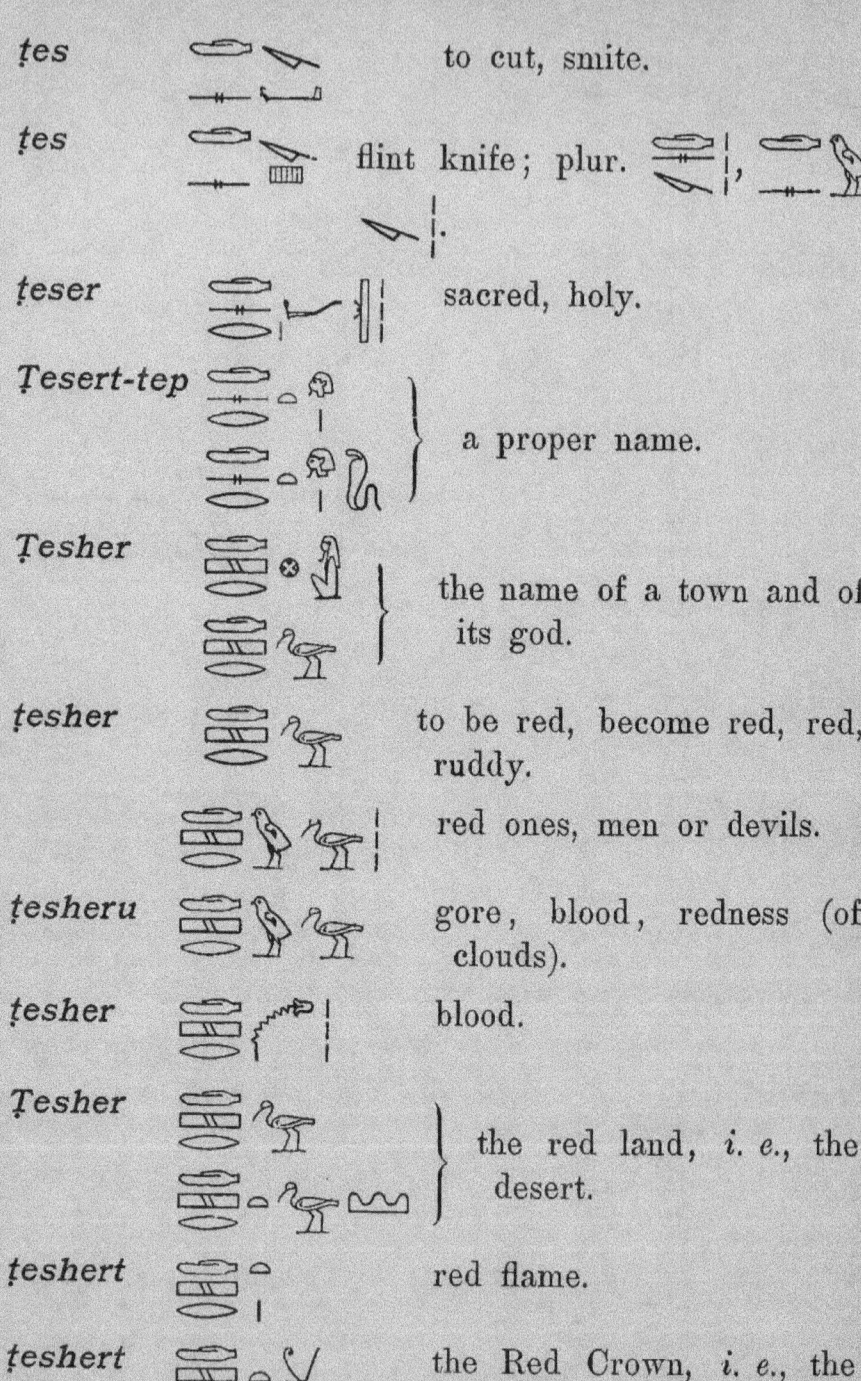

ṭeqer 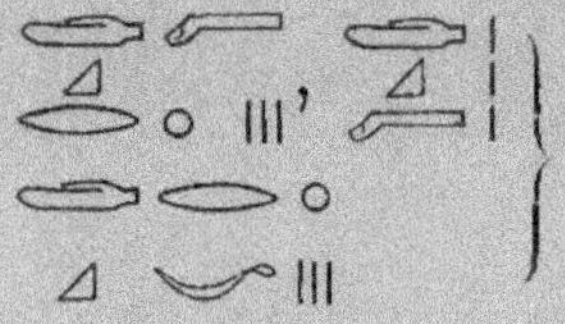 seeds, fruits.

ṭeḳa  to see.

 seeing.

 appearance.

ṭeḳaȧu  seeds, fruits (?).

ṭeḳ, ṭeḳeḳ  sight.

ṭeḳa  to hide.

ṭeḳa  plants.

ṭeḳas 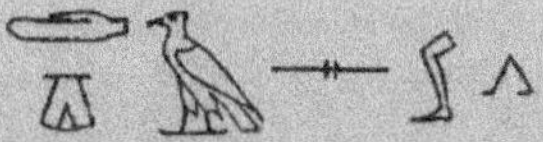 to run, walk towards.

ṭetrit  . . . . . Chap. XCIX, 12.

ṭet 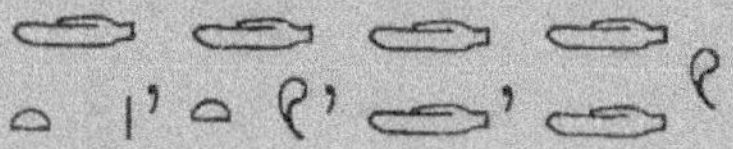 hand.

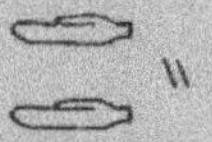 the two hands.

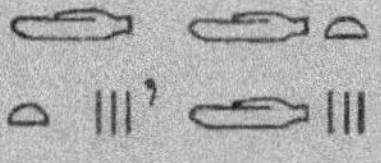 hands.

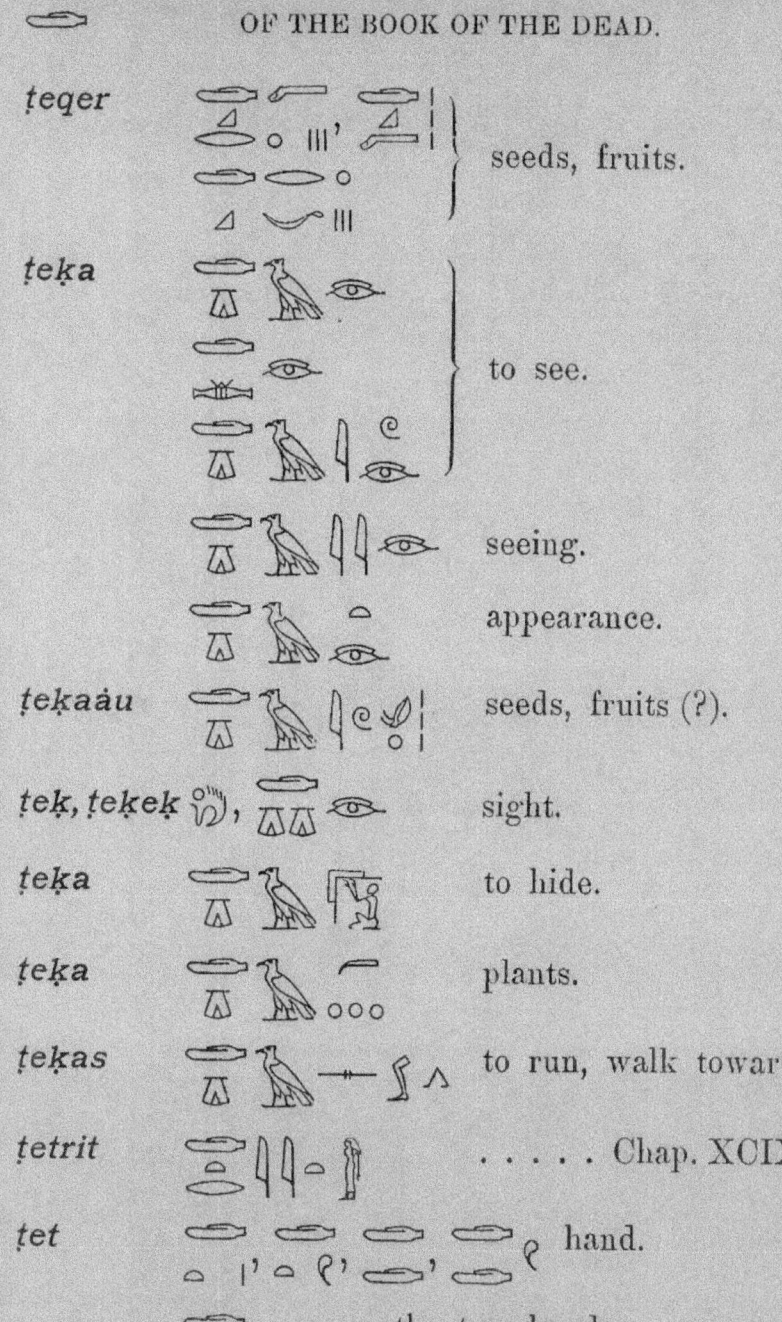

Ṭet-ent-Ȧst a proper name.

ṭeṭ, *ṭeṭṭeṭ* to stablish, be established, stable, permanent.

ṭeṭ an amulet.

ṭeṭ a figure, image, or tree trunk which was "set upright" during the festival of Osiris.

ṭeṭ a building.

Ṭeṭu the city of Busiris.

Ṭeṭt the city of Mendes.

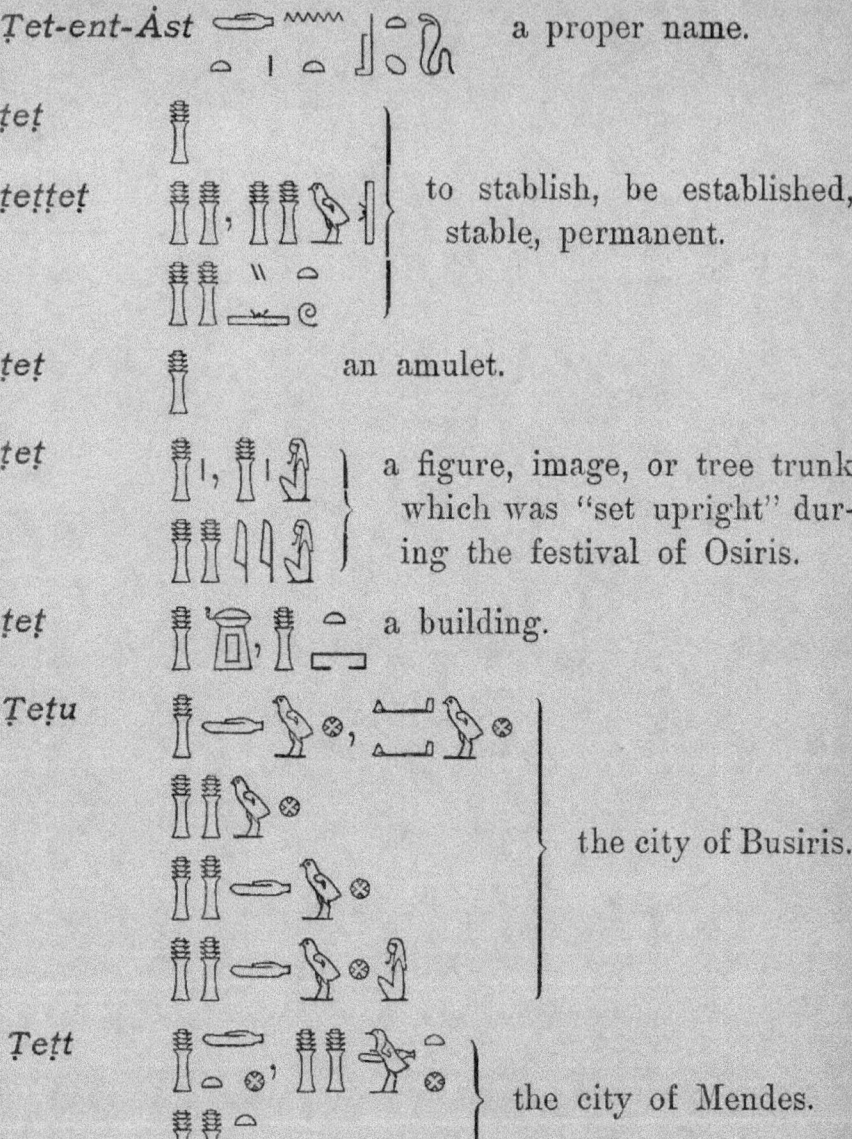

TH.

th	thee, thou, thy,
thȧ (*tȧ*)	with verbs, ..., ..., ..., ..., ..., ..., ..., etc.
Thȧnasa (*Tȧnasa*)	a proper name.
thȧthȧ	thighs.
thu	thou.
thut ȧs	behold!
thui	. . . .
theb (*teb*)	sandals.
Thefnut	the name of a goddess.
thepḥet	storehouse, cave, cavern, hole.
themes	decree, writing.

 decrees.

then  this.

then 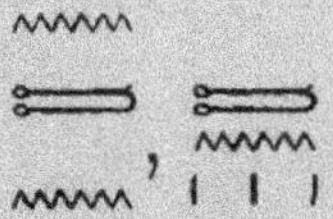 ye, you, your.

then  to be great, exalted, distinguished, worthy.

then  that.

Thena  a proper name.

Thenemi  the name of one of the Forty-two Judges in the Hall of Osiris.

Then-reṭ  the name of one of the Forty-two Judges in the Hall of Osiris.

thentchat  throne chamber.

therem  to make to weep.

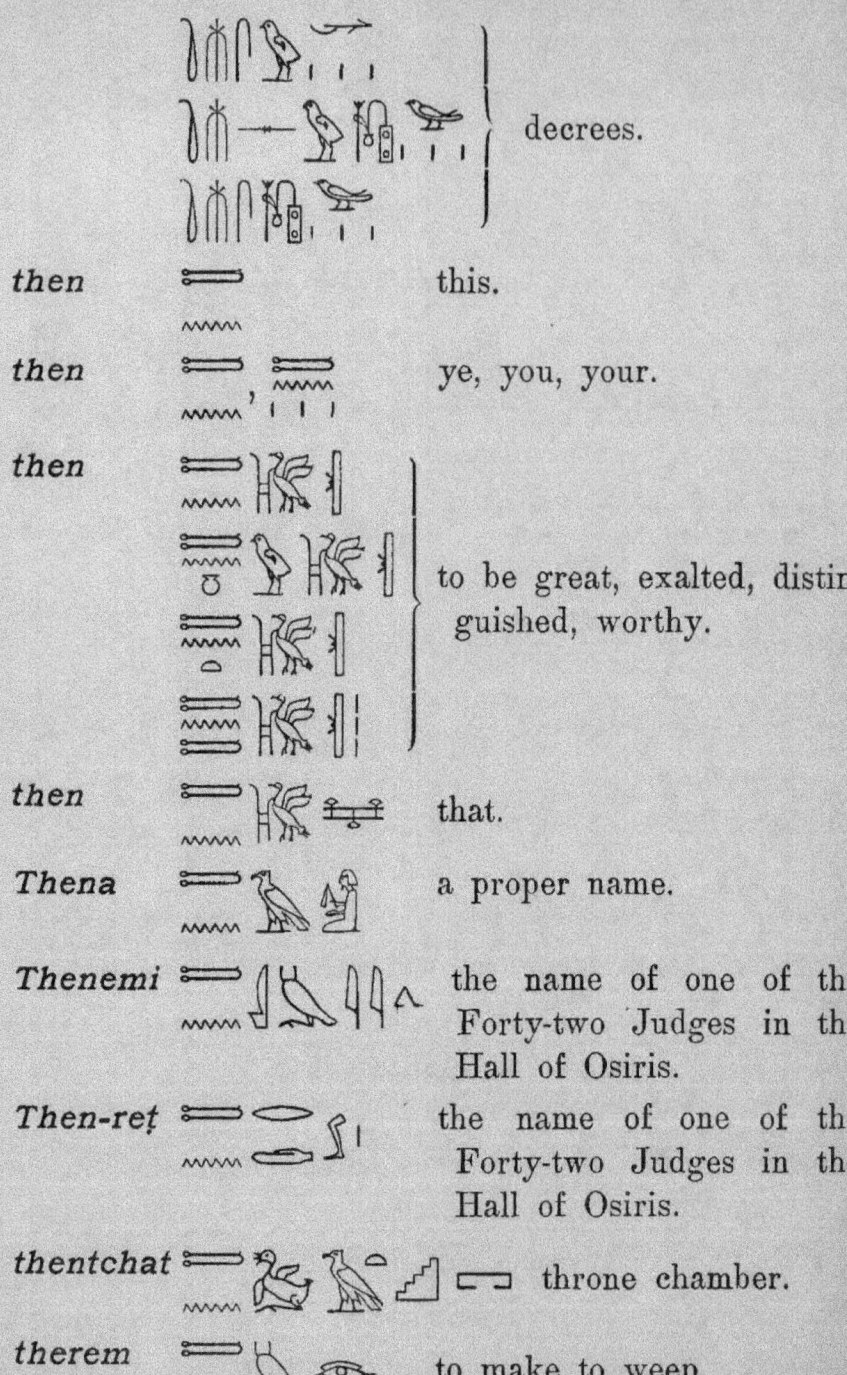

thert 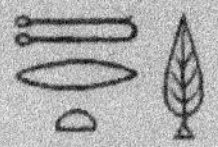 a kind of tree.

theh 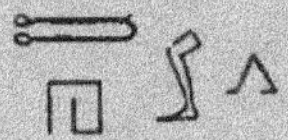 to attack.

theḥenu 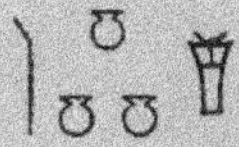 unguent.

Theḥenu, *Teḥenu* 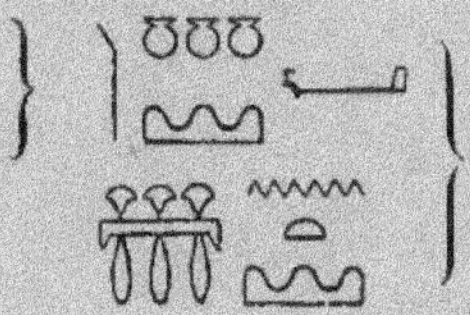 the name of a country, Libya.

theḥent 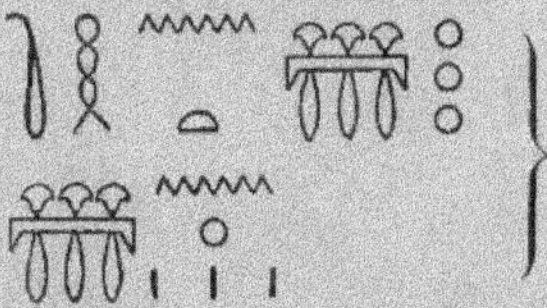 crystal (?), amber (?).

theḥen  to be yellow, or green (?); 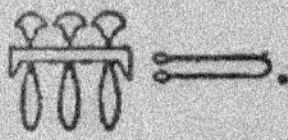.

theḥeḥ 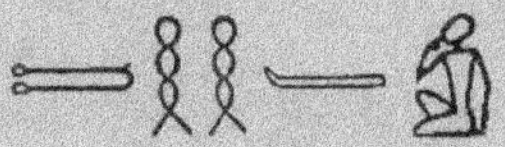 to cry out.

thes  to be strong, give orders.

thes 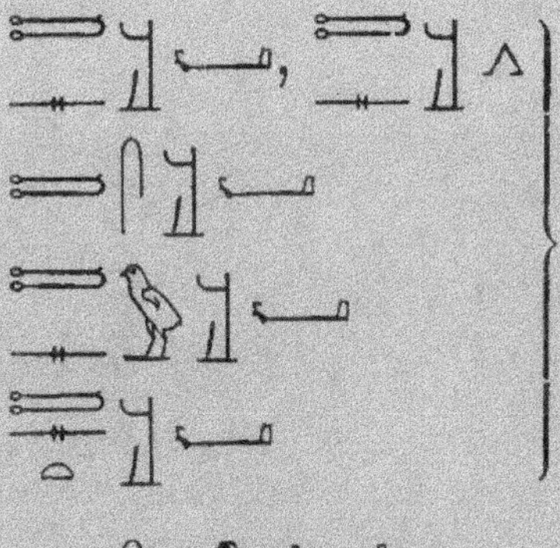 to support, lift up, raise; 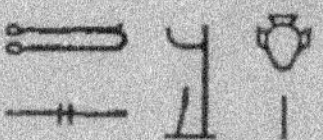 joy.

thesu, *thest*  supports, props.

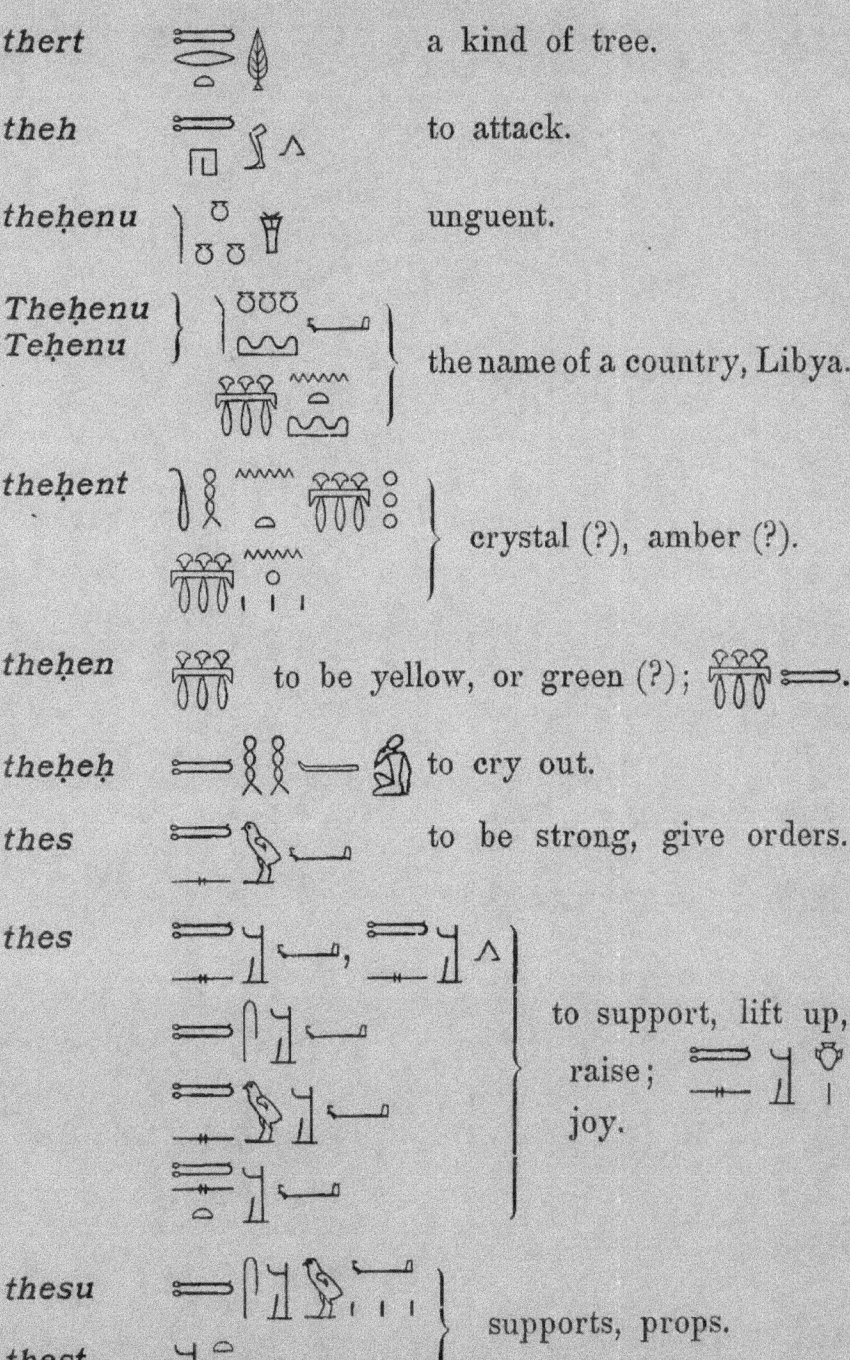

thes	to tie in a knot, knot, fetter.
	knot.
thes	vertebra.
	plur. of preceding.
thesu	word, speech, a saying, riddle.
	conversely.
thesȧu	to rule.
Thest-ur	a proper name.
thesem	dog, greyhound.
	plur. of preceding.
thesthes	a garment.
Thekem	a proper name.

thet  the name of a red stone, or faïence, amulet.

thet 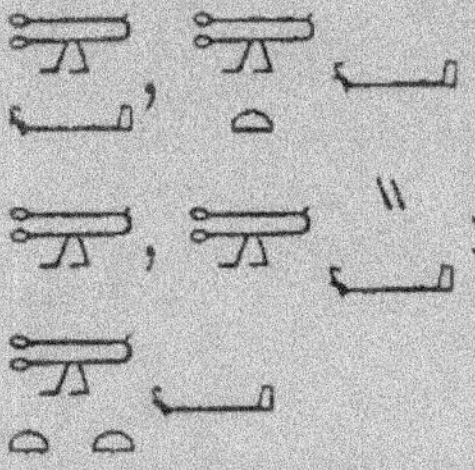 to take possession of, to seize, to carry off, conquer, acquire.

 seizers, robbers.

 ravisher of hearts.

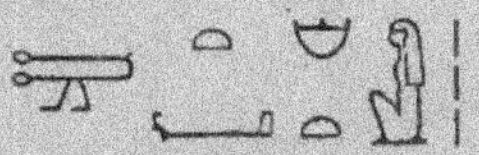 ravisher of women.

Thet-em-āua 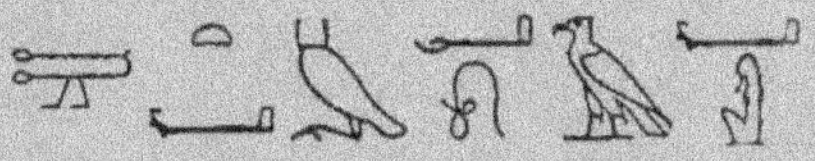 the name of a plank or peg.

thetthet 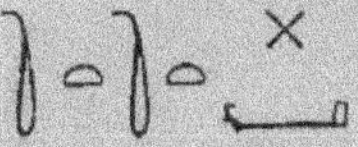 to destroy.

 TCH.

tcha  see .

tcha  safe, sound, in good case.

tcha  to split, to cut.

tcha  abyss.

tcha  to transport, to sail with something.

 one who transports.

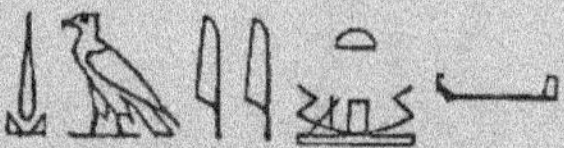 transport.

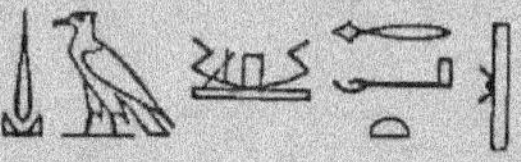 Great Boat.

tcha  to set out, go forth.

tchaau  hair.

tchau (?)  birds.

tchat  an official.

tcha  to seize, grasp, rob, ravish.

 robber.

 plunder.

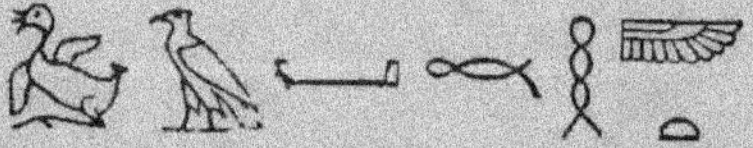 "wing-carrier", fan-bearer.

tcha  male, husband, phallus.

tchau  the west wind.

tchaui  Isis and Nephthys, the "two eagles".

tchaut  twenty; 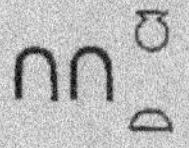 twentieth.

tchafu  flames.

Tchafi  the souls of Horus and Rā.

tchai  fiend.

tchaitiu  slaughterers.

tcham 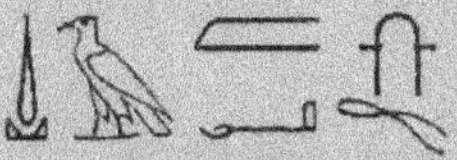 papyrus.

tchamet  coverings, garments.

tchart
tchat  strength, strong.

tchat  measure.

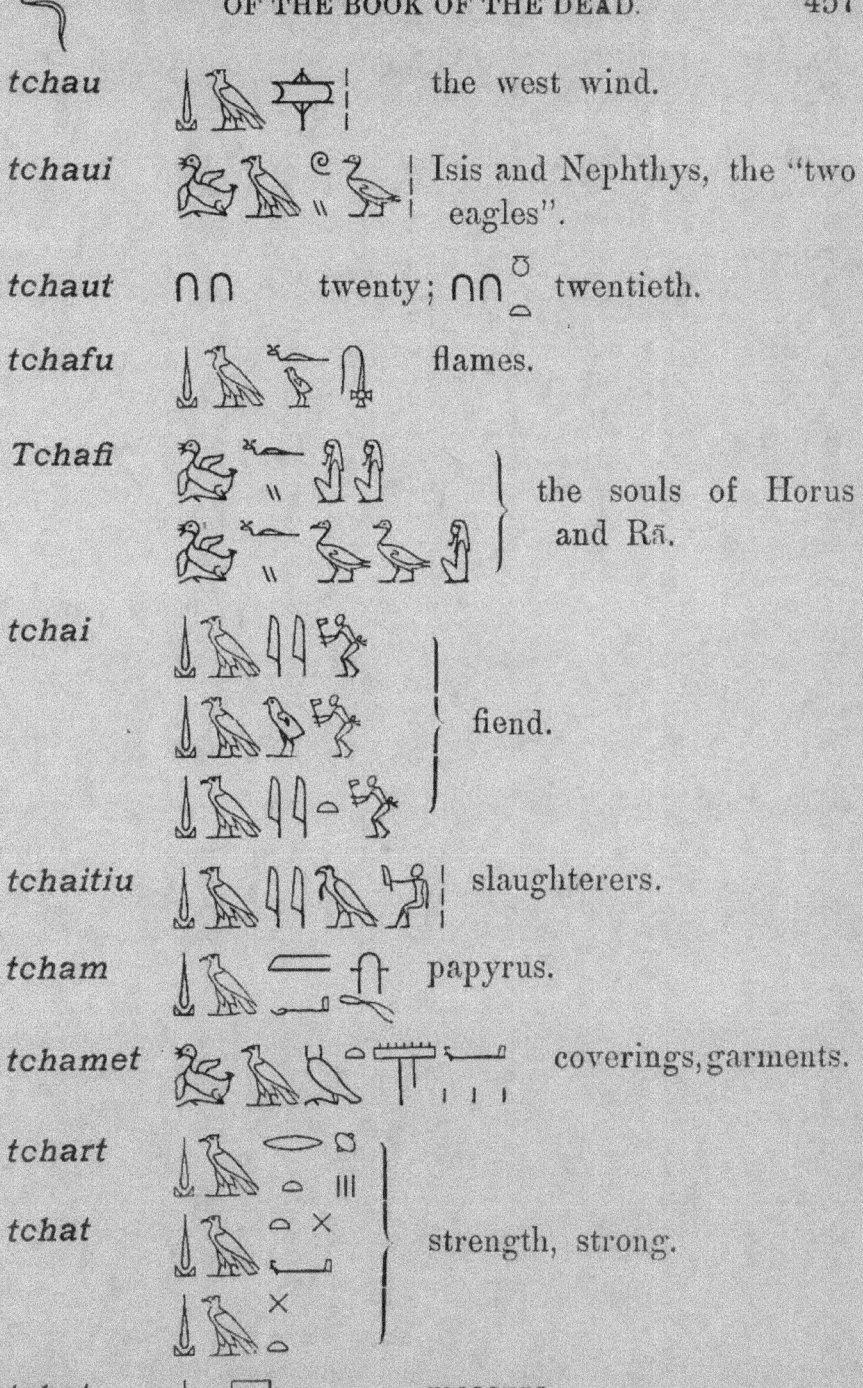

tchat 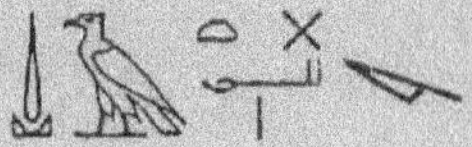 knife.

tchaut  foul things, filth.

tchaua 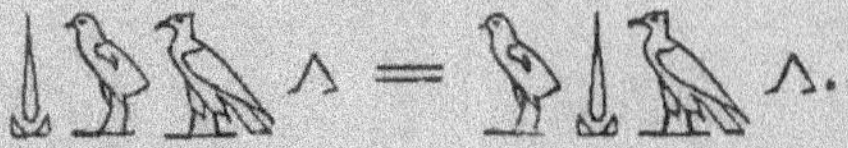

tchauu  amulet.

tchatcha  "head"; the name of the upper post.

tchatcha  head, top of anything, summit.

tchatchat 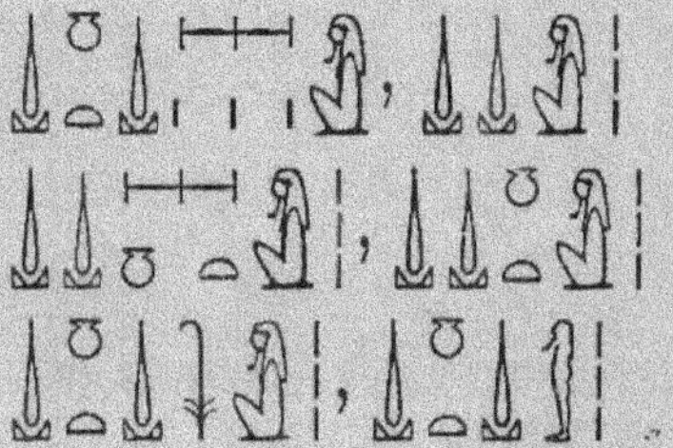 the "Heads", or "Chiefs", *i. e.*, the council of the gods in each great town of Egypt, and in the Other World. Every great god and goddess possessed a company or council of "Chiefs", *e. g.*, Osiris and Rā.

tchatchat 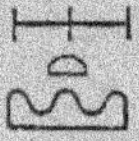 the domain of the cemetery in the hills; plur. 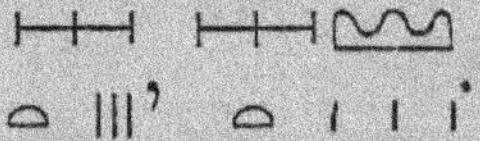

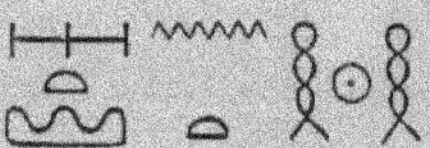 the domain of eternity, *i. e.*, the grave.

the holy domain, *i. e.*, the grave.

the domain of Ȧmenti, *i. e.*, the grave.

city boundaries.

tchāāu staves.

tchābet burning coals.

tchām sceptre; plur.

tchām gold with a very large percentage of silver mixed with it, electrum.

tchār to go about in search of, to pry into.

tchārȧ fortress.

tchebā to seal, make a reckoning (?).

tchebā finger; plur. ; fingers which seize.

Tchebā-en-Ṣekri a proper name.

Tchebā-en-Shesmu  a proper name.

Tchebāu-en-Ḥeru-semsu  name of the paddles in the magic boat.

Tchebāui-en-tepu-ā-Rā  a proper name.

tchefa 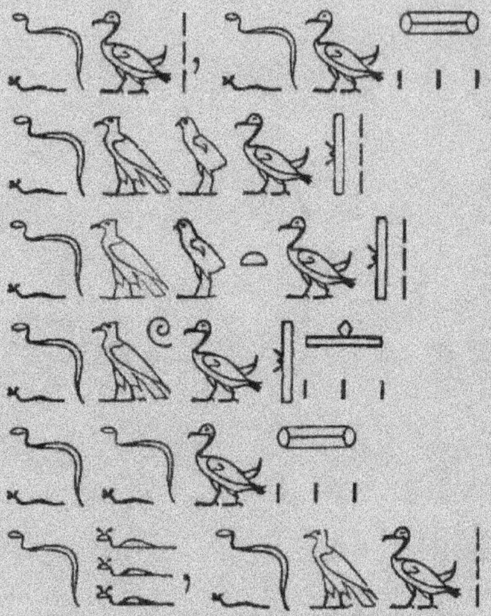 the food of the dead, sepulchral offerings.

Tchefet 

 a place and a goddess in the Elysian Fields.

Tchefit 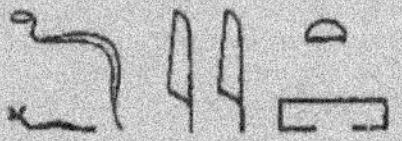

tchefetch  pupil of the eye.

 pupil of the Utchat.

tchefetch 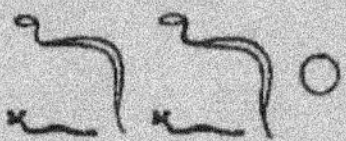 to shed.

Tchen 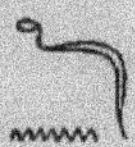 a proper name.

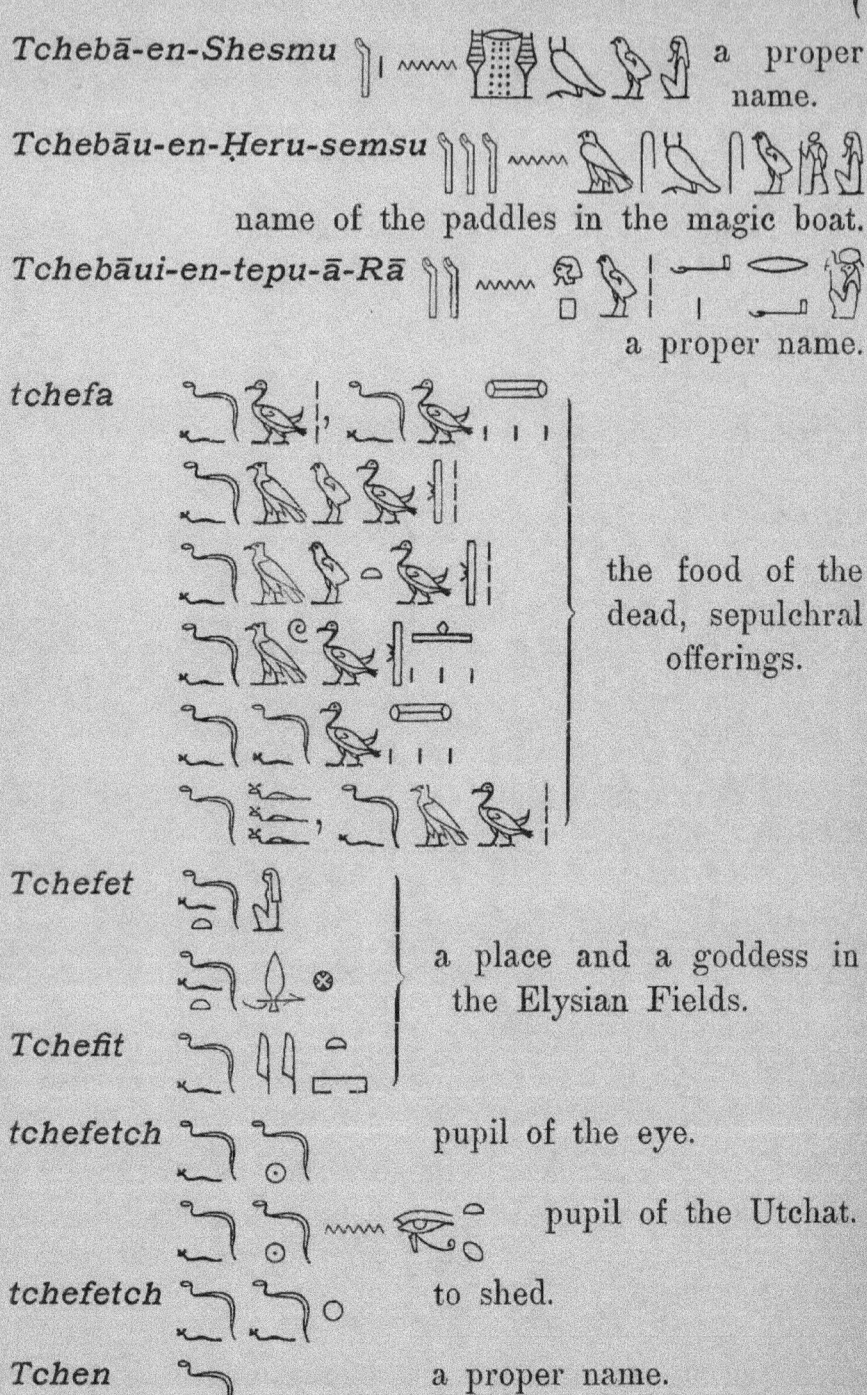

tchenḥu beams.

tchentchen to crush, break.

Tchentche[n] a proper name.

tcher to break.

tcher since, whilst, when.

tcher-ā straightway.

tcher-enti
tcher-entet } since, because.

to the limit of, all, the whole.

tcher limit, boundary; plur. , boundless.

tcheràu } to constrain, fetter.

tcherà fort, stronghold.

tcheràu } heel, hoof.

Tcheruu  the god of boundaries.

tcheru  a bird with a shrill voice.

tcheri 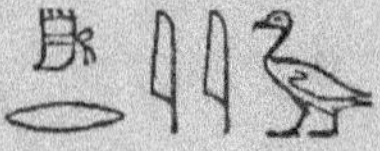 } a bird, the incarnation of Isis and Nephthys.

tcherit 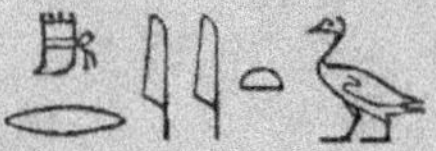

Tcherti  } Isis and Nephthys.

tcheres  abode, chamber (?).

Tcheḥes 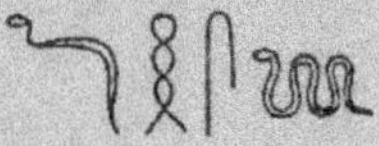 the name of a serpent.

tches 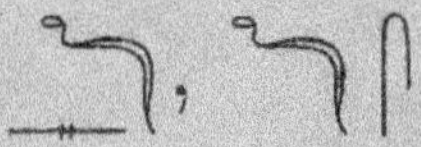 self; 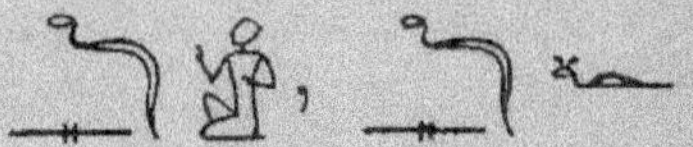, 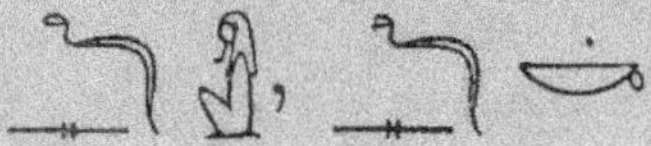 myself, himself, thyself, 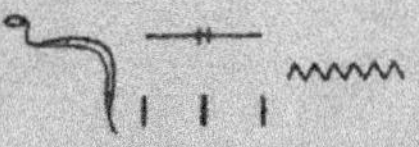 themselves.

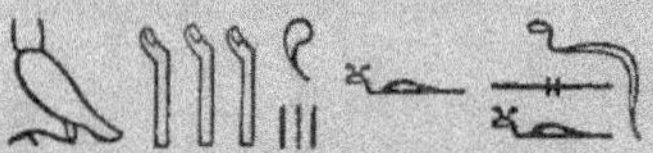 with his own fingers.

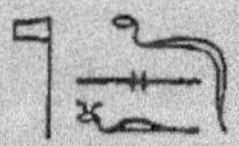 the god himself.

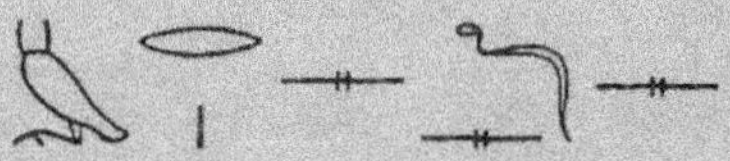 with her own mouth.

tchesef 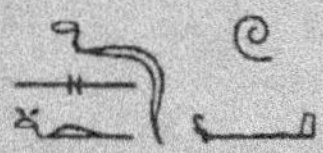 to snare.

 fowler.

tcheser — to make clear the ways, to put in good order, to be or make holy.

tcheseru — holy or beautiful things.

glorious, splendid.

Tchesert — the beautiful mountain, *i. e.*, cemetery.

Tchesert — a proper name.

Tcheser-tep — the name of one of the Forty-two Judges in the Hall of Osiris.

tchet — body, person; my own self.

tchet — house, chamber; the Ṭuat(?).

tchetta — eternity, everlastingness.

the god of eternity.

eternity and everlastingness.

tcheṭ		to say, speak, declare, recite words, converse.
em tcheṭ		saying, introducing a quotation.
tcheṭu		to declare, speak, etc.
tcheṭ-t		words, orders, things said.
tcheṭu	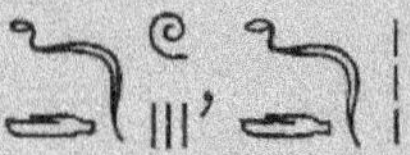	words, orders, things said.
tcheṭ meṭu	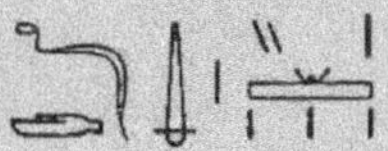	"shall be recited" [the following].
		"another reading".
tcheṭ neḥes	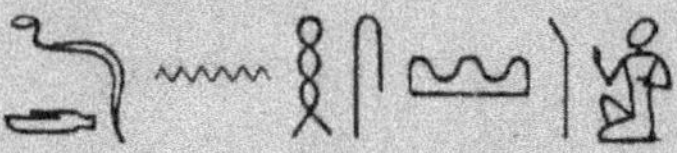	negro speech, or language.
tcheṭfet		reptiles.
tcheṭḥu		a place of restraint.
tcheṭḥu	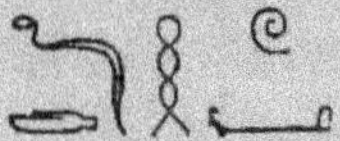 	to shut in, imprison.
tchetch	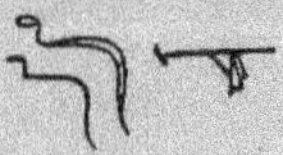	an instrument or standard.

WORDS AND SIGNS OF UNCERTAIN READING.

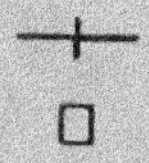
Chap. CXLV, IV, l. 16.

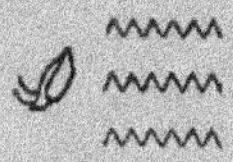
Chap. CX, l. 5.

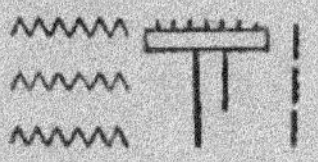
Chap. CX, l. 35.

Chap. CXXXI, 5.

Chap. XCIX, l. 38.

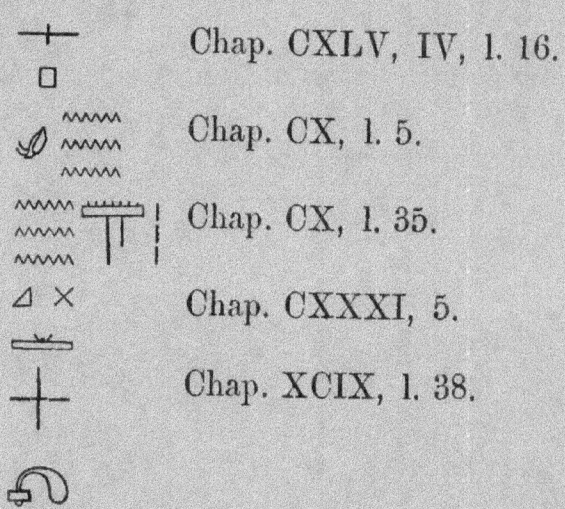

ENGLISH INDEX.

Ȧaheṭ, a god 11.
Ȧakhebit 11.
Āa-kheru 74.
Ȧaku gods 12.
Ȧamḥet 11.
Ȧaqeṭqeṭ 12.
Ȧaru 11.
Ȧat gods 11.
Ȧat-em-khut 74.
Ȧat of Amentet, souls, fire, Horus and Set, etc. 13.
Ȧats, the Fourteen 13.
Āaṭi, god 75.
Ȧb (Elephantine) 22.
Ābau-Taui 79.
Abiding 96, 174.
Abjects 68.
Able 374, 403.
Abode 42, 63, 80, 81, 86, 98, 124, 144, 245, 312, 351, 410, 411, 446, 462.
Abomination 133.
Above 229.
Ab-Rā 24.
Abt-ṭesi-ruṭu-neter 3.
Abundance 156, 353.
Abundant 291.
Āb-ur (Osiris) 78.
Ȧbu-ur 23.
Abydos 25, 426.
Abydos, god 26.
Abyss 191, 195, 249, 456.
Acacia 91, 401.
Accept 403.
Acclaim 10, 194.
Acclamation 9.
Acclamations 10, 11.
Accompany 398.
According to 158, 228, 302.
Account 26, 279, 329.
Acquire 455.
Action (battle) 72.

Actions 52.
Add 96.
Addition 252.
Address 251, 342.
Adoration 15, 195, 352.
Adorations 14.
Adore 96, 333, 353, 429, 440.
Advance 58, 72, 115, 123, 193, 211, 246, 253, 260, 353, 365, 368, 375, 378.
Adversary 318.
Adversaries 382.
Advocate 226.
Àf 33.
Afar 94, 272.
Affairs 313, 320.
Affliction 163.
Afraid 357.
Afresh 112.
After 159, 323.
Afterwards 322.
Again 112, 238.
Against 228.
Aged man 10.
Ahat, goddess 4.
Àḥi 56.
Àḥibit, god 57.
Ahit, goddess 4.
Aḥti (Osiris) 57.
Aḥu, god 5.
Aḥui gods 56.
Air 192, 206, 303.
Air-god 395.
Airless 44.
Aḳab 7.
Àḳau, god 67.
Aḳbâ 8.
Aḳeb 7.
Akeniu 66.
Akentaukhakheru 66.
Akenti 66.
Aker, Akeru, Akeriu 5, 7.
Àḳeru, gods 67.
Àḳert, Àḳertet 67.
Àḳert-khent-Àset-s, a Cow-goddess 67.
Ākesh, city 91.
Akhabiu gods 5.
Àkhen-äriti 90.
Akhmîm 28.
Àkhsesef 57.
Ākhtuset 89.
Àksi, city 66.
Ale 282, 439.
Alert 344.
Alight 71, 211, 368.
All 198, 433, 445, 461.
Allot 150.
Alone 99, 100.
Along with 264.
Also 420.

Altar 77, 120, 291.
Altogether 132.
Ambassador 29.
Amber 453.
Ȧmen 39, 393.
Ȧmen-nathek-ruthi-Ȧmen 39.
Ȧmen-nau-ȧn-ka-entek-Sharu 39.
Ȧmen-Rā 39.
Ȧmen-Rā-Ḥeru-khuti 40.
Ȧmen-ruti 40.
Ȧment, Ȧmentet, Ȧmenti 13, 41, 459.
Ames sceptre 4.
Ȧmmeḥet 39.
Ām-mit 82.
Among 31, 36, 158, 228.
Ȧmseth 42.
Ȧmsi 42.
Ȧmsu 4.
Ȧmt-ṭehen-f 42.
Amulet 75, 97, 121, 170, 280, 323, 450, 458.
Ȧm-urt 37.
Ȧn, god 45.
Ān 82.
Ȧn-ȧarruṭ-f 45.
An-ā-f 46.
Ȧn-ȧrut-f 45.
Ȧn-atf-f 46.
Ancestor, ancestors 3, 79, 431.
Ancestress 432.
And 264, 271.
Ȧn-erṭā-nef-bes-f-khenti-heh-f 45.
Ȧnes garment 283.
Anew 112.
Angry 114, 425.
Ȧn-ḥer, god 48.
An-ḥer, a warder 48.
Ȧn-ḥeri-ertisa 45.
Ȧn-ḥetep 48.
Animal, sacrificial 328, 346.
Animals 75.
Āniu 45.
Ānkhām water 172.
Ānkhet 83.
Ānkhti (Osiris) 83.
Ȧn-mut-f 47.
Announce 27, 348, 358.
Announcement 358.
Anoint 110, 424.
Another 408, 409, 411.
Ānpet 82.
Ȧnpu 47.
Ȧnreruṭ-f 47.
Ȧn-ruṭ-f, god 47.
An-ruṭ-f 210.
Answer 116.
Ānṭ 93.

Ȧn-ṭebu 50.
Ȧn-ṭes 46.
Ȧnti 49.
Āṇṭi, god 85.
Anubis 33, 47, 432.
Ȧn-urt-emkhet-uas 46.
Any 198.
Any one 100.
Apartments 29.
Ape 38, 48, 75, 415, 421.
Apes 15, 135.
Āpef 80.
Āpep 80.
Āper, Āpert 80.
Apis 253.
Apparel 152, 176, 327, 376, 430.
Appear 104, 147.
Appearance 147, 231, 449.
Appellations 69.
Applaud 10.
Apple of the eye 177.
Appoint 362, 436.
Approach 85, 184, 332, 437.
Āpshait 80.
Ȧp-shāt-taui 30.
Apsi, god 29.
Ȧpu 28.
Ȧp-uat of north and south 28.
Ȧp-ur 28.
Āqan 92.
Ȧqeh, god 66.
Āqen, god 66.
Āqennu, city 93.
Aqert-khenti-ḥet-set, a Cow-goddess 66.
Aqeṭqeṭ, god 7.
Āq-ḥer-ȧmi-unnut-f 92.
Ȧqrit, goddess 66.
Architects 67.
Archives 374.
Argue 27.
Ȧri-em-ȧb-f 52.
Ȧri-en-ȧb-f 52.
Ȧri-entuten-em-meska, etc. 52.
Ȧri-ḥetch-f 52.
Ȧri-Maāt (Osiris) 52.
Ȧri-nef-tchesef 52.
Arisi 52.
Ārits, the Seven 86.
Arm 72, 236, 414.
Arms 236.
Around 32.
Ārq-ḥeḥ 86.
Arrange 217, 263, 361, 430.
Arrangement 369.
Array 106.
Arrive 30, 85, 149, 175, 193, 342.
Arrogance 396.
Arrogant 22, 73.

Arrows of light 382.
Arthikasathika 4.
Artificer 262.
Åruhut 55.
As 158, 167, 430.
As far as 229.
As, a name(?) 57.
Åsår 59.
Ascend 294, 312.
Ascribe 438.
Aseb, Fire-god 5.
Aseb - ḥer - per - em - khet-khet 6.
Åsert, city of 62.
Åses, Åsest, city of 63.
Ashbu, god 6.
Asher, temple district 6.
Ashu, god 6.
Asia, woman of 382.
Ass 75.
Ass, Eater of 81.
Assault 8.
Assembly 345.
Assuredly 19, 253.
Astcheṭet 65.
Åsṭenu 64.
Åsṭes, god 65.
Asyûṭ 328.
At 16, 158, 228, 268.
At once 72, 100.
Åtaru - åm - tcher - qemtu-remu-par-sheta 68.
Aṭåu garment 9.
Ātch-ur 94.
Atef crown 9.
Atef-ur 9.
Åtektaukehaqheru 70.
Åten, god 69.
Återt 69.
Åtes-ḥer-mer 9.
Åthabu 70.
Åthen 71.
Ati, nome of 8.
Āti, nome of 93.
Attack 8, 328, 436, 453.
Attain 149.
Attendant 53.
Attribute 52.
Åṭu, city 70.
Åuheṭ, god 20.
Åuḳert, place and goddess 21.
Åuḳert-khentet-åst-s 21.
Åuḳeru gods 21.
Åurau-åaqer-sa-anqrebathi 19.
Åuu-ba 17.
Avenge, avenger 226.
Awake 212, 241, 359.
Award 27.

Away from 229.
Awesome 396.

Baba 128.
Babe 215, 294, 344.
Back 9, 12, 151, 319, 322, 323.
Back of head 170, 251.
Back part 149.
Backbone 151.
Bad 67, 213, 293, 411, 419.
Bake 143.
Baked meats 113.
Bakha, Bakhau, Mount 129, 440.
Balance 20, 137, 169, 267.
Baleful 135.
Bandage 148, 180, 226, 234, 377.
Banded 186.
Bandlet 377.
Bank 444.
Bank of canal 445.
Barekathà-tchaua 128.
Barley 138, 206, 358.
Base 174.
Basins 291.
Basket 434, 445.
Bast, city and goddess 129.
Basti 129.
Bath 64, 78, 415.
Bathe 133, 184.
Bati (fiend) 130.
Battle 87.
Be 16, 103.
Beams 382, 461.
Beams of light 38.
Bear, to 8, 45, 155, 198, 237.
Bear witness 189.
Beat 144, 417.
Beat down 65, 113, 248.
Beautiful 207.
Beautify 349, 352.
Bebi (god) 133.
Because 191, 229, 269, 461.
Become 103, 300.
Bed, funerary 175, 267.
Beer 67, 282.
Beetle 301.
Beetle-god 301.
Before 72, 76, 129, 158, 159, 229, 256, 313.
Beget 116, 119, 134.
Begin 392.
Beginning 256.
Behest 118.
Behind 159, 251, 319, 322.
Behold 43, 58, 63, 160, 168, 451.
Bellow 249.
Belly 293.

Belong 216.
Belonging to 53.
Beneath 313.
Benefit 329.
Bener (city) 134.
Bennu (bird) 134.
Beseech 213.
Besides 269.
Besiege 420, 421.
Best 431.
Bestow 263.
Besu-Aḥu 136.
Besu-Menu 136.
Beṭti 139.
Between 36, 228.
Bi (fiend) 132.
Bier 117, 133, 175, 209, 210, 389.
Bind 1, 49, 63, 86, 179, 196, 414.
Bind up 405.
Bird 292, 456.
Birth 184.
Birth Second, 184.
Birth, Four goddesses of 187.
Birthday 185, 250.
Birthplace 186, 373.
Bite 150.
Black 409.
Blains 396.
Blaspheme 95, 401.
Blasphemy 190.
Blaze 3, 102, 136.
Blemish 247.
Blind 68, 396.
Block 209, 443.
Block up path 265.
Blood 353, 448.
Blood relations 18.
Bloom 5.
Blossom 5, 95, 98, 105, 196, 264.
Blue-eyed 318.
Board 82, 319.
Boastful 22.
Boat 10, 30, 39, 89, 99, 114, 170, 443.
Boat of Maāt 99.
Boat of Millions of Years 99.
Boats of Rā 99.
Boat, Solar 49.
Boatman 380.
Body 18, 75, 290, 293, 373, 399, 400, 463,
Body, dead 418.
Bodyguard 398.
Body servant 398.
Boils 396.
Bold 22, 367, 416.
Bolt 135, 355, 412, 413, 418.

Bolt-hole 140.
Bone 18, 419.
Book 317, 374, 392, 393, 447.
Book of Breathings 394.
Books of Doom 54.
Book of Thoth 394.
Book of Traversing Eternity 394.
Born 147, 184.
Bough 130.
Boundary 461.
Boundaries, god of. 462.
Boundless 461.
Bow 50, 318.
Bow 410, land of 427.
Bowmen 189.
Bows of a boat 256, 348.
Bow-rope 256.
Bowls 291.
Boy 258.
Box 442.
Branch 130, 236, 346.
Brave 22, 147, 367, 416.
Bravery 216.
Breach (of the law) 17.
Bread 134, 402, 428, 443.
Bread-cakes 1, 5, 31, 157, 306, 392.
Bread offerings 353.
Breadth 115.
Break 12, 153, 194, 305, 363, 381, 386, 387, 420, 461.
Break ground 405.
Break open 155.
Break through 378.
Breast 176, 177, 256, 260, 399.
Breath 206, 402.
Breathe 351, 355, 360, 432.
Breeze 165.
Brick 443.
Bright 252, 288, 403.
Brilliance 11, 363.
Brilliant 296.
Bring 45, 85, 139, 168, 184, 383.
Bring forth 184.
Bring (gift) 120.
Bristle 218.
Broad 115, 334.
Broad-Face 115.
Broad-Horned 79.
Bronze 262.
Brother 351.
Brow 30, 231, 248.
Bubastis 129.
Build 297, 419.
Builder 67, 356.
Building 103, 327.
Building, funerary 359.

Bull 407.
Bull-god 220.
Bundle 86.
Burden 8.
Burial 345, 417, 418.
Burial-place 345.
Burn 3, 93, 102, 117, 119, 143, 243, 303, 349, 373, 382, 425.
Burning 205, burnt 196.
Burn up 325.
Burnt-offerings 291.
Burst 157.
Bury 418.
Business 313.
Busiris 8, 439, 450.
But 423.
Butcher 40, 345, 347.
Butchers of Set 346.
Buto 139, 443.
Buttocks 149, 292, 302.
By 32, 228, 268.
By the back (or, side) of 229.
Byssus 152, 336.

Cackle 194, 220.
Cairo (Old) 14.
Cake, Cakes, 92, 134, 140, 142, 148, 152, 186, 218, 230, 259, 353, 377, 393, 396, 401, 402, 415, 428, 443.
Calamity 55, 71, 132, 386, 420.
Calculate 279.
Calf 135.
Call 91, 193, 339.
Calumniate 368, 397.
Camp 42.
Canal 6, 69, 177, 197, 267.
Cannot 68.
Capsize 143.
Captive 254, 306, 384.
Capture 254.
Carcase 18, 109.
Cardinal Points 388.
Care for 253.
Carnelian 306, 360.
Carrier 354.
Carry 8, 45, 155, 198, 237, 383.
Carry away (or, off) 65, 214, 303, 455.
Carve 227.
Case 341.
Cases 320.
Cast away 290.
Cast down 119.
Castrated animals 418.
Cat 168, 258.
Cat-skin 168.

Cataract 427.
Cataract, First 3, 415.
Catch (fish) 113.
Cattle 176, 225, 422.
Cave 128, 417, 433, 451.
Cavern 128, 417, 433, 451.
Cavity 133.
Cease 23, 325.
Ceaselessly 3, 43.
Cedar 91.
Celebrant 1.
Celestial beings 269, 270.
Cemetery 111, 458, 463.
Centre 413.
Certainly 19.
Cessation 3, 22, 23.
Chain, chains 50, 95, 171.
Chamber 7, 24, 38, 42, 46, 65, 86, 102, 119, 124, 174, 246, 262, 267, 290, 323, 400, 421, 445, 462.
Change 301.
Chapel 408.
Chapter 231, 282, 432.
Character 420.
Charms 280.
Chest 80, 81, 442.
Chest, funerary, 249.
Chew 220.
Chief 71, 108, 256, 269, 270, 309, 316, 358, 400.
Chief, tribal, 235.
Chieftainess 270.
Child, children 2, 14, 57, 70, 185, 214, 215, 258, 317, 344.
Choicest 431.
Choose 384.
Circle 238, 399, 420.
Circuit 399.
Circumstance 341.
Cistern 178, 297, 405.
Citizen 197.
City 196, 444.
City-boundary 459.
City-god 222.
Clap (the hands) 257.
Claw, claws, 84, 326, 421.
Clay 329.
Clean 77, 78, 429, 442.
Clean raiment 78.
Cleanse 14, 15, 330, 429.
Clear the way 463.
Cleave 12, 128, 150, 152.
Clincher 49, 227.
Close (the eye) 89.
Cloth 31, 71, 100.
Clothe 19, 259, 386, 406.
Clothes 176.
Clothing 259.
Clouds 348.
Coals 459.

Cobra 15.
Coerce 1, 213.
Coffer 24, 442.
Coffin 117, 249, 418, 442.
Cognizance 359.
Collar 56, 115.
Collect 327, 361, 379, 445.
Collector of souls 327.
Colour 19, 37.
Columns 49.
Come 85, 123, 168, 193, 342.
Come forth (or, forward) 15, 147.
Command 118, 258, 281, 316, 432.
Commemorate 363.
Companion 307, 351, 352.
Company of gods 140, 141.
Comparative, sign of 229.
Compel 172.
Competent 374.
Complain 215.
Complete 66, 86, 181, 433.
Comprehend 81.
Compute 328.
Conceive 17, 19.
Conception 19.
Concerning 167, 228.
Condition 88, 375.
Confectionery 259.
Conformably to 302.
Confront 158.
Confuse 361.
Conquer 211, 221, 455.
Conquest 211, 216.
Consider 26, 122.
Constrain 172, 461.
Consume 31, 81, 217, 325.
Contemporary 88.
Content 249, 250, 285.
Contentment 96.
Contest 87.
Contradict 370.
Converse 226, 464.
Conversely 238, 454.
Cook 143.
Cool 380, 415.
Copies of books 374.
Copper 262.
Copper, sulphate of, 97.
Coptos 415.
Copulate 212, 219.
Copy 51, 167, 374.
Copyist 374.
Cord, cords 50, 62, 113, 196, 197, 221.
Cordage 93, 95, 196.
Corn 148, 292.
Corn-land 206, 264.
Coronation 294.
Corpse 290.

Corridors 232.
Corrupt 258, 355.
Couch (funerary) 133.
Counsel 226, 369.
Count 26, 186. 279.
Country 293, 425.
Couplet 282.
Course 260, 317.
Cover 84, 150, 253, 387, 444, 457.
Cow 263, 407.
Cow-goddess 263, 364.
Cowardly 293.
Create 50, 300, 365, 415.
Crew 419.
Cries of joy 55.
Crime 17, 137.
Crocodile 9, 91, 186, 265, 267, 268, 333.
Crocodile-god 340.
Crop, crops 6, 10.
Crowd 90, 91.
Crown 110, 166, 209, 294, 342.
Crown, to 364.
Crunch 116.
Crush 153, 461.
Cry 251, 308, 407, 453; Cry of joy 131.
Cry out 17, 91, 116, 193, 215, 249, 328, 354.
Crystal 276, 453.
Cubit 180.
Curse 361, 366, 401.
Cusae 419.
Cut 135, 280, 337, 352, 353, 363, 384, 394, 443, 448, 455.
Cut off 362, 445; cut on wood, or stone 319.

Dagger 195.
Daily 168, 233, 250.
Daily round 314.
Damage 158, 299.
Damned 173, 187, 315, 393.
Dance 46, 299.
Darkness 20, 57, 85, 90, 113, 116, 291, 317, 410, 411, 423.
Date palm 37.
Date wine 135.
Dates 135.
Daughter 322.
Dawn 136, 289, 440.
Dawn, spirits of 38.
Day 250, 372.
Daybreak 289, 440.
Dead 173, 175, 178, 189, 209, 291, 315, 389.
Dead body 293, 418.

Dead, Eater of 82.
Deaf 70, 364.
Death 173, 175.
Decay 58, 113, 178, 267, 305, 333, 355, 356, 368, 378.
Deceit 17, 265, 292, 423, 424.
Decide 122, 328.
Declare 190, 464.
Decoction 172.
Decorate 394.
Decorations 293.
Decree, decrees 26, 27, 118, 194, 221, 258, 374, 451, 452.
Deeds 52, 118, 422.
Deep 191.
Defame 386.
Defeat 298.
Defect 17, 103, 105, 137, 247.
Defective 105.
Defraud 208, 298.
Dekans, the Thirty-six 291, 299.
Delay 122.
Delight 2.
Deliver 214, 354, 405.
Delta 71, 183, 252, 426.
Den 128, 433.
Depart 94, 100, 234, 272, 339, 352, 420, 436.
Depth 191.
Deputy 71.
Descend 246, 248.
Descent 248.
Design 194, 343, 369, 376, 419.
Designer 374.
Desire 21, 22, 23, 179, 403.
Destine 392.
Destiny 392.
Destitute 49, 68.
Destroy 95, 157, 212, 287, 288, 298, 303, 305, 317, 319, 333, 363, 372, 376, 378, 446, 455.
Destruction 58, 158, 298, 303, 305.
Device 369.
Devil 193, 321.
Devour 31, 81, 217, 265, 299, 331, 349.
Dew 14.
Dhu l'ḳarnên 79.
Dhura 206.
Diadem 294.
Die 173, 175.
Dig 405.
Dignity 12.
Dilate (the heart) 2.

Diminish 155.
Dip 298, 428.
Direct 368, 378.
Directions 358.
Dirt 7, 278.
Disarrange 361.
Disaster 386.
Discover 421, 422.
Discuss 44, 226.
Disease 174, 178.
Disembark 354.
Disgust 114, 157.
Disk, solar. 69, 71.
Dislike 188.
Dismissal 326.
Disposition 381, 420.
Dispute 27.
Dissolve 134.
Distinction 385.
Distinguish 385, 387.
Distinguished 435, 446, 452.
District 94, 101, 165.
Disturb 305.
Divide 94, 150, 152, 435.
Divine 223.
Divine beings 37.
Division 71, 151, 445.
Do 50; do not 31; as one pleases 22; do away 114.
Do into writing 51.
Document 118, 374, 393, 422.
Dog 17, 454.
Domain 71, 93; of a god 13.
Dominion 281.
Doom 27.
Door 72, 231, 234, 338.
Door of Ta-qebḥ 73.
Doors of sky } 73.
Doors of truth } 73.
Door-gods 73.
Door-keeper 54.
Door-post 260.
Double 406.
Draftsman 374.
Drag 70, 383.
Draught-board 356.
Draughts 259, 356.
Draw 70, 264, 329, 343, 374, 419.
Draw out 306.
Dress 19, 106, 294, 305, 327, 386.
Drink 23, 31, 328, 331, 334, 439.
Drink-offerings 296.
Drinker of blood 331.
Drive 318, 361, 362, 409.
Drop 234.
Droppings 245.
Drown 181.

Drugs 238.
Dry 394, 395.
Dual, sign of 101.
Duck 3.
Dung 253, 258, 383, 420.
Duplicity 342.
Dwarf 209.
Dwell 262.
Dweller in 32.
Dwelling 46, 72.

Each 100, 198.
Ear 84, 188.
Ears of corn 292.
Early 431, 440.
Earth 313, 327, 425.
Earth, end of 86.
Earth-god 337, 426.
Ease 358.
East 24, 25.
East Wind 24, 249.
East, gods of 25.
Eat 31, 75, 81, 105, 116, 150, 217, 331, 417, 419; eat the heart 81.
Eater of abominations 83.
Eater of blood 31.
Eater of bones 331.
Eater of eternity 81.
Eater of livers 31.
Eater of sāḥu 31.
Eater of shades 82.
Eater of sinners 81.
Eater of souls 31, 81.
Eater of the Arm 72.
Eater of the Ass 81.
Eater of the Dead 82.
Eater of the Eye 81.
Eater of Worms 84.
Eavesdrop 189.
Ecliptic 292.
Edge 343.
Edict 387.
Effluxes 245.
Egypt 410.
Eight 304.
Eldest 350.
Electrum 459.
Elephant-city 3.
Elephantine 3, 22.
Elysian Fields 371.
Emanation 68, 234, 245, 429.
Embalm 334, 337, 359.
Embalmer 33.
Embalmment 117.
Embalmment chamber 33, 361.
Embarcation 248.
Embark 246.
Embrace 49, 56, 87, 260, 416.
Embracer, great 368.
Emission (seminal) 438.

Emissions 290.
Empty 375.
Emqeṭqeṭ 189.
Enchantments 280.
Encircle 238, 380.
Encroach 328.
End 86, 149, 175, 433, 444; to make an 409; of a book 123.
Enemy 8, 21, 193, 243, 293, 302, 316, 339, 356.
Engrave 319, 337.
Enshroud 253.
Enter 5, 66, 91, 136, 239, 246, 248, 385, 437.
Enti-ḥer-f-emm-maat-f. 221.
Entire 433, 444, 445.
Entirely 433.
Entrance 79, 92, 123, 231, 248.
Entreat 213, 214, 349.
Envoy 29.
Equal 351.
Equip 80, 387, 442.
Erṭā-hen-er-reqa 245.
Erṭa-nefu 245.
Essence 172.
Establish 349, 450.
Estates 5, 47, 326.
Estimate 122, 279.
Eternity 213, 214, 268, 277, 463.
Eternity, domain of 458.
Eternity, Eater of 81.
Eternity, god of 463.
Eternity, land of 426, 427, 428.
Even as 167.
Evening 20, 170, 436.
Eventide 170.
Everlasting abode 64.
Everlastingness 277, 463.
Everliving 83.
Every 198.
Everybody 161, 243, 245, 321.
Everyone 100, 132, 271.
Everywhere 132, 137, 198.
Everything 320.
Evidence 189.
Evil 4, 17, 67, 85, 101, 105, 131, 132, 133, 137, 220, 291, 293, 298, 327, 416, 419, 439.
Evil, god of 335, 381.
Evil beings 8.
Evil deeds 62.
Evil eye 421.
Evil hap 308.
Evil memory 334.
Evil persons 326.

Evil speech 91.
Evil things 68.
Evolution 301.
Exact 92.
Exaggeration 19.
Exalt 379, 411, 452.
Examine 328.
Exceedingly 2.
Excellent 176.
Except 43.
Executioner 330.
Excretions 136.
Exhausted 210.
Exist 16, 103, 300.
Exit 123, 147.
Expand 2.
Expedition 118.
Expel 409.
Explain 152.
Extend 2, 155, 337.
Extent 329.
Extinguish 89, 90.
Extol 388.
Eye, eyes 11, 160, 161, 403, 422.
Eye, Eater of 81.
Eyeball 137.
Eyebrows 48.
Eyelid 292, 349.
Eye paint 97, 188.
Fa-ākhu 156.
Fa-pet 156.
Face 271.
Faïence 278.
Fail 112, 247, 354.
Failure 113.
Fair-face 207.
Fall 234, 246, 248, 315, 369.
Fall away 243.
False speech 19.
Falsehood 423, 424.
Farm 5, 326.
Farm stock 176.
Fashion 50, 168, 184, 196, 300, 365, 415.
Fashioner 205.
Fasten 49, 370.
Fastening 221, 412, 413, 418.
Fat 416.
Fate 341.
Father 67, 69, 433.
Father-gods 69.
Father Kheperȧ 69.
Father Osiris 69.
Fault 62, 138, 439.
Favour 277.
Fayyûm 427.
Fear 357, 438.
Feast 361.

Feather 10, 395, 447.
Fecundity 42.
Feeble 129, 402, 422.
Feed 82, 331, 389, 417.
Fellow 351, 352.
Fenkhu 156.
Fenṭi, god 157.
Ferry 306.
Fertility 42.
Festal service (liturgy) 259.
Festival 96, 117, 246, 247, 251, 259, 291, 348, 361, 445.
Festival, to keep 51, 339.
Fetter 50, 95, 171, 191, 196, 254, 342, 379, 403, 414, 454, 461.
Field, fields 5, 56, 370, 391.
Field of Eternity 371.
Field of Fire 372.
Field of Grasshoppers 372.
Field of Offerings 371.
Field of Peace 371.
Field of Rā 371.
Field of Reeds 371.
Field of the Gods 371.
Fiend 8, 21, 62, 139, 185, 193, 206, 210, 219, 243, 291, 302, 308, 321, 339, 346, 347, 377, 383, 419, 457.
Fierce 76.
Fiery 143.
Fifth 440.
Fight 87, 378.
Fighters, the two 87.
Fighting-Faces 87.
Fig tree 212.
Figure 38, 52, 90, 376.
Filch 288.
Fill 181, 288; fill the heart 22.
Fillet 209, 377.
Filth 7, 80, 136, 253, 258, 278, 383, 420, 458.
Filthy 258.
Find 85, 421.
Fine 207, 431.
Finger 326, 459.
Finish 409.
Fire 3, 37, 95, 135, 136, 142, 169, 205, 212, 217, 239, 243, 248, 291, 297, 319, 359, 377, 397, 413, 425, 437.
Fire-altar 89, 170, 291, 293.
Fire-city 3, 218.
Fire-goddess 218.
Fire-spirits 6.
Firm 94, 234, 370.
First 431.
Firstborn 322, 350.

Fish, to 254.
Fish 22, 26, 49, 82, 94, 157, 182, 235, 259.
Fish-god 236.
Fish, land of 427.
Fish-offerings 3.
Fisherman 113, 254, 370.
Fist 302.
Fix 94, 96, 174, 349.
Flail 216.
Flame 3, 6, 37, 95, 136, 142, 205, 217, 239, 243, 250, 319, 359, 382, 397, 425, 437, 457.
Flax 31.
Flesh 18, 19, 30, 401, 414.
Flight 72, 140.
Flint knife 448.
Flood 7, 14, 132, 181, 197, 249, 259, 349, 350.
Floor 327.
Flourish 98, 234, 333, 359.
Flow 55, 102, 221.
Flower 5, 10, 12, 84, 95, 105, 118, 133, 138, 196. 213, 215, 264, 331.
Flower of Hathor 105.
Flowers of the sky 5.
Flutter 304.
Fly 79, 89, 140, 446.
Foe, foes 21, 315, 318.
Foliage 385, 447.
Folk 132, 161, 244, 245, 249, 264, 271.
Follow 116, 319, 398.
Food 5, 31, 32, 80, 81, 88, 152, 157, 286, 302, 392, 393, 396.
Food, sepulchral 460.
Foot 244.
For 16, 191.
Force 78, 172, 330.
Forebears 432.
Fore-court 79.
Forehead 30, 447.
Forget, forgetfulness 366.
Form 50, 52, 174, 196, 300, 301, 306, 365, 376, 412, 413, 415, 430.
Form of god 91.
Fort, fortress 461, 459.
Forthwith 269.
Fortifications 103.
Fortify 365.
Forty 262.
Foul 458.
Foundation 356.
Fountain head 133.
Four 30, 158.
Fowl 117, 259.
Fowler, fowlers 113, 254, 370, 462.

Frame of a net 442.
Fraternize 355.
Fraud 265, 292.
Fresh 98.
Friend 308.
Friendly 355.
Frighten 272.
From 16, 158, 228.
Front 256, 309.
Fruit, fruits 131, 237, 417, 449.
Fully 2.
Fulness 337.
Furnish 80, 442.
Furniture 443.
Furrow 119.
Fusṭât 14, 316.

Gain the mastery 367.
Gainsay 44.
Garden 279.
Garland 182.
Garment 30, 47, 48, 67, 71, 103, 106, 176, 259, 305, 327, 334, 376, 386, 401, 406, 438, 454, 457.
Gate 72, 338, 340.
Gather, gather together 327, 353, 361, 379, 445.
Geese (Kharu) 427.
Generate 39, 42.
Genetrix 184.
Genuine 164.
Giant 80.
Gift, gifts 45, 264, 438, 442.
Girdle (?) 12.
Girdle 86, 377.
Girls 207, 215, 258.
Give 38, 168, 244, 266, 438.
Give drink 5.
Glad, gladden 227, 255, 325, 357.
Gladness 2, 55, 207, 242.
Glance 160.
Glorify, glorifyings 10, 11, 15, 365.
Glorious, glory 296, 463.
Gnaw 116, 260, 446.
Go, going 123, 246, 248, 263, 265, 272, 337, 397, 436, 437.
Go about 176.
Go away 94, 195.
Go back 49, 319.
Go down 246.
Go in 91, 437.
Go forth, go on 134, 456.
Go out 120.
Go round 119, 251.
Goad 360.

Goat 85.
God 222.
God of extended arm 2.
Gods, company of 141.
Gods, three companies of 222.
Gods, false 228.
Gods, land of 427.
God-house 224.
God-offerings 224.
God-property 224.
Goddess 270.
Gold 195, 459.
Good 207.
Good condition 329.
Goods 42, 314, 320.
Goose 3, 230, 287, 349, 359, 432.
Goose-god 220.
Gore 448.
Gorge 285.
Governor 270, 281, 309.
Grace 277.
Gracious 207, 344.
Grain 57, 93, 131, 148, 206, 217, 358, 402, 417.
Grains 138.
Grain-god 206.
Grain-goddess 238.
Granary 399, 401.
Grant 38, 168, 438.
Grapes (?) 406.
Grapplers 227.
Grasp 4, 227, 252, 261, 302, 456.
Grass 12, 62.
Grasshopper 326.
Grasshopper, city of 326.
Gratification 376.
Grave 426, 458, 459.
Great 73, 107, 435, 452.
Great (of heart) 22.
Greater than 108; greatest 431.
Greatly 74.
Great Light 363.
Greeks 183.
Green 96, 98, 333, 453.
Green Eyes 98.
Green Flame 98.
Greyhound 454.
Grief 24, 62.
Grieve 24.
Groan 12.
Ground 47, 293, 327, 381, 425.
Group 430.
Grow 234; grow old 354.
Guard 54, 226.
Guardian 53, 54.
Guide 337, 375, 376.
Gullet 91.

Haȧker 246.
Haȧs 251.
Hab-em-atu 247.
Habitation 63, 144, 410, 411.
Hack in pieces 362.
Ḥa-ḥer 253.
Ha-ḥetep 247.
Hahuti-ȧm . . . 247.
Hai, god 246.
Hail 9, 123, 245, 246.
Hair 19, 46, 66, 95, 206, 257, 266, 326, 335, 353, 385, 399, 400, 420, 422, 444, 447, 456.
Hair, grey or white 378.
Hair-gods 326.
Haker 247; festival 51.
Hakheru 247.
Half 424.
Hall 86, 93, 109, 111, 115, 134.
Hand 72, 449.
Handicraft 262.
Hangings 386.
Ḥāp (Nile) 256.
Ḥāp, son of Horus 253.
Happen 315.
Happiness 96, 132, 207, 431.
Happy 207, 337.
Ḥapt-re 254.
Ḥapu-en-neb-sett 254.
Haqahakaḥer 247.
Ḥareti 254.
Ḥarîm 29.
Harm 3, 4, 17, 220.
Harpoon 171.
Ḥarpukaḳashareshabaiu 254.
Harvest 238.
Hasert 247.
Hasten 6, 277, 290.
Hate 188, 189.
Haunch 18, 109, 313.
Have 314, 423.
Hawk 131.
He 155, 206, 221, 333, 335.
He himself 333.
Head 166, 309, 430, 458.
Heads (Tchatchat) 458.
Headcloth 284.
Headdress 80.
Headrest 111.
Headsman 330.
Health 83, 352.
Healthy 120, 234, 352.
Hear 384.
Heart 22, 256, 285; abode of 63; desire of 23, 438.
Heart amulet 23.
Heart, to eat the 22, 81.

Heart-soul 23, 124.
Heat 3.
Heaven 64, 152, 153, 197, 246, 270, 370.
Ḥebt-re-f 260.
Heel 461.
Ḥeḥi 277.
Height 411, 412.
Heir 18, 19, 75.
Heirship 18.
Ḥekennut 281.
Heliopolis 46.
Helpless 111, 129, 137, 210, 303, 339, 381, 422, 424.
Ḥemaḳa 261.
Ḥemen 262.
Ḥenȧ, city 249.
Ḥenbi, god 264.
Ḥenket 267.
Ḥenku-en-ȧrp 266.
Ḥenku-en-fat-Maāt 266.
Ḥensektiu 266.
Ḥenti (Osiris) 268.
Ḥenti-requ 268.
Ḥent-khent-ta-meru 268.
Ḥenu Boat 265.
Ḥept-re 260.
Ḥept-shet 260.
Ḥepṭ-ur 260.
Ḥeq-ānṭ 282.
Ḥeqtit, goddess 282.
Her 216, 321.
Ḥer (Horus) 273.
Ḥer-ȧb-ȧrit-f 269.
Ḥer-ȧb-karȧ-f 269.
Ḥer-ȧb-uȧa-f 269.
Herakleopolis 336
Herald 348.
Herb, herbs 12, 62, 98, 349.
Herd-god 210, 211.
Ḥer-f-em-qeb 272.
Ḥer-f-ḥa-f 272.
Ḥeri-sep-f 271.
Heritage 75.
Ḥeri-uru 270.
Ḥer-k-en-Maāt 272.
Hermopolis 105, 304.
Ḥer-nefer 272.
Heron 401.
Ḥer-uā 272.
Ḥeru-khuti 274.
Ḥeru-ṭāṭāf 276.
Ḥeru-ur (Haroeris) 274.
Ḥesepti 279.
Ḥesert 280.
Ḥes-ḥer 278.
Ḥest 278, 280.
Ḥes-tchefetch 278.
Ḥetch-ȧbeḥu 289.
Ḥetch-re 289.
Ḥetem-ḥer 288.

Ḥetem-ur 288.
Ḥetep, god 286.
Ḥetep, town 287.
Ḥetep-ka 287.
Ḥetep-sekhus 287.
Ḥetep-taui 287.
Hew 227.
Hide 40, 253, 361, 377, 404, 409, 436, 449.
Hide (skin) 38.
Hieroglyphics 224.
High 411.
Hill 412, 414.
Hill-men 49.
Him 155, 206, 333.
Himself 335, 462.
Ḥi-mu 257.
Hindrance 49.
Hinge 385.
His 140, 155, 425, 429.
Ḥit 257.
Hold 314, 423.
Holdfast 227.
Hole 433, 451.
Hollow 133.
Holy 77, 396, 448, 463.
Holy apparel 78.
Holy Land 428.
Holy place 64.
Homage 199, 226, 351, 411, 447.
Homestead 326.
Honour 332.
Hoof 461.
Hook 84.
Horizon 297.
Horn 79, 196, 265, 268, 442.
Horus, Eye of 321.
Horus, Followers of 276.
Horus, Forms of 273—275.
Horus, Sons of 42, 186, 424, 441.
Hostile 267.
Hostility 316, 370.
Hot 143, 243, 359, 394, 397, 425, 437.
Hour 106, 195.
Hour-goddess 106.
House 7, 42, 46, 65, 72, 86, 87, 98, 109, 144, 282, 283, 305, 351, 463.
Hover 304.
However 50.
Ḥu, god 257.
Hu-kheru 248.
Hull 24.
Human beings and race 103, 142, 185.
Humble 209.
Humours 136, 215.
Hundred 392.
Hundred thousand 261.

Hunger 282, 362, 372.
Hunters 370.
Hurl 382.
Hurricane 355.
Hurry 6.
Husband 456.
Hut 7, 65.
Ḥu-tepa 258.
Hymn 278.
Hymns of Rā 278.

I 9, 46, 98, 193, 196, 409, 429.
Ibis 248.
Idle 114.
If 50.
Ignorant 303.
Ill 178.
Ill-luck 341.
Ill-treated 76.
Illumine 151, 363.
Image 38, 52, 167, 235, 353, 376, 380, 413, 430.
Immediately 72, 268.
Immutable 68.
Impassable 68, 373.
Implement 113.
Impost 288.
Impotence 68.
Imprison 308, 404.
In 16, 30, 32, 158, 191, 268.
In front of 76, 302.
Inasmuch 167.
Incantation 280.
Incense 138, 166, 357, 413, 416.
Incense water 172, 173.
Incline 50, 243.
Incomprehensible 377.
Incorruptible 58, 68, 378.
Increase 45, 136, 252.
Indestructible 44.
Inert 111, 339.
Inform 359.
Inhale 242.
Inherit 18, 75.
Inheritance 18, 75.
Iniquity 17.
Injure 3, 4, 9, 71, 220.
Injury 4, 8, 14, 17, 65, 193, 219, 220, 299, 308, 352, 447.
Inkjar 142, 150.
Inlay, inlaid 176, 196.
Inquire 328.
Inside 30, 159, 413.
Insolence 396.
Inspect 328.
Instruct 338.
Instrument 49, 56, 139, 184, 464.
Intelligent 403.

Intend 304.
Intent 240.
Interval 106.
Intestines 58, 136, 170.
Into 16, 30, 158, 228.
Introduce 331, 332.
Inundate 132, 181.
Inundation 132.
Invade 385.
Inventory 240.
Invert 143, 372.
Investigate 351.
Invisible 43, 44, 68, 192.
Invocation 339.
Invoke 91, 193, 214, 339, 354.
Irqai (Amen-Rā) 123.
Irresistible 68, 318.
Iron, meteoric 130, 131.
It 155, 216, 335, 337, 381.
Its 155, 321, 337, 381.

Jackal 17, 325.
Jasper 306.
Jaw 86, 215.
Jaw-bone 85, 86.
Jaw teeth 214.
Join 306, 345, 444.
Joint of meat 6, 18, 109.
Journey 22, 118, 120, 166, 193, 197, 234, 300, 306, 308, 312, 326, 373, 380, 392, 393.
Joy 55, 207, 242, 253.
Joyful 22.
Judge 26, 27, 29, 122, 328; judge hastily 22.
Judgement 26, 122, 329.
Just 92, 163.
Justice 92.
Justify 347.

Ka-priest 263.
Kaa, god 407.
Ka-àrik 408.
Kaharsapusar, etc. 408.
Ka-ḥetep 406.
Karnak 29.
Kasaika 408.
Ḳeb 337, 421.
Keen 344.
Keep guard, or watch 53, 324.
Keḥkeḥet 410.
Ḳem-ḥeru 422.
Kemkem 410.
Kem-ur 409, 422.
Kenemet 410.
Kenemti 410.
Ḳenḳenur, god 442.
Kep-ḥer 409.
Kesemu-enent 411.

Ḳestȧ 424.
Khatiu 293.
Khau-tchet-f 291.
Khemenu 304.
Khemi, god 303.
Khenememti 308.
Khnemet-em-ānkh-ȧnnuit 307.
Khnemet-urt 307.
Khennu, city 305.
Khensu 16; forms of 309.
Khenti-Ȧmenti 309.
Kher-āḥa 14, 316.
Kherefu 316.
Kher-ḥeb priest 316.
Kher-serȧu 316.
Khesef-aṭ 318.
Khesef-ḥer-āsh-kheru 318.
Khesef-ḥer-khemiu 318.
Khnemu 307.
Khu, the Four and Seven 295.
Kill 345.
Kindle 437.
Kindness 329.
King 71, 131, 335.
Kingship 335.
Kinsfolk 18, 107.
Knead 168.
Knife 65, 91, 195, 215, 217, 279, 280, 345, 394, 411, 444, 458.
Knit 388.
Knot 454.
Know 240, 304, 323.
Knowledge 240, 373.
Koḥl 188.

Labour 52, 129, 265, 408.
Labourers 178, 356, 370.
Lack 395, 420.
Ladder 166, 171; sides of 236.
Lady 198, 267.
Lair 128.
Lake 123, 178, 267, 334, 390, 405, 420, 425.
Lake, Great 390.
Lake, Land of 427.
Lake of Aḳeb 390.
Lake of Ȧqer 390.
Lake of Fire 390, 391.
Lake of Flames 390.
Lake of Geese 391.
Lake of Ḥetep 391.
Lake of Horus 391.
Lake of Light 391.
Lake of Maāti 390.
Lake of Millions of Years 391.
Lake of Natron 391.
Lake of Nu 390.
Lake of Osiris 390.

Lake of Propitiation 391.
Lake of Tchesert 391.
Lake of the Wicked 391.
Lake of Turquoise 390.
Lamentation 12, 66, 408.
Lamp 299, 437.
Land, to 175.
Land 143, 425, 444; cultivated 5.
Lands, the two 425.
Languor 157.
Lapis-lazuli 317, 318.
Large 73.
Laugh, laughter 341.
Laver 390.
Law, laws 165, 248.
Law, Land of 426.
Law-court 64.
Lawgiver 360.
Lawfulness 132.
Lay 113.
Lazy 114.
Lead 337, 375.
Leather 348, 406.
Leaves 416.
Leaves of a door 72, 234, 244.
Left (hand or side) 22, 23, 24.
Leg 166, 188, 244, 340, 344, 373.
Legality 132.
Length 1, 329.
Leopard skin 23.
Let be 38.
Letopolis 319, 366.
Libation 15, 77, 388.
Libation vessel 96, 280, 352.
Libationer 77.
Libya 453.
Lie 423, 424.
Lies 19.
Lie down 389.
Life 83, 88.
Life, hand of 426.
Lift 120, 155, 379, 387, 388, 453.
Light 1, 11, 42, 65, 85, 95, 142, 212, 252, 289, 296, 356, 363, 375, 395, 403, 435.
Light up 102.
Light-god 151.
Light (of weight) 105.
Lightness 103.
Light upon 103.
Like 158, 167, 168, 351, 420, 430.
Likeness 167.
Likewise 167, 341, 420.
Lily 376.

Limbs 19, 30, 75, 93, 165, 255, 256, 414, 421.
Limit 461.
Linen 63, 97, 148, 152, 210, 402, 403, 417.
Linen weaver 402.
Lintel 86.
Lion 163, 168.
Lion-god 232.
Lip 343.
List 240, 329.
Listen 350.
Listeners 384, 385.
Little 228, 402, 411.
Live 82.
Living people 83.
Lizard 9.
Lo 43, 63.
Load 8.
Loaf, loaves 1, 92, 289, 377.
Loathing 396.
Lock 266, 306.
Lock of hair 400.
Loin 345.
Long 1.
Longsuffering 344.
Look 154, 160.
Loose 353.
Lord 198, 288.
Loss 299.
Lot 314, 445.
Loud 315, 412.
Love 22, 179, 227.
Loved one 23.
Lowland 313.
Lowly 209.
Luck 341, 392.
Lynx 166.

Maa-ȧnu-f 161.
Maa-ȧtef-kheri-beq-f 162.
Maa-em-ḳerḥ-ȧnnef-em-hru 162.
Maa-ḥa-f 162.
Maa-ḥeḥ-en-renput 162.
Maā-kheru 163.
Maāti towns 165.
Maati-f-em-khet 162.
Maati-f-em-ṭes 162.
Maatuf-ḥer-ā 163.
Māau-taui 168.
Macerate 144.
Magic power 121.
Magical formulae 280.
Magnify 330.
Maiden 207, 258.
Majestic 396.
Majesty 263.
Maḳ stone 166.
Make 50.
Make a gift 1.

Make happen 244.
Male 456.
Man 321.
Manifest 147.
Manifestations 147.
Manifold 90.
Mankind 107, 161, 211, 241, 243, 244, 245, 264, 271, 434.
Manner 167.
Mansion 86, 144.
Mantis 2, 3, 23, 133.
Manu 166, 426.
Many 90.
March 329; march against 436, 437.
Mariners 419.
Mārqathȧ 169.
Marsh 76, 149, 415.
Marsh flowers 5.
Mason 47, 67.
Mast 319.
Master 108, 198; to act as master 316.
Mastery 95, 340.
Masturbate 196.
Matchat, Matchet 167, 171.
Māṭes 171.
Māṭet Boat 171.
Matter 134, 140.
Me 9, 98, 193.
Meadow 370.
Mean, the 189.
Measure 375, 443, 457.
Measure (land) 383.
Measuring cords 56.
Medicaments 337, 359.
Medicine 238.
Meditations 421.
Mediterranean Sea 98.
Meet 15, 318, 362.
Meeting 362.
Meḥen 33.
Meḥenet, Meḥenit, Meḥent 182.
Meḥti-sāḥ-neter 184.
Meḥt-urt 181.
Member 19, 30, 56, 75, 93, 255, 256.
Memorial services 364.
Memphis 154, 284, 427.
Memphis, high priest of 110.
Men and women 244, 245, 249, 264.
Mendes 82, 439.
Menḥu 176.
Men-kau-Rā 233.
Menkh, god 176.
Men-Maāt-Rā 233.
Menqet 177.
Mentchat 177.

Menthu, god 177.
Menu 4, 42, 174.
Merȧ 426.
Merchant 395.
Mert, goddess 179.
Meskhen 187.
Mesqen 188.
Mesqet 188.
Message 27, 29.
Messenger 29.
Mesthȧ 188.
Metal, god of (?) 127.
Metal plates 136, 218.
Meṭes-ḥer-ȧri-mer 190.
Meṭes-sen 191.
Meṭu-ta-f 190.
Micturate 116, 157.
Middle 92, 103, 268.
Middle hall 24.
Might 150, 397, 446.
Mighty 73, 107, 114, 194, 367.
Milk 11, 55, 364.
Milk vessel 169.
Million 276.
Mineral 262.
Mineral colour 312.
Ministrant 1, 47, 176.
Misery 62, 116, 137, 163, 352, 420, 421.
Misfortune 71, 386.
Misheps 172.
Mistress 198, 267.
Mixed 396.
Mnevis Bull 180.
Moisture 14.
Moment 8, 33, 106.
Monkey 75.
Monster 90.
Month 26; last day of 86.
Moon 16, 86.
Moon-god 16, 56, 309.
Moor a boat 175.
Mooring posts 175.
More than 229.
Moreover 423.
Morning 436.
Morning star 224.
Mortals 434.
Mother 173.
Motionless 111.
Mould 168, 196, 364.
Moulder 205.
Mountain 439.
Mourner 12.
Mourning 12.
Mouse 143.
Mouth 231, 432.
Move 151, 234, 253, 260, 265.
Mow 280.
Much 90.

Multitude 90, 91.
Mummify 96, 334.
Mummy bandages 96.
Mummy bed 117.
Murderous 135.
Music, instrument of 176.
Mut 173.
Muta Jambi 80.
Mutable 119.
My 9, 140, 193.
Mykerinos 233.
Myrrh 84; of women 85; water of 172.
Myself 462.
Mysterious 377, 404.
Mystery 377, 404.
Mystery, Land of 427.

Naàrrut 192.
Nāàu 193.
Nail, of body 84.
Nàk fiend 193.
Naked 252.
Name 237.
Namely 58.
Narrate 112.
Nārt 194.
Nārtiānkhemsenf 194.
Nasaqbubu 193.
Nathkerthi 193.
Natron 280.
Navel 292, 300.
Near 228, 229, 424.
Nebà 205.
Neb-ābui 199.
Neb-er-tcher, Neb-er-tchert 204.
Neb-ḥeru 201.
Neb-maāt-ḥeri-reṭui-f 204.
Neb-nebu 201.
Neb-peḥti-petpet-sebàu 204.
Neb-peḥti-thes-menment 204.
Nebeḥ bird 205.
Nebti 205.
Neck 213.
Neck ornament 115.
Needy 212, 395.
Nefer-Tem 208.
Nef-ur 206.
Negation 68, 158, 433.
Negative 43, 221.
Negro 214.
Negro speech 464.
Neḥ 213.
Neḥa-ḥāu 213.
Neḥa-ḥer 213.
Nehatu 212.
Neḥebka 214.
Neḥeb-nefert 214.
Neḥesu 213.
Neḥesui 213.

Neith 220.
Nekȧ fiend 219.
Nekhebet 215, 398.
Nekhen 215.
Nekhenu 215.
Nem 208.
Nenet, bread of 428.
Nentchā 210.
Nenunser 210.
Nepert, city 206.
Nephthys 205.
Nerȧu-ta 211.
Neri 211.
Nesersert 218.
Nesert, goddess 218.
Neshem stone 218.
Neshmet Boat 218.
Nest 373.
Net, to snare 254.
Net 14, 25, 117, 254, 370, 434.
Net frame 442.
Net posts 72.
Neṭbit 226.
Netcheb-ȧb-f 226.
Netcheḥ-netcheḥ 227.
Netchem, god 227.
Netchesti 228.
Netchet 228.
Netchfet 226.
Netchses 228.
Neter, Lake 225.
Neṭet, Neṭit 226.
Netqa-ḥer-khesef-ȧtu 225.
Netru, city 225.
Never 44, 341.
New 98, 160.
New Year's Day 431.
Nice 135.
Night 20, 57, 113, 116, 291, 410, 411, 423.
Night watchers 241.
Nile 256.
Nile Celestial 7.
Nine, ninth 151.
No 43, 68, 158, 192, 221, 433.
No time 341.
Nobleman 108.
Nome 279, 343.
None 68.
Non-existent 49.
Noonday 88.
North 183; north-west 183.
North, land of 426.
North, Lords of 183.
North wind 182, 183, 417.
Nose 157, 309, 402.
Nostrils 242, 293, 402.
Not 8, 31, 43, 68, 133, 158, 192, 221, 433.
Nourish 329.

Now 50; now as for 50.
Nu, god 195.
Nubia 49, 384, 410, 427.
Nubti 196.
Nur bird 196.
Nurse 237, 238, 307.
Nut, goddess 186.
Nut-urt 198.
Nuṭiu 198.

O 9, 57, 123, 245, 246, 248.
Oar 114, 180, 253, 260, 261, 443.
Oar-rest 75, 118.
Oasis, Northern and Southern 117.
Obelisk house 283.
Obey 384.
Objects 5.
Oblation 15.
Oblivion 267.
Observe 154, 160, 195.
Obstacle 386.
Obstruct 389.
Obstruction 49.
Occasion 341.
Ocean 270.
Ocean, Celestial 7, 421.
Odour 383.
Of 158, 191, 194, 220.
Offal 258.
Offence 17, 75.
Offend 369.
Offer 176, 266, 447.
Offer sacrifice 77.
Offerings 1, 5, 15, 45, 77, 120, 133, 140, 147, 148, 156, 182, 230, 264, 286, 436, 443, 460.
Officer 177.
Official 417, 456.
Offspring 147, 185.
Oil 182, 183, 191.
Ointment 191, 424.
Old age 10, 446.
Old man 10, 215.
Olden time 431.
Olive tree 129, 137.
Omission 342.
On 46, 158, 268.
On behalf of 229.
One 100, 321.
One (God) 99, 222.
One only 100.
Oneness 139.
Open 27, 78, 79, 103, 155, 231, 333, 355, 373, 385.
Open the face 104.
Open the mouth 27, 78.
Opener of the Earth 79.
Openers 29.

Opportunity 341.
Oppose 318, 389.
Opposite 15, 76, 158, 302.
Opposition 76, 305.
Oppress 1, 76, 163, 346.
Oppression 14, 65, 70.
Oppressor 14, 65.
Or 232.
Orbit 399, 420.
Ordain 118, 221.
Order, to 358, 453.
Order 165, 217, 221, 263, 361, 464.
Ordinances 221, 248; of heaven 369.
Ore 130.
Orion 327.
Ornament 293, 364.
Osiris 59, 326, 336.
Osiris-beings 62.
Osiris-Anubis 59.
Osiris-Begetter 59.
Osiris-Gold-of-eternity 60.
Osiris-Harmachis 60.
Osiris-Horus 60.
Osiris-Ḳeb 61.
Osiris-Khenti-Amenti 60.
Osiris, for titles of beginning with Khenti see p. 310.
Osiris-Lord-of-Life 60.
Osiris-neb-er-tcher 60.
Osiris-Orion 61.
Osiris-Ptaḥ 59.
Osiris-Seker 62.
Osiris-Taiti 62.
Osiris Teḳaiti 62.
Osiris-Un-Nefer 59.
Other 100; other things 411.
Other World 426, 441; Mountain of 440.
Out from 158.
Outcry 249.
Outside 159, 229.
Overcome 95.
Overthrow 113, 298, 303, 359, 369.
Overseer 177, 235.
Overturn 143, 416.
Owner 198.
Ox 17, 56.

Pacification 362.
Pacify 362.
Paddle 180, 253, 261, 306, 443.
Pain 114, 174, 178, 349.
Painless 68.
Paint the eyes 188.
Palace 87, 93, 111.
Palette 82, 188, 425.
Palm, a tree 38, 166.
Palm, a measure 375, 403.

Panopolis 28.
Panther skin 23.
Papyrus 395, 457.
Papyrus swamps 71.
Par 141.
Parehaqakheperu 141.
Parents 173.
Pashakasa 142.
Pass, pass by 329, 333, 337, 373, 437.
Pass away 134, 352, 356, 438.
Pass forward 58.
Passage 100, 101, 306, 337.
Pasturage 349.
Path 95, 97, 171.
Paw 72.
Pay 347.
Pay homage 196.
Pe, city 139.
Peace 285.
Peacemakers 362.
Peace offerings 45, 362.
Peasants 178.
Pectoral 115.
Pedestal 12, 174.
Pegs 21, 117, 455.
Peḳa 152.
Peḳes 152.
Pekhat, goddess 150.
Pen 194.
Penetrate 5, 24.
Pen-ḥeseb 20.
Penti, god 144.
People 107, 132, 142, 161, 169, 241, 243, 244, 245, 264, 271, 434.
Peq 152.
Per-Àsȧr 8.
Perceive 160, 323.
Perch 8, 10, 12, 304.
Perfect 66, 176, 330, 349.
Perfume 294, 384.
Perish 378.
Permanent 96, 174, 450.
Period 88, 195, 246.
Perpetuate 359.
Persea tree 65.
Persecute 1.
Person 321, 463.
Pert, season of 26, 144.
Peskheti 150.
Peti 153.
Petition 443.
Petrȧ 154.
Petrȧ-sen 154.
Peṭṭet 155.
Phallus 171, 246, 265, 456.
Pharaoh 144.
Phase of being 301.
Phoenix 134.
Physician 33, 110.

Picture 167, 194.
Pierce 135.
Pig 238, 392.
Pigment 37.
Pilfer 298.
Pillar 49, 113, 264, 369.
Pillow 111.
Pinion 182.
Pit 254.
Pitch 345.
Place, to 96.
Place 63, 80, 81, 168, 170, 171, 244, 245, 438.
Place, Great 64.
Place (in place of) 58.
Plan 343, 369, 419.
Plank 254, 319, 455.
Plants 10, 37, 62, 65, 84, 98, 130, 185, 235, 237, 264, 331, 372, 392, 395, 449.
Plaque 183.
Plate, to 364.
Plated 330.
Play draughts 259.
Play music 398.
Pleasant 134, 135, 227, 249.
Please 247, 249, 250, 341.
Pleasure 2, 250, 357.
Plentiful 291.
Pluck 306.
Plumage 46, 395.
Plunder 76, 214, 288, 456.
Plough 299, 378.
Ploughing, Ceremony of 299.
Poem 282.
Point 430.
Pointer of Balance 436.
Poison 189, 397.
Pole 93, 205, 285.
Pole, steering 261.
Poles of bier 346.
Pollute 438.
Pool 76, 78, 172, 178, 267, 334, 390, 405, 425.
Poor 209.
Porter 53, 54.
Portion 314.
Portrait figure 430.
Position 12, 88.
Possess 314, 423, 455.
Possessions 42, 174, 314, 423.
Possessor 198.
Potter-god 307.
Potter's table 214.
Powder 400.
Power 72, 83, 114, 120, 150, 212, 357, 367, 396, 397.

Power, the vital 367.
Powerful 107, 216.
Powerless 139.
Praise, to 10, 11.
Praise, praisings 9, 14, 15, 16, 195, 249, 264, 277, 280, 339, 354, 365, 384, 388, 440.
Pray 213, 353, 442.
Prayer 36, 436, 443.
Precept 432.
Predestine 392.
Preferment 12.
Pregnant 17, 19, 136.
Prepare 51, 343.
Prescription 432.
Preserves (of birds) 419.
Present 1, 77, 266.
President 270.
Pretty 207.
Prevail over 367.
Priest 1, 33, 36, 47, 77, 263, 322, 345, 263.
Prince 71, 108, 256, 316, 358, 400.
Principal 269.
Prison 308, 321.
Prithee 38, 407.
Private apartment 312.
Produce 184, 350.
Products 314.
Progeny 189, 382.
Prompting 23.
Pronouncement 190.
Props 388, 453.
Property 132, 313, 314, 320, 329.
Propitiate 362.
Propitiatory offerings 78.
Protect 51, 170, 215, 226, 295, 323, 384, 388.
Protector 308.
Proud 73.
Provide 80, 263, 288, 343.
Provisions 88, 93, 325.
Pry into 350, 459.
Ptaḥ 154.
Ptaḥ, Claw of 84.
Ptaḥ-Seker 154.
Ptaḥ-Seker-Tem 155.
Ptaḥ-Tanen 155.
Pudenda muliebris 292.
Pull 70, 329.
Pull out hair 104.
Punt, land of 142.
Pupil of the eye 460.
Pure 77, 429.
Purification 77.
Purify 14, 77, 330, 429.
Purity 132.
Purse 86.
Pus 134.

Put 244.
Putrefy 38, 412.
Pygmy 209.
Pylon 134, 338, 340.

Qabt-ent-Shu 413.
Qa-ha-ḥetep 412.
Qa-ḥer 412.
Qaḥu, god 30, 413.
Qai 413.
Qart 413.
Qebḥ-senuf 415.
Qefenu 415.
Qemḥu, god 422.
Qemḥusu, god 422.
Qen 416.
Qenqentet, Lake 417.
Qernet 417.
Qerti 418.
Qetetbu 419.
Quadrupeds 75.
Quake 386.
Quay 302.
Queen 262, 267, 336.
Quench 89, 90.
Quiet 360.

Rā, god 233.
Rā, Hymns to 278.
Rā-Harmakhis 233.
Rā-Horus 233.
Rā-Osiris 233.
Rā-Tem 233.
Radiance 1, 11, 42, 65, 85, 95, 151, 296, 363, 375, 382.
Rain-storm 14, 67.
Raise 120, 156, 387.
Raise a song 388.
Raise up 436, 453.
Ram 396.
Ram-god 128, 397.
Rameses IV 282.
Rank 12.
Rapid 6.
Rat 143.
Ravish 456.
Ravisher 455.
Rays 11, 38, 102, 151, 382.
Re-āa-urt 231.
Reach 149.
Read 366, 405.
Ready 343, 387.
Real 164.
Reap 6.
Rebel 338.
Receive 403.
Recite 51, 366, 405, 464.
Reckon 26, 122, 279, 328.
Reckoning 26, 329, 459.
Recognize 323.
Recompense 58, 228.
Records 118, 422.

Red 448.
Red Crown 448.
Red Land 448.
Redness 448.
Reed 5.
Reed pen 194.
Re-establish 349.
Refresh 360, 380, 415.
Region 47, 69, 71, 94, 101, 165.
Regularity 403.
Regularly 164.
Regulations 248.
Re-ḥent 240.
Re-ḥenent 240.
Reḥti 240.
Reḥu 239.
Reḥui (Horus and Set) 240.
Reign 246, 335.
Re-Iukasa 232.
Rejoice 46, 212, 227, 242, 246, 248, 255, 282.
Rejoicings 10, 11, 16, 55, 56.
Rejuvenate 237.
Rekhti 241.
Rekhti, Lands of 427.
Rekhti-merti 241.
Relatives 107.
Release 344.
Relieve 329.
Remain 174.
Remainder 342.
Remake 346.
Remember 363.
Remove 105, 237.
Remote 94.
Remrem 237.
Remu, town of 235.
Rend 306.
Renen 238.
Renew 112, 160, 346.
Repair 349.
Repeat 112, 416.
Repetition 238.
Report 348, 112.
Reptile 156, 464.
Repulse 318, 370, 399, 400.
Rerek 239.
Rerti 239.
Rertu-nefu 239.
Res-âb 242.
Resenet 242.
Res-ḥer 242.
Rest 30, 111, 239, 261, 285.
Re-stau 232, 383.
Restrain 1, 324.
Restraint 163, 325, 352, 358, 438, 464.
Retasashaka 243.
Retreat 251, 261, 319, 339.

Return 82, 113; in return for 58.
Revile 365.
Revolt 219, 305.
Revolve 238, 343, 398, 442.
Reward 228.
Riches 156.
Riddle 454.
Rigging 196.
Right 92, 105, 163, 164, 165, 189.
Ring 84, 134.
Rise 104, 147.
Rise (of river) 136.
Rise (of sun) 102, 294.
Rite 221.
Ritual 317.
River 69, 123, 197.
River bank 90, 302.
Road 95, 97, 171.
Roar, roaring 249.
Roast meat 6.
Rob 76, 456.
Robber 71, 76, 455, 456.
Robe 67, 327.
Rod 319.
Roof 17, 180.
Room 109.
Rope 62, 63, 93, 95. 113, 197, 256, 266.
Rope in 63.
Rot 58, 305.
Rotten 258, 368, 412.
Round about 160.
Rouse 213, 241.
Row 306.
Rudder 114, 253, 261.
Ruddy 448.
Rule 281, 454.
Run 104, 149, 263, 292, 317, 370, 449.
Runner 249, 253.
Rushes 5.
Ruṭ-en-Ȧst 235.
Ruṭu-neb-rekhit 235.
Ruṭu-nu-Tem 235.

Sȧ 328.
Sa, god 323.
Sȧa, god and city 328.
Sa-Ȧmenti-Rā 323.
Saau-ur 323.
Sabes 325.
Sacred 396, 448.
Sacrifice 77, 241, 286, 347.
Sacrificer 106.
Safe 455.
Saḥ-en-mut-f 327.
Sail, to 456.
Sail downstream 321.
Sail upstream 312.
Sail 380, 428.

Sailor 206, 306, 312, 380, 419.
Saïs, Upper and Lower 325.
Saltpetre water 172.
Salute 194, 447.
Salve 191, 281.
Sa-mer-f 322.
Sanctify 387.
Sanctuary 64, 366, 408.
Sand 393.
Sandals 289, 430, 451.
Såp 329.
Sapanemmå 322.
Sarcophagus 284, 418.
Såså 330.
Sata 322.
Sati, city 330.
Satiety 337.
Satisfy 22, 285.
Say 416, 464.
Saying 454.
Scald 102.
Scales 20, 137, 169.
Scales (armour) 136.
Scarab 301.
Scatter 104, 340, 376.
Scent 307, 387.
Sceptre 2, 29, 96, 97, 281, 319.
Scorch 3.
Scorn 327.
Scorpion 288.
Scorpion-god 288.
Scribe 374.
Sea 123.
Seal 321, 459.
Search 113, 277, 351, 459.
Season 8, 88, 106, 195, 341, 436.
Seat 63, 64, 262.
Seat of Utchat 64.
Sebå goddess 339.
Sebaku 340.
Sebek 136, 340.
Sebeḳ 340.
Sebek-en-Shesmu 340.
Sebeq-en-Tem 340.
Second 159, 351.
Secrecy 40.
Secret 40, 377, 404.
Secretary 271.
See 79, 153, 154, 160, 195, 422, 449.
Seeds 93, 138, 189, 382, 389, 449.
Seek 113, 292.
Sefekh-nebs 344.
Seḥetch-ur 363.
Seḥetemet - au - ā - em - ābet 363.
Seḥtet 363.

Seize 4, 302, 303, 455, 456.
Seker, god, city, festival 378, 379.
Seker, land of 427.
Sekhai 364.
Sekhat-Ḥeru 364.
Sekhem-em-ȧb-f 367.
Sekhem-nefer 368.
Sekhem-ur 367.
Sekhepti 365.
Sek-ḥer 378.
Sekher-āṭ 369.
Sekheriu 369, 409.
Sekher-remu 370.
Sekhet 368.
Sekhet-Ȧaru 105.
Sekhet-ḥer-āsh-āru 372.
Sekhmet 368.
Sekhmet-Bast-Rā 368.
Sekhmet-ren-s-em-ḥemut-s 368.
Seksek 379.
Sektet Boat 379.
Self 462.
Self-created 300.
Semti, king 350.
Senehpaqarha 354.
Senehaparḳana 354.
Senemti 353.
Send 246, 248.
Sentence, to 342; of death 27.
Senu, city 352.
Sep, Sepa, god 342.
Separate 150, 234, 435, 445.
Separation 71.
Sepes 343.
Sepulchre 11, 58, 180.
Sepulture 417.
Sepṭ-kheri-nehait 344.
Sepṭ-mast-ent-Reruti 344.
Sepṭu 343.
Seqebit 380.
Seqeṭ-ḥer 381.
Serȧt-beqet 358.
Serekhi 359.
Seres-ḥer 360.
Serf 37, 314, 351.
Ser-kheru 358.
Serpent 15, 156, 261, 462.
Serpent-fiends 90.
Serpent-god 364.
Serqet, goddess 360.
Sert 360.
Serṭiu 360.
Servant 37, 263, 307, 351.
Serve 129, 354.
Seshemet 376.
Seshet, town 374.
Sesheta, goddess 377.

Set 96, 244, 438; set aside 290; set fire to 102; set up 332; set (of the sun) 102, 285.
Set out 120, 456.
Set, god 381.
Setem-ȧnsi 385.
Seti I. 233.
Set-qesu 386.
Sett, goddess 382.
Seven 344, 366.
Seven Spirits 45.
Sever 353.
Sexual intercourse 388.
Shabu 392.
Shabti 392.
Shackles 220.
Shade 290, 414.
Shades, Eater of 82.
Shadow 290, 414.
Shaka 393.
Shakanasa 393.
Shake 64, 436.
Shambles 348.
Shame 396.
Shape 196.
Shapuneterȧrka 393.
Share 314, 445.
Sharshar 393.
Sharsharkhet 393.
Sharshatȧkata 393.
Shau, city of 392.
Shave 104.
She 216, 225, 321, 381.
Shebb-en-Ḳesti 396.
Shed 460.
Shenȧt-pet-utheset-neter 399.
Shenȧt-sheps-neteru 399.
Shenmu 400.
Shennu 401.
Shentit, goddess 401.
Shepherd (Osiris) 323.
Shesep-temesu 403.
Shes-khentet 404.
Shesmu 340, 404.
Sheṭ-kheru 406.
Sheta-ḥer 405.
Shetau-ā 405.
Shewbread 401.
Shine 3, 102, 113, 136, 151, 212, 252, 288, 296, 363, 403.
Shipwreck 17.
Shod 430.
Shoot 119, 120, 382.
Shore 444.
Shoulder 236, 237, 414.
Shout 246, 249.
Shrine 38, 63, 64, 104, 303, 366, 408.
Shrivel 3.

Shu 40, 239, 395.
Shuabti 392.
Shut 308.
Shut up 306.
Shut in 321, 464.
Sick 174, 178.
Sickness 174, 178, 447.
Side 322, 414, 424.
Sight 160, 449.
Sightless 68.
Silence 381.
Silent 423.
Silver 288.
Similar 430.
Similitude 167, 376, 420.
Sin 15, 17, 62, 75, 137, 138, 247, 291, 439.
Since 461.
Sing 398.
Singers 249.
Sinner 62, 137, 439.
Sinners, Eater of 81.
Sirius 343.
Sister 351.
Sistrum-bearer 56.
Sit 30, 261, 262, 358.
Siut, city 328.
Six 329.
Sketch 419.
Skilful 66, 373.
Skill 447.
Skilled 374, 403.
Skin 19, 38, 46, 137, 188, 401.
Skull 114.
Sky 152, 153, 197, 270, 395.
Sky, two halves of 70.
Sky-god 195.
Sky-goddess 197.
Slab 443.
Slander 231.
Slaughter 25, 65, 217, 241, 262, 298, 328, 345, 346, 347, 352, 394, 446, 457; place of 209.
Slaughterer 290.
Slaughter-blocks 394.
Slaughter-houses 14, 299.
Slave 263.
Slay 113, 175, 187, 317, 330, 345, 347, 372.
Sledge 170, 434.
Sleep 89, 387.
Slit 352, 423.
Slumber 420.
Smam, god and lake 347.
Smam-ur 347.
Smamti 348.
Smash 305.
Smati 348.
Smear 110, 437.

Smell 307, 308, 351, 355, 383.
Smell the earth 351.
Smell (bad) 12.
Smet-āqa 350.
Smetmet (?) 350.
Smetti 350.
Smetu 350.
Smite 257, 380, 448.
Smoke 285.
Snake 15, 261.
Snake-goddess 15, 16.
Snare 113, 117, 370, 401, 462.
Snarers 370.
Snatch at 4, 303.
Snuff the air 218, 242, 307, 355, 372, 432.
Soar 89.
Sodomy 219.
Soil 93.
Soldiers 189.
Soles of feet 430.
Solitude 100.
Son 322.
Song 249, 280, 388.
Sorry 22.
Soul, be endowed with 127.
Soul, the double 127.
Soul, the Heart 124.
Soul of Rā 134.
Souls, Eater of 81.
Soul amulet 125.
Soul-god 127, 128.
Soul-house 283.
Sound 120, 315, 337, 455.
Soundness 352.
South 242, 398; land of 427.
South wind 242.
Sovereign 71, 198, 267.
Sovereignty 281, 335.
Sow seed 104, 382.
Spacious 115.
Sparks 6, 102, 142, 143.
Speak 17, 57, 190, 342, 410, 464.
Spear 171.
Speech 190, 231, 315, 317, 432, 454.
Speech, evil 91.
Spirit-body 332.
Spirit-soul 295.
Spit 150, 151,
Splendid 463.
Splendour 11, 38, 42, 294, 296.
Split 12, 94, 135, 194, 386, 455.
Spread 89, 151.
Spread a net 370.
Sprinkle 20, 77.

Stab 443.
Stability 88.
Stable 174, 450.
Stablish 450.
Staff 2, 29, 97, 319.
Staircase 235, 244, 412.
Stairs of Osiris 319.
Stakes 21, 175.
Stalk 166.
Stand up 88, 104.
Standard 10, 12, 30, 169, 464.
Standard of Ȧp-uat 13.
Stanza 282.
Stars 5, 57, 291, 299, 338.
Stars, circumpolar and planets 20.
Star-gods 166, 378.
State 88.
Station 171, 434.
Statue 235, 353, 376, 430.
Staves 459.
Steak 6.
Steal 220, 288, 298.
Steer 114, 261.
Steering poles 114, 253, 261, 313, 316.
Steersman 54.
Steep 20.
Step, steps 208, 244, 319.
Stern of a boat 149.
Stew 113.
Steward 177.
Stibium 188.
Stick 2, 29, 97, 319.
Sting 150.
Stink 420; to make 368.
Stinking 213, 258.
Stone 48, 182.
Stone of Maāt 48.
Stop 23.
Storehouse 451.
Stores 88.
Storm 14, 219, 255, 305, 354, 355, 400, 417.
Storm-cloud 206.
Straight 163.
Straighten 370.
Straightway 72, 268, 269, 431, 461.
Stream 6, 69, 95, 101, 131, 197, 220, 259, 267, 436.
Strength 83, 114, 120, 132, 150, 212, 234, 285, 396, 397, 457.
Strengthen 227, 295, 405.
Stretch 124, 155, 166.
Stretch the legs 441.
Stride 208, 308.
Strider 436.
Strife 305.

Strike 257, 363, 417, 252, 409.
Strive 51.
Strong 66, 76, 133, 195, 211, 216, 234, 245, 330, 331, 337, 352, 354, 367, 416, 417, 453, 457.
Strong-heart 114.
Strong-mouth 121.
Strong-soul 114.
Strong-willed 356.
Stronghold 461.
Struggle 87.
Studded 236.
Stuff 140.
Subdue 248, 251, 292, 360.
Submerge 20, 181, 349.
Submission 292.
Subsist 300.
Subsistence 65.
Substance 140.
Such an one 175.
Suckle 238, 356.
Suffer 421.
Suffering 4.
Suḳaṭi 335.
Summer 397.
Summit 458.
Sun-god 233, 395.
Sunrise 436.
Sunrise, Mount of 129, 440.
Sunset 436.
Sunset, Mount of 166.
Superintendent 177, 235.
Supplicate 112, 334.
Supplication 442, 443.
Support 8. 120, 239, 453.
Supports 88, 388, 453.
Supporters 236.
Support of a god 8.
Suppress 248.
Supreme 107.
Surface 30, 172.
Surround 48, 49, 87.
Sut, Suti 335.
Suten-ḥenen 336.
Suten-ṭa-ḥetep 336.
Swallow 31, 331, 364.
Swallow (bird) 177.
Swamp 149, 178.
Swathe 406.
Swathing 180, 234, 259.
Swear 86.
Sweet 134, 227.
Swift 6, 138, 292.
Sword 345, 444.
Sycamore 211.
Syene 3, 334.
Symbolize 384.

Table of offerings 77, 120, 286.

Tablet 82, 385.
Tackle 93, 196.
Tait 428.
Take 403.
Take prisoner 380.
Talk 190, 315.
Talon 84.
Tamarisk 62.
Ta-nent 427.
Tank 178, 405.
Tar, a fiend 428.
Ta-reṭ 425.
Tarry 122.
Taste 443.
Ta-sti 49.
Ta-tchesert 33, 428.
Tatunen 429.
Taut 234.
Tax 288.
Tchafi 127, 457.
Tchaui, the Two 457.
Tchebā - en - Ḥeru - semsu 460.
Tchebā-en-Sekri 459.
Tchebā-en-Shesmu 460.
Tchebā-en-tepu-ā-Rā 460.
Tchefet, goddess and place 460.
Tchentchen 461.
Tcherti, the Two 462.
Tcheru bird 462.
Tchesert 463.
Tcheser-tep 463.
Tear 236, 306.
Ṭeb-ḥer-kehaat 442.
Tebu, city 430.
Tefnut 40, 239, 433.
Ṭehent 447.
Tekem 437.
Tell 190.
Tem, Temu 69, 434.
Tem-Harmakhis 434.
Tem-Kheperȧ 434.
Tem-Sep 434.
Ṭem-ur 444.
Temem-re 434.
Tempest 67, 219.
Temple 144, 148, 232, 283.
Ten 189.
Tenȧ 445.
Tend sheep 324.
Teni, Ṭeni 435, 446.
Ṭenpu 446.
Tent 42.
Terrify 272.
Territory 69, 93, 238, 293.
Terror 272, 328, 386, 396, 397.
Ṭesert-tep 448.
Ṭesher, god 448.
Teshtesh 437.
Testicles 314, 334.

Testify 189.
Ṭeṭ, the 450.
Tet-Ṭemui 382.
Thanksgiving 225, 441.
That 206, 433, 452.
That which 42, 225.
The 139, 425.
Thebes 96.
Thee 406, 451.
Thefnut 451.
Theft 288.
Their 94, 351, 381.
Thekem, god 454.
Them 94, 225, 335, 337, 351, 381.
Themselves 462.
Then 235, 242, 435.
Thenemi 452.
Then-re 452.
There 32.
Therefore 235.
Therein 32.
These 28, 29, 30, 195, 209.
Thet amulet 455.
They 94, 225, 335, 351, 381.
Thigh 101, 149, 174, 292, 301, 313, 340, 451.
Thing, things 5, 300, 313, 320.
Things done 52.
Things said 464.
Think 51, 304, 407.
Thirst 21, 24.
Thirty 168.
This 141, 206, 209, 435, 452.
Those 192.
Thoth 9, 447; festival of 447; city of 105.
Thoth Ḥāpi 447.
Thou 219, 225, 406, 430, 451.
Thought 36, 407, 421.
Thousand 290.
Three 304.
Threshold 327.
Thrive 359.
Throat 57, 285, 290, 317, 396.
Throne 218, 319.
Throne-chamber 452.
Through 32.
Throughout 160.
Throw 290.
Thunder, thunder-storm 219, 417.
Thus 76.
Thy 219, 406, 425, 451.
Thyself 462.
Tiara 182, 209, 377.
Tidings 358.

Tie 1, 49, 50, 86, 106, 179, 196, 226, 342, 403, 405, 414, 417, 454.
Time 88, 195, 213, 243, 246, 268, 341, 372, 436.
Timid 293, 357.
Tip 430.
Tithe 288.
Title-deeds 42.
To 16, 191, 228.
To-day 167.
Toes 326.
Toil 129, 265.
Tomb, tombs 11, 13, 58, 89, 144, 145, 180, 254, 442.
To-morrow 136, 440.
Tongue 217.
Tongue of a Balance 436.
Tool 49, 56, 86, 139, 205.
Tooth 23.
Top 430; top of anything 458; top of the head, i. e. skull 30.
Tortoise 80, 404.
Torture chamber 14, 298, 299, 348.
Total 240.
Totality 420, 444, 445.
Touch 444.
Tow along 383.
Towards 228.
Transfer 325, 330.
Transform 51.
Transformation 301.
Transport 456.
Travel 21, 193, 300, 308, 312, 313, 326, 337, 387, 388, 392, 393, 397.
Tree 37, 42, 65, 180, 208, 319, 401, 453.
Tremble 64, 386.
Tress 206, 257, 326.
Triad, solar 368.
Trial 341.
Tribe 169.
Triumphant 164, 347.
Trouble 4, 112, 305.
True 92, 163.
Truth 92, 103, 132, 189.
Truth, goddess of 165.
Ṭuamutef 441.
Ṭuat, god and place 428, 441.
Ṭu-menkh-rerek 440.
Ṭun-peḥti 441.
Turn away, or back 82, 361, 399, 400, 435; turn round 119, 170.
Turquoise 169, 170.
Turtle 80.
Ṭuṭu 439.

Twenty 457.
Twice-great 73.
Two 351.
Two-horned 79.
Type 167, 430.
Typify 384.

Ua 94.
Uāau 100.
Uaipu, goddess 95.
Uamemti 95.
Uart-neter-semsu 96.
Uatchit 98.
Ubes-ḥer-per-em-khetkhet 102.
Udder 169.
Uhem-ḥer 112.
Ui 102.
Unȧset 104.
Unbar 355.
Unbolt 355, 373.
Unclothe 252.
Uncover 105, 409.
Undecaying 68.
Under 229, 313.
Under favour of 313.
Understand 81, 241.
Undertake 403.
Undipped 44.
Undress 252, 344, 409.
Unen-em-ḥetep 105.
Unes 107.
Unguent 23, 83, 84, 93, 97, 104, 155, 210, 257, 281, 345, 354, 387, 413, 432, 453.
Uniformly 164.
Union 134, 345.
Unite 345, 444, 445.
Uniu 104.
Unknown 44, 68, 240.
Unless 43.
Unloose 105, 113, 157.
Un-nefer 106.
Un-nefer-Rā 106.
Unobserved 43.
Unquenchable 68.
Unremittingly 3.
Unresisting 43.
Unseen 43, 44.
Unsplit 44.
Unt 107.
Unti 107.
Untie 106, 157, 344, 353.
Untold 44.
Unturnable 44.
Unwashed 44.
Upon 32, 158, 159, 228, 268, 430.
Upside down 372.
Ur-ȧrit-s 109.
Ur-ḥekau 110.

Ur-ḥetchati 110.
Ur-kherp-ḥem 110.
Ur-ma 109.
Ur-maat 109.
Ur-mertus-ṭeshert-shennu 110.
Ur-peḥui-f 109.
Urine 116.
Urit 109.
Uraeus 15, 85.
Uraei 55; the living 16, 85.
Uraeus Crown 432.
Us 192.
Usekh-nemmet 115.
Usert, goddess 114.
Usṭ 116.
Utau gods 117.
Utchat 121.
Utent 118.
Utmost 2.
Utter 17, 19.
Utterance 432.
Utu-nesert 118.
Utu-rekhit 118.

Valiant 22.
Valley 49.
Valour 216, 446.
Vanquish 76, 221.
Variant reading 464.
Vase 447.
Vassal 314.
Vegetables 237.
Venerable 396.
Venerate 37.
Veneration 199.
Venom 189.
Venus 224.
Verily 123, 407, 408.
Vermify 99.
Vertebrae 8, 9, 12, 454.
Vessel 183, 250, 396, 445.
Vessel for offerings 15.
Vicar 71.
Victims 315, 347.
Victor 367.
Victory 211.
Victuals 83.
View 160.
Vigorous 98, 234, 333.
Vine 11.
Vineyard 11.
Violence 71, 76, 119, 399, 446.
Vital power 367.
Vivify 331.
Voice 315, 432, 443.
Void 120.
Vomit 136.
Voyage 380.
Vulture 211.

Wailing 12, 66.
Wailing women 12, 66.
Wake, wake up 213, 241.
Walk 104, 116, 122, 184, 208, 218, 238, 329, 352, 384, 385, 397, 430, 437, 449; walk with long strides 337.
Wall 46, 103, 327, 341, 352.
Wander 208, 265.
Want 395, 420.
War 87.
Ward 325; ward off 56.
Warder 324.
Wash 14, 77, 330.
Wash the heart 14.
Washing 15.
Waste 288.
Watch 53, 111, 195, 241, 324, 359.
Watcher 53, 359.
Water 172, 220.
Watercourse 177.
Water flood 14, 69, 102, 131, 258.
Water fowl 3.
Water-god 172.
Water house 78.
Waterless 44.
Water plant 5, 392.
Water way 95.
Watery ground 76.
Way 95, 97, 171.
Wayfarer 399.
Wax 176, 180.
We 192.
Weak 129, 130, 139, 210, 228, 339, 367, 381, 422, 424.
Weakness 136.
Wealth 156, 314.
Weapon 171, 188, 195, 205, 217, 218, 411.
Weariness 157.
Weary 129.
Weave 350.
Weep 24, 236, 328, 359, 413, 452.
Weeping 66.
Weevil 80.
Weigh 122, 169.
Weight 173, 446.
Well 120, 307, 337.
Well-doing 207.
West 41.
West, goddess of 41.
West wind 41, 457.
What? 62, 67, 143, 153.
What kind of? 435.
Wheat 206.
When 302, 461; when not yet 159.

Whence 435.
Where 67, 435.
Which 221.
Whilst 461.
Whip 216.
Whirlwind 219, 255.
White 289.
White Crown 289.
Who? 62, 67, 153, 194, 208, 221.
Whole 433, 461.
Wholly 433.
Wicked 67, 293.
Wickedness 17, 131, 288, 298, 400, 439.
Wife 262, 385.
Wig 80.
Will 22, 179.
Wind 58, 165, 192, 206, 210, 303, 402, 434.
Wind, north 414, 417; south 393; west 457; east 24.
Window 378.
Windsail 165.
Wine 55, 67.
Wing 182, 446.
Wing-carrier 456.
Wisdom 447.
Wise 240, 373, 403.
Wish 21, 22, 179.
With 31, 55, 100, 158, 228, 229, 264, 313.
Wither 305.
Within 22, 159, 184, 305.
Without 68, 221, 433.
Withstand 88.
Wolf 107, 135.
Woman 262, 322, 385.
Women, wailing 12.
Womb 293.
Wonder 131.
Wood 56, 133, 134, 319, 344.
Word 190, 315, 454.
Words of power 296, 297.
Work, works 52, 128, 129, 176, 233, 262, 408; work the heart 51.
Workman 51, 262.
World 425.
Worm 156, 157, 231, 446.
Worms, Eater of 84.
Worship 96, 195, 333, 440.
Worshipful 396.
Worthy 452.
Would that! 57.
Wound 9, 217, 280, 363, 389, 394.
Woven stuff 63.
Wreath 166.

Wretched 163, 424.
Wretchedness 62.
Write 51, 319, 343, 374.
Writing 374, 392, 393, 451.
Wrong 76, 105, 138.
Wrought 50.

Ye 221, 435, 452.
Year 237.
Yellow 453.
Yesterday 344.
Yoke 213.
You 221, 435, 452.
Young 2, 209, 237, 359.
Young man 258.
Your 452.
Youth 2, 14, 57, 237.

www.ingramcontent.com/pod-product-compliance
Lightning Source LLC
Chambersburg PA
CBHW060312230426
43663CB00009B/1671
* 9 7 8 1 6 3 9 2 3 0 1 0 5 *